PENNSYLVANIA

SCHOOL PUBLISHERS

Orlando   Austin   New York   San Diego   Toronto   London

Visit *The Learning Site!*
www.harcourtschool.com

PENNSYLVANIA

Dr. Kara Libby
Supervisor of Social Studies, K–12
Prince George's County Public Schools
Capitol Heights, Maryland

Dr. Elizabeth Mancke
Associate Professor of History
Department of History
University of Akron
Akron, Ohio

Dr. Gary Manson
Professor of Geography
Department of Geography
Michigan State University
East Lansing, Michigan

Dr. Carol McKibben
Visiting Professor
Monterey Institute of International Studies
Monterey, California

Dr. D. Mark Meyers
Chair
Department of Secondary Education
Rowan University
Glassboro, New Jersey

Dr. Ines Miyares
Associate Professor of Geography
Department of Geography
Hunter College
New York, New York

Dr. Albert Raboteau
Henry W. Putnam Professor
Department of Religion
Princeton University
Princeton, New Jersey

Dr. William Strong
Professor and Chair
Department of Geography
University of North Alabama
Florence, Alabama

Dr. Saundra McKee
Professor of Education
Clarion University of Pennsylvania
Clarion, Pennsylvania

Dr. Murry R. Nelson
Professor of Education & American Studies
Pennsylvania State University
University Park, Pennsylvania

Dr. Scott Sandage
Associate Professor of History
Carnegie Mellon University
Pittsburgh, Pennsylvania

Sandra E. Thiebaud
Teacher
Evans City Elementary School
Evans City, Pennsylvania

Pennsylvania Connections

Paula Baptiste
Teacher
Emily Brittain Elementary School
Butler, Pennsylvania

Jennifer A. Fiscus
Teacher
Rowan Elementary School
Cranberry Township, Pennsylvania

Wendy A. Gordon
Teacher
Forest Hills Elementary School
Sidman, Pennsylvania

Sara Marincic
Teacher
Memorial Elementary School
Bethel Park, Pennsylvania

Classroom Reviewers

Joan Bergamo
Teacher
Marie D. Durand Elementary School
Vineland, New Jersey

Heather Defoor
Teacher
Danville Neel Elementary School
Danville, Alabama

Julianne Frodsham
Teacher
Washington Elementary School
Medford, Oregon

Howard Itkin
Teacher
Klem South Elementary School
Webster, New York

Cheryl Kuyk
Teacher
Summerdale School
Summerdale, Alabama

Joyce Malwitz
Instructional Facilitator
Anoka-Hennepin Independent School
   District #11
Coons Rapids, Minnesota

Dr. John S. Miller
Principal
Lincoln Elementary School
Springfield, Ohio

Janet Schneider
Teacher
Windsor School
Des Moines, Iowa

Karen Todorov
Social Studies Education Consultant
Curriculum Development
Michigan Department of Education
Lansing, Michigan

Maps
researched and prepared by

Readers
written and designed by

Take a Field Trip
video tour segments provided by

ISBN 0-15-347253-7

1 2 3 4 5 6 7 8 9 10 032 13 12 11 10 09 08 07 06

Contents

· UNIT ·
1

A View of the United States

· UNIT ·

2

The Northeast

v

· UNIT ·

3

The South

· UNIT ·

4

The Middle West

PENNSYLVANIA
CONNECTION

· UNIT ·

5

The West

· UNIT ·

6

The United States Today

Reference

Features You Can Use

Time Lines

Reading Your Textbook

Getting Started

Your textbook is divided into six units.

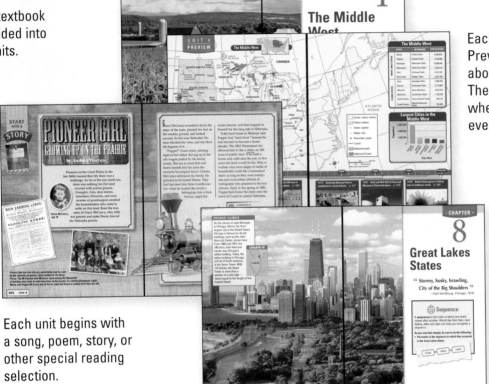

Each unit has a Unit Preview that gives facts about important events. The Preview also shows where and when those events took place.

Each unit is divided into chapters, and each chapter is divided into lessons.

Each unit begins with a song, poem, story, or other special reading selection.

The Parts of a Lesson

This statement gives you ideas to help you as you read a lesson.

This statement tells you why it is important to read the lesson.

These are the new vocabulary terms you will learn in the lesson.

· LESSON ·

1

SEQUENCE
As you read, look for the sequence of events that led the United States to expand westward.

BIG IDEA
Learn how the Great Lakes region became part of the United States.

VOCABULARY
cartographer
ally
survey
township
ordinance
frontier

The Old Northwest

1650 ———— 1775 ———— 1900

After the United States became a nation, more Americans moved inland. They settled on the rolling lands and broad river valleys of the Central Plains, west of the Appalachian Mountains. Many of them settled northwest of the Ohio River, in what is now known as the Great Lakes region. Today six states—Illinois, Indiana, Ohio, Michigan, Minnesota, and Wisconsin—make up this region. Each of these states borders at least one of the Great Lakes.

Exploring the Region

By the early 1600s, the French had built a few settlements in present-day Canada and along the Great Lakes. At the settlements they traded with Native Americans for fur. These Indians told stories about a river south of the Great Lakes, which they called the Mississippi. Hoping to discover new trade routes, French leaders sent an expedition to find and explore this river.

Marquette and Joliet explored the waterways of the Great Lakes region. Today the cities of Marquette, Michigan, and Joliet, Illinois, are named in their honor.

268

Lesson title

A time line shows the period of time in which the events in the lesson took place.

Each lesson is divided into several short sections.

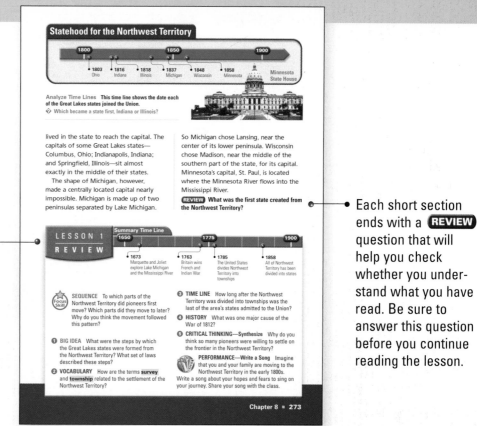

Statehood for the Northwest Territory

1800   1850   1900

• 1803   • 1816   • 1818   • 1837   • 1848   • 1858   Minnesota
Ohio   Indiana Illinois Michigan Wisconsin Minnesota State House

Analyze Time Lines This time line shows the date each of the Great Lakes states joined the Union.
➤ Which became a state first, Indiana or Illinois?

lived in the state to reach the capital. The capitals of some Great Lakes states—Columbus, Ohio; Indianapolis, Indiana; and Springfield, Illinois—sit almost exactly in the middle of their states.

The shape of Michigan, however, made a centrally located capital nearly impossible. Michigan is made up of two peninsulas separated by Lake Michigan.

So Michigan chose Lansing, near the center of its lower peninsula. Wisconsin chose Madison, near the middle of the southern part of the state, for its capital. Minnesota's capital, St. Paul, is located where the Minnesota River flows into the Mississippi River.

REVIEW What was the first state created from the Northwest Territory?

LESSON 1 REVIEW

Summary Time Line
1650   1775   1900

• 1673   Marquette and Joliet explore Lake Michigan and the Mississippi River
• 1763   Britain wins French and Indian War
• 1785   The United States divides Northwest Territory into townships
• 1858   All of Northwest Territory has been divided into states

Focus Skill **SEQUENCE** To which parts of the Northwest Territory did pioneers first move? Which parts did they move to later? Why do you think the movement followed this pattern?

❶ **BIG IDEA** What were the steps by which the Great Lakes states were formed from the Northwest Territory? What set of laws described these steps?

❷ **VOCABULARY** How are the terms **survey** and **township** related to the settlement of the Northwest Territory?

❸ **TIME LINE** How long after the Northwest Territory was divided into townships was the last of the area's states admitted to the Union?

❹ **HISTORY** What was one major cause of the War of 1812?

❺ **CRITICAL THINKING—Synthesize** Why do you think so many pioneers were willing to settle on the frontier in the Northwest Territory?

PERFORMANCE—Write a Song Imagine that you and your family are moving to the Northwest Territory in the early 1800s. Write a song about your hopes and fears to sing on your journey. Share your song with the class.

Chapter 8 ■ 273

Each lesson, like each chapter and each unit, ends with a review. There may be a Summary Time Line that shows the order of the events covered in the lesson. Questions and a performance activity help you check your understanding of the lesson.

Each short section ends with a **REVIEW** question that will help you check whether you understand what you have read. Be sure to answer this question before you continue reading the lesson.

Skills

Your textbook has lessons that will help you build your reading, citizenship, chart and graph, and map and globe skills.

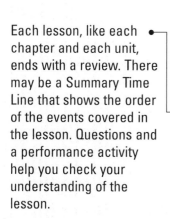

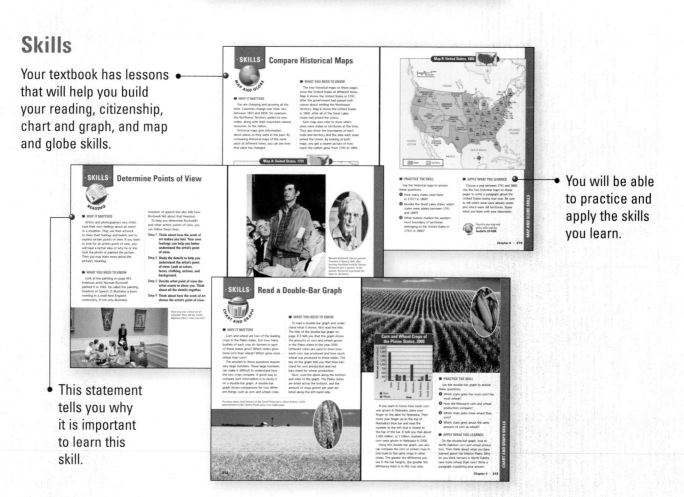

This statement tells you why it is important to learn this skill.

You will be able to practice and apply the skills you learn.

Special Features

The feature called Examine Primary Sources shows you ways to learn about different kinds of objects and documents.

The Visit feature lets you "visit" many interesting places.

Atlas

The Atlas provides maps and a list of geography terms with illustrations.

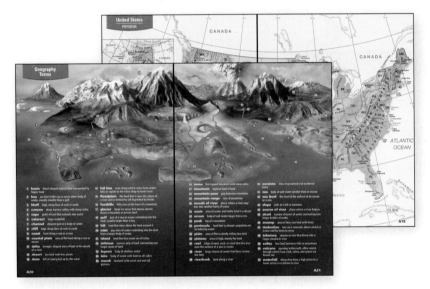

For Your Reference

At the back of your textbook, you will find the reference tools listed below.

- Almanac
- Biographical Dictionary
- Gazetteer
- Glossary
- Index

You can use these tools to look up words and find information about people, places, and other topics.

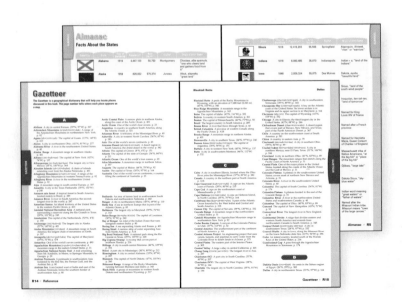

Atlas

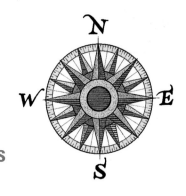

Read a Map

VOCABULARY		
grid system	locator	compass rose
inset map	map key	cardinal direction
map title	map scale	intermediate direction

▶ WHY IT MATTERS

Maps help you see where places are in the world. They show the locations of cities, states, and countries. They also show where mountains, valleys, rivers, and lakes are found. Knowing how to read a map is an important skill for learning social studies.

▶ WHAT YOU NEED TO KNOW

A map is a drawing that shows some or all of Earth on a flat surface. Mapmakers often include features that are designed to help people use maps more easily. Mapmakers sometimes include lines that cross each other to form a pattern of squares called a **grid system**. Look at the map of the United States. Around the grid

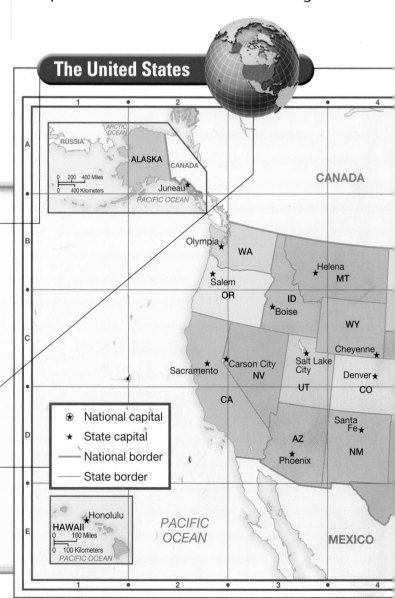

The United States

- **A map title** tells the subject of the map. The title may also help you know what kind of map it is.
  - **Political maps show cities, states, and countries.**
  - **Physical maps show kinds of land and bodies of water.**
  - **Historical maps show parts of the world as they were in the past.**

- **A locator** is a small map or picture of a globe that shows where the place shown on the main map is located.

- **A map key**, or legend, explains the symbols used on a map. Symbols may be colors, patterns, lines, or other special marks.

system are letters and numbers. The columns, which run up and down, are labeled with numbers. The rows, which run across, have letters. Each square on the map can be identified by its letter and number. For example, the top row of squares on the map includes squares A-1 to A-7.

Mapmakers may also include smaller maps called **inset maps** within larger maps. Inset maps usually show a larger view of a small area on the main map. They may also show areas not shown on the main map. Look again at the map of the United States. Alaska and Hawaii are shown on inset maps because they are located far from the area shown on the main map.

PRACTICE THE SKILL

Use the map of the United States to answer these questions.

1 What cities are located in square D-5?

2 In what direction would you travel to go from Jefferson City, Missouri, to Little Rock, Arkansas?

3 Find the map key. What symbol is used to show a state capital?

4 About how many miles is it from Washington, D.C., to Frankfort, Kentucky?

5 Look at the inset maps of Hawaii and Alaska. How are the scales different?

APPLY WHAT YOU LEARNED

Write ten questions about the United States map. You can ask questions about distance, direction, and location. Then exchange questions with a classmate. See if you can answer all your classmate's questions.

- A **map scale** is used to compare a distance on the map to a distance in the real world. It helps you find the real distance between places. Notice that the map scale shows both miles and kilometers.

- A **compass rose**, or direction marker, shows directions.

- The **cardinal directions**, or main directions, are north, south, east, and west.

- The **intermediate directions**, or directions between the cardinal directions, are northeast, northwest, southeast, and southwest.

Map scale:
0 200 400 Miles
0 200 400 Kilometers
Albers Equal-Area Projection

ND
Bismarck
MN
Lake Superior
St. Paul
WI
MI
Madison
Lansing
Des Moines
IA
IL
IN
Indianapolis
Columbus
OH
Charleston
WV
Pierre
D
NE
Lincoln
Topeka
KS
MO
Springfield
Jefferson City
KY
Frankfort
Oklahoma City
OK
AR
Little Rock
TN
Nashville
MS
AL
Atlanta
GA
Jackson
LA
Montgomery
TX
Austin
Baton Rouge
Tallahassee
FL
Gulf of Mexico

NH
ME
Augusta
Montpelier
VT
Concord
NY
Boston
Albany
MA
Providence
Hartford
RI
PA
NJ
CT
Harrisburg
Trenton
Dover
MD
DE
Annapolis
Washington, D.C.
VA
Richmond
NC
Raleigh
SC
Columbia
ATLANTIC OCEAN

N
E
W
S

ARCTIC OCEAN

80°N

Greenland
(DENMARK)

ALASKA
(U.S.)

60°N

CANADA

NORTH
AMERICA

40°N

UNITED STATES

Azores
(PORTUGAL)

Midway
Islands
(U.S.)

Bermuda
(U.K.)

ATLANTIC
OCEAN

Area of inset

20°N

Tropic of Cancer

MEXICO

CAPE VERDE

HAWAII
(U.S.)

PACIFIC
OCEAN

VENEZUELA   GUYANA
SURINAME

COLOMBIA   FRENCH GUIANA
(FRANCE)

Equator

ECUADOR

Galápagos
Islands
(ECUADOR)

BRAZIL

Tokelau
(N.Z.)

KIRIBATI

SOUTH
AMERICA

PERU

SAMOA

American
Samoa
(U.S.)

French
Polynesia
(FRANCE)

BOLIVIA

Cook
Islands
(N.Z.)

PARAGUAY

20°S

Tropic of Capricorn

CHILE

TONGA

Pitcairn
(U.K.)

Easter Island
(CHILE)

URUGUAY

Niue
(N.Z.)

ARGENTINA

Falkland
Islands
(U.K.)

40°S

PACIFIC

South
Georgia
(U.K.)

OCEAN

60°S

Antarctic Circle

80°S

180°   160°W   140°W   120°W   100°W   80°W

100°W

30°N

N
W   E
S

ATLANTIC
OCEAN

Gulf of Mexico

60°N

20°N

Tropic of Cancer

Turks and
Caicos (U.K.)

CUBA

Cayman
Islands
(U.K.)

DOMINICAN
REPUBLIC

Puerto
Rico
(U.S.)

Anguilla (U.K.)
St. Martin (FRANCE AND NETH.)

HAITI

ANTIGUA AND BARBUDA
Montserrat (U.K.)
Guadeloupe (FRANCE)

BELIZE

JAMAICA

Virgin Islands
(U.S. AND U.K.)

ST. KITTS
AND NEVIS

DOMINICA
Martinique (FRANCE)

Caribbean Sea

GUATEMALA   HONDURAS

ST. LUCIA
BARBADOS

EL SALVADOR   NICARAGUA

Aruba
(NETH.)

Netherlands
Antilles
(NETH.)

ST. VINCENT AND
THE GRENADINES

PACIFIC OCEAN

GRENADA

TRINIDAD AND
TOBAGO

10°N

Panama
Canal

10°N

| | National
border |

COSTA
RICA

A4

PANAMA

0   200   400 Miles

0   200   400 Kilometers

Azimuthal Equal-Area Projection

90°W   80°W   70°W   60°W

20°N

20°N

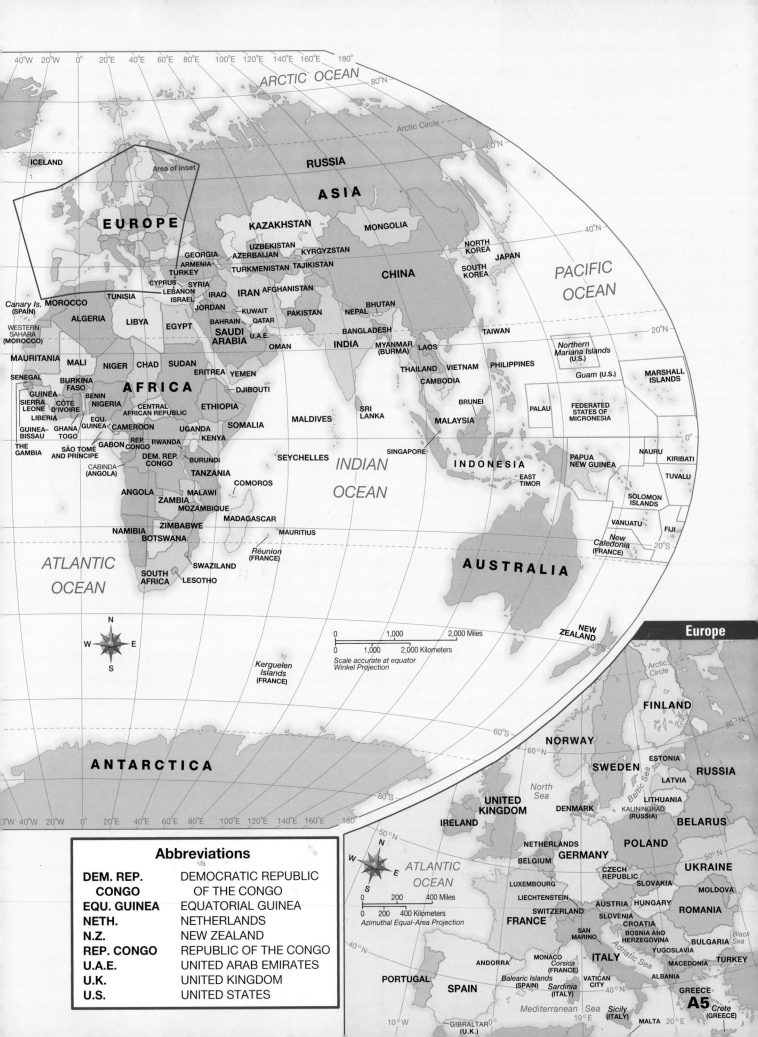

The World
PHYSICAL

Legend
- Arid
- Evergreen forest
- Grassland
- Mixed forest
- Mountains
- Tundra
- —— National border
- ▲ Mountain peak

ARCTIC OCEAN

80°N

Denali (Mt. McKinley) 20,320 ft. (6,194 m) ▲

Beaufort Sea

Queen Elizabeth Islands

Baffin Island

60°N

Bering Sea

Yukon R.

Mt. Logan 19,550 ft. (5,959 m) ▲

Great Bear Lake

Great Slave Lake

Mackenzie R.

NORTH AMERICA

Hudson Bay

Aleutian Islands

Gulf of Alaska

Vancouver Island

Columbia R.

ROCKY MOUNTAINS

GREAT PLAINS

Missouri R.

Great Lakes

Ohio R.

APPALACHIAN MTS.

Newfoundland

40°N

Mt. Whitney 14,495 ft. (4,418 m) ▲

Colorado R.

Rio Grande

Mississippi R.

Bermuda

ATLANTIC OCEAN

Gulf of California

Tropic of Cancer

20°N

Hawaiian Islands

Gulf of Mexico

Bahamas

PACIFIC OCEAN

Pico de Orizaba 18,855 ft. (5,747 m) ▲

Yucatán Peninsula

Cuba

Hispaniola

West Indies

Caribbean Sea

Equator

Polynesia

Galápagos Islands

Orinoco River

Guiana Highlands

AMAZON BASIN

Amazon R.

ANDES MOUNTAINS

SOUTH AMERICA

Brazilian Highlands

20°S

Tropic of Capricorn

Atacama Desert

Gran Chaco

Paraná River

Mt. Aconcagua 22,834 ft. (6,960 m) ▲

Pampa

40°S

PACIFIC OCEAN

Patagonia

Falkland Islands

60°S

Strait of Magellan

Cape Horn

Tierra del Fuego

Antarctic Circle

Ross Sea

Antarctic Peninsula

80°S

180° 160°W 140°W 120°W 100°W 80°W

Northern Polar Region

Sea of Okhotsk

ASIA

EUROPE

Kamchatka Peninsula

Novaya Zemlya

Severnaya Zemlya

Barents Sea

Baltic Sea

New Siberian Is.

ARCTIC OCEAN

North Pole

Svalbard

Norwegian Sea

North Sea

British Isles

Wrangel Island

Bering Sea

Bering Strait

BROOKS RANGE

Beaufort Sea

North Magnetic Pole

Queen Elizabeth Islands

Greenland

Greenland Sea

Iceland

ATLANTIC OCEAN

PACIFIC OCEAN

NORTH AMERICA

Baffin Bay

Arctic Circle

0   400   800 Miles
0   400   800 Kilometers
Azimuthal Equidistant Projection

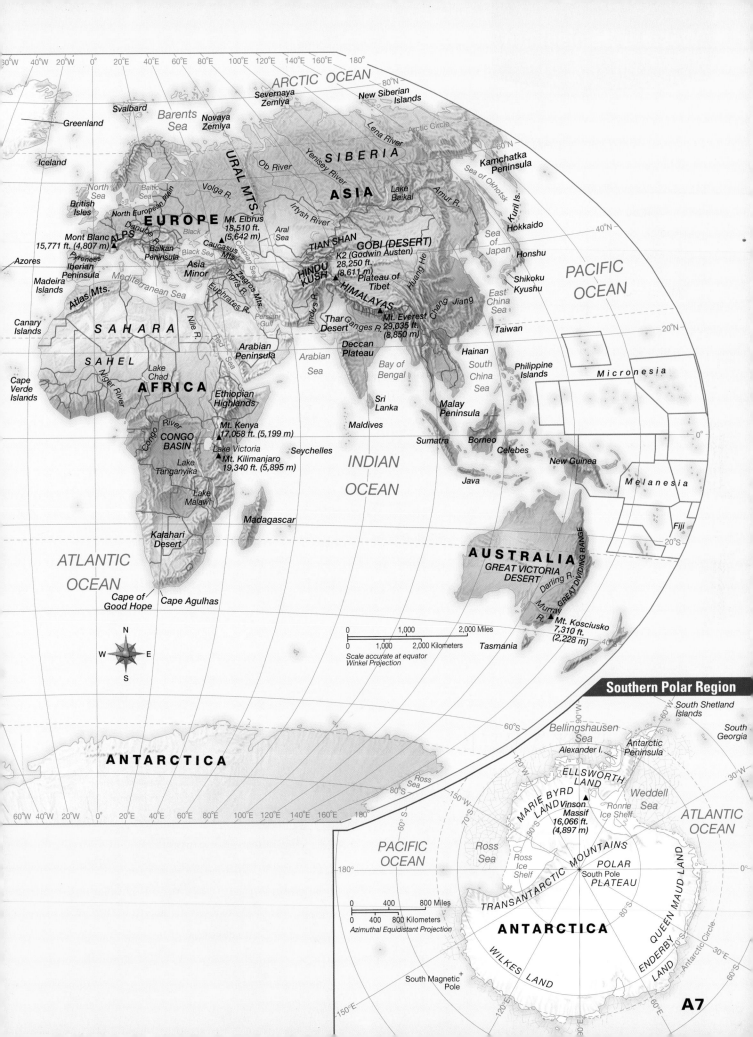

ARCTIC OCEAN

80°N

Severnaya Zemlya
New Siberian Islands

Svalbard

Novaya Zemlya

Barents Sea

Greenland

Iceland

North Sea

British Isles

Baltic Sea

North European Plain

URAL MTS.

Ob River

Yenisey River

Lena River

Arctic Circle

SIBERIA

60°N

Kamchatka Peninsula

Sea of Okhotsk

ASIA

Lake Baikal

Amur R.

Kuril Is.

Hokkaido

EUROPE

Volga R.

Danube R.

ALPS

Mont Blanc
15,771 ft. (4,807 m)

Black

Mt. Elbrus
18,510 ft.
(5,642 m)

Irtysh River

Aral Sea

40°N

Sea of Japan

Honshu

Balkan Peninsula

Pyrenees

Iberian Peninsula

Azores

Madeira Islands

Black Sea

Caucasus Mts.

Caspian Sea

Asia Minor

Zagros Mts.

Tigris R.

Euphrates R.

TIAN SHAN

HINDU KUSH

GOBI (DESERT)

K2 (Godwin Austen)
28,250 ft.
(8,611 m)

Plateau of Tibet

HIMALAYAS

Huang He

Chang Jiang

Shikoku
Kyushu

PACIFIC OCEAN

East China Sea

Atlas Mts.

Mediterranean Sea

Persian Gulf

Indus R.

Thar Desert

Ganges R.

Mt. Everest 29,035 ft.
(8,850 m)

Taiwan

20°N

SAHARA

Nile R.

Red Sea

Arabian Peninsula

Arabian Sea

Deccan Plateau

Bay of Bengal

Hainan

South China Sea

Philippine Islands

Micronesia

Canary Islands

SAHEL

Lake Chad

Niger River

AFRICA

Ethiopian Highlands

Sri Lanka

Maldives

Malay Peninsula

0°

Cape Verde Islands

Congo River

CONGO BASIN

Mt. Kenya
17,058 ft. (5,199 m)

Lake Victoria

Mt. Kilimanjaro
19,340 ft. (5,895 m)

Lake Tanganyika

Seychelles

Sumatra

Borneo

Celebes

New Guinea

Melanesia

Lake Malawi

INDIAN OCEAN

Java

Fiji

ATLANTIC OCEAN

Madagascar

20°S

Kalahari Desert

AUSTRALIA

GREAT VICTORIA DESERT

Darling R.

GREAT DIVIDING RANGE

Cape of Good Hope

Cape Agulhas

Murray R.

Mt. Kosciusko
7,310 ft.
(2,228 m)

N
W   E
S

0   1,000   2,000 Miles

0   1,000   2,000 Kilometers

Scale accurate at equator
Winkel Projection

Tasmania

60°W 40°W 20°W 0° 20°E 40°E 60°E 80°E 100°E 120°E 140°E 160°E 180°

60°S

80°S

Ross Sea

ANTARCTICA

Southern Polar Region

South Shetland Islands

Bellingshausen Sea

Antarctic Peninsula

South Georgia

Alexander I.

ELLSWORTH LAND

MARIE BYRD LAND

Vinson Massif
16,066 ft.
(4,897 m)

Ronne Ice Shelf

Weddell Sea

ATLANTIC OCEAN

PACIFIC OCEAN

Ross Sea

Ross Ice Shelf

TRANSANTARCTIC MOUNTAINS

POLAR PLATEAU

South Pole

QUEEN MAUD LAND

ENDERBY LAND

WILKES LAND

ANTARCTICA

0   400   800 Miles

0   400   800 Kilometers

Azimuthal Equidistant Projection

South Magnetic Pole

Antarctic Circle

A7

Western Hemisphere
POLITICAL

ARCTIC OCEAN

Bering Strait

Beaufort Sea

Viscount Melville Sound

Greenland
(DENMARK)

Baffin Bay

ALASKA
(U.S.)

Yukon River

Fairbanks

Anchorage

Whitehorse

Juneau

Gulf of Alaska

60°N

Bering Sea

Great Bear Lake

Mackenzie River

Liard River

Yellowknife

Great Slave Lake

CANADA

Peace River

Lake Athabasca

Edmonton

Calgary

Vancouver

Saskatoon

Regina

Saskatchewan R.

Lake Winnipeg

Winnipeg

Thunder Bay

Foxe Basin

Hudson Strait

Davis Strait

Arctic Circle

Labrador Sea

Hudson Bay

James Bay

UNITED STATES

Great Lakes

St. Lawrence River

Ottawa

Quebec

St. John's

Gulf of St. Lawrence

Seattle

Portland

Puget Sound

Boise

Columbia

Snake R.

Missouri

Toronto

Detroit

Montreal

St. John

Halifax

Albany

Boston

Great Salt Lake

Salt Lake City

Chicago

Cleveland

New York City

Philadelphia

Washington, D.C.

Reno

Denver

St. Louis

Indianapolis

Richmond

San Francisco

Las Vegas

Colorado

Memphis

Atlanta

Raleigh

Norfolk

Los Angeles

Phoenix

Charleston

San Diego

Tucson

El Paso

Dallas

Rio Grande

Houston

New Orleans

Savannah

Jacksonville

30°N

Hermosillo

Chihuahua

San Antonio

Tampa

Orlando

Miami

ATLANTIC OCEAN

Tropic of Cancer

Gulf of California

Gulf of Mexico

BAHAMAS

Nassau

Honolulu

HAWAII
(U.S.)

MEXICO

Durango

Monterrey

Havana

CUBA

HAITI

Port-au-Prince

Santo Domingo

León

Tampico

JAMAICA

Kingston

Puerto Rico **(U.S.)**

DOMINICAN REPUBLIC

PACIFIC OCEAN

Guadalajara

Mexico City

Veracruz

BELIZE

Belmopan

Puebla

Acapulco

GUATEMALA

Guatemala City

HONDURAS

Tegucigalpa

Caribbean Sea

San Salvador

EL SALVADOR

Managua

NICARAGUA

San José

COSTA RICA

San José

Panama City

PANAMA

Maracaibo

Caracas

GUYANA

SURINAME

Paramaribo

Cayenne

Medellín

VENEZUELA

Georgetown

FRENCH GUIANA **(FRANCE)**

Cali

Bogotá

COLOMBIA

0° Equator

Quito

Galápagos Islands
(ECUADOR)

Guayaquil

ECUADOR

Iquitos

Manaus

Rio Negro

Amazon R.

Belém

Fortaleza

Trujillo

PERU

Lima

Cuzco

Lake Titicaca

La Paz

Tapajós River

Xingu

Tocantins

Recife

BRAZIL

Brasília

Goiânia

Salvador

São Francisco R.

Papeete

French Polynesia
(FRANCE)

Arequipa

Sucre

BOLIVIA

Belo Horizonte

Campo Grande

Rio de Janeiro

Tropic of Capricorn

Antofagasta

PARAGUAY

Paraguay R.

Asunción

São Paulo

Curitiba

Salta

San Miguel de Tucumán

Pôrto Alegre

CHILE

Córdoba

Paraná R.

URUGUAY

30°S

Valparaíso

Santiago

Rosario

Buenos Aires

La Plata

Montevideo

Rio de la Plata

Mar del Plata

Concepción

Bahía Blanca

Valdivia

	National border
⊛	National capital
•	City

ARGENTINA

0   1,000   2,000 Miles

0   1,000   2,000 Kilometers

Miller Cylindrical Projection

N
W   E
S

Falkland Islands
(U.K.)

Punta Arenas

South Georgia
(U.K.)

A8

150°W   120°W   90°W   60°W   30°W

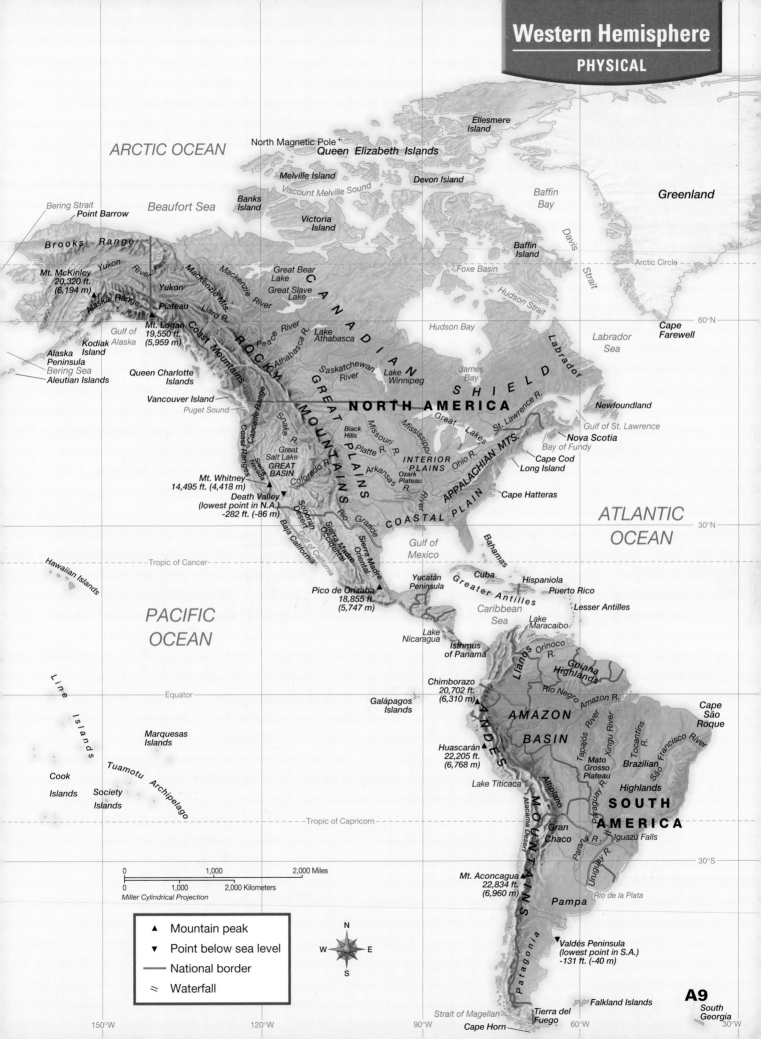

ARCTIC OCEAN

North Magnetic Pole +

Queen Elizabeth Islands

Ellesmere Island

Melville Island

Viscount Melville Sound

Devon Island

Banks Island

Beaufort Sea

Victoria Island

Baffin Bay

Greenland

Bering Strait

Point Barrow

Brooks Range

Baffin Island

Davis Strait

Arctic Circle

Mt. McKinley 20,320 ft. (6,194 m)

Yukon River

Mackenzie Mts.

Great Bear Lake

Foxe Basin

60°N

Alaska Range

Yukon Plateau

Mackenzie River

Great Slave Lake

Hudson Strait

Cape Farewell

Mt. Logan 19,550 ft. (5,959 m)

Gulf of Alaska

Coast Mountains

Liard R.

Peace River

Hudson Bay

Labrador Sea

Kodiak Island

Alaska Peninsula

Bering Sea

Aleutian Islands

Queen Charlotte Islands

Athabasca R.

Lake Athabasca

Saskatchewan River

Lake Winnipeg

James Bay

S H I E L D

Labrador

C A N A D I A N

Newfoundland

Vancouver Island

Puget Sound

Cascade Range

Coast Ranges

R O C K Y   M O U N T A I N S

G R E A T   P L A I N S

NORTH AMERICA

Great Lakes

St. Lawrence R.

Gulf of St. Lawrence

Nova Scotia

Bay of Fundy

Cape Cod

Long Island

Snake R.

Sierra Nevada

Great Salt Lake

GREAT BASIN

Black Hills

Missouri R.

Platte R.

Mississippi R.

INTERIOR PLAINS

Ohio R.

Ozark Plateau

APPALACHIAN MTS.

Cape Hatteras

ATLANTIC OCEAN

Mt. Whitney 14,495 ft. (4,418 m)

Colorado R.

Arkansas R.

Red River

Death Valley (lowest point in N.A.) -282 ft. (-86 m)

Sonoran Desert

Sierra Madre Occidental

Rio Grande

Sierra Madre Oriental

COASTAL PLAIN

30°N

Baja California

Gulf of California

Gulf of Mexico

Hawaiian Islands

Tropic of Cancer

Pico de Orizaba 18,855 ft. (5,747 m)

Yucatán Peninsula

Bahamas

Cuba

Greater Antilles

Hispaniola

Puerto Rico

Lesser Antilles

PACIFIC OCEAN

Caribbean Sea

Lake Maracaibo

Lake Nicaragua

Isthmus of Panama

Llanos

Orinoco R.

Guiana Highlands

Line   Islands

Chimborazo 20,702 ft. (6,310 m)

Galápagos Islands

Rio Negro

Amazon R.

Cape São Roque

Equator

A N D E S

AMAZON BASIN

Marquesas Islands

Huascarán 22,205 ft. (6,768 m)

Tapajós River

Xingu River

Tocantins R.

São Francisco River

Brazilian Highlands

Cook Islands

Tuamotu Archipelago

Society Islands

Lake Titicaca

Altiplano

Mato Grosso Plateau

SOUTH AMERICA

Tropic of Capricorn

M O U N T A I N S

Paraguay R.

Gran Chaco

Paraná R.

Iguazú Falls

Mt. Aconcagua 22,834 ft. (6,960 m)

Uruguay R.

Rio de la Plata

30°S

Pampa

▲ Mountain peak

▼ Point below sea level

—— National border

≈ Waterfall

N W E S

Valdés Peninsula (lowest point in S.A.) -131 ft. (-40 m)

Patagonia

Falkland Islands

A9
South Georgia

Strait of Magellan

Tierra del Fuego

Cape Horn

0   1,000   2,000 Miles

0   1,000   2,000 Kilometers

Miller Cylindrical Projection

150°W   120°W   90°W   60°W   30°W

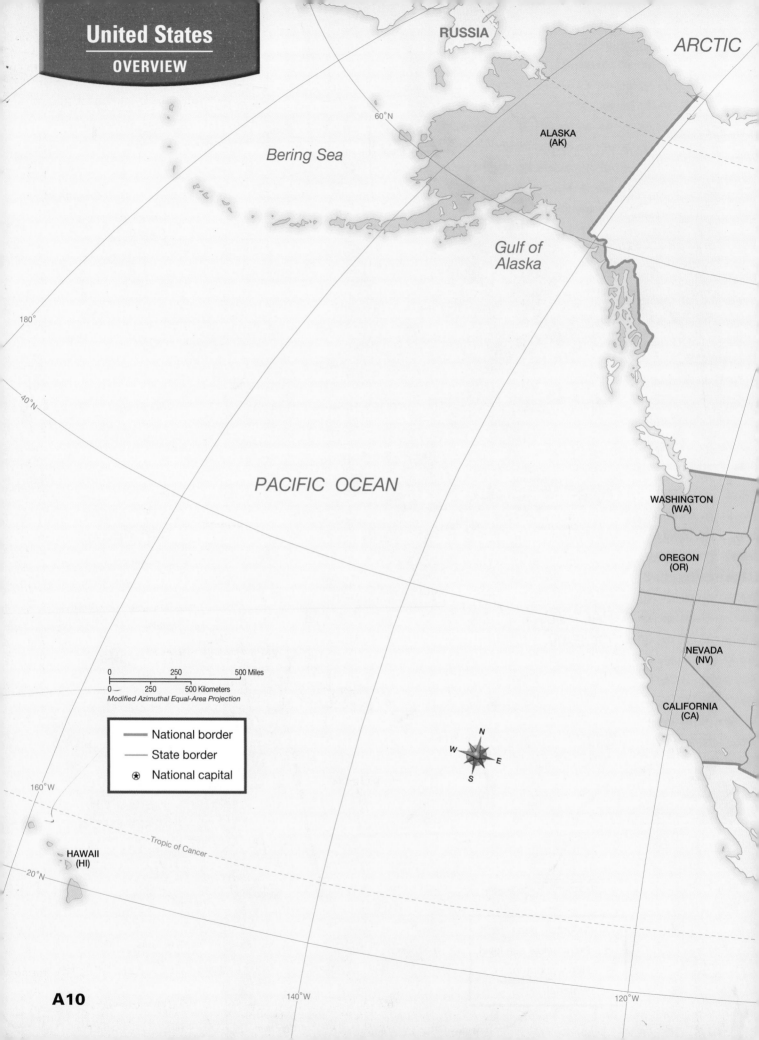

United States
OVERVIEW

RUSSIA

ARCTIC

60°N

Bering Sea

ALASKA
(AK)

Gulf of
Alaska

180°

40°N

PACIFIC OCEAN

WASHINGTON
(WA)

OREGON
(OR)

NEVADA
(NV)

| 0 | 250 | 500 Miles |
| 0 | 250 | 500 Kilometers |

Modified Azimuthal Equal-Area Projection

CALIFORNIA
(CA)

N
W   E
S

National border
State border
National capital

160°W

Tropic of Cancer

HAWAII
(HI)

20°N

140°W

120°W

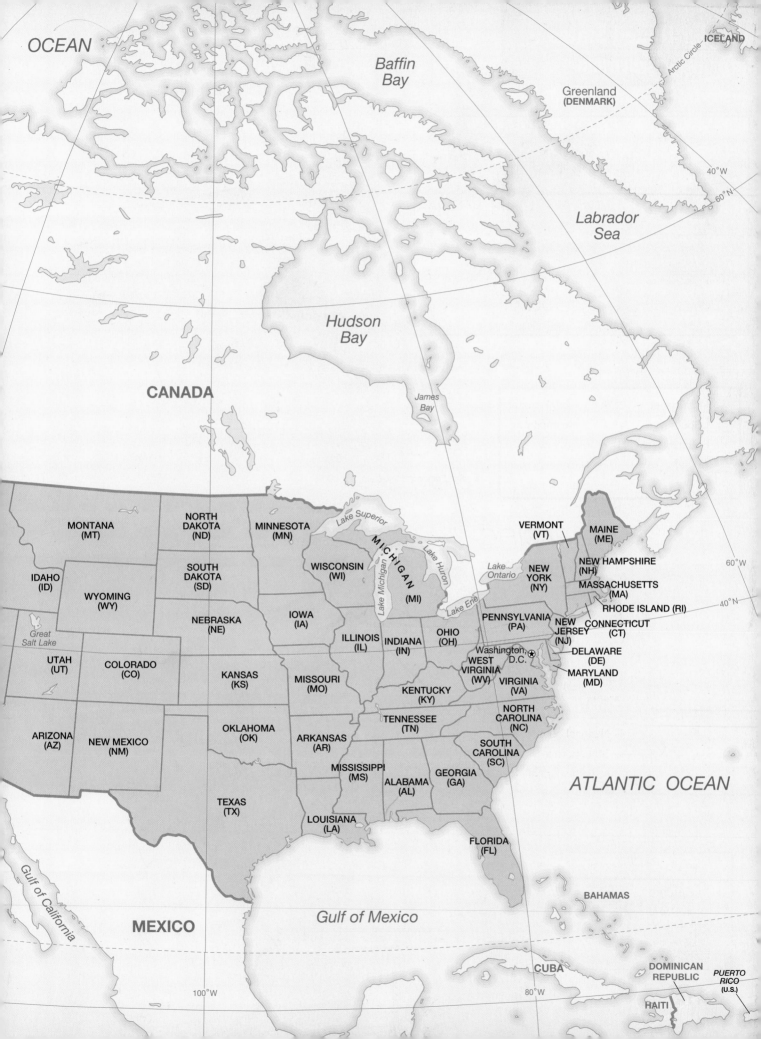

United States
POLITICAL

ARCTIC OCEAN

RUSSIA

ALASKA

70°N

120°W

Arctic Circle

Yukon River

CANADA

Fairbanks

Bering
Sea

180°

Anchorage

60°N

170°E

60°N

50°N

170°W 160°W 150°W 140°W 130°W

Gulf of
Alaska

Juneau

PACIFIC
OCEAN

| 0 | 250 | 500 Miles |
| 0 | 250 | 500 Kilometers |

CANADA

130°W   120°W   110°W

Seattle
Tacoma
Olympia
WASHINGTON

Spokane

Great Falls

Portland
Columbia River
Helena MONTANA

Salem
Billings
Eugene
OREGON
Yellowstone R.
IDAHO

Boise

Snake River
WYOMING

40°N

Pocatello

Casper

Great
Salt
Lake Ogden

NEVADA
Reno
Lake
Tahoe
Sacramento Carson City

Salt Lake City
Cheyenne
Provo

UTAH

Denver

San Francisco Oakland
San Jose

Colorado
Springs
COLORADO
Pueblo

Fresno

Colorado River

CALIFORNIA Las
Vegas

Bakersfield

PACIFIC

OCEAN

Santa Fe

Flagstaff
Albuquerque

30°N

Los Angeles San Bernardino
ARIZONA NEW MEXICO

130°W

San Diego

Phoenix
Roswell

Tucson

El Paso

Rio Grande

Legend
- Northeast
- South
- Middle West
- West
- ⊛ National capital
- ★ State capital
- • Major city
- National border
- State border

MEXICO

N
W E
S

| 0 | 250 | 500 Miles |
| 0 | 250 | 500 Kilometers |
Albers Equal-Area Projection

PACIFIC
OCEAN

160°W 155°W

Honolulu

HAWAII

20°N

Hilo

| 0 | 100 | 200 Miles |
| 0 | 100 | 200 Kilometers |

20°N

120°W   110°W

A12

United States
PHYSICAL

CANADA

RUSSIA

ARCTIC OCEAN

170°E

Brooks Range

60°N

Seward Peninsula

ALASKA

Yukon River

Arctic Circle

CANADA

St. Lawrence Island

Mt. McKinley 20,320 ft. (6,194 m)△

Alaska Range

Yukon River

60°N

Bering Sea

180°

Gulf of Alaska

250   500 Miles

0   250   500 Kilometers

Aleutian Islands

50°N

Kodiak Island

170°W   160°W   150°W   140°W   130°W

40°N

Legend

	Arid
	Evergreen forest
	Grassland
	Mixed forest
	Mountains
	Tundra
▬	National border
—	State border
▲	Mountain peak
△	Highest point
▽	Lowest point

PACIFIC OCEAN

30°N

130°W

CANADA

120°W   110°W

Range

WA

Mt. Rainier ▲ 14,410 ft. (4,392 m)

Cascade Range

Coast Ranges

▲ Mt. St. Helens 8,366 ft. (2,550 m)

Columbia River

▲ Mt. Hood 11,237 ft. (3,425 m)

OR

Columbia Plateau

Bitterroot Range

ROCKY

MT

Fort Peck Lake

Salmon River Mountains

ID

Yellowstone River

Snake River

Teton Range

Wind River Range

Bighorn Mts.

WY

Cape Mendocino

Pyramid Lake

Donner Pass

Lake Tahoe

NV

GREAT BASIN

Great Salt Lake

Uinta Mts.

Great Divide Basin

MOUNTAIN

Front Range

Sierra Nevada

Sacramento River

Central Valley

San Joaquin R.

Wasatch Range

UT

Mt. Elbert 14,433 ft. (4,399 m) ▲

Colorado River

San Juan Mts.

Sangre de Cristo Mts.

CO

▲ Mt. Whitney 14,495 ft. (4,418 m)

Death Valley ▽

CA

Mojave

-282 ft. (-86 m) ▽

Desert

Grand Canyon

Lake Mead

Lake Powell

Colorado Plateau

Point Conception

Channel Islands

Salton Sea

Imperial Valley

AZ

Sonoran Desert

NM

Baldy Peak ▲ 11,403 ft. (3,476 m)

Guadalupe Peak 8,749 ft. (2,667 m) ▲

Rio Grande

MEXICO

20°N

N
W   E
S

HAWAII

160°W   155°W

Kauai   PACIFIC OCEAN

Niihau

Oahu

Molokai

Lanai   Maui

Kahoolawe

Hawaii

20°N

Mauna Kea ▲ 13,796 ft. (4,205 m)

0   100   200 Miles

0   100   200 Kilometers

0   250   500 Miles

0   250   500 Kilometers

Albers Equal-Area Projection

20°N

120°W   110°W

A14

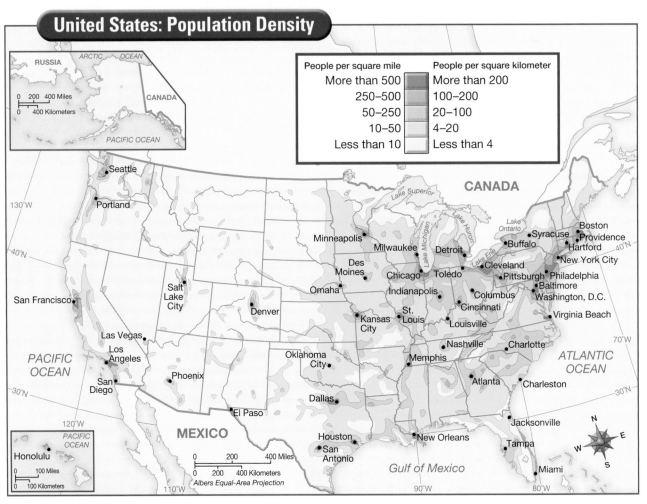

United States: Population Density

People per square mile
- More than 500
- 250–500
- 50–250
- 10–50
- Less than 10

People per square kilometer
- More than 200
- 100–200
- 20–100
- 4–20
- Less than 4

RUSSIA
ARCTIC OCEAN
CANADA
PACIFIC OCEAN
0 200 400 Miles
0 400 Kilometers

Seattle
Portland
130°W
40°N
San Francisco
PACIFIC OCEAN
Las Vegas
Los Angeles
San Diego
30°N
120°W
Honolulu
PACIFIC OCEAN
0 100 Miles
0 100 Kilometers
110°W

Salt Lake City
Denver
Phoenix
El Paso
MEXICO

CANADA
Lake Superior
Lake Huron
Lake Michigan
Lake Ontario
Lake Erie

Minneapolis
Milwaukee
Detroit
Syracuse
Boston
Providence
Buffalo
Hartford
Des Moines
Chicago
Toledo
Cleveland
New York City
Omaha
Indianapolis
Pittsburgh
Philadelphia
Columbus
Baltimore
Kansas City
St. Louis
Cincinnati
Washington, D.C.
Louisville
Virginia Beach
Nashville
Charlotte
70°W
ATLANTIC OCEAN
Oklahoma City
Memphis
Atlanta
Charleston
Dallas
Houston
San Antonio
New Orleans
Jacksonville
Tampa
Gulf of Mexico
Miami
90°W
80°W
0 200 400 Miles
0 200 400 Kilometers
Albers Equal-Area Projection
N E W S

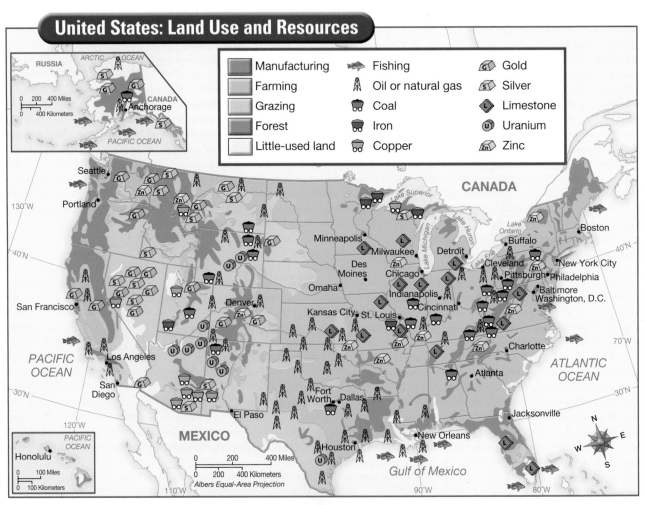

United States: Land Use and Resources

- Manufacturing
- Farming
- Grazing
- Forest
- Little-used land
- Fishing
- Oil or natural gas
- Coal
- Iron
- Copper
- Gold (G)
- Silver (S)
- Limestone (L)
- Uranium (U)
- Zinc (Zn)

RUSSIA
ARCTIC OCEAN
CANADA
Anchorage
PACIFIC OCEAN
0 200 400 Miles
0 400 Kilometers

Seattle
Portland
130°W
40°N
San Francisco
PACIFIC OCEAN
Los Angeles
San Diego
30°N
120°W
El Paso
MEXICO
Denver
Kansas City
St. Louis
Fort Worth
Dallas
Houston

CANADA
Lake Superior
Lake Huron
Lake Michigan
Lake Ontario
Lake Erie

Minneapolis
Milwaukee
Detroit
Buffalo
Des Moines
Chicago
Cleveland
New York City
Omaha
Indianapolis
Pittsburgh
Philadelphia
Cincinnati
Baltimore
Washington, D.C.
Boston
Charlotte
70°W
ATLANTIC OCEAN
Atlanta
Jacksonville
New Orleans
Gulf of Mexico
90°W
80°W
Honolulu
PACIFIC OCEAN
0 100 Miles
0 100 Kilometers
110°W
0 200 400 Miles
0 200 400 Kilometers
Albers Equal-Area Projection
N E W S

A16

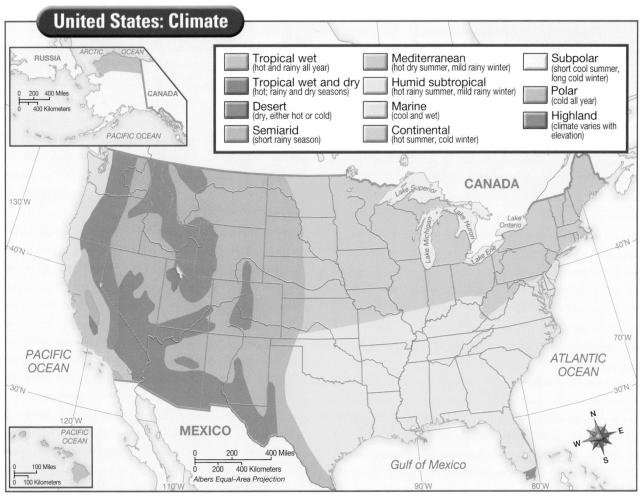

United States: Climate

Tropical wet (hot and rainy all year)
Tropical wet and dry (hot; rainy and dry seasons)
Desert (dry, either hot or cold)
Semiarid (short rainy season)
Mediterranean (hot dry summer, mild rainy winter)
Humid subtropical (hot rainy summer, mild rainy winter)
Marine (cool and wet)
Continental (hot summer, cold winter)
Subpolar (short cool summer, long cold winter)
Polar (cold all year)
Highland (climate varies with elevation)

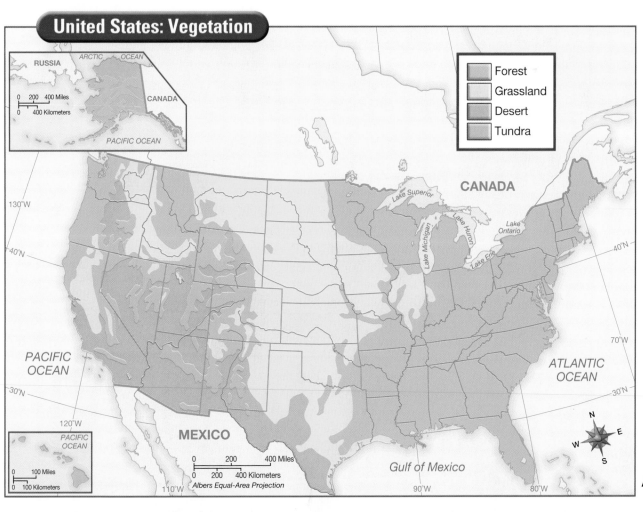

United States: Vegetation

Forest
Grassland
Desert
Tundra

A1

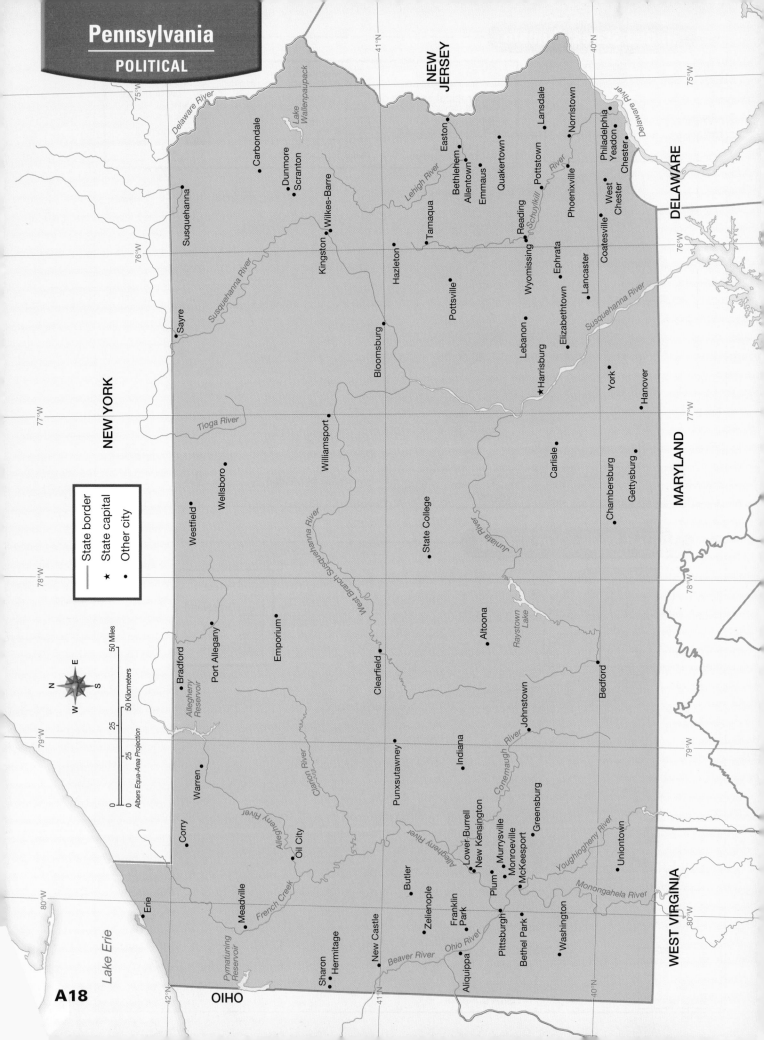

Pennsylvania
POLITICAL

NEW JERSEY

NEW YORK

DELAWARE

MARYLAND

WEST VIRGINIA

OIHO

Lake Erie

Legend:
- State border
- ★ State capital
- • Other city

50 Miles
50 Kilometers
Albers Equal-Area Projection

A18

Cities and features:

Erie
Corry
Warren
Bradford
Meadville
Sharon
Hermitage
New Castle
Oil City
Butler
Zelienople
Franklin Park
Aliquippa
Pittsburgh
Bethel Park
Washington
Plum
McKeesport
Monroeville
Murrysville
New Kensington
Lower Burrell
Greensburg
Uniontown
Johnstown
Indiana
Punxsutawney
Clearfield
Emporium
Port Allegany
Wellsboro
Westfield
Sayre
Susquehanna
Carbondale
Dunmore
Scranton
Wilkes-Barre
Kingston
Williamsport
Bloomsburg
Hazleton
State College
Altoona
Bedford
Carlisle
Chambersburg
Gettysburg
Pottsville
Tamaqua
Lebanon
Harrisburg ★
York
Hanover
Elizabethtown
Lancaster
Ephrata
Reading
Wyomissing
Easton
Bethlehem
Allentown
Emmaus
Quakertown
Pottstown
Lansdale
Norristown
Philadelphia
Yeadon
Chester
West Chester
Coatesville
Phoenixville

Rivers and water features:

Lake Erie
Pymatuning Reservoir
French Creek
Beaver River
Ohio River
Allegheny River
Clarion River
Allegheny Reservoir
Youghiogheny River
Monongahela River
Conemaugh River
Juniata River
Raystown Lake
West Branch Susquehanna River
Tioga River
Susquehanna River
Lehigh River
Schuylkill River
Delaware River
Lake Wallenpaupack

Latitude/Longitude:
41°N, 40°N, 42°N
75°W, 76°W, 77°W, 78°W, 79°W, 80°W

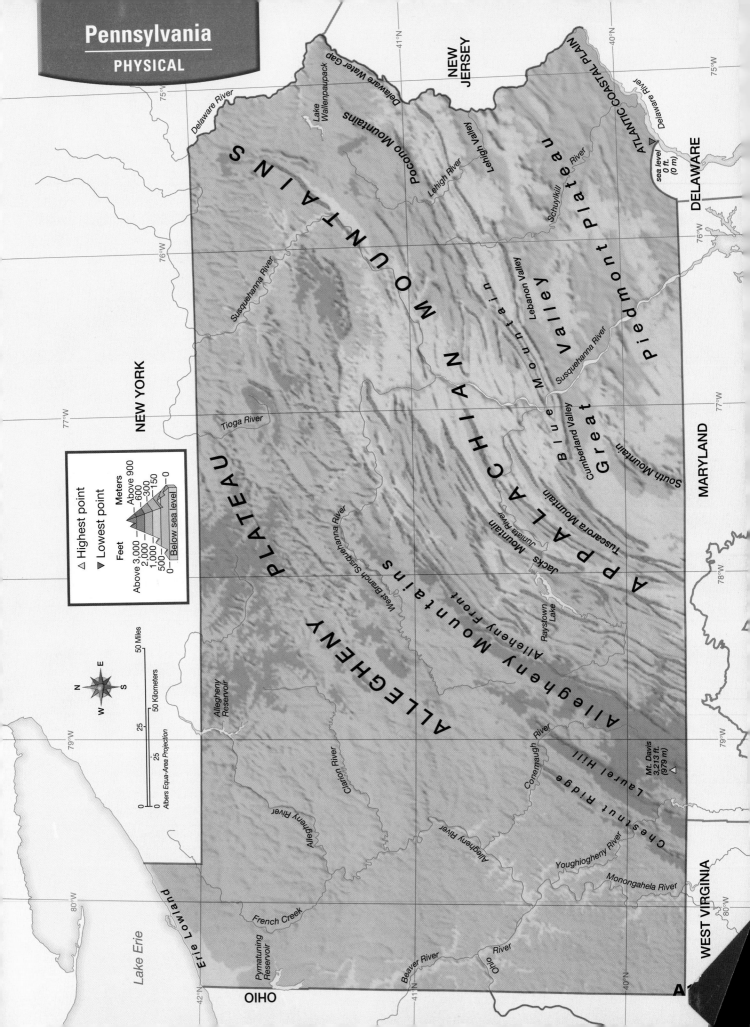

Pennsylvania
PHYSICAL

NEW JERSEY

NEW YORK

OHIO

DELAWARE

MARYLAND

WEST VIRGINIA

Lake Erie

Erie Lowland

ALLEGHENY PLATEAU

APPALACHIAN MOUNTAINS

Great Valley

Piedmont

ATLANTIC COASTAL PLAIN

Pocono Mountains

Allegheny Mountains

Allegheny Front

Chestnut Ridge

Laurel Hill

Blue Mountain

Lebanon Valley

Cumberland Valley

South Mountain

Tuscarora Mountain

Jacks Mountain

Delaware River
Lake Wallenpaupack
Delaware Water Gap
Lehigh River
Lehigh Valley
Schuylkill River
Delaware River
sea level
0 ft.
(0 m)

Susquehanna River
Susquehanna River
Tioga River
West Branch Susquehanna River
Juniata River
Raystown Lake

Allegheny Reservoir
Clarion River
Allegheny River
Allegheny River
Conemaugh River
Mt. Davis
3,213 ft.
(979 m)
Youghiogheny River
Monongahela River

Pymatuning Reservoir
French Creek
Beaver River
Ohio River
River

△ Highest point
▽ Lowest point

Feet	Meters
Above 3,000	Above 900
2,000	600
1,000	300
500	150
0	0
Below sea level	Below sea level

50 Miles
50 Kilometers
25
25
0
0

Albers Equal-Area Projection

N
S
W
E

41°N
41°N
40°N
40°N
42°N
41°N

75°W
75°W
76°W
76°W
77°W
77°W
78°W
79°W
79°W
80°W
80°W

A1

Geography Terms

1. **basin**   bowl-shaped area of land surrounded by higher land
2. **bay**   an inlet of the sea or some other body of water, usually smaller than a gulf
3. **bluff**   high, steep face of rock or earth
4. **canyon**   deep, narrow valley with steep sides
5. **cape**   point of land that extends into water
6. **cataract**   large waterfall
7. **channel**   deepest part of a body of water
8. **cliff**   high, steep face of rock or earth
9. **coast**   land along a sea or ocean
10. **coastal plain**   area of flat land along a sea or ocean
11. **delta**   triangle-shaped area of land at the mouth of a river
12. **desert**   dry land with few plants
13. **dune**   hill of sand piled up by the wind

14. **fall line**   area along which rivers form waterfalls or rapids as the rivers drop to lower land
15. **floodplain**   flat land that is near the edges of a river and is formed by silt deposited by floods
16. **foothills**   hilly area at the base of a mountain
17. **glacier**   large ice mass that moves slowly down a mountain or across land
18. **gulf**   part of a sea or ocean extending into the land, usually larger than a bay
19. **hill**   land that rises above the land around it
20. **inlet**   any area of water extending into the land from a larger body of water
21. **island**   land that has water on all sides
22. **isthmus**   narrow strip of land connecting two larger areas of land
23. **lagoon**   body of shallow water
24. **lake**   body of water with land on all sides
25. **marsh**   lowland with moist soil and tall grasses

A20

26	**mesa**	flat-topped mountain with steep sides

26 **mesa** flat-topped mountain with steep sides

27 **mountain** highest kind of land

28 **mountain pass** gap between mountains

29 **mountain range** row of mountains

30 **mouth of river** place where a river empties into another body of water

31 **oasis** area of water and fertile land in a desert

32 **ocean** body of salt water larger than a sea

33 **peak** top of a mountain

34 **peninsula** land that is almost completely surrounded by water

35 **plain** area of flat or gently rolling low land

36 **plateau** area of high, mostly flat land

37 **reef** ridge of sand, rock, or coral that lies at or near the surface of a sea or ocean

38 **river** large stream of water that flows across the land

39 **riverbank** land along a river

40 **savanna** area of grassland and scattered trees

41 **sea** body of salt water smaller than an ocean

42 **sea level** the level of the surface of an ocean or a sea

43 **slope** side of a hill or mountain

44 **source of river** place where a river begins

45 **strait** narrow channel of water connecting two larger bodies of water

46 **swamp** area of low, wet land with trees

47 **timberline** line on a mountain above which it is too cold for trees to grow

48 **tributary** stream or river that flows into a larger stream or river

49 **valley** low land between hills or mountains

50 **volcano** opening in the earth, often raised, through which lava, rock, ashes, and gases are forced out

51 **waterfall** steep drop from a high place to a lower place in a stream or river

Introduction

> **"America is a tune.
> It must be sung together."**
> —Gerald Stanley Lee,
> minister and writer (1862–1944)

Learning About the United States

Americans are proud of their country. As you read this book, you will find out why. You will learn about the four regions of the United States—the Northeast, South, Middle West, and West. You will also learn about the country's land, water, and climate. In addition, you will find out about the many different people of this country. All of these things will help you understand why people are proud to be citizens of the United States.

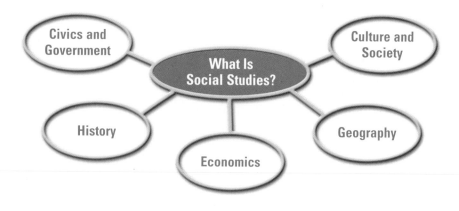

Civics and Government

Culture and Society

What Is Social Studies?

History

Economics

Geography

Why Geography Matters

The study of Earth and the people who live on it is called **geography**. People who study geography are called **geographers**. Geographers do much more than find places on maps. They learn all they can about places and the people who live there.

Themes of Geography

Geographers sometimes divide geography into five themes, or key topics. Most of the maps in this book focus on one of the five themes. Keeping the themes in mind will help you think like a geographer.

Location
Everything on Earth has its own **location**—the place where it can be found.

Human-Environment Interactions
Humans and their surroundings **interact**, or affect one another. The actions of people change the environment. The environment also affects people.

Place
Every location on Earth has features that make it different from all other locations. Features formed by nature are called **physical features**. Physical features include landforms, bodies of water, and plant life. Features created by people are called **human features**. Human features include buildings, roads, and people themselves.

Movement
People, things, and ideas move every day. Each movement affects the world in some way.

Regions
Areas on Earth whose features make them different from other areas can be called **regions**. A region can be described by its physical features or by its human features.

GEOGRAPHY THEME

Essential Elements of Geography

Geographers use six other topics to understand Earth and its people. These topics are the six essential elements, or most important parts, of geography. Thinking about the six essential elements of geography will help you learn more about the world and your place in it.

• GEOGRAPHY •

The World in Spatial Terms

Spatial means "having to do with space." Every place on Earth has its own space, or location. Geographers want to know where places are located and why they are located where they are.

Places and Regions

Geographers often group places into regions. They do this to show that all the places in a group have a similar physical or human feature.

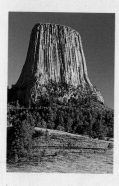

Physical Systems

Geographers study the physical parts of the surface of Earth. For example, they study climate, landforms, and bodies of water.

Human Systems

Geographers study where people have settled, how they earn a living, and what laws they have made.

Environment and Society

People's actions affect the environment. The environment also affects people's activities.

The Uses of Geography

Knowing how to use maps, globes, and other geographic tools helps people in their day-to-day lives.

REVIEW **What is geography?**

Why History Matters

VOCABULARY

history   historian   oral history   analyze
chronology   evidence   point of view

The study of **history**, or what happened in the past, is very important to the people of the United States. History teaches people how events from the past affect the present. By studying history we can find links between past and present events. These links help us understand how events in the present will affect the future.

Learning About Time

Understanding history requires knowing when events took place. The order in which events take place is called **chronology** (kruh•NAH•luh•jee). **Historians**, or people who study the past, look closely at the chronology of events. This helps them better understand how one event affects another and how the past and the present connect.

Finding Evidence

How do historians learn about the past? One way is by finding **evidence**, or proof, of when, why, where, and how things happened. Historians read books and newspapers from long ago. They study old diaries, letters, and postcards. They look at paintings and photographs from the past. They also listen to oral histories. An **oral history** is a story of an event told aloud. Historians use these different kinds of evidence to piece together the history of places and people.

Old photographs and newspapers are examples of evidence.

Identifying Points of View

Historians think about why different people of the past said or wrote what they did. They try to understand the different people's points of view. A **point of view** is how a person sees things. It can be affected by whether a person is young or old, male or female, rich or poor. Background and experiences also affect point of view. People with different points of view may have different ideas about the same event.

To understand points of view about an event, historians learn about the people who took part in the event. They find out as much as possible about how people lived long ago. This helps them get a better idea of the actions and feelings of those people.

Drawing Conclusions

After historians have identified the facts about a historical event, they still have work to do. They need to analyze the event. To **analyze** an event is to examine each part of it and relate the parts to each other. Analyzing an event allows historians to draw conclusions about how and why it happened.

REVIEW What is history?

People from different cultures and age groups often have different points of view. By studying the objects people use (left), historians can learn about their ways of life.

·SKILLS· READING

Compare Primary and Secondary Sources

VOCABULARY

primary source   secondary source

▶ WHY IT MATTERS

People who study the past look for evidence, or proof. They want to be sure they know what really happened. They look for evidence in two different kinds of sources—primary sources and secondary sources.

▶ WHAT YOU NEED TO KNOW

Primary sources are records made by people who saw or took part in an event. They may have written their thoughts in journals or diaries. They may have told their stories in letters, poems, or songs. They may have given speeches. They may have painted pictures or taken photographs. Objects made or used during an event can also be primary sources. All these primary sources are records of real words, pictures, or objects from people who saw what happened.

The official program for the opening of the Golden Gate Bridge included the bridge's toll rates (far right). Engineers inspected the Golden Gate Bridge during its construction (center).

There's No Delay The Gate Bridge Way
No Waits - No Inconvenience
The Direct Route to the Redwood Empire, Sacramento Valley and Pacific Northwest

TOLL RATES

AUTOMOBILES.... taxis, hearses, commercial or light delivery automobiles (weighing less than 3000 lbs. unladen), with driver and not to exceed four passengers.................$ .50
Additional passengers, each... .05
COMMUTE....... Passenger automobiles only, with driver and not to exceed four passengers. Thirty (30) one way trips in any sixty (60) day period, including date of sale............... 11.00
Additional passengers, each... .05
TRAILERS........ drawn by automobiles.. .50
Passengers riding trailer, each.. .05
MOTORCYCLES... or passenger tricars, with driver and one additional passenger................. .25
Additional passengers, each... .05
PEDESTRIANS..... including bicycle, each way... .05

GENERAL RULES

The Golden Gate Bridge and Highway District has erected signs, indicating each entrance to the Golden Gate Bridge. Any vehicle which passes such signs becomes immediately liable for the prescribed toll for such vehicle.
Commutation books may be purchased at the toll booths or at the office of the District at the San Francisco Toll Plaza. The coupons of any one book, when presented by driver of a car at the toll gate, whether or not he is the original purchaser of such book, will be honored to cover transit of the car he is driving at the time and no other car that may be accompanying him. The book of issue must be shown at the time of passage.
Commutation books may be redeemed at the office of the District at the San Francisco Toll Plaza at their sale price, less used coupons, if any, computed at 90 cents each, if presented by original purchaser for redemption within 60 days from their date of expiration.
The following charges will be made for special services not included in the toll rate:
Tow charge on Bridge $1.50
Tire change 1.00
Gas Delivery .... .50 first gallon.
.... .30 each additional gallon
Truck and bus pickup and tow................ 4.50 per hour
Extra work on bus or truck..................... 1.50 per hour
Inspection of vehicle subject to permit:
At Toll Plaza, San Francisco................... Free
Within 10 miles of Toll Plaza.................. $5.00
More than 10 miles from Toll Plaza....... Actual cost as determined by Golden Gate Bridge and Highway District.
All disabled cars will be picked up immediately and towed to San Francisco Toll Plaza by the District's emergency towing service. Such pickup service will be charged for at the foregoing rates. After disabled cars have been brought to the Toll Plaza, the owner may employ outside services if he so desires.

SPECIAL TRAFFIC RULES

THE GOLDEN GATE BRIDGE is a PUBLIC HIGHWAY and the provisions of the VEHICLE CODE and other laws relating to public highways are applicable thereto.
EMERGENCY PHONES have been installed along the roadway. When putting through a call, announce the number of the call box you are using.
BICYCLES will be permitted only on the Bridge sidewalks, where they may be pushed, not ridden.
VEHICLES must not cross center line strip, as indicated by reflector markers.
NO "U" TURNS shall be made on Bridge except with permission and under direction of the California Highway Patrol, or uniformed employee of the Golden Gate Bridge and Highway District.
TIRE CHANGES and repairs shall not be made on the Bridge except when authorized by a member of the California Highway Patrol and done in his presence.
SLOW-MOVING VEHICLES must keep to the extreme right side of the roadway.
NO VEHICLE MAY leave the Bridge or its approaches and enter upon army reservations except by special authority granted by the Commanding General of the Ninth Corps Area. Locked gates and guards are maintained on the reservation roadways to prevent violation of this clause.

Drive Carefully . . . . . Enjoy the Bridge Yourself and Help Others Enjoy It

Secondary sources are records written by people who were not at an event. Books written by authors who only heard about or read about an event are secondary sources. So too are magazine articles and newspaper stories written by people who did not take part in the event. Paintings or drawings by artists who did not see the event are also secondary sources.

▶ PRACTICE THE SKILL

Examine the photographs and documents about the Golden Gate Bridge in California. Most are primary sources. One is a secondary source. Can you tell which is which?

1. Which record was made by someone who saw the building of the Golden Gate Bridge?
2. Which record gives facts about the Golden Gate Bridge, such as its length and its cost?
3. How is the program for the opening of the Golden Gate Bridge a primary source?
4. What can you learn from the secondary source that you cannot learn from the primary sources?

▶ APPLY WHAT YOU LEARNED

Work with a partner to find examples of primary and secondary sources in your textbook. Discuss why you think each source is a primary source or a secondary source.

Golden Gate Bridge today (left). You can learn about the Golden Gate Bridge on some Web sites (above).

Why Economics Matters

VOCABULARY
economy   economics

Hospitals, schools, banks, and stores—these are just a few of the many places where people work. Most people work to be able to buy what they need or want and to save for the future. By working, buying, and saving, they are taking part in the economy. An **economy** is the way people use resources to meet their needs. The study of how people do this is called **economics**.

In this book you will read about how Americans make, buy, sell, and trade goods to meet their needs. You will also discover how the United States' economy has changed over time and how it came to be what it is today.

REVIEW **What is the study of how people meet their needs and wants?**

When you earn, save, or spend money, you are taking part in the economy.

Why Civics and Government Matter

VOCABULARY

government   civics

citizen

To live together peacefully, people form governments. A **government** is a system of leaders and laws that helps people live safely together in a community, a state, or a country. As a citizen of the United States, you follow the laws of your city or town, state, and country. A **citizen** is a member of a country, state, city, or town.

Harcourt Horizons: Pennsylvania tells about the role of Americans in governments. It also tells how the government of the United States came to be and how it changed over time. As you read this book, you will learn about the leaders and laws in United States history.

The study of government connects with civics. **Civics** is the study of citizenship. As you read this book, you will learn about the rights and responsibilities of citizens.

REVIEW   How are government and civics different?

When he became President, John F. Kennedy talked about the meaning of citizenship.

Why Culture and Society Matter

VOCABULARY

culture   society   heritage

As you read this book, you will find out about the people who live in the four regions of the United States. You will learn about the **culture**, or way of life, of these people. Studying the way of life of a group of people involves learning about what things they do and what ideas they believe in. It also means learning about how they dress and what they eat.

Each human group, or **society**, has a culture. Many groups of people have contributed to the United States' culture. This book gives information about the different cultures that have come together in the United States. It also describes American **heritage**, or the ways of life that have been passed down through history.

REVIEW How are culture and society related?

Traditional costumes and dances are often an important part of a culture's heritage.

A View of the United States

A modern globe

People use geography.

A View of the United States

❝ The sheer size of the United States has been an important influence on how Americans think and act. ❞

—Elizabeth Berg, *Countries of the World: USA,* 1999

Preview the Content

Scan the titles and headings in this unit. Use them to fill in a K-W-L chart like the one below. List what you know and what you want to find out about the geography and regions of the United States. As you read the unit, note what you learned.

K (What I Know)	W (What I Want to Know)	L (What I Learned)

Preview the Vocabulary

Multiple Meanings   Words often have multiple, or several, meanings. Write each vocabulary word below in a sentence to show a meaning you know. Then look up each word in the Glossary and record its social studies meaning.

basin   channel   fuel   mouth   relief   trade

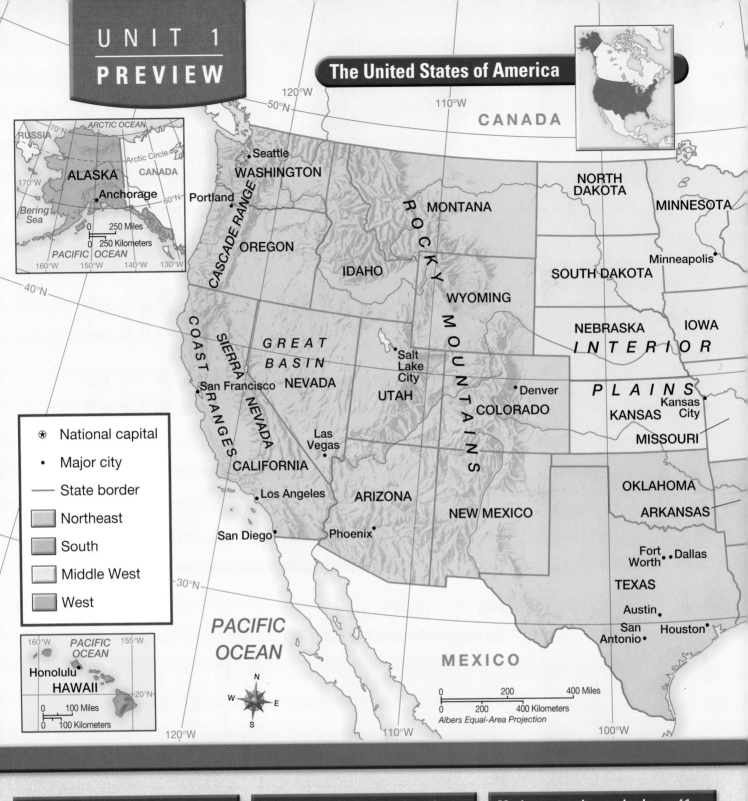

The United States of America

CANADA

Seattle
WASHINGTON

Portland

CASCADE RANGE

OREGON

IDAHO

MONTANA

ROCKY

NORTH DAKOTA

MINNESOTA

Minneapolis

SOUTH DAKOTA

WYOMING

M O U N T A I N S

NEBRASKA

IOWA

INTERIOR

GREAT
BASIN

Salt
Lake
City

NEVADA

San Francisco

SIERRA NEVADA

COAST RANGES

UTAH

Denver

COLORADO

PLAINS

KANSAS
City

KANSAS

MISSOURI

Las
Vegas

CALIFORNIA

Los Angeles

ARIZONA

NEW MEXICO

OKLAHOMA

ARKANSAS

San Diego

Phoenix

Fort
Worth • Dallas

TEXAS

Austin

San
Antonio

Houston

**PACIFIC
OCEAN**

MEXICO

0   200   400 Miles
0   200   400 Kilometers
Albers Equal-Area Projection

ALASKA (inset)
ARCTIC OCEAN
RUSSIA
Arctic Circle
ALASKA
CANADA
Anchorage
Bering
Sea
PACIFIC OCEAN
0   250 Miles
0   250 Kilometers

HAWAII (inset)
PACIFIC
OCEAN
Honolulu
HAWAII
0   100 Miles
0   100 Kilometers

Legend
- ⊛ National capital
- • Major city
- — State border
- Northeast
- South
- Middle West
- West

There are many ways to describe the locations of places on Earth.   p. 22

The United States has a variety of landforms and climates.   p. 28

Moving water changes land.   p. 41

12

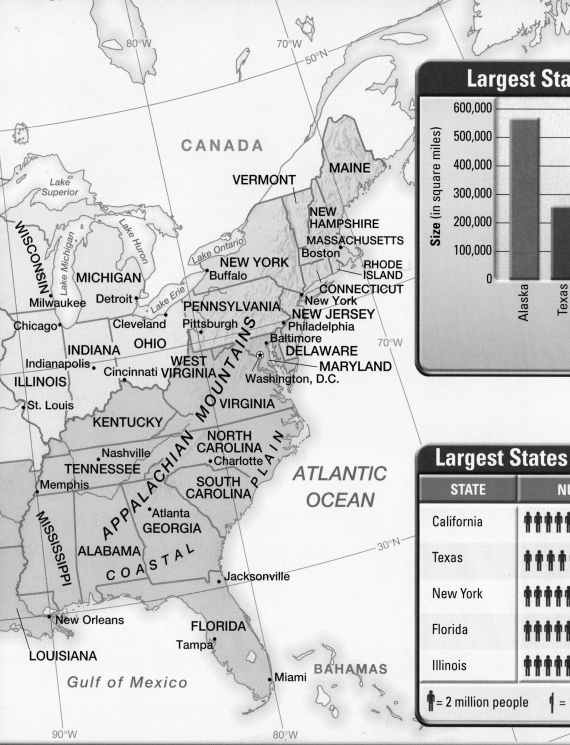

CANADA

WISCONSIN

Lake Superior

Lake Michigan

Lake Huron

Lake Ontario

Lake Erie

MICHIGAN

Milwaukee

Detroit

Chicago

Cleveland

INDIANA

OHIO

Indianapolis

Cincinnati

ILLINOIS

St. Louis

KENTUCKY

Nashville

TENNESSEE

Memphis

MISSISSIPPI

ALABAMA

GEORGIA

Atlanta

APPALACHIAN MOUNTAINS

COASTAL PLAIN

VERMONT

MAINE

NEW HAMPSHIRE

MASSACHUSETTS

Boston

NEW YORK

Buffalo

RHODE ISLAND

CONNECTICUT

New York

PENNSYLVANIA

NEW JERSEY

Pittsburgh

Philadelphia

Baltimore

DELAWARE

WEST VIRGINIA

MARYLAND

Washington, D.C.

VIRGINIA

NORTH CAROLINA

Charlotte

SOUTH CAROLINA

ATLANTIC OCEAN

Jacksonville

FLORIDA

Tampa

BAHAMAS

Miami

New Orleans

LOUISIANA

Gulf of Mexico

80°W 70°W 50°N

70°W

30°N

90°W 80°W

Largest States by Area

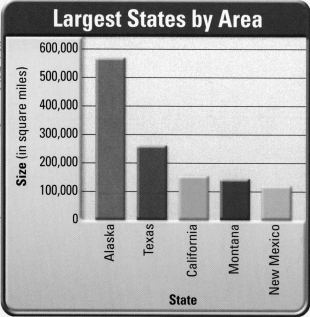

Size (in square miles)

600,000
500,000
400,000
300,000
200,000
100,000
0

Alaska | Texas | California | Montana | New Mexico

State

Largest States by Population

STATE	NUMBER OF PEOPLE
California	
Texas	
New York	
Florida	
Illinois	

👤 = 2 million people   👤 = 1 million people

People use natural resources to meet their needs. p. 49

The United States is divided into many kinds of regions. p. 60

The United States is made up of many cultures. p. 74

13

POEM

Mississippi

by Diane Siebert • illustrated by Greg Harlin

The Mississippi River, one of the longest rivers in the United States, stretches from Minnesota to the Gulf of Mexico. As the river makes its long journey through the center of the United States, it passes through many different landscapes. The "Mighty Mississippi," as it is often called, helped shape the land it flows through, and people all over the country depend on it in many ways. Read the following poem that describes the Mississippi River's journey from Minnesota to the Gulf of Mexico.

I am the river.
Come with me
And know my journey to the sea
As, cold and clear, I wander forth
From Lake Itasca in the north
Where water carves its bright designs
Upon the earth, amid the pines.

Here as a tiny creek I start
My journey through the nation's heart;
And fed by streams and lakes I grow
As north, then east, then south I flow
To Minneapolis and St. Paul
Where, strong and sure and swift, I fall
In currents harnessed for their might,
Creating power, heat, and light.

Then hugged by limestone bluffs that guide
My passage through the countryside,
My quiet currents move between
Rock Island, Davenport, Moline;
Past maples, oaks, and hickories—
The forests of the hardwood trees;
And past the farms and fields that lie
Beneath the broad midwestern sky.

Then dreaming dreams of long ago,
On down to Hannibal I flow,
Where happy memories remain
Of steamboats, and a man called Twain.

And I, the river, ever blessed
By waters from the east and west,
Now feel the great Missouri bring
Its music to the song I sing.
This river, Rocky Mountain–born,
Flows down past farms and fields of corn,
And near St. Louis, where we meet,
Its muddy rhythms, swift and sweet,
Unite with mine, and on we run—
Two mighty rivers, joined as one.

While from the east, from high plateaus,
The beautiful Ohio flows
To meet me, as do countless more;
And as these tributaries pour

Into me, all along my length,
They give to me their gathered strength
And tell me tales of history
While whispering their names to me:

The Wyaconda and the Crow.
The Wolf, the Bear, the Buffalo.
The Illinois, the Arkansas.
The Rock, the Red, the Chippewa.

I know them all and where they've been,
And faithfully I take them in,
Becoming deep, a mile-wide force
In conflict with a twisted course.

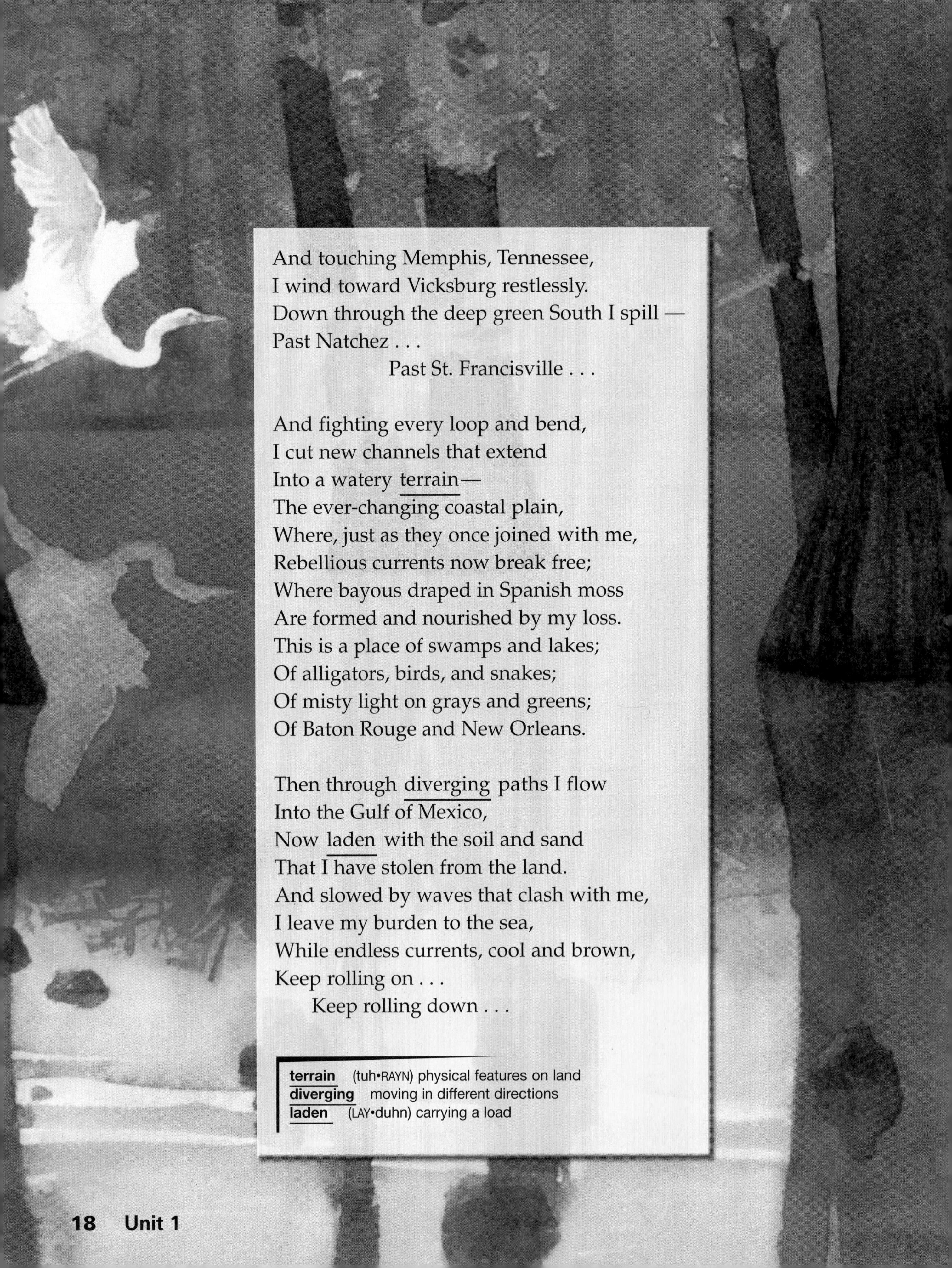

And touching Memphis, Tennessee,
I wind toward Vicksburg restlessly.
Down through the deep green South I spill —
Past Natchez . . .
                    Past St. Francisville . . .

And fighting every loop and bend,
I cut new channels that extend
Into a watery terrain—
The ever-changing coastal plain,
Where, just as they once joined with me,
Rebellious currents now break free;
Where bayous draped in Spanish moss
Are formed and nourished by my loss.
This is a place of swamps and lakes;
Of alligators, birds, and snakes;
Of misty light on grays and greens;
Of Baton Rouge and New Orleans.

Then through diverging paths I flow
Into the Gulf of Mexico,
Now laden with the soil and sand
That I have stolen from the land.
And slowed by waves that clash with me,
I leave my burden to the sea,
While endless currents, cool and brown,
Keep rolling on . . .
        Keep rolling down . . .

---

terrain   (tuh•RAYN) physical features on land
diverging   moving in different directions
laden   (LAY•duhn) carrying a load

I am the river,
Wide and deep,
Whose restless waters never sleep;
And as I move with currents strong,
I sing an old, enduring song
With rhythms wild and rhythms tame.
And Mississippi is my name.

Analyze the Literature

❶ Why do you think the author had the river describe its journey?

❷ Compare the landforms found near the Mississippi River to landforms found near a major river near you. What are the similarities and differences?

READ A BOOK

START THE UNIT PROJECT

A Travel Guide With your classmates, begin publishing a travel guide to the United States. In the travel guide describe the geography of the United States. Also write articles about the country's climate, natural resources, and economy. As you read Unit 1, write down topics that could go in your travel guide. You can use these notes as you publish the guide.

USE TECHNOLOGY

Visit The Learning Site at **www.harcourtschool.com** for additional activities, primary sources, and other resources to use in this unit.

YOSEMITE NATIONAL PARK

Located in California's Sierra Nevada, Yosemite National Park is famous for its beautiful mountain scenery. Tourists first started visiting the area in the 1850s, and Yosemite was made a national park in 1890. Today more than 4 million people visit the park each year.

LOCATE IT

Yosemite National Park

CALIFORNIA

1

Our Country's Geography

 **Pleasant it looked,
this newly created world.
Along the entire length and breadth
of the earth, our grandmother,
extended the green reflection
of her covering. . . .** **"**

—Native American myth, Winnebago tribe

Main Idea and Details

Focus Skill

The **main idea** is the most important idea in a passage. The **details** give more information that supports the main idea.

As you read this chapter, be sure to do the following.
- **List the main ideas.**
- **Under each main idea, list the supporting details.**

Main Idea

Detail   Detail

Where on Earth Is the United States?

When Christopher Columbus reached land after sailing across the Atlantic Ocean from Spain, he thought he was in Asia! Columbus described the land he found, but he could not accurately describe where on Earth he was. Could you?

Do you know where the United States is? You know that it is where you live. Suppose you had a friend in another country. Could you tell your friend where on Earth you live?

Our Global Address

To show where on Earth you live, you could use a globe. A globe is a model of Earth. Like Earth, it has the shape of a sphere, or ball. By describing where you live on Earth, you can give your global address.

To describe your global address, you might tell your friend on which half of Earth you live. Earth is a sphere; therefore, half of it is called a **hemisphere**. *Hemi* means "half." Halfway between the North Pole and the South Pole on a globe is a line called the **equator**. Every place north of the equator is in the Northern Hemisphere. Every place south of the equator is in the Southern Hemisphere. Since the United States is north of the equator, you could say to your friend that you live in the Northern Hemisphere.

FAST FACT
The world's largest globe is in Yarmouth, Maine. At its equator, this globe measures about 130 feet (40 m) around. That is about 60 times the size of your waist!

You can look at a globe to find where the United States is on Earth.

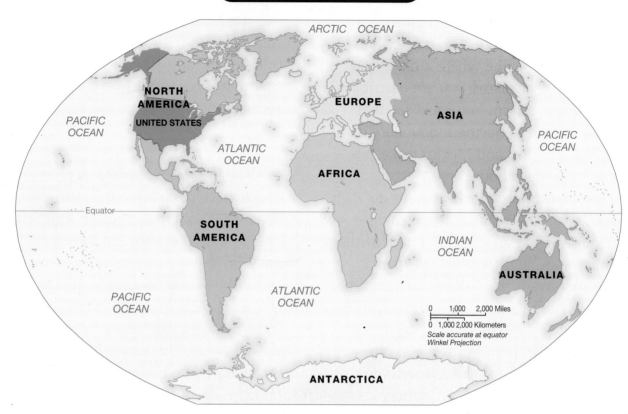

Oceans and Continents

ARCTIC OCEAN

NORTH AMERICA
UNITED STATES
EUROPE
ASIA
PACIFIC OCEAN
ATLANTIC OCEAN
PACIFIC OCEAN
AFRICA
Equator
SOUTH AMERICA
INDIAN OCEAN
AUSTRALIA
PACIFIC OCEAN
ATLANTIC OCEAN

0   1,000   2,000 Miles
0 1,000 2,000 Kilometers
Scale accurate at equator
Winkel Projection

ANTARCTICA

GEOGRAPHY THEME

Regions The Pacific Ocean is Earth's largest ocean. It covers more of Earth's surface than all the continents combined.

❖ What ocean separates North America and Europe?

Another line on the globe, called the **prime meridian**, divides Earth into the Western Hemisphere and the Eastern Hemisphere. The United States lies west of the prime meridian. Therefore, you could also tell your friend that you live in the Western Hemisphere.

To further describe your global address, you could tell your friend that you live on the continent of North America. **Continents** are the largest land areas on Earth. The seven continents, from the largest to the smallest, are Asia, Africa, North America, South America, Antarctica, Europe, and Australia.

Although the continents are large, they take up just a small part of Earth's surface. Water covers about three-fourths of the planet's surface. Most of Earth's water is in the oceans, and all of the oceans are connected. Together they make up one huge world ocean. The continents separate this world ocean into four parts—the Pacific Ocean, the Atlantic Ocean, the Indian Ocean, and the Arctic Ocean.

REVIEW What details can you use to describe the location of North America?
MAIN IDEA AND DETAILS

A North American Country

North America is made up of several countries, but three large countries cover most of the continent. You could tell your friend that the United States is one of these large countries in North America.

You could then compare the location of the United States to the locations of the two other large countries on the continent—Canada and Mexico.

When you describe where a place is in relation to other places, you are describing its **relative location**. You could say that Canada forms the northern boundary of the United States, and Mexico makes up the southwestern boundary.

You can also use bodies of water to describe relative location. The Pacific Ocean forms the western boundary of the United States, and the Atlantic Ocean shapes the country's eastern boundary. If you live in Louisiana, you might tell your friend that you live near the Gulf of Mexico. A **gulf** is a part of an ocean or sea extending into the land. The Gulf of Mexico, which is a part of the Atlantic Ocean, makes up much of the southern boundary of the United States.

What else could you tell your friend about where you live? You could name your state and describe its relative location. Most likely you live in one

of the 48 states that lie between Canada and Mexico. If you live in Alaska, you live to the northwest of Canada. People in Hawaii live in the middle of the Pacific Ocean, far west of North America.

REVIEW Where are 48 of the 50 American states located?

People from Many Places

People have been living in North America for thousands of years. The first people to live here were the American Indians, or Native Americans.

Today the Bering Strait separates North America and Asia. A **strait** is a narrow channel of water that connects two larger bodies of water. Thousands of years ago great sheets of ice covered much of Earth. So much water turned to ice that the water level in the oceans dropped. This caused an isthmus (IS•muhs) to appear between North America and Asia, where the Bering Strait is today. An **isthmus** is a narrow piece of land that connects two larger land areas.

The United States–Canada border extends 5,526 miles (8,893 km), making it the longest border in the world between two countries. This monument marks the border between the state of Washington in the United States and British Columbia in Canada.

LOCATE IT

Peace Garden

WASHINGTON

CHILDREN·OF·A·COMMON·MOTHER

Some people believe that the **ancestors**, or early family members, of Native Americans walked across this isthmus, or land bridge, from Asia. Once in North America, they moved south and east over thousands of years, settling the entire continent.

People reached North America from Europe much later. For several years Columbus and others who came after him did not realize it was another continent. Finally, an Italian explorer named Amerigo Vespucci (veh•SPOO•chee) decided that Columbus must have found a continent unknown to Europeans. In 1507 a mapmaker drew a map of the continent. He labeled it *America*, for Amerigo Vespucci. This was the first time the name America appeared on a map.

Over time people came from all over the world to live in what is now the

• SCIENCE AND TECHNOLOGY •

The Compass

A compass is the main tool used for finding directions on Earth. During the 1100s, people in both China and Europe discovered that when a metal called lodestone was floated on a stick in water, the stick tended to point north. Once people could find north, they could find any other direction. Today, sailors and airplane pilots use compasses to help them guide ships and planes around the world.

United States of America. People from so many places came that, in the 1850s, writer Herman Melville wrote, "We are not a nation so much as a world."

REVIEW How do some people believe the first people came to North America?

LESSON 1
REVIEW

 MAIN IDEA AND DETAILS What details are used to describe a global address? a relative location?

1 **BIG IDEA** Where is the United States located on Earth?

2 **VOCABULARY** Use the term **relative location** in order to describe where your community is in relation to another community, another state, or an ocean.

3 **GEOGRAPHY** Which two states are not physically connected to the other 48 states in the United States?

4 **CULTURE** Who were the first people to live in North America?

5 **HISTORY** Who is North America named for?

6 **CRITICAL THINKING—Analyze** Why do you think geographers divide Earth into hemispheres?

PERFORMANCE—Make a Globe Use a blown-up balloon to make a model of Earth, showing where the United States is. On the balloon, draw and label the equator, the prime meridian, the four hemispheres, North America, the United States, and its surrounding bodies of water. Include Alaska and Hawaii. Draw a star to show where your community is on the globe. Share your model with your classmates.

·SKILLS·

MAP AND GLOBE

Use Latitude and Longitude

<table>
<tr><td colspan="2" align="center">**VOCABULARY**</td></tr>
<tr><td>absolute location</td><td>lines of longitude</td></tr>
<tr><td>lines of latitude</td><td>meridian</td></tr>
<tr><td align="center" colspan="2">parallel</td></tr>
</table>

▶ WHY IT MATTERS

Long ago, mapmakers developed a system of lines that could be used to describe **absolute location**, or an exact position on Earth's surface. Using this system, you can give the global address for any place on Earth.

▶ WHAT YOU NEED TO KNOW

On a globe or a map, one set of lines runs east and west. These lines are called **lines of latitude** (LA•tuh•tood).

Because all the lines of latitude are the same distance apart, they are also called **parallels** (PAIR•uh•lelz). The equator itself is a line of latitude that divides Earth in half.

Find the equator on Map A. It is marked 0°. Lines of latitude are measured in degrees north and south of the equator.

Another set of lines runs north and south. They are called **lines of longitude** (LAHN•juh•tood). These lines are also called **meridians** (muh•RIH•dee•uhnz). Lines of longitude meet at the North and

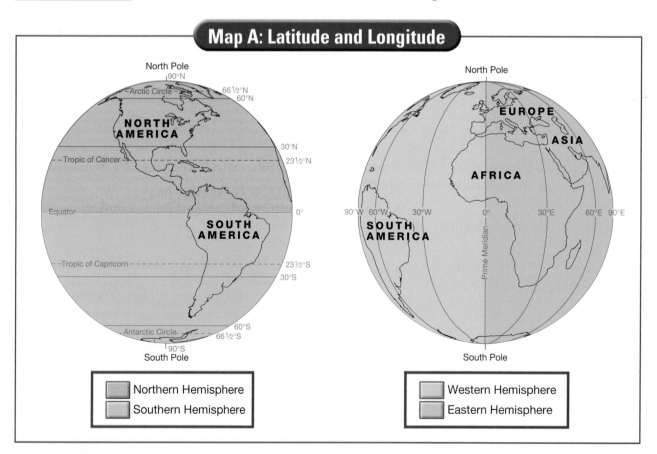

Map A: Latitude and Longitude

North Pole
90°N
Arctic Circle — 66½°N
60°N
NORTH AMERICA
30°N
Tropic of Cancer — 23½°N
Equator — 0°
SOUTH AMERICA
Tropic of Capricorn — 23½°S
30°S
Antarctic Circle — 60°S
66½°S
90°S
South Pole

| | Northern Hemisphere |
| | Southern Hemisphere |

North Pole
EUROPE
ASIA
AFRICA
90°W 60°W 30°W 0° 30°E 60°E 90°E
SOUTH AMERICA
Prime Meridian
South Pole

| | Western Hemisphere |
| | Eastern Hemisphere |

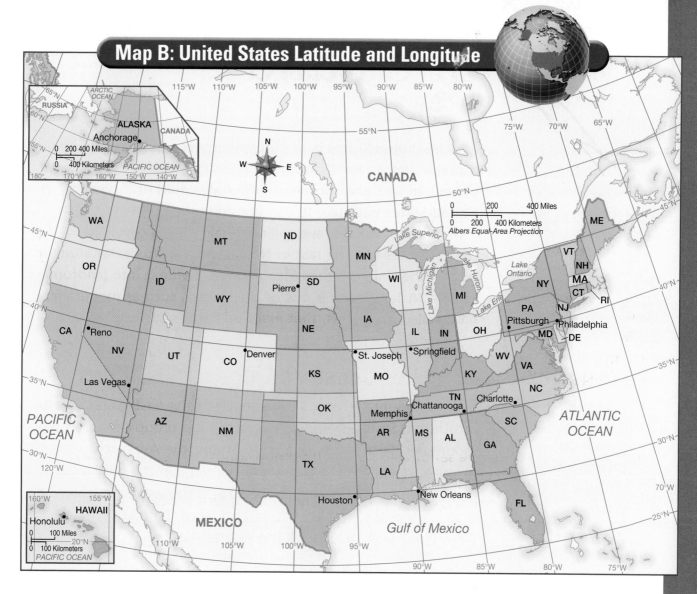

Map B: United States Latitude and Longitude

South Poles and are farthest apart at the equator. The prime meridian is a line of longitude.

Find the prime meridian on Map A. Like the equator, it is marked 0°. Lines of longitude are measured in degrees east and west of the prime meridian.

The grid formed by lines of latitude and longitude can help you describe the absolute location of any place on Earth. You can give the location by naming the line of latitude and the line of longitude closest to it. Name its latitude first and then its longitude. For example, the absolute location of Houston, Texas, is 30°N, 95°W.

▶ PRACTICE THE SKILL

Use Map B to answer these questions.

1. What city is located at 40°N, 75°W?
2. Between which lines of latitude does most of the United States lie?
3. Which lines of latitude and longitude best give the absolute location of Denver, Colorado?

▶ APPLY WHAT YOU LEARNED

Use a map of your region to find the absolute location of your community.

Practice your map and globe skills with the **GeoSkills CD-ROM**.

2

The Land

Focus Skill

MAIN IDEA AND DETAILS

As you read, identify the different kinds of landforms in the United States.

BIG IDEA

There are a variety of land-forms across the United States.

VOCABULARY

landform
mountain range
sea level
piedmont
plateau
coastal plain
peninsula
basin
canyon

The United States is the fourth-largest country in the world. It covers almost 4 million square miles (10 million square km) of land. In fact, the continent of Europe could fit inside the United States with plenty of room to spare!

Mountains, valleys, and rolling, grassy plains cover the United States and the rest of North America. To better study the land of the United States, geographers divide it into landform regions. A landform is one of the shapes, such as mountains, hills, valleys, or plains, that make up Earth's surface.

Our Country's Largest Mountains

Large mountain ranges cover much of the eastern and western United States. A mountain range is a group of connected mountains. In the eastern United States, the Appalachian (a•puh•LAY•chee•uhn) Mountains stretch about 1,500 miles (2,400 km) from Alabama to Canada. In the western United States, the Rocky Mountains extend more than 3,000 miles (4,830 km) from Mexico all the way to Alaska.

The Rocky Mountains are the second-longest mountain range in the world.

FAST FACT

The Rocky Mountain Range is so long that it could stretch all the way across the Atlantic Ocean from New York City to Paris, France!

The Appalachian National Scenic Trail

Understanding Environment and Society

One way to see all of the Appalachian Mountains is to hike the Appalachian National Scenic Trail, the longest marked walking path in the United States. It runs from Georgia to Maine. Most people use the trail for day-hikes. Every year a few hundred people hike the entire 2,167-mile (3,488-km) trail. It can take them five to seven months to complete the trip.

The Appalachian Mountains are the oldest mountains on our continent. They formed about 250 million years ago. Over time, their peaks have worn away, making the mountains appear rounded. Today most of the mountains in the Appalachians are less than 6,000 feet (1,830 m) tall. Even the tallest peak, Mount Mitchell in North Carolina, rises just 6,684 feet (2,037 m) above sea level. **Sea level** is the level at the surface of the oceans. It is used as a starting point in measuring the height and depth of landforms.

On the eastern side of the Appalachians is an area of high land that is called the Piedmont (PEED•mahnt). A **piedmont** is an area at or near the foot of a mountain. The Piedmont stretches from New Jersey to Alabama.

The Rocky Mountains formed about 90 million years ago. These mountains are much taller and more rugged than the Appalachians. More than 50 peaks in Colorado alone are higher than 14,000 feet (4,267 m). Unlike the rounded peaks of the Appalachians, the peaks of the Rocky Mountains are sharp and jagged.

In 1893 poet Katharine Lee Bates traveled up one of the peaks of the Rocky Mountains in Colorado. Upon reaching the top, she wrote, "All the wonder of America seemed displayed there." The view led Bates to write her poem "America the Beautiful."

REVIEW How do the Appalachians and the Rocky Mountains differ from each other?

The Largest Plains

From the Rocky Mountains, Bates described seeing "amber waves of grain." She was looking at America's largest plains—the Interior Plains. These low, grassy lands cover much of the middle part of the United States. They extend north from Mexico, across the middle of the United States, and into Canada.

In the eastern part of the Interior Plains, known as the Central Plains, wide rivers, grassy hills, and some forests cover the land. The Great Lakes lie in the northern part of the Central Plains. These five connected lakes—Superior, Michigan, Huron, Erie, and Ontario—are the largest group of freshwater lakes in the world.

Farther west, the Interior Plains become much flatter in what geographers call the Great Plains. Here the land has almost no trees and fewer rivers. In 1847 a woman traveling by wagon across the Great Plains described the land in her journal. She wrote, "There is nothing to see but the sky and ground. Not a tree or bush or house as far as you can see and as level as a floor."

Most of the Interior Plains are flat, but there are some hills there. In a few places, such as the Black Hills of South Dakota and the Ozark Plateau (pla•TOH) in Missouri and Arkansas, the land rises sharply. A **plateau** is mostly flat land that rises above the surrounding land. Many parts of the Ozark Plateau and the Black Hills are covered with low mountains and forests.

Another large area of plains, called the Coastal Plain, stretches inland from the Atlantic Ocean and the Gulf of Mexico. A **coastal plain** is low land that lies along an ocean or other large body of water.

Along the Atlantic Coast in Massachusetts, the Coastal Plain is a narrow strip of land only 10 miles (16 km) wide. From there it becomes hundreds of miles wide as it stretches south to include the Florida peninsula (puh•NIN•suh•luh). Land that is almost entirely surrounded by water is a **peninsula**. From Florida the Coastal Plain extends west along the Gulf of Mexico into Texas and Mexico.

REVIEW What details would you use to describe the Coastal and Interior Plains?
MAIN IDEA AND DETAILS

So much wheat and other grains grow on the Great Plains that this area is sometimes called America's "breadbasket."

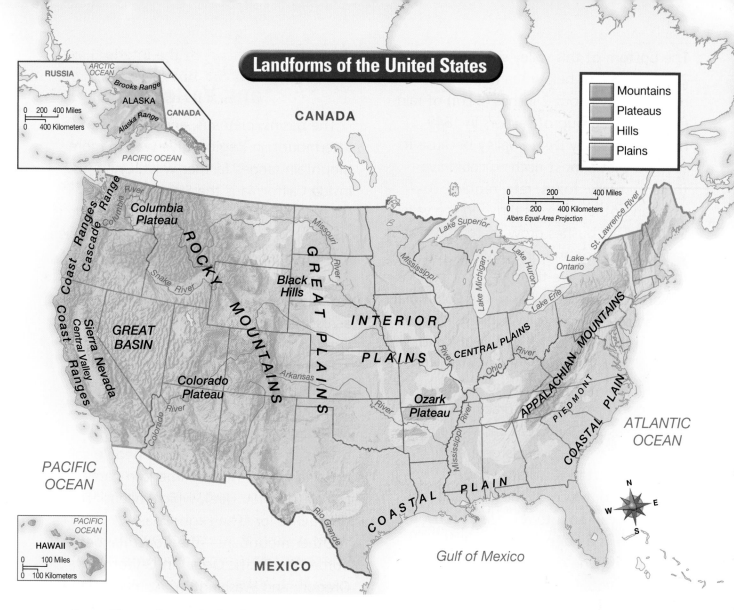

Landforms of the United States

Mountains	
Plateaus	
Hills	
Plains	

RUSSIA
ARCTIC OCEAN
Brooks Range
ALASKA
Alaska Range
CANADA
0 200 400 Miles
0 400 Kilometers
PACIFIC OCEAN

CANADA

Coast Ranges
Cascade Range
Columbia River
Columbia Plateau
ROCKY MOUNTAINS
Snake River
Missouri River
Black Hills
GREAT PLAINS
Lake Superior
St. Lawrence River
Lake Huron
Lake Michigan
Lake Ontario
Lake Erie
INTERIOR
PLAINS
CENTRAL PLAINS
Ohio River
APPALACHIAN MOUNTAINS
Sierra Nevada
Central Valley
Coast Ranges
GREAT BASIN
Colorado Plateau
Colorado River
Arkansas River
Ozark Plateau
Mississippi River
PIEDMONT
COASTAL PLAIN
ATLANTIC OCEAN

0 200 400 Miles
0 200 400 Kilometers
Albers Equal-Area Projection

PACIFIC OCEAN

HAWAII
PACIFIC OCEAN
0 100 Miles
0 100 Kilometers

Rio Grande
COASTAL PLAIN
MEXICO
Gulf of Mexico

N E S W

GEOGRAPHY THEME

Place Four major landforms in the United States are mountains, plateaus, hills, and plains.

❓ What kind of landform covers most of the middle of the country?

The Land Between the Mountains

Between the Rocky Mountains and other large mountain ranges farther west lies an area that geographers sometimes call the Intermountain Region, or "the land between the mountains." This part of the United States is dry and mostly desert.

Because the Intermountain Region is covered mostly with mountains, valleys, plateaus, and basins, it is often called the Basin and Range Region. A **basin** is low, bowl-shaped land with higher ground around it. An area called the Great Basin covers the middle of the Intermountain Region. The Great Basin stretches across Nevada and parts of five neighboring states. It is the largest desert area in the United States.

At the basin's western edge, in California, lies Death Valley. This is the lowest and driest place in North America.

Chapter 1 ▪ **31**

The bottom of this valley sits more than 280 feet (85 m) below sea level and receives only about 2 inches (5 cm) of rain each year. A group of settlers in 1849 named the valley Death Valley because it seemed that almost nothing could live there. Actually, foxes, rats, reptiles, coyotes, and other animals thrive in the valley. Some desert bushes grow there, too. The valley is too hot and dry, however, for most people to live there.

North of the Great Basin, the Columbia Plateau covers parts of Washington, Oregon, and Idaho. Mostly shrubs and grasses grow among the plateau's cliffs and gorges. The plateau also offers some good farming and grazing land.

Southeast of the Great Basin, the Colorado Plateau covers large areas of Arizona, Utah, Colorado, and New Mexico. Much of the Colorado Plateau is carved into a maze of canyons. A **canyon** is a deep, narrow valley with steep sides. One of the deepest is the Grand Canyon. It stretches 280 miles (451 km) across the Colorado Plateau in northern Arizona.

REVIEW What kind of land is found west of the Rocky Mountains?

The Pacific Mountains and Valleys

The basins, plateaus, and canyons of the Intermountain Region give way to more mountain ranges farther west. Lying just inside California is the Sierra Nevada (see•AIR•ah neh•VAH•dah). *Sierra Nevada* is Spanish for "snowy mountain range." This mountain range runs almost the entire length of California. North of the Sierra Nevada, the Cascade Range stretches across parts of northern California, Oregon, and Washington.

Farther north, in Alaska, is the Alaska Range. This range has the highest mountain peak in North America, Mount McKinley. At 20,320 feet (6,194 m) it towers above the land. Some people call the peak by its Native American name, *Denali* (duh•NAH•lee), which means "The Great One" or "The High One."

Other mountains—the Coast Ranges— border the Pacific Ocean in California, Oregon, and Washington. At many places these mountains drop sharply into the ocean. Unlike the Atlantic Coast, much of the Pacific Coast is rocky and rugged, with very little flat land.

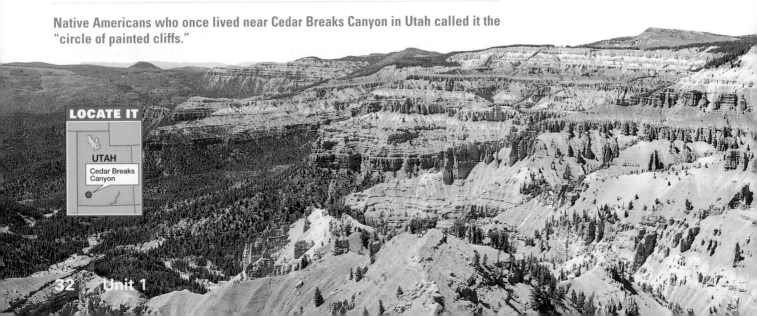

Native Americans who once lived near Cedar Breaks Canyon in Utah called it the "circle of painted cliffs."

LOCATE IT

UTAH

Cedar Breaks Canyon

The Coast Ranges give much of the Pacific coastline a rocky, rugged look.

Many fertile valleys lie between the Coast Ranges and the Sierra Nevada and the Cascade Range. The largest of these is the Central Valley in California. Other valleys include the Puget Sound Lowland in Washington and the Willamette (wuh•LA•muht) Valley in Oregon. All of these valleys have rich soil, which makes them important farming areas.

In 1868 John Muir visited this part of the United States. He loved the land here and spent much of his life fighting to preserve the western wilderness. He convinced the government to set aside parts of it for national parks, and is often called the Father of Our National Park System.

REVIEW **What four mountain ranges are nearest to the Pacific Coast?**

LESSON 2
REVIEW

 MAIN IDEA AND DETAILS What details support the idea that the Intermountain Region is also called the Basin and Range Region?

1 **BIG IDEA** What are some of the major landforms in the United States?

2 **VOCABULARY** Use the terms **sea level**, **mountain range**, and **piedmont** to describe the land between the Coastal Plain and the Interior Plains.

3 **HISTORY** Who named Death Valley? When?

4 **GEOGRAPHY** What is the largest desert area in the United States? Where is it?

5 **CRITICAL THINKING—Analyze** Why do you think fewer people live in the Intermountain Region than in other parts of the United States?

6 **CRITICAL THINKING—Evaluate** Why do you think John Muir had to fight to preserve the western wilderness?

 PERFORMANCE—Make a Model Use papier-mâché or clay to make a model of the surface of the United States. Show the major landforms discussed in the lesson. Compare your model with those of your classmates.

·SKILLS·

MAP AND GLOBE

Read an Elevation Map

▶ WHY IT MATTERS

Some parts of our country are flat. Other parts are mountainous. How would you know which parts are low or high by looking at a map? How would you know how high the mountainous areas are or how low the valleys are? To answer these questions and others, you need a map that shows elevation (eh•luh•VAY•shuhn). **Elevation** is the height of the land.

▶ WHAT YOU NEED TO KNOW

All elevations are measured from sea level, usually in feet or meters. The elevation of land at sea level is zero feet (0 m). For example, Mt. Rainier has an elevation of 14,410 feet (4,392 m) above sea level. In other words, the top of Mt. Rainier is 14,410 feet (4,392 m) above the surface of the ocean.

The elevation map of the United States on page 35 uses shading and color to show **relief** (rih•LEEF), or differences in elevation. Shaded areas on the map help you see where hills and mountains are located, but they do not give you elevations. To find elevations, you must use the map key to learn what each color stands for.

Notice that the map key does not give exact elevations. Instead, each color represents a particular area's highest and lowest elevations and all elevations in between. New Orleans, Louisiana, is in an area colored green. According to the key, this means that the elevation there is

Mt. Rainier is the tallest mountain in Washington.

LOCATE IT

WASHINGTON

Mt. Rainier

Elevations of the United States

Map legend:
- △ Highest point
- ▽ Lowest point
- ✵ National capital

Feet	Meters
Above 13,120	Above 4,000
6,560	2,000
1,640	500
655	200
0	0
Below sea level	

Albers Equal-Area Projection

ALASKA — Mt. McKinley 20,320 ft. (6,194 m)

HAWAII

Mt. Rainier 14,410 ft. (4,392 m)

Death Valley -282 ft. (-86 m)

---

between 0 and 655 feet (0 and 200 m) above sea level.

▶ PRACTICE THE SKILL

Use the elevation map to answer these questions.

1 What is the elevation of Santa Fe, New Mexico? Is the land there higher or lower than the land around Atlanta, Georgia?

2 What is the elevation of Minneapolis, Minnesota? How does its elevation compare with those of Miami and Santa Fe?

3 Which state has two large areas with elevations below sea level?

▶ APPLY WHAT YOU LEARNED

Imagine that you are planning a trip between any two cities on the map above. Lay a ruler across the map to connect the two cities. Then write the name and elevation of each city and tell the elevations of the highest and lowest land you will cross on your trip.

Practice your map and globe skills with the **GeoSkills CD-ROM**.

MAP AND GLOBE SKILLS

PRIMARY SOURCES

Tools of Geography

Geography has been called "the art of the mappable." People study different kinds of maps to gather different kinds of information. Pictures taken from airplanes and from satellites in space also help people to better understand Earth and the places where they live. Look now at four different kinds of maps of Philadelphia, Pennsylvania.

 FROM THE UNITED STATES GEOLOGICAL SURVEY

A topographic map shows the elevation and the shape of a place.

A road map shows some of the human and physical features of a place.

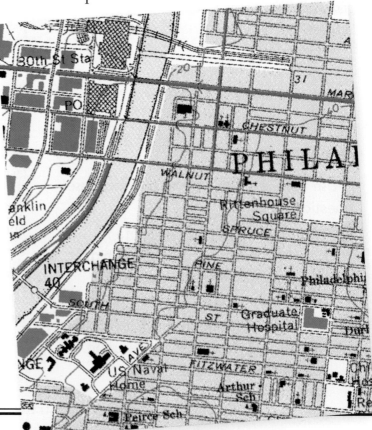

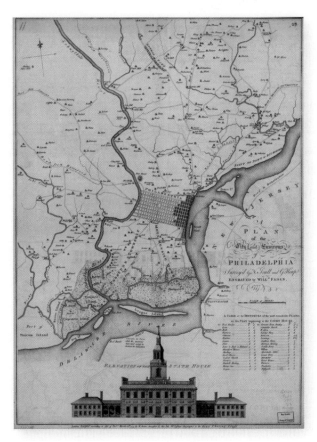

A historical map shows what a place looked like in the past. By comparing historical maps with present-day maps, people can see how places have changed over time.

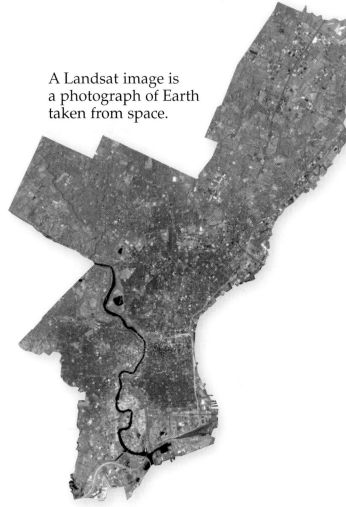

A Landsat image is a photograph of Earth taken from space.

ACTIVITY

Find Maps Look in atlases and other reference books to find three different kinds of maps of your community. In a short report, write about the different kinds of maps you found and what you learned about your community by looking at the maps together. Compare your findings with those of a classmate.

RESEARCH

Visit The Learning Site at **www.harcourtschool.com** to research other primary sources.

Analyze the Primary Source

1. What features of Philadelphia are visible in all the maps?

2. What does each map show that the others do not?

3. Which map would you choose if you wanted to get from one place to another?

3

Focus Skill

MAIN IDEA AND DETAILS

As you read, look for details that describe how rivers have helped shape the United States.

BIG IDEA

Rivers can change the land and affect people's lives.

VOCABULARY

groundwater
source
channel
mouth
tributary
river system
drainage basin
erosion
floodplain
delta

Pittsburgh has over 720 bridges, more than any other city in the United States.

LOCATE IT

PENNSYLVANIA

Pittsburgh

Looking at Rivers

Rivers, bodies of fresh moving water, cross the land in all parts of the United States, even in deserts. Some of these rivers are wide and deep and are always full of water. Others are narrow, shallow streams that may be dry for much of the year. Many rivers rush down mountains. Some wind slowly across flat land for hundreds of miles. Yet all rivers change the land.

Across the Land

Imagine that you are on your way home from school in western Pennsylvania. Large drops of rain begin to fall. Soon rain pours down on the streets and houses in your neighborhood. Where does all this water go?

Some water dries up. Some sinks into the soil and becomes **groundwater**, or the water beneath Earth's surface. The rest of the water runs down the land's surface and becomes part of the Ohio River or some other river or stream.

The place where a river begins is called its **source**. Some rivers, like the Ohio River, begin where two rivers meet. Other rivers begin high in the mountains or where lakes overflow. Some rivers begin as water bubbling out of underground springs.

No matter where or how they begin, all rivers flow from higher to lower ground. Along the way, each river carves a path, or channel, through the land. A **channel** is the deepest part of a river or another body of water. The bottom of a river is called the riverbed. The land along the sides forms its banks.

Most rivers flow into larger bodies of water, such as lakes, oceans, or other rivers. The place where a river empties into a larger body of water is called its **mouth**, or end. The mouth of the Ohio River is the Mississippi River in Illinois.

The water from most rivers eventually reaches an ocean. The Mississippi River, for example, flows into the Gulf of Mexico, which in turn empties into the Atlantic Ocean. Some rivers, however, do not flow into larger bodies of water. They flow into the low-lying land in basins. Land in the Great Basin has mountains all around it. The rivers that flow down from those mountains into the Great Basin have no place else to go. Some of the rivers flow into the desert lands and dry up. Other rivers end there as shallow pools of muddy water or empty into lakes. The largest of these lakes is the Great Salt Lake in Utah.

REVIEW What are the three main parts of a river?

Draining the Land

As rivers cross the land, tributaries (TRIH•byuh•tair•eez) may join them. A **tributary** is a stream or river that flows into a larger stream or river. Tributaries are also called branches. A river and its

Longest Rivers in the United States

This bar graph shows the lengths of the longest rivers in the United States.

Analyze Graphs This bar graph shows the lengths of the longest rivers in the United States.

❖ About how much longer is the Mississippi River than the Rio Grande?

tributaries make up a **river system**. The Ohio River system is one of our nation's largest river systems. Two rivers, the Allegheny (a•luh•GAY•nee) and the Monongahela (muh•nahn•guh•HEE•luh), meet in Pittsburgh, Pennsylvania, to form the Ohio River. From there, the Ohio River flows almost 1,000 miles (1,609 km) southwest to Cairo, Illinois. Along its route many tributaries join the Ohio River. Among these are the Kentucky, Wabash, and Tennessee Rivers.

Major Rivers of the United States

GEOGRAPHY THEME

Place   The Mississippi River forms borders for 10 states in the United States. Other rivers form borders of other states.

❓ **What river forms most of the border of Georgia and South Carolina?**

The Ohio River is itself a tributary of an even larger river system—the Mississippi River system. From its source in Lake Itasca (ih•TAS•kuh), in Minnesota, the Mississippi River flows south for 2,348 miles (3,779 km). Before emptying into the Gulf of Mexico, the Mississippi is joined by more than 250 tributaries, including the Missouri, Illinois, Arkansas, and Red Rivers.

All river systems drain, or carry water away from, the land around them. The land drained by a river system is its **drainage basin**. When a river or river system is long, its drainage basin can be very large. The Mississippi River system drains most of the land between the Rocky and Appalachian Mountains. Its huge drainage basin covers 1,200,000 square miles (3,108,000 square km)—about a third of the land in the United States. This area includes all or parts of 31 states. Nine-tenths of the fresh water that flows into the Gulf of Mexico comes from the Mississippi River system.

REVIEW What is a river system?

Wearing Down the Land

Rivers have great power to shape the surface of Earth. The erosion (ih•ROH•zhuhn) caused by flowing water in rivers has formed many of Earth's physical features. **Erosion** is the wearing away of Earth's surface.

Flowing water erodes, or wears down, the land. In a river, the current, or constantly moving water, sweeps rocks, sand, and soil down the river. As these materials tumble along in the current, they scrape along the bed of the river and its banks. This helps the river cut an even deeper and wider path.

For millions of years, the Colorado River has been carving the walls of the Grand Canyon in northern Arizona. The river has slowly cut its way deeper and deeper through the layers of rock. Parts of the canyon are now 1 mile (more than 1 km) deep and 18 miles (29 km) wide.

LOCATE IT

Grand Canyon

ARIZONA

More than 4 million people a year visit the Grand Canyon to see its spectacular beauty. To travel to the bottom of the canyon and back, on foot or by mule, takes two days.

In 1869 John Wesley Powell traveled the churning, swirling Colorado River for 277 miles (446 km) through the Grand Canyon. At times during the three-month trip, he was surrounded by high canyon walls that almost blocked out the sun.

REVIEW How do rivers wear down the land?

Focus Skill **MAIN IDEA AND DETAILS**

• BIOGRAPHY •

John Wesley Powell
1834–1902

Character Trait: Courage

John Wesley Powell was always looking for adventure. Before he was 25 years old, he had rowed down the Mississippi, Ohio, and Illinois Rivers. In 1869 Powell and a group of others set off on a 1,000-mile (1,609-km) river journey. The group's goal was to paddle down the Colorado River and to explore the Grand Canyon.

After braving miles of dangerous water, Powell and his group were the first people to reach the canyon by boat. Powell became a national hero. Two years later, he repeated the journey, mapping the Grand Canyon for the first time.

MULTIMEDIA BIOGRAPHIES
Visit The Learning Site at
www.harcourtschool.com
to learn about other famous people.

Building Up the Land

The same river materials that erode the land can also build up the land. Once a river reaches flat land, its current slows. The river begins to drop the sand and soil it has been carrying. Some of this material forms sandbars, or islands, in the river. As sandbars grow, they can block a river, forcing it to carve a new channel.

A river can also add new soil to its floodplain. A **floodplain** is the low, flat land along a river. If too much rain falls or too much snow melts at one time, the river may overflow its banks. Then, when a river floods, water spreads out over the floodplain. As the floodwaters flow back into the river's channel, they leave silt, or fine sand and soil, behind. Silt makes the soil in floodplains fertile, or good for farming.

A river can leave silt at its mouth, too. If there is no strong current to carry the silt away, it begins to build up. Over time the silt can form a delta. A **delta** is the triangle-shaped land at a river's mouth. The layers of silt that form a delta make the soil there very fertile.

REVIEW How can rivers build up the land?

Floods!

People who live near rivers have tried using human-made dams and levees (LEHV•eez) to control flooding. A levee is a high wall of earth that protects low-lying lands from rising water levels.

Protective levees along the banks of the Mississippi River were first built in the 1700s. French and Spanish settlers in New Orleans, Louisiana, built levees along parts of the river by about 1730. By the 1900s, levees lined both sides of the Mississippi River, offering some flood protection for people and property.

New Orleans, Louisiana, is the largest city in the Mississippi Delta. Much of the city was flooded when damage from Hurricane Katrina caused levees to break.

LOCATE IT

Mississippi Delta

Volunteers across the United States pitched in to help people hurt by Hurricane Katrina. Many provided food, clothing, and shelter to those whose homes were lost.

On August 30, 2005, Hurricane Katrina hit the Mississippi Delta region. It was one of the most powerful storms to ever strike the United States. Cities such as Gulfport and Biloxi, Mississippi, were badly damaged by winds of 140 miles per hour and high waves from a storm surge, or huge swell of water. The heavy rains and storm surge weakened New Orleans' levees. The next day, the city was flooded when the levees gave way.

Hundreds of people died as a result of Hurricane Katrina. As many as one million people were forced out of their homes by the storm. In the days that followed, volunteers from across the nation came to help people affected by the storm. Members of the United States Army worked hard to rebuild the New Orleans levees and to drain the floodwaters from the city.

REVIEW **How do people try to prevent rivers from flooding?**

LESSON 3
REVIEW

 MAIN IDEA AND DETAILS What details describe how rivers wear down and build up the land?

❶ **BIG IDEA** How do rivers change the land and affect people's lives?

❷ **VOCABULARY** Explain the difference between a river's **source** and its **mouth**.

❸ **GEOGRAPHY** Where does the Ohio River begin and end?

❹ **GEOGRAPHY** How did the Colorado River form the Grand Canyon?

❺ **CRITICAL THINKING—Analyze** Many cities are located on rivers. Why do you think this is so?

 PERFORMANCE—Make a Map Research a major river in your state. Find its source, channel, and mouth. Then draw a map showing the route of the river. Also show some of its tributaries. Display your map in the classroom.

MAIN IDEA AND DETAILS

As you read, look for how climate can affect people differently in various parts of the country.

BIG IDEA

There are large differences in climate across the United States.

VOCABULARY

precipitation
climate
humidity
tornado
hurricane
drought

FAST FACT

Spearfish, South Dakota, holds the record for the most extreme temperature increase in United States history. On January 22, 1943, the temperature there rose from ⁻4°F (⁻20°C) to 45°F (7°C) in just two minutes!

Climate Across the United States

How would you describe this morning's weather where you live? You could talk about how hot or cold it is by mentioning the temperature. If it is raining or snowing, you might mention precipitation (prih·sih·puh·TAY·shuhn). **Precipitation** is water in the form of rain, sleet, or snow that falls to Earth's surface. You might also describe how windy it is. The temperature, precipitation, and wind in a place on a particular day make up the weather.

A Land of Many Climates

Now how would you describe the climate where you live? **Climate** is the kind of weather a place has over a long time. For example, last winter Phoenix, Arizona, may have had rainy weather. However, the climate there is usually warm and dry.

The climate varies greatly across the United States. While people in Marquette, Michigan, are in the middle of a January snowstorm, people in Miami, Florida, might be playing on a beach. At the same time, rain might be falling in Seattle, Washington, while Las Vegas, Nevada, might be warm and dry.

In colder temperatures, water falling to Earth freezes, turning into snow or sleet. South Dakota, seen here, receives about 40 inches (102 cm) of snow each year.

HAWAII

Waiehu, Maui

The average temperature in Maui, Hawaii, is 75°F (about 24°C). The mountain areas of the island often receive 300 inches (762 cm) of rain each year.

The climate varies greatly across the United States for several different reasons. First, the United States covers an enormous area of land. Second, some places in the country are closer to the equator than others. Third, some places have higher elevations than others. Fourth, some places are located near particular landforms or large bodies of water.

REVIEW **How is climate different from weather?**

Distance from the Equator

The climate of a place depends partly on its distance from the equator. The United States is located between the equator and the North Pole. This means that temperatures in the United States are generally moderate, with warm summers and cool winters. However, because the United States is so large, temperatures can vary greatly, depending on how far a place is from the equator.

Usually, the closer a place is to the equator the warmer it is. That is because the sun's warming rays hit the equator directly throughout the year. Places farther away from the equator receive less heat from the sun, so they usually have cooler temperatures. This explains why Alaska, the state farthest from the equator, has a much colder climate than Hawaii, the state closest to the equator.

REVIEW **How does distance from the equator affect climate?**

Elevation

The climate in Hawaii is generally warm, but some mountain areas there are cold. These differences happen because elevation also affects temperature. Places at higher elevations are usually cooler than places at lower elevations. For this reason, the temperature in the mountains is usually much lower than the temperature in nearby valleys.

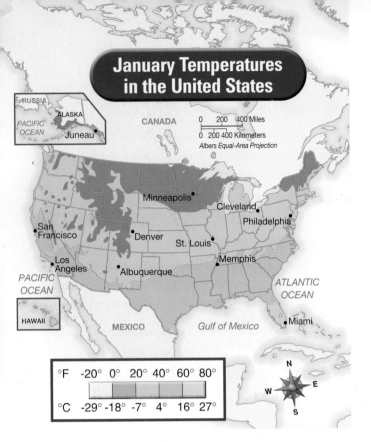

January Temperatures in the United States

°F -20° 0° 20° 40° 60° 80°
°C -29° -18° -7° 4° 16° 27°

GEOGRAPHY THEME

Place This map shows the average January temperatures in the United States.

❖ What is the average temperature in Cleveland in January?

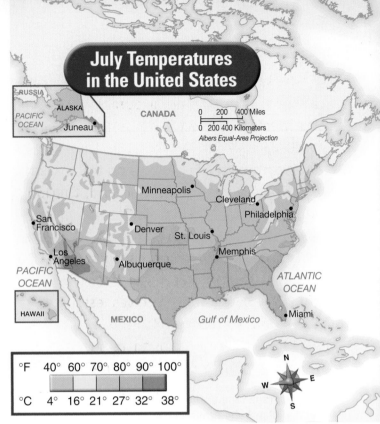

July Temperatures in the United States

°F 40° 60° 70° 80° 90° 100°
°C   4° 16° 21° 27° 32° 38°

GEOGRAPHY THEME

Place This map shows the average July temperatures in the United States.

❖ Which city is generally warmer in July, Denver or Memphis?

Albuquerque (AL•buh•ker•kee), New Mexico, and Memphis, Tennessee, are about the same distance north of the equator. The two cities have very different elevations, however. Albuquerque is nearly 1 mile (more than 1 km) above sea level. Because it is so high, Albuquerque is much cooler in both summer and winter.

REVIEW How does elevation affect climate?

MAIN IDEA AND DETAILS

Land and Water

Distance from oceans and other large bodies of water also affects climate. Because water heats and cools more slowly than land, places along coasts usually have warmer winters and cooler

summers than places farther inland.

The ocean often helps warm the land in winter and cool it in summer. Juneau, Alaska, sits farther north than Kansas City, Missouri. This Alaskan city is often warmer in the winter because it lies along the Pacific Coast. The winds that blow over the Pacific bring warmer air to Juneau.

In addition, the ocean adds humidity (hyoo•MIH•duh•tee) to the air. **Humidity** is the amount of moisture in the air. Humid places receive more rainfall than drier places. Surrounded by the Pacific, Hawaii gets more rain than any other state. Our nation's rainiest place is on Hawaii's Mount Waialeale (wy•ah•lay•AH•lay). It receives an average of 460 inches (1,168 cm) of rain a year.

REVIEW What is humidity?

Location on the Continent

The landforms that surround a place can also affect its climate. Mountain ranges in the western United States act like huge walls. They block the moist air from the Pacific from reaching places on the eastern sides of the mountains. Portland, Oregon, which lies near the Pacific Ocean, usually receives about 37 inches (94 cm) of precipitation each year. Redmond, Oregon, on the eastern side of the Cascades, receives less than 9 inches (about 23 cm) a year.

On the Interior Plains there are no mountains to block the large air masses that sometimes blow bitterly cold air southward from Canada. These cold air masses, called northers, can cause freezing temperatures in places as far south as Texas. In the summer, warm moist air blows from the Gulf of Mexico. This air often carries high temperatures and heavy rains to most of the eastern United States.

REVIEW Why does the Intermountain Region receive less precipitation than the Pacific Coast?

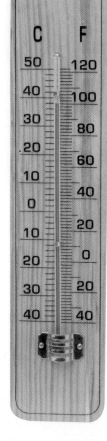

Extreme Weather

Weather and climate play an important role in people's lives. They can affect where people live, what clothes they wear, how they earn a living, and what they do for fun. Most of the time, our country's moderate climate allows people to live comfortably throughout the year.

Yet sometimes weather can be extreme. Over the years, temperatures in the United States have ranged from ⁻80°F (⁻62°C) in Prospect Creek, Alaska, to 134°F (57°C) in Death Valley, California. People cannot easily survive in such extreme temperatures.

Extreme weather can cause terrible damage to people and to property. The wind, for example, can blow so hard that it damages or destroys whatever is in its path. Winds this strong can happen in tornadoes. A **tornado** is a funnel-shaped, spinning windstorm. The wind inside tornadoes can reach speeds of more than 300 miles (483 km) per hour. Tornadoes often form over the Interior Plains.

California's Death Valley is one of the hottest, driest places in the United States. Temperatures there often soar above 100°F (about 38°C).

LOCATE IT

Death Valley

CALIFORNIA

Hurricanes can cause millions of dollars' worth of damage.

Fierce winds occur in hurricanes, too. A **hurricane** is a huge tropical storm with heavy rains and winds that can reach up to 175 miles (282 km) per hour. Most hurricanes strike the southern Coastal Plain between June and November.

Blizzards, or strong snowstorms, can knock down trees, power lines, and roofs, and block roads. Winds blowing across the Great Lakes often bring blizzards to places like Buffalo, New York. In a typical year, Buffalo receives 90 inches (229 cm) of snow.

Too little precipitation can also cause problems. A time of little or no rain is called a **drought** (DROWT). During a drought, water supplies run low, and trees and crops sometimes die. A drought can last for months or even years.

REVIEW What happens during a drought?

LESSON 4
REVIEW

MAIN IDEA AND DETAILS What are the main factors that affect weather? What are the main factors that affect climate?

1 BIG IDEA Why are there large differences in climate across the United States?

2 VOCABULARY How are **humidity** and **precipitation** related?

3 GEOGRAPHY What state receives the most rain? Why?

4 CRITICAL THINKING—Analyze How does the climate where you live affect the way you live?

5 CRITICAL THINKING—Evaluate How do you think extreme weather can affect a farmer's earnings?

PERFORMANCE—Create a Weather Chart Over a period of one week, chart the daily high temperature and precipitation level in your community. Do the same for a city in another part of the country. Based on the data, what conclusions can you draw about the climates in the two places? Compare your findings with those of classmates.

Natural Resources

The United States is a large country and is rich in natural resources. A natural resource is something found in nature that people can use. Some natural resources are soil, water, and trees. People depend on these and other natural resources to grow or make the things they need or want.

Few nations in the world have as many natural resources as the United States. However, these resources are not distributed, or spaced out, evenly. Some places have more resources than they need, while other places do not have enough. For this reason, people in different parts of the nation must depend on one another for natural resources.

A Rich, Fertile Land

The land itself is one of our most important natural resources. Many years ago, Abraham Lincoln recognized how fortunate Americans were to have such good land. He wrote:

66 We find ourselves in the peaceful possession of the fairest portion of the earth, as regards extent of territory, fertility of soil. . . . 99

MAIN IDEA AND DETAILS
As you read, look for details that explain why people should use natural resources wisely.

BIG IDEA
Many natural resources are found in the United States.

VOCABULARY

natural resource
product
scarce
mineral
fuel
conservation
renewable
recycle
nonrenewable
pollution

Corn has been grown in North America for nearly 3,000 years. Today it is the United States' largest crop.

Farmland covers about half the area of the United States. Fertile soil, generally mild climates, and plenty of fresh water help American farmers grow huge amounts of food. They grow enough food to feed the people in the United States as well as to sell to other countries. Some important food crops include wheat, corn, soybeans, fruits, and vegetables.

The land in many parts of the United States is also good for raising cattle, chickens, turkeys, hogs, and sheep. The grasslands in other parts of the country are ideal for dairy farming, which provides the nation's milk, butter, and cheese.

Forests, which cover nearly one-third of the land, are another important natural resource. Wood from trees can be used to make many products. A **product** is something people make or grow, usually to sell. Trees from some forests supply the lumber needed for building houses or making furniture, fences, and toys. Trees are used to make many other products, too, including the paper in this textbook and the pencil you use.

Like all natural resources, trees are **scarce**, or limited, and need to be used wisely. After trees are cut down to make products, many years are needed for new trees to grow. Today, thousands of trees in the United States are protected in national parks and forests. Most of these trees cannot be cut down, and many new trees are planted in the parks every year.

REVIEW Why are fertile soil and forests important natural resources?
MAIN IDEA AND DETAILS

Some redwood trees are more than 1,500 years old and more than 300 feet (91 m) tall!

Water

Water is perhaps our most important natural resource—we cannot survive without it. People need water for drinking and washing, watering crops, and even as a source of power. Lakes, rivers, streams, and groundwater supply almost all the water people use in their homes, on farms, and in factories.

Most places in the United States have enough fresh water to meet people's needs. However, people have modified, or changed, their environment to get water when water supplies are low. Often they pump water from rivers, make new lakes, and dig wells. Sometimes people lay pipes and dig ditches across the land to move water to dry areas.

Water is an important resource for other reasons, too. Power plants create electricity from the energy of moving water. That electricity is then used to light homes, run machines, and power factories.

Our water resources also make fishing an important industry in the United States. American fishers catch about 10 billion pounds of fish each year. Among their catches are tuna, salmon, oysters, shrimp, lobsters, and other kinds of shellfish from the salt waters off the nation's coasts, and many kinds of freshwater fish from lakes and rivers.

REVIEW **How do people modify the environment when water supplies are low?**

Underground Resources

Many minerals (MIN•uh•ruhlz) lie buried under our nation's land. A **mineral** is a natural substance found in rocks. Copper, gold, silver, and other metals are minerals. People use metals from mineral resources for a variety of purposes. For example, copper is used to make wire, pots, pans, and coins. Many minerals, such as iron, marble, limestone, and sand and gravel, are used as construction materials for buildings and roads.

Lake Superior is the world's largest freshwater lake. It is 350 miles (563 km) long—almost as long as Florida.

FAST FACT

The Great Lakes hold nearly all of our nation's fresh water. In fact, all the water in the Great Lakes could fill a swimming pool 9 feet (3 m) deep and the size of the entire United States!

Lying under the land in the United States are also fuels (FYOO•uhlz). A **fuel** is a natural resource, such as coal, oil, or natural gas, that is used to make heat or energy. People use fuels to cook food, heat buildings, and make machines work.

Coal, from mines mostly in Wyoming, West Virginia, and Kentucky, is one of the country's most abundant fuels. Today, one of its main uses is to create electricity. Oil, large amounts of which are found in Alaska, Oklahoma, and Texas, is another fuel that has many uses. It can be turned into gasoline, diesel fuel, or kerosene. Oil can also be used to heat homes and to make products such as nylon, shampoo, and plastic.

REVIEW How do people today use minerals and fuels?

Using Resources Wisely

As people use natural resources, they bring about change. In the past, many people believed that forests, clean water, fertile land, and other natural resources would last forever. Over time people have come to see that all resources are limited. People today understand the importance of **conservation** (kahn•ser•VAY•shuhn), or protecting natural resources and using them wisely.

Some natural resources are **renewable**. They can be replaced as they are used up. For example, forests can be renewed over time if people use them carefully. Workers can plant trees to replace the ones that have been cut down. People can **recycle** paper products, or use them again, to conserve wood. Recycling just 1 ton of paper saves 17 trees!

Other natural resources, such as minerals and fuels, cannot be replaced. They are **nonrenewable**. Once they are used up, they are gone forever. But there are many ways to conserve minerals and fuels. People can put insulation in their houses so they will lose less heat during the winter and stay cooler in the summer. They can conserve gasoline by driving their cars less or walking more often. They can recycle glass, metal, plastic, and products made from oil.

Coal is called a fossil fuel because it was formed from dead plants that lay buried for millions of years. This plant fossil was found in a coal mine.

Solar Power

Solar panels built in parts of the Mojave (moh•HAH•vay) Desert in the southwestern United States produce more solar energy than is produced in any other place in the world. The panels cover more than 1,000 acres of land. From the sun, they collect heat energy, which is then used to create electricity. The Mojave Desert panels provide enough electricity for a community of more than 150,000 people.

People can also conserve fuels by using alternative sources of energy. Scientists have already found ways to heat homes by using energy from the sun and to make electricity from wind and water power.

In addition to saving and replacing resources, people need to protect the land, water, and air from pollution. **Pollution** is anything that makes a natural resource dirty or unsafe to use. Today, people and government in the United States are aware of the dangers of pollution and are working hard to reduce it.

Natural resources have helped make the United States one of the richest countries in the world. As you read this textbook, you will learn about the natural resources found in different parts of the United States and how people throughout the nation use their resources wisely.

REVIEW **Why is it important to conserve minerals and fuels?**

LESSON 5
REVIEW

 MAIN IDEA AND DETAILS How do people change their environment when they use natural resources?

❶ **BIG IDEA** What are some of the most important natural resources in the United States?

❷ **VOCABULARY** Use the terms scarce and natural resources to explain why conservation is important.

❸ **GEOGRAPHY** What are some states where large deposits of coal and oil are found?

❹ **HISTORY** What did many people in the past think about natural resources?

❺ **CRITICAL THINKING—Synthesize** How do the natural resources found in your community affect the way you live?

❻ **CRITICAL THINKING—Hypothesize** What do you think might happen if people do not conserve natural resources?

 PERFORMANCE—Write a Riddle Make up a riddle about natural resources. Share your riddle with the rest of the class.

Use Tables to Group Information

VOCABULARY

classify

▶ WHY IT MATTERS

How many different ways can you describe the natural resources in the United States? You can describe where resources are found, how people use them, or whether they are renewable or nonrenewable.

You can organize the same information in different ways to help you find the information you want. One way to do this is to **classify**, or group, information in a table. Using a table allows you to compare numbers, facts, and other information quickly.

▶ WHAT YOU NEED TO KNOW

All tables have columns and rows. Each column contains a certain kind of information. In Table A on page 55, for example, the first column lists the names of some national forests in the United States in alphabetical order. The middle column shows their locations. The total number of acres of land that each forest covers is listed in the third column.

Table B has the same information about national forests. In this table, however, the forests are organized by size instead of alphabetically.

About 191 million acres of land in the United States are protected as national forests. The Black Hills National Forest, below, covers parts of South Dakota and Wyoming.

Table A: United States National Forests, in Alphabetical Order

NATIONAL FOREST	LOCATION	ACRES
Allegheny	Pennsylvania	513,161
Black Hills	South Dakota and Wyoming	1,000,000
Finger Lakes	New York	16,032
Hoosier	Indiana	197,000
Sequoia	California	1,192,320
Superior	Minnesota	3,000,000
Winema	Oregon	1,100,000

Table B: United States National Forests, by Size

ACRES	LOCATION	NATIONAL FOREST
3,000,000	Minnesota	Superior
1,192,320	California	Sequoia
1,100,000	Oregon	Winema
1,000,000	South Dakota and Wyoming	Black Hills
513,161	Pennsylvania	Allegheny
197,000	Indiana	Hoosier
16,032	New York	Finger Lakes

▶ PRACTICE THE SKILL

Use the tables to answer the following questions.

1 Which forest listed in the tables is the largest? In which table was it easier to find this information?

2 In which state is Hoosier National Forest located? In which table was it easier to find this information?

3 Where is Sequoia National Forest? Which table did you use to find this information? Explain why you used that table.

4 Which forest is smaller, Black Hills or Winema? Which table made it easier to answer this question?

5 In which table would it be easier to find all the information on Finger Lakes National Forest and Hoosier National Forest?

▶ APPLY WHAT YOU LEARNED

Make a table listing these national forests in alphabetical order of location. Explain how this table would be useful in comparing the information.

LOCATE IT

WYOMING · SOUTH DAKOTA

Black Hills National Forest

1 Review and Test Preparation

Use Your Reading Skills

Copy the following graphic organizer onto a separate sheet of paper. Use the information you have learned to show that you understand how the chapter's main ideas are connected.

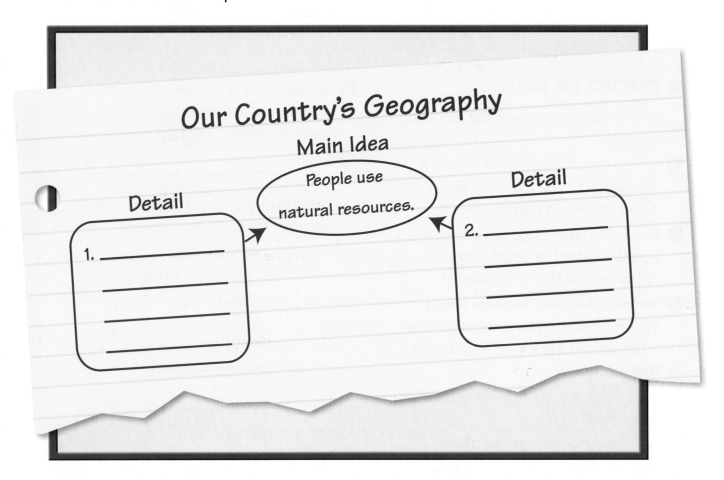

Our Country's Geography

Main Idea

People use natural resources.

Detail

1. _____
_____
_____
_____

Detail

2. _____
_____
_____
_____

THINK & WRITE

Write a Poem   Write a poem that describes the major landforms of the United States. Then use pictures or photos to illustrate your poem.

Write a Letter to the Editor   Write a letter to the editor of your local newspaper explaining why you think it is important for your community to recycle products.

USE VOCABULARY

Choose the term that matches each definition.

hemisphere (p. 22)
continent (p. 23)
plateau (p. 30)
canyon (p. 32)
erosion (p. 41)
delta (p. 42)
climate (p. 44)
drought (p. 48)
mineral (p. 51)

1 a time of little or no rain

2 mostly flat land that rises above the surrounding land

3 half of Earth

4 the wearing away of Earth's surface

5 the kind of weather a place has over a long time

6 the triangle-shaped land at a river's mouth

7 a natural substance found in rocks

8 a deep, narrow valley with steep sides

RECALL FACTS

Answer these questions.

9 What landform covers the Atlantic Coast of the United States?

10 How do floods help make soil fertile?

11 What are three kinds of precipitation?

12 Why is it important to conserve natural resources?

Write the letter of the best choice.

13 The mountain range that covers much of the eastern United States is the—
A Appalachian Mountains.
B Rocky Mountains.
C Sierra Nevada.
D Cascade Range.

14 Which of the following is *not* part of a river?
F source
G relief
H channel
J mouth

15 Which of the following is a renewable resource?
A natural gas
B oil
C trees
D coal

THINK CRITICALLY

16 Why do you think there are fewer large cities in the mountains than on the Coastal Plain?

17 How do you think climate and landforms affect the activities people do for fun?

APPLY SKILLS

Use Latitude and Longitude

18 Use the map on page 27 to give the absolute location of Springfield, Illinois.

Read an Elevation Map

19 Using the map on page 35, trace the route of the Mississippi River, and explain the change in elevations from the river's source to its mouth.

Use Tables to Group Information

20 Use the Internet or the library to research the Great Lakes. Make tables that list the five Great Lakes by their area and by their depth.

RED RIVER VALLEY, NORTH DAKOTA

A checkerboard of fields covers the Red River Valley in eastern North Dakota. Sometimes called the "breadbasket of the world," the valley is an important wheat-growing region. Other crops grown here include sugar beets, soybeans, sunflowers, and potatoes.

LOCATE IT

Red River Valley

Red River of the North

NORTH DAKOTA

Looking at Regions

" The geographer views the earth as a mosaic of regions. "

—Derwent Whittlesey,
geographer, 1943

Summarize

When you **summarize,** you retell briefly what you have read, using your own words.

As you read this chapter, summarize what you learned.

- Identify the main topic of each lesson.
- List what and who is involved, and where, how and why these events occur.
- Summarize what you read.

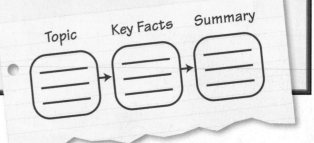

Topic   Key Facts   Summary

SUMMARIZE

As you read, look for ways that regions make it easier to study and understand large areas.

BIG IDEA

The United States is divided into different kinds of regions.

VOCABULARY

region
urban
suburb
rural
government
county
county seat

Regions Around You

In 1882, when Willa Cather was nine years old, she traveled with her family across much of the United States. Many years later, as a writer, she described her journey. She wrote, "There was nothing but land: not a country at all, but the material out of which countries are made."

Cather was saying that nature forms the physical features of the United States but people create its cities, states, and other regions. A region is an area with at least one feature that sets it apart from other areas.

Regions Where People Live

The United States is too large to study all at once, so people often divide it into smaller regions. Some of these regions are based on where people live.

Most Americans live in urban, or city, regions. In fact, more than seven out of ten people in the United States live in urban areas. No matter in what city they live, city dwellers are alike in some ways. They often live in crowded spaces. They may live close together, sometimes in tall buildings. Many people in cities walk to work or to stores rather than drive their own cars. Some ride buses, taxis, or subways, too.

Marcus, however, like many other Americans, lives in a suburb. A suburb is a town or small city built near a larger city. Marcus and his family live in Framingham, Massachusetts, a suburb of Boston. Most suburbs are filled with houses instead of factories

Marcus is a fourth-grade student in Framingham, Massachusetts. Signs like this one mark the town's boundaries.

ENTERING

INC. 1700

FRAMINGHAM

The town of Framingham is located in eastern Massachusetts, about 20 miles (32 km) west of Boston, the state's capital.

LOCATE IT

MASSACHUSETTS

Framingham

or tall buildings. People who live in suburban regions often work in nearby cities. Marcus's father travels from Framingham to Boston each day to work.

About 70 million Americans live in **rural**, or country, regions. Life in rural areas is different from urban or suburban life. Unlike homes in other regions, most homes in rural regions are built farther apart. They may be several miles from schools and businesses. People who live in rural areas often have to drive a long way to visit the doctor or to go shopping. But many enjoy outdoor activities in their free time.

People can define a region by using just about any feature based on where people live. It may be a region that shares a place, such as a neighborhood. It may also be a region that shares a government. A **government** is a system of deciding what is best for a group of people. A city

is a region that shares a government. All the residents of a city live by the same local laws and have the same city leaders.

A region that shares a government is called a political region. Political regions have exact boundaries set by law. Not everyone might agree about which street marks the end of Marcus's neighborhood, but everyone knows exactly where Framingham begins and ends. Its city limits are clearly marked with signs.

Cities can be further divided into other political regions, such as voting districts and school districts. In addition, some cities and towns are divided into fire districts, library districts, and other special districts. Just like Marcus, you also live in several different regions at the same time.

REVIEW What are the different kinds of regions city dwellers can live in at the same time? SUMMARIZE

In most counties, a sheriff runs the county jail.

Regions Within States

Regions can be any size. Some are small, such as Marcus's neighborhood and school district. Others are large, such as his state, Massachusetts. Like a city, each state has its own government and has exact boundaries set by law.

Nearly every state is divided into smaller regions called counties. A **county** is a part of a state that has its own government. There are more than 3,000 counties in the United States. The number of counties in a state range from 3 in Delaware to more than 250 in Texas. Some states have different names for this kind of region. Louisiana is divided into smaller regions called parishes. Alaska is divided into boroughs (BUHR•ohz).

The town or city that is the center of government for a county is called the **county seat**. Among the things a county government does is to take care of the county's roads and run the county's courts. Many counties have a sheriff, who makes sure that the county's laws are obeyed.

Political regions, such as cities, counties, and states, are marked by boundaries. Yet people cross boundaries like these all the time and hardly notice that they have done so. People may call one city or county home but work in

Analyze Diagrams People divide the United States into political regions of different sizes.

◈ What political region is part of a county?

Regions Within Regions

THE NATION OF THE UNITED STATES

THE STATE OF NEW MEXICO

THE COUNTY OF BERNALILLO

BERNALILLO ● Albuquerque

THE CITY OF ALBUQUERQUE

UNITED STATES

NEW MEXICO

BERNALILLO

NEW MEXICO

Regions of the United States

Scale: 200 — 400 Miles / 200 — 400 Kilometers — Albers Equal-Area Projection

ALASKA
CANADA
RUSSIA
ARCTIC OCEAN
PACIFIC OCEAN

CANADA

WASHINGTON
OREGON
IDAHO
MONTANA
NORTH DAKOTA
SOUTH DAKOTA
MINNESOTA
WISCONSIN
MICHIGAN
Lake Superior
Lake Huron
Lake Michigan
Lake Erie
Lake Ontario

NEVADA
UTAH
WYOMING
THE MIDDLE WEST
NEBRASKA
IOWA
ILLINOIS
INDIANA
OHIO

THE WEST
CALIFORNIA
COLORADO
KANSAS
MISSOURI
KENTUCKY
WEST VIRGINIA
VIRGINIA

ARIZONA
NEW MEXICO
OKLAHOMA
ARKANSAS
TENNESSEE
NORTH CAROLINA
SOUTH CAROLINA

THE SOUTH
ALABAMA
MISSISSIPPI
GEORGIA

TEXAS
LOUISIANA
FLORIDA

NEW HAMPSHIRE
VERMONT
MAINE
THE NORTHEAST
NEW YORK
MASSACHUSETTS
RHODE ISLAND
CONNECTICUT
NEW JERSEY
DELAWARE
MARYLAND
PENNSYLVANIA

PACIFIC OCEAN
ATLANTIC OCEAN

HAWAII
0 — 100 Miles / 0 — 100 Kilometers
PACIFIC OCEAN

MEXICO
Gulf of Mexico

GEOGRAPHY THEME

Regions The 50 states are often grouped into four large regions. All the states in each region are in the same part of the United States.

In which region of the United States is your state found?

Regions Within the Country

The United States is made up of 50 states. Each state is a region. It has its own government as well as its own cities and counties. Studying each state separately, however, would take a long time. For this reason, people sometimes study a group of states together. This makes it easier to compare parts of the United States.

In this textbook, the states are grouped into four large regions—the Northeast, the South, the Middle West, and the West. The states in each region are all located in the same part of the United States. Because of this, they may share the same kinds of landforms, climate, and natural resources. The people who live in those states often earn their living in the same ways, too.

As you read this textbook, you will learn about each of the four regions. You will read about important events that took place in each one. You will learn about the landforms, rivers, climates, and other physical features in each region.

Washington, D.C.

Understanding the World in Spatial Terms

Washington, D.C., is the only place in our nation that is not a part of any state. The city lies on land that was once part of Maryland. George Washington selected this spot on the Potomac River just a few miles from Mount Vernon, his home in Virginia.

PENNSYLVANIA

0   20   40 Miles
0   20   40 Kilometers

MARYLAND

NEW JERSEY

Potomac River

Mount Vernon •

WASHINGTON, D.C.

DELAWARE

Chesapeake Bay

N W E S

VIRGINIA

ATLANTIC OCEAN

You will meet some of the people who live there and find out how they live. This will help you understand how the regions are alike and how they are different. It will also help you understand your own community.

REVIEW Why do people sometimes group states into regions?

LESSON 1 REVIEW

Focus Skill

SUMMARIZE Within each of the four large regions of the United States, how are the states alike?

1 BIG IDEA What are some of the different kinds of regions in which you live?

2 VOCABULARY Describe your **county seat**, using the terms **government** and **county**.

3 CIVICS AND GOVERNMENT How is a region in which people share a government different from other kinds of regions?

4 GEOGRAPHY What is a suburb?

5 CRITICAL THINKING—Evaluate Why do you think more people in the United States live in urban regions than in rural regions?

PERFORMANCE—Make a Map Draw a map of your school. Divide the school into regions based on what is done in different parts of the school. Explain why you divided the school the way you did.

Other Kinds of Regions

People can define regions on the basis of where people live. People can also describe regions based on physical features, such as landforms, climate, or natural resources. They can also describe regions according to human features—such as culture or way of life, or how people earn a living. Even when regions are described by one feature, they may still share features with other regions.

Physical Regions

Look out the window. How would you describe the place where you live? Do you see mountains or low, flat land? Is the climate warm or cold? Is it wet or dry? What kinds of animals live nearby? What do the trees look like?

The answers to questions such as these depend on where you live. The United States does not look the same everywhere. Students in other parts of the country will probably describe a very different place from the one that you see.

Regions can be based on the kinds of wildlife that live there. The Pacific coast is our nation's only region where sea lions live.

SUMMARIZE
Summarize the physical and human features of the United States and the place where you live.

BIG IDEA
There are different ways that people divide the United States into regions.

VOCABULARY

culture
natural vegetation
economy
agriculture
manufacturing
industry
service industry
custom
ethnic group

FAST FACT

California sea lion pups weigh about 15 pounds (7 kg) when they are born. Their mothers weigh about 200 pounds (91 kg), and their fathers weigh 1,000 pounds (454 kg).

One State, Three Regions

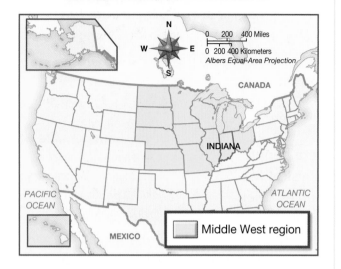

Middle West region

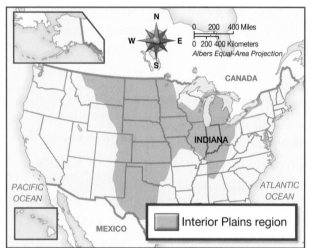

Interior Plains region

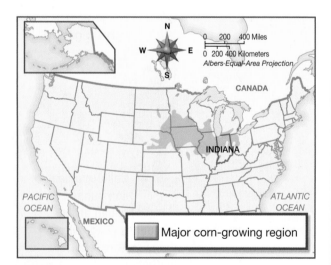

Major corn-growing region

GEOGRAPHY THEME

Regions A place can be part of more than one region at the same time. Just a few kinds of regions are shown on the maps above.

❖ What are three regions that the state of Indiana is part of?

Physical regions can be based on any kind of physical feature. Often the feature is chosen because of what people want to know. If they want to know how climate affects the way people live, they might divide the United States into regions that have similar temperatures. They might also base regions on the location of natural resources, such as coal. Landforms such as mountains or plains can also be the basis of a region.

Physical regions can be based on wildlife and natural vegetation, too. **Natural vegetation** is the plant life that grows naturally in an area. A forest ranger might divide the United States into regions based on the kinds of trees that grow in different places. Because places in the United States have different climates and soils, different kinds of trees grow across the country.

Needleleaf trees grow in many parts of the United States. They can be found in the region along the Canadian border from Maine to Minnesota. A needleleaf tree is a tree with narrow, sharp leaves that look like needles. Most needleleaf trees, such as pines and firs, stay green throughout the year.

In other parts of the country, forests of broadleaf trees grow. A broadleaf tree has wide, flat leaves. These leaves turn colors, dry up, and fall to the ground in autumn. Maple, oak, walnut, cherry, and hickory are all broadleaf trees.

Unlike cities and states, regions based on physical features do not have exact boundaries. These regions often overlap. In some places, for example, different kinds of trees can grow side by side.

REVIEW What are some physical features that can make up a region? **SUMMARIZE**

Economic Regions

Other regions in the United States are based on the **economy**, or the way people use resources to meet their needs. For example, many people in Oklahoma, Texas, and Louisiana earn their living by drilling oil or by making gasoline and other products from oil. For this reason, these states could be grouped as one economic region. This same idea can be applied to other states that produce oil. Studying these groups together can help people learn about the entire country's oil production.

People use all kinds of natural resources to earn their living. In mining regions many people work at digging from the ground rocks or resources used for fuels. For example, in the mining regions of West Virginia, Kentucky, and Tennessee, many people have jobs mining coal. In timber regions, such as Maine or Oregon, many people earn their living by cutting down trees for wood. In still other regions, people use the land for **agriculture** (A•grih•kuhl•cher), or farming.

Some economic regions are based on what product most of their factories make. The United States as a whole is the world's leading manufacturing (man•yuh•FAK•chuh•ring) region. **Manufacturing** is the making of products.

The region of California stretching from San Jose to Palo Alto is called Silicon Valley. Silicon is a material used to make computer chips. Thousands of people in this economic region have jobs making computer parts. This is the region's leading industry. An **industry** is all of the businesses that make one kind of product or provide one kind of service.

Analyze Graphs One out of every five American workers has a manufacturing job. These workers are assembling computers.

❖ What has happened to the number of manufacturing jobs since 1980?

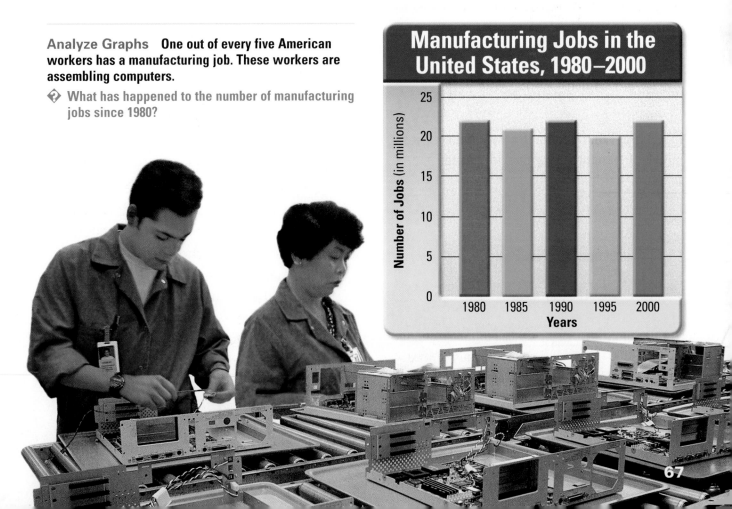

Manufacturing Jobs in the United States, 1980–2000

Number of Jobs (in millions)

Years: 1980, 1985, 1990, 1995, 2000

Service Jobs in the United States, 1980–2000

Number of Jobs (in millions)

Year	
1980	
1985	
1990	
1995	
2000	

Analyze Graphs About one-third of all workers in the United States have service jobs.

❖ How has the number of service jobs changed since 1980?

Still other economic regions in the United States are based on service industries. **Service industries** are industries in which workers are paid to do things for other people. Taking care of sick people, repairing cars, delivering mail, and serving food in restaurants are all examples of service jobs.

REVIEW What are some kinds of industries on which economic regions are based?

Cultural Regions

Another kind of region is based on culture. Dividing a place into cultural regions helps people understand the customs and beliefs of the groups that live there. A **custom** is a usual way of doing things. Shaking hands when you meet someone is a custom. When people go to live in a new place, they often take their customs with them.

Some cultural regions are based on the main ethnic group living in a place. An **ethnic group** is a group made up of people from the same country, people of the same race, or people with a shared way of life. Other cultural regions are based on people's shared religious beliefs, the foods they eat, or the language they speak.

Amish (AH•mish) communities near Lancaster, in southeastern Pennsylvania, are examples of cultural regions. Because of their religious beliefs, the Amish live very simply. They do not have electricity or telephones in their homes, and they do not use cars or tractors. Instead, they farm with plows pulled by horses and

Most Amish in Pennsylvania have German ancestors. People started calling the region Pennsylvania Dutch Country because they misunderstood the word *Deutsch,* which means "German."

LOCATE IT

PENNSYLVANIA

Lancaster

Chinese New Year

People who live in a cultural region often hold special celebrations to honor their background. Each year, thousands of Chinese Americans celebrate the Chinese New Year. During the 15-day celebration, they decorate their homes with vases of flowers, platters of oranges and tangerines, and plates of dried fruit. Families share large meals that include fish, chicken, and Chinese noodles. The Chinese New Year is celebrated on the first day of the first moon of the Chinese lunar calendar. This normally falls in late January or early February.

On the last day of the New Year celebration, children sometimes take part in a parade.

travel by horse and buggy. They dress very plainly and speak a form of German, as well as English.

In San Francisco's Chinatown, the background of most of the people is Chinese. Many people in Chinatown speak Chinese, so signs and newspapers in the neighborhood are often written in Chinese as well as English. Many people in Chinatown celebrate holidays that are important to their culture, such as Chinese New Year.

REVIEW What might people in a cultural region have in common?

LESSON 2 REVIEW

SUMMARIZE How are the regions of the United States both alike and different?

1 **BIG IDEA** In what ways do people divide the United States into physical, economic, and cultural regions?

2 **VOCABULARY** Use the terms **ethnic group** and **custom** to describe a cultural region.

3 **CULTURE** What can you learn about a place by dividing it into cultural regions?

4 **ECONOMICS** Why are Oklahoma, Texas, and Louisiana sometimes grouped into one economic region?

5 **CRITICAL THINKING—Analyze** What might cause the boundaries of a wildlife or natural vegetation region to change?

6 **CRITICAL THINKING—Evaluate** How do you think the Amish people are able to live so simply in today's world of computers and television?

PERFORMANCE—Make a Table Make a table with three columns. Label the columns *Agriculture, Manufacturing*, and *Service Industries*. In each column, list three jobs for each category. You can use reference books or the Internet to find the jobs. Then compare your lists to those of your classmates.

Use a Land Use and Resource Map

VOCABULARY

land use

➡ WHY IT MATTERS

Every day people use products made from natural resources found in the United States. Do you know where the natural resources are found that are used to make these products? Did you ever wonder where in the country these products are manufactured? You can answer these questions by using a map that shows where resources are found and how the land is used.

➡ WHAT YOU NEED TO KNOW

The map on page 71 is a land use and resource map. It uses colors to show **land use**, how most of the land in a place is used. The map does not show every forest or every farming and manufacturing region in the United States. It shows only the main ones. The map key shows the color that stands for each kind of land use.

The map uses picture symbols to show where some natural resources are found. The United States has too many resources to show on one map, so this map features only some of the important ones. Each symbol on the map is shown at or near the place where the resource is found. The map key explains what each symbol stands for.

➡ PRACTICE THE SKILL

Use the land use and resource map to answer these questions.

❶ How is most of the land used in Illinois and Iowa? How is most of the land used in Wyoming and Utah?

Iron is used to make steel frames for buildings. Here, a worker welds the parts of a steel frame together.

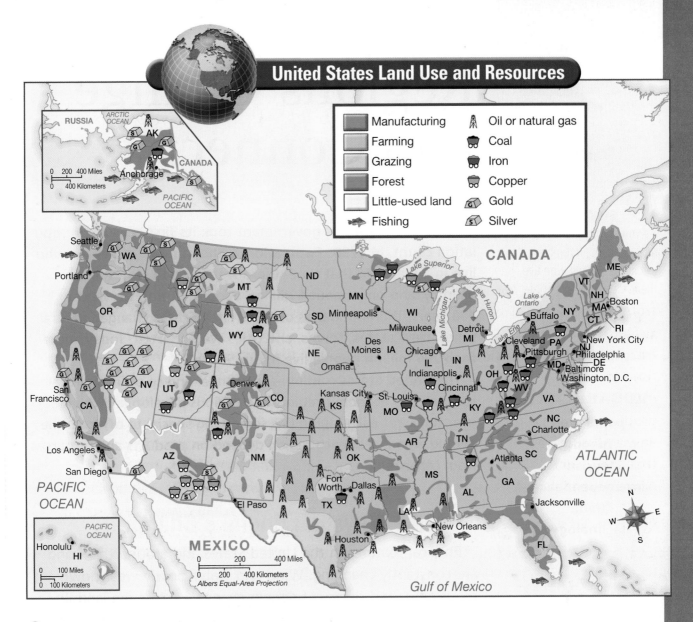

United States Land Use and Resources

Map Key

Manufacturing	Oil or natural gas
Farming	Coal
Grazing	Iron
Forest	Copper
Little-used land	Gold
Fishing	Silver

2 What important natural resources are found in northern Minnesota and Wisconsin?

3 Where does most of the manufacturing in the United States take place?

4 Which resources are found in and under the waters along the coasts of the United States?

➡ APPLY WHAT YOU LEARNED

Draw a land use and resource map for your state. Use the library or the Internet to find out how people use the land in your state and what natural resources are found there. Use colors to show the different land uses, and make a map key to tell what each color stands for. Choose different symbols for some of the important natural resources. Draw the symbols on the map, and explain what they stand for in the map key. Share your map with other students in your class. Then use it to explain land use and resources in your state to your family.

Practice your map and globe skills with the **GeoSkills CD-ROM**.

SUMMARIZE

As you read, summarize how changes in regions affect the people who live there.

BIG IDEA

Regions change over time and connect.

VOCABULARY

population
modify
tourism
interdependence
trade
technology

Regions Change and Connect

The United States government took its first census, or population count, in 1790. **Population** is the number of people who live in a place. At that time, there were just 13 states in the country, and only about 4 million people. During the next 200 years, the boundaries of the United States changed several times. New states, towns, and cities were started. Today, more than 295 million people live in our 50 states.

The United States continues to change, and so do its political, cultural, and economic regions. All regions develop and change over time. Yet each region has something special to offer, so the people who live in each region depend on products and resources from other regions.

Physical Regions Change

Physical features in the United States and around the world are constantly changing. Wind and water slowly wear down mountains, and rivers cut deeper channels across the land. In some places, floods wear down the land, while in other places they build it up. Even the oceans are constantly changing. The

bottom of the Atlantic Ocean sinks about 4 inches (10 cm) deeper every 100 years!

People also change physical regions as they **modify**, or change, the environment to meet their needs. They plow the land, mine for minerals and fuels, and cut down vegetation to clear areas for farms, buildings, and roads. They build cities and highways where there was once vacant land.

As our nation's population has grown, people have changed many physical regions to build new communities. Phoenix, Arizona, for example, is one of the fastest-growing cities in the United States today. Yet 100 years ago, only a few people lived in this part of the Sonoran (suh•NOHR•uhn) Desert. This region did not have a large enough water supply to allow large numbers of people to live there.

Over time, people started to change this region. To get more water, they drilled wells into the ground and built dams across many of the region's rivers. The dams formed lakes where only sand and rocks once covered the land. Some of the dams were used to create electricity.

More water and electricity made it possible for more people to live and work in the region. The region's warm, sunny climate also attracted people. Soon new highways, homes, and businesses were built. Phoenix is now a busy urban region that is home to one out of every five people in Arizona.

REVIEW **What causes physical regions to change over time?**

Phoenix, Arizona, has changed greatly over the years. Horses and buggies were common sights on the streets of Phoenix in the early 1900s. Today, tall buildings are part of the Phoenix skyline, and more than 1 million people live there.

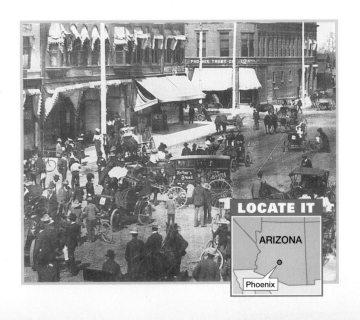

LOCATE IT

ARIZONA

Phoenix

Cultural Regions Change

Cultural regions can also change as groups of people move from place to place. People from all over the world have come to live in the United States. Each person has brought some of his or her culture to the nation.

Miami, Florida, is a good example of a changing cultural region. When Europeans came to the area in the early 1500s, only the Tequesta (teh•KES•tuh) Indians lived there. By the 1800s, people from other parts of Florida and the United States had started a settlement that would become Miami.

In the early 1900s, most people in Miami had European or African ancestors. Today, people from nearly every ethnic group in the world call Miami home. Many people who now live there have ancestors from Latin America. Latin America includes all the countries in the Western Hemisphere south of the United States.

Cuban Americans make up the largest ethnic group in Miami. Many of them live in the neighborhood called Little Havana. Many people who came to Miami from Cuba in the 1960s settled in this neighborhood. They called it Little Havana because it reminded them of Havana, the capital of Cuba. Many people there speak Spanish, so signs are written in both English and Spanish. Cuban foods, such as *empanadas* (em•puh•NAH•duhz), small pastries filled with chicken, beef, or vegetables, are among many popular foods there.

REVIEW What is the largest ethnic group in Miami today?

Economic Regions Change

Over time, economic regions change, too. The features that once made a place a part of an economic region may no longer be the same. An agricultural region may change to a manufacturing region

LOCATE IT

FLORIDA

Gulf of Mexico

Miami

Each spring, people in Little Havana take part in the Calle Ocho (KAH•yay OH•choh) Festival. Calle Ocho is the name of the main street in Little Havana.

Peanuts have become an important crop on farms such as this one in Georgia.

when businesses build factories nearby. A city may no longer be part of a manufacturing region if its industries shut down. If a new resource is found, an area may become part of a new economic region.

During the 1800s, Dothan, Alabama, like much of the South, was a cotton-growing region. Then, in the 1890s, beetles destroyed many cotton crops. As a result, many Dothan farmers switched to growing peanuts. Dothan remained an agricultural region, but it changed to a peanut-growing region.

Until the 1970s, Orlando, Florida, was also an agricultural region. Citrus fruits were an important part of the area's economy. But after several theme parks opened in the Orlando area, tourism became the most important part of the economy. **Tourism** is the selling of goods and services to people traveling for pleasure.

Most places belong to several different economic regions. Farms, factories, and service industries may all be located in the same region. However, one region cannot meet all the needs of the people who live there. The products people use each day come from factories, farms, and ranches in many different regions. Depending on one another for resources and products is called **interdependence** (in•ter•dih•PEN•duhns).

REVIEW What can cause an economic region to change over time? **SUMMARIZE**

Theme parks have made Orlando the top vacation destination in the United States.

TAXI

Elevator

SUBWAY

Information Booth

EXIT

Ticket Machine

1

Turnstile

2

3

Subway Map

3

4

Computer Controls

Connecting Regions

Interdependence among regions is possible partly because the United States has a vast transportation system. Transportation has helped regions across the nation grow, change, and connect. It allows Americans to visit friends and family in regions all over the country and the world. Millions of people travel by airplane, ship, and train. Even more people travel by car on the more than 4 million miles (6 million km) of roads in the United States. If these roads were stretched end to end, they would wrap around Earth at the equator more than 160 times! Transportation also helps **trade**, or the buying and selling of goods. It allows businesses to deliver their products to customers who live far away.

In order to trade goods, people need to know what to send and where to send it.

They find this out through communication. Like transportation, communication links businesses and people in different regions. Technology (tek•NAH•luh•jee) makes it possible for people all over the world to communicate. **Technology** is the way people use new ideas to make tools and machines.

People use regular telephones and cellular (SEL•yuh•ler) phones daily. Cellular phones use radio waves to send and receive messages. Fax machines and computers connected to telephone lines or cables also help people communicate. People stay in touch by using e-mail, or electronic mail, on the Internet.

Television is another form of communication that links people. News shows tell people about things that happen in other regions of the country and around the world. Other television shows let people see what life is like in different regions.

REVIEW How does communication connect regions? **SUMMARIZE**

LESSON 3
REVIEW

 SUMMARIZE How did Phoenix, Arizona, become a busy urban region over time?

1 **BIG IDEA** How do regions change and connect over time?

2 **VOCABULARY** Use the term **trade** to explain **interdependence** among regions in the United States.

3 **ECONOMICS** In what ways do people in different regions depend on one another?

4 **CRITICAL THINKING—Hypothesize** What do you think life might be like in the United States without good transportation and communication?

 PERFORMANCE—Write a Letter Write a letter to a fourth grader living in a different region of the United States. Describe your region's physical features, culture, and economy. Describe the different ways you could visit or communicate with each other.

Identify Cause and Effect

VOCABULARY

cause   effect

▶ WHY IT MATTERS

Regions change for many reasons. Phoenix, Arizona, changed from an empty desert region to a busy urban region. The creation of a supply of water in the desert was one of the causes of Phoenix's growth. A **cause** is an action that makes something else happen. Phoenix's change to an urban region was partly an effect of the supply of water. An **effect** is what happens because of an earlier action. Understanding causes and their effects can help you make decisions.

▶ WHAT YOU NEED TO KNOW

You can use these steps to find the causes of an effect.

Step 1 Look for the effect.

Step 2 Look for the causes of that effect.

Step 3 Think about how these causes relate to one another and to the effect.

▶ PRACTICE THE SKILL

Use the cause-and-effect chart to answer the following questions.

1. How have resources affected the growth of Phoenix?

2. How has Phoenix's climate caused growth?

3. How has transportation helped Phoenix to grow?

4. How do the different causes relate to one another and to the effect of rapid growth in Phoenix?

▶ APPLY WHAT YOU LEARNED

Interview adult family members and friends to find out how the region where you live has changed. Identify one effect, or change, and all of its causes. Organize the information in a chart like the one below. Write a short paragraph describing your findings. Then share your chart and paragraph with your classmates.

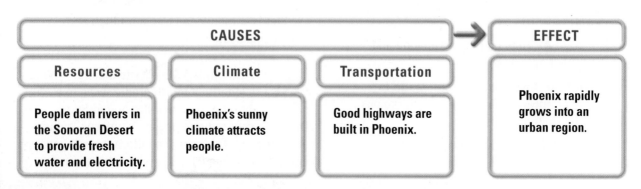

CAUSES			→	EFFECT
Resources	**Climate**	**Transportation**		
People dam rivers in the Sonoran Desert to provide fresh water and electricity.	Phoenix's sunny climate attracts people.	Good highways are built in Phoenix.		Phoenix rapidly grows into an urban region.

Regions Around the World

You already know that the United States is too large to study all at once. Imagine how hard it would be to study the whole world at one time! To make it easier to study and understand the world, people often divide it into regions.

Many of the same kinds of regions found in the United States can also be found in other places around the world. We identify physical, cultural, and political regions in all places. In this lesson, you will learn about one type of region from Asia, from Africa, and from Europe.

Physical Regions in Asia

Asia is the largest continent in the world. It stretches from the Pacific Ocean in the east to the continent of Europe in the west. It extends as far north as the Arctic Ocean and as far south as the Indian Ocean. Many of the same kinds of physical regions found in North America can also be found in Asia.

The northern part of Asia is called Siberia. This region covers almost one-third of Asia's land. The part of Siberia that borders the Arctic Ocean is a **tundra**, or large, treeless plain. South of this tundra is a vast region of evergreen forests.

LOCATE IT

CHINA

Yangshuo

SUMMARIZE
As you read, summarize information about regions around the world.

BIG IDEA
Regions around the world are similar to regions in the United States.

VOCABULARY

tundra
steppes
rain forest
heritage
tradition
currency

More than half of the world's rice is grown in Asia. The climate in Yangshuo, China, and other rice-growing regions in Asia, is similar to the climate in the rice-growing regions in the United States.

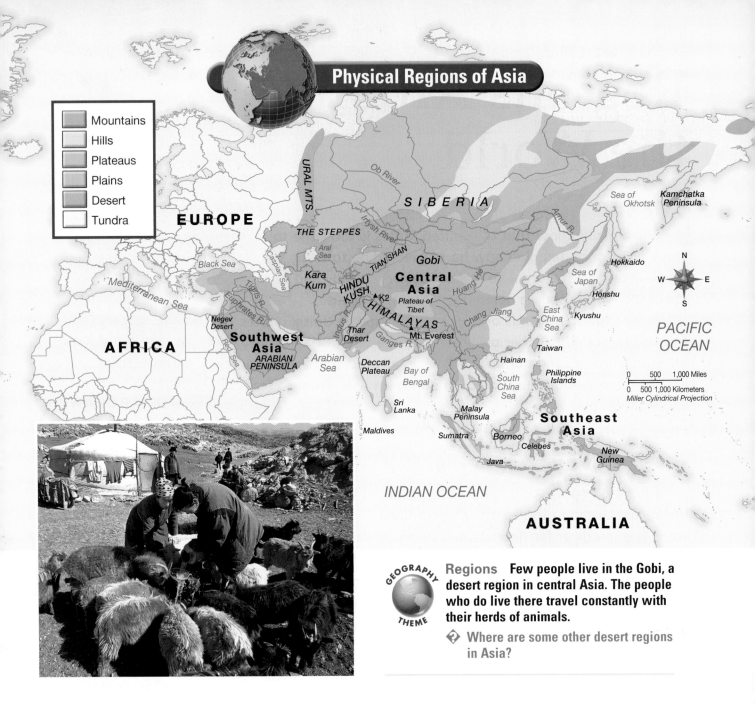

Physical Regions of Asia

Mountains
Hills
Plateaus
Plains
Desert
Tundra

EUROPE

URAL MTS.

Ob River

SIBERIA

THE STEPPES

Irtysh River

Black Sea

Aral Sea

TIAN SHAN

Gobi

Kara Kum

HINDU KUSH

Central Asia

Huang He

Sea of Okhotsk

Kamchatka Peninsula

Mediterranean Sea

Caspian Sea

Tigris R.

Euphrates R.

K2

Plateau of Tibet

Chang Jiang

Sea of Japan

Hokkaido

Honshu

HIMALAYAS

AFRICA

Negev Desert

Southwest Asia

ARABIAN PENINSULA

Red Sea

Indus R.

Thar Desert

Ganges R.

Mt. Everest

East China Sea

Kyushu

Arabian Sea

Deccan Plateau

Bay of Bengal

Taiwan

Hainan

South China Sea

Philippine Islands

PACIFIC OCEAN

N W E S

Sri Lanka

Maldives

Sumatra

Malay Peninsula

Borneo

Celebes

Java

Southeast Asia

New Guinea

0   500   1,000 Miles
0   500 1,000 Kilometers
Miller Cylindrical Projection

INDIAN OCEAN

AUSTRALIA

GEOGRAPHY THEME

Regions Few people live in the Gobi, a desert region in central Asia. The people who do live there travel constantly with their herds of animals.

◆ Where are some other desert regions in Asia?

A large region of dry, grassy plains called **steppes** (STEPS) lies south of Siberia. This region is similar to the Great Plains of the United States. Farmers on the steppes grow wheat and other crops.

Central Asia, south of the steppes, is a region of high, dry plateaus and rugged mountains. Asia's largest desert, the Gobi, covers much of central Asia.

The Himalaya (hih•muh•LAY•uh) Mountains run along the southern edge of central Asia. Their highest peak,

Mount Everest, is the world's tallest mountain. It soars to a height of 29,028 feet (8,848 m).

The tip of southeast Asia is a peninsula surrounded by thousands of islands. Rolling hills, river valleys, fertile plains, and rain forests cover much of this region. A **rain forest** is a wet area, usually warm, in which tall trees, vines, and other plants grow close together.

Deserts cover much of southwest Asia. In one of these deserts lies the Dead Sea.

At 1,312 feet (400 m) below sea level, it is the lowest place on Earth. It is also the saltiest body of water in the world.

REVIEW **What are some of the major physical features of Asia?**

 SUMMARIZE

Cultural Regions of Africa

A good place to see many cultural regions is Africa. This continent is home to more than 1,000 ethnic groups with different languages, religions, and customs.

People sometimes study Africa as five large cultural regions—North Africa, West Africa, Central Africa, East Africa, and Southern Africa. In all these regions, people value and celebrate their heritage. **Heritage** is a way of life, a set of customs, or a belief that has come from the past and continues today.

The North African cultural region lies mostly within the Sahara, the largest desert in the world. Most people speak Arabic and practice the religion of Islam. Nearly

Mosque door in North Africa

every town and city has at least one mosque (MAHSK), or Islamic place of worship.

Ancestors of people in the West African cultural region lived in some of the world's first cities. Archaeologists (ar•kee•AH•luh•jists) have discovered the ruins of the trading city of Jenné (jeh•NAY), built more than 2,000 years ago. The great city of Timbuktu (tim•buhk•TOO), a center of wealth and learning, dates from the same period.

Many archaeologists believe that the first people on Earth lived in the East African cultural region. They had their own forms of writing and traded ivory and gold.

Today, more than 100 million people live in the Central African cultural region. They

Nairobi, Kenya, is home to many international companies.

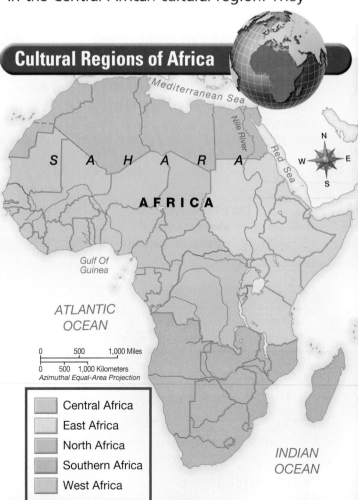

Cultural Regions of Africa

Mediterranean Sea

SAHARA

Nile River

Red Sea

AFRICA

Gulf Of Guinea

ATLANTIC OCEAN

0   500   1,000 Miles
0   500 1,000 Kilometers
Azimuthal Equal-Area Projection

Central Africa
East Africa
North Africa
Southern Africa
West Africa

INDIAN OCEAN

GEOGRAPHY THEME

Regions Each of Africa's five cultural regions contains between 6 and 15 different countries.

◆ **Which large body of water has likely had an influence on the culture of North Africa?**

belong to hundreds of different ethnic groups, but many are united in speaking what are called Bantu languages.

Although some of Africa's biggest cities are located in the Southern African cultural region, many people still live in rural villages.

Throughout Africa, in both cities and villages, the tradition of storytelling is important. A **tradition** is a way of life or an idea that has been handed down from the past.

West Africa, for example, is rich in family and cultural traditions. Playing music is one important tradition. West African musicians developed their own musical styles and invented many instruments, such as the dun-dun, or "talking drums." Today, people in cities have added other instruments such as guitars and electronic keyboards. People all over the world now listen to this popular mixture of new and traditional African music called Mande music.

REVIEW What cultural region in Africa had some of the world's first cities?

The Eiffel Tower soars above the city of Paris, the capital of France.

Political Regions of Europe

Like the United States, European countries are divided into smaller political regions. Every country in Europe has cities and towns. Some countries, such as Ireland, have counties, too. France is divided into 22 large political regions which are similar to our counties. These regions are divided into smaller regions called departments. These, in turn, are divided into the smallest political regions, communes (KAHM•yoonz).

Many political regions in Europe are connected. Four regions—England, Scotland, Wales, and Northern Ireland—make up one larger political region called the United Kingdom. Recently, many countries in Europe, including the United Kingdom, France, Germany, Italy, Spain, and Sweden, joined the European Union. The countries in this group have their own governments, but they trade freely and follow many of the same laws. They have a common **currency**, or money, that can be used in any of

LOCATE IT

Paris

FRANCE

Political Regions of Europe

Regions Ukraine is the largest country in Europe. Russia is larger, but most of it is in Asia.

❓ What body of water does Ukraine border?

these countries. This makes the European Union an economic region as well as a political region.

Transportation technology also connects political regions in Europe today. Since 1994, people have been able to travel beneath the English Channel through the Channel Tunnel, commonly called the Chunnel. This 31-mile (50-km) tunnel and the high-speed trains that run through it connect continental Europe and the island of Great Britain.

REVIEW What are some of the political regions in Europe today?

LESSON 4
REVIEW

SUMMARIZE How do the cultural regions of North Africa and West Africa compare?

1 **BIG IDEA** How are some kinds of regions around the world similar to regions in the United States?

2 **VOCABULARY** Use the terms **tradition** and **heritage** to describe a cultural region.

3 **CIVICS AND GOVERNMENT** In what ways are some political regions in Europe connected?

4 **CRITICAL THINKING—Synthesize** Southwest Asia is sometimes called a crossroads. Look at the world map on pages A6–A7. What about this region's location makes it a crossroads of continents?

PERFORMANCE—Tell a Story Practice the art of storytelling. In groups, take turns describing in stories the physical regions of Asia, the cultural regions of Africa, and the political regions of Europe.

2 Review and Test Preparation

Focus Skill Use Your Reading Skills

Copy the following graphic organizer onto a separate sheet of paper. Use the information you have learned to summarize the main topics of this chapter. For each main topic, write some important details related to the topic.

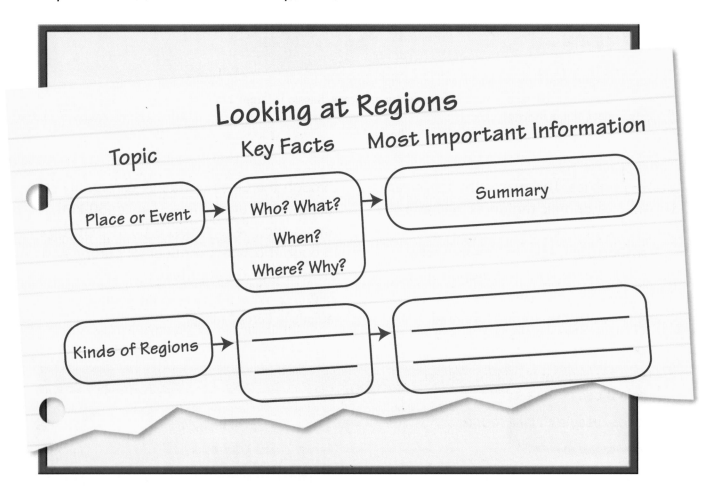

Looking at Regions

Topic — Key Facts — Most Important Information

Place or Event → Who? What? When? Where? Why? → Summary

Kinds of Regions → ___ → ___

THINK & WRITE

Write Interview Questions Write a list of questions you could ask somebody who lives in another part of the country. Ask the person about the physical features, economy, and culture where he or she lives. You may also ask why the person chose to live there.

Explain How Write a paragraph that explains how technology, transportation, and communication link the place where you live with other places in the United States. Think about how those same things might also connect you to places around the world.

USE VOCABULARY

Use each term in a sentence that helps explain its meaning.

1. **urban** (p. 60)
2. **government** (p. 61)
3. **county** (p. 62)
4. **economy** (p. 67)
5. **industry** (p. 67)
6. **trade** (p. 77)
7. **heritage** (p. 81)

RECALL FACTS

Answer these questions.

8. Why is it useful to divide a large area into smaller regions?

9. What is life like in some suburban regions?

10. Which is generally larger, a county or a state?

11. What are some of the things cultural regions can be based on?

12. How do people change regions?

13. How are regions linked?

14. What are some forms of transportation and communication?

Write the letter of the best choice.

15. Which of the following is not a political region?
    A state
    B county
    C neighborhood
    D city

16. One kind of region that is based on a physical feature is called a—
    F county.
    G cultural region.
    H suburb.
    J natural vegetation region.

17. What is another word for *farming*?
    A manufacturing
    B technology
    C agriculture
    D interdependence

THINK CRITICALLY

18. Why is it important for a region that shares a government to have exact boundaries?

19. What products do you use or consume daily that are probably provided by other regions?

20. Why are the skills and talents of every worker in the United States important?

21. How do you think the things people do for fun are affected by the regions in which they live?

APPLY SKILLS

Use a Land Use and Resource Map

22. Look at the map on page 71. Where are the major manufacturing areas in California located?

Identify Cause and Effect

23. Think about something that has happened to you at school, such as earning a good grade. List all the causes for that effect.

VISIT

Glenwood Canyon

GET READY

Glenwood Canyon, near Glenwood Springs, Colorado, is rugged and deep. Over time the rushing waters of the Colorado River have worn away rock to form the steep canyon walls. A modern highway winds through the canyon. The highway was carefully planned so that the natural environment would not be disrupted. This highway allows people to visit the canyon and enjoy its beauty. Glenwood Canyon offers many outdoor recreational activities. At the canyon, you can raft on the Colorado River, hike a scenic trail, or bicycle on paths along the river.

WHAT TO SEE

To reach Glenwood Canyon by automobile, you will pass through one of these tunnels.

LOCATE IT

COLORADO

Glenwood Canyon

THINK CRITICALLY

14 On what kinds of landforms do you think most farms are located? Why?

15 What factors affect the climate where you live?

16 What things can you and your family do to help conserve resources?

17 Why do people choose different regions to live in?

18 What is the connection between the kind of economic region a place is in and the kind of physical region it is in?

19 What things from cultures other than your own have become part of your life?

20 In what ways is your region interdependent with others in the United States?

21 How do Europe's political regions compare to those in the United States?

APPLY SKILLS

Use Latitude and Longitude
Use the map on this page to answer the following questions.

22 Which line of longitude passes near Zanesville?

23 What lines of latitude and longitude meet closest to Springfield?

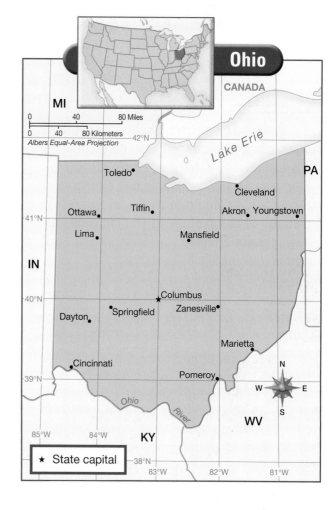

Ohio

24 What is the absolute location of Ottawa?

25 Which city's absolute location is 39°N, 82°W?

26 What is the absolute location of the capital of Ohio?

27 What city on the map lies east of 81°W?

People use natural resources to meet their needs. p. 49

The United States is divided into many kinds of regions. p. 60

The United States is made up of many cultures. p. 74

GO ONLINE

Visit The Learning Site at
www.harcourtschool.com
for additional activities.

Make a Conservation Book

Make a conservation book that explains how people can change or damage the environment as they use natural resources. Give ideas for ways people can conserve resources. To illustrate your book, draw pictures or use pictures from magazines or newspapers. Display your book where others can read it.

Make Postcards

Make a set of postcards that show how a region has changed over time. First, choose an economic, political, cultural, or physical region in the United States. Then, use the Internet or other resources to learn about the history of the region you chose. Finally, use your research to draw postcards that show the features of this region at different times in history.

VISIT YOUR LIBRARY

■ *Alice Ramsey's Grand Adventure* by Don Brown. Houghton Mifflin Company.

■ *Purple Mountain Majesties: The Story of Katharine Lee Bates and "America the Beautiful"* by Barbara Younger. Dutton Children's Books.

■ *It Happened in America: True Stories from the Fifty States* by Lila Perl. Henry Holt and Company.

COMPLETE THE UNIT PROJECT

A Travel Guide Work in groups to finish the Unit Project described on page 19—a travel guide to the United States. First, review the notes that you and the other members of your group took as you read this unit. Next, decide what information you will include in your travel guide. Also decide what articles, illustrations, photographs, and maps your travel guide will have. Remember to talk about the physical features, climate, natural resources, and economy of the United States. Share your travel guide with the rest of the class.

The Allegheny River,
Pennsylvania

Pennsylvania's Geography

" Our forests should be preserved...for [the] enjoyment of the natural beauty of Pennsylvania. "

—Governor Edward G. Rendell, 2002

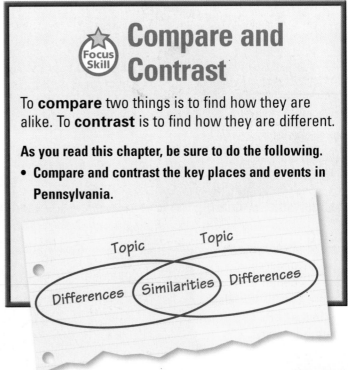

☆ Focus Skill: Compare and Contrast

To **compare** two things is to find how they are alike. To **contrast** is to find how they are different.

As you read this chapter, be sure to do the following.

- Compare and contrast the key places and events in Pennsylvania.

Topic   Topic

Differences   Similarities   Differences

COMPARE AND CONTRAST

As you read, compare and contrast communities in Pennsylvania.

BIG IDEA

Pennsylvania's location may be described in many ways.

VOCABULARY

metropolitan area
keystone
crossroad

Where Is Pennsylvania?

Pennsylvania is a beautiful state. Long ago, only Native Americans lived here. In time, people from all over the world came here to live. But, where is Pennsylvania?

A Global Address

If someone asked you to tell the relative location of Pennsylvania, what would you say? You could say that Pennsylvania is one of the 50 United States. You might also say that the state of Pennsylvania is in the Northeast region of the United States. But you could say even more.

Since most of the United States is part of the continent of North America, you could say Pennsylvania is in North America. The North American continent is in Earth's Western Hemisphere and Northern Hemisphere. Where is Pennsylvania? Pennsylvania is in the country's Northeast region. It is in North America, in the Western Hemisphere, and in the Northern Hemisphere.

REVIEW In which of Earth's hemispheres is Pennsylvania located?

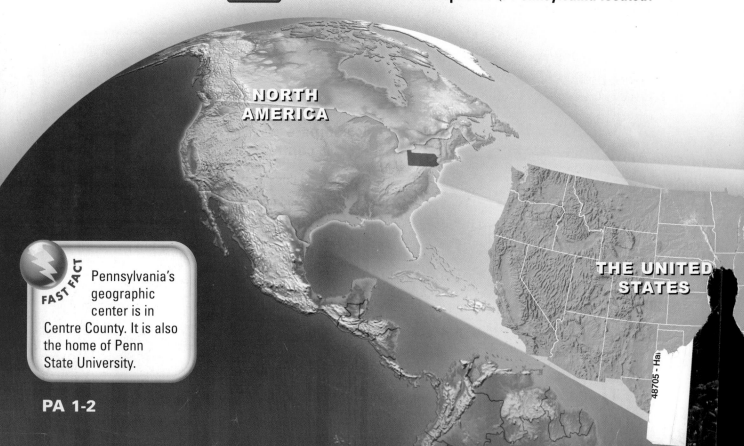

NORTH AMERICA

THE UNITED STATES

FAST FACT Pennsylvania's geographic center is in Centre County. It is also the home of Penn State University.

48705 - Ha

Pennsylvania in the United States

Pennsylvania covers more than 45,000 square miles of land. If the 50 states were lined up from largest to smallest, Pennsylvania would be thirty-third in line. That means 32 states have more land than Pennsylvania and 17 states have less land.

The state of Pennsylvania is sixth in population. More than 12 million people live in Pennsylvania. More than one-half of all Pennsylvanians live in urban, or city, areas. Philadelphia is the state's most populated city, with more than 1½ million people.

Philadelphia and nearby communities make up the sixth-largest metropolitan area in the nation. A **metropolitan area** includes a large city or cities and the surrounding communities. About six million people in four different states—New Jersey, Delaware, Maryland, and Pennsylvania—make up the metropolitan area of Philadelphia.

Pennsylvania has other metropolitan areas. Pittsburgh is Pennsylvania's second-largest city. Nearly 350,000 people live in Pittsburgh. Almost 2½ million people live in Pittsburgh's metropolitan area.

Philadelphia is the largest city in Pennsylvania.

LOCATE IT

PENNSYLVANIA

Philadelphia

Philadelphia, Pittsburgh, Allentown, Harrisburg, Scranton, and Lancaster are all among the 100 largest metropolitan areas of the United States.

Many Pennsylvanians choose to live in smaller cities and towns, such as Altoona, York, or Punxsutawney. Others live in rural, or country, areas all across the state.

REVIEW How is a metropolitan area different from a city? COMPARE AND CONTRAST

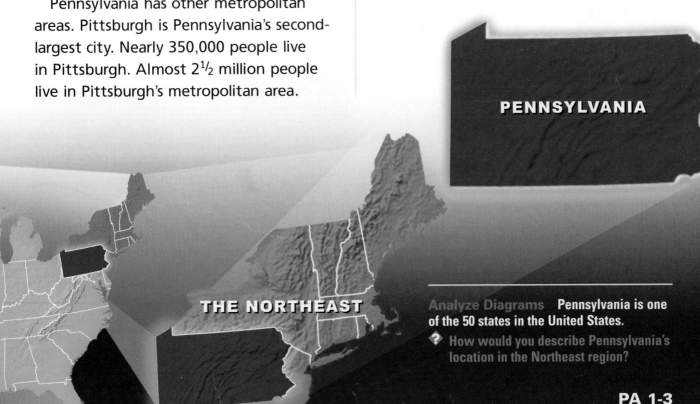

PENNSYLVANIA

THE NORTHEAST

Analyze Diagrams Pennsylvania is one of the 50 states in the United States.

? How would you describe Pennsylvania's location in the Northeast region?

The Keystone State

Pennsylvania is nicknamed the Keystone State. A **keystone** is the middle stone at the top of an arch that locks the other stones in place. Pennsylvania is called the Keystone State because of its location. The name also refers to the state's key role in early United States history.

Pennsylvania's location makes it an important crossroad for travelers and industry. A **crossroad** is a place where roads meet. A system of major highways links Pennsylvania to the Northeast and the entire United States.

In 1787, citizens from the 13 original states met in Philadelphia to write our nation's Constitution. Benjamin Franklin and Benjamin Rush helped the state earn its place in history.

Since 1701, Pennsylvanians have worked together to run the state. Today, the state capital is in Harrisburg, in the southeastern part of the state. Its location near major highways allows citizens from across the state to play a role in state government.

Citizens are also active in their local governments. Pennsylvania is divided into 67 counties. Each county has a county seat where local government meets.

REVIEW How do Pennsylvania's roads help make it the Keystone State?

GEOGRAPHY THEME

Place Every county in Pennsylvania has a county seat for government.

◆ In which county do you live? What is its county seat?

Counties of Pennsylvania

Lake Erie

NEW YORK

★ State capital
• County seat

0   25   50 Miles
0   25   50 Kilometers
Albers Equal-Area Projection

Erie
ERIE

CRAWFORD
Meadville

Warren
WARREN

McKEAN
Smethport

Coudersport
POTTER

TIOGA
Wellsboro

BRADFORD
Towanda

SUSQUEHANNA
Montrose

WAYNE
Honesdale

FOREST
Tionesta

Emporium
CAMERON

ELK
Ridgway

WYOMING
Tunkhannock

SULLIVAN
Laporte

LACKAWANNA
Scranton

PIKE
Milford

VENANGO

MERCER
Mercer

Franklin

CLARION
Clarion

JEFFERSON
Brookville

CLEARFIELD
Clearfield

CLINTON

LYCOMING
Williamsport

Lock
Haven

Wilkes-Barre
LUZERNE

MONROE
Stroudsburg

LAWRENCE
New
Castle

BUTLER
Butler

ARMSTRONG
Kittanning

INDIANA
Indiana

CENTRE
Bellefonte

COLUMBIA
MONTOUR
Danville

Bloomsburg

CARBON
Jim
Thorpe

Beaver

BEAVER

Middleburg
NORTH-
UMBERLAND

SNYDER

SCHUYLKILL
Pottsville

NORTHAMPTON
Easton

NEW
JERSEY

MIFFLIN
Lewistown

JUNIATA

LEHIGH
Allentown

UNION
Lewisburg

Sunbury

ALLEGHENY
Pittsburgh

CAMBRIA

BLAIR
Ebensburg

Huntingdon

Mifflintown

DAUPHIN

BERKS
Reading

BUCKS
Doylestown

Greensburg
WESTMORELAND

Holidaysburg

HUNTINGDON

PERRY
New
Bloomfield

LEBANON
Lebanon

★Harrisburg

MONTGOMERY
Norristown

Washington
WASHINGTON

BEDFORD
Bedford

Carlisle
CUMBERLAND

LANCASTER
Lancaster

CHESTER

PHILADELPHIA
Philadelphia

Somerset

York

West
Chester

Media
DELAWARE

FAYETTE
Waynesburg   Uniontown

GREENE

SOMERSET

FRANKLIN
McConnellsburg   Chambersburg

FULTON

ADAMS

Gettysburg

YORK

LOCATE IT

PENNSYLVANIA

Harrisburg

The state capitol in Harrisburg sits on 2 acres in a 13-acre park and has more than 600 rooms.

Pennsylvania's Borders

Six states and Lake Erie make up the borders of Pennsylvania. Our neighbor to the east is New Jersey. To the south are Delaware, Maryland, and West Virginia. Ohio shares a border with Pennsylvania on the west. Lake Erie and New York make up our state's northern border.

We also share important resources with our neighbors. Many of Pennsylvania's rivers flow into neighboring states. The Delaware River carves a natural border all along eastern Pennsylvania. Many boats carry goods on the Delaware River. The Ohio River is also a main transportation route. The shores of Lake Erie connect Pennsylvania to other states and to Canada. Many people enjoy recreational activities in and around Lake Erie. Swimming, boating, hiking, and biking are all popular activities. The Allegheny (a•luh•GAY•nee) National Forest is a beautiful place to explore.

REVIEW Which lake makes up a part of Pennsylvania's border?

LESSON 1 REVIEW

Focus Skill

COMPARE AND CONTRAST In what ways are urban and metropolitan areas alike?

1. **BIG IDEA** In which region of the United States is Pennsylvania located?

2. **VOCABULARY** Use the term **keystone** in a sentence about Pennsylvania.

3. **GEOGRAPHY** Which states share a border with Pennsylvania?

2

 COMPARE AND CONTRAST

As you read, compare and contrast physical regions in Pennsylvania.

BIG IDEA

Each of Pennsylvania's five physical regions has different landforms.

VOCABULARY

terrace

Pennsylvania's Land and Water

If you were to ride in a car from Erie to Philadelphia, you would see many different landforms. Geographers group similar landforms into physical regions. If you travel from northwestern Pennsylvania to southeastern Pennsylvania, you can visit each of the state's five physical regions.

A Land Shaped by Ice

Pennsylvania's landforms were slowly shaped by nature over a long period of time. Millions of years ago, much of what is now Pennsylvania was covered by glaciers. As the glaciers moved, they carved deep valleys into some areas of land. In other areas, the glaciers flattened the land or rounded the tops of mountains and hills.

In time, the glaciers melted, and water covered much of the land. When the water evaporated, Pennsylvania's physical regions were uncovered.

REVIEW How did glaciers shape the land in Pennsylvania?

The hills overlooking Lake Erie were left by melting glaciers millions of years ago.

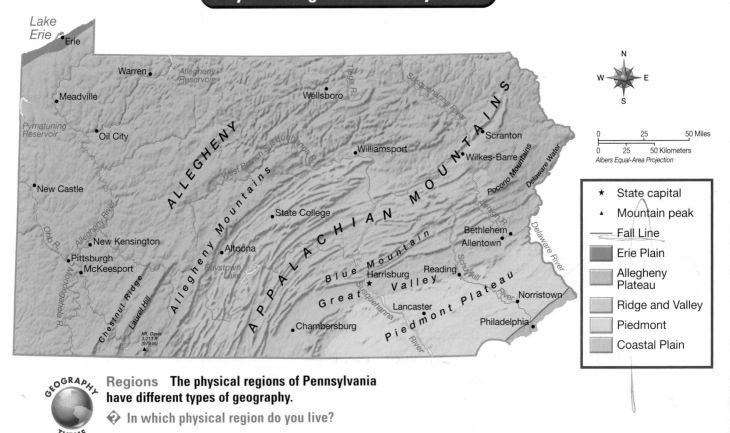

Physical Regions of Pennsylvania

Lake Erie
Erie
Warren
Allegheny Reservoir
Meadville
Wellsboro
Tioga R.
Susquehanna River
Pymatuning Reservoir
Oil City
ALLEGHENY
Scranton
Williamsport
Wilkes-Barre
New Castle
Allegheny River
Allegheny Mountains
West Branch Susquehanna
Pocono Mountains
Delaware Water
State College
APPALACHIAN MOUNTAINS
Lehigh R.
New Kensington
Altoona
Bethlehem
Ohio R.
Pittsburgh
Raystown Lake
Blue Mountain
Harrisburg
Allentown
Delaware River
McKeesport
Great
Valley
Reading
Schuylkill
Norristown
Monongahela R.
Chestnut Ridge
Laurel Hill
Lancaster
Piedmont Plateau
Susquehanna River
Philadelphia
Mt. Davis 3,213 ft. (979 m)
Chambersburg

Legend
- ★ State capital
- ▲ Mountain peak
- — Fall Line
- Erie Plain
- Allegheny Plateau
- Ridge and Valley
- Piedmont
- Coastal Plain

N W E S

0   25   50 Miles
0   25   50 Kilometers
Albers Equal-Area Projection

GEOGRAPHY THEME

Regions The physical regions of Pennsylvania have different types of geography.

❓ In which physical region do you live?

Five Physical Regions

The smallest of Pennsylvania's five physical regions is the Erie Plain. This narrow, lowland region begins at the shore of Lake Erie. As you travel east across the Erie Plain, the land gets higher. Natural **terraces**, or raised lands, increase the elevation inland, like stair steps.

The Allegheny Plateau region begins southeast of the Erie Plain. The Allegheny Plateau is Pennsylvania's largest physical region and covers more than one-half of the state. Many rivers, including the West Branch Susquehanna (suhs•kwuh•HA•nuh) and the Allegheny flow from this highland plateau.

The Appalachian Mountains are part of the landforms in the Ridge and Valley region. Mountain rivers and streams shape the valleys here. Within the Ridge

and Valley region, the Great Valley stretches south for hundreds of miles through other states.

To the east of the Ridge and Valley region is the Piedmont region. Like the Great Valley, the landforms of the Piedmont continue south through other states. Here, the Piedmont is a region of rolling hills sloping down to the southeast.

Pennsylvania's Coastal Plain region is also part of a much larger landform. The Atlantic Coastal Plain is a broad area of flat lands stretching all along the Atlantic coast of the United States. In Pennsylvania, the Coastal Plain region is small. It is only slightly larger than the Erie Plain region.

REVIEW Which of the five physical reg[...] largest? Which region is smallest?

 COMPARE AND CONTRAST

Woodlands, Mountains, and Waterways

Pennsylvania's natural resources are all around us. People living in each of the state's five physical regions use and enjoy these natural resources.

Woodlands cover about one-half of Pennsylvania. Many different kinds of trees—hickory, maple, cherry, oak, and pine—shade the state. Woodlands are also a home for wildlife. Animals such as deer, foxes, skunk, and raccoon are common.

The Allegheny Mountains are a beautiful place to enjoy outdoor activities. Mount Davis, in Somerset County, is the state's highest mountain peak at 3,213 feet.

Waterways in Pennsylvania are home to more than 150 different kinds of fish.

One of the state's most important rivers is the wide, shallow Susquehanna. The West Branch Susquehanna flows from western Pennsylvania southeast across much of the state. The Lehigh and Schuylkill rivers are in eastern Pennsylvania. Both are tributaries of the Delaware River. The Allegheny and Monongahela rivers meet in Pittsburgh and together they form the Ohio river.

In central Pennsylvania, Jacks Mountain has the Thousand Steps Trail. Visitors can see the fossils of plants and animals that lived here long ago. Nearby, Raystown Lake is part of a project to protect plant and animal habitats. Pittsburgh's Mount Washington offers a great view of the state's second-largest city.

REVIEW About how much of Pennsylvania is woodlands?

Blue Mountain Tunnel, in Franklin County, is 4,339 feet long. It is one of the seven original tunnels along the Pennsylvania Turnpike.

Blue Mountain Tunnel

BLUE MOUNTAIN

Average Temperatures in Pennsylvania

Average Temperatures in January

°F   22°   24°   26°   28°   30°

°C   -5°   -4°   -3°   -2°   -1°

Average Temperatures in July

°F   66°   70°   72°   74°   76°

°C   19°   21°   22°   23°   24°

Place The maps above show the average temperatures in Pennsylvania during the months of January and July.

❖ What is the average temperature for Harrisburg in January? in July?

Pennsylvania's Climate

Differences in landforms and elevation cause the climate to vary across the state. Some mountainous areas experience temperatures below freezing. They have snow for several months of the year.

Areas with lower elevations, such as the Piedmont and Coastal Plain, have a shorter winter. Some northern parts of the state have large changes in temperature, depending on the season. Although rainfall totals vary throughout the state, the average is about 39 inches of rain per year.

REVIEW Why does Pennsylvania's climate vary?

When snow falls in Pennsylvania, it's fun to bundle up and go sledding.

LESSON 2
REVIEW

 COMPARE AND CONTRAST How are the Erie Plain and the Allegheny Plateau alike? How are they different?

1 BIG IDEA What are the five physical regions in Pennsylvania?

2 VOCABULARY Write a sentence about landforms, using the term **terrace**.

3 GEOGRAPHY What is Pennsylvania's highest mountain peak?

COMPARE AND CONTRAST

As you read, compare and contrast places in Pennsylvania.

BIG IDEA

Pennsylvania towns and cities honor many different cultures.

VOCABULARY

borough
population center

Pennsylvania's People and Places

Today, people and places in Pennsylvania are connected to the past by culture and history. It is important to understand how different cultures shape our present and guide our future.

Pennsylvania's People

Pennsylvania is home to people from many cultures around the world. Across the state, the places where we live show the effect of these different cultures. In the past, many people moved to Pennsylvania from other countries to work on farms. Others came to work in factories. Some wanted a safe place to practice their religions. Others wanted to have a say in their government.

As new groups of people arrived, they brought their customs along with them. These customs and traditions still affect ways of life in the state. Pennsylvanians are proud of their different cultures and of all the people who make this state their home.

REVIEW **Why does Pennsylvania have many different cultures?**

Children in Pennsylvania come from many different cultural backgrounds.

In Pittsburgh, Point State Park is where the Monongahela and Allegheny rivers meet. Many bridges help cars and pedestrians get across the city's rivers.

LOCATE IT

PENNSYLVANIA

Pittsburgh

Pennsylvania's Places

In addition to its physical regions, Pennsylvania has human regions. The northwest and northcentral regions are mostly rural. Many people here work on farms or operate small businesses. Some people work at jobs in tourism. Others work in one of the many state parks, such as Ricketts Glen State Park in Benton.

Many communities around the state are towns and boroughs (BUR•ohz). A **borough** is a self-governing town that is bigger than a village. The borough of Doylestown, in Bucks County, dates back to 1745. Today, there are about 8,000 people living in Doylestown.

Philadelphia and its suburbs are in the southeast. Many people live in suburbs and travel to the city's center to work. More people live in the southeast than in any other part of the state. Because of this, Philadelphia is considered to be the state's largest **population center**, or place where many people live.

West of Philadelphia is an area known for the German settlers who arrived in the 1700s. Although they were not from the Netherlands, these immigrants came to be called Pennsylvania Dutch. The name comes from the English settlers, who did not understand the word *Deutsch*, which means "German." Many of the Pennsylvania Dutch worked on farms. They grew wheat and tobacco crops.

In central Pennsylvania, people from eastern Europe settled the Harrisburg and Hershey area. Today, state government is in Harrisburg. Nearby is Hershey, a community with a sweet history.

Pennsylvania's southwest includes Pittsburgh, the state's second-largest city. Its history and economy were built around the iron and steel industries. Many Polish and German immigrants settled in the southwest.

REVIEW How does a population center differ from a borough?

COMPARE AND CONTRAST

Caring for Cultures

Pennsylvanians have kept many traditions that honor their cultures. German immigrants built communities that looked similar to those in their homeland. Since the mid-1800s, Germantown has been part of Philadelphia. Some buildings there still feature traditional German styles.

German cooking and arts also continue. In some restaurants, you can order shoofly pie, a dessert made with brown sugar and molasses. Folk artists today combine letters with painted pictures in a kind of artwork called Fraktur.

Other German and Swiss immigrants came to be called the Mennonites and the Amish. They chose to live in Pennsylvania because they knew the state welcomed people with different religious beliefs. The Mennonites and Amish have strict religious beliefs. They live in rural areas, such as Lancaster County. In Amish communities, people wear simple,

Important events are remembered with Fraktur, handmade documents with fancy lettering.

handmade clothing. They drive horses and buggies. Children attend school in one-room schoolhouses.

Many Amish men and boys work on farms. Others run lumber mills, and some are woodworkers. Amish women teach girls how to make quilts. They gather in groups called quilting bees.

REVIEW **What German traditions are still practiced in Pennsylvania?**

• HERITAGE •

The Amish People

The Amish people of Lancaster, Pennsylvania, came to the colony in the early 1700s. Their simple way of life has remained separate from American society for almost 300 years. The Amish culture in Pennsylvania is still strong today.

As a result of their religious beliefs, the Amish choose to live without telephones or electricity. They use wood, gas, or coal for heat, light, and cooking. Windmills pump water for their homes and farms. The men wear wide-brimmed hats, and the women wear long dresses and bonnets. The Amish commitment to community traditions has produced a lasting culture.

Musicians (above) celebrate their African American heritage at an annual street festival called ODUNDE. In the Mummers' Parade, people wear unusual costumes. This mummer (right) is dressed to celebrate autumn.

Celebrating Diversity

Many communities in Pennsylvania celebrate their heritage with festivals and parades. In Philadelphia, there are several cultural celebrations. Swedish immigrants who settled in the city in the late 1600s brought their custom of holding a New Year's Day Parade. Today, the Philadelphia Mummers' Parade remains a highlight of New Year's Day. Brightly dressed mummers, or clowns, entertain large crowds.

The Chinese New Year is celebrated with a parade in Philadelphia. In June, African Americans celebrate their heritage at the Odunde Festival in Philadelphia. At Penn's Landing, people enjoy traditional foods, dancing, and music from India during the Festival of India.

In Scranton, an annual St. Patrick's Day Parade is a popular event. Scottish Highland games are held in several towns around the state. These events celebrate Scottish heritage with bagpipes and traditional dance and music.

REVIEW Who are Philadelphia's mummers?

LESSON 3
REVIEW

COMPARE AND CONTRAST How is life different for people living in Philadelphia and people living west of the city?

1 BIG IDEA Why do different places in Pennsylvania have different cultures?

2 VOCABULARY Write a sentence using the term **population center** about the city of Pittsburgh.

3 CULTURE AND SOCIETY Which immigrants started Philadelphia's New Year's Day Parade?

The Allegheny National Forest

Land for the Allegheny National Forest was set aside in 1923. It includes more than 500,000 acres. Before it was protected as a national forest, many trees in the area were cut down for timber. This deforestation led to flooding of streams and rivers. Since the Forest Service began to manage the forest, new trees have grown. Today, it is one of the world's finest hardwood forests. Protective guidelines now ensure the forest's future.

DID YOU KNOW?

One out of three people in the United States lives within a day's drive of the Allegheny National Forest.

LOCATE IT

Allegheny National Forest

PENNSYLVANIA

Allegheny National Forest, Pennsylvania

As the only national forest in Pennsylvania, the Allegheny National Forest offers many recreational opportunities. Here visitors can hike, camp, swim, bike, and boat. Many people also enjoy the scenic overlooks of the Allegheny Reservoir.

While exploring the forest, expect to see plenty of wildlife, including raccoons, gray squirrels, foxes, deer, beavers, and songbirds. Bald eagles have been seen in the Kinzua (kin·ZOO·uh) Dam area.

Safe boating on the Allegheny Reservoir

Smokey the Bear reminds us to take care of the forest.

ACTIVITY

Imagine that you work for the National Park Service. Your job is to make a brochure inviting visitors to the Allegheny National Forest. Include reasons why the Allegheny National Forest is a fun place to visit.

RESEARCH

GO ONLINE

Visit The Learning Site at **www.harcourtschool.com** to learn about other parks and scenic areas.

Review and Test Preparation

Focus Skill Compare and Contrast

Copy the Venn diagram onto a separate sheet of paper. Use it to compare and contrast Philadelphia and Pittsburgh.

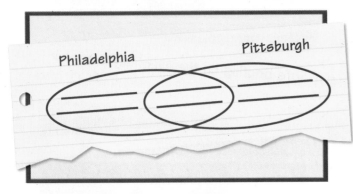

THINK AND WRITE

Write a Newspaper Article Imagine you are a newspaper reporter who travels to Pennsylvania for the first time. Describe the landforms that you see.

USE VOCABULARY

Write the word or words that correctly match each definition.

metropolitan area (p. PA 1-3)

keystone (p. PA 1-4)

terrace (p. PA 1-7)

population center (p. PA 1-11)

1 raised land

2 the middle stone at the top of an arch

3 a large city or cities and the surrounding communities

4 a place where many people live

RECALL FACTS

Answer these questions.

5 How would you describe Pennsylvania's relative location?

6 What is the state's largest city?

7 From which European country did the Pennsylvania Dutch come?

Write the letter of the best choice.

8 Which of the following is the capital of Pennsylvania?
  A Pittsburgh
  B Philadelphia
  C Lancaster
  D Harrisburg

9 Which wide and shallow river flows across much of the state?
  F the Delaware
  G the Schuylkill
  H the Susquehanna
  J the Ohio

THINK CRITICALLY

10 How do the weather and climate affect life in Pennsylvania?

11 How is the history of Pennsylvania's different groups remembered today?

PERFORMANCE

Make a Table Make a two-column table that lists Pennsylvania's physical regions in the first column. Then in the second column, describe the physical features of each region.

ast

Lightbulb invented by
Thomas Edison, 1879

New York City, New York

The Northeast

"Thine alabaster cities gleam."

—Katharine Lee Bates, "America the Beautiful," 1893

Preview the Content

In this unit you will learn how Europeans first came to the Northeast and how our nation was founded. Write five statements that you think are true about these topics. After reading the unit, change any of your statements by using what you learned.

Preview the Vocabulary

Parts of Speech   Most sentences have at least one noun and verb. In a diagram like the one below, categorize each of the vocabulary words as a noun or a verb. If you think the word can be used either way, write it in the center of the diagram. Then check your responses as you read the unit.

colony   cooperate   lock   rapid   specialize   volunteer

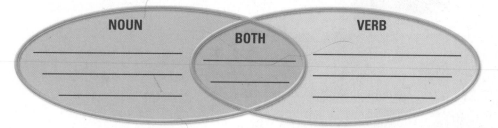

NOUN   BOTH   VERB

The Northeast

84°W   82°W   80°W   78°W   76°W   74°W   72°W

46°N

CANADA

Georgian
Bay

Lake
Huron

St. Lawrence River

VERMONT
Mt. Washington
6,288 ft.
(1,917 m)

Lake
Champlain

Adirondack   Montpelier ★
Mountains

White
Mountains

NEW
HAMPSHIRE

44°N

Lake Ontario

Rochester

New—York

State   Barge   Canal

System

NEW YORK

Niagara Falls

Buffalo

Syracuse

Concord ★

Manchester

Green Mountains

Connecticut River

Albany ★

Lowe

Boston

MI

Catskill
Mountains

MASSACHUSETTS ★

42°N

Lake Erie

Erie

Allegheny River

Hudson River

Springfield

Worcester

Hartford   Providence

CONNECTICUT   RHODE

Waterbury   ISLAND

Delaware

New Haven

Bridgeport

Allegheny Mountains

APPALACHIAN MOUNTAINS

0   50   100 Miles
0   50   100 Kilometers
Albers Equal-Area Projection

PENNSYLVANIA

Susquehanna River

Pocono
Mountains

Stamford

Paterson   Yonkers

Jersey City

Long Island

OH

Pittsburgh

Newark   New York City

Allentown   Elizabeth

40°N

Ohio River

Monongahela

Harrisburg ★

Trenton

Philadelphia

NEW
JERSEY

Wilmington

WV

Potomac

MD

Dover ★

DELAWARE

ATLANTIC
OCEAN

Delaware Bay

VA   DC

Chesapeake Bay

78°W   76°W   74°W   72°W

Key Events

1600   1650   1700   1750

1620   Pilgrims start Plymouth
Colony.   p. 102

1776   Declaration of Independence is
signed at Independence Hall.   p. 131

1838   An important shipyard is
founded in Mystic, CT.   p. 103

92

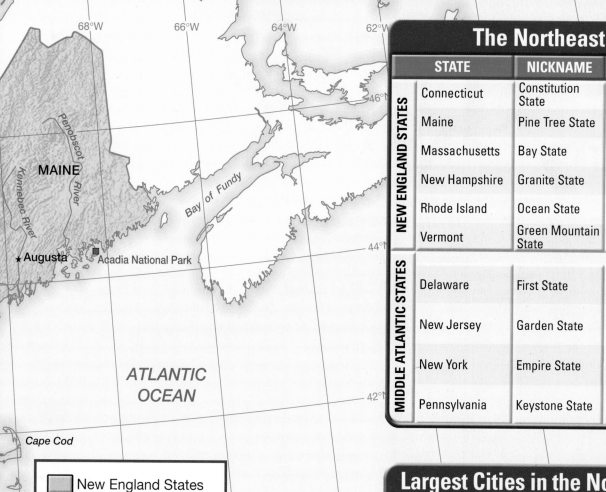

MAINE

Penobscot River

Kennebec River

Bay of Fundy

★ Augusta   ■ Acadia National Park

ATLANTIC OCEAN

Cape Cod

The Northeast

	STATE	NICKNAME	POPULATION
NEW ENGLAND STATES	Connecticut	Constitution State	3,460,503
	Maine	Pine Tree State	1,294,464
	Massachusetts	Bay State	6,427,801
	New Hampshire	Granite State	1,275,056
	Rhode Island	Ocean State	1,069,725
	Vermont	Green Mountain State	616,592
MIDDLE ATLANTIC STATES	Delaware	First State	807,385
	New Jersey	Garden State	8,590,300
	New York	Empire State	19,157,532
	Pennsylvania	Keystone State	12,335,091

Map Legend

- New England States
- Middle Atlantic States
- ★ State capital
- • Major city
- ᐱ Mountain peak
- ⊢⊢⊢ Canal
- ■ National park
- National forest

Largest Cities in the Northeast

City, State:
- New York City, New York
- Philadelphia, Pennsylvania
- Boston, Massachusetts
- Pittsburgh, Pennsylvania
- Buffalo, New York

Population (in millions): 1 2 3 4 5 6 7 8

1850   1900   1950   Present

1914 More than 1 million immigrants enter the United States. p. 143

1929 Maine's Lafayette National Park is renamed Acadia. p. 105

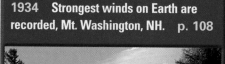

1934 Strongest winds on Earth are recorded, Mt. Washington, NH. p. 108

93

A River Ran Wild

written and illustrated by Lynne Cherry

Native Americans were the first people to live on the land that is today the Northeast region of the United States. One group, the Nashua (NA•shuh•wuh), settled along a river they called the Nash-a-way. It flowed through what are now the states of Massachusetts and New Hampshire. By this river the Nashua fished, farmed, and gathered plants.

Then Europeans began to arrive in this area. These new settlers brought with them different ways of life. They cleared forests and plowed the land. They built mills and factories along the river. Read now about ways people have depended on the river over the years.

By the Nash-a-way, Chief Weeawa's people built a village. They gathered cattails from the riverbanks to thatch their dwellings. In the forest they set fires to clear brush from the forest floor. In these clearings they planted corn and squash for eating. They made arrows for hunting and canoes for river travel.

When the Indians hunted in the forest or caught salmon in the river, they killed only what they needed for themselves for food and clothing. They asked all the forest creatures that they killed to please forgive them.

The Nashua people saw a rhythm in their lives and in the seasons. The river, land, and forest provided all they needed.

thatch   to cover with thatch, or plant materials

The Nashua had lived for generations by the clear, clean, flowing river when one day a pale-skinned trader came with a boatload full of treasures. He brought shiny metal knives, colored beads, and cooking kettles, mirrors, tools, and bolts of bright cloth. His wares seemed like magic. The Nashua welcomed him, traded furs, and soon a trading post was built.

In the many years that followed, the settlers' village and others like it grew and the Nash-a-way became the Nashua. The settlers worked together to clear land by cutting down the forests, which they thought were full of danger—wilderness that they would conquer. They hunted wolves and beaver, killing much more than they needed. Extra pelts were sent to England in return for goods and money.

The settlers built sawmills along the river, which the Nashua's current powered. They built dams to make the millponds that were used to store the water. They cut down the towering forests and floated tree trunks down the river. The logs were cut up into lumber, which was used for building houses.

The settlers built fences for their pastures, plowed the fields, and planted crops. They called the land their own. . .

Analyze the Literature

1 In what ways did the environment provide all the things the Nashuas needed?

2 What do you think were some of the long-lasting effects Europeans had on the environment?

READ A BOOK

START THE UNIT PROJECT

A Class Play As a class, begin planning a play about the growth of the Northeast region. As you read this unit, choose at least three people or events you think should be portrayed in the play. Gather additional information about each. You can use the information when you are ready to write your play's scenes.

USE TECHNOLOGY

Visit The Learning Site at **www.harcourtschool.com** for additional activities, primary sources, and other resources to use in this unit.

WOODSTOCK, VERMONT

This farm near Woodstock in Vermont stands wrapped in autumn's long shadows and golden haze. It is these brilliant leaf colors in the fall that make New England famous.

LOCATE IT

VERMONT

Woodstock

New England States

66 Hail, happy day, when, smiling like the morn, Fair Freedom rose New-England to adorn: 99

—Phillis Wheatley, *Poems on Various Subjects, Religious and Moral*, 1773

Focus Skill **Generalize**

When you **generalize** you make a statement that summarizes a group of facts and shows how they are related.

As you read this chapter, make generalizations.

• **Identify important facts.**

• **Use those facts to generalize about the New England states.**

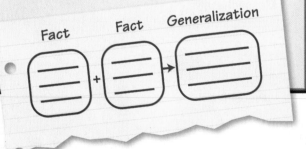

Fact   Fact   Generalization

GENERALIZE
As you read, make generalizations about ways in which past events can affect how a region develops and changes.

BIG IDEA
Since people first settled in New England, the region has changed over time.

VOCABULARY

cape
colony
colonist
harbor
industrial economy
textile mill

New England Through the Years

1600   1700   1800

In 1614 two English ships sailed along the northeast coast of what is now the United States. The explorers on the ships, led by Captain John Smith, saw a land with many natural resources. Giant whales and schools of fish swam in the Atlantic Ocean's northern waters. Bays along the coast provided places for ships to anchor, and thick forests covered a flat coastal plain.

Smith named the land New England. Convinced it would be a good place to settle, he wrote,

> **"Of all the four parts of the world that I have yet seen not inhabited, I would rather live here than anywhere."**

Today, the region of New England includes six states—Connecticut, Rhode Island, Massachusetts, New Hampshire, Vermont, and Maine.

At Plimoth Plantation in Plymouth, Massachusetts, Native Americans re-create the life of the Wampanoag people at the time when the Pilgrims arrived.

FAST FACT
In 1614, about 50,000 Wampanoag Indians lived along the New England coast. Today, several thousand Wampanoag still live in the towns of Mashpee, Aquinnah, and Manomet in Massachusetts.

LOCATE IT

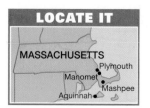

MASSACHUSETTS
Plymouth
Manomet
Mashpee
Aquinnah

Native Americans in New England

Native Americans lived throughout North America for thousands of years before Europeans arrived. Each tribe, or group, had its own culture. New England tribes were the Wampanoag (wahm•puh•NOH•ag), the Narraganset (nar•uh•GAN•suht), and the Massachuset (ma•suh•CHOO•suht).

Native Americans were farmers and shared the land and its resources. They grew corn, beans, squash, and melons and gathered roots, nuts, and berries. They hunted wild animals and, in the summer, fished along the New England coast.

Native Americans were strong, healthy people and had few diseases until the Europeans arrived. The Europeans brought new diseases that had not existed in North America. Native Americans had little defense against these diseases. Spreading quickly, the new germs often infected entire villages. Thousands of Native Americans died.

REVIEW What generalizations can you make about how Native Americans used natural resources? **GENERALIZE**

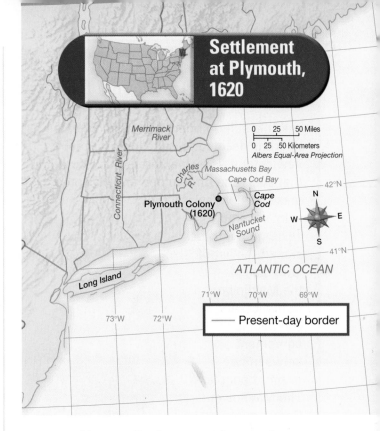

Settlement at Plymouth, 1620

0 25 50 Miles
0 25 50 Kilometers
Albers Equal-Area Projection

Merrimack River
Connecticut River
Charles R.
Massachusetts Bay
Cape Cod Bay
Plymouth Colony (1620)
Cape Cod
Nantucket Sound
Long Island
ATLANTIC OCEAN

— Present-day border

Human–Environment Interactions
The Pilgrims built their colony on a bay in what is now Massachusetts in 1620.
❖ Why might a group of settlers build their colony on a bay?

The Pilgrims Arrive

In 1620 a small ship called the *Mayflower* set sail from England with about 100 men, women, and children on board. They were sailing to North America because they were not allowed to practice their religion in England. For this reason, the travelers on the *Mayflower* came to be called Pilgrims, or people who make a long journey for religious reasons.

After sailing for two months, they saw a **cape**, or a point of land reaching out into the ocean. They sailed around the cape and anchored in a bay, near where Massachusetts is today.

Corn was an important food source for Native Americans. Native Americans in New England taught the Pilgrims how to grow and prepare it.

DEMOCRATIC VALUES
Self-Government

While still on board the *Mayflower,* the Pilgrims decided to write laws for their new colony. They wanted to make sure that everyone understood and accepted these written laws.

In November, 1620, the Pilgrims signed the list of laws, called the Mayflower Compact. A compact is an agreement between two or more people. The Mayflower Compact served as the basis for the Plymouth Colony's government. It is the first example of self-rule by colonists in the Americas.

Analyze the Value

❶ Why did the Pilgrims write the Mayflower Compact before they started their colony?

❷ In what way is the Mayflower Compact an example of self-government?

❸ **Make It Relevant** Work with a group to write the rules for a new club. Make sure that everyone in your group agrees on all the rules. Then describe your club to the class, and explain why the rules you wrote are necessary.

The Pilgrims explored the land near the bay and found fresh water, flat land for farming, and trees for building houses. They decided to stay and build their new colony there. A **colony** is a settlement started by people who leave their own country to live in another land. The Pilgrims named their colony Plymouth.

Unlike the Native Americans, the Pilgrims did not yet know how to grow food or use the natural resources in their new environment. The winter was cold, and the Pilgrims had little food. Conditions that first winter were so harsh that more than half of the Pilgrims died.

When spring arrived, two English-speaking Native Americans visited the Pilgrims. They taught the Pilgrims how to live in their new home. They showed the Pilgrims how to plant corn, catch fish, and hunt turkeys and other animals in the region. By the winter of 1621, the Pilgrims had plenty of food.

REVIEW **What did the Pilgrims need to learn to be able to survive in their new home?**

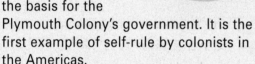

The colony had two streets.

William Bradford, the colony's leader, lived in this house.

Early Days in New England

Not long after the Pilgrims had founded Plymouth Colony, another group of people left England for North America. They, too, wanted to be free to practice their religion. In 1630, this new group, called Puritans, founded the Massachusetts Bay Colony. They built several communities near Massachusetts Bay, including Salem, Dorchester, and Boston.

Over the next ten years, about 20,000 **colonists**, or people living in colonies, came to the Massachusetts Bay area. Most were English Puritans. Later, they started the new colonies of Connecticut and Rhode Island.

Until 1630, colonists and Native Americans lived peacefully side by side. Over time, that changed. Many colonists wanted to farm more land and insisted the Native Americans change their ways and their religion. When the Native Americans refused, fighting broke out between the two groups. Although the Native Americans fought long and hard, they were outnumbered.

Most of the early colonists in New England were farmers. By the 1700s, however, Europeans had established new industries based on the region's bays and the ocean. Many colonial villages had been built on deep harbors. A **harbor** is a place where ships can dock safely. With large ships able to sail into the harbors, these villages soon became busy centers of trade.

Like other New England coastal towns, Boston was an ideal trading center. The city is located beside the deep, sheltered waters of Massachusetts Bay. From Boston, ships carried fish, furs, and lumber to places across the Atlantic Ocean. They returned with tools, clothing, and other manufactured goods from Europe. As trade increased, so did Boston's population. By 1760, about 16,000 people lived there, making it the largest city in New England.

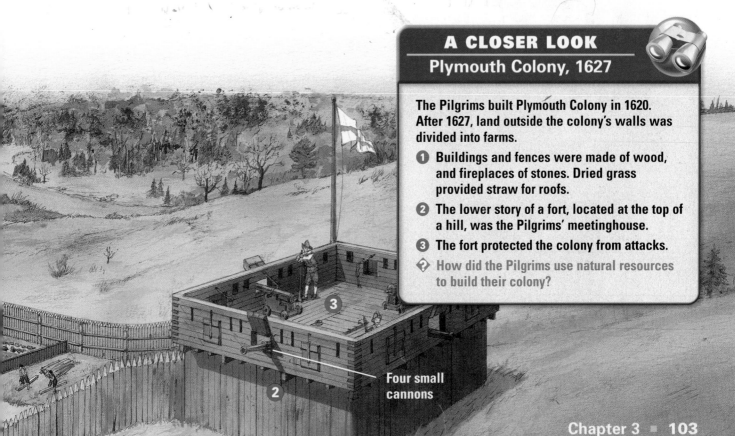

A CLOSER LOOK
Plymouth Colony, 1627

The Pilgrims built Plymouth Colony in 1620. After 1627, land outside the colony's walls was divided into farms.

1. Buildings and fences were made of wood, and fireplaces of stones. Dried grass provided straw for roofs.
2. The lower story of a fort, located at the top of a hill, was the Pilgrims' meetinghouse.
3. The fort protected the colony from attacks.

❓ How did the Pilgrims use natural resources to build their colony?

Four small cannons

Colonists in New England used the ocean in other ways, too. They caught cod, haddock, and other fish. By the early 1800s, New England was also the center of a huge whaling industry. Whale blubber, or fat, was used for its oil, which was a major source of lamp fuel in the days before electricity.

REVIEW For what reason did some people establish colonies in New England?

Industries Grow and Change

As New England's population grew, its economy changed. Fishing and trade remained important, but New England was building an **industrial economy**, or an economy in which factories and machines manufacture most of the goods.

During colonial times, most products were made by hand. Then, in 1793, Samuel Slater built a textile mill along the Blackstone River in Rhode Island.

A **textile mill** is a factory in which fibers such as cotton and wool are woven into textiles, or cloth. Slater Mill was the first factory to use waterpower in the United States. Instead of weaving cloth on hand looms, workers used machines powered by water to do this work more quickly.

Soon factories were built along other rivers near New England's coast. They also used the power of the rushing river water to run their machines. The rivers also provided a way for the factories to ship their products to markets. Eventually, machines were run on steam or electricity. This enabled people to build factories closer to the resources they used instead of on rivers.

Many people left their farms or jobs on the docks to work in the factories. Millions more moved to New England from other countries. Soon towns and cities grew up near the factories, and much of the New England coast became an urban industrial region.

Today, a variety of industries make up New England's economy. Manufacturing is still important to the region. However, textiles are no longer widely produced. New England factories now produce chemicals, computer equipment, and even helicopters. Shipping and fishing are also still a part of New England's economy.

For many years, textile manufacturing was a major industry in New England. Many young people worked in textile mills there during the late 1800s and early 1900s.

Founded in 1636 by Puritan colonists, Providence was the first city in Rhode Island. Today, it is the state's capital, and its largest city.

LOCATE IT

Providence

RHODE ISLAND

Most New Englanders today work in service industries, including health care, banking and finance, and publishing. Many people in Providence, Rhode Island, work in education. With over 50 insurance companies based there, Hartford, Connecticut, is often called the "Insurance Capital of the World."

Another important service industry in New England is tourism. Millions of tourists visit the region's cities, parks, historic sites, and beaches. Tourists also enjoy its colorful autumn leaves and ski or snowboard down its mountainsides.

REVIEW What are some important industries in New England today?

LESSON 1 REVIEW

Summary Time Line

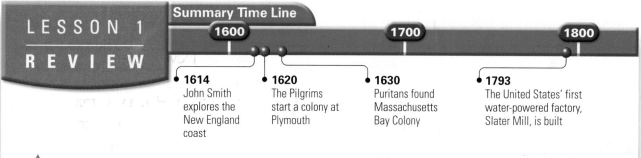

1600 — 1700 — 1800

1614 John Smith explores the New England coast

1620 The Pilgrims start a colony at Plymouth

1630 Puritans found Massachusetts Bay Colony

1793 The United States' first water-powered factory, Slater Mill, is built

 GENERALIZE What kinds of industries do you think are important in coastal communities like those in New England?

1 BIG IDEA How have places where people live along the New England coast changed over time?

2 VOCABULARY Explain the difference between a **cape** and a **harbor**.

3 TIME LINE When was Massachusetts Bay Colony founded?

4 HISTORY How did Native Americans help the Pilgrims survive?

5 GEOGRAPHY Why were New England's earliest colonies founded near the coast?

6 CRITICAL THINKING—Hypothesize How might your life be different if New England and the rest of the United States had not built an industrial economy?

 PERFORMANCE—Write a Journal Entry Imagine that you are a Wampanoag living in New England when the Pilgrims arrive. Tell what you noticed about these unfamiliar people. State what your hopes and fears are about having newcomers in your land. Share your journal entry with the class.

Read a Time Line

VOCABULARY	
time line	century
decade	millennium

➧ WHY IT MATTERS

To understand the history of New England or any other place, you need to know when important events happened. A time line can help you with this. A **time line** is a diagram that shows the order in which events took place and the length of time between them. Putting events in the order in which they took place can help you understand how one event may have led to another.

➧ WHAT YOU NEED TO KNOW

The time line below shows when some important events in the early history of New England took place. The earliest date is at the left end of the time line. The most recent date is at the right end of it.

Like a map, a time line has a scale. But the marks on a time line's scale show units of time, not distance.

Time lines can show different units of time. Some time lines show events that took place during one day, one month, or one year. Others show events that took place during a **decade**, or a period of ten years.

On the time line below, the space between the dates on the top stands for one **century**, or 100 years. The first part of the time line shows events that happened during the seventeenth century. The seventeenth century includes the years from 1601 to 1700. The next part of the time line shows the eighteenth century—from 1701 to 1800.

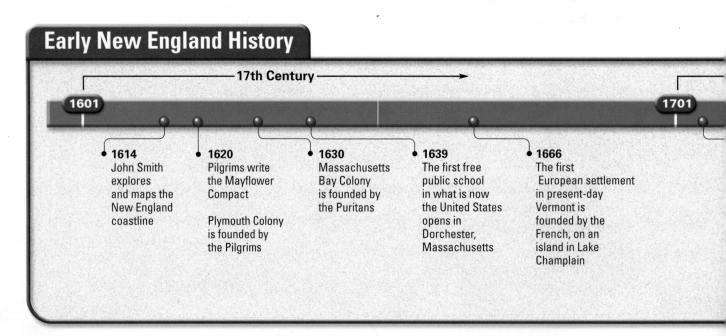

Early New England History

───── 17th Century ─────────────────────▶

1601

1701

1614
John Smith explores and maps the New England coastline

1620
Pilgrims write the Mayflower Compact

Plymouth Colony is founded by the Pilgrims

1630
Massachusetts Bay Colony is founded by the Puritans

1639
The first free public school in what is now the United States opens in Dorchester, Massachusetts

1666
The first European settlement in present-day Vermont is founded by the French, on an island in Lake Champlain

Plymouth Rock in Plymouth, Massachusetts, is engraved with the date 1620. This is the year the Pilgrims arrived in New England.

In the year 2001, people celebrated the beginning of a new millennium. A **millennium** is a period of 1,000 years. The thousand years between 1001 and 2000, for example, are a millennium. A millennium can be divided into 10 centuries, or 100 decades.

▶ PRACTICE THE SKILL

Use the time line to answer the following questions about New England's early history.

1 In what year did the first free public school in what is now the United States open?

2 How many years after the Pilgrims set up Plymouth Colony did the Puritans start the Massachusetts Bay Colony?

3 Which became a state first, Rhode Island or New Hampshire?

4 Why do you think Europeans settled in Massachusetts before going on to settle in Vermont?

▶ APPLY WHAT YOU LEARNED

Make a time line that shows one century of your state's history. Mark the decades on your time line. Then list at least five important events that took place during those years. Use reference books and the Internet to find events and their dates. You may wish to add pictures or photographs to illustrate events on your time line.

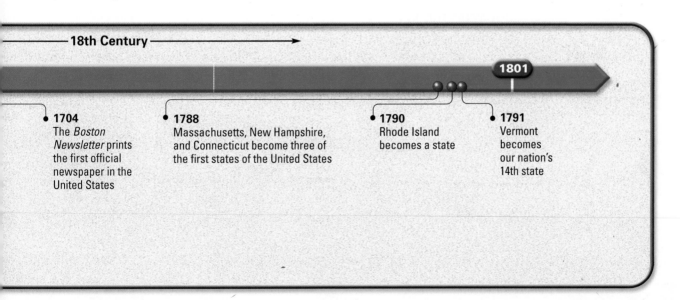

18th Century

1801

1704
The *Boston Newsletter* prints the first official newspaper in the United States

1788
Massachusetts, New Hampshire, and Connecticut become three of the first states of the United States

1790
Rhode Island becomes a state

1791
Vermont becomes our nation's 14th state

CHART AND GRAPH SKILLS

GENERALIZE

As you read, make generalizations about how people in New England and other regions of the United States use natural resources.

BIG IDEA

The landforms and natural resources of the New England countryside affect life there.

VOCABULARY

glacier
quarry

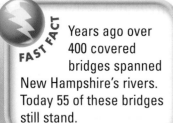

Years ago over 400 covered bridges spanned New Hampshire's rivers. Today 55 of these bridges still stand.

The New England Countryside

The earliest European colonists in New England settled along the region's Atlantic Coast. By the 1700s, many people had moved farther inland, settling along rivers in the New England countryside. Today, most New Englanders still live in busy urban areas near the Atlantic Coast or along major rivers. However, New England is also known for its quiet countryside, and many people in the region still use the land to earn a living.

The Land

New England covers the northeastern corner of the United States. Canada lies to its north, and the Atlantic Ocean forms its eastern and southern borders. The rocky coast of northern New England gives way to the Coastal Plain farther south. Inland from the coast, New England is a land of green valleys and rolling hills.

Low mountain ranges stretch across the region, too. The Green Mountains of Vermont form New England's western boundary. To the east, in Maine and New Hampshire, lie the White Mountains. Both of these ranges are part of the Appalachian Mountains. The Connecticut River flows between the White and Green Mountains through the fertile Connecticut Valley.

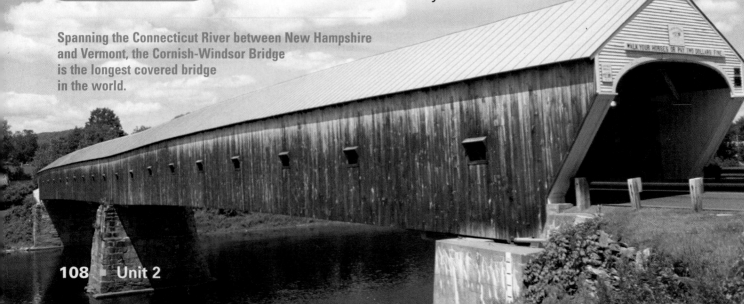

Spanning the Connecticut River between New Hampshire and Vermont, the Cornish-Windsor Bridge is the longest covered bridge in the world.

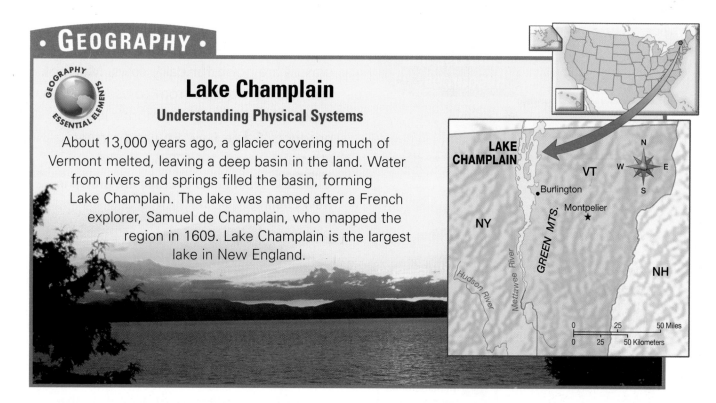

• GEOGRAPHY •

GEOGRAPHY ESSENTIAL ELEMENTS

Lake Champlain
Understanding Physical Systems

About 13,000 years ago, a glacier covering much of Vermont melted, leaving a deep basin in the land. Water from rivers and springs filled the basin, forming Lake Champlain. The lake was named after a French explorer, Samuel de Champlain, who mapped the region in 1609. Lake Champlain is the largest lake in New England.

Glaciers shaped most of New England's landforms. A **glacier** is a huge, slow-moving mass of ice. Thousands of years ago, the climate on Earth turned very cold, and glaciers covered much of the land. As the glaciers moved across New England, they wore down mountains and carried away the soil.

After the glaciers melted, many places in New England were left with rocky soil. Early settlers had to clear away the stones before they could farm the land. They often used these stones to build walls around their fields.

REVIEW What kind of soil covers much of New England?

New England Farms

Many crops do not grow well in New England's rocky soil and cool climate. Even so, agriculture is important in the region. Farmers raise the kinds of crops and animals that do well there.

In Maine, potato farming is important. Maine farmers also grow nearly all the blueberries grown in the United States. About half of the nation's cranberries come from Massachusetts. Other farms in New England grow corn, mushrooms, and greenhouse crops, such as house-plants, shrubs, and flowers.

At harvesttime, farmers flood cranberry fields and knock the berries off their vines. Workers collect the floating berries with rakes and scoops.

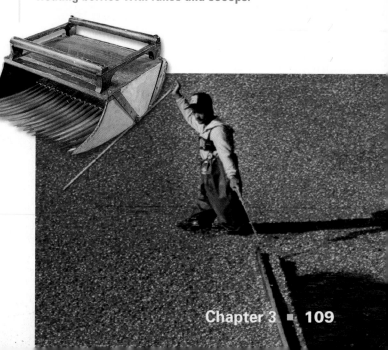

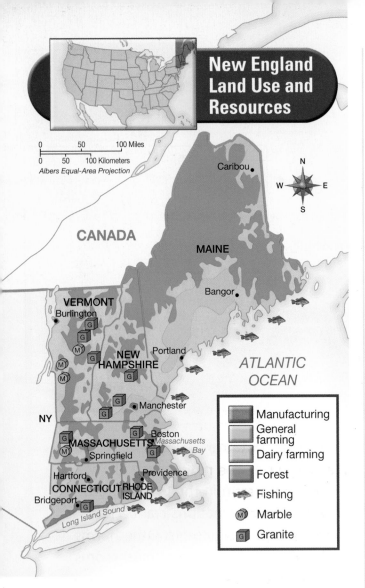

New England Land Use and Resources

0   50   100 Miles
0   50   100 Kilometers
Albers Equal-Area Projection

Caribou

N W E S

CANADA

MAINE

Bangor

VERMONT
Burlington

Portland

NEW HAMPSHIRE

ATLANTIC OCEAN

Manchester

NY

MASSACHUSETTS
Boston
Massachusetts Bay
Springfield

Hartford
CONNECTICUT RHODE ISLAND
Bridgeport
Providence
Long Island Sound

Manufacturing
General farming
Dairy farming
Forest
Fishing
Marble
Granite

GEOGRAPHY THEME

Human–Environment Interactions
Many people in New England make their living from the region's forests.

❓ How is most of the land in southern Maine used?

Pasture grasses grow well in New England's climate. The region's thick grasses are good for dairy cows. Much of the milk that comes from cows is used to make cheese, one of Vermont's leading products. Some New England farmers also raise sheep, hogs, and chickens.

REVIEW What kinds of crops are grown in New England? **GENERALIZE**

Stone Quarries

Although rocks are a problem for farmers, some people in New England earn a living working with them. New England has lots of marble, granite, and other rocks. Every state in the region has stone quarries (KWAR•eez). A **quarry** is a large, open pit cut into the ground from which stone is mined. Workers cut blocks of stone from the quarry, and then shape, polish, or crush the stone. This stone is used to construct buildings, bridges, and roads, as well as to be carved into statues.

New Hampshire has so much granite and so many granite quarries that one of its nicknames is the "Granite State." The largest granite quarries in the nation are in Vermont. Milford, Massachusetts, is famous for its unique pink granite.

To build the Vermont State House, granite had to be pulled from a quarry 10 miles (16 km) away. It took 18 hours to deliver each load.

Stone from New England has been used to build many important structures in the United States. Granite from Maine was used to build the Brooklyn Bridge in New York City. Massachusetts marble was used to build the United States Capitol Building in Washington, D.C.

REVIEW How do some New Englanders make their living from the region's rocks?

Forests and Orchards

New England's vast forests are among the region's most important natural resources. Logging has been a major industry in Maine for almost 400 years. Today, wood from Maine is used to make everything from lumber to paper products to toothpicks.

Trees in New England have another special use. Every year, people collect sap from maple trees in the region. Sap is the liquid that runs through the trunk and roots of a tree. People use the sap to make maple syrup. Native Americans made maple syrup long before European settlers

It takes more than 30 gallons (114 L) of sap to make 1 gallon (4 L) of maple syrup!

came to North America. Montpelier, Vermont, is now the largest producer of maple syrup in the nation.

Other farmers in New England raise fruit trees. New England orchards produce more than 40 different kinds of apples.

REVIEW How do people in New England use trees to earn a living?

LESSON 2
REVIEW

 GENERALIZE What physical features are found in the New England countryside?

1 **BIG IDEA** How do landforms and natural resources affect the way many people in New England's countryside live?

2 **VOCABULARY** Use the terms **glacier** and **quarry** in two sentences about New England.

3 **ECONOMICS** What are some of the crops and animals grown and raised on farms in New England's countryside?

4 **CRITICAL THINKING—Apply** How might New England's rocky soil affect your actions if you decided to become a farmer there?

 PERFORMANCE—Make a Table Work with a partner to make a two-column table showing how landforms and natural resources affect how people in New England's countryside earn a living. In the first column of the table, list natural resources. In the second column, tell how each resource is used. Share your table with your classmates.

GENERALIZE
As you read, make generalizations about the tradition of self-government in New England towns.

BIG IDEA
Learn how people in one New England town live and make decisions.

VOCABULARY
common
volunteer

A New England Town

New England is dotted with many small towns in the countryside, along the coast, and on offshore islands. Six towns are located on Martha's Vineyard, an island off the coast of Massachusetts. Tourists from around the world visit Martha's Vineyard. People who live on the island like to think, "Everything that ever happened on earth has happened on the Vineyard. And some things twice."

Oak Bluffs

Oak Bluffs is one of the six towns on Martha's Vineyard. Today, Oak Bluffs is a summer resort that people visit to enjoy the fine beaches, varied shops, and historical buildings. Before Europeans arrived on Martha's Vineyard in the 1600s, the Wampanoag Indians had farmed in the area and hunted whales off the coast of Oak Bluffs.

During the summer, many families come to Oak Bluffs to enjoy its cool ocean breezes and clean, sandy beaches.

LOCATE IT

MASSACHUSETTS

Oak Bluffs

Martha's Vineyard

On Illumination Night, porches and balconies all over Oak Bluffs are decorated with Chinese and Japanese lanterns. This annual summer tradition goes back to 1869.

In the 1600s, the English founded the town of Edgartown near present-day Oak Bluffs. As in many New England towns, the houses in Edgartown were built around an empty field in the center of the town. People in the past used this field, called the **common**, as a pasture for their animals. Now the common is used for recreation.

In 1835, a group of religious leaders started holding outdoor services in the north end of Edgartown. This central meeting place became known as the Camp Ground. Every summer, people from across New England came to stay and take part in the services. They set up tents.

By the 1850s, cottages, or small houses, surrounded the Camp Ground. The cottages were highly decorated with woodwork. As the community grew, the area became known as Cottage City.

Cottage City officially became Oak Bluffs in 1907. By then, the meeting center had become a summer resort.

REVIEW In what part of Edgartown did Oak Bluffs originate?

The People of Oak Bluffs

European settlers first arrived in the Oak Bluffs area in 1642. They were farmers who came from Massachusetts Bay Colony. They first grew corn, rye, and oats. As in other parts of New England, however, farms remained small on the island. Many people turned to fishing and whaling instead. Enslaved Africans also arrived on the island in the 1600s and were made to work on the English farms. After slavery was abolished, more African Americans moved to the area to work in the whaling industry.

By the late 1700s, whaling had become a major industry on the island. The men of Oak Bluffs sailed on whaling voyages to distant places. African American William A. Martin, captain of the whaling ship *Emma Jane*, was born in what was then Edgartown. His great-grandparents had been enslaved. Captain Martin had a long and successful career and sailed all over the world in search of whales.

Over time, technology changed people's lives in Oak Bluffs. Electricity lit the town after 1880. In the early 1900s, telephones brought much faster and better communication. By the 1930s, people began to drive automobiles to larger nearby towns to work or visit.

Oak Bluffs' economy started to change in the mid-1800s when people traveled to Oak Bluffs to take part in summer outdoor religious services. Today, most people in Oak Bluffs work in service industries, especially tourism. The town is a popular vacation spot.

REVIEW **What generalizations can you make about the ways in which people in Oak Bluffs earn their living today?** **Focus Skill** **GENERALIZE**

Government in Oak Bluffs

In New England's early days, people made decisions about their towns at town meetings. All the townspeople would gather to discuss an important issue and come to a decision. The tradition of holding town meetings continues today in many New England towns.

Oak Bluffs' first town meeting took place in 1907. To make town decisions, the people of Oak Bluffs now have a town meeting every April. The meeting is usually held at the local high school and is open to all residents of Oak Bluffs. Several hundred people usually attend.

At recent town meetings, residents have made decisions about improving the harbor, repairing downtown sidewalks, and installing a new well. They also voted on whether the town tax collector should be elected or appointed. The details of all meetings are posted in local newspapers and on the Internet. In this way, people who do not attend the meetings can learn about the decisions that are made.

Although young people cannot vote at town meetings, they can help

Shearer Cottage in Oak Bluffs was opened in 1912 by Charles and Henrietta Shearer to cater to African Americans who were not welcome as guests at other inns on Martha's Vineyard. Shearer Cottage is still owned and operated by descendants of the Shearers.

People in Oak Bluffs attend the town meeting each year. Among the issues discussed and voted on are those concerning the town's fire department.

make decisions. When some students felt that the town needed a place where young people could get together, they decided to get involved. Fourteen teenagers put together a plan for a Teen Center. They attended the town meeting and presented their plan. After some discussion, the town approved the plan. It was agreed that the Teen Center would have table tennis and pool tables as well as computers.

Many students and adults in Oak Bluffs help their community by being volunteers (vah•luhn•TIRZ). A **volunteer** is a person who does something useful without being paid for it. Recently, high school students worked as volunteers doing research for the African American Heritage Trail. The students read old documents and gathered oral histories about the people in Oak Bluffs and other towns on Martha's Vineyard. By volunteering and attending town meetings, the people of Oak Bluffs make sure their town remains a pleasant, safe place to live.

REVIEW **What have the people of Oak Bluffs discussed at recent town meetings?**

LESSON 3
REVIEW

 GENERALIZE How is life in Oak Bluffs different from life in a large city?

1 BIG IDEA How do the residents of Oak Bluffs make decisions about their town?

2 VOCABULARY Explain how students in Oak Bluffs have served as **volunteers**.

3 HISTORY How has the economy in Oak Bluffs changed over the years?

4 CIVICS AND GOVERNMENT What kinds of decisions do people in Oak Bluffs make about their community?

5 CRITICAL THINKING—Analyze Do you think town meetings would work well in a large city? Why or why not?

 PERFORMANCE—Make a Poster Draw a poster showing places and things that are important about Oak Bluffs. Your poster could include the Camp Ground and a whaling ship. Write captions about each item and why it is important. Compare your poster with those of your classmates.

Solve a Problem

VOCABULARY
cooperate

▶ WHY IT MATTERS

Think about some of the problems you may have faced in the past few weeks. Perhaps you had trouble completing one of your assignments at school. You may have argued with a brother or sister at home or with a classmate at school. How did you solve the problem?

People everywhere have problems at some time. Learning how to solve problems is an important skill that you can use now and in the future. Sometimes you may need help from others to solve a problem. Knowing how to **cooperate**, or work together, is a problem-solving skill that you will use all your life.

▶ WHAT YOU NEED TO KNOW

You can use these steps to help identify and solve problems.

Step 1 Identify the problem. If it is big, divide it into smaller parts.

Step 2 Think of ideas for solving the problem or each part of the problem.

Step 3 Compare your ideas. Ask yourself what is good and bad about each. Choose the best idea.

Step 4 Plan how to carry out your idea. Can you do it yourself, or do you need help?

Step 5 Follow your plan, and then think about how well it worked. Did it solve the problem?

Step 6 If your plan does not solve the problem, try other ideas until the problem is solved.

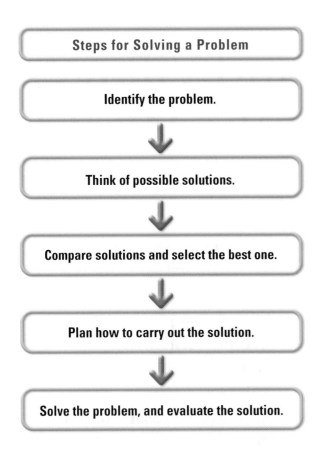

Steps for Solving a Problem

Identify the problem.

↓

Think of possible solutions.

↓

Compare solutions and select the best one.

↓

Plan how to carry out the solution.

↓

Solve the problem, and evaluate the solution.

▸ PRACTICE THE SKILL

You have read about how people in many towns in New England solve problems during town meetings. By sharing ideas and cooperating, the students in Oak Bluffs solved a problem at a town meeting. Think again about the problem the students saw and how they solved it.

1 What problem did the Oak Bluffs students see?

2 How did the students address the problem?

3 What did the students do to carry out their solution to this problem?

4 How did the students' solution help solve the problem?

5 What other solutions could the Oak Bluffs students have used to solve their problem?

▸ APPLY WHAT YOU LEARNED

Look around your school or your neighborhood. What problems do you see? Which one seems the most important to you? Working as a group, use the steps in the chart on this page to think of ways to solve that problem. Share your group's solution with the class. Then ask for and consider their suggestions. Try to think of ways you could carry out your solution.

Working together is often an important part of solving problems.

4

GENERALIZE

As you read, make generalizations about ways early settlers can affect the development of a place.

BIG IDEA

Small towns in New England and other parts of the world are both alike and different.

VOCABULARY

recreation
specialize
fish farm

Towns and Villages Around the World

Many places in New England look very much like places in England. Most of New England's colonists brought their language and traditions with them from England. For this reason, people in both places often live in similar ways, too.

An English Village

The village of Hawkshead is located in the English countryside, in a region called the Lake District. Like many towns in New England, Hawkshead lies on rolling hills covered with grassy fields and trees. Mountains and lakes surround the village.

The first settlers in Hawkshead Village arrived more than 1,000 years ago. Like the first colonists in New England, these early settlers were farmers. They discovered that the land in their region was rocky. So most farmers in Hawkshead began raising sheep instead of crops. For 600 years, wool was the village's most important product.

Hawkshead Village lies near Lake Windermere, the largest lake in England. For centuries boats carried wool from Hawkshead across the lake to nearby textile mills.

LOCATE IT

Hawkshead

UNITED KINGDOM

The Tenterfield Railway Station opened in 1868. Today it is a museum.

LOCATE IT

AUSTRALIA

Tenterfield

Many buildings in Hawkshead were built around town squares, which were similar to commons in New England towns. Hawkshead also has many old buildings. The oldest building in the village, the courthouse, was built about 700 years ago!

Like many New England towns, Hawkshead is in a beautiful setting. People visit Hawkshead and the Lake District for recreation (reh•kree•AY•shuhn). **Recreation** is what people do to have fun. Near Hawkshead, people can swim, fish, boat, and hike in the countryside.

As in Oak Bluffs, tourism is Hawkshead's main industry. Visitors stroll along the village's winding cobblestone streets, where cars are not permitted. They enjoy its teashops, bookstores, and museums, including the Beatrix Potter Gallery. The writer Beatrix Potter used Hawkshead for ideas and illustrations for *The Tale of Peter Rabbit* and other children's books.

REVIEW In what ways is the arrangement of buildings in Hawkshead similar to the arrangement of buildings in many New England towns? GENERALIZE

An Australian Town

Like the region of New England, the country of Australia was once an English colony, and its first settlers came from England. As a result, people in Australia speak English, and their towns are similar to towns in England and New England. The region along the southeastern Pacific Coast of Australia is even called New England!

The countryside of Australia's New England has many small towns and villages. Tenterfield, founded in 1848, was one of the first towns settled in the region. Most of Tenterfield's early residents were farmers. They grew apples and oats and raised dairy cows and sheep. Wool production was the major industry in Tenterfield for many years.

Several of Tenterfield's original buildings still stand today, including the town's first meetinghouse and school. One of the oldest buildings is a cottage. It has been turned into a museum that shows how the town's first settlers lived.

The koala diet consists almost entirely of eucalyptus leaves. Because the leaves have little nutritional value, koalas do not have much energy. Koalas usually sleep about 22 hours a day!

Koalas live along Australia's eastern coast.

The people of Tenterfield and other Australian towns today participate in their local government by attending town meetings. Wildfires are a special safety concern for Australian towns. Many plants that grow there, such as grasses and eucalyptus (yoo•kah•LIP•tus) trees, burn easily when there has been little rain. At a recent town meeting in Tenterfield, people passed a wildfire safety plan. As part of the plan, people

in Tenterfield have agreed not to plant eucalyptus trees near buildings.

REVIEW How is town government in Tenterfield similar to town government in the New England region of the United States?

A Canadian Coastal Town

Parts of Canada were also once English colonies. As a result, some towns in Canada, especially those near the Atlantic Coast, are very much like coastal towns in England and New England in the United States. One of those Canadian towns is St. Andrews. It is located only a few miles north of Maine. In fact, European settlers from Castine, Maine, founded St. Andrews in 1783.

The oldest part of St. Andrews sits at the top of a hill overlooking the town's harbor on the Bay of Fundy. The area contains several town squares, which the

So many old buildings stand in St. Andrews that the entire town is a Canadian National Historic Site.

LOCATE IT

St. Andrews

CANADA

community uses for markets, festivals, and concerts.

Like they have been in New England coastal towns, shipping and trading have always been important to the economy of St. Andrews. As many people who live along coasts do, some people in St. Andrews also specialize (SPEH•shuh•lyz) in fishing. To **specialize** is to work at only one kind of job and do it well. Fishers can specialize because they do not also have to grow wheat for bread or make gasoline for fuel. They can depend on workers in other regions for those products.

As in the United States, much of St. Andrews' fishing industry now relies on fish farms. A **fish farm** is a closed-off area of water in which people raise fish. These fish farms have added millions of dollars to the local economy and created many new jobs.

Like Oak Bluffs, St. Andrews has been a popular tourist spot for many years. Beginning in the 1930s, overnight trains from Boston brought people to St. Andrews to escape New England's hot summer weather. Some popular tourist activities in St. Andrews today include fishing, water sports, and bird and whale watching.

REVIEW How do people in Canadian coastal towns use their water resources to earn a living?

Whale watching is a popular tourist activity in St. Andrews, as well as in parts of New England. More than 15 different kinds of whales feed and mate in the Bay of Fundy.

LESSON 4 REVIEW

GENERALIZE What makes some small towns attractive to tourists?

1 **BIG IDEA** How is life in some towns and villages around the world similar to life in some towns and villages in New England?

2 **VOCABULARY** How do **fish farms** help people in coastal communities **specialize** in fishing industries?

3 **GEOGRAPHY** What physical features of the towns and villages discussed in this lesson make their economies similar?

4 **CRITICAL THINKING—Apply** How does life in the towns and villages discussed in this lesson compare with life in your own community?

PERFORMANCE—Make a Poster Choose the town discussed in this lesson in which you would most like to live. Make a poster showing life in the town, including drawings of buildings, people working, and recreational activities. Write captions for your drawings. Display your poster in the classroom.

3 Review and Test Preparation

Summary Time Line

1600

1614
John Smith explores the
New England coast

1620
The Pilgrims
start a colony
at Plymouth

Generalize

Copy the following graphic organizer onto a separate sheet of paper. Use the information you have learned to make a generalization based on the facts below.

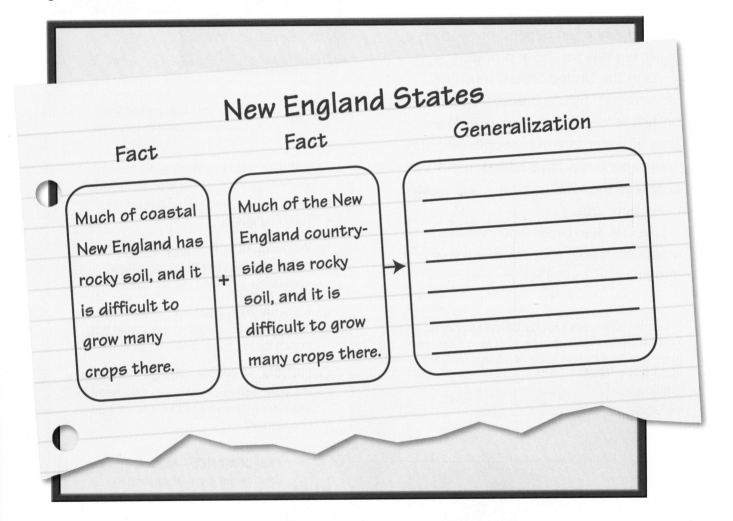

New England States

Fact

Much of coastal New England has rocky soil, and it is difficult to grow many crops there.

+

Fact

Much of the New England country-side has rocky soil, and it is difficult to grow many crops there.

→

Generalization

_____
_____
_____
_____
_____

THINK & WRITE

Plan a Meal   Imagine you are cooking a meal with a New England theme. Think of the foods grown, raised, caught, or produced in New England. Describe a meal that you could serve using these foods.

Write a Magazine Article   Write an article for a travel magazine describing the New England countryside. To persuade people to visit the region, include descriptions of the landscape, town life, and tourist attractions.

1630
Puritans found
Massachusetts Bay Colony

1793
Samuel Slater builds a
waterpowered textile
mill in Rhode Island

USE THE TIME LINE

1 When did John Smith explore the New England coast?

2 Which was founded first, Plymouth Colony or Massachusetts Bay Colony?

USE VOCABULARY

Choose a term from this list to complete each of the sentences that follow.

colony (p. 102)

industrial economy (p. 104)

glacier (p. 109)

volunteer (p. 115)

recreation (p. 119)

specialize (p. 121)

3 A _____ offers to do something without being paid.

4 People who work at only one kind of job and do it well _____.

5 In an _____, factories and machines manufacture most goods.

6 A huge, slow-moving mass of ice is called a _____.

7 A settlement started by people who leave their own country to live in another land is called a _____.

RECALL FACTS

Answer these questions.

8 Which explorer named New England?

9 Where was Plymouth Colony?

10 Why did people build most early factories along rivers?

11 Where do most people in New England live?

12 What is a town meeting?

Write the letter of the best choice.

13 Which of the following states is *not* part of New England?
 A Massachusetts
 B New York
 C New Hampshire
 D Vermont

14 A place where ships can dock safely is a—
 F cape.
 G glacier.
 H village.
 J harbor.

THINK CRITICALLY

15 Why do you think it is important for people to participate in their local governments?

16 Farmers in New England plant crops that grow in cool climates and rocky soil. How do people adapt to the geography of the place where you live?

17 How has the economy of New England changed over the years?

APPLY SKILLS

Read a Time Line

18 Look at the time line on pages 106–107. How many years after Europeans founded their first settlement in Vermont did Vermont become a state?

Solve a Problem

19 Think of a problem that you have. Then list the steps that you might follow to solve that problem.

PHILADELPHIA, PENNSYLVANIA

Philadelphia, in southeastern Pennsylvania, is considered the birthplace of the United States. The Declaration of Independence and the United States Constitution were signed in the city. The word *philadelphia* means "brotherly love" in Greek, and Philadelphia is often called the City of Brotherly Love.

LOCATE IT

PENNSYLVANIA

Philadelphia

4

Middle Atlantic States

" **The United States was born in the country and moved to the city.** "

—Richard Hofstadter,
The Age of Reform, 1960

Focus Skill: Cause and Effect

A **cause** is an event or action that makes something else happen. An **effect** is what happens as a result of that event or action.

As you read this chapter, look for causes and effects.

- **List the causes and effects of important events in the Middle Atlantic states.**

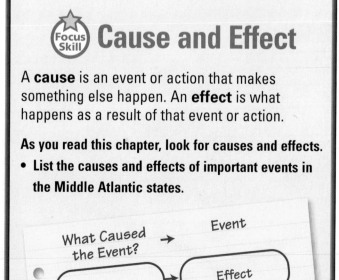

What Caused the Event? → Event

Cause → Effect

Chapter 4 ■ 125

The Middle Atlantic Colonies

CAUSE AND EFFECT

As you read, look for ways in which early settlers in the Middle Atlantic Colonies affected American life today.

BIG IDEA

A variety of people settled the Middle Atlantic Colonies.

VOCABULARY

confederation

treaty

port

generation

representation

independence

revolution

declaration

1600	1700	1800

Not long after the Pilgrims arrived in New England, other Europeans began settling in what are often called the Middle Atlantic Colonies. These colonies later became the states of Delaware, New Jersey, New York, and Pennsylvania. Unlike the New England Colonies, people from many different countries settled in the Middle Atlantic Colonies.

A Mix of People

One of the first Europeans to explore the Middle Atlantic region was Henry Hudson. In 1609 Hudson sailed his ship, the *Half Moon*, along the entire Middle Atlantic coast. During the voyage, the crew saw many rivers and deep bays.

Native American longhouses on Manhattan Island (present-day New York City) in the 1500s

FAST FACT

An Iroquois longhouse could be as long as a football field. Several families, called a clan, shared one. Each family had its own section. The eldest woman was in charge of the clan.

Hudson steered the *Half Moon* inland along one of these rivers, which now bears his name—the Hudson River. He claimed all the land along this river for Holland.

In 1625 the Dutch started a colony on the lands Hudson had claimed. They built their colonial capital, New Amsterdam, on an island at the mouth of the Hudson River.

The Dutch welcomed people from many European countries who wanted to settle in their colony. Among them were people from Sweden, Belgium, Denmark, France, Italy, and Spain.

The settlers traded with Native Americans in the region. Many of the tribes living there at the time belonged to the Iroquois (IR•uh•kwoy) or Delaware confederations. A **confederation** is a loosely united group of governments working together. Each tribe governed itself. The leaders of the confederation made decisions about matters that were important for all the tribes, such as war and trade.

In 1664 England took control of the Dutch colony in the Middle Atlantic region. The English split the land into two colonies, giving them their present-day names of New York and New Jersey. The Dutch capital of New Amsterdam became New York City.

Many houses in New York were built in the Dutch style, using bricks of different colors.

Thousands of English colonists soon moved to the Middle Atlantic Colonies. Among them were members of the Society of Friends, a religious group also known as Quakers. In 1682 a Quaker named William Penn founded the colony of Pennsylvania. Penn decided his colony would offer freedom of speech and "would stand above the differences of religion." From its beginning, Pennsylvania welcomed people of all religions and backgrounds, including free Africans, Irish Catholics, German and Scottish Protestants, and Jewish people from many different countries.

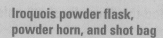

Iroquois powder flask, powder horn, and shot bag

German colonists settled in what is now Bethlehem, Pennsylvania, in 1741. This painting of Bethlehem, made only 16 years after the German colonists arrived, shows large farms along the Lehigh (LEE•hy) River.

Like all Quakers, Penn believed that problems should be solved peacefully. He signed a treaty with the Native Americans to buy land. A **treaty** is an agreement between countries or groups of people. Although fighting broke out between Indians and colonists in other parts of the region, the Quakers generally maintained good relations with the Indians.

REVIEW What was the capital of the Dutch colony in the Middle Atlantic region?

The Breadbasket Colonies

The Middle Atlantic Colonies soon had a mix of people, religions, and cultures. The Middle Atlantic region differed from New England in another important way, too. Unlike the poor, rocky soil in much of New England, the soil in eastern New York, Pennsylvania, Delaware, and New Jersey is generally very fertile. "The land," Henry Hudson wrote about the region, "is the finest for cultivation that I ever in my life set foot upon, and it also abounds in trees."

Descriptions of the rich land in the Middle Atlantic Colonies attracted many farmers to the region. The region's flat plains, rolling hills, and grassy meadows were good places to start farms. Its climate was also good for growing many crops, especially wheat. In fact, the Middle Atlantic Colonies soon produced so much wheat that they became known as the "breadbasket" colonies.

Middle Atlantic colonists used their rich land to raise more than just wheat. Cattle and dairy cows thrived on the thick grasses in the region. Hogs roamed in the forests, growing fat on acorns and wild strawberries and grapes. All these animals provided the colonists with plenty of meat, milk, butter, and cheese.

The fertile soil also allowed settlers in the Middle Atlantic Colonies to grow rye, corn, tobacco, vegetables, and fruit. Travelers through the region saw corn "eight feet high, . . . orchards full of peach trees," and "pears larger than a fist."

REVIEW Why were the Middle Atlantic Colonies called the "breadbasket" colonies?

A Time of Growth

Religious freedom, fertile land, trade opportunities, and good jobs brought thousands of people to the Middle Atlantic Colonies. Several early settlements along the region's coast grew into busy port cities. A **port** is a trading center where ships are loaded and unloaded.

Some port cities in the Middle Atlantic region were built on harbors where rivers flow into the Atlantic Ocean. New York City, for example, grew at the mouth of the Hudson River. Many other port cities in the region also grew along rivers. Dover, Delaware, is located a few miles inland on the St. Jones River. Several other large port cities developed on the Delaware River, which empties into the Delaware Bay. These cities include Trenton, New Jersey, and Philadelphia, Pennsylvania.

Philadelphia quickly became the busiest trading center in the region. Farmers near Philadelphia traveled to the city to sell their goods. Dock workers loaded grain, flour, meat, lumber, and furs onto ships in the city's harbor. Merchants then sold these goods in other colonies and in cities around the world.

By 1760, more than 20,000 people lived in Philadelphia, making it the largest city in the British colonies in North America.

Carpenters, bakers, tailors, blacksmiths, printers, and other skilled workers moved to the region. Many, including Benjamin Franklin, set up shops in towns and port cities throughout the region. Franklin moved to Philadelphia when he was 17 years old and, after a few years, opened his own printing business.

• BIOGRAPHY •

Benjamin Franklin
1706–1790

Character Trait: Inventiveness

Benjamin Franklin was a printer, writer, and world-famous scientist and inventor. Franklin conducted an experiment using a kite to show that lightning is electricity. He then invented the lightning rod, a piece of metal used to protect homes and buildings from lightning. Franklin also invented bifocal eyeglasses and a stove for heating homes. He also started the first fire insurance company.

MULTIMEDIA BIOGRAPHIES
Visit The Learning Site at
www.harcourtschool.com
to learn about other famous people.

He later started Philadelphia's first hospital and founded its first volunteer fire department and public library. He also became one of the most important political leaders in the British colonies.

By 1733 Britain governed 13 colonies along the Atlantic Coast of North America. Many families had been living in these colonies for several generations (jeh•nuh•RAY•shuhnz). A **generation** is the average time between the birth of parents and the birth of their children. After so many years in North America, many people in the colonies began to feel more American than British.

REVIEW What caused many Middle Atlantic settlements to grow into large cities?

CAUSE AND EFFECT

A New Nation

During the 1760s Britain passed the first of several laws that made it more difficult for the colonists to trade. Other laws forced the colonists to pay new taxes. Many colonists did not see why they should pay taxes they had not agreed to. After all, they had no **representation** in the British government, which meant that they could not elect leaders to speak or act for them. Throughout the colonies, people began to shout,

❝ No taxation without representation! ❞

Some colonists used newspapers and printed pamphlets to protest, or speak out against, the taxes.

The Liberty Bell is a symbol of freedom for Americans.

Others refused to buy British goods. Some colonists even began to talk about **independence**, or the freedom to govern themselves. They said that the time had

POINTS OF VIEW
Independence

THOMAS PAINE, American colonist and author of the pamphlet *Common Sense*

❝ Our . . . trade will always be . . . secure. I challenge [anyone] to show a single advantage [the colonies] can reap by being connected with Great Britain. . . . Our corn will fetch its price in any market in Europe. ❞

CHARLES INGLIS, American colonist and minister of the Church of England

❝ Past experience shows that Britain is able to defend our trade, and our coasts. . . . These advantages . . . derive from our connection with Great Britain. . . . But as soon as we declare independence, every prospect of this kind must vanish. Ruthless war . . . will ravage our once happy land—our seacoasts and ports will be ruined, and our ships taken. ❞

Analyze the Viewpoints

❶ What view about American independence from Britain did each person hold?

❷ How did Paine and Inglis use the issue of trade to support their views?

❸ **Make It Relevant** Write a short paragraph explaining what advantages you think your state gains from being part of the United States.

This painting shows the signing of the Declaration of Independence in 1776. The colonial representatives met in Philadelphia, in Pennsylvania's State House, known today as Independence Hall. Can you find Benjamin Franklin in the painting?

come for the 13 colonies to break away from British rule and start their own country.

Fighting between the colonists and British troops broke out in Massachusetts in 1775. Soon after that, the American Revolution (reh•vuh•LOO•shuhn) began. A **revolution** is a large, sudden change in government or in people's lives.

Representatives from all of the colonies gathered in Philadelphia to decide what to do. After a long and heated debate, they decided to form a committee to write a **declaration** (deh•kluh•RAY•shuhn), or an official statement, of independence.

Each member of the committee added ideas about what the declaration should

say. But one young representative from Virginia, Thomas Jefferson, did most of the writing. When it was finished, the Declaration of Independence stated that all people have certain rights, which include

❝ Life, Liberty and the pursuit of Happiness. ❞

A printed copy of the Declaration of Independence

Not all colonists wanted to go to war with Britain. Throughout the colonies, people were divided over which side to support in the American Revolution. The colonists who wanted to remain part of Britain were called Loyalists. Those who wanted to fight for independence were called Patriots. Still other colonists remained neutral, or chose not to take sides.

After eight long years of fighting, the Americans defeated the British. A treaty signed in 1783 officially ended the war and defined the borders of the United States. The new nation stretched from about present-day Florida on the south to present-day Canada on the north. The Atlantic Ocean formed its entire eastern border, while the Mississippi River shaped its western boundary.

REVIEW What was the colonists' main complaint against the British?

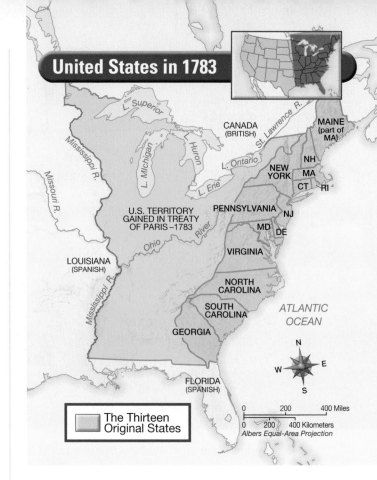

United States in 1783

The Thirteen Original States

 Regions This map shows the United States in 1783.

❖ How many states made up the new nation?

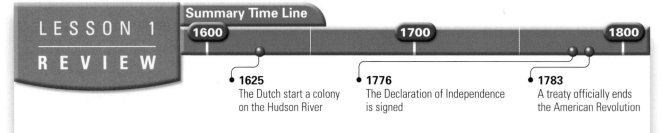

LESSON 1 REVIEW

Summary Time Line

1600 — 1700 — 1800

• **1625** The Dutch start a colony on the Hudson River

• **1776** The Declaration of Independence is signed

• **1783** A treaty officially ends the American Revolution

 CAUSE AND EFFECT How did the new laws passed by the British in the 1760s lead to the American Revolution?

1 **BIG IDEA** Who settled in the Middle Atlantic Colonies?

2 **VOCABULARY** Use the terms **confederation** and **treaty** to describe relations between Native Americans and Middle Atlantic colonists.

3 **TIME LINE** When was the Declaration of Independence signed?

4 **GEOGRAPHY** What were the boundaries of the United States after the American Revolution?

5 **CRITICAL THINKING—Evaluate** What do you think the colonists meant when they wrote in the Declaration of Independence that all people have the rights of "Life, Liberty and the pursuit of Happiness"?

 PERFORMANCE—Create a Hall of Fame Research a signer of the Declaration of Independence. Use the Internet or the library to learn about that person's life. Then draw a portrait, and write a short paragraph explaining what that person did. Display your biography in the classroom to create an Independence Hall of Fame.

·SKILLS· READING

Identify Fact and Opinion

VOCABULARY

fact
opinion

▶ WHY IT MATTERS

Every day, you get information from many sources, including people, books, television, and newspapers. Whenever you get a piece of information, you must decide whether it is a fact or an opinion. A **fact** is a statement that can be checked and proved to be true. An **opinion** is a statement that tells what someone thinks or believes. Knowing how to tell fact from opinion can help you understand what you hear or read.

▶ WHAT YOU NEED TO KNOW

The Atlantic Ocean borders New Jersey. This statement is a fact. You could prove the fact by visiting New Jersey or by doing research at the library or on the Internet.

I think New Jersey is the most beautiful place in the world. This sentence gives someone's opinion. There is no way to prove what is the most beautiful place in the world.

An opinion tells what a speaker or writer believes. Looking for some clues can help you know

when a statement is an opinion. Certain key words, such as *I think*, *I believe*, *in my opinion*, and *I doubt*, tell you that you are reading or hearing an opinion. Words such as *beautiful*, *happy*, *best*, *worst*, and *greatest* are often part of an opinion.

▶ PRACTICE THE SKILL

Identify each statement below as fact or opinion.

1 People from Europe settled in the Middle Atlantic Colonies.

2 I think the colonists were right to demand independence from Britain.

3 Maryland, Pennsylvania, New Jersey, and the Atlantic Ocean border Delaware.

4 Life in the Middle Atlantic Colonies was better than life in the New England Colonies.

▶ APPLY WHAT YOU LEARNED

Look through several newspapers and find at least three statements of fact and three statements of opinion. Be prepared to explain to the class how you identified each statement as fact or opinion.

A lighthouse on the New Jersey shore

2 Transportation and Growth

CAUSE AND EFFECT

As you read, look for the ways in which changes in transportation affect life in every region of the United States.

BIG IDEA

Improvements in transportation helped the Middle Atlantic states grow and change.

VOCABULARY

waterway
navigable
rapid
canal
lock
competition
turnpike

In the years following the country's independence from Britain, the Middle Atlantic states grew and changed rapidly. The region's economy shifted from agriculture to manufacturing. Many industries grew up around the eastern ports. The growth of those industries led to an increased need for the natural resources of the Appalachian Mountains in the west. To get the resources to ports in the east, the Middle Atlantic states had to build transportation systems to connect all places in the region.

Early Transportation

In the early years of the United States, the Middle Atlantic region and the rest of the nation lacked a good transportation system. There were only two ways to move people and goods—on water or on roads.

Transporting goods by horse and wagon was hard, slow work. Most early roads were mainly dirt paths full of tree stumps and holes. Road transportation also cost a lot of money. Wagons pulled by horses were slow and could carry only small amounts of goods at one time. As a result, they often had to make many trips between places to deliver their goods.

Because road travel was so difficult, most farmers and traders preferred water travel. It was faster, easier, and cheaper. Also, boats were usually larger than wagons and could carry more goods each trip.

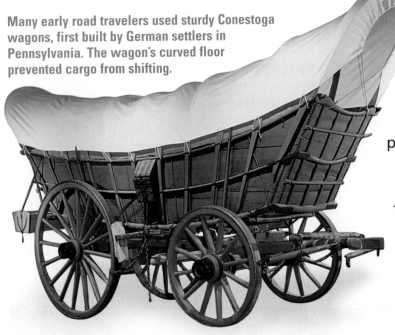

Many early road travelers used sturdy Conestoga wagons, first built by German settlers in Pennsylvania. The wagon's curved floor prevented cargo from shifting.

Boats, pulled by horses or mules, traveled in groups through the Erie Canal. The first boat hung lanterns, like the one shown at the left, on its deck. The number of lanterns showed how many boats were traveling together.

The Middle Atlantic region has many wide rivers and other **waterways**, or bodies of water that boats can use. In the east, there are deep harbors along the Atlantic Ocean. In the west, past the Appalachian Mountains, two of the five Great Lakes form part of the region's border. Lake Ontario and Lake Erie lie along the western edge of New York. Lake Erie also borders northwestern Pennsylvania. Many navigable (NA•vih•guh•buhl) rivers flow into the Great Lakes and the Atlantic Ocean. A **navigable** river is a river that is deep and wide enough for ships to use.

The region's waterways, however, were not all connected. The Appalachian Mountains separated rivers that flowed into the Great Lakes from those that flowed into the Atlantic Ocean. There was no good way to move goods from the Great Lakes to the Atlantic Ocean without using some kind of land transportation. Only one river, the St. Lawrence River, connected the Great Lakes to the coast.

This river, however, was not entirely navigable because it contained rapids. A **rapid** is a rocky place in a river where a sudden drop in elevation causes water to be fast-moving and dangerous.

Ships could not even travel from one end of the Great Lakes to the other. On the Niagara River, between Lake Ontario and Lake Erie, for example, the water dropped about 167 feet (51 m), forming Niagara Falls.

REVIEW Why were ships on the Great Lakes not able to reach the Atlantic Ocean?

Linking Waterways

In 1817 the state of New York decided to link the Great Lakes to the Atlantic Ocean by building a canal. A **canal** is a waterway dug across the land. The Erie Canal connected the New York cities of Buffalo, on Lake Erie, and Troy, on the Hudson River. From Troy, ships sailed down the Hudson to Albany and New York City and on to the Atlantic Ocean.

To build the Erie Canal, workers had to cut through 363 miles (584 km) of forests and hills in New York's countryside. They also had to build more than 80 locks on the canal. A **lock** is a part of a canal in which the water level can be raised or lowered. Changing the water level brings ships to the level of the next section of the canal. Locks had to be built on the Erie Canal because the elevation of Lake Erie is 572 feet (174 m) higher than the elevation of the Hudson River at Troy.

When the Erie Canal was finished in 1825, it was the longest canal in the world. From the start, the canal increased trade, agriculture, and manufacturing in the region. New York City, at the end of the canal and river network, became the leading trading city in the United States. The Erie Canal also offered settlers an easier way to move west.

Today other waterways connect the Great Lakes with the Atlantic Ocean. One is the St. Lawrence Seaway. It stretches about 450 miles (724 km) from the eastern end of Lake Erie to Montreal, Canada. The St. Lawrence Seaway, which includes the Welland Ship Canal built between Lake Ontario and Lake Erie, links several inland ports on the Great Lakes to ports along the Atlantic Ocean. In good weather, a ship can travel the entire route of the seaway in one and a half days.

The St. Lawrence Seaway helped make Buffalo and Rochester, in New York, and Erie, in Pennsylvania, important manufacturing centers in the Middle Atlantic states. Buffalo is one of the nation's largest producers of flour. Rochester produces cameras and film. Factories in Erie produce heavy machinery.

REVIEW **How did the Erie Canal affect trade in the Middle Atlantic region?**

CAUSE AND EFFECT

How a Canal Lock Works

Analyze Diagrams   This diagram shows how a ship is raised or lowered in a canal lock.

❶ A ship enters the lock and gates close behind the ship.

❷ Water is pumped into the lock to raise the ship or pumped out of the lock to lower the ship.

❸ Gates open in front of the ship, and it leaves the lock.

❖ What causes a ship to rise when it is in a lock?

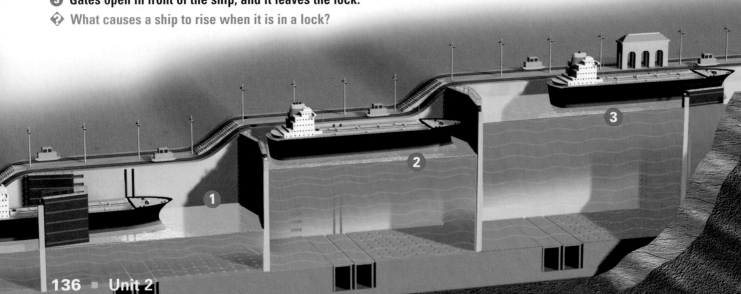

Elijah McCoy
1844–1929

Character Trait: Inventiveness

Elijah McCoy's parents had been enslaved in Kentucky before escaping to freedom in Canada. Born in 1844, Elijah McCoy studied in Scotland and later moved to Detroit, Michigan. His first invention was a device to oil steam engines. The invention enabled machines to be oiled while in motion. McCoy's new oiling device revolutionized the machine industry. In his lifetime, McCoy obtained 57 patents for products he invented. Among his many inventions was a lawn sprinkler.

MULTIMEDIA BIOGRAPHIES
Visit The Learning Site at www.harcourtschool.com
to learn about other famous people.

New Industries

By the early 1900s, roads, waterways, and railroads linked the eastern and western parts of the Middle Atlantic region. Business owners in the region could now easily and quickly ship their products to customers. They could also build factories closer to the natural resources they used. Often those resources were in the Appalachian Mountains. In the Middle Atlantic states, several smaller mountain ranges make up the Appalachians. There are the Allegheny (a•luh•GAY•nee) Mountains in western Pennsylvania, the Poconos (POH•kuh•nohz) in eastern Pennsylvania and southeastern New York, and the Catskills in eastern New York.

With transportation now connecting resources, businesses, and customers, many new industries started in the Middle Atlantic states. The steel industry, for example, began in the mountain regions of western Pennsylvania, near Pittsburgh. To make steel, people need iron, coal, and limestone. Surrounded by all three of these resources, western Pennsylvania became the center of the nation's steel industry.

As the United States grew, steel became more important. Large amounts of it were needed to build railroad tracks, bridges, ships, buildings, tools, and machines. By the 1920s the United States was producing nearly three-fifths of the world's steel. About half of that steel was created in the mills of western Pennsylvania. In fact, so much steel was produced in Pittsburgh that it became one of the largest industrial cities in the nation.

Smoke from steel mills in Pittsburgh during this time caused the city to be polluted. Author Anna Egan Smucker wrote about growing up in Pittsburgh with all the steel mills:

66 We went to school across from the mill. The smoke-stacks towered above us and the smoke billowed out in great puffy clouds of red, orange, and yellow, but mostly the color of rust. Everything—houses, hedges, old cars—was a rusty red color. 99

Today Pennsylvania steel mills no longer make as much steel. Steel mills in other cities can do the same job more cheaply. The steel industry also faces strong competition (kahm•puh•TIH•shuhn) from steelmakers in other countries. In business, **competition** is the contest among companies to get the most customers or sell the most products. Partly

because of competition, many steel mills in this region have closed.

Still, the Middle Atlantic states remain leaders in manufacturing. In addition to steel, the region's factories produce food products, chemicals, computer equipment, and machinery. The largest chemical company in the world is located in Wilmington, Delaware. New York City is the center of the nation's publishing industry. Making chocolate is a major industry in Hershey, Pennsylvania.

REVIEW What industries in the Middle Atlantic states grew as a result of new transportation links?

Connecting Cities

Many cities, like Pittsburgh, grew around factories in the Middle Atlantic states. Other cities, like New York City and Buffalo, continued to develop as ports along the region's waterways. Today service industries make up the largest part of the region's economy, and most of them are also based in cities.

Transportation helped Middle Atlantic cities grow. Today it helps the cities connect with one another. A vast system of highways, including Interstate 95, links all the Middle Atlantic cities. *Inter* means "between" or "among." An interstate highway is a highway that goes through more than one state. These highways are wide, divided roads that connect large cities. Because interstate highways usually do not have traffic lights, people can

Some steel mills still operate in Pittsburgh. Andrew Carnegie (above) was a leader in the steel industry in the 1900s and one of the richest people in the world.

About half a million vehicles drive on the New Jersey Turnpike every day.

travel long distances on them quickly. One of the busiest parts of Interstate 95 is called the New Jersey Turnpike and links Philadelphia and New York City. A **turnpike** is a road that drivers must pay to use. Another such road, the Pennsylvania Turnpike, extends across the entire state of Pennsylvania.

Other roads connecting the region are called state highways and United States highways. State highways link places within one state. Like interstate highways, United States highways go from state to state. However, United States highways have traffic lights and lower speed limits.

People also use airplanes and trains to travel between Middle Atlantic cities. Airlines offer many flights each day between major cities. A new, high-speed train, called the Acela (ah•SELL•uh) Express, links Boston, New York City, and Washington, D.C. Traveling up to 150 miles (241 km) per hour, the Acela speeds between Washington, D.C., and New York City in less than three hours.

REVIEW How do people travel between the Middle Atlantic states today?

LESSON 2
REVIEW

 CAUSE AND EFFECT How did improved transportation in the early 1900s lead to the development of the steel industry in the Middle Atlantic region?

1. **BIG IDEA** How did new forms of transportation help the Middle Atlantic states grow and change?

2. **VOCABULARY** Use the terms **navigable** and **rapid** to explain why people in the Middle Atlantic region built **canals**.

3. **HISTORY** Why did the state of New York decide to build the Erie Canal?

4. **GEOGRAPHY** Why did western Pennsylvania become a center for the nation's steel industry?

5. **CRITICAL THINKING—Analyze** How was early road travel in the United States different from traveling by road today?

 PERFORMANCE—Conduct an Interview Interview older family members or people you know about the changes that they have witnessed in transportation in their community. Do they know about a part of your community that was once covered with forests and fields and that is now paved with roads? Share what you learn with your classmates.

Use a Road Map and Mileage Table

VOCABULARY

mileage   mileage table

▶ WHY IT MATTERS

Imagine that this is the first day of your family's vacation in Pennsylvania. An hour into the car trip, your brother asks, "How much farther do we have to go?"

To answer this question, you can use a road map of Pennsylvania like the one on this page. A road map shows the routes between places. You can also use a road map to find the driving distance, or **mileage**, between places.

Road maps give other important information, too. They show the locations of cities and towns. They may also show physical features, such as mountains, bodies of water, and forests. Many road maps show where to find parks, museums, and other points of interest.

Road Map of Pennsylvania

Lake Erie
Erie
NY
NY
CT
Allegheny National Forest
Susquehannock State Forest
Wilkes-Barre
Scranton
Williamsport
PENNSYLVANIA
OH
Allegheny Portage Railroad Natl. Hist. Site
State College
Altoona
Allentown
Bethlehem
Pittsburgh
Johnstown
Harrisburg
Reading
Pottstown
Lebanon
Philadelphia
NJ
Chambersburg
Lancaster
York
Gettysburg Natl.Mil. Park
WV
MD
DE

0 15 30 Miles
0 15 30 Meters
Albers Equal-Area Projection

★   State capital
🌟 Metropolitan area
⬡35⬡ Interstate highway
⟨57⟩ U.S. highway
⟨44⟩ State highway
■ State forest
■ Point of Interest

Index to Major Cities

Allentown...........B-5   Pittsburgh.........B-2
Erie..................A-2   Scranton............A-5
Harrisburg..........C-4   State College.....B-3
Lancaster...........C-4   Wilkes-Barre......B-5
Reading.............C-5   Williamsport......B-4
Philadelphia.......C-5   York..................C-4

Pennsylvania Road Mileage

	Erie	Harrisburg	Lancaster	Pittsburgh	Scranton	Uniontown	York
Erie		298	340	126	317	183	341
Harrisburg	298		44	205	119	200	25
Lancaster	340	44		242	130	237	26
Pittsburgh	126	205	242		301	48	220
Scranton	317	119	130	301		315	143
Uniontown	183	200	237	48	315		214
York	341	25	26	220	143	214	

▶ WHAT YOU NEED TO KNOW

Road maps also provide information about the kinds of roads that connect places. Different kinds of lines on a road map stand for different kinds of roads. Knowing the kinds of roads helps you choose good routes.

On most road maps, places on main highways have small numbers next to them. These show the number of miles between places on the highways. Usually each place is marked with a wedge called a distance marker.

An easier way to find the distance between cities is to use a mileage table such as the one shown on this page. A **mileage table** gives the number of miles between its listed cities. Suppose you want to find the mileage between Erie and Lancaster. Find the box where the row and column for those two cities cross. You will see that the driving distance is 340 miles.

▶ PRACTICE THE SKILL

Use the road map, map key, and mileage table to answer these questions.

❶ If you want to travel quickly west across all of Pennsylvania, which highway should you use?

❷ What road connects Harrisburg and York? What is the mileage between those two places?

❸ What two highways cross at Williamsport?

▶ APPLY WHAT YOU LEARNED

Use the road map to write directions between two places in Pennsylvania. See if a classmate can follow the route and figure the mileage.

Practice your map and globe skills with the **GeoSkills CD-ROM**.

Interstate highways that run east and west have even numbers, like Interstate 80. Interstate highways that run north and south have odd numbers.

MAP AND GLOBE SKILLS

3

Cities Grow and Change

CAUSE AND EFFECT

As you read, look for ways in which the growth of a city affects the people who live there.

BIG IDEA

Cities in the Middle Atlantic states grew in similar ways.

VOCABULARY

metropolitan area
megalopolis
immigrant
urban growth
commute

FAST FACT

About 100 million people living in the United States today can trace their heritage to an ancestor who came by way of Ellis Island in New York Harbor.

Nearly 90 million people live in the Middle Atlantic states today. Most of them live in cities. These include New York City and Buffalo in New York; Philadelphia and Pittsburgh in Pennsylvania; Wilmington, Delaware; and Trenton and Newark in New Jersey. Every city in the United States is different, but most have grown in similar ways. As a result, cities across the country often share similar features, as well as similar problems.

A Region of Cities

The Middle Atlantic region has many big cities, but New York City is by far the largest. In fact, with more than 8 million people, New York City is the largest city in the United States. Only 10 states have larger populations.

Like New York City, many large cities in the Middle Atlantic region were built near the coast. As these cities grew larger, their boundaries also grew closer and closer together. Eventually, New York City became the center of the largest metropolitan (meh•truh•PAH•luh•tuhn) area in the United

During its busiest year, 1907, Ellis Island welcomed more than 1 million newcomers to the United States. Today Ellis Island is part of the Statue of Liberty National Monument.

States. A **metropolitan area** is a large city together with its suburbs. More than 20 million people, or about one out of every 14 Americans, live in this metropolitan area.

Years ago empty countryside stood between New York City and other cities along the coast. Today those cities almost blend into one another. In fact, it is sometimes hard to tell where one city ends and the next one begins.

A long, wide string of cities stretches more than 500 miles (805 km) from southern New Hampshire to northern Virginia. Together, these cities make up the nation's largest megalopolis (meh•guh•LAH•puh•lihs). A **megalopolis** is a huge urban region formed when two or more metropolitan areas grow together. The word *megalopolis* means "great city."

REVIEW What is a megalopolis?

Megalopolis in the Northeast

Lake Ontario

0 50 100 Miles
0 50 100 Kilometers
Albers Equal-Area Projection

NY   VT   NH   ME
· Manchester
MA   · Boston
· Springfield
Hartford ·   Providence ·
CT   RI

Scranton ·
PA   Newark ·   Long Island
New York City
Trenton ·
Philadelphia ·   NJ
Wilmington ·   ATLANTIC
WV   Baltimore ·   OCEAN
MD   DE
Washington,   N
D.C.   W   E
VA   S

Megalopolis

GEOGRAPHY THEME

Regions Part of the largest megalopolis in the United States is in the Middle Atlantic states.

◆ What large cities in New Jersey are part of the megalopolis?

Immigrants Crowd into Cities

New industries were a major reason many Middle Atlantic cities grew so large. Factories in cities needed workers. During the 1800s and early 1900s, thousands of Americans left their farms and small towns in search of jobs in cities. Many were African Americans. They were often forced to live in separate neighborhoods because landlords in some areas refused to rent to them. Many worked as laborers, cooks, and nurses.

At the same time, many immigrants came to America's cities. An **immigrant** is a person who comes to live in a country from another country. Most immigrants arrived by boat in New York Harbor. Their first stop was Ellis Island, the nation's largest immigration center. From 1892 to 1954, more than 12 million immigrants from over 50 countries entered the United States by way of Ellis Island.

Millions of immigrants stayed in New York City. They often

These immigrant children came to the United States from Italy in 1905.

settled in immigrant neighborhoods, such as Little Italy or Chinatown. Many Jewish immigrants from Russia, Poland, and other European countries lived in an area called the Lower East Side.

Because immigrants had little money, many of them had to live in run-down apartment buildings called tenements (TEH•nuh•muhnts). As many as 20 people sometimes lived in just two rooms. Most immigrants had to work long hours to afford even these tiny apartments and to feed their families. Adults and children often worked 14-hour shifts in the city's factories, making clothing and other goods.

As more immigrants arrived, many Middle Atlantic cities grew larger and more crowded. Between 1800 and 1900, for example, New York City's population grew from just 60,000 people to more than 3 million. By

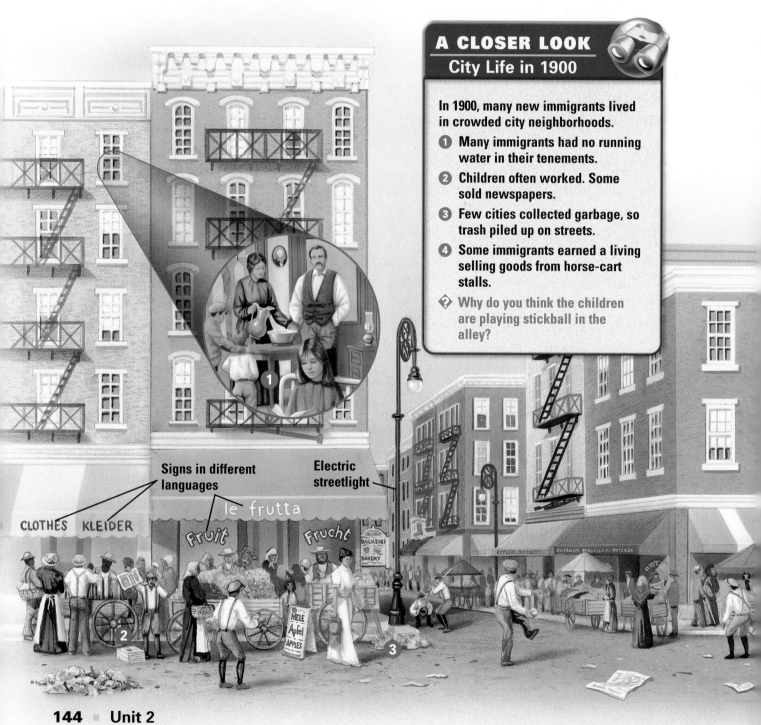

A CLOSER LOOK
City Life in 1900

In 1900, many new immigrants lived in crowded city neighborhoods.

1. Many immigrants had no running water in their tenements.
2. Children often worked. Some sold newspapers.
3. Few cities collected garbage, so trash piled up on streets.
4. Some immigrants earned a living selling goods from horse-cart stalls.

❓ Why do you think the children are playing stickball in the alley?

Signs in different languages

Electric streetlight

CLOTHES KLEIDER
le frutta
Fruit
Frucht
BACKEREI BAKERY
MELE Apfel APPLES

1930 nearly 7 million people lived in New York City, making it the largest city in the world at the time.

REVIEW How did immigrants change many Middle Atlantic cities?
CAUSE AND EFFECT

Living in Cities Today

Today, about four out of every five people in the Middle Atlantic states live in or near cities. Some people are attracted by the job opportunities that cities offer. Others attend colleges and universities in cities. Still others just want to be part of the excitement and opportunities of city life.

In the past, manufacturing and shipping industries caused much of the region's **urban growth**, or growth of cities. Thousands of people in the region continue to manufacture products in city factories. Others still work in ports in cities. The New York–New Jersey port in Elizabeth, New Jersey, is the third-largest port in the nation.

However, most people in Middle Atlantic cities today work in service industries. New York City, for instance, is the nation's center for banking and finance. Princeton, New Jersey, and many other Middle Atlantic cities are scientific research centers. Health care, education, and insurance are other large service industries in Middle Atlantic cities.

Many city residents have government service jobs, too. With such large populations, cities need to provide certain services. Millions of people work in city schools and in police and fire departments. Others have jobs repairing and improving city water pipes, sewers, roads, and bridges. Still others help run public transportation.

Today's transportation lets people travel quickly and easily between Middle Atlantic cities. As a result, people no longer have to live in the city where they work. Instead, they can live in the suburbs and **commute**, or travel back and forth, to the city each day.

Transportation also allows more people to visit cities, making tourism another major service industry in Middle Atlantic cities. Each year millions of people visit New York City's many attractions, such as the Ellis Island Museum, the Statue of Liberty, and the Empire State Building. Both city residents and tourists can attend the theater, visit museums and art galleries, and watch professional sports teams play. One place in New York City, Coney Island, even has beaches, an amusement park, and an aquarium.

Because people of many ethnic groups live in most cities, cities also offer many different kinds of foods, dance, and music. Thousands of immigrants continue to move to Middle Atlantic cities. Today most of them arrive by airplanes rather than by ships. Instead of coming from Europe, these immigrants now come mainly from Asia, Africa, and Latin American countries. As in the past, many of these new arrivals first settle in city immigrant neighborhoods.

Many city residents still live close together in small apartments. Parks offer an escape from the busy city streets and a place to enjoy nature. People gather in city parks to picnic, ride bikes, walk their dogs, or talk to neighbors. New York City's Central Park has tennis courts, baseball fields, and lakes with boats to rent. Other parks have zoos and even wildlife preserves.

REVIEW **Why do many people choose to live in or near cities?**

The Problems of Crowding

There are many advantages to living in cities. However, growing cities also present problems. City residents must learn how to live with these problems, or they must work together to solve them.

Traffic is a major problem in most cities, including those in the Middle Atlantic states. Many of the region's cities are among the oldest in the United States. In Philadelphia, New York City, and many other cities, the streets are often narrow. They were first built for horses and carriages. They were never meant to handle the large numbers of cars, trucks, and buses that now use them.

Pollution can be a problem in cities, too. Smoke from factories, and the fumes from cars and trucks jamming the streets, can pollute the air. Sometimes the air becomes hazy and dirty. Breathing such air can harm people's health. To help reduce traffic and pollution, most cities

Philadelphia's Fairmount Park is one of the largest city parks in the world.

LOCATE IT

PENNSYLVANIA

Philadelphia

The New York City subway system carries nearly 4 million passengers a day.

provide public transportation systems. New York City, for example, has a sprawling 733-mile (1,179-km) subway network. Another way cities deal with pollution is to pass laws to protect their air and water.

Providing necessary services for city residents, such as police protection, schools, water, electricity, and trash removal, is a challenge for many cities. People in the United States throw away huge amounts of trash. People faced this problem by creating organized garbage collection services. Many cities now have recycling programs as well.

In these and other ways, cities are meeting the challenges of growth and crowding. By working together, people are making their cities cleaner, safer, and better places to live.

REVIEW What are some problems many cities face?

LESSON 3 REVIEW

CAUSE AND EFFECT How does over-crowding cause problems in many cities?

1 BIG IDEA What are the reasons the Middle Atlantic states make up a region of cities?

2 VOCABULARY Write a paragraph that shows how the terms **metropolitan area**, **megalopolis**, and **commute** are related.

3 ECONOMICS How did new industries help cause urban growth in the Middle Atlantic states?

4 CULTURE From where do most immigrants in cities in the Middle Atlantic states now come?

5 CRITICAL THINKING—Hypothesize What do you think will happen if metropolitan areas in the Middle Atlantic states continue to grow?

PERFORMANCE—Make a Tourism Brochure Choose a Middle Atlantic city you would like to visit. Use the library or the Internet to find out more about that city. Then create a brochure to try to persuade people to visit the city. Make sure you explain where the city is and describe its physical features. Mention some of its attractions, such as historical sites, museums, and theaters. Present your brochure to your class to try to convince them to visit the city.

The Immigrant Experience

Between 1892 and 1954, more than 12 million immigrants entered the United States at the immigration station on Ellis Island, in New York Harbor. Almost half of the people living in the United States today have ancestors who were among the immigrants who came through Ellis Island. Fritz Neumann, of Leipzig, Germany, was one of these immigrants. He arrived at Ellis Island on January 30, 1922, at the age of 25, on the ship *America*. Today, members of the family he started in the United States live in Florida and Louisiana.

FROM THE STATUE OF LIBERTY–ELLIS ISLAND FOUNDATION, INC., NEW YORK, NEW YORK

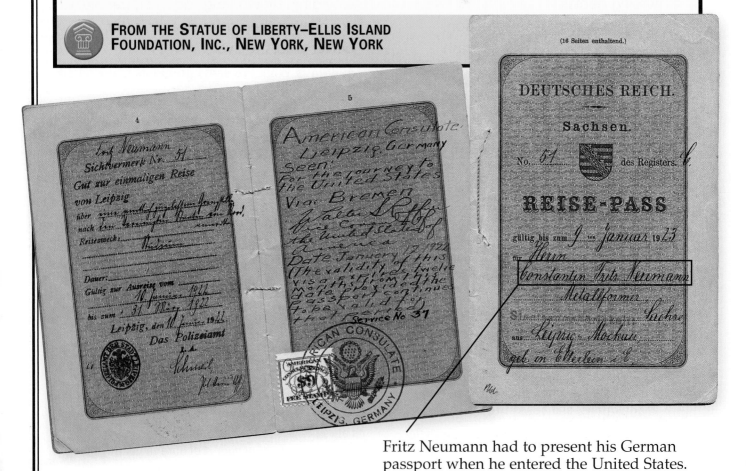

Fritz Neumann had to present his German passport when he entered the United States.

Fritz Neumann is listed on line 13 of the *America's* manifest, or their list of passengers.

Many immigrants, including Fritz Neumann, became United States citizens.

Analyze the Primary Source

1. **What kinds of documents are shown on these pages?**

2. **What kind of information is given in these documents?**

ACTIVITY

Conduct an Interview Identify someone in your school or neighborhood who has immigrated to the United States. Write five questions that you would like to ask about his or her experiences. Then use your questions to interview the person. Share your interview with the class.

RESEARCH

Visit The Learning Site at **www.harcourtschool.com** to research other primary sources.

Focus Skill

CAUSE AND EFFECT

As you read, look for the causes and effects of challenges that all cities face.

BIG IDEA

Explore what life is like in some cities around the world.

VOCABULARY

unemployment

urban sprawl

Cities Around the World

Cities in every part of the world have grown rapidly. In fact, about half of the world's population now lives in urban areas, and each day the numbers increase. Around the world, as in the United States, people have moved to cities for job and educational opportunities, services, and excitement.

Regardless of their locations, cities around the world have much in common. They also face many of the same challenges. Yet each city has unique features that make people want to live there.

Low Land in Amsterdam

The first Europeans to settle in the Middle Atlantic region of the United States came from Holland, a country in north-western Europe. They named their colonial capital New Amsterdam, after Amsterdam, the capital city they had left behind in Holland.

Many buildings in Amsterdam are close together and narrow, like these houses built along the city's canals.

LOCATE IT

Amsterdam

NETHERLANDS

Major Cities of the World

ARCTIC OCEAN

NORTH AMERICA

PACIFIC OCEAN

Los Angeles
Chicago
UNITED STATES
Montreal
New York
Miami

Guadalajara
Mexico City

ATLANTIC OCEAN

Bogotá
SOUTH AMERICA
Lima
Rio de Janeiro
São Paulo
Santiago
Buenos Aires

Equator

PACIFIC OCEAN

ATLANTIC OCEAN

Amsterdam
London
Paris
Barcelona
Casablanca

St. Petersburg
Moscow
Berlin
EUROPE
Milan
Istanbul
Athens
Cairo

ASIA
Beijing
Seoul
Tokyo
Shanghai
Taipei
Tehran
Bagdad
Delhi
Karachi
Kolkata (Calcutta)
Hong Kong
Chennai (Madras)
Bangkok
Manila

AFRICA
Lagos
Kinshasa

Jakarta

INDIAN OCEAN

PACIFIC OCEAN

AUSTRALIA
Sydney
Melbourne

N
W   E
S

0   1,000   2,000 Miles
0 1,000 2,000 Kilometers
Scale accurate at equator
Winkel Projection

ANTARCTICA

Location Large cities are found on most of Earth's continents.

GEOGRAPHY THEME

❖ **Why do you think many major cities are located near coasts?**

Today Holland is known as the Netherlands, which means "low land." This name certainly fits, as much of the country lies at or below sea level. Preventing floods and finding enough dry land to live on are two of the greatest challenges facing the Netherlands.

Only about 700,000 people live in Amsterdam today, but the city seems crowded because there is not enough dry land for its population to spread out. In fact, water once covered the land where Amsterdam is today.

To drain their land, the Dutch built about 1,500 miles (2,414 km) of dikes across the Netherlands. Like a levee, a dike is an earthen structure that holds back water. Once the dikes were built, the Dutch used huge, powerful windmills to pump out the water. They also built dams as well as hundreds of canals to drain the land and control flooding.

In Amsterdam the streets are often narrow. This means that traffic can be a problem, just as in other cities around the world. Amsterdam has a public transportation system to help move people around the city. However, people in Amsterdam have come up with some special ways to get around. Since canals cut through many parts of the city, many residents ride canal boats instead of driving cars. During the winter, some people even ice skate to work or to school on frozen canals!

Bicycling is another popular way to travel in the city. One out of every five people in Amsterdam bicycles to work.

More than 1 million bicycles are sold in the Netherlands every year.

covers an area the size of 75 football fields! Every day it ships 15 million cut flowers to cities around the world.

A wide, deep channel connects the port of Amsterdam to the North Sea, a part of the Atlantic Ocean. Like many people in port cities in the Middle Atlantic region of the United States, many people in Amsterdam also work in shipping and in trade industries. Others have jobs in the fishing and shipbuilding industries. Thousands of people in Amsterdam also work in factories, producing furniture, automobiles, and food products.

REVIEW How do people in Amsterdam use canals?

To encourage even more people to ride bikes, Amsterdam started a special program called White Bikes. At stations throughout the city, people can pick up a white bike owned by the city. They can then pedal to their destination and leave the bike at the nearest station.

People in Amsterdam especially enjoy bicycling in spring, when the red, orange, purple, and yellow tulips are in bloom. In April, Amsterdam holds tulip festivals with parades and parties. Many people make their living by growing and selling tulips. A huge flower market near the city

Mexico's Capital City

Mexico City is one of the oldest cities in the Western Hemisphere. Located in the southern region of central Mexico, the city was founded by Spanish explorers in 1521. It was built on the site that was once the capital city of the powerful Aztec Indians.

Today Mexico City is the capital of the nation of Mexico. In both area and population, Mexico City is one of the largest cities in the world. More than 18 million people live in Mexico City, and many more arrive from the countryside every week.

A huge square called the Zócalo (ZOH•cah•loh) is at the heart of Mexico City.

LOCATE IT

Mexico City

MEXICO

Tall mountains surround Mexico City.

FAST FACT Mexico City has one of the world's largest subway systems. Planning its route was not easy. The ruins of an ancient Aztec city lie below the surface of Mexico City. Engineers had to make sure the subway tracks went around the ruins.

Like many cities around the world, Mexico City is an exciting place to live. There are sports arenas where city residents can watch soccer games or other sporting events. Throughout the city, museums such as the Palace of Fine Arts are filled with Mexican art. Every September 16, people in the city celebrate Mexico's Independence Day with fireworks, parades, and fiestas.

Like cities everywhere, Mexico City also faces many challenges. In recent years, the city's economy has suffered. There are often not enough jobs for the growing population. The result for people is **unemployment**, or being without a job. However, Mexico City remains the manufacturing center of the nation. In fact, factories in the Mexico City metropolitan area produce about half of all the goods made in Mexico.

Just as many other large cities do, Mexico City has a serious pollution problem. At one time the city was famous for its clean air. But overcrowding, traffic, and factories have increased pollution in Mexico's capital. The mountains surrounding the city trap the pollution, making the problem worse. Several times a year, pollution becomes so bad that the city has to set up roadblocks to stop vehicles from entering it.

To deal with the problem, Mexico City has improved public transportation and passed laws to reduce pollution. Every day more than 4 million people use Mexico City's subway system. Many others use buses or shared taxis to travel around the city.

Recently, Mexico City started a program to reduce its traffic.

El Angel, a statue of liberty honoring Mexico's independence from Spain in 1821, stands in the center of Mexico City.

Every car in the city now has a specially marked license plate. The plates have symbols showing one day each week when that car cannot be driven on the city's streets.

REVIEW What are some of the causes of air pollution in Mexico City?

CAUSE AND EFFECT

Crowding in Tokyo

Japan is a small island nation in eastern Asia. It is about twice the size of New Jersey. Steep mountains cover much of Japan, so most people live in coastal cities such as Tokyo, Japan's capital and largest city. In fact, two out of every five people in Japan—more than 28 million—live in Tokyo. This makes Tokyo one of the world's most crowded cities.

From its center at the Imperial Palace, the home of the emperor of Japan, Tokyo spreads out in all directions. Over time, more and more land around Tokyo has been used for new houses, apartment buildings, shopping malls, roads, and businesses. As a result, Tokyo's metropolitan area has spread out farther into the surrounding countryside. This spreading of urban areas and the growth of new centers of business and shopping are called **urban sprawl**.

Over time, Tokyo and many other Japanese cities on Honshu Island grew closer together. Like New York City, Tokyo is now the center of its nation's largest megalopolis. This urban region includes five large metropolitan areas around Tokyo Bay, as well as many suburbs and smaller islands near Tokyo.

Because of urban sprawl, many Tokyo workers commute very long distances to and from work—often traveling more than four hours a day! To avoid traffic, many Tokyo workers take trains instead of driving to work. Since 1964 Tokyo has been linked to every major city in Japan by high-speed trains called "bullet trains." These trains travel across Japan at about 130 miles (209 km) per hour.

Some people who live in the suburbs also rent "sleeping capsules" in Tokyo during the workweek and return home only on the weekends. Offered by hotels,

Main Street in Tokyo's Ginza district is often crowded with shoppers. Ginza is one of the largest centers of business in Tokyo.

LOCATE IT

JAPAN

Tokyo

FAST FACT Finding addresses in Tokyo can be hard. Only the main streets have names. Buildings are not numbered in order, as those in the United States are. They are numbered according to the year they were built.

About 10 million people cram into Tokyo's trains and subways every day. At some stations, official "pushers" squeeze people into the trains to let the doors shut.

these sleeping capsules are stacks of small spaces just big enough for one person to sleep in.

Many of these commuters work in Tokyo's electronics industry, producing televisions and computers. Like New York City, Tokyo is also a world center of banking and finance. Nearly every company in Japan has its main offices in Tokyo.

Because land is scarce in Tokyo and its suburbs, housing is expensive. People often apply to live in apartments months before they are built. Most apartments in Tokyo are tiny. In their small apartments, people in Japan have few pieces of furniture. In many Tokyo homes people sit on pillows instead of chairs. They store futons (FOO•tahnz), or mattresses, in closets and unroll them at night for sleeping. No matter where they live, people in Japan leave their shoes at the door. This is a traditional sign of respect for one's home.

REVIEW **Where do most people live in Japan?**

LESSON 4
REVIEW

 CAUSE AND EFFECT What causes urban sprawl?

1 BIG IDEA How does life in cities around the world compare with life in cities in the United States?

2 VOCABULARY Write a sentence using the term **unemployment** to describe a problem many cities around the world face today.

3 CULTURE What are some of the cultural traditions practiced in Mexico City?

4 ECONOMICS How does Amsterdam's location affect the way many people in that city earn a living?

5 CRITICAL THINKING—Apply What solutions to certain problems in cities around the world might also work in cities in the United States?

 PERFORMANCE—Write a Letter
Write a letter to a fourth grader living in Amsterdam, Mexico City, or Tokyo. Describe your community's location relative to that of the city that you choose. Then explain what life is like where you live. Be sure to point out any similarities or differences between the two communities. Share your letter with a classmate.

4 Review and Test Preparation

Summary Time Line

1600

1625
The Dutch build
New Amsterdam

1682
William Penn
founds the colony
of Pennsylvania

Cause and Effect

Copy the following graphic organizer onto a separate sheet of paper. Use the information you have learned to show that you understand the causes and effects of key events in the history of the Middle Atlantic states.

Middle Atlantic States

Cause

Many colonial settlements in the Middle Atlantic region were built along rivers near the Atlantic Ocean.

→

Effect

_____
_____
_____

THINK & WRITE

Express a Viewpoint   Write a short statement explaining why you think some people want to live in cities, while others prefer to live in small towns or in the country. In which would you prefer to live? Why?

Write a Journal Entry   Imagine you are an immigrant arriving in New York City. Think about what your life will be like in the United States. Then write a journal entry describing your first day in the city.

1800			Present

1776
The Declaration of Independence is signed

1783
A treaty officially ends the American Revolution

1825
The Erie Canal is completed

1954
Ellis Island closes as an immigration center

USE THE TIME LINE

1 When was the Erie Canal completed?

2 Which was founded first, New Amsterdam or the colony of Pennsylvania?

USE VOCABULARY

For each group of terms, write a sentence or two explaining how the terms are related.

3 port (p. 129), immigrant (p. 143)

4 independence (p. 130), declaration (p. 131)

5 waterway (p. 135), canal (p. 135), lock (p. 136)

6 metropolitan area (p. 143), megalopolis (p. 143)

7 urban growth (p. 145), urban sprawl (p. 154)

RECALL FACTS

Answer these questions.

8 Why was the Erie Canal built?

9 Why do Pennsylvania steel mills produce less steel than they did in the past?

10 How has urban sprawl changed cities?

11 In what kind of region do most people around the world live?

Write the letter of the best choice.

12 Who were the first Europeans to settle in the Middle Atlantic Colonies?
 A the Dutch
 B the English
 C the Spanish
 D the Germans

13 The Declaration of Independence was signed in—
 F New York City, New York.
 G Philadelphia, Pennsylvania.
 H Washington, D.C.
 J Boston, Massachusetts.

14 Which of the following mountain ranges does **not** run through the Middle Atlantic states?
 A Allegheny Mountains
 B Catskill Mountains
 C Adirondack Mountains
 D Rocky Mountains

THINK CRITICALLY

15 Without fertile farmland nearby, could cities along the Middle Atlantic coast have grown so large? Explain your answer.

16 Why do you think it is important that people in cities work together to solve problems that urban areas face?

17 How have the many ethnic groups that now live in the United States affected the country?

APPLY SKILLS

Identify Fact and Opinion

18 Write three statements of fact and three statements of opinion about the Middle Atlantic states.

Use a Road Map and Mileage Table

19 Using a road map of your state, describe a route from your city or town to your state's capital or to another city that you would like to visit. Then tell the mileage between those two places.

VISIT The Erie Canal

GET READY

In the 1800s the Erie Canal played an important role in the shipping of goods from the Great Lakes to New York City. Today the Erie Canal is part of the New York State Canal System. This waterway is still used to move goods. However, it is also used for recreation, including boating on the canals and biking on the nearby trails.

On a visit to the Erie Canal, you can stop by the Erie Canal Village, a restored community from the 1800s. Here actors show what everyday life was like in one community along the canal.

WHAT TO SEE

A boat ride lets you experience the Erie Canal's early days if you travel in a canal boat pulled by a mule.

LOCATE IT

Erie Canal

NEW YORK

A hotel at the Erie Canal Village shows where visitors in the past might have stayed. At the Erie Canal Village, a printer (above) works in his shop and villagers (below) work together to rake hay.

This barge is going through a lock on the New York State Canal System.

TAKE A FIELD TRIP

A VIRTUAL TOUR
Visit The Learning Site at **www.harcourtschool.com** to find virtual tours of historic places in the United States.

A VIDEO TOUR
Check your media center or classroom library for a videotape tour of the Erie Canal.

·UNIT·

2 Review and Test Preparation

Visual Summary

Write Generalizations Study the pictures and captions below to help you review Unit 2. Then from your observations, write four sentences in which you generalize about the Northeast.

Use Vocabulary

Use each term in a sentence that helps explain its meaning.

1. **colony** (p. 102)
2. **industrial economy** (p. 104)
3. **volunteer** (p. 115)
4. **independence** (p. 130)
5. **unemployment** (p. 153)

Recall Facts

Answer these questions.

6. Why did the Pilgrims think Plymouth Bay was a good place to build their colony?
7. Why was it important to link waterways in the Northeast?
8. What is the largest city in the United States?
9. How has urban sprawl changed cities?

Write the letter of the best choice.

10. The first Europeans to settle in the Middle Atlantic region were the—
    A Pilgrims.
    B Puritans.
    C Dutch.
    D Spanish.
11. A large city together with its suburbs is called a—
    F megalopolis.
    G county seat.
    H metropolitan area.
    J population.
12. Which of the following is not a problem caused by urban growth?
    A crowding
    B war
    C traffic
    D pollution

Visual Summary

1600 | 1650 | 1700 | 1750

1620 **Pilgrims start Plymouth Colony.** p. 102

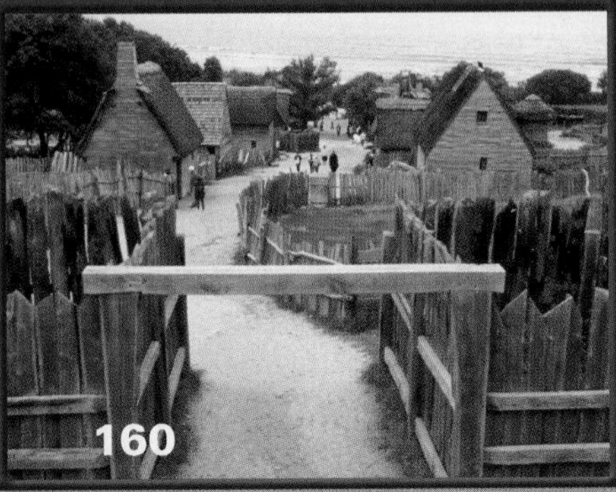

1776 **Declaration of Independence is signed at Independence Hall.** p. 131

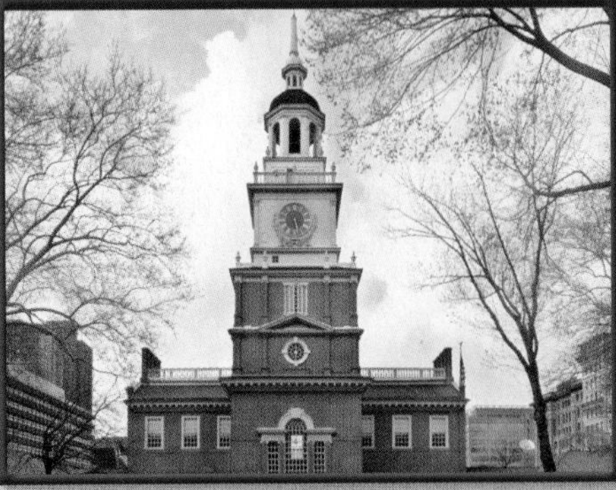

1838 **An important shipyard is founded in Mystic, CT.** p. 103

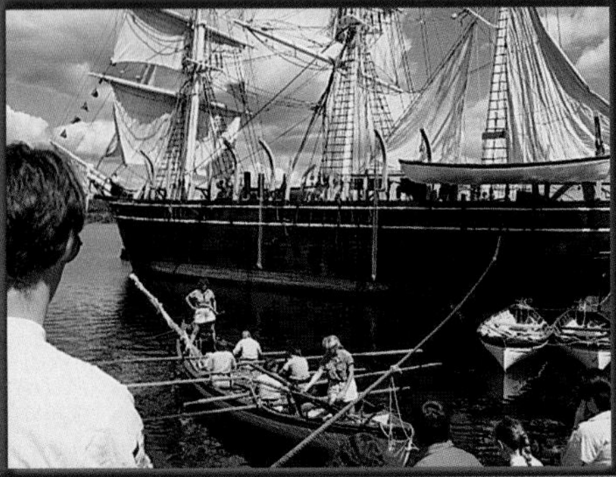

THINK CRITICALLY

13 How do many people in coastal locations earn a living?

14 Why do you think the Northeast region is so crowded with cities?

15 How might life be different today if the United States had not built an industrial economy?

16 Would you rather live in a city or in the countryside of the Northeast? Explain your answer.

17 If you had been a colonist in the 1700s, would you have wanted independence from Britain? Why?

APPLY SKILLS

Use a Road Map and Mileage Table
Use the map and the table to answer the following questions.

18 How many miles is it from Quidnick to Newport?

19 What interstate highway passes through Providence?

20 If you wanted to travel east from Providence to the Atlantic Ocean, which United States highway could you take?

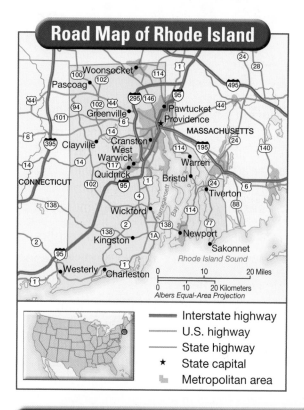

Road Map of Rhode Island

	Interstate highway
	U.S. highway
	State highway
★	State capital
	Metropolitan area

Rhode Island Road Mileage

	Newport	Providence	Quidnick
Newport		34	21
Providence	34		14
Quidnick	21	14	

21 About how many miles is it from Newport to Providence? Explain why you used either the map or the mileage table to find the answer.

| 1850 | 1900 | 1950 | Present |

1914 More than 1 million immigrants enter the United States. p. 143

1929 Maine's Lafayette National Park is renamed Acadia. p. 105

1934 Strongest winds on Earth are recorded, Mt. Washington, NH. p. 108

Unit Activities

Create a Mural

Work in a group to create a mural of an early New England or Middle Atlantic colony, a New England town or Middle Atlantic city today, or a farming or factory scene in the Northeast. Use the Internet or other resources to gather ideas for your mural.

Draw a Map

Draw an outline map of the Northeast on a large sheet of paper. Use two colors to group the New England states and the Middle Atlantic states into separate regions. Label the bodies of water, landforms, and large cities found in each region. Draw symbols to show some of each region's major resources. Use the map to take the class on a "tour" of the Northeast.

GO ONLINE Visit The Learning Site at www.harcourtschool.com for additional activities.

VISIT YOUR LIBRARY

- *Life in America's First Cities* by Sally Senzell Isaacs. Heinemann Library.

- *Squanto's Journey: The Story of the First Thanksgiving* by Joseph Bruchac. Silver Whistle.

- *The Amazing Impossible Erie Canal* by Cheryl Harness. MacMillan Books for Young Readers.

COMPLETE THE UNIT PROJECT

A Class Play Finish the Unit Project described on page 97—a play about the colonization and growth of the Northeast. As a class, decide on the people and events you want to have in your play. Then form small groups. Each group will write one scene about a person, a group of people, or an important event. As a class, perform the play for invited guests in your school or the community.

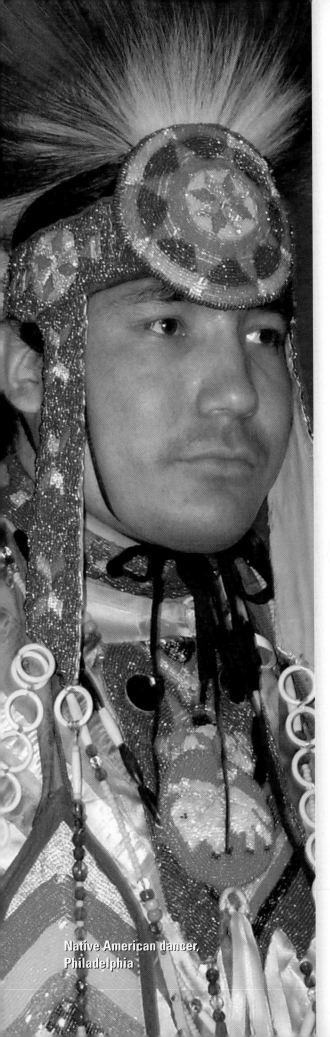

Native American dancer, Philadelphia

Pennsylvania Long Ago

" We, Iroquois Nations, compose but one cabin; we maintain but one fire. "

—Mohawk Orator, 1654

Summarize

When you **summarize,** you retell briefly what you have read, using your own words.

As you read this chapter, summarize what you learned.

- Identify the main topic of each lesson.
- List what and who is involved, and where, how and why these events occur.
- Summarize what you read.

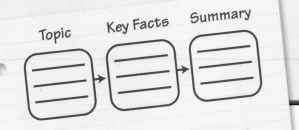

Topic   Key Facts   Summary

Focus
Skill
SUMMARIZE

As you read, summarize information about early people in Pennsylvania.

BIG IDEA

Native American groups were the first people to live in what is now Pennsylvania.

VOCABULARY

dugout
peacemaker

Early People in Pennsylvania

Long ago, early people migrated into what is now Pennsylvania. These Native Americans lived mostly by gathering wild plants and by hunting. After many generations, Native Americans began to lead more settled lives.

Early People and the Environment

Agriculture changed the way early people lived. To care for crops, people began to stay in one place and form villages. Often, they chose to live alongside a river or stream. Native American culture groups grew from these villages.

The first people to live in what is now Pennsylvania were the Allegwi people. They lived in what is now western Pennsylvania near the Allegheny River. The word *Allegheny* comes from the Allegwi people.

The Allegwi used many resources from the forests and rivers. They traveled to trade. The Allegwi were careful not to take chances when dealing with other Native Americans. They were said to be strong warriors who guarded their villages closely.

REVIEW **How did agriculture affect ways of life for early people?**
 SUMMARIZE

FAST FACT The Meadowcroft Rockshelter in western Pennsylvania contains the remains of some of North America's earliest cultures. Visitors can see remains of tools and campfires used by early people.

These copies of Delaware wigwams show how the Delaware used natural materials to build their homes.

Delaware People

The largest Native American group lived in the east near the Delaware River. They were the Lenni Lenape (LEN•ee len•AH•pay) and are known today as the Delaware people. Like the Allegwi, the Delaware hunted nearby forests and fished in nearby waterways.

The Delaware built large villages of shelters known as wigwams. Delaware women grew crops, such as corn, squash, beans, and sweet potatoes. They made clothing out of deerskins and decorated it with beads, feathers, and porcupine quills.

Delaware men carved **dugouts**, canoes made from trees and used to travel on rivers. The Delaware traded with Native Americans

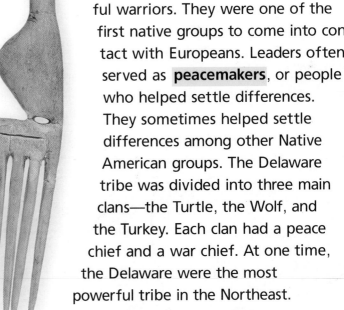

Susquehannock comb

in the north and west for copper. They used copper to make tools and jewelry. The Delaware also made pottery, beads, and feather ornaments.

The Delaware were known as skill-ful warriors. They were one of the first native groups to come into contact with Europeans. Leaders often served as **peacemakers**, or people who helped settle differences. They sometimes helped settle differences among other Native American groups. The Delaware tribe was divided into three main clans—the Turtle, the Wolf, and the Turkey. Each clan had a peace chief and a war chief. At one time, the Delaware were the most powerful tribe in the Northeast.

REVIEW How did the Delaware get from one place to another?

PA 2-3

Native American Place-Names

Many place-names in Pennsylvania come from Native American words. For example, the word *Monongahela* (muh•nahn•guh•HEE•luh) was a Native American name for the river. It meant "high banks breaking off and falling down at places." The Native American word *Pocono* means "stream between the mountains." Some places are named after Native American leaders. The city of Aliquippa is named for a Native American queen (right) who lived in the 1700s. The name *Lackawanna* is an Algonquian word that means "where the streams meet." Lackawanna is a county in northeastern Pennsylvania. The borough of Connoquenessing is in western Pennsylvania, in Butler County.

EVANS CITY – 5
CONNOQUENESSING
FROM THE INDIAN
"A LONG WAY STRAIGHT"
FOUNDED
1792

Delaware Ways

The Delaware people spoke an Algonquian (al•GAHN•kwee•uhn) language. They were greatly respected by other Algonquian groups of the Northeast. Many thought of the Delaware as grandfathers. This was because many groups had Delaware ancestors.

The Delaware honored their elders and believed that with age came wisdom. Villages were governed by a council of male leaders chosen by the oldest women. Village leaders wore a single eagle feather in their hair to show their important role. **REVIEW** **Why were the Delaware thought of as grandfathers?**

LESSON 1
REVIEW

⭐ **Focus Skill** **SUMMARIZE** How did Native Americans use natural resources?

1 **BIG IDEA** Who were the first people to live in what is now Pennsylvania?

2 **VOCABULARY** Why were Delaware leaders called **peacemakers**?

3 **CIVICS AND GOVERNMENT** How were Delaware council members chosen?

The Iroquois People

Native American cultures included many different groups. Each group shared a common language and way of life. Today, one of the largest cultures is known as the Iroquois (IR•uh•kwoy).

Focus Skill SUMMARIZE
As you read, summarize information about Iroquois ways of life.

BIG IDEA
The Iroquois shared a common culture and government.

VOCABULARY
palisade
longhouse
extended family
confederation

A Common Language

There were many Native American groups that spoke the Iroquois language. At one time, Iroquois was the most common language in the Northeast. However, the different Iroquois groups did not always get along.

The Susquehannock (suhs•kwuh•HAN•ahk) people and the Erie people were both Iroquois groups. They fought each other in many wars. The wars left few people alive. Yet both groups continue to be remembered in Pennsylvania today. The Susquehanna River, Lake Erie, and the city and county of Erie are named for these Native Americans.

REVIEW How are Native American groups remembered in Pennsylvania? **Focus Skill** SUMMARIZE

Many Native American groups made pots and used them to store food (below). During the mid-1600s, the Susquehannocks were involved in conflicts with other native groups.

People of the Longhouse

The different Iroquois groups shared a common way of life. Their villages were often large, with several hundred people living in a single village.

Each village was surrounded by a well-built **palisade**, or fence made of tall wooden poles. Within the palisade, the people lived in **longhouses**—long, narrow buildings with a curved roof.

Iroquois women built the longhouses. They used wooden poles cut from young trees. The poles were bent into a frame that was covered with bark. At each end of the longhouse was a door. In the center, there was a cooking fire. Holes in the roof let smoke escape.

Longhouses were big. Some were more than 100 feet long! Most were about 50

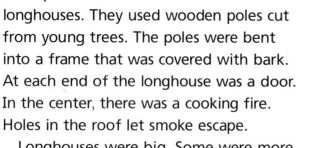

The Three Sisters

feet long and 20 feet wide. The large size allowed the home to be shared by an extended family. Children, parents, aunts, uncles, cousins, and grandparents make up an **extended family**. Often, parents and children shared an area within the longhouse.

The Iroquois thought the longhouse was the most important part of their culture. They called themselves Haudenosaunee (hoh•dee•noh•SHOH•nee), which means "people of the longhouse."

The Iroquois depended on agriculture, hunting, and trade. Iroquois women planted corn, beans, and squash. They called these foods the Three Sisters. Men fished nearby waters and hunted deer and other animals to eat in winter. Children helped with the planting, and older boys learned to hunt and fish.

REVIEW Why were longhouses large?

GEOGRAPHY THEME

Place **Several culture groups lived on the land that became Pennsylvania.**

Which native culture had the most land?

Native American Groups in Pennsylvania

Lake Erie

ERIE

WENRO

French Creek

Allegheny River

Clarion River

Tioga R.

Susquehanna River

West Branch Susquehanna R.

Allegheny River

Conemaugh River

Ohio R.

Monongahela R.

Youghiogheny River

SUSQUEHANNOCK

Juniata River

Lehigh R.

Delaware River

DELAWARE

Schuylkill River

Susquehanna River

MONONGAHELA

0   25   50 Miles
0   25   50 Kilometers
Albers Equal-Area Projection

N W E S

Algonquian group

Iroquoian group

Poorly known

Present-day border

The painting (above) of an Iroquoian village shows many longhouses enclosed by a palisade. Iroquois leaders (right) meet inside a longhouse to make decisions.

The Iroquois League

For many years, neighboring peoples battled one another. To end the fighting among themselves, they joined together. At first, five northern groups—the Cayuga, Mohawk, Oneida, Onondaga, and Seneca—agreed to form a confederation. In a **confederation**, separate groups form a single government in order to work on common problems. A sixth group, the Tuscarora, later joined the confederation. The confederation was known as the Iroquois League.

A Grand Council of leaders met to make decisions affecting all of the groups. Each group had a single vote on the Grand Council. A special council of "peace chiefs" settled larger differences. By joining together, all the people were stronger.

REVIEW Why did the Iroquois form a confederation? SUMMARIZE

LESSON 2 REVIEW

⭐ **Focus Skill** **SUMMARIZE** Describe an Iroquois village.

1 **BIG IDEA** What did the different Iroquois groups have in common?

2 **VOCABULARY** Write a sentence about the importance of the **longhouse** in Iroquois culture.

3 **CIVICS AND GOVERNMENT** Who were the members of the Iroquois League?

SUMMARIZE
As you read, summarize the information about European explorers and settlers.

BIG IDEA
European countries struggled for control of land and trade in North America.

The First Europeans Arrive

About 500 years ago, ships carrying European explorers sailed to North America. About 100 years later, England started a permanent colony at Jamestown, Virginia. One of the English settlers explored lands north of the Chesapeake Bay.

Cultures Meet

Captain John Smith of Virginia may have been the first European to arrive in what is now Pennsylvania. Smith wrote of meeting Susquehannock people in 1608. One year later, in 1609, explorer Henry Hudson sailed into part of Delaware Bay.

At the same time, an explorer named Étienne Brulé (ay•tee•EN bru•LAY) came from France to learn about the land and the native people here. Brulé traveled the length of the Susquehanna River.

This modern copy of Henry Hudson's *Half Moon* is closely based on the original ship. Hudson's boat was designed to carry a crew of 20.

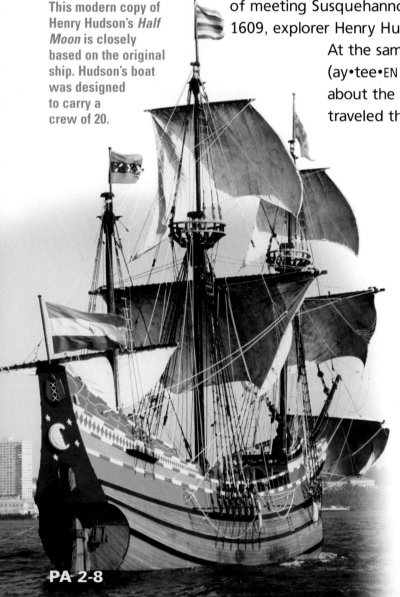

Hudson was English, but his ship and crew were Dutch. They were from the European country of Holland, also called the Netherlands. Hudson's crew met with an Algonquian group near the northern part of the Delaware River. All the lands Hudson explored were claimed by the Netherlands. The Dutch were leaders of trade in Europe. They hoped that there would be business opportunities in North America.

REVIEW Who were the first Europeans to arrive in Pennsylvania?
SUMMARIZE

European Colonies

In 1624, the Dutch built a permanent settlement. They called the settlement New Amsterdam, and they called the colony New Netherland. Today, they are New York City and the state of New York.

By 1626, hundreds of settlers had arrived at New Amsterdam. The immigrants brought illness and diseases. Native Americans could not fight these diseases, and millions died within a few years. Many others died in battles with Europeans.

In 1638, settlers from Sweden founded the colony of New Sweden. They chose Tinicum (TIH•nih•kum) Island for their main settlement. It was on the Delaware River, near what is now Philadelphia.

By the mid-1600s, only a few Native American villages remained near New Sweden. Yet, leaders of New Sweden signed treaties with the Delaware who still lived in the area. The settlers and their Native American neighbors got along well.

REVIEW **What colony was founded at Tinicum Island?**

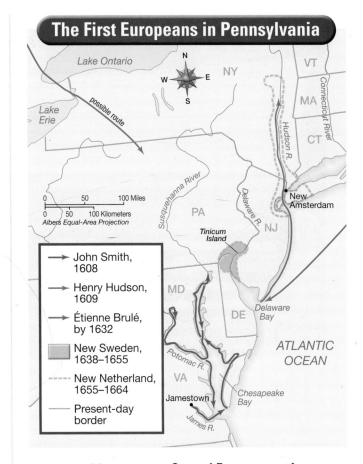

The First Europeans in Pennsylvania

John Smith, 1608
Henry Hudson, 1609
Étienne Brulé, by 1632
New Sweden, 1638–1655
New Netherland, 1655–1664
Present-day border

Movement **Several European explorers came to Pennsylvania in the early 1600s.**

❓ **What body of water did John Smith travel on to get to Pennsylvania?**

This painting appears on the ceiling of the American Swedish Historical Museum. It shows an artist's idea of the first meeting between Native Americans and settlers from Sweden in 1638.

This log cabin is the only remaining cabin from New Sweden. Swedish settlers cleared the land and used the logs to build cabins. They also made stools and chairs from the logs.

Conflict with New Netherland

In the late 1640s, Dutch traders set up trading posts along the Delaware River. Leaders of New Netherland wanted to control all trade in the area.

Competition for trade turned to conflict in 1654. The governor of New Sweden led an attack on a Dutch trading post. New Netherland's governor, Peter Stuyvesant (STY•vuh•suhnt), led colonists to defeat the settlers of New Sweden.

New Sweden and its people became part of New Netherland. Few Dutch settlers moved to the area. In 1664, the English forced the Dutch to surrender New Netherland. The English renamed the colony New York. By 1680, fewer than 700 Europeans were living in what is now Pennsylvania.

REVIEW How did conflicts lead to English control of Pennsylvania? **SUMMARIZE**

LESSON 2 REVIEW

SUMMARIZE Why did European settlers come to North America?

1 **BIG IDEA** Why did Europeans want to control trade in North America?

2 **CIVICS AND GOVERNMENT** Why was there conflict between New Sweden and New Netherland?

3 **HISTORY** What caused the deaths of many Native Americans in the 1600s?

The First Africans Arrive

People from West Africa and Central Africa were with the Europeans who sailed to North America. One African man spent years exploring parts of North America. He is known by his Spanish name, Estevanico (es•tay•vahn•EE•koh).

Africans in the Northeast

When Henry Hudson first sailed into Northeast waterways, his crew may have included Africans. The Dutch were among the first Europeans to use trading routes from Africa to North America.

The Europeans needed many settlers to build their colonies. However, settlers had to pay shipowners for their passage. Most people did not have enough money to pay. Some Europeans offered people a paid passage in exchange for a work contract. Workers were freed at the end of the contract, usually seven years. These workers were called **indentured servants**. The first Africans to settle in the Northeast were probably indentured servants.

> **REVIEW** Why did people become indentured servants?
> **SUMMARIZE**

 SUMMARIZE
As you read, summarize what you learn about early Africans living in North America.

BIG IDEA
Africans first came to Pennsylvania with European settlers.

VOCABULARY
indentured servant
apprentice

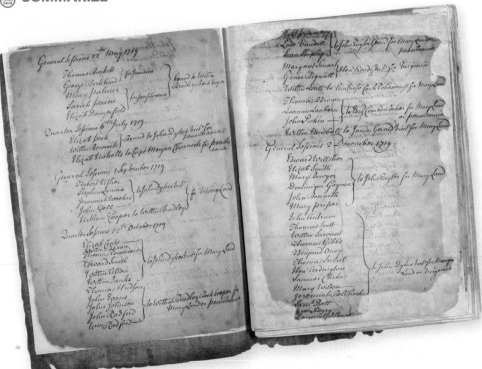

This register of indentured servants lists the names of young men and women who left London to work in Pennsylvania, Maryland, and Jamaica.

Africans in New Sweden

Africans arrived in New Sweden as early as 1639. They were enslaved people from West and Central Africa. The Africans were forced to work for European colonists without pay. The lack of workers caused the colonists to use enslaved Africans to do much of the work.

Many Africans were like Anthoni Swartz, who was born in what is now Angola. As a young man, he was captured, enslaved, and brought to New Sweden. Swartz proved to be a valuable part of the colony.

Swartz learned different languages. In addition to his native African language, he spoke Swedish, Dutch, English, and Algonquian. All were helpful in doing business in the early colonies.

At first, Swartz was the only African living in the settlement of Fort Christina, New Sweden. Because of his skill in communicating, Swartz was sent to work for the governor at Tinicum. No one knows if Swartz was freed when the Dutch took over the colony.

REVIEW **Where did the first Africans in New Sweden come from?**

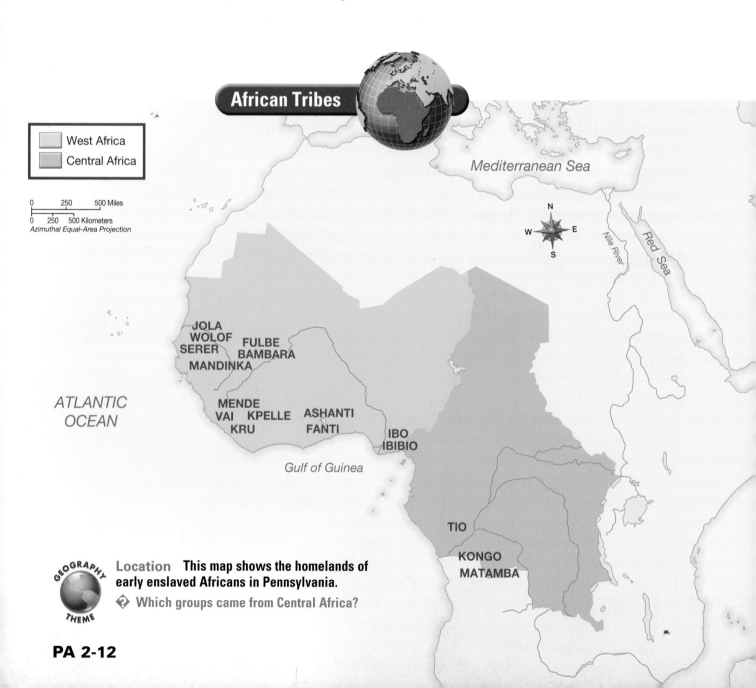

African Tribes

West Africa
Central Africa

0   250   500 Miles
0   250   500 Kilometers
Azimuthal Equal-Area Projection

Mediterranean Sea

Nile River

Red Sea

JOLA
WOLOF
SERER   FULBE
         BAMBARA
MANDINKA

ATLANTIC
OCEAN

MENDE
VAI   KPELLE   ASHANTI
KRU   FANTI

IBO
IBIBIO

Gulf of Guinea

TIO

KONGO
MATAMBA

Location **This map shows the homelands of early enslaved Africans in Pennsylvania.**

Which groups came from Central Africa?

PA 2-12

Alice of Dunk's Ferry   1686–1802

Character Trait: Trustworthiness

Alice was born an enslaved African American in 1686, in Philadelphia. She was the daughter of one of the first enslaved Africans who arrived in 1684 from Barbados. She worked for more than 40 years, collecting tolls and managing the ferry boats at a Delaware River crossing. Late in her life, Alice shared stories of meeting important people, such as William Penn. She was known for her honesty and her sharp memory. Many early historians spoke with Alice to learn about the early days of the colony. Alice lived to be 116 years old.

MULTIMEDIA BIOGRAPHIES
Visit The Learning Site at **www.harcourtschool.com**
to learn about other famous people.

 GO ONLINE

More Africans Arrive in the Colonies

There were already many Africans in New Netherland. The Dutch brought enslaved Africans to work in the colony. Some were farmworkers. Others were highly skilled blacksmiths and carpenters.

In time, a few enslaved Africans gained their freedom. Together, they built a small, free African community. They bought land. Many joined the official church of New Netherland, the Dutch Reformed Church.

Laws in the colony kept enslaved children from learning to read and write. Free black children could be educated. They often worked as **apprentices** (uh•PREN•tuhs•iz), people who work for others in order to learn a trade.

In 1664, the English took control of New Netherland. All of England's colonies used enslaved workers. Some settlers on the Delaware River began to trade with Dutch or English merchants for enslaved Africans.

REVIEW What gains did enslaved Africans win when they became free? **SUMMARIZE**

LESSON 4 REVIEW

⭐ **Focus Skill** **SUMMARIZE**   How did indentured servants settle in the colonies?

❶ **BIG IDEA**   How did Africans come to live in the early colonies?

❷ **VOCABULARY**   How were enslaved workers and **indentured servants** different?

❸ **HISTORY**   How did the African colonist Anthoni Swartz help the governor of New Sweden?

Native American Paths to Modern Highways

Sometimes Native Americans needed to travel long distances overland. To do this, they used well-traveled footpaths that crossed mountains and rivers. When European settlers arrived in what is now Pennsylvania, they followed Native American paths and built settlements on the frontier. Today, many of Pennsylvania's most used highways follow routes that were once Native American paths.

DID YOU KNOW?

Nearly 180 million cars and trucks travel the Pennsylvania Turnpike each year.

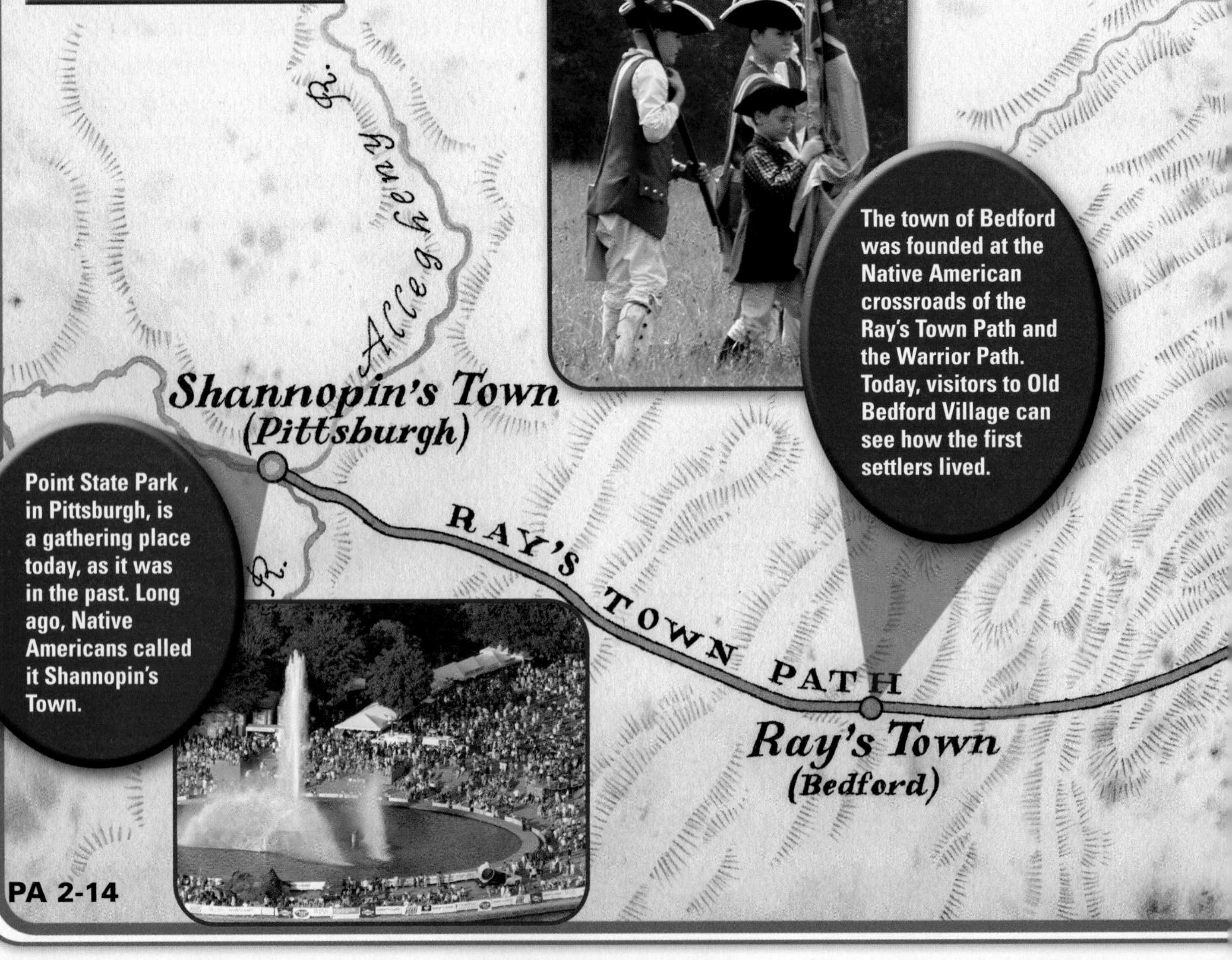

The town of Bedford was founded at the Native American crossroads of the Ray's Town Path and the Warrior Path. Today, visitors to Old Bedford Village can see how the first settlers lived.

Allegheny R.

Shannopin's Town (Pittsburgh)

Point State Park, in Pittsburgh, is a gathering place today, as it was in the past. Long ago, Native Americans called it Shannopin's Town.

RAY'S TOWN PATH

Ray's Town (Bedford)

Native Americans traveling between Shannopin's Town and the village of Shackamaxon used two main paths. The Ray's Town Path went from what is now Pittsburgh to present-day Harrisburg. The Old Trading Path continued on to present-day Philadelphia.

European settlers widened the paths into roads for their horses, oxen, and wagons. In 1741, people began to call the Old Trading Path by a new name, the Great Wagon Road. Today, the road is a part of Interstate Highway 76, but most people call it the Pennsylvania Turnpike.

ACTIVITY

Use the library or Internet to research highways near your home. Choose one and make a time line of events from its history. Include names the highway has had from early settlement to the present day. Share your time line with your classmates.

RESEARCH

GO ONLINE

Visit The Learning Site at **www.harcourtschool.com** to learn about other places of interest.

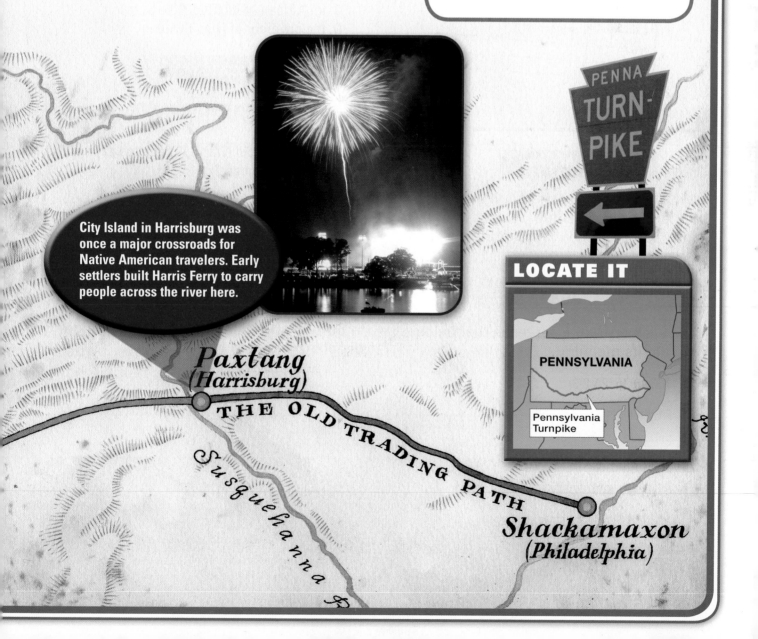

City Island in Harrisburg was once a major crossroads for Native American travelers. Early settlers built Harris Ferry to carry people across the river here.

PENNA TURN-PIKE

LOCATE IT

PENNSYLVANIA

Pennsylvania Turnpike

Paxtang
(Harrisburg)

THE OLD TRADING PATH

Susquehanna R.

Shackamaxon
(Philadelphia)

Review and Test Preparation

 **Summarize**

Copy the graphic organizer onto a separate sheet of paper. Use it to write a summary of the first people who lived in Pennsylvania and how they interacted with the environment.

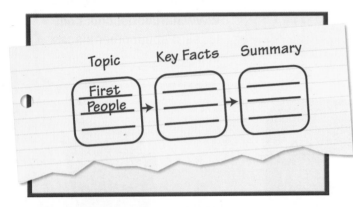

Topic   Key Facts   Summary

First People

THINK AND WRITE

Write a Journal Entry Imagine you are a settler in New Sweden. Write a journal entry to describe what your life is like in the new colony.

USE VOCABULARY

Use each term in a sentence that helps explain its meaning.

1. **dugout** (p. PA 2-3)

2. **peacemaker** (p. PA 2-3)

3. **palisade** (p. PA 2-6)

4. **longhouse** (p. PA 2-6)

5. **confederation** (p. PA 2-7)

6. **apprentice** (p. PA 2-13)

RECALL FACTS

Answer these questions.

7. What is another name for the Lenni Lenape?

8. Which native culture group did the Erie people belong to?

Write the letter of the best choice.

9. Who was Anthoni Swartz?
   A the governor of Tinicum
   B an explorer
   C an African brought to New Sweden
   D the governor of New Sweden

THINK CRITICALLY

10. How do we know that Native Americans used trade?

11. In what ways did Native Americans depend on the environment?

12. Why do you think free African Americans wanted their children to learn how to read and write?

PERFORMANCE

Make a Flier Create a flier that someone in Europe might have used to encourage people to move to New Sweden.

The South

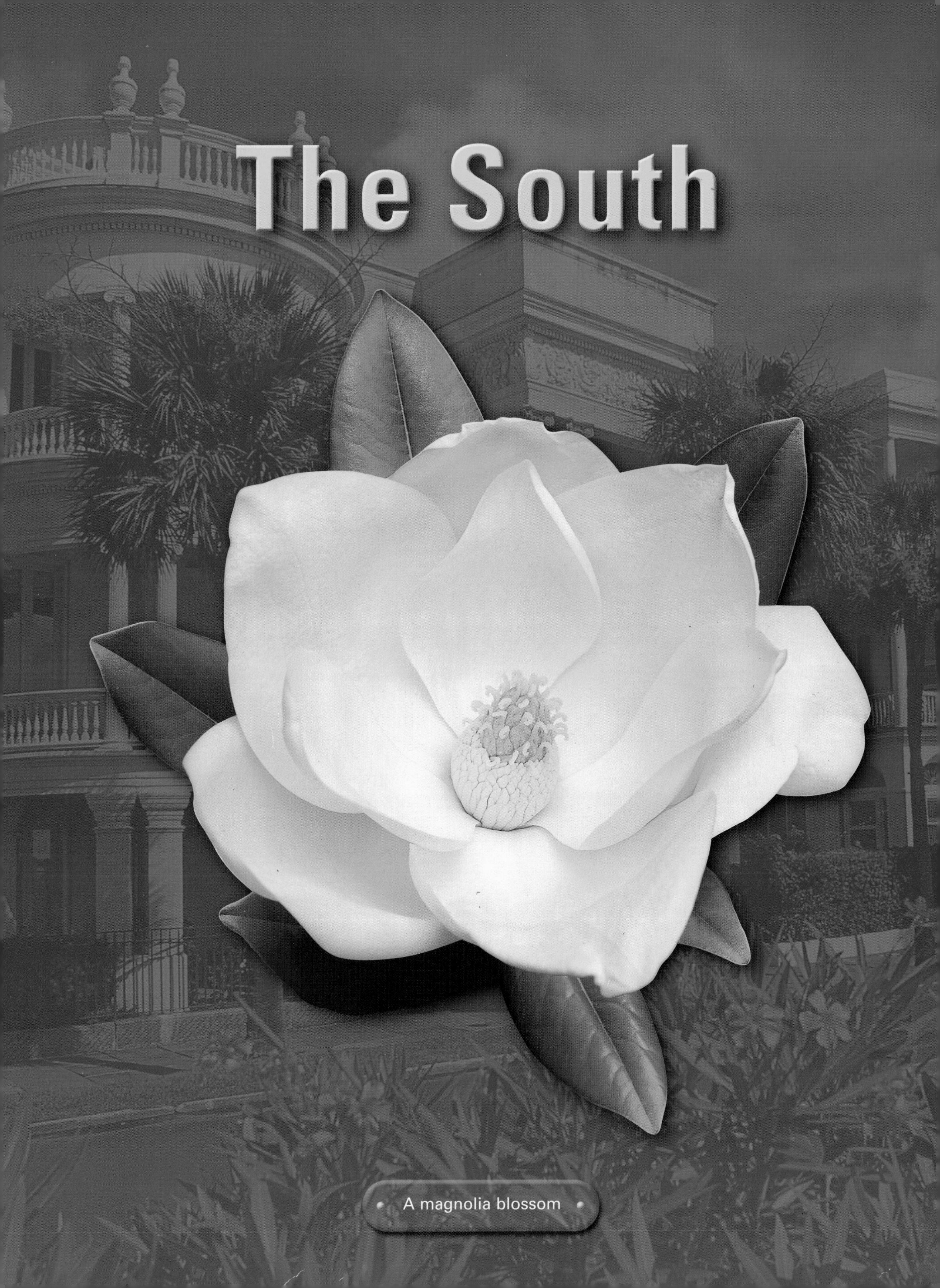

A magnolia blossom

Charleston, South Carolina

The South

> ❝ Heritage, tradition, and a strong sense of place are woven into the fabric of Southern life. ❞
>
> —Suzan Hall, *America,* 1994

Preview the Content

Discuss with a partner what you know about the differences and similarities between the northern part of the United States and the southern part of the United States.

Preview the Vocabulary

Related Words   Related words often have something in common. Use a graphic organizer like the one below to describe what the vocabulary words in each group have in common.

WORDS	WHAT THEY HAVE IN COMMON
bayou, swamp, marsh	_____
import, export, international trade	_____
mainland, coral, reef	_____

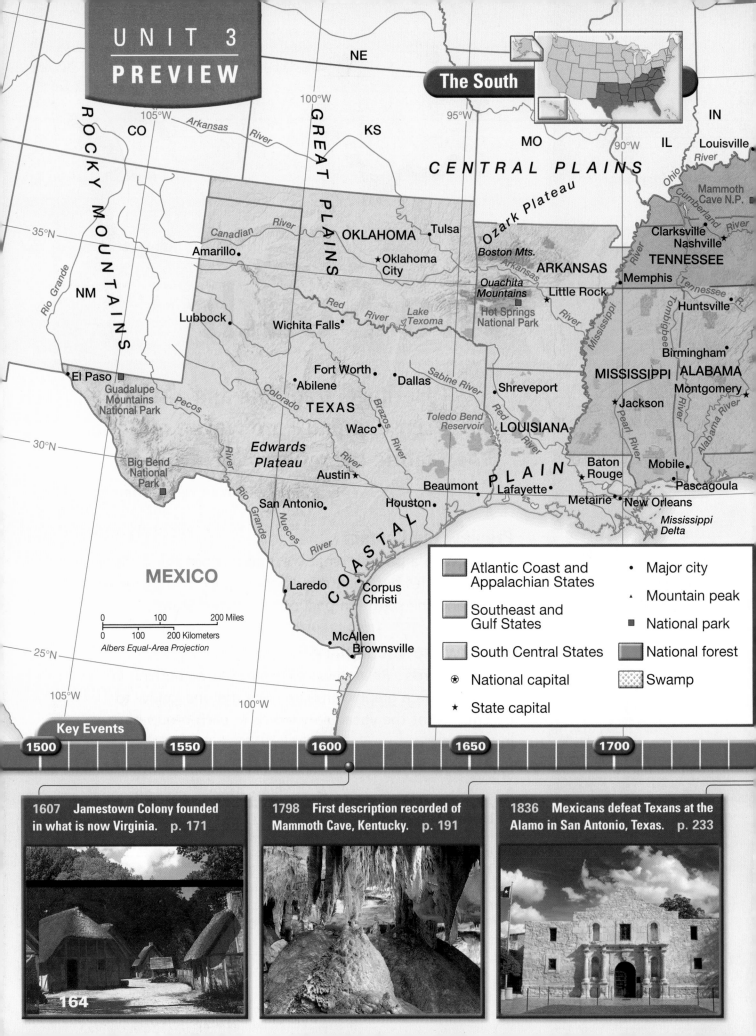

The South

NE

100°W

CO

105°W

Arkansas River

35°N

Canadian River

Amarillo

ROCKY MOUNTAINS

NM

Rio Grande

Lubbock

El Paso

Guadalupe Mountains National Park

Pecos River

30°N

Colorado River

Edwards Plateau

Big Bend National Park

Rio Grande

MEXICO

Nueces River

105°W

100°W

25°N

GREAT PLAINS

KS

OKLAHOMA

Tulsa

★Oklahoma City

Red River

Lake Texoma

Wichita Falls

Fort Worth

Abilene

TEXAS

Waco

Brazos River

Austin ★

San Antonio

Laredo

Corpus Christi

McAllen

Brownsville

95°W

MO

90°W

CENTRAL PLAINS

IL

IN

Louisville

Ohio River

Mammoth Cave N.P.

Ozark Plateau

Boston Mts.

ARKANSAS

Ouachita Mountains

Hot Springs National Park

Arkansas River

Little Rock ★

Clarksville
Nashville ★

TENNESSEE

Memphis

Tennessee R.

Huntsville

Mississippi River

Birmingham

MISSISSIPPI

ALABAMA

Tombigbee River

Shreveport

Dallas

Sabine River

Red River

Toledo Bend Reservoir

LOUISIANA

COASTAL PLAIN

Beaumont

Houston

Lafayette

Baton Rouge ★

Metairie

New Orleans

Mississippi Delta

Jackson ★

Pearl River

Montgomery

Alabama River

Mobile

Pascagoula

Scale:
0   100   200 Miles
0   100   200 Kilometers
Albers Equal-Area Projection

Legend:
- Atlantic Coast and Appalachian States
- Southeast and Gulf States
- South Central States
- ⊛ National capital
- ★ State capital
- • Major city
- ▲ Mountain peak
- ■ National park
- National forest
- ▨ Swamp

Key Events

1500   1550   1600   1650   1700

1607   Jamestown Colony founded in what is now Virginia.   p. 171

1798   First description recorded of Mammoth Cave, Kentucky.   p. 191

1836   Mexicans defeat Texans at the Alamo in San Antonio, Texas.   p. 233

OH

PA
80°W
40°N
NJ

Baltimore
DE
Annapolis
Washington, D.C.
Alexandria
MARYLAND
WEST
VIRGINIA
Shenandoah
National Park
Chesapeake
Bay
Charleston
Richmond
Frankfort
Lexington
James River
Ohio
River
KENTUCKY
Newport News
Norfolk
VIRGINIA
Virginia Beach
Cumberland
Gap
Great
Dismal
Swamp
Greensboro
Durham
Holston River
Roanoke
Outer Banks
Knoxville
Winston-
Salem
Raleigh
35°N
Great
Smoky
Mts. N.P.
Mt. Mitchell
6,684 ft.
(2,037 m)
NORTH
CAROLINA
Cape
Hatteras
Chattanooga
Charlotte
Cape Fear River
Cape
Lookout
SOUTH CAROLINA
Savannah River
Columbia
Cape Fear
Athens
Stone Mountain
Atlanta 1,683 ft.
(513 m)
Augusta
Charleston
Macon
GEORGIA
Hilton Head Island
Columbus
Ocmulgee River
Altamaha
River
Savannah
ATLANTIC
OCEAN
Chattahoochee River
Okefenokee
Swamp
APPALACHIAN MTS.
Blue Ridge Mts.
COASTAL PLAIN
Jacksonville
30°N
Tallahassee
St. Johns River
Daytona Beach
Cape Canaveral
Orlando
FLORIDA
Clearwater
Tampa
St. Petersburg
Lake
Okeechobee
Fort Myers
Big
Cypress
Swamp
Everglades
Fort Lauderdale
Miami
Biscayne
National Park
Everglades National Park
Dry Tortugas
National Park
Florida Keys
BAHAMAS
25°N
85°W
80°W

N
W   E
S

The South

	STATE	NICKNAME	POPULATION
ATLANTIC COAST & APPALACHIAN STATES	Kentucky	Bluegrass State	4,092,891
	Maryland	Old Line State	5,458,137
	North Carolina	Tar Heel State	8,320,146
	Tennessee	Volunteer State	5,797,289
	Virginia	Old Dominion	7,293,542
	West Virginia	Mountain State	1,801,873
SOUTHEAST & GULF STATES	Alabama	Heart of Dixie	4,486,508
	Florida	Sunshine State	16,713,149
	Georgia	Empire State of the South	8,560,310
	Mississippi	Magnolia State	2,871,782
	South Carolina	Palmetto State	4,107,183
SOUTH CENTRAL STATES	Arkansas	Land of Opportunity	2,710,079
	Louisiana	Pelican State	4,482,646
	Oklahoma	Sooner State	3,493,714
	Texas	Lone Star State	21,779,893

Largest Cities in the South

CITY, STATE	POPULATION
Houston, Texas	👤👤👤👤👤👤👤👤👤👤
Dallas, Texas	👤👤👤👤👤👤
San Antonio, Texas	👤👤👤👤👤╎
Jacksonville, Florida	👤👤👤╎
Austin, Texas	👤👤👤╎

👤 = 200,000 people   ╎ = 100,000 people

1800   1850   1900   1950   Present

1861   First shots of Civil War fired at Fort Sumter, South Carolina. p. 204

1937   Cape Hatteras is designated first national seashore. p. 191

1947   *The Everglades: River of Grass* is written. p. 210

First Impressions of the South

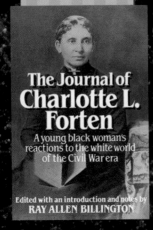

The Journal of
Charlotte L. Forten

A young black woman's
reactions to the white world
of the Civil War era

Edited with an introduction and notes by
RAY ALLEN BILLINGTON

From
The Journal of Charlotte L. Forten

Charlotte Forten was a young woman from Philadelphia, Pennsylvania. During the early days of the Civil War, she went to St. Helena, an island off the coast of South Carolina. She wanted to help the island people who had been enslaved and were now free to learn to read and write. She kept a journal of her experiences. Read her impressions of her first day on St. Helena. Think about how this place might be like other parts of the South.

Wednesday, October 29, 1862

[We drove to the school], which is beautifully situated in a grove of live oaks. Never saw anything more beautiful than these trees. It is strange that we do not hear of them at the North. They are the first objects that attract one's attention here. They are large, noble trees with small glossy green leaves. Their great beauty consists in the long bearded moss with which every branch is heavily draped. . . .

We went into the school and heard the children read and spell. The teachers tell us they have made great improvement in a very short time, and I noticed with pleasure how bright, how eager to learn many of them seem. . . .

As we drove homeward I noticed that the trees are just beginning to turn; some beautiful scarlet berries were growing along the roadside; and everywhere the beautiful live oak with its moss drapery.

> **grove** a small group of trees

Analyze the Literature

1 What feature of the landscape does Charlotte Forten like best?

2 How might St. Helena Island be like other places in the South?

READ A BOOK

START THE UNIT PROJECT

An Atlas Working in a small group, make an atlas of the South. Include at least four different kinds of maps, such as a physical map, a land use and resource map, or a map of historic sites. As you read about the South, take notes on the kind of information that should go on each map.

USE TECHNOLOGY

Visit The Learning Site at **www.harcourtschool.com** for additional activities, primary sources, and other resources to use in this unit.

GREAT SMOKY MOUNTAINS NATIONAL PARK

The Great Smoky Mountains stretch across eastern Tennessee and western North Carolina. Here they show the pale blue haze that gave them their name. Great Smoky Mountains National Park, set up in 1934, covers 800 square miles (2,072 sq km). In 1983 the park was declared a World Heritage Site.

LOCATE IT

TENNESSEE   NORTH CAROLINA

Great Smoky
Mountains
National Park

Atlantic Coast and Appalachian States

" *Shaconage,*
the place of blue smoke "

—Cherokee description of the
Great Smoky Mountains

Fact and Opinion

A **fact** is a statement that can be proved. An **opinion** is a statement that tells what a person thinks or believes. It cannot be proved.

As you read this chapter, identify facts and opinions.

- Identify the facts by asking, *Can the idea be proved true by testing*?
- Look for phrases and words such as *think, feel, worst,* and *best* to identify opinions.

1

Early Settlement

1500	1600	1700	1800

Although many English colonists settled in the New England and Middle Atlantic regions, they built their first settlement in a region farther south. Today that region is called the Atlantic Coast and Appalachian region of the United States. Six states make up this region—Maryland, Virginia, North Carolina, Kentucky, Tennessee, and West Virginia.

Geography and Native American Settlement

Native Americans had lived along the broad plain of the Atlantic Coast and in the mountains of the Appalachian region for thousands of years. They built settlements along the many rivers that flow from the Appalachian Mountains across the Coastal Plain and into Chesapeake (CHEH•suh•peek) Bay and the Atlantic Ocean. The flat, rich lands along these rivers were good for farming.

The Native American village of Pomeiock in North Carolina was drawn in 1585 by John White, an English colonist. In his drawing, he cut away the walls of some of the houses to show how they had been built.

Large coastal marshes form where the fresh water from the rivers mixes with the salt water from the ocean. A **marsh** is low, wet land where cattails, tall grasses, and other, similar plants grow. Marshes cover large areas of Maryland, Virginia, and North Carolina. The Piedmont, an area of low hills, lies west of the Coastal Plain. West of the Piedmont are the tree-covered Appalachian Mountains.

Several mountain ranges make up the Appalachians as they stretch across the middle of the region. The Blue Ridge Mountains, the easternmost range, extend from North Carolina to West Virginia. To the west, reaching from Virginia to Maryland, are the Allegheny Mountains. Between the mountain ranges are long, narrow valleys. One of the largest is the Shenandoah (sheh•nuhn•DOH•uh) Valley, which lies between the Blue Ridge and the Allegheny Mountains in Virginia and West Virginia.

Native Americans traveled across the Appalachians on footpaths they made through the mountains. European colonists later followed these paths to the High Cumberland Plateau and present-day Kentucky and Tennessee. From the plateau, the land gradually falls into hills and valleys, giving way to the rolling lands of the Central Plains. The fertile land along the Mississippi River marks the region's western edge.

REVIEW What are some physical features of the Atlantic Coast and Appalachian region?

FAST FACT The first English child in North America was born in 1587 on Roanoke Island. She was named Virginia, because her birthplace was then part of the Virginia Colony.

The only trace left by the "Lost Colony" of Roanoke was the word *CROATOAN* carved on a tree.

Early English Settlements

The first attempt by the English to colonize the Atlantic Coast and Appalachian region took place in 1587. That year, a group of colonists landed on Roanoke (ROH•uh•nohk) Island, off the coast of what is now North Carolina. When supply ships returned in 1590, all the Roanoke settlers had vanished. Even today, no one knows why this first colony disappeared. For this reason, Roanoke is often called the "Lost Colony."

In 1607 another group of English colonists came to the region. From Chesapeake Bay they sailed up a broad river that they named the James River. Not far from the river's mouth, in present-day Virginia, the colonists chose a site for their settlement. They called it Jamestown. This became the first lasting English settlement in North America.

Pocahontas 1595?–1617

Character Trait: Kindness

Pocahontas (poh•kuh•HAHN•tuhs) was the daughter of Chief Powhatan. In 1607, John Smith was taken prisoner and brought before Powhatan. Smith later claimed that Pocahontas begged her father to spare his life. No one knows if the story is true. We do know that Pocahontas often visited the Jamestown colonists, bringing food supplies and messages from her father.

MULTIMEDIA BIOGRAPHIES
Visit The Learning Site at www.harcourtschool.com
to learn about other famous people.

Algonquian (al•GAHN•kwee•uhn) Indians were already living in the area in about 200 villages. Powhatan (pow•uh•TAN) was their powerful chief. The Algonquians farmed, growing corn, beans, and squash. They hunted deer in the nearby woods and fished in the rivers. The Jamestown colonists, however, often faced starvation. They had come to North America to find riches and spent most of their time searching for gold instead of farming.

Powhatan and his people saved the lives of the English colonists. They brought corn and bread to Jamestown when the colonists ran out of food. Captain John Smith's leadership also helped the colonists survive. He organized the colonists into groups to grow food, collect fresh water, and build houses. Smith also built a friendship with Chief Powhatan.

The Jamestown colonists never found gold in Virginia. They also lacked a major

Map of Jamestown

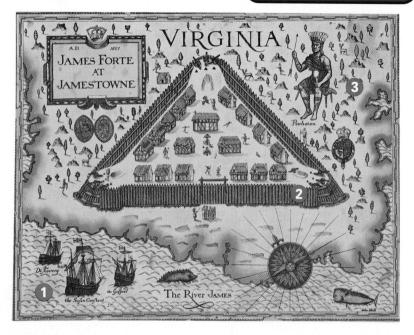

Analyze Primary Sources

This map pictures Jamestown in 1607. It shows the triangular shape of the fort where the first settlers lived.

❶ The three ships that carried the first settlers are shown sailing along the James River.

❷ Cannons were placed at each corner of the Jamestown fort.

❸ Chief Powhatan is shown sitting outside the fort.

◆ Why do you think the first Jamestown settlers lived behind the fort's walls?

crop to sell in Europe. Then people planted a new kind of tobacco seed. Virginia's soil proved perfect for growing this crop. Soon people cleared more and more land to plant tobacco.

This crop earned a lot of money for colonists and helped Virginia prosper. At the same time, ships began crossing the Atlantic Ocean regularly, bringing more people to the region. As Virginia grew, colonists moved south, starting farms in present-day North Carolina.

A group of English Catholics started the colony of Maryland, north of Virginia, in 1632. Like many other religious groups, Catholics could not freely practice their religion in England. From its beginning, Maryland welcomed people of many different religions.

REVIEW How were the settlers of Jamestown able to survive?

FACT AND OPINION

Colonists Move West

By the 1700s, farms and towns covered the Coastal Plain. Many were along the broad rivers that flow across the region. Over time, colonists followed those rivers upstream, where they started new farms

and towns. Others used the rivers to take them farther inland, toward the Appalachian Mountains. On most rivers, however, waterfalls blocked the way to the mountains.

Where the Piedmont meets the Coastal Plain, the elevation of the land drops suddenly. This steep drop causes waterfalls to form on the rivers along what geographers call the Fall Line. A **fall line** is a place where rivers drop from higher to lower land. People who wanted to travel west beyond the Fall Line had to carry their supplies overland around the waterfalls.

As a result, thousands of people decided to settle at the Fall Line. There they built mills and factories that used **waterpower**, or energy produced by rushing water. To use this power, people built waterwheels on the rivers. The river water flowing over the wheel caused it to turn. The turning wheel could then run machines connected to it.

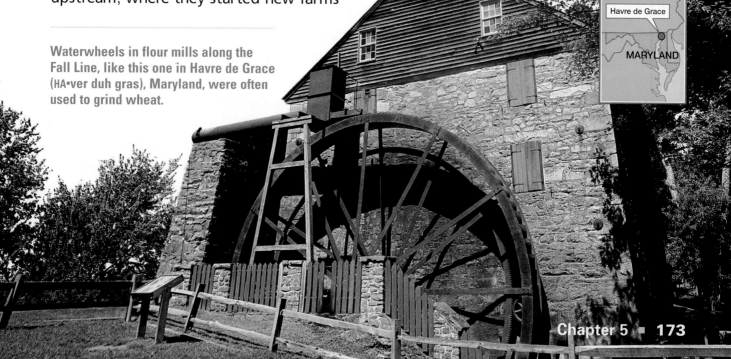

Waterwheels in flour mills along the Fall Line, like this one in Havre de Grace (HA•ver duh gras), Maryland, were often used to grind wheat.

LOCATE IT

Havre de Grace

MARYLAND

The Fall Line

0   100   200 Miles
0   100   200 Kilometers
Azimuthal Equal-Area Projection

PA
OH
IN
WV
KY
Ohio River
Harrodsburg
Boonesborough
Cumberland Gap
TN
AL
Tennessee River
Macon
Montgomery
Columbus
Chattahoochee River
Ochlockonee River
Oconee River
Ocmulgee River
Altamaha River
GA
FL
Trenton
New York City
Havre de Grace
NJ
MD
DE
Washington, D.C.
VA
James River
Richmond
Roanoke River
Piedmont
Appalachian Mountains
NC
Raleigh
Salisbury
Congaree R.
Saluda R.
SC
Columbia
Cape Fear R.
Santee R.
Coastal Plain
Coastal Plain

- - - - Fall Line
——— Boone's Trail
——— Wilderness Road
——— Present-day border
⊛ National capital

Feet   Meters
Above   Above
1,640   500
            200
655
0   0
Below sea level

N W E S

GEOGRAPHY THEME
Movement Waterfalls at the Fall Line blocked early settlers from traveling upstream by boat. For example, the Potomac River drops about 76 feet (23 m) at the Fall Line, forming nearly a mile of cascades and rapids called the Great Falls.

❖ Through how many states does the Fall Line pass?

Cities, including Richmond, Virginia; Raleigh, North Carolina; and Havre de Grace, Maryland, grew along the Fall Line. After settlers crossed the Appalachians, these Fall Line cities became useful trading points. They linked the new western settlements with the region's eastern colonial settlements.

REVIEW How did people use rivers along the Fall Line?

Crossing the Mountains

When people talked about "the West" during the 1700s, they meant the land between the Appalachian Mountains and the Mississippi River. Traders and explorers told people about the West's fertile land, good hunting grounds, and dense forests. To reach this land, however, pioneers had to cross the Appalachian Mountains. A **pioneer** is a person who leads the way to a new place.

In 1750 a group of explorers from Virginia discovered a natural pass, or gap, in the Appalachian Mountains. A **pass** is an opening between high mountains. The pass they found crosses at the point where the present-day states of Kentucky, Tennessee, and Virginia meet. They named the pass the Cumberland Gap.

Hunters and traders began using this pass to travel to what are now Kentucky and Tennessee. Pioneer Daniel Boone made his first trip from North Carolina through the Cumberland Gap in 1767. He later described what he had seen. "Thousands of buffalo roamed the Kentucky hills," Boone wrote, "and the land looked as if it never would become poor."

Many pioneers wanted to move west to this rich land, but traveling over the pass was difficult. At the time, the only way to cross the

Daniel Boone (above) helped pioneers travel through the Cumberland Gap (left).

Cumberland Gap was by a narrow path through thick bushes and rocks. In 1775 Boone and other pioneers cut down trees and bushes along the path to make more room for wagons. This path became known as the Wilderness Road. Nearly 300,000 people had traveled the road by 1800.

Eventually farms and towns covered the lands west of the Appalachians all the way to the Mississippi River. By 1796 those areas had become the states of Kentucky and Tennessee, the first two states west of the Appalachian Mountains.

REVIEW How did many people cross the Appalachian Mountains?

LESSON 1 REVIEW

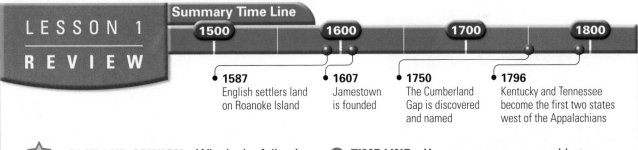

Summary Time Line

1500 — 1600 — 1700 — 1800

- **1587** English settlers land on Roanoke Island
- **1607** Jamestown is founded
- **1750** The Cumberland Gap is discovered and named
- **1796** Kentucky and Tennessee become the first two states west of the Appalachians

FACT AND OPINION Why is the following statement an opinion? *The Chesapeake Bay region is the most beautiful place in the United States.*

1 **BIG IDEA** How did the geography of the Atlantic Coast and Appalachian region affect how it was settled?

2 **VOCABULARY** Use the term **waterpower** to explain why many people in the Atlantic Coast and Appalachian region built factories along the **Fall Line**.

3 **TIME LINE** How many years passed between the discovery of the Cumberland Gap and the time that both Kentucky and Tennessee became states?

4 **HISTORY** What was the first lasting English settlement in North America?

5 **CRITICAL THINKING—Apply** How do you think interdependence among people affected the growth of cities along the Fall Line?

PERFORMANCE—Make a List Imagine that you are planning to settle in Kentucky or Tennessee in the 1700s. Make a list of 20 items you and your family will take with you. Explain why you chose those items.

PRIMARY SOURCES

Photographs of the Past

Between 1927 and 1934 Doris Ulmann traveled throughout the Appalachian Mountains of North Carolina and Kentucky. During that time she took thousands of photographs. Ulmann captured in her pictures the people, the crafts, and the landscape of the time and the region.

 FROM BEREA COLLEGE DEPARTMENT OF ART, BEREA, KENTUCKY

Posing for a picture
Top of Turkey, North Carolina, 1934

Grinding corn with a hand mill
Pine Mountain, Kentucky, 1933

Analyze the Primary Source

1. What are the people doing in each photograph?

2. What do the photographs tell you about life in Appalachia in the 1930s?

3. Why is taking photographs a good way of recording history?

Spinning and weaving
Shottin' Creek, North Carolina, 1934

ACTIVITY

Compare and Contrast Describe the people, the crafts, and the landscape of Appalachia today. If Doris Ulmann were taking pictures today, how would they differ from the older pictures? What might be the same?

RESEARCH

Visit The Learning Site at **www.harcourtschool.com** to research other primary sources.

Exploring the inside of a tin can,
South Carolina, 1929

Read a Line Graph

VOCABULARY

line graph

▶ WHY IT MATTERS

The population of the Atlantic Coast and Appalachian region has grown since the arrival of the Jamestown settlers. But just how much and how quickly did the population grow?

The numbers that show such changes are often very large and may be hard to understand. Sometimes putting large numbers, such as population, on a line graph makes them easier to understand. A **line graph** is a graph that uses a line to show changes over time. In this way, the differences between such numbers can easily be seen.

▶ WHAT YOU NEED TO KNOW

Look at the line graph on page 179. To read this line graph and understand the information it shows, first read the title. It tells you that this graph shows the population of the Atlantic Coast and Appalachian region between 1800 and 2000.

Then read the labels across the bottom of the graph. These dates tell you the years the population was counted. If you want to know the population for 1850, for example, place your finger on that year's label and move up until you reach that dot on the red line.

Baltimore, Maryland, has the largest population of any city in the Atlantic Coast and Appalachian states. More than 650,000 people live there.

LOCATE IT

Baltimore

MARYLAND

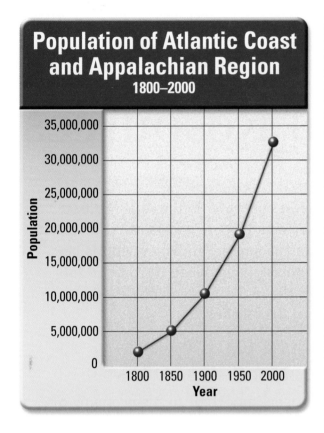

Population of Atlantic Coast and Appalachian Region
1800–2000

The labels on the left side of the graph give the numbers of people living in the region each year. To find the number of people living in the region in 1850, move your finger to the left from the dot until you touch that year's population number. This tells you that

about 5 million people lived in the region in 1850.

The direction the line on the graph moves tells you how the population changed in each 50-year period. If it rises up to the right, the population increased, or went up. If it drops down to the right, the population decreased, or went down. The steeper the line slants up, the quicker the population grew.

▶ PRACTICE THE SKILL

Use the line graph on this page to answer these questions.

❶ About how many people lived in the Atlantic Coast and Appalachian region in 1900?

❷ In what 50-year period did the greatest change in population take place?

❸ In which year was the population the lowest? the highest? What general statement can you make about the region's population based on the line graph?

▶ APPLY WHAT YOU LEARNED

Work with a partner to make a line graph that shows how your state's population changed over time. Use almanacs or the Internet to find the number of people living in your state in five different years. Use graph or grid paper to make a line graph showing that information. Remember to give your graph a title and to label its left and bottom sides. Then write a paragraph that describes the changes in your state's population during those years. Report your findings to your class.

2

People Use Natural Resources

 FACT AND OPINION

As you read, identify the resources that help make the economies of regions across the United States unique.

BIG IDEA

People in the Atlantic Coast and Appalachian region use natural resources to earn their livings.

VOCABULARY

reservoir
hydroelectric power
aluminum
reclaim

The landforms and bodies of water in the Atlantic Coast and Appalachian region affected where early settlers first lived. So did the region's natural resources. People farmed the land, used the wood from the forests, and mined the ground for minerals and fuels. Today, the region's geography continues to affect how people earn their livings.

Industries and Resources

Agriculture has always been important to the economy of the Atlantic Coast and Appalachian region. Since colonial days, tobacco has been the region's leading crop. Other major crops in the region include peanuts, soybeans, sweet potatoes, and cotton. Some farms in the region specialize in raising turkeys, chickens, dairy cows, and hogs. Farmers raise more turkeys in North Carolina than in any other state.

Horses thrive on the region's grassy pastures, and horse farms have long been an important part of its economy. Many horses are raised in the central part of Kentucky, where fields of thick bluegrass grow. Maryland, Virginia, and Tennessee are also famous for raising horses.

Many people earn a living by fishing on Chesapeake Bay. They catch oysters, blue crabs, clams, flounder, bass, and other fish.

Land Use and Resources in the Atlantic Coast and Appalachian States

Legend:
- Manufacturing
- Fruits and vegetables
- General farming
- Dairy farming
- Forest
- Little-used land
- Coal
- Iron ore
- Oil or natural gas
- Zinc
- Limestone

ATLANTIC OCEAN

GEOGRAPHY THEME

Human–Environment Interactions The maple, walnut, and oak trees in the Atlantic Coast and Appalachian region are used to make furniture, such as grandfather clocks (below).

❖ Where in the region are most of the forests located?

Several industries in the Atlantic Coast and Appalachian states manufacture products that use the region's natural resources or the crops grown there. For example, textile mills use cotton grown in the region to make clothing. Greensboro, North Carolina, has one of the largest denim factories in the world. Some factories in the region produce canned fish and crab, frozen vegetables, chicken, and other food products.

More than half of the region's land is covered with forests. People use the trees to make lumber, paper, hardwood flooring, pencils, and other kinds of wood products. North Carolina is the top furniture-producing state. In fact, so much furniture is made in High Point, North Carolina, that the city is sometimes called the "Furniture Capital of America."

Factories manufacture most of the products made in the region,

but many people still make some goods by hand, using traditional methods. Before there was modern transportation, travel and trade in the Appalachian Mountains was difficult. Because they were often unable to get goods from other places, people in this part of the region used the resources around them to make most of what they needed. They made pots, baskets, furniture, and other goods from clay, trees, and plants. They made cloth from sheep's wool, and they sewed their own clothes and blankets. Today, many people who live in Appalachia, or the southern areas of the Appalachian Mountains, continue to practice and pass on the crafts of basket weaving, quilting, pottery making, and wood carving.

REVIEW What are some products made from the natural resources of the Atlantic Coast and Appalachian region?

Using Rivers

People in the Atlantic Coast and Appalachian region use the large rivers there for travel and to transport many of the region's crops, minerals, and manufactured goods. Rivers also provide fresh water for people and businesses.

To make good use of some rivers, people often build dams across them. Dams form reservoirs (REH•zuh•vwahrz) behind them. A **reservoir** is a lake formed by the water held back by a dam. Like rivers, reservoirs provide fresh water for people to drink and use every day.

Dams help produce electricity, too. Water from reservoirs can be used to turn the machines that create electricity. **Hydroelectric power** is electricity made by waterpower.

People have built many dams across rivers flowing west of the Appalachians, especially along the Tennessee River and its tributaries. These rivers used to flood often, and rapids made travel on them difficult. To help control the flooding, improve navigation, and provide electricity, the national government in the 1930s set up the Tennessee Valley Authority, or TVA. Workers for TVA built several dams in the Tennessee River drainage basin.

TVA also built power plants near the dams to produce electricity. These plants

1 Reservoir

2

3 Generator

Power Plant

Turbine

4

brought electricity to many people in the Tennessee Valley for the first time. Before TVA, only 1 out of every 30 farms in Tennessee had electricity.

This large, inexpensive source of electricity also attracted new industries to the region. Several aluminum factories, which require large amounts of electricity, opened in Tennessee and Virginia. **Aluminum** is a metal used to make things that need to be strong and light, such as airplane parts. Other factories used TVA power to make food, timber products, and chemicals. Thousands of people moved to the region to work in these factories.

REVIEW Why do people build dams across rivers? **FACT AND OPINION**

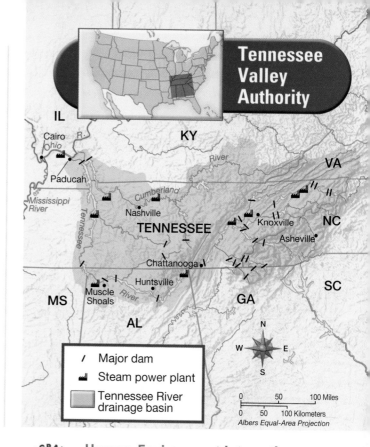

Tennessee Valley Authority

IL
Cairo
Ohio R.
Paducah
KY
River
VA
Mississippi River
Tennessee
Cumberland
Nashville
TENNESSEE
Knoxville
NC
Asheville
Chattanooga
SC
Muscle Shoals
River
Huntsville
GA
MS
AL

N
W E
S

Legend:
/ Major dam
⊶ Steam power plant
▭ Tennessee River drainage basin

0   50   100 Miles
0 50 100 Kilometers
Albers Equal-Area Projection

GEOGRAPHY THEME

Human–Environment Interactions
TVA operates about 35 dams in Tennessee and supplies nearly all the state's electricity.

❓ How many major TVA dams are in Kentucky?

A CLOSER LOOK
Hydroelectric Power

Water rushing through dams provides waterpower needed to make electricity.

1 Water is stored in a reservoir.
2 Pipes carry water to the power plant.
3 Water turns the machines that make electricity.
4 Water returns to the river.
5 Power lines carry electricity to users.

❓ What two machines are used to make electricity?

5 Power Lines

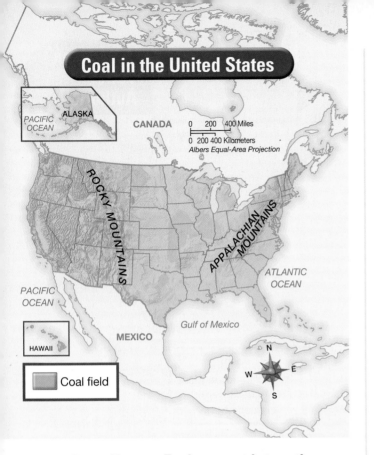

Coal in the United States

PACIFIC OCEAN

ALASKA

CANADA

0   200   400 Miles
0 200 400 Kilometers
Albers Equal-Area Projection

ROCKY MOUNTAINS

APPALACHIAN MOUNTAINS

ATLANTIC OCEAN

PACIFIC OCEAN

Gulf of Mexico

MEXICO

HAWAII

Coal field

N E S W

GEOGRAPHY THEME

Human–Environment Interactions
After China, the United States is the largest coal-producing nation in the world.

◆ **Where is most of the coal in the eastern part of the United States?**

Coal Mining

Hydroelectric plants cannot produce all the electricity people need. To create more energy, businesses have also built coal-fired steam plants. In these plants, coal is burned to heat water, which forms steam. The steam is used to run machines that produce electricity. About half of the nation's electricity now comes from power plants that burn coal. Coal is also used to produce steel.

Much of the coal mined in the United States comes from the Atlantic

Coast and Appalachian states. During the 1800s and early 1900s, coal mining was the largest industry in Appalachia. Coal is still an important part of the economy there. After Wyoming, the two largest coal-producing states are West Virginia and Kentucky. In a recent year, these two states produced nearly one-third of the nation's coal.

When coal lies near the surface, bulldozers remove the soil and rocks covering the coal. Then miners use huge mechanical shovels to dig out the coal. Because these surface mines strip away layers of soil and coal, they are sometimes called strip mines.

In the past, strip mines destroyed or badly damaged parts of Appalachia. When the coal was gone, mining companies left the mines and moved on. Because trees and grasses had been removed to mine the coal, the land quickly eroded. Today, however, mining companies must **reclaim** the land, or return it to a natural condition. By law, strip mines must be filled in with soil, and the land must be replanted.

When coal is buried far below the surface, mine holes, or shafts, must be dug deep in the ground. One shaft is used to let miners and their tools in and out of the mine. Another shaft is used to

In a recent year, Kentucky and West Virginia produced 317 million tons of coal—nearly one-third of the nation's total.

People plant trees to reclaim the land damaged by strip mines (left).

take out the coal. Miners dig low tunnels branching out from these main shafts. As coal is removed, the tunnels grow longer, sometimes stretching for miles.

The first miners who went underground worked by hand, using shovels and picks. Today, machines do much of the work. They carve tunnels and dig the coal and haul it out of the mines. With the help of machines, a worker today can mine three times as much coal as a miner working 40 years ago.

Even with improved technology, underground coal mining is hard work. The miners ride an elevator down a shaft early in the morning and may not see the sun all day. One miner explained, "It's like crawlin' under your kitchen table on your hands and knees eight hours a day . . . draggin' 50-pound sacks of rock dust and shovelin' coal." It takes strength and courage to work in these dark, cramped mines.

REVIEW What are two kinds of coal mines?

LESSON 2
REVIEW

Focus Skill **FACT AND OPINION** How could you prove that the following statement is a fact? *Much of our nation's coal comes from the Appalachian Mountains.*

1 BIG IDEA How do some people in the Atlantic Coast and Appalachian region use natural resources?

2 VOCABULARY Explain how **reservoirs** are used to produce **hydroelectric power**.

3 ECONOMICS How do people in the Atlantic Coast and Appalachian states use the region's forests?

4 CULTURE Why did making baskets, quilts, pottery, and other craft products become a tradition in Appalachia?

5 CRITICAL THINKING—Hypothesize What do you think would happen if all the nation's coal were used up?

PERFORMANCE—Write a Description Write a paragraph describing what working in an underground mine might be like. Describe the mine, and explain how you feel as the elevator takes you under the ground. Share your description with the class.

3

BIG IDEA

Cities have grown and industries have changed in the Atlantic Coast and Appalachian region.

VOCABULARY

hub
occupation
high-tech
resort

LOCATE IT

VIRGINIA

Hampton Roads

Cities Grow and Industries Change

Until the 1900s the typical family in the Atlantic Coast and Appalachian region lived and worked on a farm. Although many people in the region continue to live in rural areas today, most people now live in urban areas. As cities have grown and transportation has improved, new kinds of industries have changed the way most people in the region earn their livings.

Centers of Shipping and Trade

Most older cities in the Atlantic Coast and Appalachian region began along rivers or the Atlantic Ocean. Shipping and trading became important industries in many of these cities. Today, many of the region's largest cities still serve as centers of shipping and trade.

Some of these cities are located where rivers empty into the Chesapeake Bay. Baltimore, Maryland, for example, grew at the mouth of the Patapsco (puh•TAP•skoh) River. Hampton, Newport News, and Norfolk all developed at the mouth of the James River, in Virginia. Today, Baltimore and Norfolk are two of the nation's busiest ports. They ship steel, crops, machinery, chemicals, and other goods produced in their states.

The Port of Hampton Roads, in Virginia, includes the harbors of Newport News, Norfolk, and Portsmouth. About $40 billion in goods are shipped through the port every year.

Packages are loaded into airplanes at Louisville International Airport 24 hours a day. After the packages are loaded, workers deliver them all over the world.

Several cities that grew inland, along the Fall Line or on the Piedmont, also became leading centers of shipping and trade. Richmond, Virginia, is a trading center for much of the region's tobacco crop. Charlotte and Raleigh, the two largest cities in North Carolina, are distribution centers for their state's furniture, clothing, crops, and other goods.

Many cities west of the Appalachian Mountains are centers of shipping and trade, too. Memphis, the largest city in Tennessee, has been an important Mississippi River port since the early 1800s. Another large river port, Louisville, Kentucky, is located on the Ohio River. Because the Ohio is a tributary of the Mississippi River, businesses in both Memphis and Louisville can use rivers to ship tobacco, cotton, coal, textiles, and manufactured goods downstream to ports along the Gulf of Mexico.

Some cities in Tennessee, such as Knoxville and Chattanooga, are linked to the Ohio River by the Tennessee River system. The Tennessee River flows into the Ohio River at Paducah, Kentucky. These same cities are also connected to the Gulf of Mexico by the Tennessee–Tombigbee Waterway.

Improved transportation helped some cities in the region become centers for new kinds of shipping and trade. Both Louisville and Memphis are major air shipping hubs for package-delivery companies. A **hub** is a city where trains or planes stop on their way to other places. Packages from all over the country and the world are flown to Louisville or Memphis before being flown to other places. Memphis International Airport is the largest air shipment center in the world.

REVIEW Why are many cities in the region located on rivers?
FACT AND OPINION

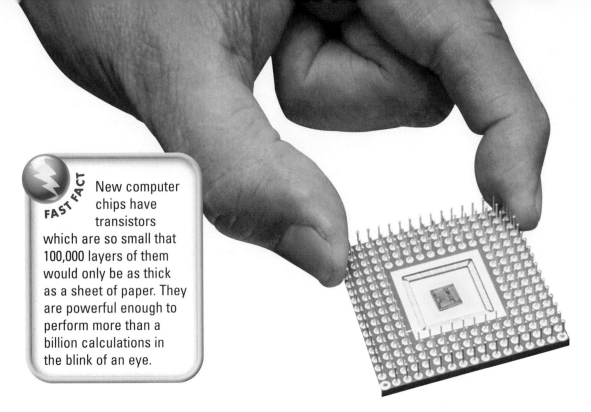

Workers in Raleigh, North Carolina, manufacture computer parts and other high-tech products.

Centers of New Industries

In the past few decades, the economy of the Atlantic Coast and Appalachian states has changed as new industries have started in the region. Many people's occupations have also changed. An **occupation** is what a person does for a living.

One out of every five people in the Atlantic Coast and Appalachian region now has a manufacturing job. Some work in automobile factories that have opened in the smaller cities that surround Nashville, Tennessee, and Lexington and Louisville, Kentucky. As a result, these cities' metropolitan areas have grown rapidly.

New high-technology, or "high-tech," industries are also now part of the region's economy. **High-tech** industries are those that invent, build, or use computers and other kinds of electronic equipment. In northern Virginia, for example, more than 1,000 companies make or sell computer products.

In North Carolina, an area known as the Research Triangle is one of the nation's largest high-tech centers. The cities of Chapel Hill, Durham, and Raleigh form the three corners of this triangle-shaped area. Many research companies, universities, and high-tech businesses are located there. With more than 1 million people, the Chapel Hill–Durham–Raleigh metropolitan area is now one of the fastest-growing places in the United States.

REVIEW What are two large high-tech areas in the Atlantic Coast and Appalachian region?

Centers of Government

As in every part of the country, service industries are growing in the Atlantic Coast and Appalachian region. Thousands of people in the region work in education, publishing, transportation, and entertainment. However, the largest service industry today is government.

Some cities in the region grew because they are state capitals. This helps a city grow in many ways. State governments provide jobs for workers. Many companies have offices in state capitals. Business-people like being close to the government leaders and offices that affect their work. They also use the services available in capital cities, such as communications, transportation, banking, and hotels.

To better serve the entire state, many states have chosen central locations for their capitals. Some states have even moved their capitals as people settled more of the state's land. For example, Virginia and North Carolina moved their capitals from coastal cities to Piedmont cities along the Fall Line. This helped the cities of Richmond and Raleigh grow.

Other cities in the region have grown because of the national government in Washington, D.C. Both Virginia and Maryland border Washington, D.C., so many nearby cities in those states have grown. The Baltimore–Washington–Virginia metropolitan area is now the fourth largest in the nation. Hundreds of thousands of the people who live there commute to government jobs in Washington, D.C., each day.

Other government workers have jobs in the many military bases in the Atlantic Coast and Appalachian region. Norfolk, Virginia, is home to the largest naval base in the world. Fort Bragg, in North Carolina, is one of the largest Army bases in the United States. Our nation's training center for navy officers has been in Annapolis, the capital of Maryland, for more than 150 years. The Pentagon, in Arlington, Virginia, is the headquarters for our nation's Department of Defense.

REVIEW How does being a state capital help a city grow?

Several United States Army special forces units are stationed at Fort Bragg, North Carolina.

LOCATE IT

NORTH CAROLINA

Fort Bragg

Centers of Tourism

Tourism has become another major service industry in the Atlantic Coast and Appalachian region. Every year many tourists visit Jamestown, Williamsburg, and Yorktown in Virginia. For a time, Williamsburg was Virginia's colonial capital. Yorktown was the site of the battle that ended the American Revolution. Visitors to these places can see how people lived and worked during colonial days.

There are also many historical sites for tourists to visit in Washington, D.C. People from all over the world travel there to see the White House, the Washington Monument, the Jefferson Memorial, the Lincoln Memorial, and the Smithsonian museums.

Music also draws people to the Atlantic Coast and Appalachian region, which is known as the birthplace of country music. Early settlers in Appalachia brought folk music with them from Great Britain that developed into country and later bluegrass music. Today so much country music is recorded in Nashville that the city is often called the "Capital of Country Music." Each year millions of tourists visit the city's Grand Ole Opry and the Country Music Hall of Fame and Museum.

The Atlantic Coast and Appalachian region is popular with race fans, too. More than 100,000 tourists visit Louisville every year for the most famous horse race in the nation, the Kentucky Derby. Charlotte, North Carolina, hosts some of the biggest auto races in the country.

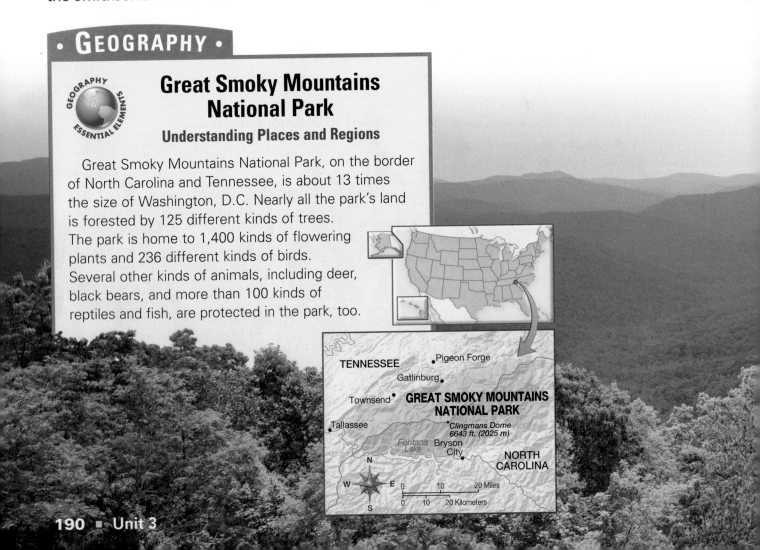

· GEOGRAPHY ·

Great Smoky Mountains National Park

Understanding Places and Regions

Great Smoky Mountains National Park, on the border of North Carolina and Tennessee, is about 13 times the size of Washington, D.C. Nearly all the park's land is forested by 125 different kinds of trees. The park is home to 1,400 kinds of flowering plants and 236 different kinds of birds. Several other kinds of animals, including deer, black bears, and more than 100 kinds of reptiles and fish, are protected in the park, too.

TENNESSEE
Pigeon Forge
Gatlinburg
Townsend · **GREAT SMOKY MOUNTAINS NATIONAL PARK**
Tallassee
Clingmans Dome 6643 ft. (2025 m)
Fontana Lake
Bryson City
NORTH CAROLINA

N
W E
S
0   10   20 Miles
0   10   20 Kilometers

Many tourists visit the region's resorts along the Atlantic Ocean, such as Virginia Beach, Virginia. A **resort** is a place where people go to relax and have fun. The Outer Banks, the low, narrow islands off the coast of North Carolina, are popular surfing and vacation spots. The Cape Hatteras Lighthouse there is also a popular attraction.

Some of our nation's largest and most popular national parks are found in this region, too. Great Smoky Mountains National Park in North Carolina and Tennessee receives more visitors than any other park in the country. Virginia is home to Shenandoah National Park. Many of the region's parks have spectacular waterfalls, such as Fall Creek Falls, Tennessee. Mammoth Cave in Kentucky is the longest cave system in the world.

REVIEW What are some of the tourist attractions in this region?

The Grand Ole Opry is the longest-running live radio program in the world. The show has broadcast every Friday and Saturday night since 1925.

LESSON 3
REVIEW

 FACT AND OPINION Rewrite the following statement so it is a fact instead of an opinion. *Great Smoky Mountains National Park is the best park in the nation.*

1 BIG IDEA Why did different cities in the Atlantic Coast and Appalachian region grow?

2 VOCABULARY Where might you find a **resort** in the Atlantic Coast and Appalachian region? Why?

3 GEOGRAPHY Why did two states in this region move their state capitals?

4 CIVICS AND GOVERNMENT In what kinds of cities are state governments based? In what city in the Atlantic Coast and Appalachian region is the national government based?

5 ECONOMICS What kinds of jobs might people have in a hub city?

6 CRITICAL THINKING—Analyze On a map of the United States, find Louisville and Memphis. Other than being located on major waterways, what do you notice about their locations that might have contributed to these cities' growth as trade centers?

 PERFORMANCE—Make a Postcard Choose a place in this region you would like to visit, and learn more about it. On one side of an index card, draw a postcard picture of that place. On the other side, write about it.

BIG IDEA

Learn about some national parks in other parts of the world.

VOCABULARY

wildlife refuge
habitat
endangered
extinct
reef
coral

National Parks Around the World

You have just read about some of the national parks in the Atlantic Coast and Appalachian region. Like parks in the United States, parks around the world serve different purposes. Many parks preserve natural resources, such as coastal areas and forests. Some parks are protected homes for wildlife. Still others preserve important cultural or historical sites.

Kruger National Park

Like Great Smoky Mountains National Park in Tennessee and North Carolina, Kruger National Park is the most visited park in its country, South Africa. Both parks also share the same purpose—preserving their regions' plants and animals.

Kruger is the largest park in South Africa. Nearly the entire state of New Jersey could fit inside this park! Much of the park

Zebras, giraffes, and wildebeests (WIL•duh•beests) are just a few of the animals that live in Kruger National Park in South Africa.

LOCATE IT

Kruger National Park

SOUTH AFRICA

Baobab tree trunks store water to help the tree survive in South Africa's dry climate.

is flat, grassy plains. Bushes, vines, and more than 300 kinds of trees cover other areas of the park. Some baobab (BAY•uh•bab) trees in the park may be more than 2,000 years old. The largest of these trees can measure more than 64 feet (20 m) around. That is about 30 times the size of your waist!

Kruger National Park also serves as a **wildlife refuge**, or an area of land set aside to protect animals and other living things. In the park, elephants, hippopotamuses, and rhinoceroses cool off by wading in muddy pools. Zebras, antelopes, lions, and other animals come to the pools to drink.

REVIEW What is the purpose of Kruger National Park?

Wolong Natural Reserve

Many parks protect habitats for animals. A **habitat** is a region where a plant or an animal naturally grows or lives. Some parks protect just one kind of animal. Wolong (WOH•long) Natural

Reserve in China is one such park, preserving the habitat of giant pandas.

Giant pandas live in the mountain regions of central Asia, where bamboo forests grow. Bamboo is practically all that giant pandas eat, and they need enormous amounts of it to survive. However, much of the giant panda's habitat has been damaged to clear land for farms, houses, and businesses.

As more of their habitats were damaged or destroyed, giant pandas became endangered animals. **Endangered** animals are ones that are few in number and whose survival is uncertain. For this reason, in 1975 China set aside large areas in its southwestern mountains for the Wolong Natural Reserve. Even with this protected habitat, fewer than 1,000 giant pandas now live in the wild.

Giant pandas spend an average of ten hours a day eating more than 35 pounds (16 kg) of bamboo.

LOCATE IT

Wolong Natural Reserve

CHINA

Without parks like Wolong, giant pandas could become extinct. Animals are **extinct** when all of their kind have died out. With wildlife organizations around the world, people in China are working hard to save the giant pandas. More than six out of every ten giant pandas living in the wild today were born in zoos or research centers. About 100 pandas live in zoos, including the National Zoo in Washington, D.C.

REVIEW **What is the natural habitat of giant pandas?**

Great Barrier Reef Marine Park

Some national parks, such as the Great Barrier Reef Marine Park in Australia, protect marine, or coastal, areas. This **reef**, or ridge of rocks, sand, or coral near the surface of the sea, extends more than 1,250 miles (2,000 km) along Australia's eastern Pacific Coast. **Coral** is a stony

More than 400 kinds of coral are protected in the Great Barrier Reef Marine Park.

material formed by the skeletons of tiny sea animals. The Great Barrier Reef Marine Park, first established in 1975, is the largest underwater park in the world.

The protected waters surrounding the reef are so clear that people at the surface can see marine life more than 100 feet (30 m) down. Brightly colored sea sponges, shrimp, and lobsters live among the park's coral reefs. Schools of more than 1,500 kinds of fish also live there. Humpback whales and dolphins feed on the fish, algae (AL•jee), and forests of sea grasses along the reef.

Visitors to the Great Barrier Reef Marine Park can view the sea life from glass-bottomed boats. Some visitors swim and dive along the reef. Visitors can learn about protecting coastal areas at the park's museum.

REVIEW **What is the purpose of the Great Barrier Reef Marine Park?**

FACT AND OPINION

Australia's Great Barrier Reef is the world's largest group of coral reefs.

LOCATE IT

AUSTRALIA

Great Barrier Reef Marine Park

The Maya built the city of Palenque on a high hill so that people traveling to it from the coast could see it for days.

LOCATE IT

Palenque
National Park

MEXICO

Palenque National Park

Many parks are dedicated to preserving a nation's culture or history. Some provide a glimpse of Native American life. One of the most famous of these historical parks is Palenque (pah•LENG•kay) National Park, in Mexico.

This park covers about 750 acres of rain forest along the Yucatán (yoo•kuh•TAN) Peninsula. A Native American group called the Maya built a large city here. Hundreds of years ago, the Maya abandoned the city and over time rain forest grew over it.

In the late 1700s the city of Palenque was rediscovered, and since then, scientists have been studying its ruins. Experts believe that the Mayan people built Palenque almost 2,000 years ago without metal tools, wheels, or pack animals. Although no one knows why the Mayan culture declined, the city contains evidence of their knowledge of astronomy and mathematics as well as the earliest writing system in the Americas.

REVIEW Who built and lived in the ancient city of Palenque?

LESSON 4
REVIEW

FACT AND OPINION Is the following statement a fact or an opinion? Explain your answer. *National parks are found in many places all over the world.*

1. **BIG IDEA** Where are some of the important national parks in the world?

2. **VOCABULARY** Use the terms **habitat**, **endangered**, and **extinct** to describe the purpose of Wolong Natural Reserve.

3. **GEOGRAPHY** Why is the location of Wolong Natural Reserve important to the survival of giant pandas?

4. **CULTURE** What did scientists learn about the Maya at Palenque?

5. **CRITICAL THINKING—Hypothesize** What do you think might happen to some plants, animals, and historical sites if they were not part of national parks?

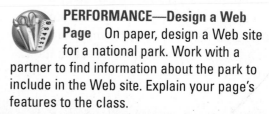

PERFORMANCE—Design a Web Page On paper, design a Web site for a national park. Work with a partner to find information about the park to include in the Web site. Explain your page's features to the class.

5 Review and Test Preparation

Summary Time Line

1500 — 1600

1587
Settlers from England
land on Roanoke Island

1607
Jamestown
colony
is founded

Fact and Opinion

Copy the following graphic organizer onto a separate sheet of paper. Use the information you have learned to write facts and opinions about the Atlantic Coast and Appalachian States.

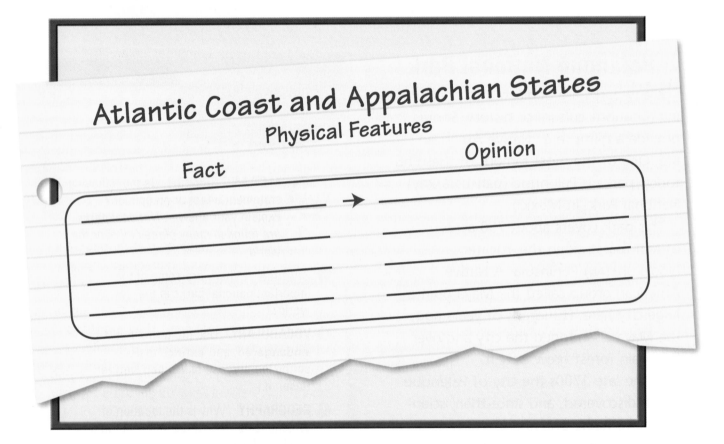

Atlantic Coast and Appalachian States
Physical Features

Fact → Opinion

THINK & WRITE

Make a Decision Imagine that you are a pioneer in the Atlantic Coast and Appalachian region. You are traveling upstream on a river. At the Fall Line, you must decide whether to settle there or go on. Explain your decision and the reasons for it.

Write a Song Write a short song that describes the land in the Atlantic Coast and Appalachian states. You can describe the entire region's physical features, or choose a certain place to describe. The lines to your song do not have to rhyme.

1700   1800   1900   **Present**

1775
Wilderness Road is built
through the Cumberland Gap

1933
Tennessee Valley
Authority is created

1934
Great Smoky Mountains
National Park opens

USE THE TIME LINE

1 When was the Wilderness Road built?

2 What two events on the time line happened within a year of each other?

USE VOCABULARY

Use each term in a sentence that helps explain its meaning.

3 **marsh** (p. 171)

4 **pass** (p. 174)

5 **reservoir** (p. 182)

6 **reclaim** (p. 184)

7 **hub** (p. 187)

8 **wildlife refuge** (p. 193)

RECALL FACTS

Answer these questions.

9 On what landforms did Native Americans and English colonists build settlements in the Atlantic Coast and Appalachian region?

10 How did Daniel Boone make travel easier for early settlers crossing the Appalachians?

11 How do people use forests in the Atlantic Coast and Appalachian states?

12 How are surface coal mines different from underground coal mines?

13 Why are many of the largest cities in the Atlantic Coast and Appalachian region important centers of shipping and trade?

14 Why do people create national parks?

Write the letter of the best choice.

15 Which of the following is **not** a reason people build dams?
 A to provide fresh water
 B to control flooding
 C to prevent ships from traveling on rivers
 D to produce electricity

16 Coal from United States coal mines is used to—
 F produce electricity.
 G produce gasoline.
 H reclaim land.
 J strip the top layer of soil.

THINK CRITICALLY

17 How do farmers in the Atlantic Coast and Appalachian states help other people in the region earn a living in manufacturing, mining, or service industries?

18 Do you or any members of your family make crafts in a traditional way? How are these crafts important to you and your family?

19 Where is your state capital located? Why do you think that location was selected for your state's capital?

APPLY SKILLS

Read a Line Graph

20 Use the information below to make a line graph that shows how the population of West Virginia changed between 1800 and 2000.

Year	Population
1800	78,592
1900	958,800
2000	1,808,344

MOBILE, ALABAMA

Mobile has done well since its beginning in 1702. Its deep bay and harbor area made it a natural shipping port. The resulting international trade allowed even the earliest settlers to enjoy imports from Europe, England, the Mediterranean, and Asia.

LOCATE IT

ALABAMA

Mobile

6

Southeast and Gulf States

" O land and soil, red soil
and sweet-gum tree,
So scant of grass, so
profligate of pines . . . "
—Jean Toomer, "Song of the Son," 1923

Compare and Contrast

To **compare** two things is to find how they are alike. To **contrast** is to find how they are different.

As you read this chapter, be sure to do the following.
- **Compare and contrast the key places and events in the Southeast States and Gulf States.**

1

 Focus Skill

COMPARE AND CONTRAST

As you read, compare and contrast the economies and ways of life in the North and South in the past.

BIG IDEA

Farming was important to the early economy of the southeastern United States.

VOCABULARY

slavery
growing season
plantation
cash crop
abolish
Union
secede
Confederacy
civil war

Settlement and Early Life

| 1500 | 1700 | 1900 |

About 100 years before the English founded their first colony in North America, Spanish explorers and soldiers conquered parts of Central and South America. As a result, the Spanish gained huge amounts of gold and silver. Hoping to find more riches, they traveled to North America.

The Southeast and Gulf region was the first place they explored. The Spanish did not find gold there, but many people eventually went to the region to live. They settled in what became the states of South Carolina, Georgia, Florida, Alabama, and Mississippi.

Exploring the Region

The first Spanish explorer to set foot on what is now the United States was Juan Ponce de León (POHN•say•day•lay•OHN). In 1513 he landed near the present-day city of St. Augustine. He named the land *La Florida*, which means "full of flowers" in Spanish.

Founded in 1565, St. Augustine, Florida, is the oldest city in the United States. It was founded 42 years before Jamestown, Virginia.

LOCATE IT

St. Augustine — FLORIDA

Other Spanish explorers soon followed. In 1539 Hernando de Soto (day SOH•toh) arrived on the west coast of Florida. From Florida, de Soto's army marched north to what are now Georgia, South Carolina, Alabama, and Mississippi. De Soto believed he would find treasures. He did not find gold, but he claimed the land of the Native Americans for Spain.

Native Americans at first welcomed the new arrivals. Soon, however, they grew to mistrust them. The Spanish raided food supplies and forced Native Americans into slavery to work as servants. **Slavery** is the practice of holding people against their will and making them work without pay.

Native Americans fought back. For example, Indian guides misled the Spanish explorers and set fire to their camps. Native Americans also united in revolt against the Spanish. Thousands of Native Americans died in these battles as well as from the diseases the Spanish brought. The Native Americans had little defense against these diseases, which were new to them.

REVIEW What was the main reason the Spanish explored the Southeast and Gulf region?

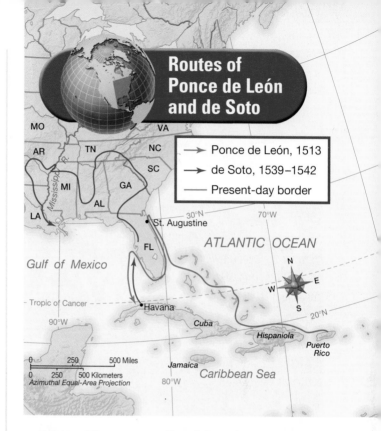

Routes of Ponce de León and de Soto

→ Ponce de León, 1513
→ de Soto, 1539–1542
— Present-day border

MO
VA
AR
TN
NC
SC
MI
GA
AL
LA
Mississippi
St. Augustine
30°N
70°W
ATLANTIC OCEAN
FL
Gulf of Mexico
N
W   E
S
Tropic of Cancer
Havana
20°N
90°W
Cuba
Hispaniola
Puerto Rico
80°W
Jamaica
Caribbean Sea
250   500 Miles
0
250   500 Kilometers
Azimuthal Equal-Area Projection

GEOGRAPHY THEME

Movement Spanish explorers traveled through the Southeast and Gulf region during the 1500s.

❖ In what order did de Soto explore the present-day states in this region?

FAST FACT

The Castillo de San Marcos in St. Augustine is the oldest stone fort in North America. To build it, the Spanish colony used all its funds. A year after it was completed in 1695, there was no money left to pay the Spanish soldiers in the fort.

A Region for Farming

Spain was not the only European nation to claim land in the Southeast and Gulf region. France and Britain also claimed different parts of the region at different times. So did the United States, after it became a country.

Regardless of which nation claimed the land or where settlers came from, the region proved to be an excellent place for farming. Although the Appalachian Mountains run through northwestern South Carolina and northern Georgia and Alabama, most of the region has gently rolling or flat land. In fact, the Coastal Plain covers more than half of the land in the region. Settlers found especially rich soil on the broad floodplains along the region's rivers and on the Mississippi Delta.

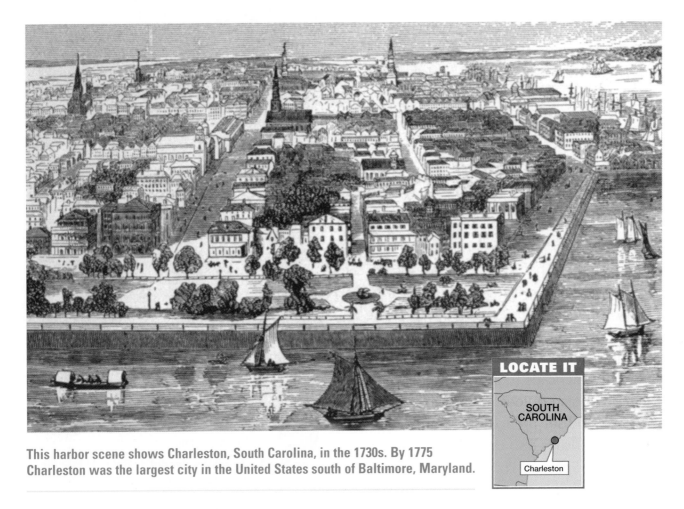

This harbor scene shows Charleston, South Carolina, in the 1730s. By 1775 Charleston was the largest city in the United States south of Baltimore, Maryland.

The region's climate is excellent for farming, too. In most years, 40 to 50 inches (102 to 127 cm) of rain fall on the southern Coastal Plain. Winters are generally short and mild. In the southern parts of the region, temperatures stay warm throughout the year. As a result, most of the region has a long growing season. A **growing season** is the time during which the weather is warm enough for plants to grow.

Plentiful rainfall and a long growing season allowed settlers in the Southeast and Gulf region to grow cotton, rice, and other crops that require wet, warm climates. Cotton, for example, needs about 180 frost-free days to grow, while rice needs about 120 days. To grow these crops, some settlers in the region started huge farms called **plantations**.

The region's rivers and harbors provided a way for plantation owners and other farmers to ship their crops to markets. Located at the mouth of the Ashley and Cooper Rivers, Charleston, South Carolina, became one of the region's largest ports. Farther south along the Atlantic Coast, near the mouth of the Savannah River, was the port city of Savannah, Georgia. In Alabama, settlers used the Mobile River system to ship goods to the port at Mobile. In Mississippi, people used the Mississippi River and smaller rivers for shipping and trade. In Florida, they used the St. Johns and other rivers in the same way.

REVIEW What comparisons can you make about farming in the Southeast and Gulf region?

COMPARE AND CONTRAST

Cash Crops

By the early 1800s, farms covered much of the Southeast and Gulf region. Most people in the region lived on small farms, where they raised livestock and grew food to feed their families. Some also grew cash crops. A **cash crop** is a crop people raise to sell to others rather than to use themselves. Among the region's leading cash crops were cotton, rice, and indigo. Indigo is a plant used to make blue dye for clothing.

Most cash crops in the region were grown on large plantations. Plantation owners grew different crops depending on where they lived. For example, sugarcane, a plant used to make sugar, needs a very warm, wet climate to grow. So most sugarcane plantations were in Florida. In the region's marshy areas farther north, many plantation owners grew rice and indigo. By the early 1800s, however, cotton had become a leading cash crop in all the Southeast and Gulf states. Georgia became the largest cotton producer in the world.

It took many workers to raise and harvest cash crops. On plantations in the Southeast and Gulf region and across the rest of the South, enslaved African Americans did most of the work. Not everyone in the region owned enslaved workers. Still, many people in the Southern states believed that slavery was necessary.

REVIEW Where were most of the region's cash crops grown?

A Nation Divided

By the mid-1800s, people in the Northern and Southern states had developed different ways of life. In the South most people earned their living from agriculture. There were few factories.

The 107th United States Colored Troops was just one of many African American regiments that fought for the Union during the Civil War.

ABRAHAM LINCOLN, President of the United States of America, 1861–1865

❝I believe this government cannot endure permanently half slave and half free. . . . It will become all one thing, or all the other . . . in all the States . . . North as well as South.❞

JEFFERSON DAVIS, President of the Confederate States of America, 1861–1865

❝The inhabitants of an organized Territory of the United States, like the people of a State . . . [must] decide for themselves whether slavery . . . shall be maintained or prohibited.❞

Analyze the Viewpoints

1. What did each person believe about the right of the states to decide for themselves whether or not they wanted to permit slavery?

2. **Make It Relevant** Abraham Lincoln was hoping to be a United States senator when he expressed this viewpoint in 1858. Do you think it is still important for leaders to hold debates before elections? Explain your answer.

Most people in the North were farmers, too, but more people there were moving to cities to work in manufacturing industries. Meanwhile, Southerners depended on enslaved African Americans to help run their farms and businesses.

Since colonial times, Americans had argued about whether states should allow slavery. Many Northerners believed that slavery was wrong and wanted the government to **abolish** (uh•BAH•lish), or end, it. Other Northerners thought the government should stop slavery from spreading to new states. Most Southerners, however, felt that each state had the right to decide for itself about such things as slavery. These differences soon tore the country apart.

In 1860 Abraham Lincoln was elected President. Lincoln opposed the spread of slavery to new states joining the **Union**, or United States. Many people in the South feared that he would try to end slavery everywhere.

After Lincoln's election, eleven Southern states decided to **secede** (sih•SEED) from, or leave, the Union. These states formed their own country, called the Confederate States of America, or the **Confederacy**. The United States was now divided into two parts.

On April 12, 1861, Confederate soldiers fired shots at Union forces at Fort Sumter, in Charleston Harbor in South Carolina. This event marked the beginning of the American Civil War. A **civil war** is a war between groups of people in the same country. For the next four years, the Union and the Confederacy fought the bloodiest war in United States history. More than 600,000 soldiers died.

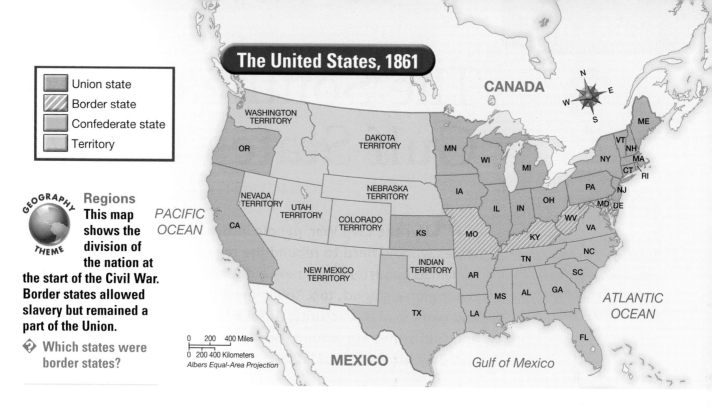

The United States, 1861

Union state
Border state
Confederate state
Territory

CANADA

WASHINGTON TERRITORY

OR

DAKOTA TERRITORY

MN

WI

MI

ME

VT
NH
NY
MA
CT
RI

PACIFIC OCEAN

NEVADA TERRITORY
UTAH TERRITORY

CA

NEBRASKA TERRITORY

COLORADO TERRITORY

KS

IA

IL IN

MO

OH

KY

PA

WV

VA

NJ
MD DE

NC

NEW MEXICO TERRITORY

INDIAN TERRITORY

AR

TN

SC

TX

MS AL GA

LA

FL

ATLANTIC OCEAN

MEXICO

Gulf of Mexico

GEOGRAPHY THEME

Regions This map shows the division of the nation at the start of the Civil War. Border states allowed slavery but remained a part of the Union.

❖ Which states were border states?

0   200   400 Miles
0 200 400 Kilometers
Albers Equal-Area Projection

The Confederate army surrendered on April 9, 1865, saving the Union. In 1863, Lincoln had issued the Emancipation Proclamation, an order freeing all African Americans in areas still fighting against the Union. With the Union victory, more than 4 million enslaved African Americans gained their freedom.

REVIEW How was the United States divided during the Civil War?

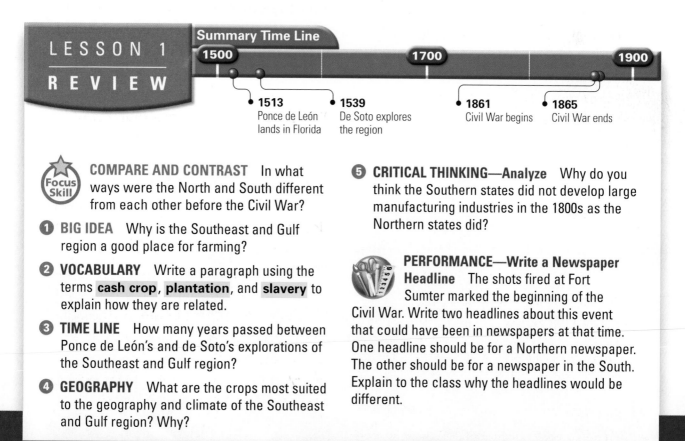

LESSON 1
REVIEW

Summary Time Line

1500 — 1700 — 1900

1513 Ponce de León lands in Florida

1539 De Soto explores the region

1861 Civil War begins

1865 Civil War ends

Focus Skill

COMPARE AND CONTRAST In what ways were the North and South different from each other before the Civil War?

1. **BIG IDEA** Why is the Southeast and Gulf region a good place for farming?

2. **VOCABULARY** Write a paragraph using the terms **cash crop**, **plantation**, and **slavery** to explain how they are related.

3. **TIME LINE** How many years passed between Ponce de León's and de Soto's explorations of the Southeast and Gulf region?

4. **GEOGRAPHY** What are the crops most suited to the geography and climate of the Southeast and Gulf region? Why?

5. **CRITICAL THINKING—Analyze** Why do you think the Southern states did not develop large manufacturing industries in the 1800s as the Northern states did?

PERFORMANCE—Write a Newspaper Headline The shots fired at Fort Sumter marked the beginning of the Civil War. Write two headlines about this event that could have been in newspapers at that time. One headline should be for a Northern newspaper. The other should be for a newspaper in the South. Explain to the class why the headlines would be different.

2

COMPARE AND CONTRAST

As you read, compare and contrast how the resources and economy of the Southeast has changed over time.

BIG IDEA

The location and resources of the Southeast and Gulf states have helped the region become one of the fastest-growing in the nation.

VOCABULARY

food processing
pulp
fertilizer
raw material
import
export
international trade
Sun Belt
swamp

The Southeast and Gulf States Today

After the Civil War, people in the Southeast and Gulf states worked hard to rebuild the region's economy. Agriculture remained important, but new industries also developed. Life in the region changed, too. Today most people live in urban areas and work in manufacturing or service industries. The Southeast and Gulf states are among the nation's fastest-growing states, and they have some of its largest cities.

Resources and Industries

Fewer people in the Southeast and Gulf states work on farms today than in the past, but they still use the region's land to grow millions of tons of crops each year. Georgia and Alabama are the nation's leading producers of peanuts. South Carolina grows more peaches than any other state. Florida grows the most sugarcane and oranges in the nation and is the leading grapefruit producer in the world. Georgia raises more chickens than any other state.

More than 7 out of 10 oranges grown in the United States come from Florida.

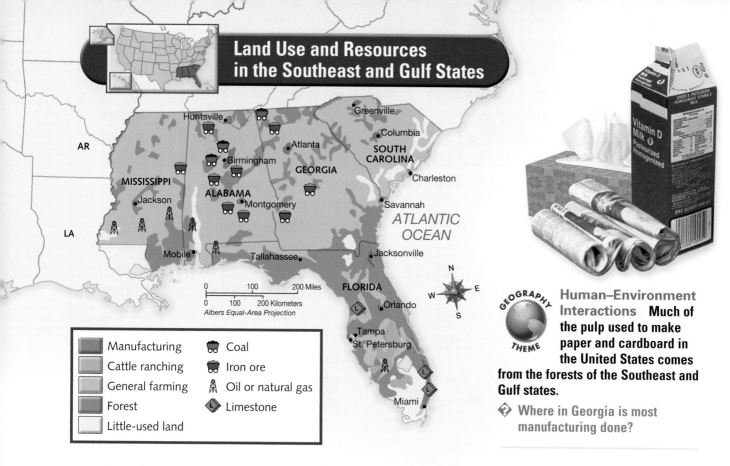

Land Use and Resources in the Southeast and Gulf States

Map Legend:
- Manufacturing
- Cattle ranching
- General farming
- Forest
- Little-used land
- Coal
- Iron ore
- Oil or natural gas
- Limestone

Map labels: AR, LA, MISSISSIPPI, Jackson, ALABAMA, Montgomery, Mobile, Huntsville, Birmingham, Atlanta, GEORGIA, Tallahassee, FLORIDA, Orlando, Tampa, St. Petersburg, Miami, Greenville, Columbia, SOUTH CAROLINA, Charleston, Savannah, ATLANTIC OCEAN, Jacksonville

Scale: 0 100 200 Miles / 0 100 200 Kilometers / Albers Equal-Area Projection

Human–Environment Interactions Much of the pulp used to make paper and cardboard in the United States comes from the forests of the Southeast and Gulf states.

◆ Where in Georgia is most manufacturing done?

Many of the region's manufacturing industries are related to agriculture. Food processing, for example, is a major industry in every state in the region. **Food processing** is the cooking, canning, drying, or freezing of food and the preparing of it for market. Workers in this region process the crops grown there to make such products as peanut butter, sugar, and orange juice.

Another industry related to agriculture in the region is the textile industry. Textile workers use cotton grown in the region to produce denim and other kinds of cloth.

Other manufacturing industries in the Southeast and Gulf states depend on the region's pine forests. Paper mills and furniture factories operate throughout the region. Georgia is the largest producer of lumber and wood pulp east of the Mississippi River. **Pulp** is a soft mixture of ground-up wood chips and chemicals and is used to make paper.

Mining is another important industry in some Southeast and Gulf states. Georgia produces more granite than any other state, and nearly all the nation's phosphate (FAHS•fayt) comes from Florida. Phosphate is a mineral that is used mainly to manufacture **fertilizers**, or materials added to the soil to make it more fertile. Workers in Birmingham, Alabama, use that state's deposits of coal, iron, and limestone to manufacture steel. As a result, Alabama is the largest supplier of cast-iron and steel pipe products in the country.

There are other kinds of manufacturing industries in the Southeast and Gulf states, too. Workers in Dalton, Georgia, for example, produce carpeting. Factories in this region also manufacture machinery, automobiles, tires, dyes, and ships.

REVIEW How does the use of agricultural products in the Southeast today differ from their use in the past?

COMPARE AND CONTRAST

A Region of Ports

Because the Southeast and Gulf states have two coastlines and many rivers that flow from the interior, they are also known for their busy ports. Some cities, such as Charleston, South Carolina, and Savannah, Georgia, have been busy Atlantic Ocean ports since colonial times. Other cities, such as Jacksonville and Miami in Florida, became major ports more recently. Large port cities along the Gulf of Mexico include Tampa, Florida; Mobile, Alabama; and Pascagoula (pas•kuh•GOO•luh), Mississippi.

Many of the ships that sail into and out of these ports carry goods from one part of the United States to another. Some ships carry food, fuels, and raw materials. A **raw material** is a resource, such as a mineral, that can be used to manufacture a product. Other ships carry products made in factories.

Ports also link the Southeast and Gulf states with other countries. Each day, imports from all over the world arrive in ports in the United States. An **import** is a good brought into one country from another country, most often to be sold.

The United States also uses its ports to send exports to other countries. An **export** is a good shipped from one country to another. Many businesses in the United States make money exporting goods to people in other countries.

International trade, or trade among nations, allows people to buy goods that their countries do not make or grow. Most of those goods are carried from country to country by ship. Businesses rely on ships because they hold more goods and are less expensive to use than airplanes.

Because Miami sits at the southern tip of the Florida peninsula, much of its trade is with countries in Latin America. The Port of Miami is sometimes called the "Gateway of the Americas." It is also the nation's largest cruise-ship port. Passengers board ships in Miami that take them to places around the world.

REVIEW How do ports in the Southeast and Gulf states link the United States with other countries?

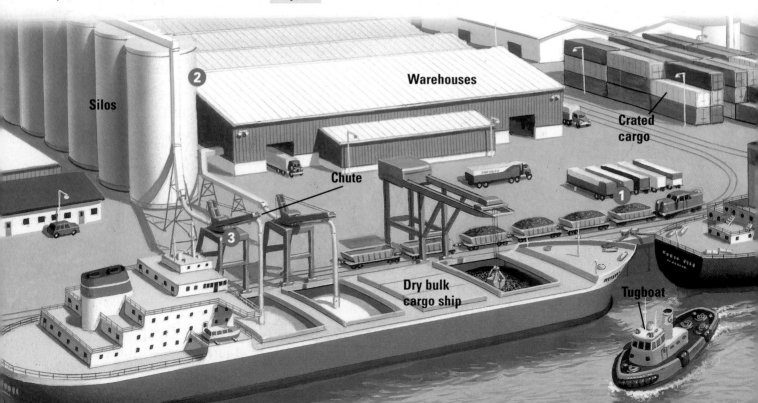

Silos

② Warehouses

Crated cargo

Chute

③

Dry bulk cargo ship

Tugboat

①

A Fast-Growing Region

The mild climates and growing economies of the Southeast and Gulf states attract thousands of new residents each year. Much of the nation's population growth is taking place there and in other states that make up an area called the Sun Belt. The **Sun Belt** is a wide area in the southern part of the United States that has a mild climate all year. It stretches from Virginia in the east to California in the west.

Among the many people moving to the Sun Belt are retired people, or people who no longer hold paid jobs. Many of them have moved to the Southeast and Gulf states, especially Florida. Today, almost one of every five people living in Florida moved there after retiring.

As the Southeast and Gulf region's population has grown and changed, so has its economy. Because everyone who moves to the region needs a home, many people work in construction and

real estate industries. To help meet the other needs of a growing population, many people have jobs in health care, banking, and other service industries.

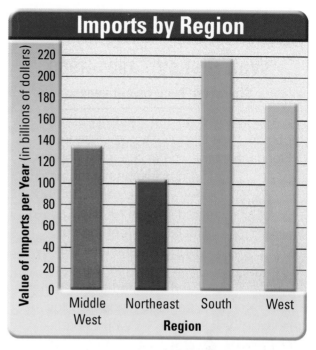

Imports by Region

Value of Imports per Year (in billions of dollars)

Region: Middle West, Northeast, South, West

Analyze Graphs The South region imports more goods than any other region in the United States.

❖ How much more does the South region import per year than the Northeast region?

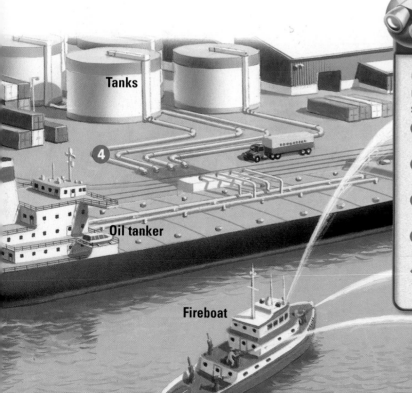

Tanks

4

Oil tanker

Fireboat

A CLOSER LOOK
A Port

Cargo from all over the world is loaded and unloaded in port cities in the Southeast and Gulf states.

1. Trains and trucks carry goods to and from the port docks.
2. Goods are stored in warehouses, tanks, and silos on the docks.
3. Chutes load or unload grains, sugar, coal, and other dry bulk cargo.
4. Tankers and other ships are filled with such liquids as oil and chemicals.

❖ What kinds of goods are shipped in dry bulk cargo ships?

As in other regions of the United States, more people in the Southeast and Gulf states now work in service industries than in any other kind of industry.

The fastest-growing industry in the region today is tourism. Florida alone attracts more than 50 million tourists each year. Some tourists to the Southeast and Gulf states visit the region's swamps. **Swamps** are low, wet areas where trees and bushes grow. The largest swamps in the United States include the Okefenokee (oh•kuh•fuh•NOH•kee) Swamp, in Georgia and Florida, and the Big Cypress Swamp, also in Florida. Another large area of low, wet land, called the Everglades, covers much of southern Florida. Founded in 1947, Everglades National Park was the first national park in the United States started for the purpose of preserving wildlife.

Golf is a popular sport for tourists and retired people alike in Florida.

Atlanta

GEORGIA

Nearly 5 million people live in the Sun Belt city of Atlanta and its metropolitan area. Because of urban sprawl, Atlanta workers have the longest commute in the nation.

High-tech, communication, and transportation industries in the region have developed rapidly, too. Florida is a leader in film and television production, and one of the largest cable television networks in the world is based in Atlanta, Georgia. Atlanta, with the world's busiest airport, is also a hub city.

Elsewhere in the region, thousands of researchers, engineers, and computer scientists work in the space industry. In fact, Huntsville, Alabama, is known as Rocket City. Workers in Huntsville build most of the nation's space rockets. All United States space shuttles are tested and launched from the Kennedy Space Center in Florida.

REVIEW How has the region's mild climate helped the Southeast and Gulf states grow?

LESSON 2 REVIEW

 COMPARE AND CONTRAST   How does the economy of the Southeast and Gulf region today compare with its economy in the past?

1 **BIG IDEA**   How have the resources and location of the Southeast and Gulf states helped the region grow?

2 **VOCABULARY**   Use the terms **import** and **export** to explain **international trade**.

3 **GEOGRAPHY**   Where is the Sun Belt?

4 **ECONOMICS**   How has the large number of people moving into the region helped the economy of the Southeast and Gulf states?

5 **CRITICAL THINKING—Evaluate**   In your opinion, has growth been good or bad for the Southeast and Gulf states? Explain.

 PERFORMANCE—Make a Map
Draw a map of the Southeast and Gulf states. Label all the states and at least ten places named in this lesson. Use your map to explain why those places have grown quickly.

Compare Maps with Different Scales

▶ WHY IT MATTERS

Have you ever helped your family plan a trip? You could have used a map and its scale to find out how far you had to travel. A map scale compares a distance on a map with a distance in the real world.

Map scales are necessary because no map is as large as the part of Earth it shows. Map scales are determined by the size of the land area to be shown compared to the size of the map. This means that different maps are drawn to different scales. Knowing about map scales can help you choose the best map for gathering certain information.

▶ WHAT YOU NEED TO KNOW

Suppose you wanted to know how far it is from Natchez to Biloxi, Mississippi. Using a ruler and a map scale, you can find the real distance in miles or kilometers between any two places on a map.

Look at the maps of Mississippi on these pages. Find the map scale on Map A. Use a ruler to measure the exact length of the scale bar. You can see that 1 inch stands for 80 miles (129 km). Now use your ruler to measure the number of inches from Natchez to Biloxi on Map A. Because it measures about $2\frac{1}{4}$ inches, the

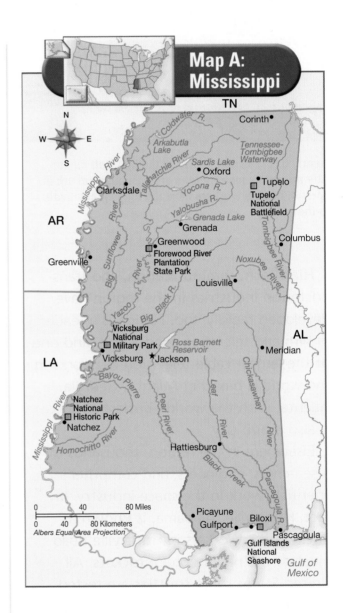

Map A: Mississippi

distance between the two cities is about 180 miles (about 290 km).

If you do not have a ruler, you can also use a strip of paper to measure distances on a map. Place the paper below the map scale. With a pencil, mark the distances in either miles or kilometers. Move the strip of paper to the left and keep marking equal distances. Then write the correct number of miles or kilometers next to each mark. To measure distances in miles, your strip of paper for Map A should look something like this:

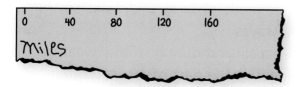

On Map B, you see that 1 inch stands for 120 miles (193 km). The distance between Natchez and Biloxi on Map B is about $1\frac{1}{2}$ inches—180 miles or about 290 kilometers.

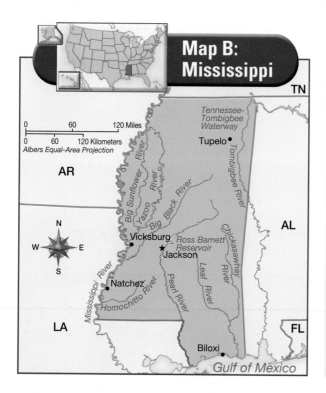

The scale used for a map depends on the amount of information to be shown. Map A is drawn to a smaller scale, so it shows many more details about Mississippi than Map B can. Map B would be very crowded if it showed all the same information as Map A.

▶ PRACTICE THE SKILL

Use Map A and Map B to answer these questions.

1 About how many miles separate Gulfport and Tupelo? How many kilometers?

2 Which map would you use to find the distance between Sardis Lake and Grenada Lake?

3 What information is shown on Map A that is not shown on Map B?

4 Which map would you take with you on vacation to Mississippi? Why?

▶ APPLY WHAT YOU LEARNED

Look through your textbook to find two different maps that show the same state or region. Compare the scales on the two maps. Then measure the distance between any two places shown on both maps. Is the distance the same? What kinds of things are shown on one map but not on the other? Why is it useful to draw maps to two different scales? Share your findings with the class.

Practice your map and globe skills with the **GeoSkills CD-ROM**.

3

Focus Skill

COMPARE AND CONTRAST

As you read, compare and contrast the special challenges faced by people who live on islands.

BIG IDEA

Learn about life on islands that lie off the coasts of the Southeast and Gulf states.

VOCABULARY

**barrier island
mainland
territory
commonwealth
tropics**

Islands and People

Hundreds of islands lie along the Atlantic and Gulf Coasts of the southeastern United States. Each of those islands is different. Yet the people who live there face many of the same challenges.

Barrier Islands

Barrier islands line much of the Atlantic and Gulf Coasts of the Southeast and Gulf region. **Barrier islands** are low, narrow islands near a coast. They are made of sand, shells, and soil dropped by rivers or ocean waves.

Barrier islands protect the mainland during stormy weather. The **mainland** is the continent or the part of a continent nearest to an island. Barrier islands help block ocean winds and pounding waves from reaching the mainland. This is especially important during hurricanes.

While barrier islands have many similarities, they can be different in many ways. Some barrier islands are wildlife refuges. For example, part of Dauphin Island, Alabama, is set aside as an Audubon Bird Sanctuary. Many, such as Hilton Head,

Dauphin Island is a small barrier island off of Alabama's Gulf Coast in Mobile Bay.

LOCATE IT

ALABAMA

Dauphin Island

This Gullah woman is making a basket out of sweetgrass, using a technique passed down by her African ancestors. The Gullah have been making baskets this way for more than 300 years.

South Carolina, are popular vacation spots, too. Some barrier islands have large cities on them, such as Daytona Beach and Miami Beach in Florida.

In the past, some barrier islands were isolated, or cut off, from the mainland. People who lived on them sometimes developed their own unique cultures. For example, descendants of enslaved African Americans, known as the Gullah (GUH•luh) people, live on several islands off the coasts of South Carolina and

Georgia. They developed their own language, music, foods, and arts. Nearly 6,000 African words have been identified in the Gullah language.

Have you ever watched a space shuttle launch on television? If you have, you have seen the John F. Kennedy Space Center. The center lies along the Atlantic Coast of Florida, on Cape Canaveral and Merritt Island. This barrier island lies between the mainland and Cape Canaveral.

REVIEW How do the barrier islands protect the mainland in the Southeast and Gulf region?

COMPARE AND CONTRAST

· GEOGRAPHY ·

John F. Kennedy Space Center

Understanding Human Systems

All of our nation's space shuttles are tested, repaired, and launched into space from the John F. Kennedy Space Center, located on Florida's Cape Canaveral and Merritt Island. The National Aeronautics and Space Administration, or NASA, chose this coastal site because its surrounding waters provide the isolation needed for dangerous space launches.

The space shuttle *Discovery* lifts off from the John F. Kennedy Space Center.

Map labels:

95
1
Canaveral National Seashore
ATLANTIC OCEAN
Indian River
Shuttle Landing Facility
Titusville
JOHN F. KENNEDY SPACE CENTER
Vehicle Assembly Building
Shuttle Launch Complex
Titan IV Complex
CAPE CANAVERAL AIR STATION
U.S. Astronaut Hall of Fame
405
Spaceport U.S.A.
407
3
Cape Canaveral
Merritt Island
Banana R.
401
Space and Missile Museum
520
528
Cocoa
Cape Canaveral
Merritt Island
95
0 4 8 Miles
0 4 8 Kilometers
1
PATRICK AIR FORCE BASE
N W E S

The Florida Keys

Islands of another kind rise from the ocean waters at the tip of the Florida peninsula. They are the Florida Keys, a chain of small islands that stretches about 150 miles (241 km) along the north side of the Straits of Florida. These straits connect the Atlantic Ocean and the Gulf of Mexico.

The Florida Keys are made of layers of coral and limestone that have built up over time. Lying near the islands are several coral reefs. In the past, many ships sank after hitting the reefs. People still recover goods from those ships—some of which sank more than 400 years ago.

Key Largo is the largest island in the Florida Keys, but Key West is the largest city. The city of Key West lies about 100 miles (160 km) southwest of the mainland, on the island of Key West. Except for cities in Hawaii, Key West is the southernmost city in the United States. Only about 25,000 people live in Key West, but the island is crowded. Key West is only 4 miles (6 km) long and about 1 mile (less than 2 km) wide. Space is such a problem that some buildings on the island now reach the water's edge.

GEOGRAPHY THEME

Location The Florida Keys stretch southwest from the Florida peninsula. More than 600 kinds of fish live in the coral reefs around the Florida Keys.

❓ What body of water lies north of the Florida Keys?

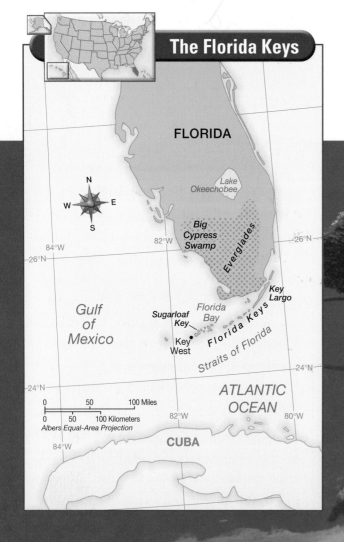

The Florida Keys

FLORIDA

Lake Okeechobee

Big Cypress Swamp

Everglades

Gulf of Mexico

Key Largo

Florida Bay

Sugarloaf Key

Florida Keys

Key West

Straits of Florida

84°W 82°W 26°N 24°N 82°W 80°W

0   50   100 Miles
0   50   100 Kilometers
Albers Equal-Area Projection

ATLANTIC OCEAN

CUBA

The Overseas Highway is now part of U.S. Highway 1. Using this highway, people can drive from Key West all the way to Maine.

Some people in the Florida Keys earn their living by catching fish and shrimp. However, most people earn their living from tourism. Thousands of people visit the Keys every year, especially in the winter months. Tourism helps the islands' economy, but it makes crowding there worse. Crowding adds to the pollution, harming nearby coral reefs. Many reefs are now protected in parks, such as the Florida Keys National Maritime Sanctuary.

REVIEW What is the largest city in the Florida Keys?

Links to the Mainland

About 100 years ago, the only way to reach the Florida Keys and most of the barrier islands in the Southeast and Gulf region was by boat. People in Key West had closer ties with the island nation of Cuba than they did with the United States. After all, Cuba is located just 90 miles (145 km) to the south.

In the early 1900s, people built bridges and roads to connect some islands with the mainland. In 1912 a business leader named Henry Flagler built a railroad over several concrete bridges from Miami to Key West. Using the railroad, thousands of tourists could reach the Keys. It also made trade between Key West and the mainland easier.

In 1935 Flagler's link to the mainland was destroyed in one day when a powerful hurricane hit the Florida Keys. But just three years later, a new link connected the islands to the mainland. That link was the Overseas Highway. It was, and still is, the longest road in the world to run partly over water. The highway extends more than 100 miles (160 km) and has 42 bridges. The longest bridge stretches 7 miles (11 km)!

Getting enough fresh water, food, and electricity to most islands is another challenge. Today a 130-mile (209-km) pipeline carries about 15 million gallons (57 million L) of fresh water from the Florida mainland to Key West every day! Much of the food that people in the Keys eat must be brought from the mainland, too. Because water and food must be shipped in, these items often cost much more on the islands than they cost on the mainland. The electricity that most people in the islands use reaches them from the mainland through undersea cables.

REVIEW How did Henry Flagler improve travel between the mainland and the Florida Keys?

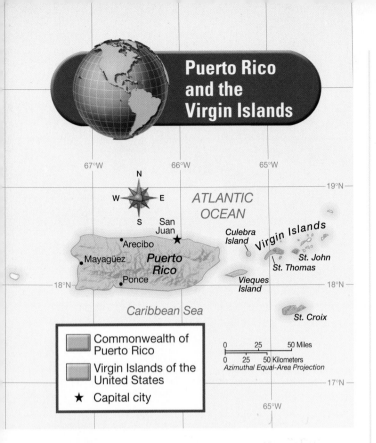

Puerto Rico and the Virgin Islands

Location The Atlantic Ocean and Caribbean Sea surround Puerto Rico and the Virgin Islands.

◆ Which city in Puerto Rico lies nearest to 66°W?

Puerto Rico

Other islands of the Southeast and Gulf region lie much farther from the mainland than Key West does. One of these islands is Puerto Rico, which means "Rich Port" in Spanish. It lies about 1,000 miles (1,609 km) southeast of Miami, Florida. Puerto Rico is crowded with nearly 4 million people. San Juan (sahn HWAHN) is Puerto Rico's capital and largest city.

Founded in 1521, San Juan is now a busy, modern port city.

Puerto Rico is made up of the peaks of underwater mountain ranges. Unlike flat barrier and coral islands, Puerto Rico has a variety of landscapes. Mountains, valleys, beaches, swamps, and rain forests are all found on Puerto Rico. Along its coast lies a wide, fertile plain. Sugarcane, coffee, and bananas thrive on farms dotting the plain.

In 1898, after a war between Spain and the United States, Puerto Rico became a territory (TAIR•uh•tohr•ee) of the United States. A **territory** is a place owned and governed by a country. Later, the people of Puerto Rico became citizens of the United States.

In 1952 Puerto Rico became a commonwealth of the United States. A **commonwealth** is a territory that governs itself. As a commonwealth, Puerto Rico has close ties to the United States, but it has its own government. People who live in Puerto Rico do not have voting representatives in the national government. They cannot vote for President, either.

REVIEW How is Puerto Rico's geography different from that of barrier and coral islands?

The Virgin Islands

The Virgin Islands of the United States, or U.S. Virgin Islands, lie about 60 miles (97 km) east of Puerto Rico. Like Puerto Rico, these islands are the peaks of ancient mountains.

About 50 islands make up the U.S. Virgin Islands. The three largest are St. Croix (saynt KROY), St. Thomas, and St. John. However, all the islands are small. Puerto Rico is about 17 times larger than all the U.S. Virgin Islands combined.

The United States bought its Virgin Islands from Denmark in 1917. Since that time, the islands have been a United States territory. Like Puerto Ricans, the people of the U.S. Virgin Islands are citizens of the United States.

The Virgin Islands and Puerto Rico are all located in the **tropics**, a band of warm climate that circles Earth near the equator. In this location, the islands enjoy year-round warm weather. This pleasant climate, combined with beautiful beaches,

Many tourists and residents in the U.S. Virgin Islands shop for fruits, nuts, baskets, wood carvings, and other craft products in outdoor markets.

makes tourism the major industry on the islands.

About 100,000 people live on the tiny U.S. Virgin Islands. There is not enough fresh water on the islands to meet the needs of all the people who live or visit there. As on other islands, most fresh water and food are imported.

REVIEW Why must the Virgin Islands import fresh water?

LESSON 3 REVIEW

COMPARE AND CONTRAST How do the rights of citizens in Puerto Rico differ from those of other United States citizens?

1 BIG IDEA How do islands affect the lives of the people living on them?

2 VOCABULARY Write one or two sentences using the terms **barrier island** and **mainland** to describe the coasts of the Southeast and Gulf states.

3 CIVICS AND GOVERNMENT Which island in the Southeast and Gulf region is a commonwealth? Which island group is a territory?

4 CRITICAL THINKING—Evaluate What would you like most about living on an island? What would you like least?

PERFORMANCE—Create a Travelogue Imagine you have visited one of the islands off the coasts of the Southeast and Gulf states. Create a travelogue, or a lecture, about your travels there, describing some of the unusual features. Then deliver your lecture to the class. Use pictures or photos of the places you describe.

COMPARE AND CONTRAST

As you read, compare and contrast the challenges faced by people who live in coastal regions around the world.

BIG IDEA

Coastal regions around the world are both alike and different.

VOCABULARY

monsoon
cyclone
legend

Coastal Regions Around the World

Like the Southeast and Gulf states, many places in the world border the sea. In fact, some nations are completely surrounded by water. People in coastal regions often use their resources in similar ways. They farm on coastal plains and use the ocean for fishing, trade, and transportation. People who live in coastal regions in every part of the world also face many of the same challenges.

Islands of India

Like the United States, India is a large country with many different physical features. Within its borders are snow-capped mountains, deep valleys, fertile plains, vast deserts, and thick rain forests. Mostly surrounded by water, India also has large coastal regions lined with islands.

Many people on the Lakshadweep Islands, off the coast of India, live in small cottages covered with palm leaves. When it is hot, they lift the palm leaves off the walls to let in the ocean breezes.

LOCATE IT

INDIA

Lakshadweep Islands

Monsoons in India can cause great hardship. These villagers were among 5 million affected by a monsoon in 1999.

One special group of islands off the coast of India is the Lakshadweep (luhk•SHAD•weep) Islands. They lie in the Arabian Sea about 185 miles (298 km) off the southwestern coast of mainland India. All the Lakshadweep Islands are small, and people live on only ten of them. In their language, *Lakshadweep* means "Hundred Thousand Islands."

Like many islands around the world, the Lakshadweep Islands can experience strong storms. From November to April in India, seasonal winds called **monsoons** blow dry air from the north. During this dry season, much of coastal India suffers from scorching heat and lack of water. With the hot summers, however, monsoons reverse direction and blow moist air and rainstorms from the Indian Ocean.

Many farmers in India depend on the monsoon rains to water their crops. But the heavy rains can cause terrible damage, too. Crops, homes, and even entire communities can be wiped out by severe flooding. During the summer monsoons, cyclones (SY•klohnz) may cause even worse flooding and destruction in India's coastal areas.

A **cyclone** is an intense storm with strong winds and heavy rains. The hurricanes that sometimes strike the coastal regions of the south-eastern United States are examples of cyclones.

As on some islands in the Southeast and Gulf states, life on the Lakshadweep Islands is often different from life on the mainland.

Fishers on India's islands often use nets to catch shark, perch, tuna, shrimp, stingrays, and eels in the Arabian Sea.

In the past, Lakshadweep Island communities took care of their own needs, growing and making almost everything they used. People there rarely had contact with outsiders. Even today, farmers on the islands grow only one cash crop—coconuts. Fishing is the other major source of income for islanders. Recently, outsiders have begun to visit the remote Lakshadweep Islands. However, tourism has not become a major industry there.

REVIEW **What kinds of storms hit India's coastal regions?**

A Brazilian Port City

Like the United States and India, the nation of Brazil is one of the largest countries in the world. In both size and population, Brazil is the largest country in South America. It also has the longest coastline on the continent. The Atlantic Coast of Brazil is about 4,600 miles (7,400 km) long. Four out of five Brazilians live within 200 miles (322 km) of the Atlantic Coast.

Like the Southeast and Gulf states, Brazil has many busy ports along its coast. The city of Rio de Janeiro (REE•oh day zhuh•NER•oh) in southeastern Brazil is one such port city. Rio de Janeiro lies along the deep harbor of Guanabara (gwah•nuh•BAR•uh) Bay. Explorers from the European nation of Portugal claimed the area in 1502. The first colonists arrived in the 1520s.

Since its founding, Rio de Janeiro has been a busy port city, shipping Brazilian goods all over the world. Many ships that leave Rio de Janeiro's docks are loaded with agricultural products, such as coffee, bananas, sugarcane, and nuts. Brazil also exports timber and other raw materials, such as diamonds, gold, iron, and tin. The mountains along Brazil's coast have rich deposits of these minerals.

Brazil is one of the United States' largest trading partners. From ports such as Rio de Janeiro, Brazil exports about $11 billion in goods to the United States each year. In return, the United States exports about $25 billion in goods to Brazil. Bananas are among Brazil's biggest exports.

Sugarloaf Mountain towers over Rio de Janeiro.

LOCATE IT

BRAZIL

Rio de Janeiro

Brazil exports many manufactured products, too. Factories in Brazil produce high-tech equipment, textiles, rubber, processed foods, and chemicals. Most of these products are shipped to other countries from Rio de Janeiro. Ships from other countries arrive in Rio de Janeiro, loaded with imports such as oil, machinery, coal, and food.

Rio de Janeiro is more than just a busy port. It is Brazil's second-largest city, and many people think it is the country's most exciting city. Rio de Janeiro's beaches are always crowded. Apartment buildings, hotels, and restaurants line the beaches. Each year millions of Brazilians and tourists visit the city for Carnival. During this four-day celebration, people in Rio de Janeiro throw an enormous festival, with parades and parties.

Like many port cities in the United States, Rio de Janeiro faces many challenges today. Because Rio de Janeiro is surrounded by mountains and crowded with more than 11 million people, thousands of cars, and hundreds of factories, its air is often polluted. However, Brazil's government is trying to protect its coastal environment. Rio de Janeiro is one of the few cities in the world that has a rain forest national park within its city limits. The Tijuca (tee•ZHOO•kuh) Forest is the largest urban forest in the world.

REVIEW Why is Rio de Janeiro's location good for a port? COMPARE AND CONTRAST

The Coastal Nation of Greece

Greece is a small country—about the size of Alabama. Yet its coastline is one of the longest in the world. Most of Greece lies on a peninsula that juts out from southern Europe into the Mediterranean (med•uh•ter•RAY•nee•uhn) Sea. The sea's waters cut deeply into the coast, so no place in Greece is more than 50 miles (80 km) from the coast.

The Olympic Games

Every four years, nations all over the world compete in the Olympic Games. The first such games took place in Greece more than 2,700 years ago. The modern Olympic Games began in Athens, Greece, in 1896. The games have been a common celebration of heritage for countries around the world ever since. The lighting of the Olympic torch officially opens the games.

About 2,000 islands dot the waters surrounding the Greek mainland. Together, the islands make up nearly one-fifth of the nation's area. The largest island, Crete (KREET), is almost as large as Puerto Rico.

Like the Southeast and Gulf states, Greece has warm summers and mild winters. However, the land in Greece is not very fertile. Most of the mainland and islands are rocky and mountainous, making farming difficult. Even so, Greeks have been raising olives, wheat, grapes, and citrus fruits for thousands of years.

More Greeks make their living from the sea than from the land. Greek ships have been traveling the Mediterranean Sea for 4,000 years. Many Greek legends describe heroes making sea voyages. A **legend** is a story that has come down from the past. Parts of the story may or may not be true.

The sea continues to provide Greeks with fish, transportation, and trade routes today. Greece has one of the largest shipping fleets in the world, and shipping is one of the country's most important industries.

As it is in coastal areas in the Southeast and Gulf states, tourism is the fastest-growing industry in Greece. Millions of tourists travel to the Greek islands to enjoy the beautiful beaches and clear blue waters. Others visit the many historical sites in Athens, the capital of Greece and

Because of lack of land, buildings on many Greek islands such as Santorini are built close together up the sides of rocky cliffs.

LOCATE IT

GREECE

Santorini

A Trireme

Analyze Primary Sources

The Greeks invented a ship called a trireme (TRY•reem) about 2,650 years ago. This picture of a trireme appears on a piece of ancient Greek pottery.

1 Triremes had large square sails made of canvas.

2 Lines of about 170 rowers sat in three rows at the bottom of the ship.

3 In later years, the pointed beak of the prow, or front of the ship, was used to ram enemy ships.

❖ Why do you think the boat used both a sail and rowers?

its largest city. About four out of every ten people in Greece now live in the coastal city of Athens.

Like many countries, Greece is working to protect its coastal regions. Years of overfishing have hurt Greece's fishing resources. Recently, the Greek government passed laws to limit fishing. Greece is also working to protect its coastal plants and animals. Several Greek islands now have wildlife refuges, including one for endangered loggerhead sea turtles.

REVIEW What major industries in Greece depend on the sea?

LESSON 4
REVIEW

COMPARE AND CONTRAST How do India, Brazil, and Greece compare in size?

1 **BIG IDEA** How are the coastal regions discussed in this lesson similar to the coastal regions of the Southeast and Gulf states?

2 **VOCABULARY** Use the terms **monsoon** and **cyclone** to describe India's coastal climate.

3 **ECONOMICS** How do people around the world use coastal resources to earn a living?

4 **CULTURE** How do legends help tell the history of the Greeks?

5 **CRITICAL THINKING—Evaluate** Why do you think much of the world's population lives near coastal regions?

PERFORMANCE—Plan a Route Use a map of the world to plan a sea voyage. Choose a site in the Southeast and Gulf states to begin your journey. Then find each of the coastal regions discussed in this lesson. Now plan your sailing route to visit them all, naming the major bodies of water you would cross. Share your route with a classmate. How do your voyages compare?

6 Review and Test Preparation

Summary Time Line
1500   1600

1539
Hernando de Soto begins
to explore the region

Focus Skill — Compare and Contrast

Copy the following graphic organizer onto a separate sheet of
paper. Use the information you have learned to compare and
contrast the Southeast states and Gulf states.

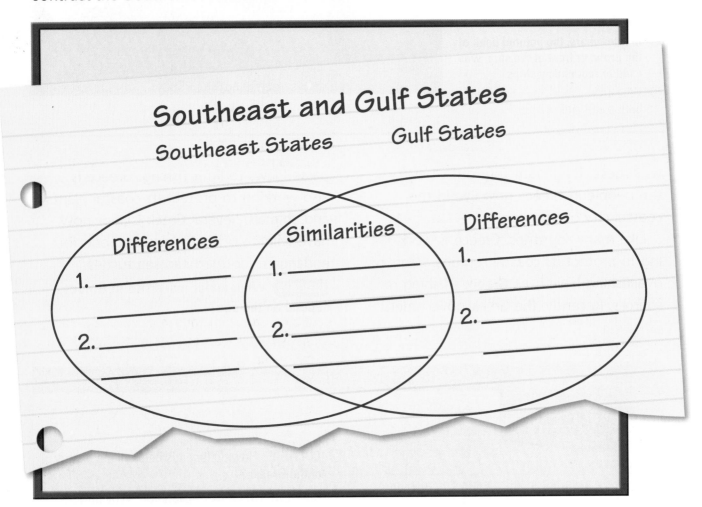

Southeast and Gulf States

Southeast States   Gulf States

Differences   Similarities   Differences

1. _____   1. _____   1. _____

2. _____   2. _____   2. _____

THINK WRITE

Write a Business Plan   If you owned
land in the Southeast and Gulf states, what
business would you open on it? Write a plan
describing the crop, product, or service you
would provide. Explain why this region would
be a good place for your business.

Describe a Trip   Which of the Southeast
and Gulf states would you most like to visit?
Write a short explanation of why that state is
interesting to you. Describe a trip you would
take to that state. Tell about the state's
location and its physical features.

1861
Civil War begins

1912
Henry Flagler builds
a railroad from
Miami to Key West

1947
Everglades National
Park founded in
Florida

1952
Puerto Rico becomes
a commonwealth of
the United States

USE THE TIME LINE

1. When did the Civil War begin?

2. Which event in Florida history happened first, the founding of Everglades National Park or the building of a railroad from Miami to Key West?

USE VOCABULARY

For each sentence below, write C if it is correct. If it is not, change the underlined word or words to correctly complete the sentence.

3. A growing season is the time when the <u>weather</u> is warm enough for plants to grow.

4. Cash crops in the Southeast and Gulf states include <u>granite and iron</u>.

5. A soft mixture of ground-up <u>wood chips and chemicals</u> that is used to make paper is called pulp.

6. <u>The U.S. Virgin Islands are</u> a commonwealth of the United States.

7. The Sun Belt can be described as a wide area in the <u>northern</u> part of the United States that has a mild climate all year.

RECALL FACTS

Answer these questions.

8. Why are farmers in the Southeast and Gulf states able to grow many kinds of crops?

9. What caused the Southern states and Northern states to disagree during the mid-1800s?

10. How are the Florida Keys different from barrier islands?

Write the letter of the best choice.

11. The states that seceded during the Civil War formed the—
    A Union.
    B Emancipation Proclamation.
    C Confederacy.
    D Commonwealth.

12. Which of the following is **not** an industry that uses natural resources found in the Southeast and Gulf states?
    F agriculture
    G television production
    H food processing
    J iron and steel production

THINK CRITICALLY

13. What do you think are the advantages and disadvantages of rapid growth in the Southeast and Gulf region?

14. Why do you think tourism is an important industry in the Southeast and Gulf states and in many coastal regions all over the world?

APPLY SKILLS

Compare Maps with Different Scales

MAP AND GLOBE SKILLS

Use the maps on pages 212 and 213 to answer these questions.

15. About how many miles is it from Gulfport to Greenville? Which map did you use? Why?

16. About how far is it from Jackson to Tupelo? Which map did you use? Why?

BIG BEND NATIONAL PARK

The walls of Mariscal Canyon tower more than 1,400 feet (427 m) over these rafters on the Rio Grande. The canyon stretches 6 miles (about 10 km) through Big Bend National Park in Texas. Activities such as boating, hiking, riding, and camping attract more than 300,000 visitors a year to the park.

LOCATE IT

TEXAS

Big Bend
National Park

South Central States

" A river seems a magic thing.
A magic, moving, living part of
the very Earth itself. "

—Laura Gilpin
The Rio Grande, 1949

 Categorize

To **categorize** information is to classify, or to arrange, the data into similar groups so that it is easier to understand and compare.

As you read this chapter, categorize information about the South Central states.

• **Classify what you read into the following categories: geography, history, economy, and culture.**

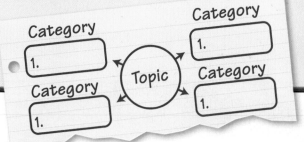

1

Settling the South Central Region

Focus Skill CATEGORIZE

As you read, categorize the physical features of the South Central region.

BIG IDEA

The South Central region is a place of great variety.

VOCABULARY

inlet
expedition
bayou
land grant

FAST FACT

Arkansas is the only state to pass a law about how to pronounce its name. In 1881 the state's government ruled that the final *s* should be silent.

About 500 years ago, Spanish explorers reached what is now the South Central region of the United States. They were the first Europeans to describe its great variety of physical features. Over time, people from all over the world settled in the area. They made their homes in what became the states of Arkansas, Louisiana, Oklahoma, and Texas. Together, these states are the South Central states.

A Region of Variety

The South Central region has varying climates and land-forms. The region's lowest and wettest lands lie along the Gulf of Mexico. These lowlands are part of the Coastal Plain. They cover all of Louisiana, eastern Texas, and southern Arkansas.

Along the Gulf Coast are barrier islands, broad beaches, marshes, and shallow inlets. An **inlet** is a narrow strip of water leading into the land from a larger body of water. A few miles inland from the coast are many large lakes and dense pine and hardwood forests.

The Ozark Plateau covers 50,000 square miles (129,500 sq km) of northwest Arkansas and neighboring states.

LOCATE IT

Ozark Plateau
MISSOURI
ARKANSAS

To reach underground water, roots of some mesquite (muh•SKEET) bushes (left) in western Texas extend 60 feet (18 m) below the desert. Horned lizards (above) that live in the desert get most of their water from insects and plants they eat.

Farther inland, parts of the Central Plains reach into northern Arkansas, eastern Oklahoma, and central Texas. Rolling hills and forests run through much of this part of the region, especially in a high area called the Ozark Plateau. There the low Boston Mountains rise sharply above the Arkansas River. To the south of the river are the Ouachita (WAH•shuh•taw) Mountains.

West of the Central Plains, in western Oklahoma and northwestern Texas, the land is very flat, and the climate is drier. This area of the South Central region is part of the Great Plains. As these grass-covered plains stretch west across the region, the elevation of the land gradually rises.

The highest and driest part of the South Central region is in western Texas. Here small ranges of the Rocky Mountains surround the Chihuahuan (chee•WAH•wahn) Desert. Winters in the desert are cool, while summers are extremely hot. The region's highest point, Guadalupe (gwah•dah•LOO•pay) Peak, is here, towering 8,749 feet (2,667 m) above the desert land.

REVIEW What is the highest point of the South Central region? **CATEGORIZE**

Claiming the Land

The Spanish were the first Europeans to explore and claim parts of the South Central region. They were also the first Europeans to meet some of the Native American groups already living there.

The Natchez, Caddos (KAD•ohz), and most other Native American groups on the Coastal Plain lived by hunting and farming. On the drier lands of the Great Plains, most Indians, such as the Comanches (kuh•MAN•cheez), gathered wild plants and hunted animals.

By the late 1500s, Spain had claimed much of the southern part of the South Central region. Almost a century passed, however, before Spanish colonists from Mexico settled there. In 1682 they built their first settlement, near where El Paso, Texas, is today.

While the Spanish settled mostly in what is now Texas, the French, who had already claimed parts of present-day Canada and the Great Lakes, sent their own expeditions to the South Central region. An **expedition** is a journey into an area to learn more about it. René-Robert Cavelier (ka•vuhl•YAY), known as Sieur de La Salle (SER duh luh SAL), led one of the expeditions.

United States, 1803

- United States
- Louisiana Purchase, 1803

0   200   400 Miles

0   200 400 Kilometers
Albers Equal-Area
Projection

OREGON COUNTRY

ROCKY MOUNTAINS

LOUISIANA PURCHASE

Mississippi River

APPALACHIAN MOUNTAINS

UNITED STATES

OZARK PLATEAU

El Paso
Guadalupe Peak

Natchitoches

MEXICO (SPAIN)

Rio Grande

San Antonio

New Orleans

FLORIDA (SPAIN)

CHIHUAHUAN DESERT

Laredo

GEOGRAPHY THEME

Regions After the Louisiana Purchase, the United States was one of the largest countries in the world.

❖ How did the Louisiana Purchase affect much of the South Central region?

In 1682 La Salle and his group explored the lower Mississippi River. Near the Gulf of Mexico, the explorers entered the huge Mississippi Delta. There the river divides into smaller channels. In each channel are muddy islands and bayous (BY•ooz). A **bayou** is a slow-moving body of water.

La Salle claimed the Mississippi River valley for France. He named the region *Louisiana,* in honor of the king of France, Louis XIV. By the early 1700s the French had built several settlements there. The largest of these, New Orleans, was made the capital of Louisiana

in 1722. Located near the mouth of the Mississippi River, the city became the region's leading port.

In 1803 the United States paid France about $15 million for Louisiana. The purchase of this huge area, known as the Louisiana Purchase, doubled the size of the United States. The United States now stretched from the Mississippi River all the way to the Rocky Mountains.

REVIEW What two European countries once claimed land in the South Central region?

Becoming States

In 1812 Louisiana became the first state formed out of the Louisiana Purchase. In 1836 Arkansas became a state. The other states that now make up the South Central region—Texas and Oklahoma—joined the United States later.

In the early 1800s, Texas still belonged to Spain. Then, in 1821, Mexico won its independence from Spain, making Texas a part of Mexico. The Mexican government began offering **land grants**, or gifts of land, to people who were willing to settle in Texas.

By 1830 most of the more than 20,000 settlers in Texas were from the United States. The Mexican government worried that it would lose control of Texas to the settlers. So it passed several laws raising taxes in Texas and limiting new settlement there. Many people in Texas thought these new laws were unfair.

CAVELIER DE LA SALLE · 300TH ANNIVERSARY

CAVELIER DE LA SALLE · 300E ANNIVERSAIRE

5

CANADA

La Salle's role in North American history was honored on this Canadian postage stamp.

At first, most Texans hoped to solve their problems with the Mexican government peacefully. In 1833 Texas leader Stephen F. Austin went to Mexico to convince Mexico's leaders to change the laws. Instead, they put Austin in jail. When he returned to Texas two years later, Austin declared, "We must defend our rights, ourselves, and our country." So began the Texas fight for independence from Mexico. In 1836 the Texans defeated the Mexican army, and Texas became an independent country. Nine years later, in 1845, it joined the United States as a state.

Meanwhile, the land that is now Oklahoma was called the Indian Territory. At first, the United States government allowed only Native Americans to live there. The government made most of the Cherokees and other tribes living east of the Mississippi River leave their homes and move to the Indian Territory.

In the late 1800s, however, the government opened almost 2 million acres of the Indian Territory to settlers. On April 22, 1889, land was to be given to anyone willing to live on it for five years. The first person to reach each piece of open land could claim it.

That morning, between 50,000 and 100,000 men and women waited at the starting line. At exactly twelve o'clock the signal was given, and the rush for land was on! People raced on horses and in covered wagons. Some settlers even ran on foot to get the land they wanted.

One of the most important battles of the Texas Revolution was at the Alamo, in San Antonio.

LOCATE IT

TEXAS

San Antonio

CITIZENSHIP

DEMOCRATIC VALUES
Liberty

One of the most important battles in the Texas war for independence took place at the Alamo in San Antonio. In March 1836, about 2,000 Mexican soldiers attacked the Alamo. Defending it were fewer than 200 Texans and other volunteers. The defenders of the Alamo fought bravely, but nearly all of them were killed. During the next long year of fighting, "Remember the Alamo!" became a battle cry for the Texas army. Today the Alamo continues to have a special meaning in both Texas and United States history. To some, it stands for the high price people sometimes pay for liberty.

Analyze the Value

1. Why does the Alamo have special meaning for some Americans?

2. **Make It Relevant** In what ways do you think the Texas fight for independence was similar to the American Revolution?

Within hours, every inch of free land was taken by settlers. Over the next few years, other land rushes were held, bringing more settlers. In 1907 Oklahoma finally became a state.

REVIEW What is one reason so many people settled in Texas and Oklahoma during the 1800s?

A Variety of Cultures

Over the years, people from all over the world moved to the South Central region. They added a variety of cultures to the region, including many different traditions and languages.

French colonists founded the city of New Orleans in 1718. Today it is the largest city in Louisiana, with almost 500,000 residents. The different styles of buildings in the city show a blend of cultures.

LOCATE IT

LOUISIANA

New Orleans

Native Americans were the first people to live in the region, and thousands still live there today. After California, Oklahoma has the largest Native American population in the United States. Many Native Americans in the South Central region honor their cultures by teaching their children Indian languages and by celebrating events with traditional dance, music, and art.

People from Spain and Mexico also added much to the region's cultural heritage, especially in Texas. Many people living there today have Hispanic ancestors, and they speak Spanish as well as English. Cinco de Mayo (SEENG•koh day MAH•yoh), the fifth of May, is an important holiday for Mexican Americans. It honors a battle in 1862 in which Mexican soldiers defeated an invading French army.

A special way of life has also grown up along the bayous of Louisiana. This is partly due to two groups who settled there, the Creoles (KREE•ohlz) and the Cajuns (KAY•juhnz). The Creoles' ancestors were French and Spanish settlers. The Cajuns' ancestors were French colonists who came from Canada.

These two groups have given much of Louisiana its unique heritage. Today many Creoles and Cajuns speak both English and a form of French, and many places in Louisiana have French names. The Creoles and Cajuns brought Mardi Gras (MAHR•dee grah) to the region. People take part in parades during this springtime celebration.

People with English, German, Irish, Scottish, and African American ancestors have also contributed to the culture of the South Central region. These groups also have traditions that they practice today. Many people in the region celebrate June 19, or "Juneteenth," the day in 1865 when enslaved African Americans in Texas learned that they were free.

Many traditions found in the South Central region today formed when different cultures mixed together. For example, Tejano (tay•HAH•noh) music, popular in Texas, blends Spanish and Mexican guitars and singing with accordion music brought by German and Polish settlers. A popular stew in the Mississippi Delta, called gumbo, mixes ingredients from French, Spanish, and African cultures.

REVIEW What two groups have given Louisiana much of its unique heritage?

• **HERITAGE** •

Jazz

In the South Central region, musical traditions from several cultures combined to form a uniquely American style of music called jazz. This music blends African rhythms, spirituals, and blues with European musical styles. New Orleans, home to Louis Armstrong and other famous jazz musicians, is known as the birthplace of jazz. Many people visit the city every year to listen to the many jazz musicians who perform there.

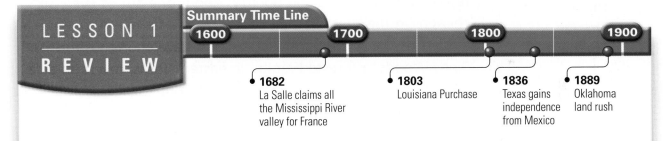

Louis Armstrong

LESSON 1
REVIEW

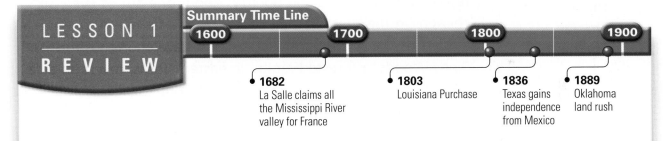

Summary Time Line

| 1600 | 1700 | 1800 | 1900 |

1682 La Salle claims all the Mississippi River valley for France

1803 Louisiana Purchase

1836 Texas gains independence from Mexico

1889 Oklahoma land rush

CATEGORIZE Make a list of the region's major physical features. Then divide the list into two categories, features that appear in the eastern part of the region and features that appear in the western part.

1 BIG IDEA In what ways is the South Central region a region of variety?

2 VOCABULARY Use the terms **inlet** and **bayou** to describe the Coastal Plain of the South Central region.

3 TIME LINE How many years after La Salle claimed the Mississippi River valley for France did the Louisiana Purchase occur?

4 GEOGRAPHY In what part of Texas is the highest point in the South Central region?

5 HISTORY Why did Louisiana and Arkansas become states before Texas?

6 CRITICAL THINKING—Synthesize Why do you think more people in the South Central region live on the Coastal Plain than farther west?

PERFORMANCE—Plan a Festival Work with a group of three or four classmates to plan a festival celebrating one of the many cultures present in the South Central region. Think about what kinds of activities, music, and food from each culture can be a part of your festival. Work together to create a poster advertising your festival. Then share your ideas and poster with the class.

2

Focus Skill

CATEGORIZE

As you read, categorize the kinds of jobs available in the South Central region and the products and services they provide.

BIG IDEA

The economy of the South Central region has changed over time.

VOCABULARY

diverse economy
petroleum
crude oil
refinery
dredge
aerospace

A Diverse Economy

Until the early 1900s, most people in the South Central region worked on farms or ranches. Then people discovered oil in the region, and drilling for that natural resource became an important industry. Today the South Central region has a **diverse economy**, or one that is based on many kinds of industries. People in the region still farm, ranch, and drill for oil. However, they also work in many other businesses, including manufacturing, shipping, and service industries.

Crops, Lumber, and Fish

Much of the South Central region has fertile soil and a long growing season. This allows farmers there to raise large crops of cotton, wheat, rice, soybeans, sugarcane, and citrus fruits. Texas produces more cotton than any other state, and Arkansas is the nation's leading rice producer. Many farmers in the region also raise hogs and poultry. About one out of every six chickens in the United States comes from a farm in Arkansas.

Parts of the South Central states also have enormous forests. Piney Woods, a forested region in eastern Texas, covers an area the size of West Virginia. Nearly half of Louisiana is covered with cypress, oak, and other trees. In Arkansas, pine, elm, and maple trees thrive on the Ozark Plateau and the state's mountainsides. Loggers in all those states harvest trees to make lumber, furniture, and paper products.

Fishing is another leading industry in the South Central states. Louisiana is the nation's largest producer of

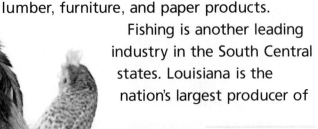

Poultry farmers in Arkansas sell more than 1 million chickens every year.

shrimp and oysters. Fishers along the Gulf of Mexico catch large amounts of crab, red snapper, and tuna. The many inlets and bayous cutting into the coast provide nearly all the nation's crawfish— the tiny, lobsterlike shellfish cooked in gumbo and other dishes.

REVIEW What are three industries that use natural resources in the South Central region? **CATEGORIZE**

Ranching

Ranching has long been a leading industry in the South Central region. At one time, however, there were no cattle in this region or anywhere else in the Americas. Spanish settlers brought cattle with them from Europe. Over time, some of those cattle wandered away and became wild. The wild cattle then spread across the grasslands of the southern Great Plains. Early settlers in the southern part of Texas rounded up these cattle and started ranches. The land there was too dry for most crops, but it was good for grazing cattle.

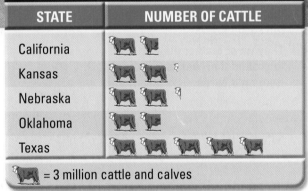

Leading Cattle-Producing States

STATE	NUMBER OF CATTLE
California	🐄🐄
Kansas	🐄🐄
Nebraska	🐄🐄
Oklahoma	🐄🐄
Texas	🐄🐄🐄🐄🐄

🐄 = 3 million cattle and calves

Analyze Graphs Each year ranchers in Texas, like the one pictured above, raise more than 14 million cattle and calves.

❖ Which two states shown on the graph raise about 5 million cattle and calves each?

In the late 1800s, cattle in Texas sold for only about $4 each. But in cities elsewhere in the country, they sold for ten times as much! For many years, there was no easy way for Texas ranchers to get their cattle to those markets. That changed when railroads reached the Great Plains.

The new railroads, however, lay far to the north of Texas, in Missouri, Kansas, and Nebraska. To reach them, the ranchers drove, or walked, their cattle from Texas to towns along the railroads. There, the cattle were loaded onto railroad cars and were shipped by train to market.

Cowboy Clothing and Equipment

Analyze Primary Sources

Cowhands wear special clothing and use special equipment when they work on cattle ranches.

1. Cowhands wear chaps to protect their legs from brush and to provide warmth in winter.

2. They use braided ropes with lassos to round up cattle.

3. The wide-brimmed hats keep the sun off their faces during long days on the range.

4. Cowhands wear boots with heels so that their feet do not slip through the stirrups.

5. They wear leather gloves to protect their hands from rope burns.

◆ Why do you think special clothing is necessary to work on cattle ranches?

Between 1867 and 1890, Texas ranchers drove about 10 million head of cattle to railroad towns. Within a few years, railroads were also built through Texas. This meant that long cattle drives were no longer necessary. Ranchers could now ship their cattle by train from the South Central region to cities all over the United States.

Today, Texas is the leading cattle-producing state in the United States. Ranching is an important industry in Oklahoma, too. Beef cattle are the largest source of ranching income in those states, but ranchers also raise other animals, such as sheep and goats.

REVIEW How did railroads help the cattle industry?

Oil!

Sometimes a single resource can influence a region's economy and growth. In the South Central region, that resource is oil, or **petroleum** (puh•TROH•lee•uhm). Over the past 100 years, oil has greatly changed the way many people earn a living there.

The region's oil-based economy began at Spindletop, an oil field near the Texas and Louisiana border. On January 10, 1901, workers at Spindletop were busy drilling for oil. Suddenly the ground began to shake. With a roar, oil shot nearly 200 feet (61 m) into the sky. People had never seen a gusher like this before. It took workers nine days to cap the well.

News of Spindletop spread quickly, and thousands moved to the region to buy land and start drilling. Wherever oil was found, cities grew nearby. Houston and other towns in Texas, such as Dallas and Galveston, grew rapidly. So did Oklahoma City and Tulsa, in Oklahoma.

Today the South Central states produce about one-third of the nation's petroleum. Much of this oil comes from offshore wells located in the waters of the Gulf of Mexico. In the state of Louisiana alone, there are about 20,000 oil wells. To remove oil from a well, workers may drill more than 1 mile (almost 2 km) underground. The petroleum pumped from the ground is called **crude oil**.

The same forces in Earth that made oil millions of years ago also created natural gas. Like oil, natural gas is a fuel resource used to supply energy. Texas and Louisiana are now the leading producers of natural gas in the United States.

Many people in this region have jobs drilling for natural gas as well as for oil. Other workers build pipelines that take both resources to other places. Still others work in refineries. A **refinery** is a factory that turns crude oil into useful products, such as gasoline and other fuels. Houston is the largest center for oil refining in the United States. Many people in the region also work in factories that manufacture products from oil, such as paint, plastic, and tires.

REVIEW **What are the two major fuel resources found in the South Central region?**

Shipping the Goods

Many people in cities along the Gulf coast of the South Central region work in shipping and trade. The nation's busiest port is the Port of South Louisiana, near the mouth of the Mississippi River. New Orleans and Baton Rouge are other busy ports upstream on the Mississippi.

Analyze Graphs Huge platforms, called rigs, make offshore oil drilling possible along the coast of the South Central region.

◈ About how much oil do the South Central states shown on the graph produce each year altogether?

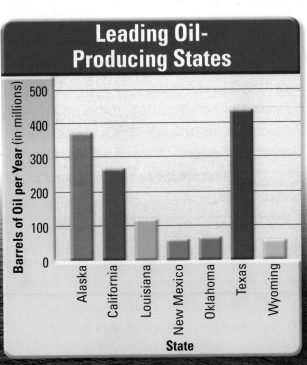

Leading Oil-Producing States

Barrels of Oil per Year (in millions)

State: Alaska, California, Louisiana, New Mexico, Oklahoma, Texas, Wyoming

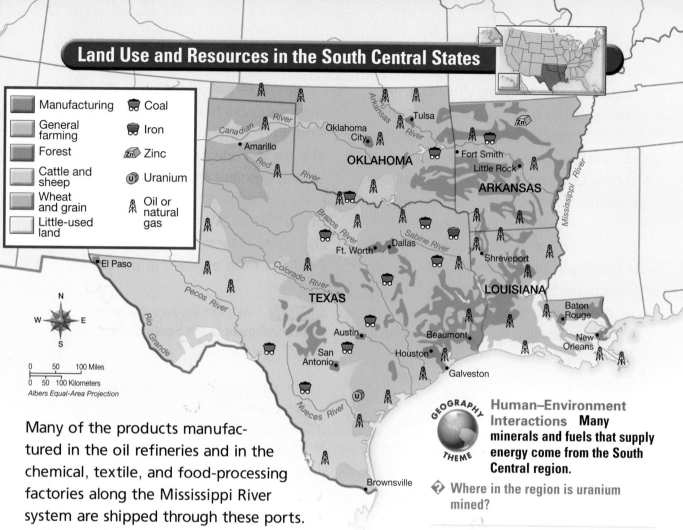

Land Use and Resources in the South Central States

Legend:
- Manufacturing
- General farming
- Forest
- Cattle and sheep
- Wheat and grain
- Little-used land
- Coal
- Iron
- Zinc
- Uranium
- Oil or natural gas

0 50 100 Miles
0 50 100 Kilometers
Albers Equal-Area Projection

GEOGRAPHY THEME

Human–Environment Interactions Many minerals and fuels that supply energy come from the South Central region.

? Where in the region is uranium mined?

Many of the products manufactured in the oil refineries and in the chemical, textile, and food-processing factories along the Mississippi River system are shipped through these ports.

Houston is the second-busiest port in the nation. A century ago, however, only small boats could sail up the shallow bayou that connected Houston to the Gulf of Mexico. To improve navigability, the city dredged the bayou. To **dredge** is to dig out the bottom and sides of a waterway to make it deeper and wider. The 57-mile (92-km) Houston Ship Channel finally opened in 1914. It links Houston to Galveston Bay and the Gulf of Mexico.

REVIEW What are the two busiest ports in the United States?

A Changing Economy

Rich land, wide rivers, petroleum, and other natural resources helped the South Central states grow. Today the region's diverse economy also includes many service and high-tech industries.

People in every state in the region work in education, health care, government, hotels, and other service industries. The largest department store chain in the United States has its headquarters in Bentonville, Arkansas. Austin, the capital of Texas, is a major high-tech center.

The Lyndon B. Johnson Space Center near Houston has made aerospace (AIR•oh•spays) an important industry in the region. The **aerospace** industry builds and tests equipment for air and space travel. Workers at the center oversee space shuttles during flight. Astronauts train at the center, too.

Tourism is a major industry throughout the South Central states. Many people visit the region to experience its different

FAST FACT

Astronaut Neil Armstrong spoke the first words from the moon to Mission Control. He said, "Houston, Tranquillity Base here. The *Eagle* has landed." The spacecraft that landed on the moon was called the *Eagle*.

Experts in Mission Control at the Johnson Space Center near Houston help control the flights of space shuttles.

cultures and to see its historical sites, such as the French Quarter in New Orleans, Louisiana, or the Alamo in San Antonio, Texas. Some visitors to Oklahoma tour the Cowboy Hall of Fame or the Cherokee Heritage Center.

Tourists also visit the region's national parks and forests. Many people travel to the Ozark National Forest in Arkansas to view the autumn colors. Others hunt for treasures in North America's only active diamond mine at Crater of Diamonds State Park in Arkansas. Thousands of people vacation at Padre Island National Seashore near Corpus Christi, Texas. This park sits on the longest barrier island in the United States.

REVIEW **From which city are our nation's space shuttles overseen?**

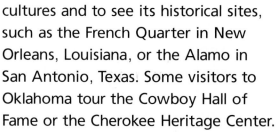

LESSON 2
REVIEW

Focus Skill

CATEGORIZE Of all the natural resources people in the South Central region use to earn a living, which ones are renewable?

1 **BIG IDEA** What factors have caused the South Central region's economy to change over the years?

2 **VOCABULARY** Use the terms **petroleum** and **crude oil** to explain what happens in a **refinery**.

3 **HISTORY** How did the Houston Ship Channel affect Houston's growth?

4 **CRITICAL THINKING—Evaluate** Why do you think it is important for the South Central states to have a diverse economy rather than to rely entirely on the oil industry?

PERFORMANCE—Make a Time Capsule Imagine that you work at Johnson Space Center and need to prepare a time capsule to send into space. What would you put in your capsule to describe living and working in the South Central region today? Make a list of items you would place in the capsule. Then share your list with the class and explain what each object represents.

3

CATEGORIZE

As you read, categorize ways in which sharing resources can cause people to both cooperate and disagree.

BIG IDEA

People in the United States and Mexico work together to protect and share the Rio Grande.

VOCABULARY

arid
irrigation
conflict
compromise
runoff

Sharing a River

The entire South Central region lies in the fast-growing Sun Belt. Its natural resources and mild climate have attracted many people and industries. More than 30 million people now live in the region—and all of them need water. While water is generally plentiful in the eastern half of the region, it becomes more scarce in the western parts, especially in the Rio Grande valley. The people who live along the Rio Grande depend on the river for their water. They work together to protect and use this resource. However, they do not always agree on the best ways to share the river.

Meeting Water Needs

The Rio Grande is the fourth-longest river in the United States. Its name is Spanish for "Large River." People in Mexico call it the Rio Bravo, or "Bold River." The Rio Grande begins its long journey in the Rocky Mountains of Colorado, where melting snow forms a small stream. From there the river grows wider as it flows 1,885 miles (3,034 km) to its mouth at the Gulf of Mexico.

Near its mouth, the Rio Grande passes through the warm, moist Coastal Plain. Upstream, however, the river cuts through canyons and high plateaus. Much of that land is **arid**, or dry. This part of the Rio Grande valley has the lowest precipitation levels in the South Central region. The area also has some of the region's highest temperatures.

Giant sprinklers help farmers grow crops in the dry climate of the upper Rio Grande valley.

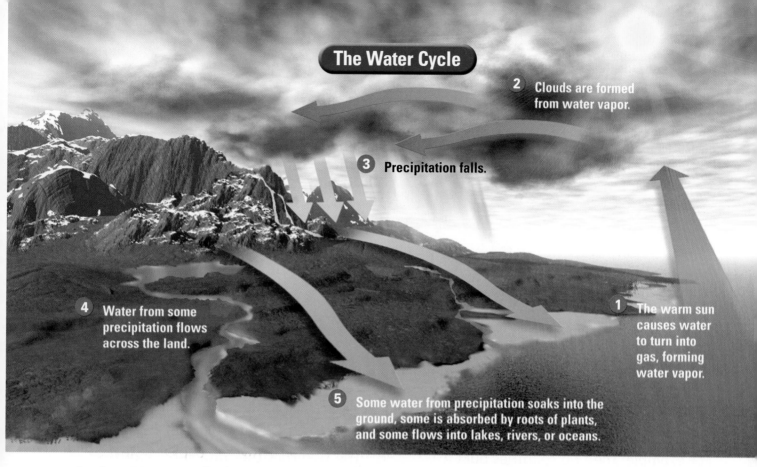

The Water Cycle

2 Clouds are formed from water vapor.

3 Precipitation falls.

4 Water from some precipitation flows across the land.

1 The warm sun causes water to turn into gas, forming water vapor.

5 Some water from precipitation soaks into the ground, some is absorbed by roots of plants, and some flows into lakes, rivers, or oceans.

Analyze Diagrams Earth's water is constantly moving from the oceans to the air to the ground and finally back to the oceans. This process is called the water cycle.

◈ In what form does water from the air return to the ground?

As in other regions, water in the Rio Grande valley has affected the area's development. "Wherever there is any water, there is a ranch," noted one settler in the valley. Today, many farmers rely on the Rio Grande for irrigation. **Irrigation** is the use of canals, ditches, or pipes to move water to dry areas. Without irrigation, farmers would not be able to grow crops in these arid lands.

Getting enough water has always been a problem in the Rio Grande valley. People in Colorado and New Mexico use so much of the river's water that by the time it reaches El Paso, Texas, its riverbed is sometimes dry. People downstream often blame those living upstream for using too much water. When the water runs out and harvests are poor, conflicts

can arise. A **conflict** is a disagreement between two or more people or groups.

To make sure there is enough water downstream, the United States government has built several dams across the Rio Grande. People, farms, and businesses can use the water stored in reservoirs behind these dams. During dry times, water can be released into the river.

The water used upstream also affects people in Mexico. The Rio Grande supplies water for more than half of all irrigated land in Mexico. To protect Mexico's use of the river, the United States has agreed that a certain amount of water must reach Mexico.

To help solve their water problems, the United States and Mexico together built additional dams on the Rio Grande.

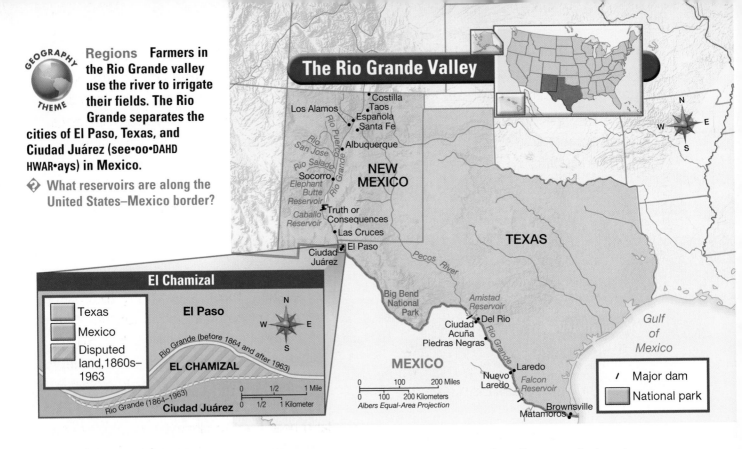

Regions Farmers in the Rio Grande valley use the river to irrigate their fields. The Rio Grande separates the cities of El Paso, Texas, and Ciudad Juárez (see•oo•DAHD HWAR•ays) in Mexico.

◈ What reservoirs are along the United States–Mexico border?

El Chamizal

- Texas
- Mexico
- Disputed land, 1860s–1963

El Paso

Rio Grande (before 1864 and after 1963)

EL CHAMIZAL

Rio Grande (1864–1963)   Ciudad Juárez

0   1/2   1 Mile
0   1/2   1 Kilometer

NEW MEXICO

Costilla
Taos
Los Alamos
Española
Santa Fe
Albuquerque
Rio San Jose
Rio Salado
Socorro
Elephant Butte Reservoir
Truth or Consequences
Caballo Reservoir
Las Cruces
Ciudad Juárez
El Paso

TEXAS

Pecos River

Big Bend National Park

Amistad Reservoir
Ciudad Acuña
Piedras Negras
Del Rio

MEXICO

Nuevo Laredo
Laredo
Falcon Reservoir

Brownsville
Matamoros

Gulf of Mexico

0   100   200 Miles
0   100   200 Kilometers
Albers Equal-Area Projection

⁄ Major dam
National park

For example, the two countries built a dam to create Falcon Reservoir, about 50 miles (80 km) downstream from Laredo, Texas. Water from this reservoir is used to irrigate citrus groves and vegetable and cotton fields on both sides of the river.

REVIEW How have people along the Rio Grande worked together to share its water?

Border Conflicts

For about 1,200 miles (1,931 km) of its long journey, the Rio Grande forms a natural border between the United States and Mexico. However, rivers sometimes change course. That happened to the Rio Grande in the 1860s. After some floods, the channel of the river moved south. Land that had been part of Mexico was now north of the Rio Grande. Mexico said it still owned the land. The United States, however, said the land had become part of the state of Texas.

The two countries disagreed about which country owned this small piece of land, called El Chamizal (chah•mee•SAHL). Because neither side was willing to give up its claim to the land, the conflict dragged on for almost 100 years. Finally, Mexico and the United States agreed to a compromise. In a **compromise**, each side in a conflict gives up some of what it wants in order to reach an agreement. In 1963, the United States agreed to give El Chamizal back to Mexico. In return, Mexico gave the United States some land that had been on the north side of the Rio Grande's original channel.

As part of the agreement, Mexico and the United States worked together to move the river's channel north. To make sure that the Rio Grande would not change course again, they lined the new riverbed with concrete. All the land south of the Rio Grande now belongs to Mexico, and all the land north of the river belongs to the United States. Today

El Chamizal is an international park shared by Mexico and the United States. To honor the peaceful settlement, the United States also built the Chamizal National Memorial in El Paso, Texas, in 1966.

REVIEW What caused Mexico and the United States to disagree over their border?

CATEGORIZE

Cooperating in Other Ways

Agreement was reached over the United States–Mexico border, but other problems remain. Sharing the Rio Grande means that the United States and Mexico must cooperate in many ways. They must work together to handle important issues on both sides of the river.

Millions of people now live in the Rio Grande valley. Many have moved to the area for jobs in the new factories that are located in cities along the Rio Grande. While economic development helped the region grow, it also increased pollution. In fact, the Rio Grande became one of North America's most polluted rivers.

Runoff from irrigation and rainwater carries pollutants from city streets, sub-urban lawns, and nearby farms into the river. **Runoff** is surface water that does not soak into the ground. Air pollution also damages the Rio Grande. When air pollution falls back to the surface of Earth in precipitation, it seeps into the soil and flows underground to the river.

Pollution affects people living on both sides of the Rio Grande, so the United States and Mexico are working together to clean up the river. Both countries have passed laws against dumping harmful wastes. Plans are underway to build new wastewater treatment plants in towns along the border. In addition, some of the land near the Rio Grande is now protected in Big Bend National Park and Amistad National Recreation Area in Texas.

The Rio Grande flows through Amistad National Recreation Area.

• GEOGRAPHY •

Amistad National Recreation Area

Understanding Environment and Society

At Amistad Reservoir, created by a dam built by the United States and Mexico, is Amistad National Recreation Area. At the park, visitors can enjoy beautiful scenery and water sports all year round. The reservoir attracts a wide variety of wildlife, including lizards, jackrabbits, wild pigs, and white-tailed deer. Native American artifacts and rock art, some dating back more than 12,000 years, have been discovered at the park.

Recently, the United States named the Rio Grande an American Heritage River. This means that the United States government has pledged to protect this vital resource and help communities along the river solve problems. As they plan for future growth, both the United States and Mexico will continue to cooperate and to share and conserve the waters of the Rio Grande.

REVIEW What are the United States and Mexico doing about pollution in the Rio Grande?

These plaques, on a bridge between Laredo, Texas, and Nuevo (NWAY•voh) Laredo in Mexico, mark the border between the United States and Mexico.

LESSON 3
REVIEW

 CATEGORIZE Classify actions by the United States and Mexico involving the Rio Grande as either conflicts or compromises.

1 BIG IDEA When countries share a river, why must they work together to protect and use it?

2 VOCABULARY Explain why **irrigation** is necessary in **arid** regions such as the upper Rio Grande valley.

3 GEOGRAPHY Why do farmers in the lower Rio Grande valley sometimes find too little water in the Rio Grande for irrigation?

4 ECONOMICS How do people use irrigation to change their environment and earn a living?

5 CRITICAL THINKING—Evaluate Do you think the compromise the United States and Mexico made about El Chamizal and their shared border was fair to both sides? Explain your answer.

 PERFORMANCE—Design a Bumper Sticker Imagine that your job is to encourage people to visit the Rio Grande. Think of a catchy slogan, or saying, about the Rio Grande. Then write your slogan on a strip of paper to make a bumper sticker. Illustrate your work and share it with the class.

·SKILLS· CITIZENSHIP

Resolve Conflicts

VOCABULARY

resolve

▶ WHY IT MATTERS

Most people work well together when they agree. But people can have different ideas about how things should be done. This can lead to conflict. There are many ways to **resolve**, or settle, a conflict. Compromising is one such way.

▶ WHAT YOU NEED TO KNOW

To resolve a conflict through compromise, you can follow these steps.

Steps for Resolving Conflict

> Identify what is causing the conflict.

⬇

> Tell the people on the other side what you want.
> Listen to what they want.

⬇

> Decide which things are most important to you.

⬇

> Present a plan for compromise.
> Let the people on the other side present their plan.
> Talk about the differences in the two plans.

⬇

> Present a second plan for a compromise,
> giving up one of the things that is important to you.
> Ask the other side to do the same thing.
> Look for a way to let each side have
> most of what it wants.

⬇

> Keep talking until you agree.

⬇

> Plan your compromise so that
> it will work for a long time.

▶ PRACTICE THE SKILL

Being able to compromise and resolve conflicts is important for people. It is important for countries, too. The United States and Mexico compromised about the land called El Chamizal and the border they share along the Rio Grande. Think again about what happened.

1. What caused the conflict between the United States and Mexico?

2. What did each country give up to make the compromise work?

3. What did the two countries do to make sure that a similar conflict would not happen in the future?

4. On what other issues have the United States and Mexico compromised?

▶ APPLY WHAT YOU LEARNED

Suppose the school board wants students to wear uniforms to school every day, but students want to be able to choose what they wear. Using the steps on this page, work with a classmate to come to an agreement and resolve the conflict. One of you should take the side of the school board, and the other, the side of the students. Compare your compromise with those of other students.

CITIZENSHIP SKILLS

4

Oil Resources Around the World

Focus Skill

CATEGORIZE

As you read, categorize the kinds of natural resources that make up a nation's economy.

BIG IDEA

People in different parts of the world use oil resources.

VOCABULARY

wealth
petrochemical

Like the South Central region of the United States, regions in some other countries around the world also have large amounts of oil under their lands. Those oil resources have had a major effect on the economy of each of those nations. They have also changed the way many people in those countries earn a living.

Deserts and Oil in Saudi Arabia

Whenever you ride in your family's car or listen to a CD, you might be using a product made from oil that came from Saudi Arabia. This country is the world's largest oil producer. Every day, its wells pump out about 9 million barrels of oil. About one-fourth of all the oil imported to the United States is shipped from Saudi Arabia.

The Kingdom of Saudi Arabia covers nearly four-fifths of the Arabian Peninsula, a huge peninsula in southwestern Asia. While Saudi Arabia is a very large country, nearly all its land is desert. Fresh water is so scarce and oil is so plentiful in arid Saudi Arabia that water costs more than gasoline!

Saudi Arabia was once one of the poorest countries in the world. Most people there made a living raising small herds of sheep, camels, or goats. Then, in the 1930s, life in Saudi Arabia changed forever when huge oil deposits were discovered buried beneath the desert. Those petroleum resources brought enormous **wealth**, or riches.

FAST FACT

Saudi Arabia has so little fresh water that it takes salt water from the ocean to meet its needs. Large factories along the coast heat sea water to remove the salt. The process removes so much salt that workers need to add some salt back to make the water taste better.

LOCATE IT

Saudi Arabia

Much of Saudi Arabia's oil lies beneath its vast deserts. The world's largest sand desert is in southern Saudi Arabia and is the size of Texas.

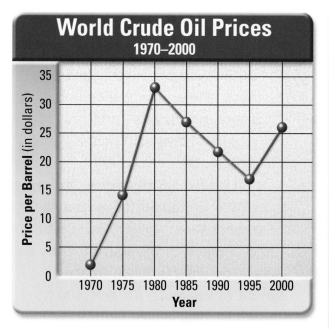

World Crude Oil Prices
1970–2000

Analyze Graphs World oil prices affect the economies of countries around the world.

◈ About how much did a barrel of oil cost in 2000?

Cities grew in the desert, and many people in Saudi Arabia found jobs drilling, shipping, and trading oil. Money from oil exports built schools, hospitals, roads, and airports in the country.

Yet people in Saudi Arabia know that their oil resources will not last forever. They are working hard to build a more diverse economy to prepare for the future.

REVIEW Why does water cost more than gasoline in Saudi Arabia?

Oil on the Nigerian Coast

Like Saudi Arabia, the country of Nigeria has vast oil resources. Nigeria is located on the Atlantic Coast of Africa, along the Gulf of Guinea (GIH•nee). It covers an area about the same size as Texas and Oklahoma combined.

Oil resources have had a great effect on Nigeria's economy in recent years. For centuries, most Nigerians were farmers and ranchers. Then, in 1956, drilling crews discovered large oil deposits in the Niger (NY•juhr) River Delta in southern Nigeria. Drilling for oil quickly became the leading industry in the country, producing more than two and a half million barrels of oil a day.

Just as they did in the South Central region of the United States, cities near the oil wells in Nigeria grew rapidly. More than 10 million people now live in the port city of Lagos (LAY•gahs), Nigeria's and Africa's largest city.

Some people in Nigeria work in factories that manufacture petrochemicals (peh•troh•KEH•mih•kuhlz). A **petrochemical** is a chemical made from oil, used to make many products, including asphalt, plastics, and some medicines.

Many people in Nigeria work on offshore oil rigs in the Gulf of Guinea.

LOCATE IT

Nigeria

Many products we use every day, such as paint and CDs, are made from petroleum.

Parts of your sneakers and the school bus, and even the ink used in this book, may have been made from petrochemicals.

Today Nigeria has the largest and most urban population in Africa. Like people in the South Central region of the United States, some people in Nigeria are still farmers and ranchers. Unlike the economy of the South Central region, however, Nigeria's economy depends almost entirely on exporting oil. To reduce the country's dependence on oil, the Nigerian government is trying to build up agriculture, food processing, and other parts of the nation's economy.

REVIEW How has Nigeria's economy changed over the years? CATEGORIZE

Oil on the Russian Plains

Russia is the largest country in the world. It covers almost as much land area as the United States and Canada combined. It is part of two continents—Asia and Europe.

Like the South Central region of the United States, Russia has a great variety of physical features and climates. In the south there are large deserts, while frozen tundra covers much of the country's northern area. The largest landforms, however, are plains. The flat Siberian Plain in central Russia is the world's largest area of plains.

The Siberian Plain holds most of Russia's oil and natural gas deposits. Russia has about one-third of the world's total. The Russian government drilled many oil wells on the Siberian Plain. It also created cities for oil workers to

Drilling oil in Russia's icy Siberian Plain is difficult work. Snow covers the ground nine months a year, and some places there are always frozen.

LOCATE IT

Russia

live in and large ports on the Baltic Sea to ship the oil around the world.

Today Russia is the world's third-largest oil producer. Each day, wells in Russia pump nearly 6 million barrels of oil. Only Saudi Arabia and the United States produce more oil than Russia. Unlike Saudi Arabia and Nigeria, however, Russia has developed a diverse economy. Drilling oil and mining other resources are important parts of Russia's economy, but so are agriculture, manufacturing, and service industries.

Many people all over the world depend on oil from Russia, Saudi Arabia, Nigeria, and other countries. They use the oil resources to provide fuel for transportation and manufacturing. They also use products made from oil resources.

REVIEW Where are most of Russia's oil and natural gas reserves found?

• SCIENCE AND TECHNOLOGY •

Cars of the Future

Many people all over the world depend on cars for transportation, and cars use large amounts of oil for fuel. Because oil is a nonrenewable resource, people in the future will need to depend less on oil. Automobile manufacturers are now building lighter cars that use less gasoline. They are also developing cars that run on other fuels, such as natural gas or alcohol made from sugarcane and other plants. Many people around the world now drive electric cars that run on batteries. Some cars today are even powered by solar energy. In addition to conserving oil, these cars of the future cause less pollution.

HYBRID ELECTRIC VEHICLE

LESSON 4
REVIEW

CATEGORIZE List the countries discussed in this lesson in alphabetical order, and then in order of greatest to least daily oil production. Explain how each grouping would be useful for comparing information.

1 **BIG IDEA** How do people in Saudi Arabia, Nigeria, and Russia use their oil resources?

2 **VOCABULARY** Use the term **petrochemical** to describe some of the products you see in your classroom.

3 **HISTORY** When was oil discovered in Saudi Arabia?

4 **GEOGRAPHY** Where are most of Nigeria's oil wells located?

5 **CRITICAL THINKING—Synthesize** How do oil resources around the world affect your life?

6 **CRITICAL THINKING—Apply** Based on the countries discussed in this lesson, what conclusion can you reach about how landforms and climate affect oil resources?

PERFORMANCE—Make a Poster Work with a partner to make a poster showing different products made from oil. Label each product you draw. Then write a paragraph describing how your life might be different without these products.

Review and Test Preparation

Focus Skill — Categorize

Copy the following graphic organizer onto a separate sheet of paper. Use the information you have learned to categorize facts about the South Central states.

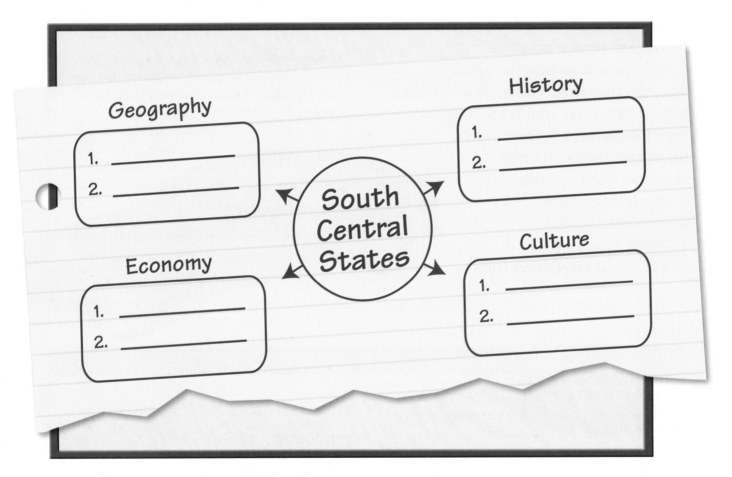

Geography
1. _____
2. _____

History
1. _____
2. _____

South Central States

Economy
1. _____
2. _____

Culture
1. _____
2. _____

THINK & WRITE

Write a Description   Suppose oil were discovered in the community where you live. Write a description of how you think this would affect your life and the lives of your neighbors.

Write About Conflict   Write a paragraph describing something that causes conflict in your community or state. Tell how people are trying to resolve that conflict through compromise.

| 1700 | | 1800 | | | 1900 | | Present |

1682
La Salle claims all of the
Mississippi River valley
for France

1803
The United States
purchases Louisiana
from France

1836
Texas gains
independence
from Mexico

1889
Oklahoma
land rush

1901
Oil is discovered
in Texas

1963
Mexico and the United
States set the Rio Grande
as their official border

USE THE TIME LINE

1 How many years after Texas gained its independence from Mexico was oil discovered there?

2 When did the United States and Mexico set the Rio Grande as their official border?

USE VOCABULARY

Use terms from the list to complete the paragraphs that follow.

inlets (p. 230)
expedition (p. 231)
bayous (p. 232)
petroleum (p. 238)
dredge (p. 240)
arid (p. 242)
irrigation (p. 243)
petrochemical (p. 249)

Along the coast of the South Central region are such waterways as **3** ⎯⎯ and **4** ⎯⎯. In some cases it has been necessary to **5** ⎯⎯ these waterways for ships to use them.

Many South Central farmers use **6** ⎯⎯ to grow crops in the more **7** ⎯⎯ parts of the region. Other people in the region have jobs drilling for **8** ⎯⎯ along the coast.

RECALL FACTS

Answer these questions.

9 How does the climate in the South Central region change from east to west?

10 Where are the lowest lands in the South Central region? the highest lands?

11 Where did Creole and Cajun people first settle in the South Central region?

12 What country is the largest oil producer in the world?

Write the letter of the best choice.

13 The South Central state that was once an independent country is—
A Arkansas.
B Louisiana.
C Oklahoma.
D Texas.

14 Which of the following is ***not*** a product made from petroleum?
F paper
G paint
H gasoline
J plastic

THINK CRITICALLY

15 In which part of the South Central region would you most like to visit or live? Give reasons for your answer.

16 Do you think the way Oklahoma was opened up to new settlement was fair? Explain.

17 Most regions in the United States have a variety of cultures. In what ways does your community celebrate its mix of cultures?

18 Why must the United States and Mexico work together to reduce pollution in the Rio Grande?

19 In what ways can you help the world conserve oil resources?

APPLY SKILLS

Resolve Conflicts

20 Describe the steps you could take to resolve a conflict you might have with a friend or family member. Explain how compromise is part of your solution and why it is fair to both sides in the conflict.

CITIZENSHIP SKILLS

THE OKEFENOKEE SWAMP

GET READY

Located in southern Georgia and northern Florida, the Okefenokee Swamp is almost 700 square miles (1,813 km) of low, wet land. Part of the swamp has been set aside as a National Wildlife Refuge. This means that the land may not be used for human development. Many kinds of plants and animals live in this watery ecosystem. On a visit to the Okefenokee Swamp, you can take a boat tour through water trails bordered by towering bald cypress trees. These trails lead to wide "water prairies," where you can see wood storks, woodpeckers, squirrels, alligators, and other animals. Once you have visited the Okefenokee Swamp, you will understand why it is most important to preserve this freshwater wilderness.

LOCATE IT

GEORGIA

Okefenokee Swamp

FLORIDA

WHAT TO SEE

American egret

The swamp's waterways can be enjoyed by canoe.

Bald cypresses grow in low, wet areas such as the Okefenokee Swamp. Their branches are often draped with Spanish moss, an air plant common in tropical regions.

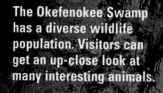

The Okefenokee Swamp has a diverse wildlife population. Visitors can get an up-close look at many interesting animals.

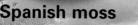

Spanish moss

Black bear

Cottonmouth snake

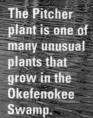

The Pitcher plant is one of many unusual plants that grow in the Okefenokee Swamp.

TAKE A FIELD TRIP

GO ONLINE

A VIRTUAL TOUR
Visit The Learning Site at www.harcourtschool.com to find virtual tours of parks and scenic areas in the United States.

CNN Turner Le@rning

A VIDEO TOUR
Check your media center or classroom library for a videotape tour of the Okefenokee Swamp.

3 Review and Test Preparation

Write a Journal Entry Study the pictures and captions below to help you review Unit 3. Imagine you live near one of the places shown. Write a journal entry describing the physical features you see around you and a typical day in your life there.

USE VOCABULARY

Write a description of the South's economy by using the following terms.

1 **food processing** (p. 207)

2 **international trade** (p. 208)

3 **diverse economy** (p. 236)

4 **refinery** (p. 239)

5 **aerospace** (p. 240)

RECALL FACTS

Answer these questions.

6 How have people in the South changed rivers there?

7 How is most coal in the United States used?

8 How does a long growing season affect farming in the South?

9 Why are food and water often more expensive on islands than on the mainland?

10 Which states in the South border the Gulf of Mexico?

Write the letter of the best choice.

11 The oldest city in the United States is—
A Plymouth Colony.
B St. Augustine.
C Jamestown Colony.
D New Amsterdam.

12 Nearly all of the South is part of the—
F Sun Belt.
G tropics.
H rain forest.
J Research Triangle.

13 Which state in the South has desert areas?
A Florida
B Tennessee
C Texas
D West Virginia

Visual Summary

1500   1550   1600   1650   1700

1607 Jamestown Colony founded in what is now Virginia. p. 171

1798 First description of Mammoth Cave, Kentucky. p. 191

1836 Mexicans defeat Texans at the Alamo in San Antonio, Texas. p. 233

256

THINK CRITICALLY

14 Why did lumber and paper industries develop in the South?

15 How did different ways of life cause conflict between people in the North and people in the South during the 1800s?

16 What are some advantages of living in a fast-growing region like the South? What do you think might be some problems created by fast growth?

17 Why do you think tourism is such an important industry in the South?

18 How did improved transportation affect life in Appalachia and on islands?

APPLY SKILLS

Compare Maps with Different Scales

Use the maps on this page to answer the questions. Tell which map you used to answer each question and explain why.

19 About how many miles is it from Rock Hill to Spartanburg?

20 How far is it from the capital of South Carolina to the capital of North Carolina?

21 Which city is closer to the capital of South Carolina, Florence or Camden?

Map A: South Carolina

★ State capital

Map B: South Carolina and North Carolina

★ State capital

22 About how many miles separate Charleston and Myrtle Beach?

23 How far would you travel to get from Greenville, South Carolina, to Charlotte, North Carolina?

1800   1850   1900   1950   Present

1861 First shots of Civil War fired at Fort Sumter, South Carolina.   p. 204

1937 Cape Hatteras is designated first national seashore.   p. 191

1947 *The Everglades: River of Grass* is written.   p. 210

257

Unit Activities

Visit The Learning Site at www.harcourtschool.com for additional activities.

Make a Collage

In groups make a collage that shows how people in the South depend on natural resources. Label one half of a large sheet of paper *Renewable Resources* and the other half *Nonrenewable Resources*. Then, draw pictures or cut out magazine photographs that show people using resources. Paste your pictures onto the paper under the correct heading. Display the collage and talk about ways to conserve natural resources.

Make a Class Magazine

As a class, put together a magazine about tourism in the South. Decide what articles and illustrations to include. Then, form small groups and assign each group a different part of the magazine to publish.

VISIT YOUR LIBRARY

■ *An Island Scrapbook: Dawn to Dusk on a Barrier Island* by Virginia Wright-Frierson. Simon and Schuster Books for Young Readers.

■ *Appalachia: The Voices of Sleeping Birds* by Cynthia Rylant. Harcourt Brace Jovanovich.

■ *Going to School During the Civil War: The Confederacy* by Kerry A. Graves. Blue Earth Books.

COMPLETE THE UNIT PROJECT

An Atlas Finish the Unit Project described on page 167—an atlas of the South. First, make at least four outline maps of the South. Then use your textbook and other resources to create different maps of the South, such as a physical map, a land use and resource map, and a map of historic sites. Remember to include labels on your maps and to give your maps titles. Also, be sure to define any symbols on your maps in map keys.

Independence Hall,
Philadelphia

From Colony to Commonwealth

" Governments, like clocks,
go from the motion [people]
give them. "

—William Penn, 1682

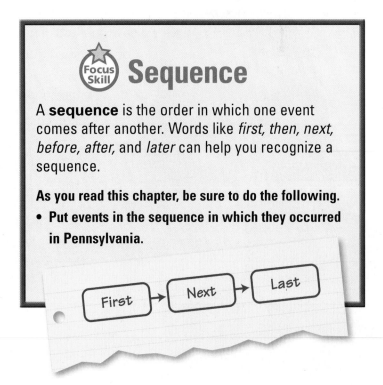

Focus Skill — Sequence

A **sequence** is the order in which one event comes after another. Words like *first, then, next, before, after,* and *later* can help you recognize a sequence.

As you read this chapter, be sure to do the following.

- Put events in the sequence in which they occurred in Pennsylvania.

First → Next → Last

Focus Skill

SEQUENCE
Read to learn the sequence
of events in early
Pennsylvania history.

BIG IDEA
William Penn founded a
colony that allowed
religious freedom.

VOCABULARY

charter
proprietor

The Pennsylvania Colony

In 1664, English warships on the Hudson River forced the Dutch to give up the New Netherland colony. Renamed New York, the colony gave England control of the Northeast. Like other Europeans, the English knew it would take many settlers to protect their land claims.

The Religious Society of Friends

William Penn was born to a wealthy English family. His father was an admiral in the English navy and a friend of King Charles II. In England, the king was the head of the government and of the official religion. The Penn family belonged to the Church of England, known as the Anglican Church.

By 1667, Penn had left the Anglican Church and became a leader of the "Friends." The Religious Society of Friends believed that all people—free and enslaved—were equal. Members of the Religious Society of Friends were known as Quakers. They refused to fight in wars. They believed people should govern themselves. As a result, Quakers did not respect the king's power.

William Penn began to talk about starting a Quaker colony in North America. Penn hoped that in his colony, Quakers could live and worship in peace.

REVIEW Which event happened first—Penn's decision to join the Quakers or Penn's decision to start a colony? **Focus Skill SEQUENCE**

William Penn's belief in religious freedom marked a major change in the colonies. For many years, Pennsylvania was known as the most peaceful and most welcoming of the colonies.

William Penn's
LAST
FAREWEL
TO
ENGLAND:
BEING AN
EPISTLE
Containing a
SALUTATION
TO ALL
Faithful Friends,
A REPROOF to the Unfaithful,
AND A
Visitation to the Enquiring,
In a Solemn FAREWEL to them all in the
Land of my Nativity.

London, Printed for Thomas Cooke, 1682.

William Penn met with native groups (left) to encourage them to have peaceful relationships with colonists. Delaware chief Tamanend gave the Treaty Wampum Belt (above) to William Penn in 1682.

Penn's Colony

In 1670, Penn received his family's wealth when his father died. Admiral Penn had loaned money to his friend, King Charles II. William Penn offered to accept land in North America as repayment for the loans. The king agreed and gave Penn a charter for a new colony in North America. The **charter** was a written document that made Penn the owner of the colony.

The Charter of 1681 named William Penn **proprietor** (pruh•PRY•uh•ter), or owner, of a huge land grant. The land was located between the Maryland and New York colonies. Penn wanted to call his colony *Sylvania*, which means "woods." King Charles II felt that the name should honor his friend, Admiral Penn. They agreed on *Pennsylvania*, which means "Penn's woods."

As proprietor, Penn could use and rule the land as he wished. He advertised to get more settlers to move to the new colony. He wrote letters to European settlers and Native Americans already living there. Penn wanted them to stay and live in peace with the new Quaker settlers.

Using the Quaker idea of equality, Penn wrote a plan for governing the colony. Known as the First Frame of Government, it called for a deputy governor, an Assembly of representatives, and a council of advisers.

In 1682, Penn arrived in the colony aboard the ship *Welcome*. He was greeted warmly by both the settlers and the Native Americans. Penn set to work organizing the colony.

In just four days, the Assembly wrote a new document called the Great Law. It set up a court system and gave people the right to freely practice any religion. However, only those with Christian beliefs could be elected to public office.

Penn also met and signed treaties with leaders of nearby Native American tribes. He dealt fairly with them.

REVIEW How did William Penn get land in North America for a colony?

Philadelphia

William Penn named his colony's capital city *Philadelphia*, which means "City of Brotherly Love." The name expressed Penn's hopes for the future. Philadelphia was a port city, centrally located in the colonies. It was the best-planned city of the time.

While still in England, Penn and his surveyor, Thomas Holme, made a street plan for the city. They laid out a grid of rectangular blocks. There were four public squares and a central square, where City Hall was later built. Streets that ran north and south were numbered; streets that ran east and west were named.

In the early 1700s, about 1,000 immigrants arrived in the city each year. Many of them settled in Philadelphia, including Benjamin Franklin. Many came for religious freedom. Others wished to buy land at low prices and pay low taxes. Those who wanted their own land moved west. They started farms in the Piedmont region.

Penn offered religious freedom to the Dutch, Swedes, Finns, and the Delaware. These groups had already settled on the land included in the charter. English, German, and Dutch Quakers joined the colony. Huguenots (HYOO•guh•nahts), or French Protestants, and German Lutherans came to live in Philadelphia. Swiss Amish and German Mennonites also moved to the colony. Many Europeans paid for their passage by becoming indentured servants.

When Penn arrived, Philadelphia was more than a year old and already successful. By the 1760s, it was the largest city in the colonies. Philadelphia was also a major center for business and culture.

REVIEW **What was Penn and Holme's plan for Philadelphia's streets?**

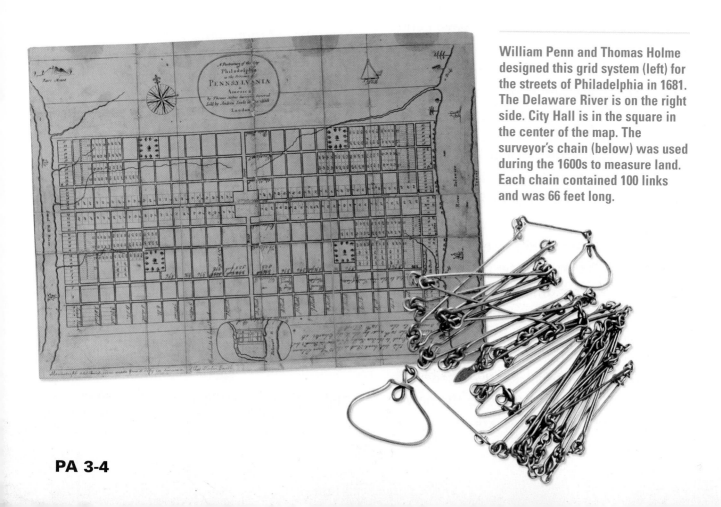

William Penn and Thomas Holme designed this grid system (left) for the streets of Philadelphia in 1681. The Delaware River is on the right side. City Hall is in the square in the center of the map. The surveyor's chain (below) was used during the 1600s to measure land. Each chain contained 100 links and was 66 feet long.

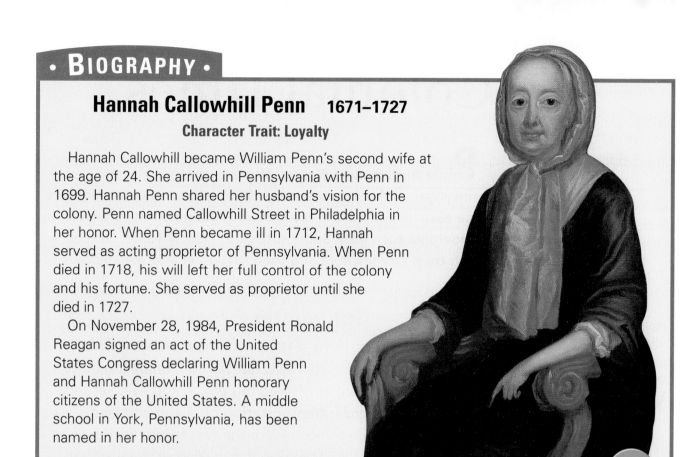

Hannah Callowhill Penn   1671–1727

Character Trait: Loyalty

Hannah Callowhill became William Penn's second wife at the age of 24. She arrived in Pennsylvania with Penn in 1699. Hannah Penn shared her husband's vision for the colony. Penn named Callowhill Street in Philadelphia in her honor. When Penn became ill in 1712, Hannah served as acting proprietor of Pennsylvania. When Penn died in 1718, his will left her full control of the colony and his fortune. She served as proprietor until she died in 1727.

On November 28, 1984, President Ronald Reagan signed an act of the United States Congress declaring William Penn and Hannah Callowhill Penn honorary citizens of the United States. A middle school in York, Pennsylvania, has been named in her honor.

MULTIMEDIA BIOGRAPHIES
Visit The Learning Site at www.harcourtschool.com
to learn about other famous people.

GO ONLINE

The Charter of Privileges

In 1684, Penn received word that he was needed in England. Family and Quaker business kept him away from Pennsylvania for 15 years. When he returned in 1699, Penn and the Assembly began to write a new constitution. They agreed on a form of government that protected individual freedoms.

In 1701, the Assembly adopted the Charter of Privileges. The charter gave the Assembly the power to make laws. The proprietor, or governor, could veto an unfair law. The new constitution protected people's religious beliefs.

REVIEW What was the Charter of Privileges?

LESSON 1 REVIEW

SEQUENCE Did William Penn become the colony's proprietor before or after the Charter of Privileges was adopted by the Assembly?

❶ **BIG IDEA** What freedom did the Great Law give to Pennsylvania colonists?

❷ **VOCABULARY** Use the terms **charter** and **proprietor** in a paragraph about Pennsylvania.

❸ **CIVICS AND GOVERNMENT** What power did the Charter of Privileges give to the Assembly?

Focus Skill

SEQUENCE
Read to learn the sequence of events that led to war in western Pennsylvania.

BIG IDEA
Population growth led to conflicts on Pennsylvania's frontier.

VOCABULARY

keelboat
abolitionist
emancipation
neutral

FAST FACT Where possible, the rivers in western Pennsylvania were used to move goods and people. Keelboats could be poled upstream against the current.

Colonial Times

People from many different places came to live in the Pennsylvania colony. In the early 1700s, about 1,000 immigrants came each year. By 1750, several thousand newcomers arrived in Philadelphia each year. Some settled in Pennsylvania. Others began their journey here and then settled in another colony.

Settling the Frontier

In the early years, most settlers lived near Philadelphia or in other towns in eastern Pennsylvania. As the population grew, the vast western frontier offered more places to live. Settlers found ways to improve transportation on water and land.

Early settlers from Sweden were the first to use keelboats to travel into the frontier. A **keelboat** is a shallow freight boat moved by poles or oars. Keelboats allowed settlers to carry heavy loads upriver against the current.

German settlers later invented a wagon that could carry heavy loads over rough frontier trails. The Conestoga wagon had large wheels and was curved on the bottom to keep loads from shifting. By the 1750s, wagon roads to new settlements were being carved through the wilderness.

REVIEW Which was first used in Pennsylvania—the keelboat or the Conestoga wagon? **Focus Skill** SEQUENCE

At the Ligonier Highland Games in the Laurel Highlands, people of Scottish background celebrate their heritage. The boy (below) is playing a bagpipe, a traditional Scottish instrument.

Into the Piedmont

German immigrants were among the first to settle the Piedmont region of Pennsylvania. Many were farmers and skilled craftworkers. By 1750, about 70,000 Germans were living in the colony.

German settlers introduced farming methods that protected the soil. They planted in different fields each year. They grew several kinds of crops and used natural fertilizers.

Between 1718 and 1775, about 100,000 Scots-Irish immigrants traveled from Northern Ireland to Pennsylvania. The Scots-Irish were farmers, craftworkers, and traders. As before, some people arrived as indentured servants. From Philadelphia, most Scots-Irish moved west to the Susquehanna Valley. They settled on frontier lands and started farms.

By 1720, many farmers in Pennsylvania depended on Scots-Irish and German immigrants who had come as indentured servants. About half of the new immigrants paid for their ocean voyage in this way. Many indentured servants worked on small farms throughout the colony.

REVIEW What farming methods did German settlers introduce?

Slavery and Abolition

During the mid-1700s, European countries were fighting each other in Europe and North America. These wars slowed the arrival of indentured servants from Europe. Many farmers turned to using enslaved Africans for labor. Merchants began to bring enslaved people from the Caribbean islands to Philadelphia. Pennsylvania's enslaved population grew from 5,000 in 1721 to about 30,000 in 1766.

Pennsylvania was known as an abolitionist, or antislavery, colony. In 1688, Quakers in Germantown had held the first abolitionist meeting in North America. They wrote an antislavery petition. Even though Quakers believed in equality, some used enslaved workers.

The issue of slavery began to divide the Quakers. In the 1750s, Quakers stopped accepting people who traded enslaved Africans into the Religious Society of Friends. In 1767, a Pennsylvania law made it illegal to bring enslaved people into the colony. In the mid-1770s, Quakers refused to allow people who used enslaved workers into their meetings.

Pennsylvania passed a law granting gradual, or slow, emancipation in 1780. Emancipation is freedom from someone else's power. The law said that children born enslaved after 1780 would be free at age 28. The law also gave free Africans many rights. Pennsylvania was the first state to make slavery against the law.

REVIEW To whom did farmers turn for labor in the mid-1700s?

Benjamin Rush (right) was a well-known medical doctor in Philadelphia. He was one of the most outspoken members of the Pennsylvania Abolition Society. He wrote a pamphlet (below) against using enslaved workers.

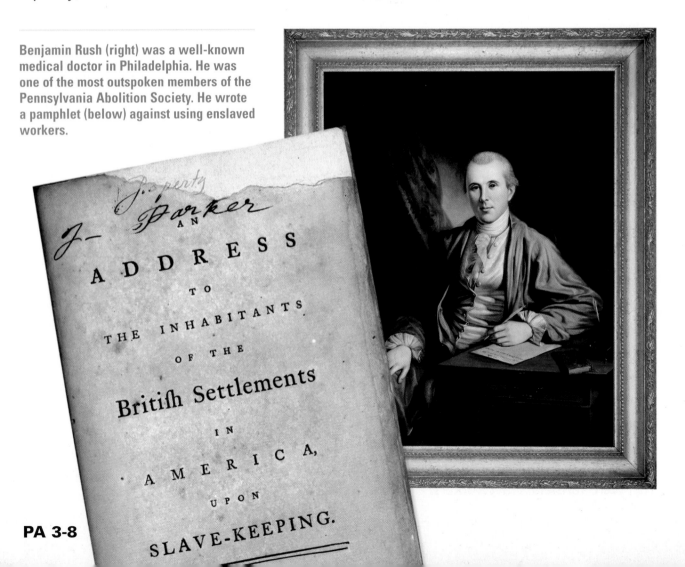

J. Parker

AN

ADDRESS

TO

THE INHABITANTS

OF THE

Britiſh Settlements

IN

AMERICA,

UPON

SLAVE-KEEPING.

The Walking Purchase

Sometimes, the European settlers gained land from the Native Americans through unfair practices. In 1737, William Penn's sons presented an old, unsigned version of a document to the Delaware people. Penn's sons said that the document permitted settlers to have as much land as they could walk in a day and a half. Thomas Penn hired the three fastest walkers in the colony. One man ran the path and crossed more than twice the land the Delaware had expected to lose. As a result, Pennsylvania settlers gained 1,200 square miles of land from the Native Americans.

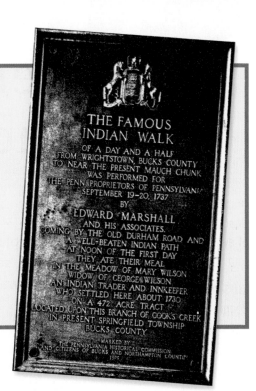

The French and Indian War

The arrival of European settlers forced many Native Americans to migrate. Some native people were angry with the colonists.

The French held huge land claims in what is now Canada and in land west of the English colonies. The French used these land claims for trade with Native Americans. In 1754, the French built Fort Duquesne (doo•KAYN) where the Ohio, Allegheny, and Monongahela rivers meet. The settlement that grew up there became Pittsburgh.

The English sent General Edward Braddock to force the French out of the Ohio Valley. On their way to Fort Duquesne, the English troops were attacked by French soldiers and their Native American allies. Braddock and more than half of his soldiers were killed.

This started a war known as the French and Indian War. During this conflict, Native American groups were divided. Some were French allies. Others were English allies. Some stayed neutral. To be **neutral** means to take no side in a war.

After nine years, the war ended in 1763. France was defeated and had to surrender its land claims east of the Mississippi River to the English.

REVIEW Who built Fort Duquesne?

LESSON 2
REVIEW

SEQUENCE Which event happened first—the first abolitionist meeting or the passage of the gradual emancipation act?

1 **BIG IDEA** How did population growth cause conflicts with Native Americans?

2 **VOCABULARY** Use **abolitionist** in a sentence about **emancipation**.

3 **HISTORY** Which invention allowed settlers to carry heavy loads over frontier trails?

SEQUENCE
Read to learn the sequence of events that led to the forming of a new nation.

BIG IDEA
People and places in Pennsylvania were important to the American Revolution.

VOCABULARY
delegate
ratify

Pennsylvania's Independence

After the French and Indian War, Pennsylvania and the other colonies had hard times. England, or Britain as it became known, said colonists had to pay new taxes to cover the costs of the war.

The Continental Congress

In the early 1770s, Britain began to pass new tax laws for the colonies. Many Pennsylvania colonists did not think the taxes were fair. Some angry colonists refused to pay.

In 1774, **delegates**, or elected representatives, from each colony met in Philadelphia for the First Continental Congress. Only Georgia did not attend. The delegates discussed the problems their colonies had with Britain.

Although many Pennsylvanians were unhappy with British rule, some people still supported the British. Some of these were Quakers, who did not believe in fighting wars. Others were successful business owners who made money trading with Britain.

The Second Continental Congress met in 1775 at the State House in Philadelphia. Then Patriots began to call for changes in Pennsylvania's government, too.

REVIEW Did Britain pass new tax laws before or after the First Continental Congress?
SEQUENCE

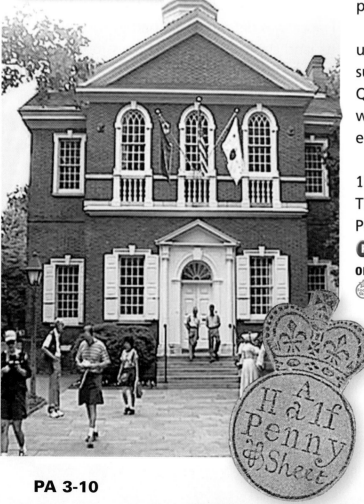

Visitors can tour the building where the First Continental Congress met in 1774. Reenactors dress in clothing from colonial times (far left). This is one of the stamps that showed the British tax was paid.

Elections in Philadelphia were held at the Court House, at Market and Second Streets. Voters handed their ballots through the windows.

A New Pennsylvania Constitution

In 1776, the Second Continental Congress said that colonial governments, which got their powers from the king, should no longer rule. Colonists who wanted change stopped the Pennsylvania Assembly from meeting. For the first time since 1701, Pennsylvanians wrote a new constitution. They reorganized the government and created a new Assembly for the Commonwealth of Pennsylvania.

Benjamin Franklin became the president of the new Assembly. A council replaced the governor. Political power shifted away from wealthy eastern landowners. Settlers from western counties and middle-class merchants and craftworkers gained a stronger voice.

The new constitution included a Declaration of Rights. It gave citizens certain rights and said that the Assembly could not make laws that blocked those rights. Citizens were promised freedom of religion, freedom of speech and of the press, trial by jury, and free elections. The Pennsylvania Constitution of 1776 and its Declaration of Rights later became models for the United States Constitution.

As a delegate to the Second Continental Congress, Benjamin Franklin helped write the Declaration of Independence for the new nation. It was accepted in July 1776. Patriots soon learned, however, that there was much more to independence than meetings.

REVIEW **What was Benjamin Franklin's role in the Assembly for the Commonwealth of Pennsylvania?**

The American Revolution

Pennsylvania played an important role during the American Revolution. When the 13 colonies formed the United States, Philadelphia became its first capital city. Pennsylvania's citizens served in the Continental Army and fought in many battles. The first Navy ships were built in Philadelphia. Citizens from all over Pennsylvania, including African Americans, sailed those ships.

Pennsylvania's farms, factories, and mines supplied products to the Continental Army, which was led by General George Washington. The state government and its citizens gave money for the war.

At first, the war did not go well for Washington's army. The British won battles at Brandywine and Germantown. In the summer of 1777, the British captured Philadelphia. Washington and his troops suffered through the cold winter of 1777–1778 at Valley Forge.

Washington let African Americans join the Continental Army. About 5,000 African Americans fought for the United States. Soldiers who were enslaved before the war were given their freedom. Yet, most African Americans were still enslaved after the war.

The British were forced to leave Philadelphia in the spring of 1778. With their Iroquois allies, the British attacked Pennsylvania's frontier. Colonists defeated the Native Americans in 1781.

In the same year, American and French troops won a battle against the British at Yorktown, Virginia. That victory ended the war. The Treaty of Paris, signed in 1783, recognized the United States as an independent nation.

REVIEW **Where were the first United States Navy ships built?**

LOCATE IT

PENNSYLVANIA

Valley Forge

Valley Forge, 22 miles northwest of Philadelphia on the Schuylkill River, was where General Washington's army spent the winter of 1777–1778. Reenactors (below) gather at Valley Forge to remember the soldiers who fought for independence.

At the Constitutional Convention in Philadelphia, 55 delegates met for about 4 months to write the United States Constitution.

A New Nation

In 1787, a Constitutional Convention was held in Philadelphia. Delegates wrote a new constitution for the United States of America. Pennsylvania was the second state to **ratify**, or vote to accept, the document. From 1790 to 1800, the nation's capital remained in Philadelphia.

More than half of the state's population lived in or near Pittsburgh or Philadelphia. Most of the state's 6,500 free African Americans lived in Philadelphia.

To encourage growth in Pennsylvania's north and west, the government gave land grants to soldiers who had fought in the war. The land office also sold land at low prices to other settlers and to new immigrants.

After battling Native Americans for many years, the government purchased land from the Iroquois. Pennsylvania gained a western port city on the Great Lakes. Both the lake and the city were named Erie for the Native American group who had once lived in the area.

REVIEW Where did most Pennsylvanians live in 1800?

LESSON 3 REVIEW

 Focus Skill **SEQUENCE** What events led up to the signing of the Declaration of Independence?

1 **BIG IDEA** What role did Pennsylvanians play in the American Revolution?

2 **VOCABULARY** Use the term **delegate** in a sentence about a Continental Congress.

3 **HISTORY** What happened at Valley Forge?

The Call to Liberty

DID YOU KNOW?

By 1779, about one of every seven Patriot soldiers in Washington's army was an African American.

In the 1700s, many colonists grew unhappy with Britain's rule. Colonial leaders met in Philadelphia to work for the cause of liberty. Pennsylvania had been founded on ideas of self-government and freedom. During the American Revolution, it became the heart of a new nation.

On September 11, 1777, a battle took place along Brandywine Creek, about 25 miles southwest of Philadelphia. Thanks to the leadership of General George Washington, few Patriots were injured. However, the Battle of Brandywine was a victory for the British.

Haym Salomon (HAH•yim SAHL•uh•muhn) was a Jewish immigrant from Poland. By the time of the American Revolution, Salomon was a Philadelphia Patriot. He raised much of the money needed to fight the long war. In 1975, the United States honored Salomon on a ten-cent postage stamp.

At the beginning of the American Revolution, Native Americans in the Iroquois League were British allies. However, Seneca chief Cornplanter began to support the Patriots near the war's end. In 1791, Cornplanter's people were granted land in western Pennsylvania. President Washington, who admired the courage of his former enemy, gave him a peace medal. The medal shows Washington meeting Cornplanter.

Margaret Corbin of Franklin County, helped Patriot soldiers both in and out of battle. When Corbin's husband was killed in battle, she took his place firing a cannon until she was injured and could no longer fight. Corbin is honored on a monument at the United States Military Academy.

ACTIVITY

Use the library or Internet to learn more about Pennsylvania's Patriot leaders. Then, write a one-page biography of the leader you find most interesting. Be sure to give the dates that tell when the leader lived, and include details about his or her role in the American Revolution.

RESEARCH

GO ONLINE

Visit The Learning Site at **www.harcourtschool.com** to learn about other historic places and people.

Review and Test Preparation

Sequence

(Focus Skill)

Copy the graphic organizer onto a separate sheet of paper. Then put events from Pennsylvania's history in the order in which they occurred.

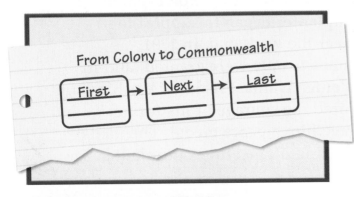

From Colony to Commonwealth

First → Next → Last

THINK AND WRITE

Write an Advertisement Write an advertisement inviting Europeans to come to William Penn's new colony in North America.

USE VOCABULARY

Use each word in a sentence that helps explain its meaning.

1. **charter** (p. PA 3-3)
2. **proprietor** (p. PA 3-3)
3. **keelboat** (p. PA 3-6)
4. **abolitionist** (p. PA 3-8)
5. **emancipation** (p. PA 3-8)
6. **neutral** (p. PA 3-9)
7. **delegate** (p. PA 3-10)
8. **ratify** (p. PA 3-13)

RECALL FACTS

Answer these questions.

9. Why did King Charles II give William Penn a charter for Pennsylvania?
10. What contributions did German settlers make to farming in Pennsylvania?
11. How were Philadelphia streets laid out?
12. How did Pennsylvania contribute to the American Revolution?

Write the letter of the best choice.

13. What was the first capital city of the United States?
    A Washington, D.C.
    B Boston
    C New York
    D Philadelphia

THINK CRITICALLY

14. How did William Penn's Quaker beliefs affect the Pennsylvania colony?
15. Why did slavery increase in the 1700s?

PERFORMANCE

Create a Skit Write a skit showing what happened when William Penn arrived in the colony. Include dialogue between Penn and the settlers and Native Americans who greeted him. Perform your skit for the class.

The Middle West

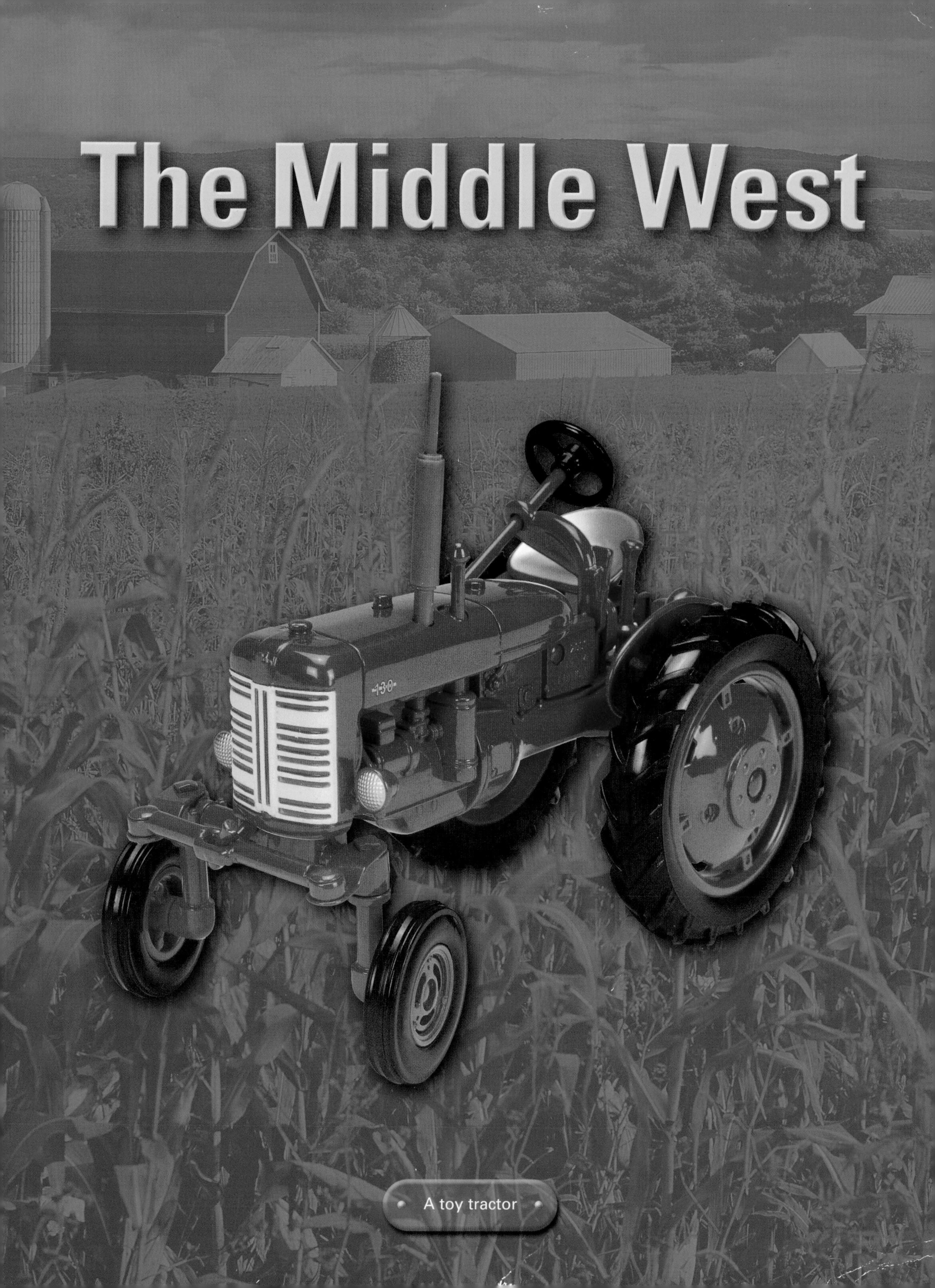

A toy tractor

Farm near Baraboo, Wisconsin

The Middle West

> " I am the Heartland, Great and wide,
> I sing of hope. I sing of pride. "
> —Diane Siebert, *Heartland,* 1989

Preview the Content

Using the chapter and lesson titles, make an outline of this unit. Write down any questions that occur to you about the Middle West.

Preview the Vocabulary

Synonyms   Synonyms are words with the same or similar meanings. Scan through the unit to find a vocabulary word to match each synonym below. Make a chart to record your responses. Use each vocabulary word in a sentence.

SYNONYM	VOCABULARY WORD	SENTENCE
friend; partner	_____	_____
user	_____	_____
measure	_____	_____
desire	_____	_____
cargo; shipped goods	_____	_____

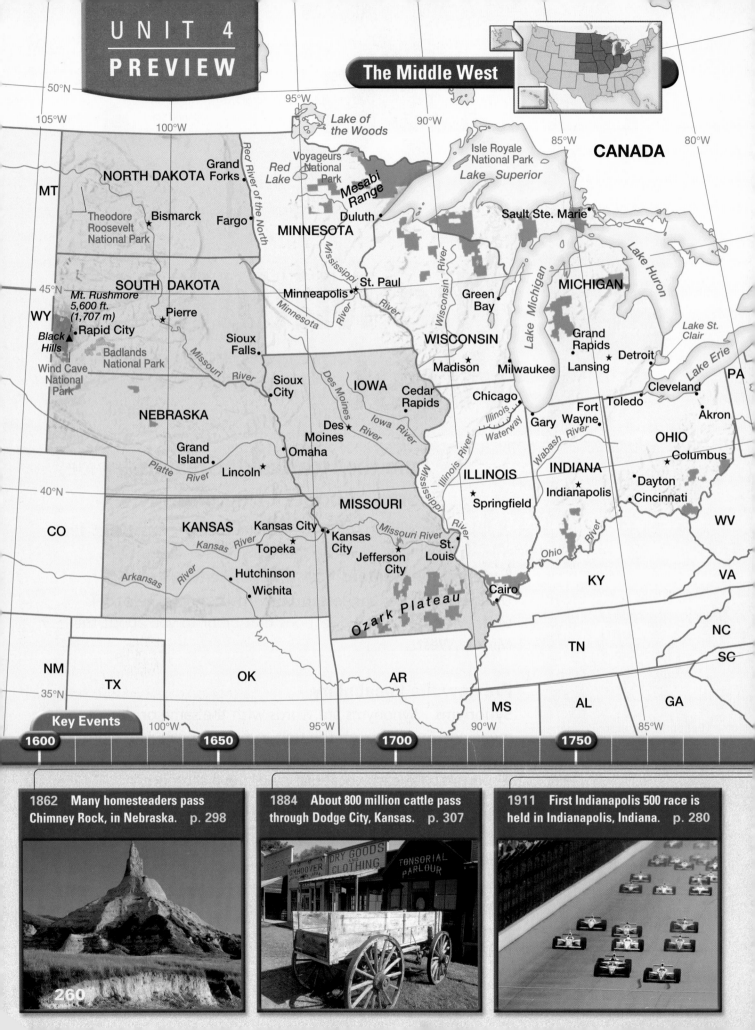

The Middle West

CANADA

NORTH DAKOTA

MT

50°N

105°W

100°W

95°W

90°W

85°W

80°W

Lake of the Woods

Grand Forks

Red Lake

Red River of the North

Voyageurs National Park

Mesabi Range

Isle Royale National Park

Lake Superior

Sault Ste. Marie

Theodore Roosevelt National Park

★ Bismarck

Fargo

Duluth

MINNESOTA

45°N

SOUTH DAKOTA

Mt. Rushmore 5,600 ft. (1,707 m)

★ Pierre

Minneapolis

St. Paul

Mississippi River

Minnesota River

Wisconsin River

Green Bay

MICHIGAN

Lake Michigan

Lake Huron

Lake St. Clair

WY

Black Hills

• Rapid City

Badlands National Park

Sioux Falls

WISCONSIN

Madison ★

Grand Rapids

Lansing ★

Detroit

Wind Cave National Park

Missouri River

Sioux City

Des Moines River

IOWA

Cedar Rapids

Milwaukee

Chicago

Lake Erie

PA

Cleveland

NEBRASKA

Iowa River

Des Moines ★

Illinois Waterway

Fort Wayne

Toledo

Akron

Grand Island

Omaha

Gary

OHIO

Platte River

Lincoln ★

INDIANA

Wabash River

Columbus ★

40°N

CO

Springfield ★

Indianapolis ★

Dayton

Cincinnati

MISSOURI

Illinois River

Mississippi River

ILLINOIS

WV

KANSAS

Kansas City

Kansas River

Topeka ★

Kansas City

Missouri River

Jefferson City

St. Louis

Ohio River

KY

VA

Hutchinson

Wichita

Cairo

Ozark Plateau

TN

NC

NM

OK

AR

SC

35°N

TX

MS

AL

GA

100°W

95°W

90°W

85°W

1600   1650   1700   1750

1862 Many homesteaders pass Chimney Rock, in Nebraska. p. 298

1884 About 800 million cattle pass through Dodge City, Kansas. p. 307

1911 First Indianapolis 500 race is held in Indianapolis, Indiana. p. 280

260

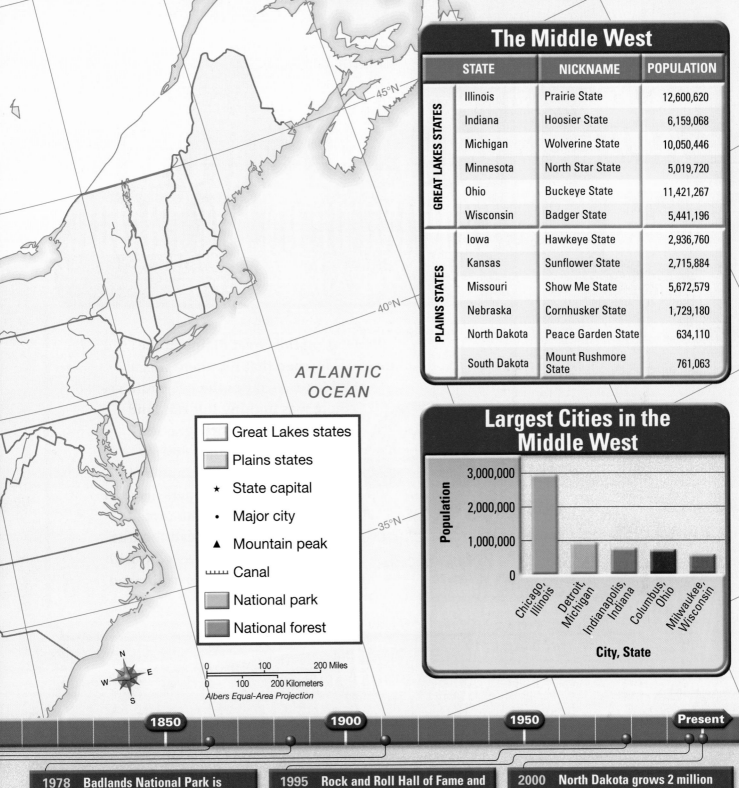

The Middle West

	STATE	NICKNAME	POPULATION
GREAT LAKES STATES	Illinois	Prairie State	12,600,620
	Indiana	Hoosier State	6,159,068
	Michigan	Wolverine State	10,050,446
	Minnesota	North Star State	5,019,720
	Ohio	Buckeye State	11,421,267
	Wisconsin	Badger State	5,441,196
PLAINS STATES	Iowa	Hawkeye State	2,936,760
	Kansas	Sunflower State	2,715,884
	Missouri	Show Me State	5,672,579
	Nebraska	Cornhusker State	1,729,180
	North Dakota	Peace Garden State	634,110
	South Dakota	Mount Rushmore State	761,063

ATLANTIC OCEAN

- Great Lakes states
- Plains states
- ★ State capital
- • Major city
- ▲ Mountain peak
- ⊔⊔⊔⊔ Canal
- National park
- National forest

0 100 200 Miles
0 100 200 Kilometers
Albers Equal-Area Projection

Largest Cities in the Middle West

Population vs. City, State

Chicago, Illinois — nearly 3,000,000
Detroit, Michigan
Indianapolis, Indiana
Columbus, Ohio
Milwaukee, Wisconsin

1850   1900   1950   Present

1978   Badlands National Park is established in South Dakota.   p. 317

1995   Rock and Roll Hall of Fame and Museum in Cleveland opens.   p. 279

2000   North Dakota grows 2 million tons of sunflower seeds.   p. 306

261

PIONEER GIRL
GROWING UP ON THE PRAIRIE
by Andrea Warren

Pioneers on the Great Plains in the late 1800s learned that life there was a challenge. As far as the eye could see, there was nothing but flat land covered with prairie grasses. Droughts, fires, dust storms, tornadoes, blizzards, and even swarms of grasshoppers awaited the homesteaders who came to settle on this land. Read the true story of Grace McCance, who with her parents and sister Florry, braved the Nebraska prairie.

Grace McCance, age 10

RICH FARMING LANDS!
ON THE LINE OF THE
Union Pacific Railroad!
Located in the GREAT CENTRAL BELT of POPU-
LATION, COMMERCE and WEALTH, and
adjoining the WORLD'S HIGHWAY
from OCEAN TO OCEAN.

12,000,000 ACRES!
3,000,000 Acres in Central and
Eastern Nebraska, in the Platte Valley, now for sale!

We invite the attention of all parties seeking
a HOME, to the LANDS offered for sale by this Company

Posters like this one (above), advertising land for sale by the railroad companies, drew settlers to the Great Plains. The McCances from Missouri were among the thousands of families who came to start new lives on the prairie. In a family photograph (right), Mama and Poppie McCance are at the far right and Grace is seated third from the left.

Grace McCance scrambled down the steps of the train, planted her feet on the muddy ground, and looked around. So *this* was Nebraska! No trees blocked the view, and she liked the bigness of it. . . .

"Poppie!" Grace cried, catching sight of her father driving up in the old wagon pulled by the family mules. She ran to meet him and threw herself into his arms the moment he jumped down. Charles McCance embraced his family. He grinned as he kissed Mama. They had last seen him three months earlier when he loaded the family's belongings into a train boxcar, urged the mules aboard, and then hopped in himself for the long ride to Nebraska.

Folks back home in Missouri said Poppie had "land fever" because he had decided to become a homesteader. The 1862 Homestead Act allowed him to file a claim on 160 acres of public land. If he built a house and cultivated the soil, in five years the land would be his. Men or women who were single or heads of households could file a homestead claim as long as they were twenty-one and were either citizens or immigrants who planned to become citizens. Early in the spring of 1885, Poppie had found his claim near the town of Cozad in central Nebraska.

claim a statement of ownership of a piece of land

Locomotives like this one brought settlers to Nebraska in the 1880s.

He paid the ten-dollar filing fee and set to work. His first task had been to build a house so he could send for his family—and now they were here.

Everyone settled into the wagon, and Poppie turned the mules toward the northwest. When they stopped several hours later, Grace woke up from a nap. She thought they must be in the middle of nowhere. She recalled in her memoir, "I can still see the homestead as it looked when we pulled into it that day—just two naked little soddies squatting on a bare, windswept ridge. . . . Not another building in sight, not a tree, not an animal, nothing but grassy flats and hills."

The "soddies" were built of blocks of compacted sod Poppie had cut from the earth. The smaller one was a stable. The other was a twelve-by-fourteen-foot room: their new home. It was smaller than Grandmother Blaine's parlor in Missouri. Grace stared at the tiny house. The wind whipped around them, its sound a mournful wail. For a moment she felt unsure about this new place.

Then she saw her cat, Old Tom, who had made the trip with Poppie and the mules, and a moment later she and Florry were running through the prairie grass, laughing. Darting ahead of Mama and Poppie, they explored the house, happy to see the cookstove and the familiar belongings from their old house.

A family of homesteaders (above) is resting in St. Louis before leaving for Kansas. These homesteaders (right) are planting corn.

Later they walked with Mama and Poppie to see the field Poppie was readying for corn planting. Poppie kept saying this was land where anything would grow. Mama was quiet. The only thing she asked about was a school, but Poppie said the girls were still too young for school, and by the time they were old enough, he figured there would be one.

Thinking back on that first day, Grace realized that, for herself and Florry, "it was all new and interesting, but to Mama it must have seemed poor and desolate. She had grown up among the green fields and woods of Missouri, where she lived in a big white house. She liked nice things, good food, pretty clothes, handsome furniture. I know she must have been nearly crushed by the unexpected bigness of the prairie, the endless blue of the sky, our rough, homemade furniture, and the almost total lack of neighbors."

Analyze the Literature

❶ How did the McCance family get its land in Nebraska?

❷ How was life on the Great Plains different from life in Missouri for the McCance family?

READ A BOOK

START THE UNIT PROJECT

A Mural Work in groups to plan a mural that shows what the Middle West is like. As you read the unit, make a list of places and activities that are important in the region. Take notes, and draw simple sketches to go with them.

USE TECHNOLOGY

Visit The Learning Site at **www.harcourtschool.com** for additional activities, primary sources, and other resources to use in this unit.

CHICAGO, ILLINOIS

On the shores of Lake Michigan is Chicago, Illinois, the third-largest city in the United States. Chicago is famous for its tall buildings, such as the John Hancock Center, shown here. From 1968 until 1973, the 100-story John Hancock Center was Chicago's tallest building. Today, the tallest building in Chicago, and all of North America, is the Sears Tower. With 110 stories, the Sears Tower is more than a quarter of a mile high—nearly equal to the length of five football fields!

LOCATE IT

Chicago

ILLINOIS

Great Lakes States

" Stormy, husky, brawling,
City of the Big Shoulders "
—Carl Sandburg, *Chicago*, 1916

Sequence

A **sequence** is the order in which one event comes after another. Words like *first, then, next, before, after,* and *later* can help you recognize a sequence.

As you read this chapter, be sure to do the following.
- **Put events in the sequence in which they occurred in the Great Lakes States.**

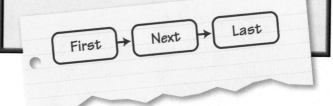
First → Next → Last

The Old Northwest

| 1650 | 1775 | 1900 |

SEQUENCE

As you read, look for the sequence of events that led the United States to expand westward.

BIG IDEA

Learn how the Great Lakes region became part of the United States.

VOCABULARY

cartographer
ally
survey
township
ordinance
frontier

After the United States became a nation, more Americans moved inland. They settled on the rolling lands and broad river valleys of the Central Plains, west of the Appalachian Mountains. Many of them settled northwest of the Ohio River, in what is now known as the Great Lakes region. Today six states—Illinois, Indiana, Ohio, Michigan, Minnesota, and Wisconsin—make up this region. Each of these states borders at least one of the Great Lakes.

Exploring the Region

By the early 1600s, the French had built a few settlements in present-day Canada and along the Great Lakes. At the settlements they traded with Native Americans for fur. These Indians told stories about a river south of the Great Lakes, which they called the Mississippi. Hoping to discover new trade routes, French leaders sent an expedition to find and explore this river.

Marquette and Joliet explored the waterways of the Great Lakes region. Today the cities of Marquette, Michigan, and Joliet, Illinois, are named in their honor.

This horn, used to carry gunpowder, belonged to a British officer during the French and Indian War. It is engraved with a map showing some of the war's major battles.

Leading the expedition were Louis Joliet (LOO•ee zhohl•YAY) and Jacques Marquette (ZHAHK mar•KET). Joliet was a fur trader and **cartographer** (kar•TAH•gruh•fer), or a person who makes maps. Marquette was a Catholic priest who knew several Native American languages.

In 1673 the explorers set out from the northern shores of Lake Michigan. They paddled across the lake and up the Fox River. Then they had to carry their canoes and supplies overland from the Fox to the Wisconsin River, a tributary of the Mississippi. For four months, the explorers canoed about 1,000 miles (about 1,600 km) down the Mississippi River.

The expedition encouraged further exploration of the Great Lakes region. As a result, more French traders moved into the area. Over time, their trading posts grew into towns and cities.

One trader named Jean Baptiste Point du Sable (JAHN bah•TEEST PWAN do SAH•bluh)

started a trading post where the Chicago River empties into Lake Michigan. That trading post later became the city of Chicago, Illinois. Today Chicago is the largest city in the Great Lakes region.

France claimed all the lands along the Great Lakes and the Mississippi River. At the same time, Britain claimed all the lands stretching inland from the Atlantic Coast. Both countries, however, claimed the lands in the Ohio River valley.

Fighting soon broke out over ownership of the valley. Both the French and the British were helped by their Native American **allies**, or friends, in what came to be called the French and Indian War. In 1763 the British defeated the French and gained control of the French lands, including most of the Great Lakes region.

At the end of the American Revolution in 1783, most of the Great Lakes region became part of the United States. The government named the region the Northwest Territory. It included the lands west of Pennsylvania, north of the Ohio River, east of the Mississippi River, and south of the Great Lakes. Thousands of settlers soon poured into the Northwest Territory.

REVIEW How did the Marquette and Joliet expedition affect the Great Lakes region?

FAST FACT
Jean Baptiste Point du Sable, the founder of Chicago, built Chicago's first permanent home in the 1770s. In that log cabin, the first marriage in Chicago was performed, and the city's first election and trial were held.

Townships and Settlers

Settlers were moving to the Northwest Territory, but there was no plan for how the land should be divided. Different people sometimes claimed the same land, and they often disagreed about who really owned it. To better plan for the division of these western lands, in 1785 the United States decided to **survey**, or measure, the Northwest Territory.

The Northwest Territory was divided into squares called **townships**. Each side of a township measured 6 miles (10 km). Each township, in turn, was divided into 36 smaller square sections to be sold to settlers. One section in each township

Tools such as sextants were used to survey the Northwest Territory.

was set aside for a school. In 1787 the United States government passed the Northwest Ordinance. This **ordinance**, or set of laws, set up a plan for governing the Northwest Territory.

The ordinance also banned slavery in the Northwest Territory. This ban, however, did not apply to enslaved people already there. In 1800 only a few hundred enslaved people lived in the Northwest Territory. But by 1820 thousands of free African Americans had made a new home there. They had few rights, however. They could not vote, serve on juries, or attend public school. To encourage even more people to move to the Northwest Territory, the United States government sold land there for as little as a dollar per acre, and thousands of pioneers headed west. Many journeyed overland in wagons. Others traveled by water on the Great Lakes or the Ohio River.

In the early 1800s Jeannette Mitchell moved with her family from New York to present-day Illinois. Life on the **frontier**, or lands beyond settlement, was hard for pioneer families like Jeannette's. Surrounded by wilderness, they had to build their own homes. To do so, most chopped down trees from the forests

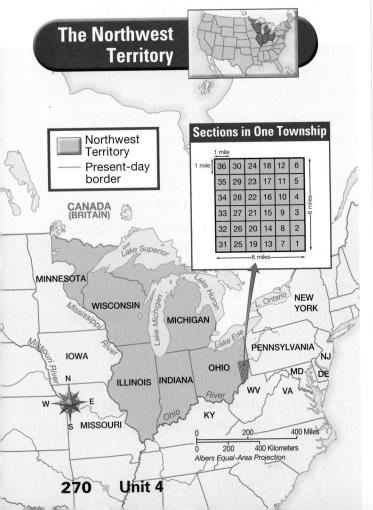

The Northwest Territory

Legend:
- Northwest Territory
- Present-day border

CANADA (BRITAIN)

Lake Superior

MINNESOTA
WISCONSIN
Lake Michigan
MICHIGAN
Lake Huron
L. Ontario
NEW YORK
Lake Erie
PENNSYLVANIA
NJ
IOWA
OHIO
MD
DE
ILLINOIS INDIANA
WV
VA
Ohio River
KY
MISSOURI
Mississippi River
Missouri River

N
E
W
S

0   200   400 Miles
0   200   400 Kilometers
Albers Equal-Area Projection

Sections in One Township

36	30	24	18	12	6
35	29	23	17	11	5
34	28	22	16	10	4
33	27	21	15	9	3
32	26	20	14	8	2
31	25	19	13	7	1

1 mile
6 miles
6 miles

GEOGRAPHY THEME

Place This map shows how the Northwest Territory was divided into townships and sections.

◆ Where do you think it was difficult to divide the land into perfect squares?

In the 1800s pioneer families in the Northwest Territory built and lived in log cabins. This photo shows the log cabin of Abraham Lincoln's parents in Charleston, Illinois.

of oak and hickory then covering parts of the Northwest Territory. In her journal, Jeannette described how her family built their one-room log cabin.

> **The logs were cut the desired length, each end being . . . notched, so as to bring them as near together as possible. . . . A wide fireplace was cut out of one end of the cabin.**

After building their cabins, settlers had to clear more trees and bushes before they could plant their crops. Corn and other crops grew well in the fertile soil of the Central Plains. Livestock grazed on the thick grasses. Settlers also hunted deer, rabbits, and other animals in the forests.

As more pioneers moved to the Northwest Territory, many Native Americans grew angry because they were losing so much of their land. Fighting often broke out between the settlers and the Indians. Many settlers blamed the Indian attacks on Britain, which now controlled Canada. They thought the British were encouraging the Indians to fight.

This belief, along with other issues, was one reason the United States and Britain were on the brink of war in the early 1800s. These conflicts led to the War of 1812. Many of the largest battles of the war took place in the Northwest Territory, where British soldiers and their Indian allies fought the settlers. The war ended in 1814, but neither side clearly won. However, the young United States had proved itself equal to a great European nation.

REVIEW How did the government organize settlement of the Northwest Territory?

SEQUENCE

Westward Expansion

0   150   300 Miles
0   150   300 Kilometers
Albers Equal-Area Projection

CANADA

Lake Superior

Lake Michigan

Lake Huron

Lake Ontario

Lake Erie

Mississippi River

Missouri River

Arkansas River

Red River

Tennessee River

Ohio River

APPALACHIAN MTS.

MAINE
(part of
Massachusetts
until 1820)

NEW
HAMPSHIRE

NEW
YORK

MASSACHUSETTS
Boston

RHODE ISLAND
CONNECTICUT

PENNSYLVANIA
New York City
NEW JERSEY
Philadelphia
Pittsburgh
DELAWARE
MARYLAND

Richmond
VIRGINIA

NORTH
CAROLINA

SOUTH
CAROLINA

ATLANTIC
OCEAN

GEORGIA
Atlanta
Charleston
Savannah

St. Augustine

Gulf of Mexico

Minneapolis★
St. Paul

Madison★

Lansing★

Detroit

Des
Moines

Chicago

Cleveland

Springfield★

Indianapolis★
Cincinnati

Columbus

St. Louis

Louisville

Nashville

Dallas

Houston

New Orleans

N E S W

Settled by 1790
Settled by 1820
Settled by 1850
Settled by 1860

- - - The 13 colonies
——— Present-day border

Movement During the 1800s more and more people moved west of the Appalachian Mountains.

GEOGRAPHY THEME

❖ By what year was most of the land along the Ohio River settled by pioneers?

Statehood for the Old Northwest

Before the War of 1812 began, one state, Ohio, had already been formed from land in the Northwest Territory. It became a state in 1803.

The Northwest Ordinance of 1787 described the steps by which new states would be formed in the Northwest Territory. First, the land was divided into separate territories. Once a territory had 60,000 people, it could become a state. Each new state would be equal to the other states in the Union in every way.

In general, pioneers settled first in the eastern part of the Northwest Territory. Eventually others moved farther north and west in the territory. By 1858 all of the Great Lakes states had been formed and admitted into the Union.

In the original states, the capital city was usually the largest city in the state or an important port city. People in the Great Lakes region, however, usually chose a central location for state capitals. That made it easier for the people who

• HERITAGE •

Land of 10,000 Lakes

Each state chooses symbols to represent its history, geography, and heritage. These symbols may include state flags, songs, birds, flowers, and nicknames. The people of Minnesota chose "Land of 10,000 Lakes" for one of their state's nicknames. In fact, Minnesota has more than 20,000 lakes! The state has so many lakes that many share the same name.

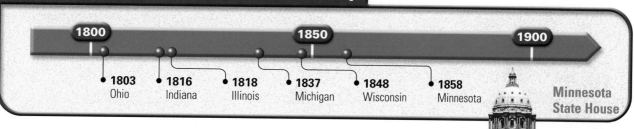

Statehood for the Northwest Territory

1800

- **1803** Ohio
- **1816** Indiana
- **1818** Illinois
- **1837** Michigan

1850

- **1848** Wisconsin
- **1858** Minnesota

1900

Minnesota State House

Analyze Time Lines This time line shows the date each of the Great Lakes states joined the Union.

❖ Which became a state first, Indiana or Illinois?

lived in the state to reach the capital. The capitals of some Great Lakes states—Columbus, Ohio; Indianapolis, Indiana; and Springfield, Illinois—sit almost exactly in the middle of their states.

The shape of Michigan, however, made a centrally located capital nearly impossible. Michigan is made up of two peninsulas separated by Lake Michigan.

So Michigan chose Lansing, near the center of its lower peninsula. Wisconsin chose Madison, near the middle of the southern part of the state, for its capital. Minnesota's capital, St. Paul, is located where the Minnesota River flows into the Mississippi River.

REVIEW What was the first state created from the Northwest Territory?

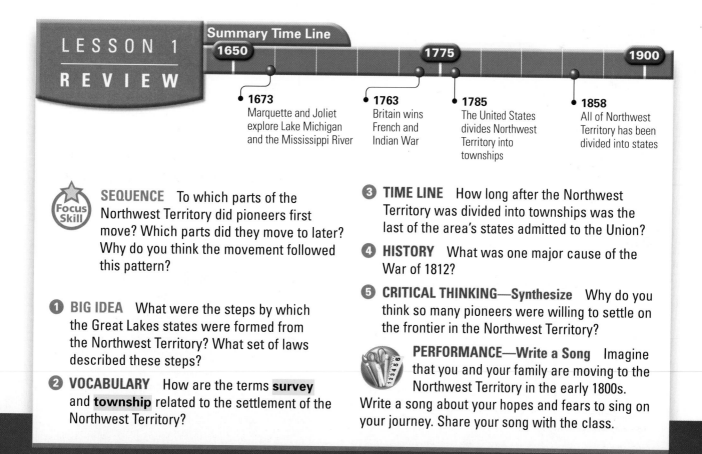

LESSON 1 REVIEW

Summary Time Line

1650

- **1673** Marquette and Joliet explore Lake Michigan and the Mississippi River

1775

- **1763** Britain wins French and Indian War
- **1785** The United States divides Northwest Territory into townships

1900

- **1858** All of Northwest Territory has been divided into states

(Focus Skill) SEQUENCE To which parts of the Northwest Territory did pioneers first move? Which parts did they move to later? Why do you think the movement followed this pattern?

1 BIG IDEA What were the steps by which the Great Lakes states were formed from the Northwest Territory? What set of laws described these steps?

2 VOCABULARY How are the terms **survey** and **township** related to the settlement of the Northwest Territory?

3 TIME LINE How long after the Northwest Territory was divided into townships was the last of the area's states admitted to the Union?

4 HISTORY What was one major cause of the War of 1812?

5 CRITICAL THINKING—Synthesize Why do you think so many pioneers were willing to settle on the frontier in the Northwest Territory?

PERFORMANCE—Write a Song Imagine that you and your family are moving to the Northwest Territory in the early 1800s. Write a song about your hopes and fears to sing on your journey. Share your song with the class.

Compare Historical Maps

▶ WHY IT MATTERS

You are changing and growing all the time. Countries change over time, too. Between 1803 and 1858, for example, the Northwest Territory added six new states, along with their important natural resources, to the nation.

Historical maps give information about places as they were in the past. By comparing historical maps of the same place at different times, you can see how that place has changed.

▶ WHAT YOU NEED TO KNOW

The two historical maps on these pages show the United States at different times. Map A shows the United States in 1791, after the government had passed ordinances about settling the Northwest Territory. Map B shows the United States in 1860, after all of the Great Lakes states had joined the Union.

Each map uses color to show which areas were states or territories at the time. They also show the boundaries of each state and territory and the date each state joined the Union. By looking at both maps, you get a clearer picture of how much the nation grew from 1791 to 1860.

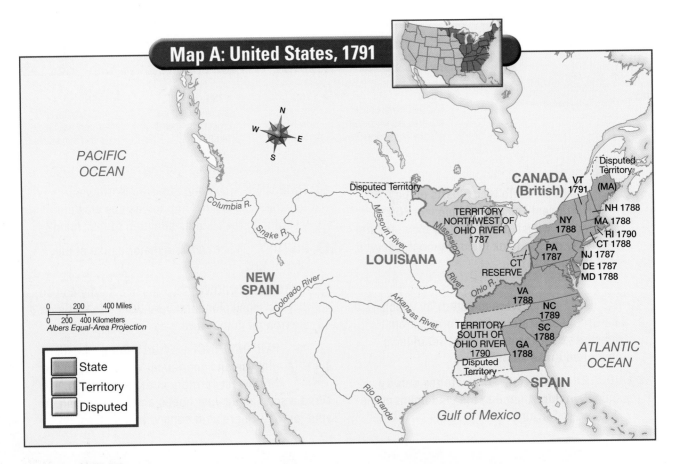

Map A: United States, 1791

PACIFIC OCEAN

Columbia R.

Snake R.

NEW SPAIN

Colorado River

Rio Grande

0   200   400 Miles
0   200   400 Kilometers
Albers Equal-Area Projection

Disputed Territory

Missouri River

Mississippi River

Arkansas River

LOUISIANA

Ohio R.

TERRITORY NORTHWEST OF OHIO RIVER 1787

CT RESERVE

TERRITORY SOUTH OF OHIO RIVER 1790
Disputed Territory

CANADA (British)

VT 1791   (MA)

Disputed Territory

NH 1788
NY 1788   MA 1788
PA 1787   RI 1790
CT 1788
NJ 1787
DE 1787
MD 1788

VA 1788

NC 1789

SC 1788

GA 1788

SPAIN

ATLANTIC OCEAN

Gulf of Mexico

State
Territory
Disputed

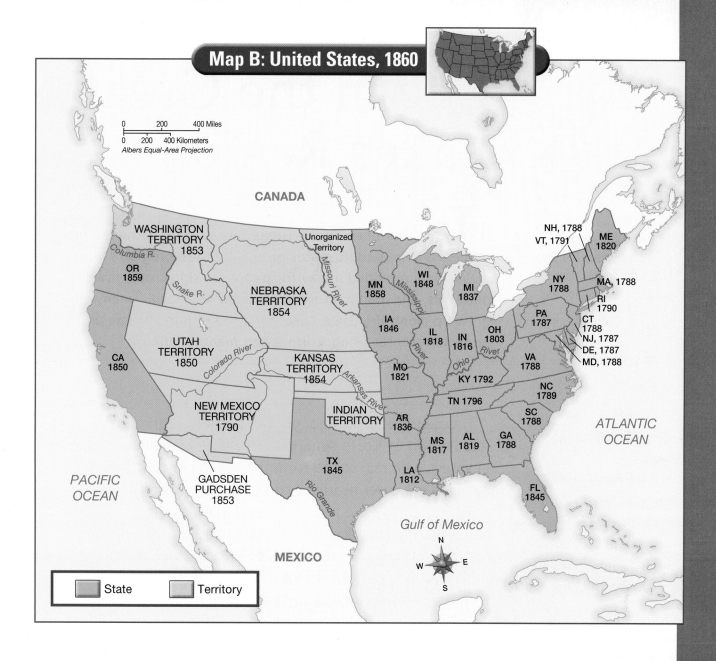

Map B: United States, 1860

0 200 400 Miles
0 200 400 Kilometers
Albers Equal-Area Projection

CANADA

WASHINGTON TERRITORY 1853

Columbia R.

OR 1859

Snake R.

NEBRASKA TERRITORY 1854

Unorganized Territory

Missouri River

MN 1858

WI 1848

Mississippi River

MI 1837

NH, 1788
VT, 1791

ME 1820

NY 1788

MA, 1788

RI 1790

UTAH TERRITORY 1850

Colorado River

IA 1846

IL 1818

IN 1816

OH 1803

PA 1787

CT 1788
NJ, 1787
DE, 1787
MD, 1788

CA 1850

KANSAS TERRITORY 1854

Arkansas River

MO 1821

Ohio River

KY 1792

VA 1788

NEW MEXICO TERRITORY 1790

INDIAN TERRITORY

AR 1836

TN 1796

NC 1789

SC 1788

ATLANTIC OCEAN

PACIFIC OCEAN

GADSDEN PURCHASE 1853

TX 1845

Rio Grande

MS 1817

AL 1819

GA 1788

LA 1812

FL 1845

Gulf of Mexico

N W E S

MEXICO

☐ State   ☐ Territory

▶ PRACTICE THE SKILL

Use the historical maps to answer these questions.

1 How many states were there in 1791? in 1860?

2 Besides the Great Lakes states, which states were added between 1791 and 1860?

3 What feature marked the western-most boundary of territories belonging to the United States in 1791? in 1860?

▶ APPLY WHAT YOU LEARNED

Choose a year between 1791 and 1860. Use the two historical maps on these pages to write a paragraph about the United States during that year. Be sure to tell which areas were already states and which were still territories. Share what you learn with your classmates.

MAP AND GLOBE SKILLS

Practice your map and globe skills with the **GeoSkills CD-ROM**.

2 Life in the Great Lakes Region

 SEQUENCE

As you read, look for events that made the Great Lakes states important centers of agriculture and manufacturing in the United States.

BIG IDEA

Large cities and agriculture and manufacturing industries have grown up in the Great Lakes region.

VOCABULARY

ore
skyscraper
mass production
interchangeable part
assembly line

The rich farmland in the Great Lakes region attracted many settlers and helped its states grow. So did the region's waterways. They provided a way for people to ship crops, raw materials, and manufactured products. As a result, many cities grew up along the Great Lakes, and the region became an important center of agriculture and manufacturing.

Rich Farmland

Thousands of years ago, glaciers pushed south over the middle part of North America. They flattened hills and filled in valleys with rich soil to form the Central Plains. These low, rolling plains cover nearly all of the Great Lakes region.

The region's fertile soil has helped make all the Great Lakes states leaders in agriculture. Farmers there grow many kinds of crops, including corn, wheat, soybeans, and oats. Ohio, Indiana, Illinois, and Minnesota are among the nation's leading producers of corn and soybeans in most years. Farmers in the Great Lakes region also raise large numbers of livestock. In fact, Wisconsin has more cows than it has people!

Everyone enjoys cherries from Michigan, where about 250 million pounds (113 million kg) are grown yearly.

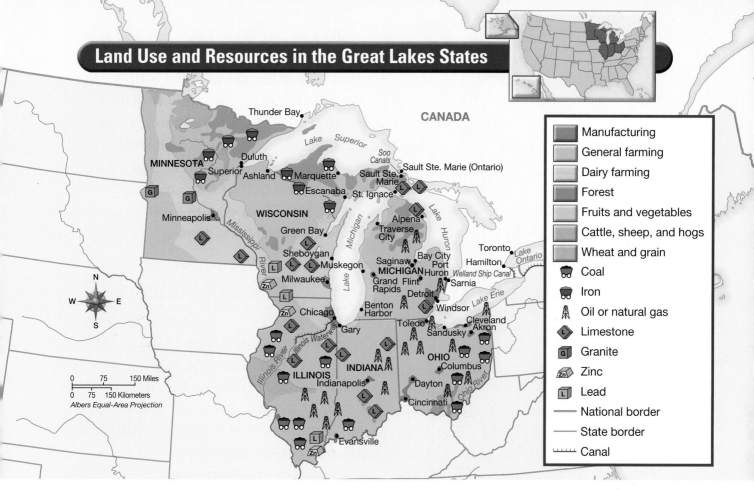

Land Use and Resources in the Great Lakes States

Manufacturing
General farming
Dairy farming
Forest
Fruits and vegetables
Cattle, sheep, and hogs
Wheat and grain
Coal
Iron
Oil or natural gas
Limestone
Granite
Zinc
Lead
National border
State border
Canal

Human–Environment Interactions Before the Illinois Waterway was built, ships could not reach the Mississippi River system from the Great Lakes.

❓ What waterways link the Mississippi River and Lake Michigan?

The cool, damp climate along the Great Lakes is very good for growing fruit and vegetables, too. Michigan produces more cherries than any other state. Minnesota grows the most sugar beets and green peas. After Massachusetts, Wisconsin is the top cranberry-growing state.

REVIEW How were the Central Plains formed? 🔺 SEQUENCE

Great Lakes Ports

The same glaciers that formed the Central Plains also created the Great Lakes. The glaciers scraped out five huge holes in the ground. As the ice melted, water left behind filled the holes and

formed the Great Lakes. Four of these lakes—Erie, Huron, Michigan, and Superior—border Great Lakes states.

The Great Lakes are among the most important waterways in North America. Many rivers flow into and out of the Great Lakes. Long ago, ports were built at the mouths of some of the larger rivers. Over time, some of these ports grew into large cities, such as Detroit, Michigan; Chicago, Illinois; Milwaukee, Wisconsin; Cleveland, Ohio; and Duluth, Minnesota.

Ships can travel all over the world from these Great Lakes ports, even though some of the ports lie more than 1,000 miles (1,609 km) from the Atlantic Ocean. The St. Lawrence Seaway makes this possible.

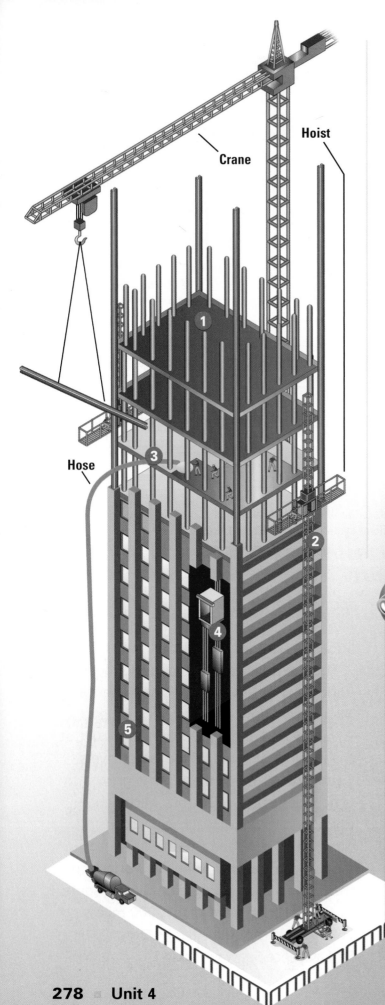

Crane

Hoist

Hose

Ships on the Great Lakes can also reach the Gulf of Mexico. The Illinois Waterway links Lake Michigan with the Illinois River, which flows into the Mississippi River. Using the Illinois Waterway and those rivers, ships can move goods between ports on the Great Lakes and ports on the Gulf of Mexico.

REVIEW How can ships travel all over the world from Great Lakes ports?

Centers of Industry

Few places in the world have as many navigable rivers and lakes as the Great Lakes region. These waterways provide a means of transportation that industries need. As a result, the Great Lakes region has become one of the largest industrial areas of the United States.

Many factories in the Great Lakes states use the region's farm goods to process cereal, flour, and dairy products. In the forested areas around the Great

A CLOSER LOOK
Building a Skyscraper

Before steel was available, buildings could not be taller than 4 or 5 stories. Bricks and wood were not strong enough to support higher buildings. Some skyscrapers today are more than 100 stories tall.

❶ A steel frame holds most of the skyscraper's weight.

❷ Workers, tools, and materials are lifted by a hoist to higher floors.

❸ As each story is built, concrete is mixed and then poured for the floors.

❹ Electric elevators are installed.

❺ The building begins to look finished when workers add glass, metal, or stone walls.

❖ Why do you think skyscrapers need elevators?

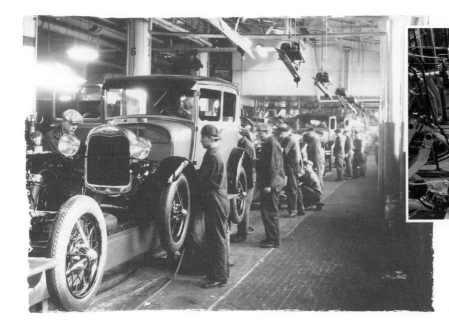

Early automobile factories (left) needed many workers. Today, robots (above) and other machines do much of the work.

Lakes, workers manufacture furniture, paper, and musical instruments.

Many industries use the Great Lakes region's mineral resources. For example, the steel industry uses coal and iron ore found in the region. **Ore** is rock that contains one or more kinds of minerals. Large deposits of iron ore are in Minnesota's Mesabi (muh•SAH•bee) Range. Coal and limestone, also needed to make steel, come from Illinois, Indiana, and other nearby states. To be nearer these resources, the steel industry built steel mills in Gary, Indiana; Chicago, Illinois; Cleveland, Ohio; and other cities along the Great Lakes.

The steel industry grew rapidly in the early 1900s, as people used steel to build railroads, bridges, and tall buildings. In 1885 an engineer named William Jenney used steel and iron to build the 10-story Home Insurance Company Building in Chicago. It was the world's first steel-frame **skyscraper**, or very tall building.

Steel mills in the Great Lakes states no longer make as much steel as they once did. However, steel production is still an important industry in the region. Nearly three-fourths of the nation's steel now comes from the Great Lakes states.

REVIEW What helped the steel industry grow in the Great Lakes states?

Industries Connect

Sometimes one industry helps other industries grow. That is what happened with the automobile and steel industries. When automobile makers began producing large numbers of cars in the early 1900s, the steel mills along the Great Lakes grew by supplying automobile makers with the steel they needed.

Detroit, Michigan, quickly became the center of the automobile industry. One reason for this was Detroit's location on the Detroit River. The river made it easy to ship steel and automobiles in and out of the Detroit area.

The reason why automobile makers began producing large numbers of cars was that they began to manufacture cars by mass production. In **mass production**, many products that are alike can be made quickly and cheaply using machines.

Products made by mass production are the same. Their parts are the same, too. For example, the parts from one mass-produced car will fit another car of the same model and year. This use of **interchangeable parts** makes building and repairing cars easier and less expensive.

The assembly line made mass production of automobiles and many other products possible. An **assembly line** is a line of workers along which a product moves as it is put together one step at a time. In 1913 a business leader named Henry Ford set up one of the nation's largest assembly lines in his automobile factory in Detroit. This method produced cars much faster and more cheaply.

Today the Detroit area still produces more cars and trucks than anywhere else in the United States. In most automobile factories, a computer-controlled assembly line now moves an unfinished car past workers. Robots, or machines controlled by computers, also do much of the work on assembly lines today.

The auto industry helped other industries in the Great Lakes region grow, too. Some factories in the region now produce car parts, tires, and glass for windows. New factories in Detroit build robots and computer equipment for other factories.

REVIEW What methods of production helped the automobile industry grow?

 FAST FACT In 1908, before Ford set up his assembly line, his Model T car cost about $950 and took more than 12 hours to build. By 1927, his factory assembly line could turn out a Model T that cost just $290 in less than two hours!

LESSON 2 REVIEW

Focus Skill **SEQUENCE** What route would a ship follow from Chicago on Lake Michigan to the Gulf of Mexico? Name all the bodies of water the ship would pass through, in the correct order.

1 BIG IDEA Why did many large cities and manufacturing industries grow up in the Great Lakes region?

2 VOCABULARY How are **mass production** and **assembly lines** related?

3 ECONOMICS Why are fruits and vegetables a large part of the agriculture industry in the Great Lakes region?

4 CRITICAL THINKING—Analyze How do you think the faster and cheaper production of automobiles affected life for many Americans?

PERFORMANCE—Write a Newspaper Article Imagine that you are a newspaper reporter in 1913. Write an article about Henry Ford's use of the assembly line. Explain how this new method will affect people.

River Transportation

The Great Lakes have helped shipping, trade, and manufacturing grow in the Great Lakes states. The region's large rivers have also been important to the region's growth. Long ago, American Indians traveled on rivers in canoes to trade goods. Settlers later used the same rivers to reach the region and to ship their products to markets. Today people still use rivers as transportation and trade routes between different parts of the United States.

The Mississippi River System

The names of many bodies of water in the Great Lakes region are drawn from Native American languages. For example, the name of Lake Michigan comes from the Ojibwa (oh•JIB•way) word for "great lake." The Ojibwa Indians lived throughout the Great Lakes region. Many lived in present-day Minnesota, near Lake Itasca, the source of the Mississippi River. The Ojibwa helped name this river, too. Their words *misi sipi* mean "big water."

SEQUENCE
As you read, identify the events that led to the development of transportation routes on the rivers in the Great Lakes region.

BIG IDEA
Discover how the Mississippi River system has been used as a transportation and trade route.

VOCABULARY
migration
flatboat
keelboat
steamboat
freight
barge

Native Americans, explorers, and early traders used canoes made from birchbark or hollowed-out logs to travel through the Great Lakes region. These boats were light enough to be carried around waterfalls and rapids or overland between rivers.

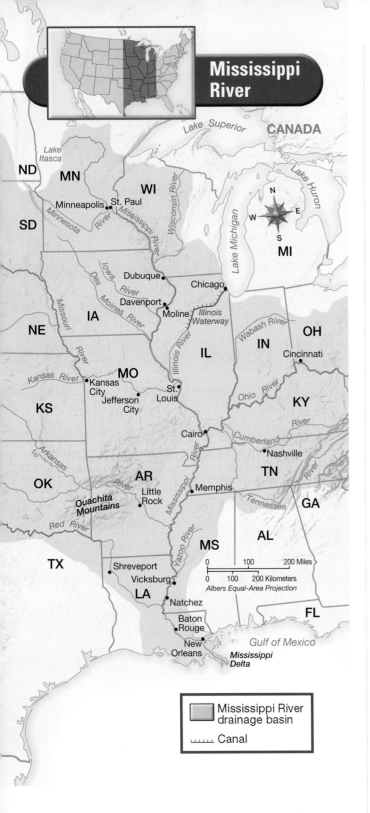

Mississippi River

Movement The Mississippi River system is the world's longest inland waterway. The Mississippi River and its tributaries drain an area of more than 1 million square miles (2.5 million sq km).

➔ What route would a ship or boat follow to reach the port of St. Paul, Minnesota, from Cincinnati, Ohio?

This name seems to be a good description of the mighty Mississippi River. It is North America's largest river, winding 2,348 miles (3,779 km) through the center of the continent. In fact, the Mississippi is so large that a raindrop falling into the river at its source will not reach its mouth at the Gulf of Mexico for 60 days!

At its source, the Mississippi is only a tiny stream. As it flows south, however, about 250 tributaries join the Mississippi, adding to the river's size. In all, the Mississippi River system includes about 14,000 miles (22,530 km) of navigable waterways.

Because the Mississippi River system is so large, geographers often divide it into three regions—upper, middle, and lower. The Great Lakes region lies mainly along the upper Mississippi, which includes the part of the river from its source to an area north of St. Louis, Missouri. The middle Mississippi begins just north of St. Louis. There the Missouri and Illinois Rivers flow into the Mississippi. The lower Mississippi begins where the Ohio River joins the Mississippi at Cairo, Illinois. From Cairo, the lower Mississippi winds along flat land, forming rich floodplains and finally the Mississippi Delta.

REVIEW **Near what cities do the Missouri and Ohio Rivers join the Mississippi?**

Using River Highways

Before paved roads were built in the United States, rivers were used as highways. Water travel was much easier than overland travel through thick forests and rugged mountains. Instead of hauling their goods overland in wagons, settlers and traders could load boats and rafts and float to their destinations.

Rivers carried early settlers inland from the Atlantic Coast, and then farther west from the Appalachian Mountains. The Ohio, Mississippi, and Missouri Rivers became water highways for a huge westward migration. A **migration** is the movement of many people who leave one country or region to settle in another.

Many pioneers used the Ohio River to travel west into the Great Lakes region. Pioneer families carried a lot of goods with them to start their lives on the frontier. When they reached the Ohio River in Pittsburgh, they often boarded flatboats. A **flatboat** is a large raft made of boards that are tied together.

Because flatboats were low and flat, they could carry large amounts of cargo, or goods, even in shallow waters. One person traveling down a river on a flatboat in 1788 described it as "pretty close crowded having 27 men on board, 5 horses, 2 cows, 2 calves, 7 hogs, and 9 dogs besides 8 tons of baggage."

Farmers and traders also used flatboats to carry crops and manufactured goods downstream to ports along the rivers. However, once people unloaded their goods, they could not use the flatboats to travel back upstream, against the current. These boats were usually broken up and sold for lumber. New Orleans, near the end of the Mississippi River system, had many sidewalks made from discarded flatboat wood.

Soon keelboats joined flatboats on the rivers. **Keelboats** were similar to flatboats, except that they were pointed at both ends and sometimes used sails. Unlike flatboats, they could travel upstream by being poled or sailed. However, poling, or pushing, upriver was slow, hard work. It took more than three months to travel upstream on a keelboat from New Orleans to Cincinnati, Ohio.

REVIEW How were rivers part of the westward migration of the United States?
SEQUENCE

Changes in River Travel

As population and industries grew in the United States, the need for faster transportation also increased. The steamboat was developed to help meet this need. A **steamboat** is a boat powered by a steam engine that turns a large wheel.

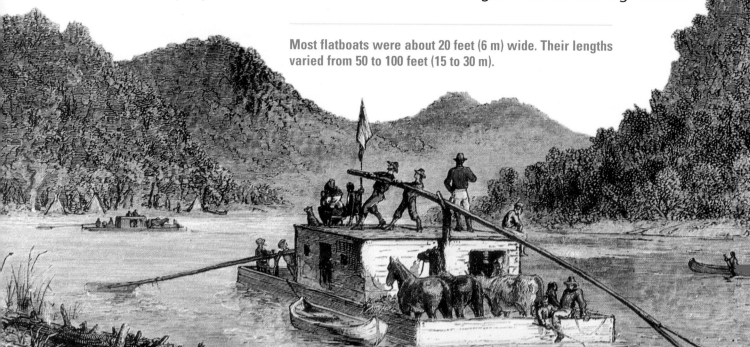

Most flatboats were about 20 feet (6 m) wide. Their lengths varied from 50 to 100 feet (15 to 30 m).

The steamboats *Robert E. Lee* and *Natchez* raced from New Orleans to St. Louis on the Mississippi River in 1870.

As the paddle wheel turns in the water, it causes the steamboat to move. These boats had enough power to travel upstream, against a river's current.

In the summer of 1807, inventor Robert Fulton took his steamboat, the *Clermont,* on a trip up the Hudson River, in New York. Another Fulton steamboat, the *New Orleans,* made an even longer voyage in 1812. The boat traveled more than 2,000 miles (3,219 km) on the Ohio and Mississippi Rivers to the Gulf of Mexico.

By the 1820s steamboats had become one of the main forms of transportation in the United States. They greatly increased the speed at which goods were shipped. Steamboats from New Orleans could reach Cincinnati in just about a week.

Because steamboat transportation was faster, shipping prices dropped, and river trade increased. As a result, several port cities grew up along the Mississippi River system. Cincinnati, Ohio; Minneapolis and St. Paul, Minnesota; and many other cities on rivers in the Great Lakes region became major ports during this time.

REVIEW How did steamboats change river travel and trade?

Using Rivers Today

Rivers are just as important today for moving goods from one region of the country to another. The Mississippi River

The writer Mark Twain, whose real name was Samuel Clemens, worked as a steamboat pilot on the Mississippi as a young man. He later described the work in *Life on the Mississippi*.

alone carries more than half the **freight**, or transported goods, shipped on inland waterways in the United States.

Large ships that sail the oceans can go up the Mississippi River from the Gulf of Mexico as far as Baton Rouge, Louisiana. Smaller boats and barges can travel all the way to Minneapolis, Minnesota— a distance of more than 1,800 miles (2,897 km). A **barge** is a large, flat-bottomed boat used mostly on rivers and other inland waterways.

A single barge can hold tons of cargo. On the Mississippi River system, barges often carry crops grown on farms in the Middle West. They haul industrial products made in the region's factories, coal from Appalachia, and raw materials such as iron ore, sand, and gravel. Barges are also used to ship petroleum and petrochemicals from the Gulf Coast to the Great Lakes states.

To increase shipping and trade, people have modified the Mississippi River in some places. For example, people have built 29 locks and dams on the upper Mississippi to create a more navigable route to Minneapolis.

Often several barges are joined to form units called tows, which are pushed and pulled up and down a river by tugboats.

With such good water transportation available, many industries grew up in cities along the Mississippi River system, just as they did along the Great Lakes. Factories in Minneapolis and St. Paul, for instance, manufacture clothing, metal, paper, and food products. In Cincinnati, workers produce soap, tools, and even jet airplane engines.

REVIEW What kind of boat carries most of the goods on the Mississippi River system today?

LESSON 3 REVIEW

 SEQUENCE List the different kinds of boats in the order in which they came to be used on the Mississippi River.

1 BIG IDEA What are some of the ways the Mississippi River system has been used as a transportation and trade route?

2 VOCABULARY Use the terms **freight** and **barge** to describe shipping and trade on the Mississippi River system today.

3 ECONOMICS How did the invention of the steamboat affect the economy of the Great Lakes region?

4 CRITICAL THINKING—Hypothesize What might happen to the price of food and other goods if the Mississippi River system could no longer be used as a shipping route?

 PERFORMANCE—Make a List Imagine that you are about to travel on a flatboat to settle in the Great Lakes region. You must choose ten things to take with you. Explain to classmates why you chose those items.

4

SEQUENCE

As you read, look for ways in which rivers have become important in different countries around the world.

BIG IDEA

Rivers around the world are both similar to and different from those in the United States.

VOCABULARY

paddy

deforestation

Flat-bottomed sailboats called feluccas (fuh•LOO•kuhz) have been cruising on the Nile for thousands of years.

LOCATE IT

Nile River in Egypt

Rivers Around the World

Like many people in the United States, people in other countries often choose to live along rivers. They farm the fertile floodplains and deltas or live and work in cities along the rivers. They also use rivers to travel and to transport their goods. Yet all rivers in the world are different, and people around the world use rivers in their own ways.

The Nile River

The Nile River is the longest river in the world. Beginning in the mountains of east-central Africa, the Nile flows north 4,187 miles (6,738 km). In the country of Egypt, the Nile River ends where it empties into the Mediterranean Sea.

The Nile is the most important source of fresh water in all of Egypt. For this reason, most of Egypt's people live in the fertile, green Nile Valley and Nile Delta. Many people in both of these areas earn a living by farming.

For thousands of years, Egyptian farmers depended on Nile River floods to water their fields. The floods left behind rich silt along the river's banks. Each summer, after the Nile flooded, farmers planted their seeds. For irrigation, they also trapped water left behind from the floods by digging basins.

Major Rivers of the World

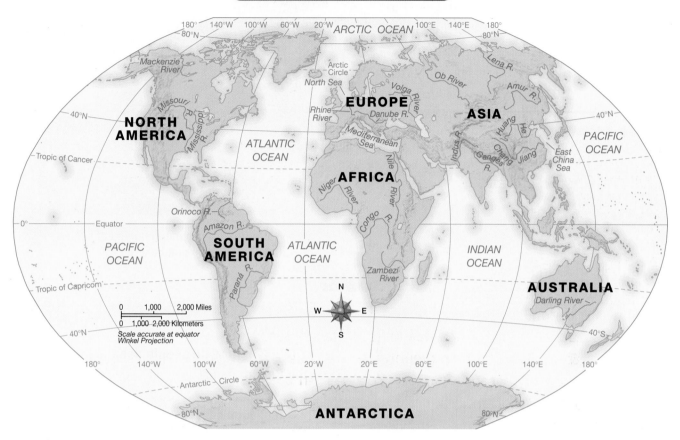

Location Like most rivers in the United States, most rivers around the world eventually reach the oceans.

❖ Into which ocean does the Ganges River flow?

Today, however, the Aswan High Dam in Egypt stops the Nile from flooding. The water stored behind the dam has allowed people to irrigate millions of acres of new farmland. The dam also provides drinking water and electricity for Egypt's people and industries.

Not everyone agreed about building the Aswan High Dam, however. Some people argue that the dam prevents important silt from reaching the floodplain downstream. As a result, most Egyptian farmers must now add fertilizer

to the soil in order for their crops to grow. Others feel that such challenges are a small price to pay for a dependable source of water and power.

REVIEW Why is the Nile River important for Egypt? SEQUENCE

This ancient painting shows early Egyptian farmers harvesting a field.

The Chang Jiang

The Chang Jiang (CHAHNG jee•AHNG) in China is the third-longest river in the world. In fact, the name *Chang Jiang* means "long river." It flows for more than 3,400 miles (5,472 km) across China.

Near the Chang Jiang's mouth lies the city of Shanghai (shang•HY). It is China's largest and most industrial city and busiest port. Many other cities and industries line the banks of the Chang Jiang.

Farmers in China grow many crops along the Chang Jiang. Miles and miles of rice fields, or **paddies**, stretch from the banks of the river. This helps make China the world's leader for rice production. Cotton, wheat, and other crops also grow well along the river.

To get these crops to markets, the Chinese have been modifying the Chang Jiang for centuries. More than 1,000 years ago, the Chinese started building a system of canals to link the Chang Jiang to other rivers in China. Today, that waterway is called the Grand Canal.

Water from the Chang Jiang is often used to flood nearby rice paddies.

It is the longest human-made waterway in the world.

REVIEW How do people use the land along the Chang Jiang?

The Ganges River

The Ganges River flows 1,560 miles (2,511 km) through the southern part of Asia. For much of its course, the Ganges crosses the country of India.

The Ganges River, like other major rivers, provides transportation, water for farming and drinking, and deposits of rich soil along its banks. The delta

Varanasi, India, is one of the seven holy cities for Hindus. More than 1 million pilgrims visit this city on the Ganges each year.

LOCATE IT

INDIA

Varanasi

formed by the Ganges is the largest in the world. It is about twice the size of the Mississippi Delta.

The Ganges is very different from other rivers around the world in one way. For Hindus, people who follow the religion of Hinduism, the Ganges is a holy river. Each year thousands of Hindus go to the Ganges to bathe in its waters. They believe the water will purify and heal them. "The Ganges is more than a river," says Raghubir Singh of India. "It is a . . . force that holds 5,000 years of history, culture, and tradition."

REVIEW What makes the Ganges different from other rivers?

The Amazon River

The Amazon River is South America's longest river. It begins in the mountains of Peru near the Pacific Ocean. From this source, it flows east across Brazil to the Atlantic Ocean. The Amazon's total length is about 4,000 miles (6,400 km). It carries more water than any other river in the world.

Many areas in the Amazon River basin receive more than 100 inches (254 cm) of rain a year. Because most of this land lies near the equator, the Amazon River basin also is hot all year. This climate has produced the world's largest rain forest along the Amazon River. One tour guide explains, "You can walk . . . for six months and still be in the rain forest."

Few people live along the Amazon River. For many, the climate is just too hot and humid. Still, there are a few small cities and ports on the river. About 2 acres of the Amazon rain forest are now being cleared every second to make room

for farms and grazing land. Many people are worried about **deforestation**, or the clearing of forest land by cutting down trees. People around the world are working hard to protect these important resources for the future.

REVIEW Why do few people live along the Amazon River?

• GEOGRAPHY •

GEOGRAPHY ESSENTIAL ELEMENTS

The Amazon Rain Forest
Understanding Physical Systems

The Amazon rain forest covers an area more than half the size of the United States! Its thick vegetation extends across about one-third of South America, mostly in Brazil. More kinds of trees live in the Amazon rain forest than in any other place on Earth. The forest also is home to millions of different kinds of insects, birds, fish, and animals.

Macaws live in the Amazon rain forest.

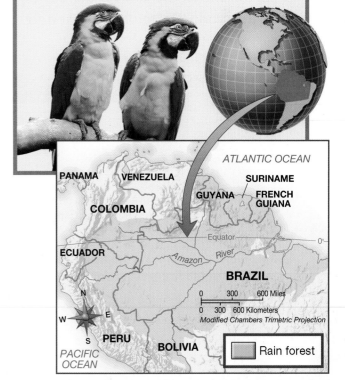

Several old castles, like this one in Germany, line the banks of the Rhine River.

The Rhine River

The Rhine River is the most important inland waterway in Europe. Starting in the mountains of Switzerland, the Rhine flows 865 miles (1,392 km) northwest through the continent. In the Netherlands, the Rhine empties into the North Sea, a part of the Atlantic Ocean.

The Rhine River is like many navigable rivers in the United States. It connects inland cities to an ocean port, Rotterdam. This port in the Netherlands is the busiest port in the world. Rotterdam is linked to the North Sea by a 19-mile (31-km) canal called the New Waterway.

Industries in many European countries use the Rhine River to transport raw materials and finished products to Rotterdam for shipment around the world. About one-fifth of the world's chemical industries are located along the Rhine. As on the Mississippi River, long lines of barges travel on the Rhine River each day.

REVIEW **Why is the Rhine River Europe's most important inland waterway?**

LESSON 4
REVIEW

 SEQUENCE Before dams were built on the Nile River, what did farmers do after the Nile flooded?

1 BIG IDEA In what ways are rivers around the world similar to rivers in the United States?

2 VOCABULARY Use the term **paddy** to describe farming along the Chang Jiang.

3 CULTURE What religion considers the Ganges a holy river?

4 CRITICAL THINKING—Evaluate Why do you think so much of the world's population lives along rivers?

 PERFORMANCE—Make a Table Make a table that has four columns labeled *River, Continent, Length,* and *Major Uses.* Fill the table with information about the rivers discussed in this lesson. Next, write questions that can be answered from the table. Then exchange papers with a partner and answer each other's questions.

· SKILLS ·

Make a Thoughtful Decision

VOCABULARY

consequence

▶ WHY IT MATTERS

You make decisions every day. Some are easy, like deciding what to eat for breakfast. Others are more difficult, such as deciding what college to attend. Difficult decisions require more thought because your choices may have lasting consequences (KAHN•suh•kwen•suhz). A **consequence** is what happens because of an action.

▶ WHAT YOU NEED TO KNOW

To make thoughtful decisions, you can follow these steps.

Step 1 Identify a goal and make a list of choices that might help you reach your goal.

Step 2 Think about possible consequences for each choice.

Step 3 Decide which choice you think will have the best consequences, and then follow your choice.

▶ PRACTICE THE SKILL

Being able to make thoughtful decisions is important for governments, too. In 1970 the government of Egypt decided to build the Aswan High Dam across the Nile River. Think again about arguments for and against building the dam and some of the consequences of the government's decision.

1 What arguments did people use for and against building the dam?

2 Explain the good and bad consequences of building the Aswan High Dam.

3 If it had been your decision to make, would you have built the dam? Explain.

▶ APPLY WHAT YOU LEARNED

Think about a decision that you made recently. What were the consequences of your decision? Do you think your decision was a thoughtful one? Explain.

Aswan High Dam in Egypt

CITIZENSHIP SKILLS

8 Review and Test Preparation

Summary Time Line

1600   1700

1682
France claims all
land drained by the
Mississippi River

⭐ (Focus Skill) Use Your Reading Skills

Copy the following graphic organizer onto a separate sheet of
paper. Use the information you have learned to sequence
events that have occurred in the Great Lakes states. Complete
it by writing the event in the appropriate date's box.

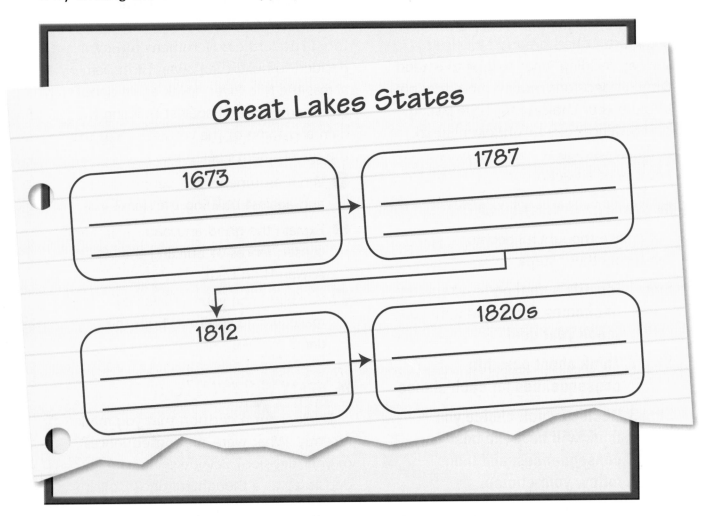

Great Lakes States

| 1673 | 1787 |
| 1812 | 1820s |

THINK & WRITE

Describe a River   Choose one of the
rivers discussed in this chapter. Write a
paragraph describing its location, its source
and its mouth, and how it is used.

Write Questions   Write questions about
people or places that were part of the history
of the Great Lakes region. Phrase your
questions as "Who am I?" or "Where am I?"

1800		1900	Present

1763
French and
Indian War ends

1803
Ohio becomes the first
Great Lakes state

1885
First skyscraper in the world is
built in the Great Lakes region

1971
Aswan High Dam is
completed on the
Nile River

USE THE TIME LINE

Use the chapter summary time line to answer these questions.

1 When did the French and Indian War end?

2 Which was built first, the Aswan High Dam or the world's first skyscraper?

USE VOCABULARY

Choose the letter of the definition that best matches each term.

3 **survey**
A to trade
B to measure
C to build

4 **frontier**
A lands near a large metropolitan area
B lands beyond settlement
C lands along a river

5 **ore**
A rock that contains one or more kinds of minerals
B a manufactured good made from a raw material
C petroleum pumped from the ground

RECALL FACTS

Answer these questions.

6 Why did French leaders send an expedition to explore the Mississippi River?

7 How can ships sailing from ports along the Great Lakes reach the Atlantic Ocean?

8 How did steamboats affect the growth of cities and industries along the Great Lakes?

9 What is the longest river in the world? Where is it?

Write the letter of the best choice.

10 Which of these lakes does **not** border any of the Great Lakes states?
A Lake Erie
B Lake Huron
C Lake Superior
D Lake Ontario

11 The city on one of the Great Lakes that had the world's first skyscraper is—
F Cleveland, Ohio.
G Chicago, Illinois.
H Minneapolis, Minnesota.
J Detroit, Michigan.

THINK CRITICALLY

12 What do you think Native Americans living in the Great Lakes region thought of the Northwest Ordinance of 1787? Explain.

13 If you could visit any river in the world, which would you choose? Why?

APPLY SKILLS

Compare Historical Maps

14 Look at the historical maps on pages 274 and 275. How did Virginia change from 1791 to 1860?

Make a Thoughtful Decision

15 Imagine that you have been offered a choice of two jobs. You can be a riverboat captain or a worker on a factory assembly line. Make a thoughtful decision about which job you would choose. Consider all the consequences of the decision. Explain your decision.

NEBRASKA SAND HILLS

Covering almost one-fourth of Nebraska, the Sand Hills region is the largest tract of sand dunes in the Western Hemisphere. Though dunes up to 300 feet (91 m) tall are found there, the Nebraska Sand Hills also has many small lakes, rivers, and miles of grasses. In fact, the Sand Hills is part of the largest area of undisturbed grasslands in the United States.

LOCATE IT

NEBRASKA

Nebraska Sand Hills

Plains States

**" The grass is the country,
as the water is the sea. "**

—Willa Cather,
My Ántonia, 1918

Draw Conclusions

A **conclusion** is a decision reached by thoughtful study. When you draw a conclusion, you combine new facts with facts you already know to make a general statement about an idea or an event.

As you read each lesson in this chapter, be sure to do the following.

- List facts you already know about an event or topic relating to the Plains states.
- Add new facts about that subject.
- Use your list to draw a conclusion about that event or topic.

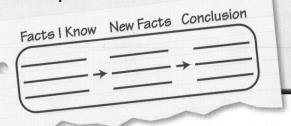

Facts I Know   New Facts   Conclusion

1

As you read, draw conclusions about how the environment of the Interior Plains affected early ways of life.

BIG IDEA

Read to learn how people long ago used the resources of the Plains region.

VOCABULARY

prairie

sod

self-sufficient

adapt

tepee

FAST FACT

The Missouri River earned the nickname "Big Muddy" because it carries so much silt and mud. People often say the river is "too thin to plow, too thick to drink."

Early Days on the Interior Plains

1600	1700	1800	1900

After the Great Lakes states were established, Americans moved farther west in the Middle West region. They first settled on the fertile, rolling lands west of the Mississippi River, in what are now the states of Missouri and Iowa. These lands are part of the Central Plains. Later, pioneers moved even farther west onto the dry, flat lands of the Great Plains. Kansas, Nebraska, South Dakota, and North Dakota lie mostly in the Great Plains. Together, all these states make up the Plains region of the United States.

Pioneers on the Central Plains

Like the Great Lakes states, much of what are now the Plains states was once claimed by France. As a result, the French were the first Europeans to explore and settle in the region.

Trees dotted the Central Plains in what is now Council Bluffs, Iowa. Many pioneer trails met there to cross the Missouri River.

They came from Canada in the north and up the Mississippi River from the south. Even today, many cities in the Plains region—such as Des Moines (dih MOYN), Iowa, and St. Louis, Missouri—have French names.

Several French settlements in the Plains region began as fur trading posts along rivers. St. Louis, for example, was founded in 1764 by a French fur trader from New Orleans. Its location, about 10 miles (16 km) south of where the Missouri River joins the Mississippi River, helped St. Louis become the busiest trading post in the region.

With the Louisiana Purchase in 1803, the Plains region became part of the United States. Soon, thousands of Americans headed west, hoping to start farms and businesses on the Central Plains. There they found large rivers cutting through rolling hills, some areas of forests, and dark, rich soil.

To begin their new lives on the Central Plains, settlers had to make a long, hard journey. Most pioneers had to travel in wagons overland.

During much of their journey west, pioneers traveled over miles of prairie (PRAIR•ee). A **prairie** is an area of flat or rolling land covered mostly with wildflowers and grasses.

In some places on the Central Plains the grasses rose above the pioneers' heads. The first pioneers to see this tall-grass prairie described it as "a sea of grass." Those grasses helped make the area's soil very dark and fertile. When the grasses died, they rotted and left behind matter that enriched the soil.

REVIEW How did the Plains region become part of the United States?

LOCATE IT

NEBRASKA

Willa Cather Memorial Prairie

• BIOGRAPHY •

Willa Cather   1873–1947

Character Trait: Individualism

Many of Willa Cather's books, such as *O Pioneers!* and *My Ántonia*, describe the Plains region and the individualism of the pioneers who settled there. Much of Cather's writing was drawn from her own childhood experiences on the Nebraska frontier. "I was . . . homesick and lonely," she later remembered. "[But] by the end of the first autumn the shaggy grass country had gripped me with a passion that I have never been able to shake." Today, people can learn about Cather's love of the plains at the Willa Cather Memorial Prairie in Nebraska.

MULTIMEDIA BIOGRAPHIES
Visit The Learning Site at
www.harcourtschool.com to
learn about other famous people.

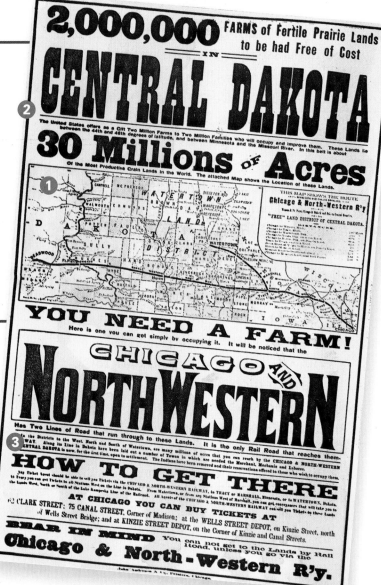

A Railroad Poster

Analyze Primary Sources

This poster from the 1870s advertised free land to people willing to move to the area that is now South Dakota.

1. A map on the poster showed the area where the land was available.

2. The poster explains that the United States government was giving away the land.

3. Directions for taking trains to the area were listed on the poster.

◆ Where do you think posters like this one were displayed?

Life on the Great Plains

Farther west, on the drier Great Plains, the prairie grasses grew short and stubbly. For miles the flat land looked much the same. At first, few settlers wanted to move onto the Great Plains. They thought the entire region was a vast, treeless wasteland that was too dry to farm or live on.

To encourage settlement on the Great Plains, the United States government passed the Homestead Act in 1862. Under this law, any person over 21 who was the head of a family could receive 160 acres of land at no cost. That person had to live on the land, called a homestead, for five years and make improvements to it.

The government also gave millions of acres of land on the Great Plains to railroad companies. In return, the companies agreed to build railroads there. Even before the railroads were completed, the railroad companies advertised their new routes in newspapers all over the United States and in other countries.

Thousands of settlers soon made their way to the Great Plains. Some came from farms and cities in the East. Many were African Americans from the South. Even though slavery had ended, conditions in the South were still harsh and unfair. More than 15,000 African Americans migrated to Kansas in just one year. They called themselves Exodusters because they made an exodus, or mass departure, to a freer land. Newcomers to the Plains also included farming families from Sweden, Norway, Germany, Ireland, and other countries. After making the journey west, settlers had to build a new life on the frontier. They soon learned that living on the Great Plains presented special challenges.

Most pioneers on the frontier had to build their own houses. Since few trees grew on the Great Plains, most settlers built their houses out of sod. **Sod** is a layer of soil held together by the roots of grasses. It took about an acre of sod from the prairie to make a one-room "soddy," as sod houses were called.

Sod houses had some good points. In the summer they stayed cool, like a cave. In the winter their thick walls kept the houses warm inside. Each spring, flowers sprouted from some of the sod roofs! And sod houses did not burn easily. This was important on the prairie, where there were sometimes dangerous grass fires. Soddies had bad points, too. They were damp and dirty, of course. Leaky roofs were a common problem, as were insects and small animals. One woman wrote,

> **66** I remember it—bugs and snakes and mice were always dropping down from the ceiling. . . . Mama used to hang sheets over the tables and beds so that things wouldn't fall on them. **99**

Homes on the frontier of the Great Plains were often a long way from a town and stores. Even the closest neighbors could be miles away. Because of this, pioneer families had to be self-sufficient. **Self-sufficient** means able to do almost everything for yourself, with no help from other people.

Besides building sod houses, settlers on the Great Plains found other ways to use available resources. They built fences with rocks and dirt. They slept on mattresses filled with straw or cornhusks. To make fires, they burned corncobs, straw, and dried manure called buffalo chips.

Families on the frontier made just about everything they needed. They grew their own food—usually corn, beans, and potatoes. From their farm animals, they had milk, meat, eggs, wool and hides, and materials to make soap and candles. To get water on the dry Great Plains, settlers dug deep wells and built large windmills to pump water from them.

REVIEW **Why did settlers on the Great Plains need to be self-sufficient?**
DRAW CONCLUSIONS

This photo shows the Shores family in 1888 in front of the sod buildings of their farm in Nebraska.

Native Americans on the Great Plains rode on horseback and used arrows and spears to hunt buffalo.

Plains Indians and Lifeways

Long before the pioneers arrived on the Great Plains, the Sioux (soo) and other Native American groups lived there. During the 1600s, many of the Sioux left the forests and lakes of present-day Wisconsin and Minnesota. They settled farther west, where North Dakota and South Dakota are today. These Sioux called themselves Lakota.

Like the pioneers, the Sioux had to **adapt**, or fit their ways of living, to their new environment. There are few rivers on the Great Plains, so the Sioux had to give up canoes as a means of travel. Instead, they learned to use horses.

Spanish explorers first brought horses to the Americas in the 1500s. Some of those horses ran away and lived wild. Over time, the number of wild horses increased. The Sioux captured and tamed some of the horses and learned to ride

them. This changed the way of life for the Sioux and for many other Plains Indians. On horses the Indians could travel long distances to hunt buffalo.

Instead of building permanent homes and farming the land, the Sioux moved from place to place, following herds of buffalo. In order to travel quickly, the Sioux built shelters that were easy to move. These shelters, called **tepees**, were cone-shaped tents made of poles and covered with animal skins. Because trees were scarce on the Great Plains, the Sioux often went to the Rocky Mountains to get wooden poles long enough for their tepees.

The Sioux depended on the buffalo for most of their needs. They ate buffalo meat, and they made tepees, clothing, and ropes from buffalo skins and hair. They used the bones for tools and arrow-heads. As the settlers would do later, the Sioux burned buffalo chips for fire.

In the 1860s about 15 million buffalo lived on the Great Plains. "The plain was alive with thousands of buffalo," wrote one early traveler through the region. "The swelling prairie was darkened with them to the very horizon." The Indians killed only as many buffalo as they needed to survive. As white settlers used more of the land for farming and hunting, however, the buffalo began to disappear. Also, the railroad companies hired hunters to shoot buffalo to feed railway workers and to sell the valuable hides. By 1880 nearly all the buffalo were gone. As a result, the traditional way of life for the Sioux and other Plains Indians eventually disappeared.

REVIEW How did the Sioux meet many of their needs on the Great Plains?

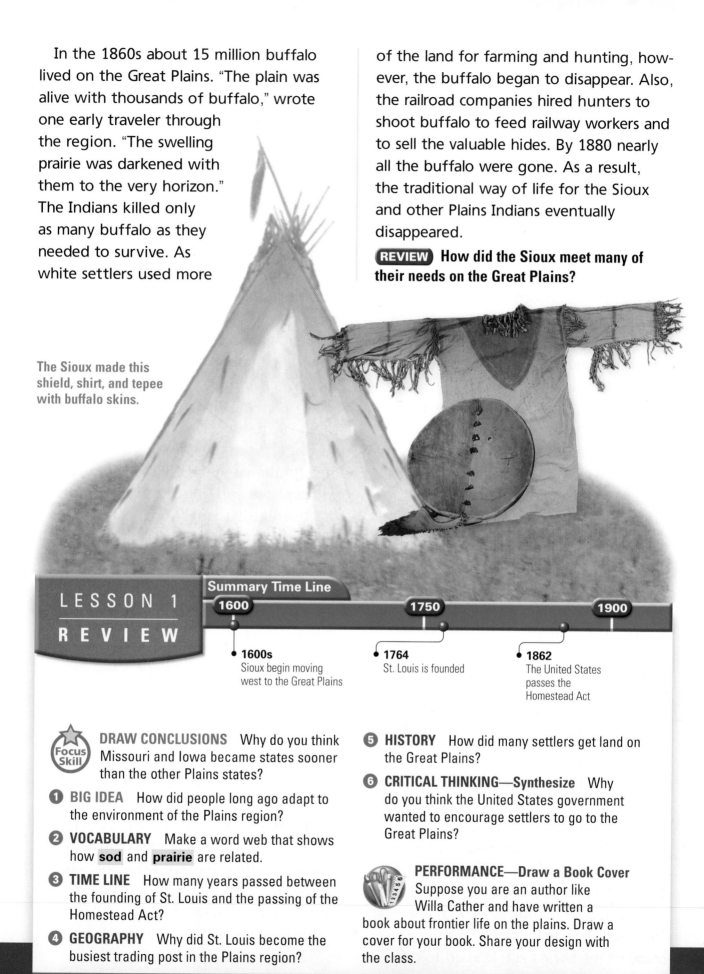

The Sioux made this shield, shirt, and tepee with buffalo skins.

LESSON 1 REVIEW

Summary Time Line

1600 — 1750 — 1900

1600s Sioux begin moving west to the Great Plains

1764 St. Louis is founded

1862 The United States passes the Homestead Act

(Focus Skill) DRAW CONCLUSIONS Why do you think Missouri and Iowa became states sooner than the other Plains states?

1 BIG IDEA How did people long ago adapt to the environment of the Plains region?

2 VOCABULARY Make a word web that shows how **sod** and **prairie** are related.

3 TIME LINE How many years passed between the founding of St. Louis and the passing of the Homestead Act?

4 GEOGRAPHY Why did St. Louis become the busiest trading post in the Plains region?

5 HISTORY How did many settlers get land on the Great Plains?

6 CRITICAL THINKING—Synthesize Why do you think the United States government wanted to encourage settlers to go to the Great Plains?

PERFORMANCE—Draw a Book Cover Suppose you are an author like Willa Cather and have written a book about frontier life on the plains. Draw a cover for your book. Share your design with the class.

Use a Cultural Map

▶ WHY IT MATTERS

You have read about the Sioux Indians and how they lived. To know exactly where they lived, you can use a cultural map. A cultural map shows where people with similar ways of life live.

The culture of each Native American group was often affected by where the group lived and what natural resources were nearby. Studying where a Native American group lived can help you understand how the group's environment and culture are related.

▶ WHAT YOU NEED TO KNOW

The cultural map on page 303 shows where some Native American groups lived in the Plains region during the 1700s. By looking at the map, you can see where the Sioux lived and which tribes were their neighbors.

The map also shows some of the physical features of the Plains region, such as major rivers. It shows what areas are covered mostly by the Central and Great Plains, too. Having both physical features and cultural regions of an area on the same map allows you to compare the two. It also can help you draw conclusions about how culture and environment can be related.

An Oglala Sioux poses in front of his tepee in January 1891.

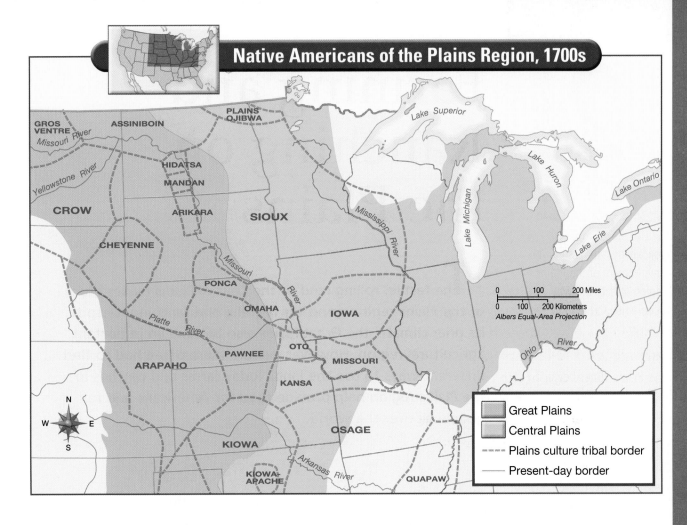

Native Americans of the Plains Region, 1700s

GROS VENTRE
ASSINIBOIN
PLAINS OJIBWA
Lake Superior
Missouri River
Yellowstone River
HIDATSA
MANDAN
CROW
ARIKARA
SIOUX
Lake Huron
Lake Michigan
Lake Ontario
CHEYENNE
Mississippi River
Lake Erie
Missouri River
PONCA
OMAHA
IOWA
Platte River
OTO
ARAPAHO
PAWNEE
MISSOURI
Ohio River
KANSA
Arkansas River
KIOWA
OSAGE
KIOWA-APACHE
QUAPAW

0   100   200 Miles
0   100   200 Kilometers
Albers Equal-Area Projection

Great Plains
Central Plains
- - - Plains culture tribal border
——— Present-day border

▶ PRACTICE THE SKILL

Use the cultural map to answer these questions.

❶ What tribes labeled on the map lived mostly on the Great Plains?

❷ What tribes labeled on the map lived mostly on the Central Plains?

❸ Which tribes had names similar to the names of today's states?

❹ Along what river running through the Great Plains did many Native American groups settle?

❺ How do you think life on the Interior Plains affected the tribes' cultures?

▶ APPLY WHAT YOU LEARNED

Choose one of the Native American groups labeled on the map above. Use the library or the Internet to learn more about the group's lifeways. Then write a few paragraphs explaining how life on the Interior Plains affected how these Native Americans lived. Share with your family your map, paragraphs, and what you have learned.

Practice your map and globe skills with the **GeoSkills CD-ROM**.

2

DRAW CONCLUSIONS

As you read, draw conclusions about how the environment of the Plains region affects the way people use the land to earn a living.

BIG IDEA

The Plains states became an important farming and ranching region.

VOCABULARY

entrepreneur
blizzard
hailstorm
windbreak

FAST FACT The first horse-drawn combines were introduced in Michigan in 1836. Machine-driven combines appeared a century later. Modern combines feature dust-free, air-conditioned cabs with CD players, and can harvest more than 100 acres of grain per day.

Farming and Ranching on the Plains

The fertile, rolling land of the Central Plains makes much of the Plains region good for farming and ranching. Despite its drier climate, the Great Plains also became an important agricultural region. However, people there often had to find different ways to use the land. Today farms and ranches in the Plains region help provide food for Americans and for people all over the world.

Two Plains, Two Crops

In 1913 Willa Cather described much of the land in the Middle West as "a vast checkerboard, marked off in squares of wheat and corn." For many years, corn was the largest farm product on the Central Plains, and wheat was the largest on the Great Plains. The main reason for this is the difference in climate between the two parts of the Plains region.

Farmers today use large machines called combines (KAHM•bynz) to harvest wheat. A combine can cut the wheat and separate the grain from the stems in one step.

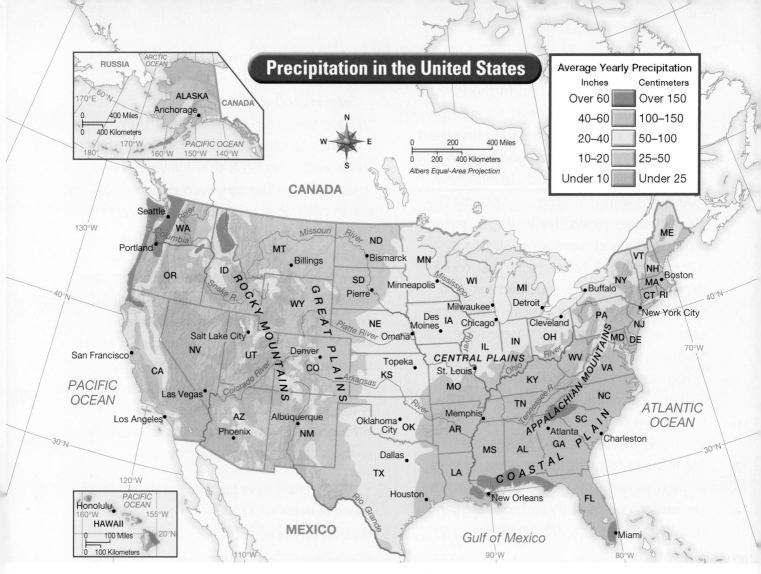

Precipitation in the United States

Average Yearly Precipitation

Inches		Centimeters
Over 60		Over 150
40–60		100–150
20–40		50–100
10–20		25–50
Under 10		Under 25

Regions **Missouri receives more precipitation than any other Plains state.**

Which two Plains states receive the least precipitation?

The rainier climate of the Central Plains is ideal for growing corn. In most years, Iowa is the top corn-growing state in the nation, and Nebraska is not far behind. Together, they produce about one-third of all the corn in the United States. Most of this corn is not the kind that people can eat right off the cob. It is dent corn. Dent corn makes good feed for livestock. It is also used to manufacture many products.

The drier climate on the Great Plains is better suited to growing wheat. Early farmers on the Great Plains first had success growing wheat when Russian

Mennonites (MEH•nuh•nyts) moved there in the late 1800s. From Russia they brought winter wheat, which grows well in dry climates.

Today miles of wheat fields cover the Great Plains. In most years, North Dakota and Kansas are the leading wheat-producing states. Most of this wheat is used to make flour. Farmers on the Great Plains also grow durum (DUR•uhm) wheat, which is used to make spaghetti and other kinds of pasta.

REVIEW **Why is more wheat than corn grown on the Great Plains?**

Changing Farms

Farmers who first settled in the Plains region needed new kinds of tools to break up the soil. The iron plows they had used in the East were not very good at turning over the prairie's thick sod. Several new inventions improved the way people farmed. Steel plows, for example, cut through the sod more easily. Using a machine called a reaper, a farmer could harvest five times as much wheat as a farmer could by hand. Another machine, called a thresher, then separated the grain from the stems.

Farming methods continue to change. Today's technology allows farmers to raise more crops on each acre of land than ever before. It also makes it possible for farmers to plant larger areas of land. In fact, most farms in the United States are now more than three times bigger than they were in 1900. Some farms in the Plains region are now owned by large businesses and are run like factories.

Farmers today add fertilizers to the soil to help their crops grow. Often they use airplanes or other machines to spray their fields with chemicals that kill weeds and insects. Some farmers even use computers to plan when to plant and harvest their crops, and to check crop prices.

The crops grown in the Plains region have also changed. In addition to corn and wheat, sorghum is now another leading crop in the region. Nearly half the country's sorghum comes from Kansas. In North Dakota, farmers grow more barley and oats than in any other state, while Iowa is top in soybean production. Farmers throughout the region also raise livestock, such as cattle, sheep, and chickens.

REVIEW How have farms in the United States changed in recent years? **DRAW CONCLUSIONS**

POINTS OF VIEW
Prairie Dogs

Prairie dog burrows can damage farmland and ranchland on the Great Plains. Yet some people think prairie dogs are important.

JONATHAN PROCTOR, Wildlife Program Associate, Predator Project

66 Prairie dogs are a food source for many other animals and create homes for them by digging deep burrows. Their digging helps make the soil healthy and helps plants grow. We need prairie dogs to protect the health and wildlife of the Great Plains. 99

SANDRA WATKINS, Great Plains rancher and farmer

66 Prairie dogs build mounds in the middle of our fields that injure our farm animals and damage our farming equipment. Our farming costs have increased because of the never-ending battle to rid our land of these varmints. 99

Analyze the Viewpoints

❶ What viewpoint does each person hold about prairie dogs?

❷ **Make It Relevant** Ranchers and wildlife workers are trying to compromise over prairie dogs. Work with classmates to think of possible solutions to the conflict.

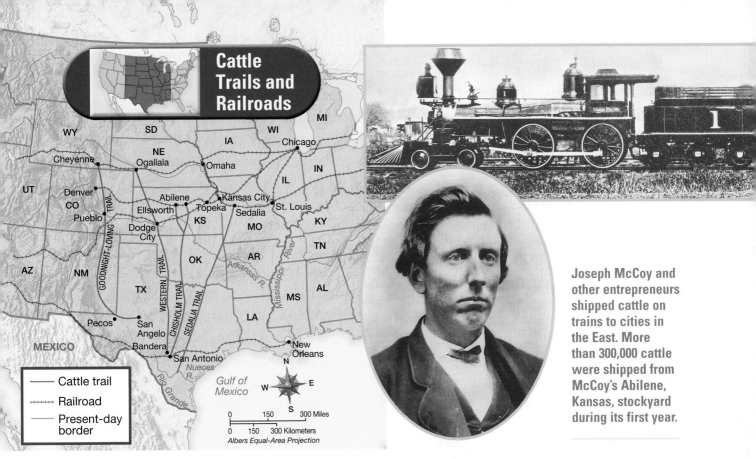

Cattle Trails and Railroads

Joseph McCoy and other entrepreneurs shipped cattle on trains to cities in the East. More than 300,000 cattle were shipped from McCoy's Abilene, Kansas, stockyard during its first year.

GEOGRAPHY THEME

Movement **It often took ranchers three months to drive their cattle north to the railroads in the Plains region.**

Which cattle trail led to Missouri?

Railroads and Ranches

In the late 1800s, railroad companies built miles of railroad lines across the Plains region. The trains helped cities in the region grow and connected them with cities in other parts of the country. The railroads also helped the ranching industry grow in the region.

Among the cities that grew were Topeka and Abilene, in Kansas, and Omaha, Nebraska. People in those cities and others soon found ways to make money by using the railroads.

One of these people was a cattle trader named Joseph McCoy. McCoy was an **entrepreneur** (ahn•truh•pruh•NER), or a person who starts a new business. In 1867 McCoy built a stockyard near Abilene to ship beef cattle in railroad cars to markets in cities in the East. He then advertised his stockyard all over Texas.

Texas ranchers moved their herds in great cattle drives to McCoy's and other stockyards. Several cattle trails led from Texas through Oklahoma, north to the railroads in Kansas, Nebraska, and Missouri. The most famous of these trails was the Chisholm (CHIH•zuhm) Trail. It went from San Antonio, Texas, to Abilene and Ellsworth, Kansas.

Ranching eventually spread north across the Great Plains. Today ranching is a leading industry in all the Great Plains states. After Texas, Nebraska and Kansas are the two top cattle-producing states in the country. Ranching is most important where the land is too rough or too dry for farming. Both cattle and sheep graze on those lands.

REVIEW How did railroads help the ranching industry grow in the Plains states?

Danger on the Plains

The flat, treeless land in much of the Plains region offers little protection from big storms. Farmers and ranchers there must watch the weather closely. A whole year's crop can be wiped out by a single storm, and livestock can be hurt.

Schools all over the United States have fire drills. In the Plains region, many students also have to participate in tornado drills. Tornadoes, Earth's strongest winds, happen frequently in this part of the United States. At the center of some tornadoes, also called cyclones or twisters, winds can reach speeds of 500 miles (805 km) per hour! Twisters move over the land in a short time, often destroying everything in their paths.

Most tornadoes occur in spring or summer, but winter can bring extreme weather to the Plains region, too. Winds blowing from the north can cause **blizzards**, snowstorms driven by strong freezing winds.

Another frozen danger is a hailstorm. A **hailstorm** drops hail, or lumps of ice, that can destroy crops and property. A major hailstorm took place in Kansas on September 3, 1970. That day, hailstones weighing almost 2 pounds (1 kg)—the size of bowling balls—fell on the plains!

Droughts are another danger on the plains. The worst drought in United

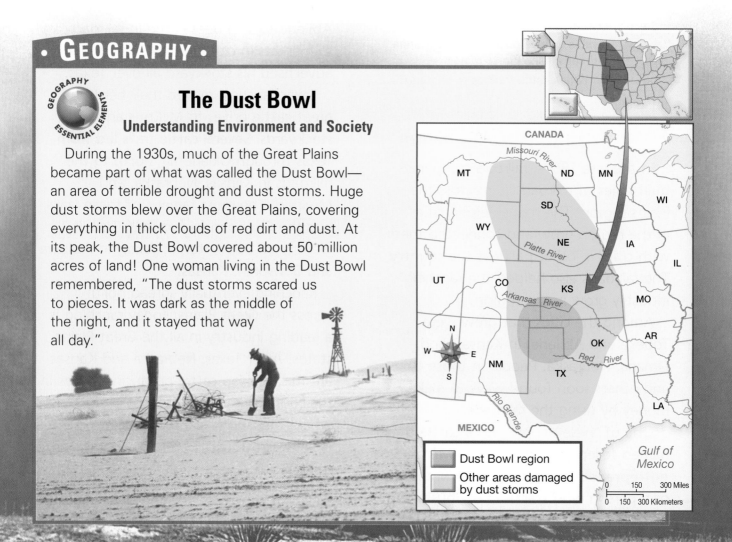

• GEOGRAPHY •

GEOGRAPHY ESSENTIAL ELEMENTS

The Dust Bowl
Understanding Environment and Society

During the 1930s, much of the Great Plains became part of what was called the Dust Bowl—an area of terrible drought and dust storms. Huge dust storms blew over the Great Plains, covering everything in thick clouds of red dirt and dust. At its peak, the Dust Bowl covered about 50 million acres of land! One woman living in the Dust Bowl remembered, "The dust storms scared us to pieces. It was dark as the middle of the night, and it stayed that way all day."

CANADA
Missouri River
MT · ND · MN · WI
SD
WY · NE · IA · IL
Platte River
UT · CO · KS · MO
Arkansas River
N · W · E · S
NM · OK · AR
Red River
TX · LA
Rio Grande
MEXICO · Gulf of Mexico

☐ Dust Bowl region
☐ Other areas damaged by dust storms

0   150   300 Miles
0   150   300 Kilometers

States history hit parts of the Plains region in the 1930s. Some places had no rain at all for months. Strong winds blew across fields that had been plowed for crops. With no prairie grasses to help hold the soil in place, the wind carried the soil away in huge dust storms. These dust storms filled homes with choking dust, killed cattle, and destroyed many farms.

Over time, people changed their farming methods to better protect the soil from wind erosion and help prevent dust storms. Many farms now have rows of large trees, called **windbreaks**, between fields to help block the wind. On hilly land, farmers usually plow their fields across the side of a hill, rather than up and down. This helps keep the soil from washing away. Some farmers today use farming methods that allow them to plant crops without having to plow fields.

REVIEW Why can storms in the Plains states be especially bad for farmers or ranchers?

Much of the Plains region is known as Tornado Alley because many tornadoes form there. This tornado is blowing across Nebraska.

LESSON 2
REVIEW

 DRAW CONCLUSIONS Why do you think ranchers wanted to ship their cattle to cities in the East?

1 BIG IDEA How have new farming methods helped make the Plains states an important agricultural region?

2 VOCABULARY Explain why many farmers in the Plains states now plant **windbreaks**.

3 HISTORY When and why did people start farming wheat on the Great Plains?

4 GEOGRAPHY Why does much of the Plains region sometimes have dangerous storms?

5 CRITICAL THINKING—Apply How do you think a drought in the Plains states might affect you and your family?

 PERFORMANCE—Make a Time Line Use the library or the Internet to find the dates when steel plows, reapers, and threshing machines were invented. Then present that information on a time line. Illustrate your time line with drawings or photographs. Compare your time line with those of your classmates.

PRIMARY SOURCES

Inventions and Inventors

Many items that we use today were invented in the 1800s. This new technology changed how people worked, traveled, and lived their daily lives in cities and in the countryside. Many of these inventions have been improved and updated for the twenty-first century, but their initial impact brought about major change.

**FROM THE SMITHSONIAN INSTITUTION
NATIONAL MUSEUM OF AMERICAN HISTORY**

Edison patented the electric light bulb (below) in 1880s.

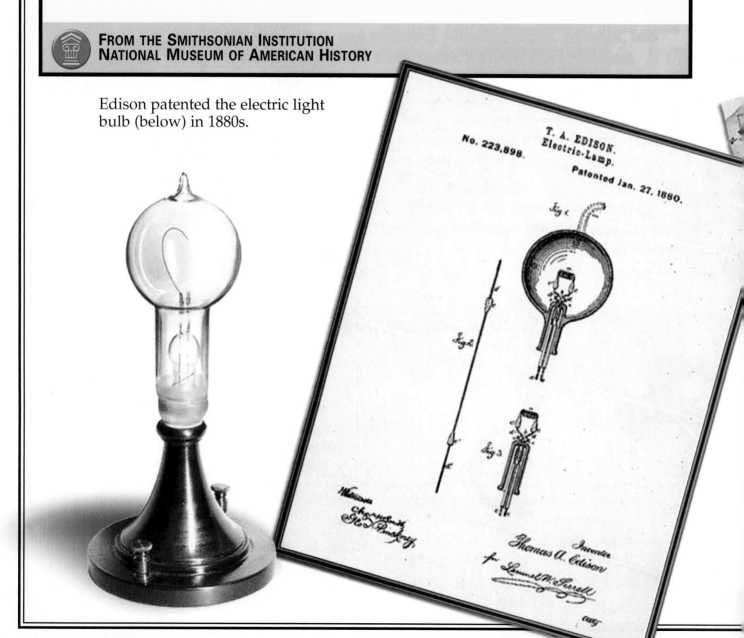

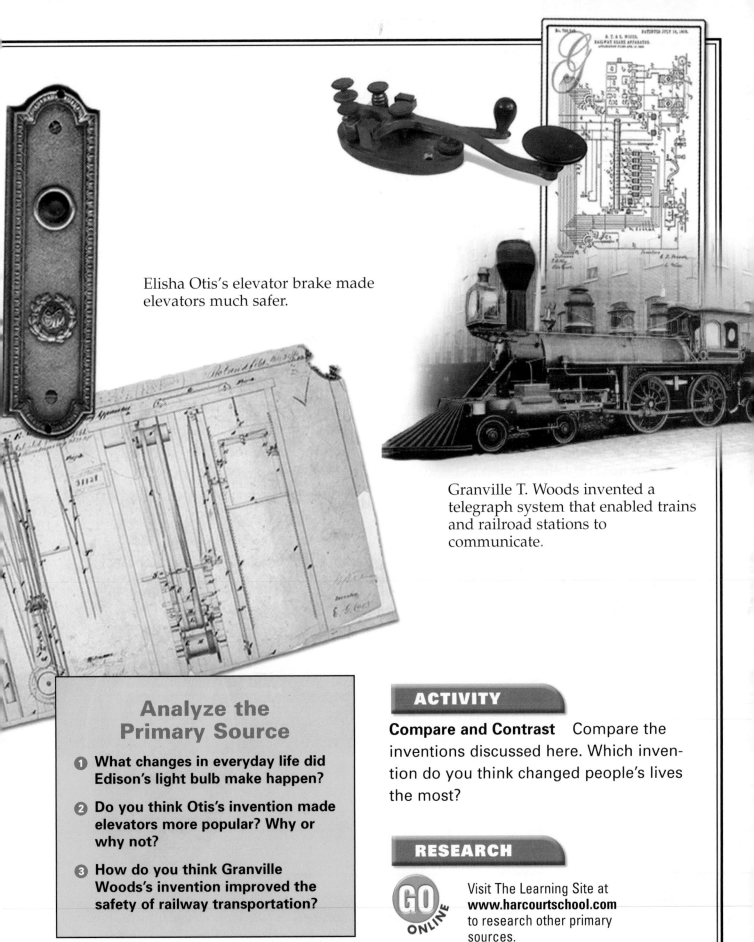

Elisha Otis's elevator brake made elevators much safer.

Granville T. Woods invented a telegraph system that enabled trains and railroad stations to communicate.

Analyze the Primary Source

1. What changes in everyday life did Edison's light bulb make happen?

2. Do you think Otis's invention made elevators more popular? Why or why not?

3. How do you think Granville Woods's invention improved the safety of railway transportation?

ACTIVITY

Compare and Contrast Compare the inventions discussed here. Which invention do you think changed people's lives the most?

RESEARCH

GO ONLINE Visit The Learning Site at **www.harcourtschool.com** to research other primary sources.

Read a Double-Bar Graph

▶ WHY IT MATTERS

Corn and wheat are two of the leading crops in the Plains states. But how many bushels of each crop do farmers in each of these states grow? Which states grow more corn than wheat? Which grow more wheat than corn?

The answers to these questions require very large numbers. These large numbers can make it difficult to understand how the two crops compare. A good way to compare such information is to study it on a double-bar graph. A double-bar graph shows comparisons for two different things, such as corn and wheat crops.

▶ WHAT YOU NEED TO KNOW

To read a double-bar graph and understand what it shows, first read the title. The title of the double-bar graph on page 313 tells you that the graph shows the amounts of corn and wheat grown in the Plains states in the year 2000. Different colors are used to show how much corn was produced and how much wheat was produced in those states. The key on the graph tells you that blue bars stand for corn production and red bars stand for wheat production.

Next, read the labels along the bottom and sides of the graph. The Plains states are listed across the bottom, and the amount of crops grown per year are listed along the left-hand side.

For many years, most farmers on the **Great Plains** grew wheat (below), while most farmers on the **Central Plains** grew corn (right page).

Corn and Wheat Crops of the Plains States, 2000

Bushels per year (in millions)

2,000
1,750
1,500
1,250
1,000
750
500
250
0

Iowa | Kansas | Missouri | Nebraska | North Dakota | South Dakota

State

■ Corn
■ Wheat

If you want to know how much corn was grown in Nebraska, place your finger on the label for Nebraska. Then move your finger up to the top of Nebraska's blue bar and read the number at the left that is closest to the top of the bar. It tells you that about 1,000 million, or 1 billion, bushels of corn were grown in Nebraska in 2000.

Using this double-bar graph, you also can compare the corn or wheat crops in one state to the same crops in other states. The greater the difference you see in the bar heights, the greater the difference there is in the crop sizes.

▶ **PRACTICE THE SKILL**

Use the double-bar graph to answer these questions.

1 Which state grew the most corn? the most wheat?

2 How did Missouri's corn and wheat production compare?

3 Which state grew more wheat than corn?

4 Which state grew about the same amount of corn as wheat?

▶ **APPLY WHAT YOU LEARNED**

On the double-bar graph, look at North Dakota's corn and wheat production. Then think about what you have learned about the Interior Plains. Why do you think farmers in North Dakota raise more wheat than corn? Write a paragraph explaining your answer.

DRAW CONCLUSIONS

As you read, draw conclusions about ways in which people who live in cities and on farms and ranches depend on one another.

BIG IDEA

The economy of the Plains region today is diverse.

VOCABULARY

urbanization
demand
meat packing
free enterprise
consumer
supply

The Plains States Today

Farming and ranching are major parts of the Plains region's economy, and they use much of the region's land. But most people in the Plains states now live in towns and cities. Some of them own their own businesses, while others have jobs in one of the region's diverse industries. Regardless of where they live, however, people in cities and on farms and ranches depend on one another.

Linking Farms and Cities

As in other parts of the United States, factories and manufacturing became more important to the economy of the Plains states during the 1900s. Improved farming methods and machinery meant that fewer farmworkers were needed to produce the same amount of crops. Today fewer than 2 out of every 100 people in the United States live and work on farms. However, most farms actually produce more goods now than

Kansas City, Missouri, grew from a small trading post on the Missouri River to become a major transportation center of almost half a million people.

they did in the past—even with fewer people working on them.

Many of the people who left farms and ranches moved to cities in search of jobs, mostly in factories. At the same time, immigrants also moved to cities for factory jobs. This growth of city populations compared to rural populations is called **urbanization** (er•buh•nuh•ZAY•shun).

Urbanization continues today. Cities in the Plains states, just like cities all over the nation, are growing rapidly. So are the suburbs surrounding those cities. However, without farms and ranches, urbanization would be impossible. The millions of people who live in urban areas all need food. Many of the factories in cities depend on farms and ranches for raw materials.

Many industries in the Plains states use the resources that nearby farmers and ranchers supply. For example, flour milling is a large industry in the Plains states today. At first, farmers on the Great Plains sent their wheat to mills in the East.

But those mill owners did not like to grind the hard winter wheat that farmers grew on the Great Plains. This meant there was a demand for the service of grinding hard wheat. In business a **demand** is a need or desire for a product or service that people are willing to pay for. Some businesspeople in the Plains region met that demand by building their own flour mills near the wheat farms.

Being close to sources of raw materials has helped food-processing industries thrive in the Plains states. Factories there use corn and wheat to make breads, cereals, pastas, popcorn, syrups, and margarine. Other factories use corn to make building materials, paints, paper goods, and even fuels!

The raising of cattle and hogs in the Plains states has helped another industry grow—meat packing. **Meat packing** is the preparing of meat for market. Most meat-packing businesses are in cities near ranches. Omaha, Nebraska, is a large center for this industry.

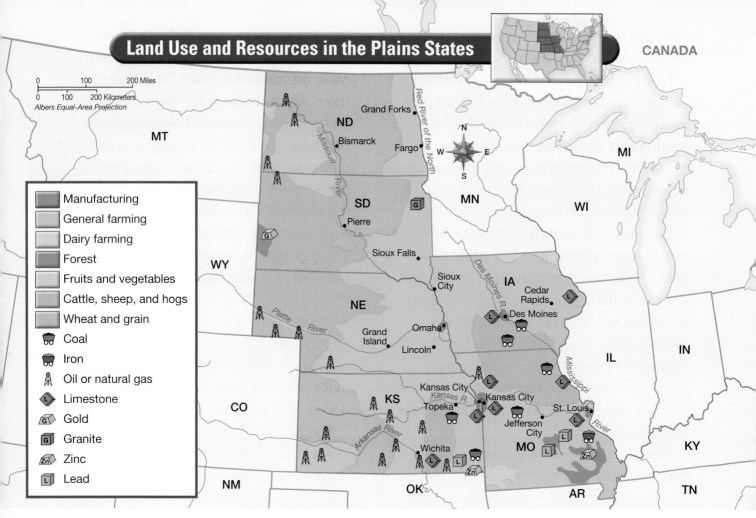

Land Use and Resources in the Plains States

CANADA

0   100   200 Miles
0   100   200 Kilometers
Albers Equal-Area Projection

Legend:
- Manufacturing
- General farming
- Dairy farming
- Forest
- Fruits and vegetables
- Cattle, sheep, and hogs
- Wheat and grain
- Coal
- Iron
- Oil or natural gas
- Limestone
- Gold
- Granite
- Zinc
- Lead

MT, ND, Grand Forks, Bismarck, Fargo, MI, SD, Pierre, MN, WI, Sioux Falls, Sioux City, IA, Cedar Rapids, Des Moines, WY, NE, Grand Island, Omaha, Lincoln, IL, IN, KS, Kansas City, Topeka, Kansas City, St. Louis, Jefferson City, CO, Wichita, MO, KY, NM, OK, AR, TN

Missouri River, Red River of the North, Des Moines R., Platte River, Arkansas River, Kansas R., Mississippi River

---

Human–Environment Interactions **Kansas is the largest producer of oil and natural gas in the Plains states.**

❷ What is the main land use for most of North Dakota?

Being close to customers is good for most businesses. So industries that supply products to ranchers and farmers started businesses in the Plains states to be near their customers. Factories there produce farm machinery, fertilizers, and other chemicals that the region's farmers use.

Farmers, in turn, depend on workers in cities. Without city workers, farmers would not have tractors, plows, and other machines they need to plant and harvest their crops. They would not have telephones, computers, or fertilizers either.

REVIEW Why are certain businesses likely to be in cities in the Plains states?

 **DRAW CONCLUSIONS**

Other Products and Industries

Not all industries in the Plains states are related to farming or ranching. Like most parts of the United States, the economy of the Plains states continues to become more diverse. In addition to having fertile land, the Plains region is rich in other kinds of natural resources. South Dakota has the largest gold mine in the country, and Missouri is a leading producer of lead. Kansas produces oil and natural gas, helium, salt, chalk, and coal. North Dakota has large deposits of oil, coal, and uranium.

In Missouri, manufacturing aerospace and transportation equipment is a bigger industry than food processing. Wichita, Kansas, is a high-tech center for the region, as well as a world leader in airplane manufacturing. Nebraska and South Dakota both have large printing and publishing industries.

As in other regions, service industries are the fastest-growing businesses in the Plains states today. Kansas City, Missouri, is the financial center of the Plains region.

It has many large banks and other financial businesses. Nebraska and Iowa are major insurance centers.

Tourism is another leading service industry in the Plains states. The Black Hills of South Dakota is a popular place to visit. About 2 million people visit Mount Rushmore National Memorial there every year. Just a few miles away, tourists can also see the Crazy Horse Memorial or view the spectacular landscapes of the Badlands National Park.

• GEOGRAPHY •

GEOGRAPHY ESSENTIAL ELEMENTS

Mount Rushmore National Memorial

Understanding Places and Regions

Artists have carved an enormous monument into the side of a mountain in the Black Hills of South Dakota, Mount Rushmore. By doing so, they have used the geography of the Plains states to honor great people in history.

Mount Rushmore National Memorial honors four Presidents of the United States—George Washington, Thomas Jefferson, Theodore Roosevelt, and Abraham Lincoln. Four hundred workers spent 14 years carving the faces of the Presidents into the side of Mount Rushmore. The carved faces are 60 feet (18 m) tall.

WYOMING

Black Hills National Forest
Black Hills

Black Hawk
Rapid City
Box Elder
90
385
16
79
Rapid Creek
44

■ **MOUNT RUSHMORE NATIONAL MEMORIAL**
▲ Harney Peak 7,242 ft. (2,207 m)

Custer
16
40

Jewel Cave National Monument
385
Wind Cave National Park

79

National Cemetery

Mammoth Site
18
Hot Springs
385
Cheyenne River

0   5   10 Miles
0   5   10 Kilometers

N W E S

DEMOCRATIC VALUES
Equal Opportunity

Because of our free enterprise economy, people in the United States have the right to run their own businesses. Our nation's laws also provide certain rights to people who do not want to open a business, but choose to work for someone else instead. By law, no business can refuse to hire people because of their race, religion, national origin, or gender. In other words, people in the United States have the right to equal employment opportunities. As a result, people in the United States have the freedom to succeed in the career of their choice.

Analyze the Value

1 What does *equal employment opportunity* mean?

2 Why do you think it is important to have employment laws?

3 **Make It Relevant** Think about the kind of job you would like to have in the future. Do you want to open your own business or do you want to work for a business someone else owns? Make a list of the skills and qualifications you think you will need for your chosen job and how you can gain those requirements. Share your ideas with the class.

The northwest corner of Iowa is another major resort area in the Plains states. The six large lakes there are often called the Iowa Great Lakes. Visitors to North Dakota's Theodore Roosevelt National Park can see wild buffalo and horses still roaming freely across the plains. Many tourists interested in history visit the Homestead National Monument near Beatrice, Nebraska, which celebrates the first land claim of the Homestead Act in 1862. Missouri is home to the Mark Twain National Forest. Other tourists travel to Missouri to visit the Gateway Arch in St. Louis.

REVIEW **What city is the financial center for the Plains states?**

Building Businesses

In the United States, a person is free to become an entrepreneur and start a new business. Having that right is an important part of our nation's free enterprise economy. A **free enterprise** economy is one in which people own and run their own businesses with only limited control by the government.

In some countries around the world, governments tell owners how to run their businesses. They tell them exactly what to make and how much to charge. In the United States, however, the owners of businesses decide those things mostly on their own. Consumers in the United States are also free to make choices about what to buy. A **consumer** is a person who buys a product or service.

People are often interviewed before they are hired for a job.

A free enterprise economy means that people have the freedom to do well in business. It also means freedom to fail. For example, a business owner in the Plains states who specializes in surfboards is likely to fail. There is little demand for surfboards in a region so far from the ocean. On the other hand, a business that sells farm equipment has a much better chance of success in an agricultural region like the Plains states.

To do well, a business must offer goods or services that people want to buy. A good or service that a business offers for sale is called a supply. The cattle that a rancher offers for sale is a supply that meets the demand for beef. The supply of a good or service usually rises or falls to meet a demand. This means a business will produce more of something if consumers want to buy a lot of it. If consumers do not want to buy much of a supply, a business will produce less of it.

REVIEW In a free enterprise economy, who makes most of the decisions about a business?

This printing company in Missouri takes part in free enterprise by making books that people want to buy.

LESSON 3
REVIEW

DRAW CONCLUSIONS You read that about 2 million people visit Mount Rushmore each year. What conclusion can you draw about the number of people who visit South Dakota each year? Explain your answer.

1 **BIG IDEA** In what ways do the Plains states have a diverse economy today?

2 **VOCABULARY** Explain the difference between **supply** and **demand**.

3 **ECONOMICS** Why are there many flour mills in the Plains states?

4 **GEOGRAPHY** Where in the Plains states are most meat-packing industries located?

5 **CRITICAL THINKING—Synthesize** Why does a free enterprise economy give you more choices about what to buy and where to buy it?

PERFORMANCE—Make a Sequenced Chart Do further research on an industry that you read about in this lesson. Make a chart showing the sequence of how that industry makes its products. Show the raw materials and supplies used by the industry and the finished products shipped by the industry. Then share your chart with the class and explain each step.

Plains Around the World

Focus Skill

DRAW CONCLUSIONS

As you read, draw conclusions about the world's plains and the way people live on them.

BIG IDEA

People live in different plains regions around the world.

VOCABULARY

gaucho
estancia
station

Just as in the Plains region of the United States, plains are found all over the world. In fact, plains are Earth's most common landform. No matter where they are, all plains are broad, mostly flat lands. Yet, not all plains regions are alike. Depending on their location and climate, plains can be very different. Still, most people around the world have found ways to use the plains where they live.

The Pampas

In 1912 an American named W. J. Holland traveled through South America. He wrote, "I have crossed the prairies of . . . the Dakotas, of Kansas and Nebraska . . . but in none of them have I seen such absolutely level lands." The plains he was describing are the Pampas, which cover much of the country of Argentina. In Spanish, the word *pampa* means "level land."

Like the Coastal Plain of the United States, the Pampas stretch inland from the Atlantic Ocean. They spread west for

FAST FACT

Gauchos have been herding cattle on the Pampas for centuries. Many words Americans associate with ranching come from Spanish, including the word *ranch* itself. The words *lasso, corral,* and *bronco* also come from Spanish.

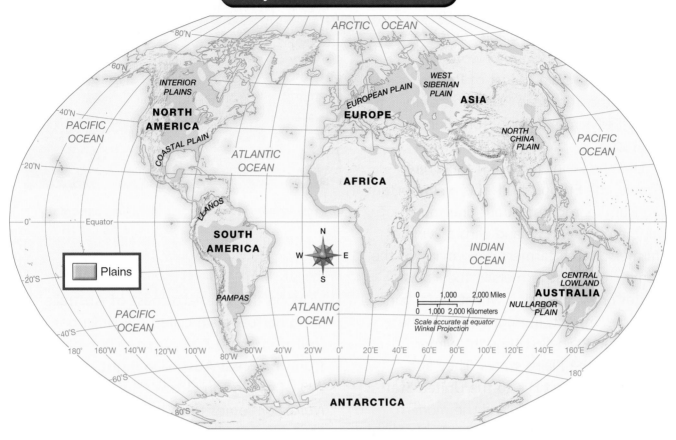

ARCTIC OCEAN

80°N

60°N

INTERIOR
PLAINS

WEST
SIBERIAN
PLAIN

EUROPEAN PLAIN

ASIA

40°N

NORTH
AMERICA

PACIFIC
OCEAN

EUROPE

NORTH
CHINA
PLAIN

PACIFIC
OCEAN

COASTAL PLAIN

ATLANTIC
OCEAN

20°N

AFRICA

Equator

0°

LLANOS

SOUTH
AMERICA

N

W   E

S

INDIAN
OCEAN

20°S

Plains

PAMPAS

CENTRAL
LOWLAND

AUSTRALIA

NULLARBOR
PLAIN

ATLANTIC
OCEAN

0   1,000   2,000 Miles

PACIFIC
OCEAN

0   1,000 2,000 Kilometers

Scale accurate at equator
Winkel Projection

40°S

180° 160°W 140°W 120°W 100°W   80°W   60°W   40°W   20°W   0°   20°E   40°E   60°E   80°E 100°E 120°E 140°E 160°E

80°W

60°S

180

ANTARCTICA

80°S

GEOGRAPHY THEME

Regions   Plains are found on most of Earth's continents.

❔ What two large plains regions are in South America?

hundreds of miles toward the Andes (AN•deez) Mountains. As on the Interior Plains of the United States, the amount of rain decreases from east to west on the Pampas. The eastern part gets plenty of rain, while the western half is much drier.

The Pampas have some of the world's richest soil. Corn grows well on the wet northern and eastern Pampas. On the southern and western Pampas, where the climate is drier, wheat is the leading crop.

Long ago, Spanish settlers brought horses and cattle to the Pampas. Millions of cattle once roamed the western Pampas, grazing on the region's thick grasses. Skilled riders, called **gauchos** (GOW•chohz), rode the open plains and herded the cattle for food and hides. Today many gauchos continue to herd cattle, but now they work as ranch hands on **estancias** (es•TAHN•see•ahs), or large ranches.

Many farm and ranch products from the Pampas are exported to other countries. Most are shipped out of the port of Buenos Aires (BWAY•nohs EYE•rays), which is located on the Pampas. Buenos Aires is the capital and largest city in Argentina.

REVIEW   How do many people on the Pampas use the land to earn a living?

LOCATE IT

ARGENTINA

Pampas

Chapter 9   ■   **321**

The European Plain

Poland is a country in eastern Europe. The name *Poland* comes from the Slavic (SLAH•vik) word that means "plain." Most of Poland lies on the European Plain. This plain stretches across Europe from France to Russia.

Like the Plains region of the United States, the European Plain is an important agricultural region. About one-fourth of all the people in Poland earn a living as farmers. Polish farmers grow many of the same crops that farmers in the Plains states grow, including wheat, oats, barley, and rye. In fact, immigrants from the European Plain first brought winter wheat to the Plains states. They also brought the first rye to the United States.

Some farmers in Poland use modern machinery and farming methods. However, most Polish farms are very small compared to American farms—usually covering less than 12 acres of land. Many farmers there still plant and harvest their crops by hand. The machines that could do this work are too expensive to use on such small farms.

REVIEW On what plain does most of Poland lie?

Most farmers in Poland raise more than one crop.

The Nullarbor Plain

Along the southern coast of Australia lies a narrow plain called the Nullarbor (nuh•luh•BAWR) Plain. It stretches inland from the Great Australian Bight, a large bay of the Indian Ocean. The name *Nullarbor* comes from the Latin words for "no trees." It is a good description, since most of this vast, flat plain is completely treeless.

The dry climate and poor soil of the Nullarbor Plain are the main reasons why few trees grow there. Nearly all of the plain is covered with limestone, a hard rock similar to coral. In most years, the Nullarbor Plain receives less than 10 inches (25 cm) of rain, and it never snows there. Any rain that does fall

A farmer in Poland piles hay to feed his cows.

LOCATE IT

POLAND

LOCATE IT

AUSTRALIA

Nullarbor Plain

on the plain quickly disappears as it soaks into the limestone ground. There are no major rivers on the Nullarbor Plain, either.

Because of its dry environment, few people live on the Nullarbor Plain, and there are no large cities there. However, ranching is an important industry in parts of the plain, as it is elsewhere in Australia. In fact, Australia leads the world in wool production. People in Australia call their sheep and cattle ranches **stations**. Stations on the Nullarbor Plain must be very large in

Signs posted along Eyre (AYR) Highway on the Nullarbor Plain warn drivers to look out for crossing kangaroos and other animals.

order to provide enough grazing land and water for the animals.

Other than ranching, there are few industries on the Nullarbor Plain. Along the Great Australian Bight, some people fish, but cliffs along the coast make shipping difficult there. Farther inland are a few nickel and uranium mines. This flat, empty area, however, is perfect for aerospace testing. The Nullarbor Plain is the site of a major rocket research center for Australia.

REVIEW How do most people on the Nullarbor Plain earn their living? DRAW CONCLUSIONS

LESSON 4 REVIEW

 DRAW CONCLUSIONS What conclusions can you make about how climate affects life on plains around the world?

1 BIG IDEA How do people around the world live on plains?

2 VOCABULARY Write a poem using the term **gaucho** to describe working on the Pampas.

3 GEOGRAPHY Why are many of the world's plains regions important agricultural areas?

4 CULTURE How have people from Spain affected ranching elsewhere in the world?

5 CRITICAL THINKING—Analyze Many of the world's largest cities are on plains. Why do you think this is so?

 PERFORMANCE—Draw a Scene Draw a scene showing the geography and way of life in one of the plains regions you just read about. Write a title and a description for your scene. Display your scene in the classroom.

Review and Test Preparation

Summary Time Line

1600 — 1650 — 1700

1600s
Sioux begin moving
to the Plains region

 Use Your Reading Skills

Copy the following graphic organizer onto a separate sheet of paper. Use the information you have learned to draw conclusions about the Plains states. To complete it, read the new fact. Then write any related facts you already know. Finally, draw a conclusion based on your listed facts.

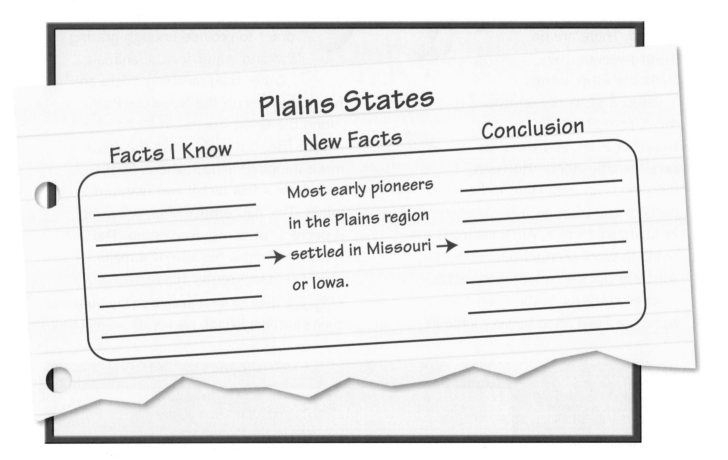

Plains States

Facts I Know	New Facts	Conclusion
	Most early pioneers in the Plains region → settled in Missouri or Iowa. →	

THINK & WRITE

Write an Advertisement   Imagine that the year is 1820. Write an advertisement that urges people in the East to move to the Great Plains. List reasons why someone might want to leave the East and settle on the plains. Describe what settlers will find there.

Write Cargo Lists   Make a cargo list of things a train might carry from the Plains states to the East. Then make a list of cargo a train might carry from eastern cities to the Plains states. Explain the differences between the two lists.

1764
St. Louis is
founded

1803
Plains region becomes part
of the United States with
the Louisiana Purchase

1831
The reaper is
invented

1867
McCoy opens
a stockyard in
Abilene, Kansas

1930s
The Great Plains suffers
terrible droughts and
dust storms

USE THE TIME LINE

Use the chapter summary time line to answer these questions.

1 When did the Plains region become part of the United States?

2 Did McCoy open his stockyard in Abilene before or after the reaper was invented?

USE VOCABULARY

Use each term in a sentence that helps explain its meaning.

3 **self-sufficient** (p. 299)

4 **adapt** (p. 300)

5 **tepee** (p. 300)

6 **entrepreneur** (p. 307)

7 **hailstorm** (p. 308)

8 **urbanization** (p. 315)

9 **meat packing** (p. 315)

10 **free enterprise** (p. 318)

RECALL FACTS

Answer these questions.

11 Why did many settlers on the Great Plains use sod to build their homes?

12 How did horses change the way of life for Plains Indians?

13 What is the main difference between the Central Plains and the Great Plains?

14 How did the invention of the reaper, thresher, and steel plow affect American farmers?

15 What is the most common landform on Earth?

Write the letter of the best choice.

16 What did many people call the Great Plains in the 1800s?
  A the Dairyland
  B the Great American Desert
  C the Badlands
  D the Crossroads of America

17 The Plains region provides most of our nation's—
  F wheat.
  G rice.
  H berries.
  J oranges.

THINK CRITICALLY

18 Why do people today no longer need to be as self-sufficient as they were in the past?

19 Why do you think many Sioux moved from Wisconsin and Minnesota and settled on the Great Plains of North Dakota and South Dakota during the 1600s?

APPLY SKILLS

Use a Cultural Map

20 Look at the map on page 303. Which tribe labeled on the map lived on the largest area of land? Which tribes lived on both the Great Plains and the Central Plains?

Read a Double-Bar Graph
Use the double-bar graph on page 313 to answer these questions.

21 Which state grew more corn, Kansas or Missouri?

22 About how much more corn was grown in Iowa than in Nebraska?

The Gateway Arch

GET READY

The Gateway Arch is a monument that rises above the western bank of the Mississippi River in St. Louis. It honors Meriwether Lewis and William Clark's exploration of the Louisiana Territory, which opened the West to settlement.

On a visit to the Gateway Arch, you will see a smooth curve made of steel, standing 630 feet (192 m) tall. The Gateway Arch is taller than any other monument in the National Park system!

If you like adventure, you can go up to the observation deck at the top of the arch. From there you can gaze out over the Mississippi River and the city of St. Louis. Maybe you will feel the spirit that urged American pioneers to journey westward.

WHAT TO SEE

LOCATE IT

St. Louis

MISSOURI

Visitors can ride up 63 stories to the top of the Gateway Arch in a special kind of tram. The tram cars run inside the legs of the arch.

Construction of the Gateway Arch began in 1963. **❶** Workers took great care in building the legs of the arch. Large sections were placed one on top of the other and then welded together. **❷** Special equipment was needed to put the last piece into place at the top of the arch. **❸** The Gateway Arch was completed in 1965.

TAKE A FIELD TRIP

GO ONLINE

A VIRTUAL TOUR
Visit The Learning Site at **www.harcourtschool.com** to find virtual tours of other monuments and national parks.

CNN Turner Le@rning

A VIDEO TOUR
Check your media center or classroom library for a videotape tour of the Gateway Arch in St. Louis.

4 Review and Test Preparation

VISUAL SUMMARY

Write a Travel Magazine Article
Study the pictures and captions below to help you review Unit 4. Then, based on what is shown in the scenes, write an article about the Middle West for a travel magazine.

USE VOCABULARY

Use each term in a sentence that helps explain its meaning.

1. **cartographer** (p. 269)
2. **frontier** (p. 270)
3. **interchangeable part** (p. 280)
4. **migration** (p. 283)
5. **prairie** (p. 297)
6. **tepee** (p. 300)
7. **blizzard** (p. 308)
8. **windbreak** (p. 309)
9. **consumer** (p. 318)

RECALL FACTS

Answer these questions.

10. Why did the steel industry spread to cities along the Great Lakes?

11. How do different amounts of precipitation on the Central Plains and the Great Plains affect farming?

12. How is demand different from supply?

13. How are most of the world's plains used?

Write the letter of the best choice.

14. What kinds of boats did early explorers use to travel on the Mississippi River?
    A canoes
    B barges
    C flatboats
    D steamboats

15. Who were the first Europeans to claim most of the Middle West?
    F the British
    G the French
    H the Dutch
    J the Spanish

Visual Summary

| 1600 | 1650 | 1700 | 1750 |

1862 Many homesteaders pass Chimney Rock, in Nebraska. p. 298

1884 About 800 million cattle pass through Dodge City, Kansas. p. 307

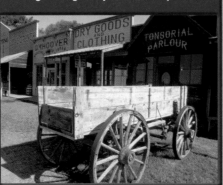

1911 First Indianapolis 500 race is held in Indianapolis, Indiana. p. 280

THINK CRITICALLY

16 Why do you think Native Americans fought on both sides in the French and Indian War?

17 In the early 1800s most people in the Middle West lived on farms or in rural areas. Today most live in urban areas. How has this change affected the region?

18 Why do more people live along the Rhine River than along the Amazon River?

19 How has technology changed farming in the Middle West over the years?

20 How might life have been different in the Middle West without the introduction of railroads?

APPLY SKILLS

MAP AND GLOBE SKILLS

Compare Historical Maps
Use the two historical maps on this page to answer the following questions.

21 How did the Middle West region change between 1800 and 1900?

22 Which map would you use to find the part of the Middle West that France once claimed? Why?

23 By 1900, what states had been formed out of parts of the Indiana Territory?

Map A: Middle West, 1800

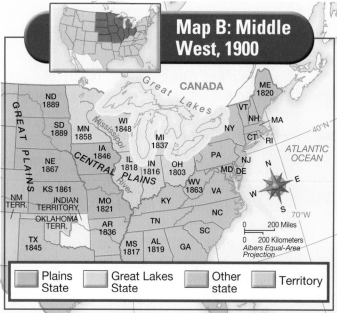

Map B: Middle West, 1900

1850   1900   1950   Present

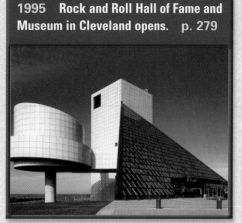

1978 Badlands National Park is established in South Dakota. p. 317

1995 Rock and Roll Hall of Fame and Museum in Cleveland opens. p. 279

2000 North Dakota grows 2 million tons of sunflower seeds. p. 306

Unit Activities

Visit The Learning Site at
www.harcourtschool.com
for additional activities.

Make Dioramas

Work with a group to make two dioramas that show different kinds of houses used by pioneers in the Middle West. One should show a log cabin on the Central Plains and the other should show a soddy on the Great Plains. Include in your models what the environment of each home may have looked like and the kinds of work that pioneers there had to do. Display your finished dioramas in the classroom and point to different parts of them as you talk to your classmates about pioneer life in the Middle West.

Give a Weather Report

As a class, give a weather report for the Middle West. Work in groups to collect information from the Internet or the library about the typical weather for different months in the region, including average temperatures, precipitation levels, and likelihood of storms. Display the information on maps, graphs, and posters. Then take turns presenting your month's weather report to the class. Finally, as a class, use the different reports to describe the climate of the Middle West.

VISIT YOUR LIBRARY

■ *If You're Not from the Prairie* by David Bouchard. Raincoast Books.

■ *Mark Twain and the Queens of the Mississippi* by Cheryl Harness. Simon and Schuster Books for Young Readers.

■ *Homesteading on the Plains: Daily Life in the Land of Laura Ingalls Wilder* by Mary Dodson Wade. The Millbrook Press.

COMPLETE THE UNIT PROJECT

A Mural Work in small groups to finish the Unit Project described on page 265. First, review the lists you and the other members of your group made as you read the unit. Then decide what scenes you will show in your mural. Fasten a large sheet of paper to a wall in your classroom. Use pencils to sketch the scenes, and use paints, crayons, or markers to color them. Each group member should write facts about a place or an activity shown in the scene. Present the mural and facts to your class.

Steamtown
National Historic
Site, Scranton

Pennsylvania and the New Nation

" This land which we have
watered with our tears
is now our mother country. "

—Richard Allen, 1827

 **Generalize**

When you **generalize,** you make a statement
that summarizes a group of facts and shows how
they are related.

As you read this chapter, make generalizations.

- **Identify important facts.**
- **Use these facts to generalize about Pennsylvania.**

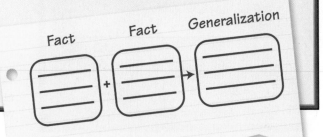

Fact + Fact → Generalization

Early Pennsylvania Industries

GENERALIZE
As you read, make generalizations about Pennsylvania's early industries.

BIG IDEA
New people and technology helped Pennsylvania's economy grow.

VOCABULARY
traditional economy
command economy
market economy

In the early 1800s, Pennsylvania's economy was growing and changing quickly. Pennsylvania needed better ways to move its many new people and products.

Freedom of Opportunity

As a colony, Pennsylvania had a **traditional economy**, or one that changes little over time. In this kind of economy, people spend most of their time growing food for themselves and their families. Manufacturing is done mostly by individuals in small workshops or in their homes.

Some European countries, such as Russia, had a command economy at the time. In a **command economy**, the government controls production. Farmers are told which crops to grow. Craftworkers are told what products to make.

There are three questions all economic systems answer. What goods and services should be produced? How will they be produced? Who will use or buy the goods and services?

People in the new state and nation wanted a market economy. In a **market economy**, the people decide which goods and services to produce. This kind of economy is also known as a free enterprise system. Many immigrants to early Pennsylvania came for the freedom to make their own economic choices.

REVIEW Why do you think people in Pennsylvania wanted a market economy? GENERALIZE

This painting, *Pat Lyon at the Forge,* shows a blacksmith at work in his Philadelphia shop. The boy on the left worked as an apprentice, learning the craft until he was old enough to open his own shop.

This advertisement (right) from 1837 shows that people could use the train and canal service to get from Philadelphia to Pittsburgh in three and one-half days. Horseshoe Curve (above) still brings many tourists to the Altoona area.

New Ways to Travel

By the early 1800s, Pennsylvania was no longer a wilderness. Communities all over the state were growing quickly. People needed to travel and ship their goods. To meet this need, Pennsylvanians built new roads, canals, and railroads.

Many early roads followed old trading paths. Villages connected by the paths grew to be towns. Often, the people who took care of a road charged a toll, or fee, for its use. On some roads, a wooden pike, or roadblock, was turned after the toll was paid. These roads were called turnpikes.

Wagons carried goods and passengers over the roads. People also rode horses and walked. Some roads were paved in stone and gravel, but most were dirt roads. Journeys were slow and tiring. Settlers living in towns offered travelers places to rest, eat, and make wagon repairs. By

1832, the state had more than 3,000 miles of roads. It was the most of any state in the nation.

Travel by water was also improving. Philadelphian John Fitch had designed a steamboat in 1787. Over the next 50 years, the state's canals linked many rural areas and cities. More than 1,300 miles of canals connected Pennsylvania's eastern and western regions.

Railroads spread in the 1830s and 1840s. The Pennsylvania Railroad from Philadelphia to Pittsburgh was completed in 1854. In the same year, Horseshoe Curve opened near Altoona. This curving section of railway allowed trains to cross the Allegheny Mountains. By the 1860s, Pennsylvania had more railroad tracks than any other state.

REVIEW How did improvements in transportation affect the state? **GENERALIZE**

New Industries

Pennsylvania's natural resources encouraged the growth of industries. Its fertile farmland, river system, and rich supply of iron, coal, and timber created a strong economy.

The Pittsburgh and Ohio Valley regions were rich in natural resources, such as bituminous (buh•TYOO•mih•nuhs) coal. This soft coal can be burned as a source for heat. In 1792, George Anschutz built a furnace for making iron. Manufacturing iron became Pittsburgh's main industry.

From 1810 to 1830, as the iron industry grew, the population of Pittsburgh tripled. Pittsburgh supplied area farms with iron products, such as nails, horseshoes, and farm tools.

By the 1830s, mining and manufacturing were successful industries. Anthracite (AN•thruh•syt) coal was found in eastern Pennsylvania. Anthracite is a hard natural coal that provides high heat. This coal was used to fuel trains and steamboats, run factories, and heat homes. Workers in Pottstown, Hazleton, and Scranton mined anthracite coal.

In the early 1800s, Philadelphia was the largest city in the nation. Its industries included ironworks and factories that made paper, gunpowder, and carriages.

Towns, such as Williamsport, were settled in north-central Pennsylvania near timber camps. The Schuylkill Valley was an early center of the iron industry. Erie had a growing shipbuilding industry. The Piedmont region was the state's agricultural center.

The drawing below shows industries in Pittsburgh in 1852. The small drawing on the left shows a plan to build the city on land where the Allegheny and Monongahela Rivers meet. Notice that the names of the city and the rivers are spelled differently today.

Many people worked at the Keystone Silk Mill in Emmaus, just south of Allentown.

Different regions had special products. Eastern Pennsylvania was known for dairy products, while the western part of the state mined coal and made iron. Pittsburgh produced 100 steam engines a year. Better transportation increased the demand for products because people could buy goods made in faraway places.

The growing industries changed the way people worked. Factory production began to replace home crafts in the making of cloth, or textiles, furniture, and farm tools. Mass production used machines and standard parts to produce goods quickly and cheaply.

Farmers began to use improved equipment, such as threshers, plows, and scythes. They used them to grow crops to sell and then bought factory-made goods with their earnings.

Pennsylvania's cities and towns grew quickly. The anthracite coal, iron, and textile industries brought European immigrants to Philadelphia and Pittsburgh. Many people moved from rural areas to work in the cities. Some cities became crowded.

REVIEW How did growing industries change where people worked? **GENERALIZE**

LESSON 1
REVIEW

GENERALIZE How did natural resources in Pennsylvania help industries grow?

1 **BIG IDEA** How did new people and technology help Pennsylvania's economy?

2 **VOCABULARY** Write a paragraph using the terms **traditional economy** and **market economy**.

3 **ECONOMICS** In a free enterprise system, who decides what products will be made or grown?

Focus
Skill
GENERALIZE
As you read, make
generalizations about
changes in early
Pennsylvania.

BIG IDEA
New people and new
industries affected
society in Pennsylvania.

VOCABULARY
labor union
social reform

The Cornwall Iron Furnace
in Lebanon County was
the state's leading
producer of iron from 1742
until 1883. Today, you can
visit and see the original
buildings where workers
made many kinds of iron
products.

Society in the Early Commonwealth

Pennsylvania, and the Northeast region of the United States, grew rapidly. Thousands of new European immigrants came to eastern cities. Many more moved inland. Cities and towns, such as Allentown, Scranton, Altoona, and Erie, grew quickly.

Growth and Change

Throughout the early 1800s, ships arrived at Philadelphia carrying immigrants. Many newcomers had sold everything they owned to pay for their passage. They arrived with little money and few skills. Many immigrants had children.

Factories, mills, and mines offered jobs to immigrants and their children. The mill and mine owners made a lot of money. Workers did not share in this wealth. They did not make much money even though they worked long hours in poor conditions. Many feared losing their jobs if they spoke out.

Some workers formed **labor unions**, groups that aim to improve the workplace. They asked for shorter hours, better pay, and a safer workplace. The unions had some success. In 1849, the General Assembly passed laws to protect children. No child under 12 years old could work in a Pennsylvania textile mill. Children could work for only ten hours a day, six days a week.

REVIEW Why did immigrants accept low-paying jobs?
Focus
Skill **GENERALIZE**

Environmental Sciences

In the early 1800s, Philadelphia led the United States in scientific studies. Scientists at the Academy of Natural Sciences were pioneers in studying the natural world. Since 1812, the academy's scientists have studied plants, animals, and ecosystems around the world.

Today, understanding ecosystems and caring for the environment are the academy's focus. In the children's nature center, called "Outside-In," visitors learn about different land and water habitats. Scientists and volunteers teach young people about Earth's environment. The hands-on exhibits feature live animals, including insects, birds, reptiles, and rodents. For nearly 70 years, the academy has worked with schools to educate young people about nature.

Science and Education

From colonial times, Philadelphia was a center for science and invention. In 1812, the Academy of Natural Sciences was founded. The members of the academy shared a common interest in studying the natural world.

In 1824, the Historical Society of Pennsylvania was started. This group gathered important papers that showed the state's leading role in the new nation.

The state government was playing a more important role in education. In 1790, the General Assembly passed a new state constitution. It set up the state senate as a second house in the legislature and made changes in the job of governor. The Constitution of 1790 required free schools for poor children in Pennsylvania.

In 1830, Western University was started in Pittsburgh. In 1834, the Free School Act set up a public education system. By 1840, there were almost 3,000 public elementary schools in Pennsylvania. In 1852, a teachers' association was formed. The Normal School Act of 1857 called for programs to train teachers. Education in Pennsylvania had become possible for everyone.

REVIEW How did the Constitution of 1790 affect education in the state? GENERALIZE

Social Reforms

The Pennsylvania constitution did not give rights to African Americans, Native Americans, women, or children. Some white men in the state worked together to gain citizens' rights for these groups.

Many people in the state called for **social reforms**, or changes to improve society. Lucretia Mott was a white woman, a Quaker minister, and a teacher. She spoke out against slavery. Mott led the American Anti-Slavery Society that started in Philadelphia in 1833. Mott also belonged to the Philadelphia Female Anti-Slavery Society. That group included African American women and white women.

African American communities within Pennsylvania cities were growing. In 1787, two African American ministers, Absalom Jones and Richard Allen, started the Free African Society in Philadelphia. The group wanted to help African Americans improve their lives.

In 1794, Reverend Jones started the St. Thomas African Episcopal Church. It was the first African church in Philadelphia. In 1822, the African American church was started in Pittsburgh. In 1837, the Institute for Colored Youth was started in Philadelphia. Now called Cheyney University, this school was one of the first to educate African Americans.

Thousands of new immigrants made the cities crowded. There was not enough clean water, and illnesses spread quickly. In 1751, Dr. Thomas Bond and Benjamin Franklin had opened Pennsylvania Hospital in Philadelphia. By 1804, doctors were performing surgery.

In 1847, Dr. Nathan Davis started the American Medical Association in Philadelphia to set rules for doctors. The Western Pennsylvania Hospital opened in 1848 and was Pittsburgh's first public hospital.

REVIEW What was the Free African Society?

Philadelphians such as Lucretia Mott (first row, second from the right) were members of the executive committee of the Pennsylvania Anti-Slavery Society. Women played a key role in the movement to end slavery.

Octavius Catto (right) led the campaign to pass a state law requiring railroad and streetcar companies in Pennsylvania to carry all passengers, regardless of race. Pittsburgh's first streetcar line (above) opened in 1859.

Abolitionist Movement

Pennsylvania was the first state to pass an emancipation act in 1780. Yet, not all African Americans in the state were free until 1850. By 1860, Pennsylvania was home to 57,000 free African Americans. Philadelphia was the center of this community.

Abolitionists were men and women, African American and white, who worked to end slavery. African Americans led the fight. James Forten and Robert Purvis worked through the political system. John and George Vashon wrote and published their antislavery opinions. Octavius Catto was a schoolteacher who started the Equal Rights League.

Several Pennsylvanians, including free African Americans Robert Porter and William Still, led the Underground Railroad. This secret effort helped enslaved Africans escape to Canada by walking at night and staying in "safe houses," private homes that provided shelter. Most runaway slaves from Virginia and Maryland entered southeastern Pennsylvania and headed north to freedom.

REVIEW **What did abolitionists want to do?**
GENERALIZE

LESSON 2 REVIEW

 GENERALIZE How did immigrants change life in big cities?

1 **BIG IDEA** How did ways of life in Pennsylvania change in the early 1800s?

2 **VOCABULARY** Use **social reform** to describe two improvements in Pennsylvania in the early 1800s.

3 **CULTURE AND SOCIETY** What was the purpose of the Underground Railroad?

GENERALIZE

As you read, make generalizations about Pennsylvania's role in the Civil War.

BIG IDEA

Differences between the North and the South led to the Civil War.

VOCABULARY

political party
assassinate

Civil War and Reconstruction

By the mid-1800s, people in the United States disagreed about national government, society, and economics. These differing views led to forming political parties. A **political party** is a group of people with the same point of view about many issues. Members of a political party work together to elect government officials who share the group's views.

Republicans and Democrats

In 1846, Pennsylvania's David Wilmot introduced a bill in the United States Congress. This famous antislavery bill became known as the Wilmot Proviso. Wilmot wanted to stop the spread of slavery into new United States territories. Most Pennsylvanians agreed with Wilmot. However, the United States Senate voted against making the bill into a law.

Abolitionists formed the Republican party in 1856. That same year, James Buchanan, a Democrat and a native Pennsylvanian, was elected President of the United States. Democrats were divided over slavery. President Buchanan said states and territories should decide if they wanted slavery. Voters in the South agreed and helped elect him.

REVIEW What was the Wilmot Proviso?

GENERALIZE

David Wilmot represented Pennsylvania in the United States Congress.

James Buchanan 1791–1868

Character Trait: Loyalty

Much of James Buchanan's life was spent in public service. He served the people of Pennsylvania as a state representative, as a member of Congress in the House of Representatives, and as a United States Senator. He was also an ambassador to Russia and later to Britain and was secretary of state for President James K. Polk. Then in 1856, James Buchanan was elected President of the United States. He is the only Pennsylvanian to serve as President.

President Buchanan believed that civil war could be avoided through communication and trade between the North and the South. However, only a few weeks before his presidency ended in 1861, several Southern states seceded from the Union. He returned to his home in Lancaster, where he died on June 1, 1868.

 MULTIMEDIA BIOGRAPHIES
Visit The Learning Site at **www.harcourtschool.com** to learn about other famous people.

The Civil War

By 1860, the antislavery Republicans were the strongest party in the state and nation. Pennsylvanians elected a Republican governor, Andrew Gregg Curtin. Republican Abraham Lincoln was elected President. Soon after the election, 11 Southern states seceded from the Union and formed the Confederacy.

Most of the state's border between Pennsylvania and Maryland was called the Mason-Dixon Line. The line had been drawn in the mid-1700s to settle an argument over land. During the Civil War, most states south of the Mason-Dixon Line joined the Confederacy. Maryland, Delaware, West Virginia, Kentucky, and Missouri were border states. These states tried to remain neutral.

President Lincoln asked for support from Governor Curtin. The governor asked the General Assembly to organize the Reserve Corps. These troops fought in many battles during the war.

Pennsylvanians were important in fighting and winning the Civil War. General George G. Meade and General George B. McClellan were both from Pennsylvania. They led the Union army of the Potomac, which fought battles in the East.

The state provided the Union army with money, weapons, uniforms, food, and railroad transportation. Fort Pitt Ironworks made more than 2,000 cannons. Companies in Philadelphia made more than 1,000 rifles a month.

Pennsylvania supplied most of the Union's iron and all of its anthracite coal. Pennsylvanians built ships for the Union navy. The state also provided railroad locomotives, freight cars, and new tracks to move soldiers and supplies.

REVIEW How did Pennsylvanians support the Union?  **GENERALIZE**

On to Gettysburg

More than 400,000 Pennsylvanians fought for the Union, including 8,600 African Americans. Camp Curtin in Harrisburg was the first Union army camp to be set up.

There were hundreds of battles in the Civil War, but most of them were fought in the South. Confederate troops entered Pennsylvania three times from Virginia. In 1862, Confederate General J.E.B. Stuart attacked the Union army supply center in Chambersburg.

On January 1, 1863, the Emancipation Proclamation went into effect. This document, signed by President Lincoln, freed all enslaved people living in Confederate states. In June 1863, the Union began to accept African Americans soldiers. Camp William Penn was set up north of Philadelphia. It was the nation's first training center for African American soldiers. By the end of the war, almost 11,000 soldiers had trained there.

In July 1863, Confederate General Robert E. Lee led 75,000 soldiers into Pennsylvania. Citizens in Pittsburgh and Harrisburg built defenses for their cities.

The Battle of Gettysburg was a turning point of the war. The South had won several battles before this one. Here, Lee did not defeat General Meade's Union troops and was forced to retreat.

Almost a third of Meade's army was made up of Pennsylvanian soldiers. More than 40,000 Confederate and Union soldiers were killed or wounded in the Battle of Gettysburg. It was decided that the battlefield should be a place to honor those who died.

President Lincoln spoke at the dedication ceremony of the Soldiers' National Cemetery. His Gettysburg Address was made on the battlefield on November 19, 1863. Although only ten sentences long, it was one of Lincoln's greatest speeches. In the first sentence of the speech, Lincoln reminded people about the American Revolution.

> **Four score and seven years ago our fathers brought forth on this continent, a new nation, conceived in Liberty, and dedicated to the proposition that all men are created equal.**

REVIEW Why did President Lincoln come to Gettysburg?

African Americans relax alongside Union soldiers two years after the Battle of Gettysburg. These men gathered to build the Soldiers' National Monument.

THE FIFTEENTH AMENDMENT

1 Reading Emancipation Proclamation
2 Life Liberty and Independence
3 We Unite the Bonds of Fellowship
4 Our Charter of Rights the Holy Scriptures
5 Education will prove the Equality of the Races.
6 Liberty Protects the Marriage Altar
7 Celebration of Fifteenth Amendment May 19th 1870
8 The Ballot Box is open to us.
9 Our representive Sits in the National Legislature
10 The Holy Ordinances of Religion are free
11 Freedom unites the Family Circle
12 We will protect our Country as it defends our Rights.
13 We till our own Fields
14 The Right of Citizens of the US to vote shall not be denied or abridged by the U S or any State on account of Race Color or Condition of Servitude 15th Amendment

This poster celebrates the passage of the Fifteenth Amendment, which gave voting rights to African American men. In 1870, more than 600 African Americans were elected to Southern legislatures.

Reconstruction

President Lincoln was reelected in 1864. His plan to bring the nation together again was cut short on April 14, 1865. Lincoln was **assassinated**—murdered in a sudden attack—at Ford's Theatre in Washington, D.C. Vice President Andrew Johnson became President. He, too, had a plan for Reconstruction, or rebuilding, of the South.

Thaddeus Stevens of Pennsylvania, served on Congress' Joint Committee on Reconstruction. He had worked hard to end slavery. He and other Republicans passed laws to help African Americans in the South.

In 1865, Congress set up the Freedmen's Bureau to provide jobs, health care, and education to African Americans. The Thirteenth Amendment abolished all slavery in 1865. The Fourteenth Amendment was passed by Congress in 1866 and ratified by the states in 1868. It said that all people born in the United States are citizens of the nation and of the state where they live. The Fifteenth Amendment, passed in 1870, gave all male citizens the right to vote.

REVIEW How did Reconstruction affect those living in Pennsylvania?

LESSON 3 REVIEW

 GENERALIZE What social changes did the Civil War bring about?

1 **BIG IDEA** Why did the North and the South fight the Civil War?

2 **VOCABULARY** Use **political party** in a sentence about elections.

3 **HISTORY** What was Reconstruction?

PENNSYLVANIA CONNECTION

HISTORIC LANDMARKS

Pennsylvania is rich in historic landmarks. Many are from Civil War times. One of the most famous landmarks is the Gettysburg National Military Park. In 1863, President Abraham Lincoln gave a speech known as the Gettysburg Address. In it, he dedicated the battlefield as a national memorial. Landmarks in the form of monuments, memorials, and parks help Pennsylvanians today remember the people and events of the past.

DID YOU KNOW?

The Gettysburg National Military Park has more than 1,400 monuments, markers, and memorials.

Gettysburg National Military Park

LOCATE IT

PENNSYLVANIA

Gettysburg National Military Park

The growth of industries in the United States depended on coal to power factories. This statue, near Minersville, honors the contributions of thousands of workers in Pennsylvania's coal mines.

The Pennsylvania Monument is one of the largest monuments at Gettysburg. Statues and carvings around the monument honor Pennsylvanians who fought at the Battle of Gettysburg.

A pyramid near Mercersburg marks the birthplace of the fifteenth President of the United States, James Buchanan. He was a key figure in events leading to the Civil War and the only Pennsylvanian to serve as President.

In 1890, a memorial was planned to honor the Civil War veterans of Allegheny County, Pennsylvania. Today, the Soldiers and Sailors National Military Museum and Memorial is located in Pittsburgh. The memorial honors men and women of the United States military from the Civil War to the present day.

ACTIVITY

Use the library or Internet to learn more about historic landmarks in Pennsylvania. Then, create a map of Pennsylvania showing the locations of five landmarks. Number each location and create a key with information about why each was important to Pennsylvania's history.

RESEARCH

Visit The Learning Site at **www.harcourtschool.com** to learn about other historic sites.

Review and Test Preparation

Generalize

Focus Skill

Copy the graphic organizer onto a separate sheet of paper. Use the facts you have learned to write a generalization about early Pennsylvania.

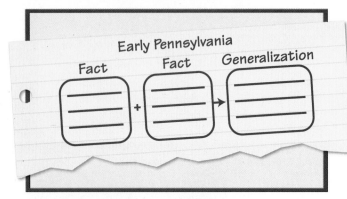

Early Pennsylvania

Fact + Fact → Generalization

THINK AND WRITE

Write a Diary Entry Describe a trip on Pennsylvania's early roads.

USE VOCABULARY

Write the word that correctly matches each definition.

market economy (p. PA 4-2)

labor union (p. PA 4-6)

social reform (p. PA 4-8)

political party (p. PA 4-10)

assassinate (p. PA 4-13)

1 changes to improve society

2 producers decide which goods to make

3 to murder in a sudden attack

4 group with the same point of view on issues

5 group that wants to improve the workplace

RECALL FACTS

Answer these questions.

6 Why was Horseshoe Curve important?

7 For what was anthracite coal used?

8 What was the Underground Railroad?

Write the letter of the best choice.

9 What was a turning point of the Civil War?
   A the Wilmot Proviso
   B the Battle of Gettysburg
   C the Emancipation Proclamation
   D Camp Curtin

THINK CRITICALLY

10 Why do you think population growth caused problems for cities?

11 How did better transportation affect Pennsylvania's economy in the 1800s?

12 Why was Reconstruction important to the Southern states?

PERFORMANCE

Make a Brochure Make a brochure to describe the growth of one of Pennsylvania's industries in the 1800s. Tell what roles location, natural resources, and people had in the growth of your industry. Be sure to include illustrations.

William Clark's compass, 1804

Olympic National Park, Washington

The West

❝ **Great joy in camp. We are in view of the ocean, this great Pacific Ocean.** ❞

—Journal of William Clark, November 7, 1805

Preview the Content

Scan the headings, captions, graphs, charts, diagrams, maps, and time lines throughout this unit. Use them to answer the following questions: *Who* and *what* is the unit about? *Where* are the places you will study? *When* did the events occur? *Why* are the events important?

Preview the Vocabulary

Compound Words A compound word is made up of two or more smaller words. Use the meanings of the smaller words below to write a possible meaning for each compound vocabulary word. Make a chart to record your responses.

SMALLER WORD		SMALLER WORD		COMPOUND/ VOCABULARY WORD	POSSIBLE MEANING
boom	+	town	=	boomtown	_____
cross	+	roads	=	crossroads	_____
earth	+	quake	=	earthquake	_____
wet	+	lands	=	wetlands	_____

CANADA

50°N

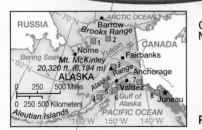

RUSSIA
70°N
ARCTIC OCEAN
Barrow
Brooks Range
1
2
Nome
Mt. McKinley
20,320 ft. (6,194 m)
3
Fairbanks
Yukon
CANADA
Bering Sea
60°N
ALASKA
Alaska Range
Anchorage
7
Valdez
5
6
Gulf of Alaska
8
Juneau
0   250   500 Miles
0   250 500 Kilometers
Aleutian Islands
PACIFIC OCEAN
160°W   150°W   140°W

ALASKA'S NATIONAL PARKS

1 Kobuk Valley National Park
2 Gates of the Arctic National Park
3 Denali National Park
4 Katmai National Park
5 Lake Clark National Park
6 Kenai Fjords National Park
7 Wrangell-St. Elias National Park
8 Glacier Bay National Park

Olympic National Park
Olympia
Puget Sound
North Cascades National Park
Seattle
Grand Coulee Dam
Spokane
Glacier National Park
Missouri River

WASHINGTON
Mt. Rainier National Park
Mt. Rainier 14,410 ft. (4,392 m)
Columbia River
Helena
Butte
MONTANA
Billings
Yellowstone River

Portland
Salem
Coast Ranges
Cascade Range
Mt. Hood 11,235 ft. (3,427 m)
Eugene
OREGON
Columbia Plateau
Boise
IDAHO
Idaho Falls
Snake River
Pocatello
Yellowstone National Park
Grand Teton National Park
WYOMING
N. Platte River
Casper
Cheyenne
Laramie

ROCKY MOUNTAINS
GREAT PLAINS
ND
SD
NE

Redwood National Park

40°N

Crater Lake National Park

Lassen Volcanic National Park
Reno
Carson City
NEVADA
Sacramento
Yosemite National Park
Great Basin National Park
GREAT BASIN
Great Salt Lake
Salt Lake City
Provo
UTAH
Arches National Park
Capitol Reef National Park
Bryce Canyon National Park
Zion National Park
Canyonlands National Park
Lake Powell
Colorado Plateau
Mesa Verde National Park
Rocky Mountain National Park
Boulder
Denver
COLORADO
Aspen
Mt. Elbert 14,433 ft. (4,399 m)
Colorado Springs
Pueblo
Arkansas River
N. Platte River
40°N

Sierra Nevada
Lake Tahoe
Coast Range
Sacramento River
San Joaquin River

San Francisco
San Jose

Kings Canyon National Park
Sequoia National Park
Death Valley National Park
Mt. Whitney 14,495 ft. (4,418 m)
Las Vegas
Lake Mead
Hoover Dam
Colorado River
Grand Canyon National Park
Painted Desert
Flagstaff
Petrified Forest National Park
Wheeler Peak 13,161 ft. (4,011 m)
Santa Fe
Gallup
Albuquerque
NEW MEXICO
Clovis
Roswell
Pecos River
TX

PACIFIC OCEAN

Channel Islands National Park
Los Angeles
Joshua Tree National Park
San Diego
CALIFORNIA
Mojave Desert
Bullhead City
ARIZONA
Sun City
Phoenix
Mesa
Yuma
Salton Sea
Gila River
Salt River
Gila River
Casa Grande
Tucson
Saguaro National Park
Sonoran Desert
Rio Grande
Las Cruces
Chihuahuan Desert
Carlsbad Caverns National Park

160°W   Kauai   155°W
Niihau   Oahu   Molokai   Haleakala N.P.
Honolulu   Maui
HAWAII
PACIFIC OCEAN
Lanai   Mauna Kea 13,796 ft. (4,205 m)
Kahoolawe   Hawaii
20°N
0   100 Miles
0   100 Kilometers
Hawaii Volcanoes N.P.

30°N
120°W
110°W
MEXICO

Key Events

| 1200 | 1600 | 1650 | 1700 | 1750 |

1200s Native Americans settle at Mesa Verde, in Colorado. p. 368

1610 Spanish build the city of Santa Fe, in New Mexico. p. 369

1915 A motion picture industry starts in Hollywood, California. p. 408

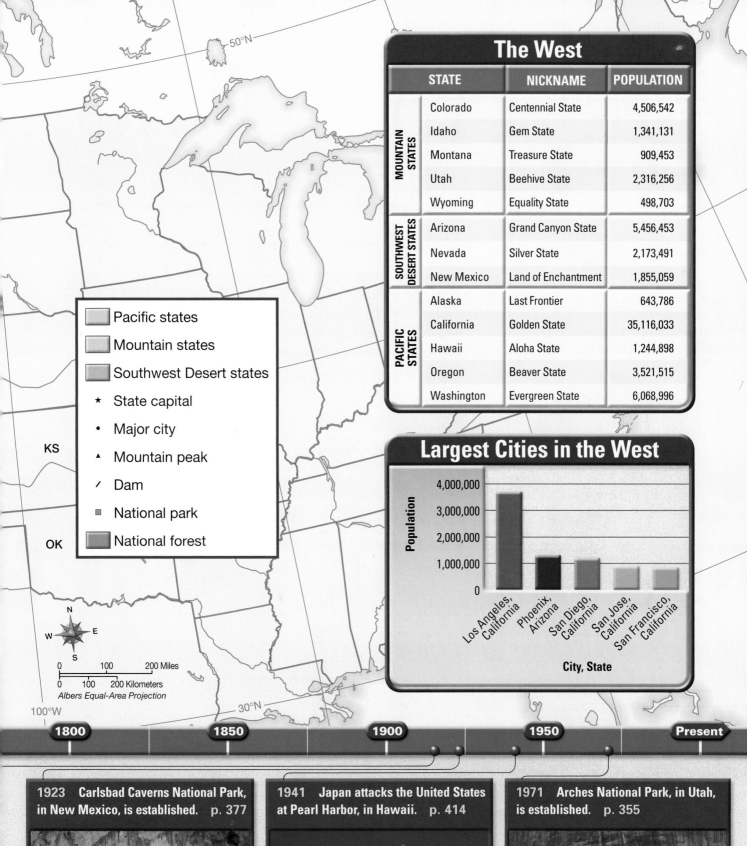

The West

STATE		NICKNAME	POPULATION
MOUNTAIN STATES	Colorado	Centennial State	4,506,542
	Idaho	Gem State	1,341,131
	Montana	Treasure State	909,453
	Utah	Beehive State	2,316,256
	Wyoming	Equality State	498,703
SOUTHWEST DESERT STATES	Arizona	Grand Canyon State	5,456,453
	Nevada	Silver State	2,173,491
	New Mexico	Land of Enchantment	1,855,059
PACIFIC STATES	Alaska	Last Frontier	643,786
	California	Golden State	35,116,033
	Hawaii	Aloha State	1,244,898
	Oregon	Beaver State	3,521,515
	Washington	Evergreen State	6,068,996

Pacific states

Mountain states

Southwest Desert states

★ State capital

• Major city

▲ Mountain peak

╱ Dam

▪ National park

National forest

KS

OK

50°N

100°W

30°N

N
W · E
S

0   100   200 Miles
0   100   200 Kilometers
Albers Equal-Area Projection

Largest Cities in the West

Population

4,000,000
3,000,000
2,000,000
1,000,000
0

Los Angeles, California · Phoenix, Arizona · San Diego, California · San Jose, California · San Francisco, California

City, State

1800   1850   1900   1950   Present

1923   Carlsbad Caverns National Park, in New Mexico, is established.   p. 377

1941   Japan attacks the United States at Pearl Harbor, in Hawaii.   p. 414

1971   Arches National Park, in Utah, is established.   p. 355

333

Grand Canyon
Exploring a Natural Wonder

written and illustrated by Wendell Minor

On a trip to the Grand Canyon, artist Wendell Minor created an artist's journal. In it he sketched or painted some of the things he saw. He also wrote down his thoughts and feelings about this natural wonder. Read now about what inspired Minor on his trip to the Grand Canyon.

The Grand Canyon is one of the most visited national parks in the United States. More than 5 million people from all over America and more than 120 countries come to Arizona to enjoy its beauty every year. The canyon is 277 miles long, 600 feet to 18 miles wide, and in some places more than a mile deep! It has been called "a mountain range in a ditch," and it is hard to believe that the Colorado River—which runs through it—is responsible for creating this spectacular chasm carved by erosion over millions and millions of years.

The average visitor spends only 3 to 4 hours in this natural wonder, but my first trip to the Grand Canyon lasted 12 days. I wanted to explore and record my impressions of the canyon with on-the-spot sketches, as did the famous artist Thomas Moran (1837–1926) more than 120 years ago. In a time before color photography, Moran's watercolor field sketches of Yellowstone helped motivate Congress to establish it as the first national park in 1872. His sketches and large studio paintings of the Grand Canyon did much the same to inspire America to preserve it as the fifteenth national park in 1919.

In the spirit of Moran, I brought along my watercolors, sketch pads, and pencils, and found many quiet spots to observe and record nature at her best.

---

chasm   (KA•zuhm) a deep crack or gorge

The images in this book are now my visual diary of a very special experience at one of the world's truly remarkable places.

I arrive at Moran Point just as the first rays of light are peeking over the horizon. I am so taken with the silence and beauty that I just watch in wonderment as the shadows quickly change, minute by minute. The sun strikes a wall of Kaibab limestone across from where I stand. I decide to capture the moment with my watercolors. I must work very fast before the light changes too much, or I will not remember the shadow patterns. It is hard to believe that the rocks I am painting are 250 million years old.

A rush of wind whistles, just over my head. I look up, and three white-throated swifts zoom past like miniature jets in formation.

Weather changes very quickly over the canyon. Within a matter of minutes, a storm can build. I watch with great anticipation as the dark clouds roll in. Suddenly a thin sliver of lightning appears to tear through the sky beyond a distant butte. Thunder echoes from one canyon wall to another, creating the most marvelous sounds. A cool breeze sweeps across the spot where I'm painting. A plateau lizard scurries over my boot, looking for a place to hide. I must hurry to finish.

butte (BYOOT) a steep hill of rock with a flat top

As I paint a butte called The Battleship, I am facing Powell Memorial, a large stone monument honoring John Wesley Powell. In May of 1869, Powell led the first documented expedition of the full length of the canyon by traveling the Colorado River with a crew of nine men in four small wooden boats. On his second expedition in 1872, Powell and his men became the first to chart and record important information about the Canyon of the Colorado for geological surveys commissioned by the United States government.

But it was the artist's eye that gave America its first view of the western wilderness frontier. Field sketches and paintings by artist-explorers Karl Bodmer, George Catlin, and Thomas Moran spoke to the imagination more clearly than words, and provided a preview of the beauty of the American West to the entire country through reproductions in books, magazines, and prints.

Of the numerous wildflowers found along the edge of the canyon, I think Indian paintbrush is my favorite. The brilliant vermilion color demands attention like the waving of little red flags. It amazes me that so many bright and beautiful flowers bloom in the spring from the tiniest cracks in the rocks and parched ground. While I am painting, a large bee fly stops by to investigate.

vermilion   red

He hovers like a small helicopter at the edge of my paint water jar and takes a drink.

I have always been fascinated by the basic shapes and forms found in nature, and the Grand Canyon offers an endless feast for the eye. Every butte, plateau, rock, tree, and shrub creates a stunning pattern of color, texture, and design. The canyon is so enormous that I must remind myself not to overlook its simple details.

Bright Angel Trail is busy this early morning as hikers and riders on muleback wind their way down the eight-mile trek to the river, almost 4,700 feet below the canyon rim.

I find a spot just off the path about one mile from the trail head, and I get ready for the first sketch of the day.

The wildlife is busy, too: below me, two desert bighorn ewes pass by, and just behind me, three young rock squirrels are chasing one another among the fallen boulders. All of a sudden, one pops up beside me to see what all the fuss is about. A busy morning, indeed!

One of the most striking buttes I discover in the canyon is called Sinking Ship. I can almost imagine the captain ordering his crew to abandon his vessel, while he, honoring the tradition and folklore of the sea, goes down with his sinking ship.

As I paint, I sit beneath an ancient, twisted juniper tree, wondering how many centuries it has been here. If it could tell its life story, what a history lesson that would be!

It is believed that some 11,000 years ago, the Paleo-Indians were the first to see the canyon. Indeed, the Native Americans of this high, dry desert place have an ancient and proud heritage.

All around me, I sense the presence of the past in this timeless place.

Analyze the Literature

1 Why did the artist sometimes have to paint his scenes very quickly?

2 Think about your favorite places. What about them makes them special to you?

READ A BOOK

START THE UNIT PROJECT

A 3-D Time Line With a few classmates, make a three-dimensional time line of the history of the West. As you read the unit, take notes on when and where important events took place, who was there, and why the events are important to the region's history. Then pick five events to include on the time line.

USE TECHNOLOGY

Visit The Learning Site at **www.harcourtschool.com** for additional activities, primary sources, and other resources to use in this unit.

BLACKTAIL BUTTE, WYOMING

Skiers enjoy the scenery from Blacktail Butte, in Wyoming's Grand Teton National Park. Grand Teton towers in the distance. At 13,770 feet (4,197 m), this mountain is the tallest peak in the Teton Range of the Rocky Mountains.

LOCATE IT

Teton Range

WYOMING

Blacktail Butte

10

Mountain States

" **Everything in the West is on a grander scale, more intense, vital, dramatic.** "

—Edward Weston,
diary entry, c. 1937

Generalize

A **generalization** is a statement that summarizes a group of facts and shows the relationship between them.

As you read this chapter, make generalizations.
• **Identify and list important facts.**
• **Then use those facts to make generalizations about the Mountain states.**

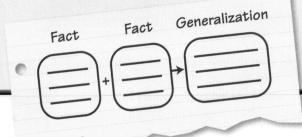

1

People and Mountains

1800   1850   1900

 GENERALIZE

As you read, make generalizations about the journey made by early settlers across the Rocky Mountains to the West.

BIG IDEA

The Rocky Mountains affected early travel and settlement in the Mountain region.

VOCABULARY

Continental Divide
barrier
wagon train
boomtown
suffrage

The Rocky Mountains stretch like a giant wall across much of the western United States. With their high, jagged peaks, the Rockies have helped shape our country's history. This has been especially true in the present-day states of Colorado, Idaho, Montana, Utah, and Wyoming. Although plains, plateaus, and basins cover parts of these states, mountains are the most common landform there. The Rocky Mountains affected how people reached the Mountain region, where they settled, and the ways they earned a living.

After crossing the Rocky Mountains, Lewis and Clark canoed on the Columbia River. Sacagawea, their guide, used sign language to greet the Native Americans they met.

FAST FACT During their expedition, Lewis and Clark recorded 178 kinds of plants and 122 kinds of animals that most Americans had never seen before.

York 1770?–1832?

Character Trait: Endurance

York was an important member of the Lewis and Clark expedition. Clark's journal of the expedition records York's contributions. One day, Clark, Sacagawea and her baby son, John Baptiste, and her husband, Toussaint, were caught in a sudden storm. They were nearly washed into the Missouri River. York, not thinking of his own safety, immediately rushed to help them.

Clark's journal also records that York took care of those who got sick along the way. When the expedition returned home, York was acclaimed a hero.

MULTIMEDIA BIOGRAPHIES
Visit The Learning Site at www.harcourtschool.com
to learn about other famous people.

Exploring the Mountains

When the United States bought Louisiana from France in 1803, Americans knew very little about that part of the country. They knew even less about the Rocky Mountains or the lands west of them. What kinds of resources did the area offer? Was it possible to take a wagon across the Rockies? To answer these and other questions, President Thomas Jefferson chose Meriwether Lewis to explore the region. Lewis asked William Clark to join him.

In May 1804 Lewis and Clark, with a small group of explorers called the Corps of Discovery, set out from St. Louis, Missouri. They spent the summer and fall traveling up the Missouri River. That winter, the explorers camped at a Mandan Indian village in present-day North Dakota. There Lewis and Clark hired a trapper to help them find a way through the Rocky Mountains. Sacagawea (sa•kuh•juh•WEE•uh), the trapper's wife,

was a Shoshone (shoh•SHOH•nee) Indian. She, too, would serve as a guide for the explorers.

In the spring of 1805, the group left its winter camp and continued across the Great Plains. When they reached the eastern Rockies in September, they also reached Sacagawea's homeland. The Shoshone people there agreed to show the explorers an old trail across the Rocky Mountains. Even with a guide and horses to carry supplies, the journey was very difficult.

The explorers spent 11 days traveling through heavy snow. They had to walk in a single line on the trail, cutting their way through thick trees. Clark reported, "I have been wet and as cold in every part as I ever was in my life." At last, with their supplies nearly gone, the group made its way out of the Rocky Mountains. After another two months traveling west, the explorers reached the Pacific Ocean in November 1805.

A few weeks before Lewis and Clark returned to St. Louis, President Jefferson sent Zebulon Pike to the southern Rocky Mountains. Pike reached present-day Colorado in 1806. He set out to climb a peak of the Rockies there, but it was November, and the mountainside was covered with snow. Exhausted and running out of supplies, Pike gave up the attempt. Today that mountain is called Pikes Peak in his honor.

Zebulon Pike

REVIEW Why did President Jefferson send explorers to the Rocky Mountains?

GENERALIZE

Mountains Divide the Continent

The Rocky Mountains stretch across the length of North America. They are very young mountains, so erosion over time has not smoothed their peaks. As a result, the Rockies have some of the highest and sharpest peaks on the continent. Several ranges make up the Rocky Mountains. Among these are the Front Range in Wyoming and Colorado, the Teton Range in Wyoming, and the Bitterroot Range in Idaho and Montana. Many of their peaks rise more than 14,000 feet (4,267 m) above sea level.

Running north and south along the peaks of the Rockies is an imaginary line, called the **Continental Divide**. From this line, rivers flow west or east. Most rivers that begin west of the Continental Divide, such as the Yukon, the Columbia, and the Colorado, flow into the Pacific Ocean. Those that begin east of the Continental Divide, such as the Missouri and the Rio Grande, flow into the Mississippi River or the Gulf of Mexico and eventually reach the Atlantic Ocean.

The Rocky Mountains not only affect the flow of many rivers but also separate the Interior Plains from the Intermountain Region and the Pacific Coast. Like Lewis and Clark and Pike, other people from the East looked for ways to cross the Rockies and reach the West.

REVIEW How do the Rocky Mountains divide the continent?

Zebulon Pike first saw what is now called Pikes Peak when he was about 150 miles (240 km) away.

LOCATE IT

COLORADO

Pikes Peak

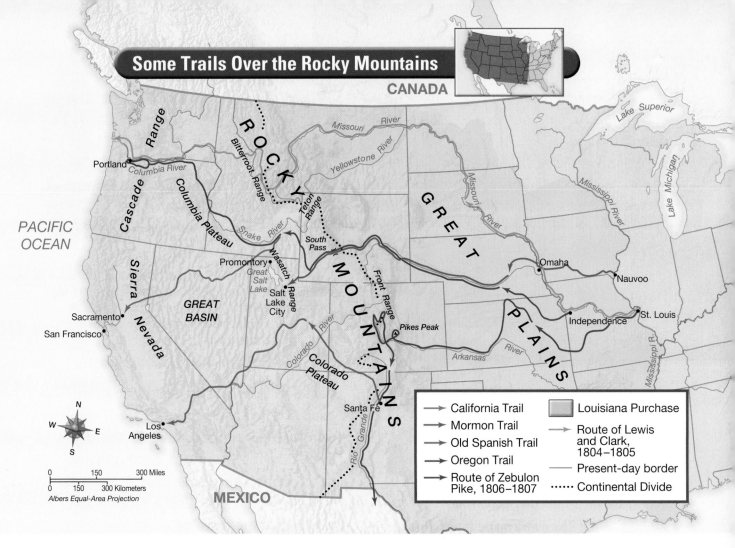

Some Trails Over the Rocky Mountains

CANADA

Lake Superior

ROCKY

Missouri River

Bitterroot Range

Yellowstone River

Teton Range

Missouri River

Lake Michigan

GREAT

Mississippi River

Columbia River

Portland

Cascade Range

Columbia Plateau

Snake River

South Pass

Wasatch Range

PACIFIC OCEAN

Sierra Nevada

Promontory

Great Salt Lake

Salt Lake City

GREAT BASIN

Colorado River

Front Range

Pikes Peak

PLAINS

Omaha

Nauvoo

Independence

St. Louis

Sacramento

San Francisco

Colorado Plateau

MOUNTAINS

Arkansas River

Mississippi R.

N W E S

Los Angeles

Santa Fe

Rio Grande

0   150   300 Miles
0   150   300 Kilometers
Albers Equal-Area Projection

MEXICO

→	California Trail		Louisiana Purchase
→	Mormon Trail	→	Route of Lewis and Clark, 1804–1805
→	Old Spanish Trail		Present-day border
→	Oregon Trail		
→	Route of Zebulon Pike, 1806–1807	·····	Continental Divide

GEOGRAPHY THEME

Movement   **Explorers and pioneers followed several trails west across the Rocky Mountains.**

❓ **As shown on the map, which of the trails went through the South Pass to cross the Rockies?**

Mountain Travel

Early explorers discovered that the Rocky Mountains form a great barrier to travel. A **barrier** is something that blocks the way or makes it hard to move from one place to another. The high, rugged Rockies made early travel in the Mountain region slow, hard, and often dangerous. Rock slides and blizzards could happen without warning. The narrow passes through the Rockies were often steep and covered with snow. Even so, pioneers soon began to cross the

Rocky Mountains. Trappers had found a wide, level gap in the Rockies near where the states of Wyoming, Utah, and Colorado meet. They named the gap South Pass. This pass opened the way for wagon travel in the Mountain region.

The first wagon train traveled through the South Pass in 1843. A **wagon train** is a group of wagons, each pulled by horses, mules, or oxen. During the next 70 years, about 400,000 pioneers crossed the Rockies by using the South Pass. Most of them traveled with covered wagons, which carried their belongings.

Thousands of Mormons traveled in wagon trains through the South Pass (above). In 1847 they began building the Salt Lake Temple (left), which now stands in the center of Utah's capital city.

After crossing the Rockies, pioneers still faced harsh conditions in the hot, dry climates of the Great Basin and the Columbia Plateau. In these arid regions west of the Rockies, water was scarce, making travel there difficult, too.

REVIEW What discovery made it possible for wagons to travel through the Rockies?

Life in the Mountain States

As pioneers traveled across the Mountain region's high mountains and arid plateaus and basins, most thought the land was too harsh for settlement. As a result, only a few of them chose to stay in the Mountain region.

Members of a religious group called the Mormons were among the earliest pioneers in the region. They headed to the West in search of religious freedom. After making their way through the South Pass, the first wagon train of Mormon settlers reached the desert lands of present-day Utah in 1847.

One of the first things the Mormons did after settling along the shores of the Great Salt Lake was to build irrigation canals. These canals brought fresh water from the nearby mountains to this dry land. Soon the Mormons were growing grains, fruits, and vegetables. The settlement they built eventually became Salt Lake City, the capital of Utah.

After gold and silver were discovered in the Mountain region, thousands of miners rushed there, hoping to strike it rich. Wherever gold or silver was found, towns sprang up almost overnight. Because these towns grew so fast, they were called **boomtowns**. Most boom-towns, however, did not last. When minerals in the area were used up, people moved away. Yet, some miners stayed in the region, and several boomtowns survived. In fact, two of those towns are now capital cities in the Mountain region. Helena, Montana, was once a gold-mining town, and Denver, Colorado, started as a supply center for miners.

Very few of the early settlers in the Mountain region were women, especially in mining towns. In Wyoming, for example, there were only about 1,000 women by 1869. That same year, Wyoming's leaders passed a law that they hoped would encourage more women to settle there. The law gave women the right to vote. This was one of the first victories in the fight for women's **suffrage** (SUH•frij), or the right to vote, in the United States.

Another event of 1869 brought even more settlers—both men and women—to the Mountain region. That year a railroad was completed, connecting the region to both the East and West coasts. Thousands of people now used the trains to move west and settle in the region. Farms, towns, and cities soon sprang up throughout the Mountain region. By 1896 all the Mountain states had become part of the United States.

REVIEW How did mining affect the settlement of the Mountain region?

DEMOCRATIC VALUES
The Right to Vote

On December 10, 1869, Wyoming lawmakers approved suffrage for women. Nowhere else in the United States at this time did women have the rights to vote and hold office. Women throughout the country worked hard to win those same rights. Finally, in 1920, all women in the United States were given the right to vote.

Analyze the Value

❶ Where in the United States did women first gain the right to vote?

❷ **Make It Relevant** Work together with a group to make a list of the reasons why voting is an important right and why every American citizen should have this right.

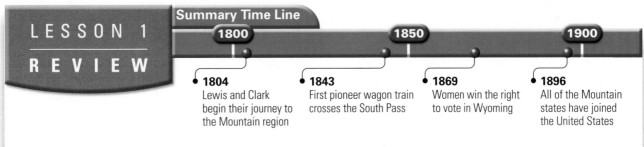

LESSON 1 REVIEW

Summary Time Line

1800	1850	1900

1804 Lewis and Clark begin their journey to the Mountain region

1843 First pioneer wagon train crosses the South Pass

1869 Women win the right to vote in Wyoming

1896 All of the Mountain states have joined the United States

GENERALIZE In general, how can travel be affected by geography?

❶ **BIG IDEA** Why were the Rocky Mountains a barrier to travel and settlement?

❷ **VOCABULARY** Describe the meaning of each word part of **Continental Divide** and how this relates to the meaning of the whole term.

❸ **TIME LINE** Which event occurred first, women winning the right to vote in Wyoming, or Lewis and Clark's journey?

❹ **GEOGRAPHY** Where is the South Pass?

❺ **CULTURE** What religious group settled near the Great Salt Lake in Utah?

❻ **CRITICAL THINKING—Analyze** Why do you think some people were willing to face danger in order to settle in a new place, such as the West?

PERFORMANCE—Draw a Coin Design Sacagawea's role in American history is honored with a portrait on the United States dollar coin. Draw a design for a coin to celebrate the history of the Mountain states. Share your design with the class and explain its meaning.

· SKILLS ·

CHART AND GRAPH

Read a Cutaway Diagram

VOCABULARY

cutaway diagram

▶ **WHY IT MATTERS**

To know how something works, we sometimes need to know how it looks on the inside. However, it is often not possible to see inside an actual object.

When you need to know what is inside an object, a cutaway diagram can help

you. A **cutaway diagram** is a kind of drawing that shows both the outside and the inside of an object. In a cutaway diagram, the artist "cuts away" part of the drawing to make a kind of window. Looking through the window, you can see inside the object. Around the window, you can see the outside of the object, too.

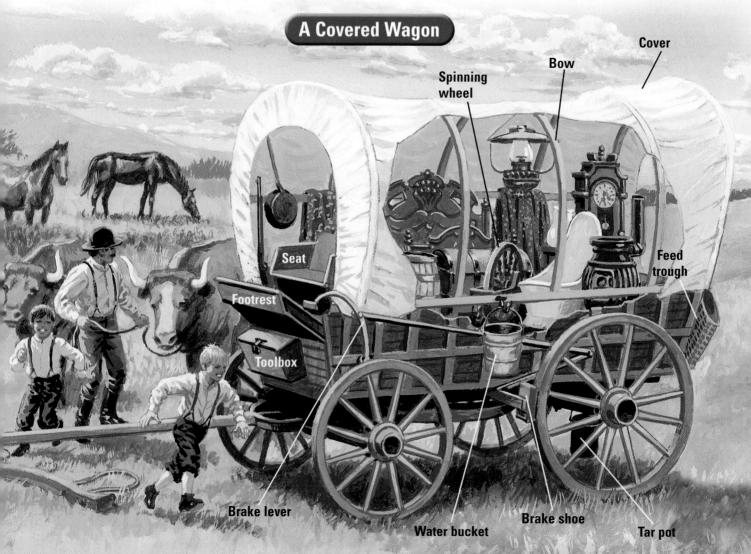

A Covered Wagon

Cover

Bow

Spinning wheel

Feed trough

Seat

Footrest

Toolbox

Brake lever

Water bucket

Brake shoe

Tar pot

WHAT YOU NEED TO KNOW

The cutaway diagram on page 348 shows the inside and outside of a covered wagon. This wagon is the kind that settlers used when they moved west to the Mountain region. Such wagons were nicknamed prairie schooners, because they "sailed" across the grassy "seas" of the Great Plains. A schooner is a kind of sailboat.

Settlers packed as many household items in their wagons as they could. They also packed tools and seeds that they would need to begin their lives on the frontier. To protect their belongings from the weather, settlers used wagon covers. These covers were usually made of cotton or canvas. Settlers rubbed oil on the covers to make them waterproof. Wooden hoops, called bows, held up the covers.

Teams of horses, mules, or oxen pulled the wagons. To stop a wagon, the driver pulled on the reins of the team and on the brake lever. The brake lever pushed the brake shoe against the rear wheel.

PRACTICE THE SKILL

Use the cutaway diagram to answer the following questions.

1 What equipment hung on the outside of the wagon?

2 What parts did the driver use to stop the wagon?

3 What held up the wagon cover? What was the cover made of?

4 What household items are in this covered wagon?

5 Why might a toolbox be important to pioneers?

APPLY WHAT YOU LEARNED

Look in an encyclopedia, in library books, or on the Internet to find out how a piece of equipment works—perhaps a flashlight or a camera. Then draw a cutaway diagram of that object. Use the diagram to explain to classmates how the object works.

GENERALIZE

As you read, generalize how people today depend on the Mountain states' natural resources to earn a living.

BIG IDEA

People in the Mountain states have adapted to the geography of their region.

VOCABULARY

satellite
timberline
geyser
public land

The Mountain States Today

Even though the Rocky Mountains often made settlement challenging, thousands of people eventually moved to Colorado, Idaho, Montana, Utah, and Wyoming. Once there, they had to adapt to the different climates of the Mountain region. They also had to adapt to the region's landforms. Today the Rocky Mountains and the region's other landforms continue to affect how people in the Mountain states travel and communicate, where they live, and what they do for a living.

Across the Rockies Today

Traveling across the Rocky Mountains today is much easier than it was in the past. People can now fly in airplanes above the mountains. They can use a system of modern trains and highways, too. But just as early pioneers discovered, Rocky Mountain weather still can make travel challenging.

Today's trains can travel through the steep Rocky Mountains.

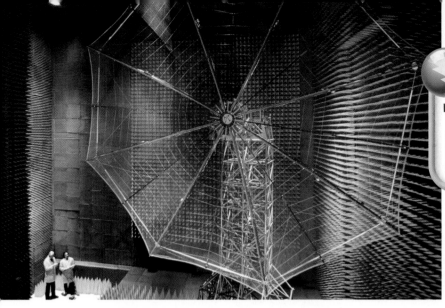

FAST FACT Today about 2,670 satellites circle Earth in space. Some fly more than 22,000 miles (about 35,000 km) above Earth's surface.

Technicians prepare a communication satellite before its launch into space.

Elevation varies greatly across the Mountain states. Temperatures vary greatly, too. In fact, temperatures drop about 3°F (almost 2°C) for every 1,000 feet (305 m) in height. On the same day, a valley might have warm temperatures and showers, while places higher in the mountains might have sleet or snow.

This mountain weather can make driving on roads at higher elevations dangerous or impossible. As a result, some of the region's highest roads are closed during winter months. Even in June, drivers often pass between walls of snow 8 feet (more than 2 m) high!

Mountains can make communication difficult, too. Both radio and television reception can be poor because the mountains block signals. Communication satellites, however, can improve reception. A **satellite** is an object that orbits Earth. Traveling high above Earth, communication satellites can send their signals over the mountains.

A gold nugget

REVIEW Why is mountain travel easier today than in the past?

GENERALIZE

Mining in the Mountain States

Years ago, people were willing to face the challenges of mountain travel because the Rocky Mountains held gold, silver, lead, and other minerals. Many people in the Mountain states still make their living from minerals and fuels.

Early miners in the Mountain region discovered gold near Pikes Peak, along Montana's Yellowstone River, and in the mountains of Idaho. People in the region also found silver, copper, and lead.

Today Idaho has several large lead mines and produces nearly half of the nation's silver. One of the world's largest copper mines is at Butte, Montana.

All the Mountain states are also rich in minerals and fuels that supply energy. Workers drill for oil and natural gas in Colorado, Wyoming, and Montana. These states also have rich stores of coal. Wyoming produces more coal than any other state. Mines in Utah, Idaho, and Wyoming hold most of the country's uranium, a mineral used to make nuclear energy.

REVIEW What resources mined in the Mountain states supply energy?

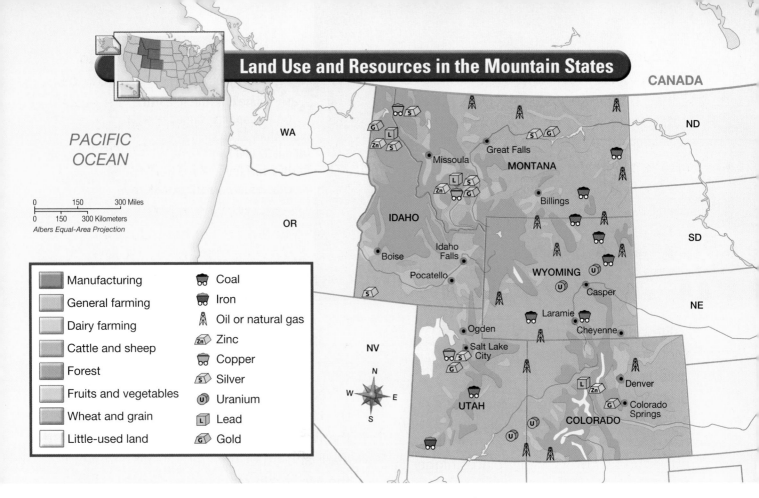

CANADA

PACIFIC OCEAN

WA

ND

OR

NV

SD

NE

Missoula

Great Falls

MONTANA

Billings

IDAHO

Boise

Idaho Falls

Pocatello

WYOMING

Casper

Laramie

Cheyenne

Ogden

Salt Lake City

Denver

Colorado Springs

UTAH

COLORADO

0   150   300 Miles
0   150   300 Kilometers
Albers Equal-Area Projection

	Manufacturing		Coal
	General farming		Iron
	Dairy farming		Oil or natural gas
	Cattle and sheep	Zn	Zinc
	Forest		Copper
	Fruits and vegetables	S	Silver
	Wheat and grain	U	Uranium
	Little-used land	L	Lead
		G	Gold

Human–Environment Interactions People in every Mountain state use part of their state's land for cattle and sheep ranching.

❓ In which Mountain state is the largest area of little-used land?

Ranches, Farms, and Lumber

People in the United States depend on the Mountain states for many metals, minerals, and fuels. They also depend on the region for food and wood. Mountains cover much of this region, but people there have found ways to use the more fertile areas to earn their livings.

Most ranches in the Mountain states are located on the Great Plains, east of the Rockies, or on the Columbia Plateau, west of the mountains. In both places, large herds of cattle and sheep graze on huge ranches.

Smaller ranches also lie in valleys between the mountains. Many ranchers in the region use computers and satellites to track their animals and predict weather changes. Some even use helicopters to herd their livestock.

Mountain land is generally too steep and rocky for most farming, and much of the Mountain region is arid. But people do farm the land on plains, plateaus, and river valleys. To provide enough water for the crops, every Mountain state has dams and reservoirs. The dams also supply power for homes and businesses.

Through irrigation, the once dry Snake River valley in Idaho has been turned into productive farmland. The valley is best known for producing potatoes. In fact, farmers in Idaho grow more potatoes than in any other state. Irrigation is especially important in western Utah and Colorado. Farmers there are now able to grow large crops of apples, peaches, pears, sugar beets, and potatoes.

The environment of the Mountain region also affects lumber industries. Because the climate in the mountains changes at different elevations, plant life there changes, too. The Rockies, like all high mountains, have a clear **timberline**. Above this elevation line, temperatures are too low for trees to grow. Just below the timberline, however, there are dense forests of firs, spruce, and pine.

These trees are used to produce lumber, pulp, and other wood products. Factories in the region make paper, plywood, pencils, and telephone poles. Like farmers and ranchers, lumber workers closely watch the changing mountain weather. In dry times, especially in hot summers, forest fires can spread quickly, killing thousands of trees.

REVIEW How do people in the Mountain states use the land to earn a living?

A CLOSER LOOK
Fighting Forest Fires

Most forest fires begin naturally when lightning strikes a dry area. To battle these blazes, crews of firefighters work on the ground and in the air.

1. Ground crews clear vegetation and dig ditches around the edges of the fire.
2. Other ground crews spray water or foam from fire trucks.
3. Helicopters drop water from tanks.
4. Air tankers spread chemicals across the burning area to slow the spread of the fire.
5. To reach areas that ground crews cannot reach, helicopters drop equipment and specially-trained firefighters into the area.

◈ Why do you think firefighters clear vegetation and dig ditches around the edges of the fire?

Denver is the largest city in the Mountain states. Its elevation of 5,280 feet (1,609 m) above sea level has earned Denver the nickname Mile High City.

LOCATE IT

Denver

COLORADO

Cities and Industry

Mountain regions generally have smaller populations than most other kinds of physical regions. This is true of the Mountain region of the United States, too. Only about 9 million people live in the Mountain states, and no cities there have more than 600,000 residents.

Most steep mountain slopes are not well suited for building large cities. So people in the Mountain states adapt to the environment by building their cities away from the slopes. In the Mountain states, most cities are built in valleys between mountains or on plains and plateaus. For example, Denver, the capital of Colorado, is built on the Great Plains. In fact, all of the capitals and largest cities in this region are in areas east or west of the mountains.

Mountain slopes are not good places for building factories, either. So, the region's manufacturing centers are located in the same kinds of places as its cities. Factory workers in Salt Lake City make transportation and high-tech equipment. Plants in Boise, Idaho, produce machinery and chemicals. In Denver, Colorado, workers make medical instruments, computers, and office equipment.

Most jobs in the Mountain states today, however, are in service industries. Stores, offices, and restaurants operate just about anywhere people want or need their services. Since more than seven out of ten people in the Mountain states live in urban areas, most of the region's service industries are also based in cities.

REVIEW Where are most of the large cities in the Mountain states?

A Land of Beauty

The beautiful scenery of the Mountain states has made tourism the region's fastest-growing industry. Tourists come to hike, climb mountains, camp, and fish in the spring and summer. In winter, they ski at resorts such as Sun Valley, Idaho; Aspen, Colorado; and Park City, Utah.

National parks and forests are major tourist attractions in the Mountain states, too. Yellowstone National Park covers parts of Idaho, Wyoming, and Montana. Founded in 1872, it is the oldest national park in the United States. Here visitors can see bubbling pools of mud and geysers. A **geyser** is a spring that shoots steam and hot water into the air. Wyoming is home to our nation's first national forest—Shoshone National Forest. At Colorado's Rocky Mountain National Park visitors might see sure-footed mountain goats and bighorn sheep climbing the high peaks.

Old Faithful geyser at Yellowstone National Park erupts nearly 20 times a day, sending a stream of boiling water more than 100 feet (31 m) into the air.

Many of these wild and beautiful places in the Mountain states remain so because much of the land is now **public land**, or land that is owned by the government. To use this land, ranchers, farmers, and lumber companies must rent it from the government.

REVIEW **Why is tourism a fast-growing industry in the Mountain states?**

LESSON 2
REVIEW

Focus Skill

GENERALIZE Why are there usually few large cities in mountain regions?

1 **BIG IDEA** What are some of the ways people today in the Mountain states adapt to the geography of the region?

2 **VOCABULARY** Explain how a **timberline** relates to the lumber industry.

3 **ECONOMICS** What makes farming possible in the arid parts of this region?

4 **CRITICAL THINKING—Evaluate** How do you think farmers, ranchers, and lumber company owners feel about having to rent land from the government?

PERFORMANCE—Write "Where Am I?" Questions Write three questions, each describing a place in the Mountain states. End each question with "Where Am I?" Then exchange papers with a partner and answer each other's questions.

3

Mountains Around the World

GENERALIZE

As you read, generalize how people in mountain regions around the world have adapted to their environments.

BIG IDEA

Living in mountain regions affects people in other parts of the world.

VOCABULARY

terrace

bartering

LOCATE IT

CHINA

NEPAL

INDIA

Mt. Everest

The Rocky Mountains are just one of Earth's mountain ranges. Wide bands of mountains cross all the continents. Snow covers many of their highest peaks, and powerful winds rush between them. Even at lower elevations, most mountain land is steep and rocky. These factors make traveling and living in most mountain regions difficult. Yet, like people in the Mountain states, people all over the world have learned ways to adapt to their mountain environments.

The Himalayas

The Himalayas are the world's highest mountain range. They form a barrier across southern Asia 5 miles (8 km) high. The tallest mountain in the world, Mount Everest, is part of the Himalayas. It rises 29,035 feet (8,850 m) high. The name *Himalaya* comes from an ancient word meaning "house of snow." Because the Himalayas are so high, many of their peaks are bitterly cold and covered with snow all year.

However, people do live in the Himalayas. Among them are the Sherpas. The Sherpas live in Nepal (nuh•PAWL), a country between China and India. Like farmers in the Mountain states, Sherpas in Nepal farm in small valleys at lower elevations. There they grow potatoes, rice, and soybeans, and herd animals.

All 35 of the highest mountains in the world are found in Asia, including Mount Everest, the highest point on Earth. The first people to reach the top of Mount Everest made the climb in 1953.

Major Mountain Ranges of the World

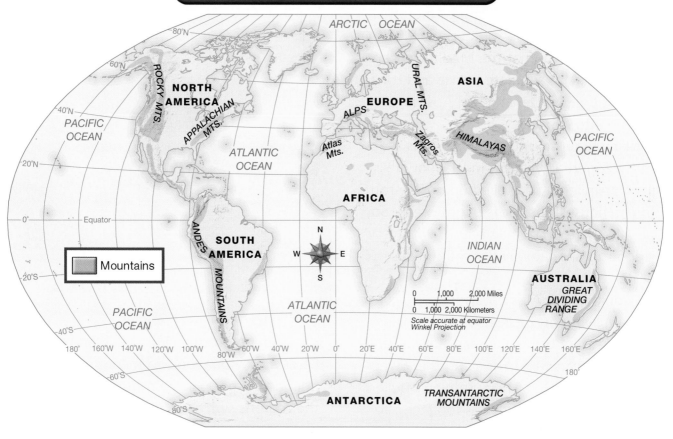

Regions   **Mountain ranges cross all the continents.**

◆ **What mountain range divides Europe from Asia?**

For many of their needs, the Sherpas depend on long-haired oxen called yaks. These animals have thick coats of fur that help them live in the region's cold climate. Sherpas often use yaks to transport goods and supplies across the Himalayas. Tilen, a Sherpa, says, "Life would be impossible here without the yaks. They give yogurt and cheese, butter, . . . hide for shoes, wool for blankets. . . . They carry our loads. They take care of us."

Even for experienced climbers like the Sherpas, travel in the Himalayas is slow and difficult. Most passes between the mountains are very high, and snow often blocks them. Many of the Himalayan peaks are so tall that

building roads and railroads over them is impossible. Yet several modern highways cross the lower ranges of the Himalayas today. Nepal now has an international airport, too.

REVIEW **What is the highest mountain range in the world?**

Many people in the Himalayas use yaks as pack animals.

The Alps

The Alps are Europe's largest mountain range. They cross the southern part of the continent. Starting at the Mediterranean Coast, the Alps separate France and Italy, run through Switzerland and Austria, and extend into Albania.

Many high mountains in the Alps are snowcapped all year. So much snow falls in the Alps that, if it piled up on the roofs of the houses, the roofs might break. So, people there build their houses with very steep roofs. That way the snow slides off more easily.

People in the Alps have found ways to make a living on their mountainous land. Farmers there grow grapes, potatoes, and sugar beets in valleys or along the lower slopes of the Alps. They use plows pulled by horses to till land that is too steep for tractors. Many farmers also herd sheep, goats, cattle, and other animals. They bring their livestock to grassy mountain slopes and valley pastures to graze.

Mining and manufacturing make up a large part of the economy in the Alps.

LOCATE IT

Switzerland

This house in Switzerland is typical of many houses built in the Alps.

Mines there produce iron, coal, and salt. Forests provide wood to manufacture pulp and other paper products. Dams on the region's swift-running rivers produce hydroelectric power to run factories in the valleys and foothills. As in the Mountain states, tourism is the fastest-growing industry in the Alps. Millions of tourists travel to the Alps each year to ski or just to enjoy the beautiful scenery.

The Swiss, who are famous for their dairy products, raise cattle in Alpine valleys and on grassy slopes.

For many years, however, the Alps stood as a barrier to travel in Europe. They separated people living in different parts of the mountains. As a result, people in the Alps adopted different customs and languages. Switzerland, for example, has three national languages—German, French, and Italian.

Today modern highways, railroads, and airports connect most places in the Alps. The Swiss Alps have the longest road tunnel in the world—the St. Gotthard Tunnel. The Swiss are also constructing the world's longest railroad tunnel. When it is complete, high-speed trains will travel through a tunnel more than 35 miles (56 km) long.

REVIEW How are homes in the Alps suited to the mountain environment? **GENERALIZE**

The Atlas Mountains

The Atlas Mountains curve about 1,200 miles (1,931 km) through north-western Africa. As in the Mountain region of the United States, the climates in the Atlas Mountains vary greatly.

On the northern side of the Atlas Mountains, nearest to the Atlantic and Mediterranean Coasts, the climate is mild. Because enough rain falls there, forests cover the mountainsides. Farther north, between the mountains and the sea, is a narrow coastal plain. Farmers on the plain grow large crops of wheat, barley, grapes, olives, potatoes, and citrus fruits.

The land to the north of the Atlas Mountains is the most crowded area in this part of Africa. Adding to the crowds are many tourists. They go to enjoy the mild, coastal climate and to shop in the ancient outdoor marketplaces.

The land to the south of the Atlas Mountains, however, is very different. Because the southern slopes get less rain, they are mostly dry and rocky. Here lies the Sahara, the world's largest desert. The few farms on this arid side of the Atlas Mountains are tiny, growing small crops of dates and grains. Some people in the Atlas Mountains also work as miners. The area holds almost two-thirds of the world's phosphate. Iron, copper, lead, natural gas, and zinc also come from the Atlas Mountains.

REVIEW How do climates vary in the Atlas Mountains?

People sell blankets and vegetables at outdoor markets in the Atlas Mountains.

The Quechuas use methods learned by their ancestors to farm on the slopes of the Andes.

The Andes Mountains

The Andes (AN•deez) Mountains stretch along the entire length of South America, near the Pacific Coast. They are the world's longest mountain range, extending 5,500 miles (8,851 km) from Venezuela to the southern tip of Chile.

Like the Rocky Mountains, the Andes are young mountains. So, they also are high, rugged, and steep. Wind and water have not yet worn down their peaks.

Among the Andes are many high, dry plateaus. People have lived on these lands for thousands of years. One group that lives there is the Quechua (KEH•chuh•wuh) Indians.

Most Quechuas herd animals and farm. Farming, however, is difficult in the Andes. Water is scarce and the soil is rocky. To grow crops on their steep mountain land, the Quechuas have built terraces. A **terrace** is a flat "shelf" dug into a mountainside. From far away, the terraces look like steps up the mountains.

Among the few crops that can grow in the high elevations of the Andes are beans, potatoes, and a grain called *quinoa* (KEEN•wah). The Indians who lived in this region long ago were the first people to grow potatoes. The Quechuas keep potatoes from spoiling the same way their ancestors did. They leave the potatoes on the ground to freeze at night and dry in the sun the next day. After several days and nights, the dried potatoes are ground into a meal called *chuña* (CHOON•ya). Chuña keeps for many months.

For many of their needs, the Quechuas depend on llamas (LAH•muhz). The llama

The Quechuas use llama hair to make wool, which they weave and dye for clothing and blankets.

La Paz, Bolivia

Understanding Places and Regions

La Paz is the capital of Bolivia, a country in western South America. It lies on a plateau high in the Andes Mountains. The center of La Paz is 12,001 feet (3,658 m) above sea level. This elevation makes La Paz the world's highest capital city. It is more than twice as high as the United States' highest capital city—Denver.

looks a little like a camel without a hump. Its coat provides wool for clothing and blankets. The llama is an excellent pack animal. It can carry heavy loads over long distances through the mountains. Like camels, llamas can go for long periods with little water—a great help for travel in arid areas of the Andes.

Some Quechuas use llamas to carry goods to market, while others use trucks and trains. For many years, the Quechuas bartered to get the things they needed. **Bartering** is trading one kind of good for another without using money. Today, however, the Quechuas use money to buy goods. Mining is another way that many Quechuas earn a living. Silver, tin, and copper are some of the important metals mined in the Andes Mountains.

REVIEW How do the Quechuas farm the steep land of the Andes mountainsides?

LESSON 3
REVIEW

GENERALIZE List some things that Sherpas and Quechas have in common. Then use this information to write a general statement about living in mountain regions.

1. **BIG IDEA** How do mountains affect the way people around the world live?

2. **VOCABULARY** Name a synonym and an antonym for the term **bartering**.

3. **CULTURE** How did the Alps affect the languages people speak in Switzerland?

4. **GEOGRAPHY** Which mountain range runs along most of South America's Pacific Coast?

5. **CRITICAL THINKING—Apply** How do you think modern transportation is changing life in mountain regions?

PERFORMANCE—Make a Bar Graph Research the name and height of the highest mountain on each continent. Make a bar graph displaying this data. You may wish to illustrate your graph. Write a question about your graph. Trade graphs with a classmate, and answer each other's questions.

10 Review and Test Preparation

Summary Time Line

1800

1805
Lewis and Clark cross
the Rocky Mountains

1847
Mormons found
Salt Lake City

Focus Skill Generalize

Copy the following graphic organizer onto a separate sheet
of paper. Use the information you have learned to make a
generalization based on the facts below.

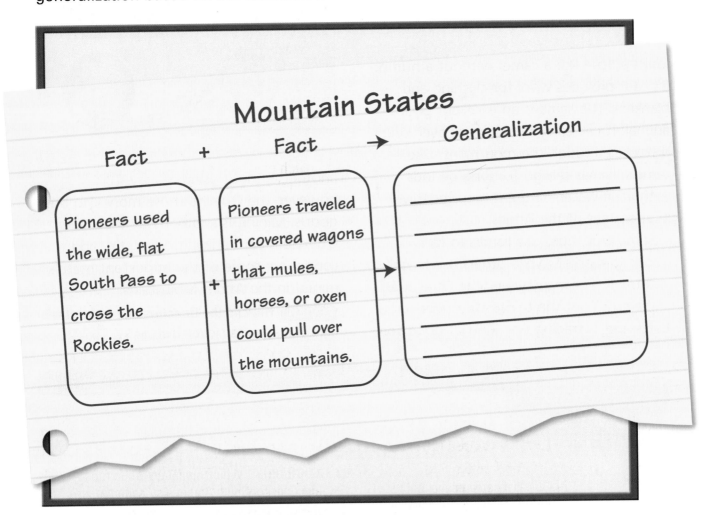

Mountain States

Fact + **Fact** → **Generalization**

Fact		Fact
Pioneers used the wide, flat South Pass to cross the Rockies.	+	Pioneers traveled in covered wagons that mules, horses, or oxen could pull over the mountains.

THINK & WRITE

Write a Letter Imagine that you are a
pioneer who has just traveled through the
Rocky Mountains. Write a letter to your family
and friends in the East describing what you
saw and how you felt during your journey.

Write a Television Commercial
Choose a mountain range that you have read
about in this chapter. Write a script for a
television commercial to attract visitors to
the mountains you have chosen.

1900   Present

1872
Yellowstone National Park opens

1896
All of the Mountain states
have joined the United States

1953
People climb to the top of
Mount Everest for the first time

USE THE TIME LINE

Use the chapter summary time line to answer these questions.

1 When did Yellowstone National Park open?

2 How many years after Lewis and Clark crossed the Rockies did Mormons found Salt Lake City?

USE VOCABULARY

Match each term to the correct definition.

barrier (p. 345)

suffrage (p. 347)

satellite (p. 351)

timberline (p. 353)

public land (p. 355)

terrace (p. 360)

bartering (p. 361)

3 the right to vote

4 a flat "shelf" dug into a mountainside to make farming there possible

5 an object that orbits Earth

6 something that blocks the way or makes it hard to move from place to place

7 land that is owned by the government

8 on a mountain, the elevation above which the temperatures are too low for trees to grow

RECALL FACTS

Answer these questions.

9 Why do most mountain regions have fewer large cities than other regions do?

10 Why did ranching become an important industry in the Mountain states?

11 How are some public lands in the Mountain states used?

12 What are some forms of transportation people use to cross mountains?

Write the letter of the best choice.

13 What was the name given to a town that grew up quickly near mines?
A capital
B port
C boomtown
D suburb

14 The mountain range covering northwestern Africa is the—
F Alps.
G Andes Mountains.
H Atlas Mountains.
J Himalayas.

15 Which of the following is *not* a major industry in the Mountain states?
A mining
B ranching
C tourism
D shipping

THINK CRITICALLY

16 What would you like most about living in a mountain region? What would you like least?

17 How do satellites help you know about current events in places all over Earth?

18 Why do you think so much land in the Mountain region is owned and managed by the government?

APPLY SKILLS

Read a Cutaway Diagram

19 Draw a cutaway diagram that shows either your classroom inside your school or a room inside your home. Add labels to your diagram.

CHART AND GRAPH SKILLS

Chapter 10 ▪ 363

ORGAN PIPE CACTUS NATIONAL MONUMENT

Organ Pipe Cactus National Monument in Arizona was established in 1937 to protect the unique plants and animals of the Sonoran Desert. Here, desert wildflowers bloom below the saguaro cactus (right), the state flower of Arizona, and the rare organ pipe cactus (far right), which grows nowhere else in the United States.

LOCATE IT

Organ Pipe Cactus National Monument

ARIZONA

11

Southwest Desert States

" Be still and the earth will speak to you. "

—Ancient Navajo Proverb

 Make Inferences

When you make an **inference**, you use facts and your own experiences to form a reasonable opinion or conclusion.

As you read this chapter, be sure to do the following.

- **List the facts about the Southwest Desert states.**
- **List information from your own experiences.**
- **Use the two lists to make inferences about the region.**

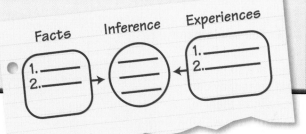

The Southwest Desert Long Ago

| 2000 Years Ago | | 1525 | 1725 | 1925 |

MAKE INFERENCES

As you read, make inferences about ways in which Native American, Spanish, and Mexican settlers of the past greatly influenced life in the Southwest Desert region today.

BIG IDEA

People lived in the Southwest Desert region long ago.

VOCABULARY

mesa
butte
nomad
adobe
pueblo
mission
society
reservation

In the 1500s, after the Spanish conquered what is now Mexico, they heard stories about great treasures that were said to lie to the north. One story even described seven cities built of gold! To find these and other riches, Spanish explorer Francisco Vásquez de Coronado (kawr•oh•NAH•doh) left Mexico in 1540. More than 1,300 soldiers and workers went with him. One of the first areas the group explored is now part of the Southwest Desert region of the United States. Today this region is made up of three states—Arizona, Nevada, and New Mexico.

The Desert Landscape

Coronado spent more than two years exploring parts of the Southwest Desert region and the surrounding lands. While doing so, he observed that different places in the region have very different climates and landforms. However, just as its name suggests, much of the region is dry land, or desert. In fact, all of our country's largest deserts lie in the Southwest Desert region.

When early Spanish explorers saw the bands of bright colors in this desert in Arizona, they called it *El Desierto Pintado,* which means "The Painted Desert."

FAST FACT
The sands in the Painted Desert are so colorful that at times they cause the air above them to appear to glow with a pink or purple haze. Navajo Indians in the area use the colorful sand for their famous sand paintings.

LOCATE IT

ARIZONA | Painted Desert

Landforms and Elevations in the Southwest Desert States

NEVADA
Reno
Lake Tahoe
Carson City
Great Basin
Humboldt River

ROCKY MOUNTAINS

GREAT PLAINS

Colorado Plateau
Four Corners
Lake Mead
Las Vegas
Grand Canyon
Colorado River
Painted Desert
Santa Fe
Albuquerque
Flagstaff
ARIZONA
Phoenix
Salt River
Gila River
Gila River
NEW MEXICO
Rio Grande
Pecos River
Sonoran Desert
Tucson
Chihuahuan Desert

MEXICO

0   100   200 Miles
0   100   200 Kilometers
Albers Equal-Area Projection

→ Route of Coronado, 1540–1542
— Present-day border

Feet	Meters
Above 13,120	Above 4,000
6,560	2,000
1,640	500
655	200
0	0
Below sea level	

GEOGRAPHY THEME

Place The highest parts of the Southwest Desert region are the Rockies and the Colorado Plateau.

❯ Near what present-day city on the Rio Grande did Coronado (above) pass?

When Coronado and his expedition reached what is now Arizona, they could find little food or water. With their supplies running low, the group turned east near the Painted Desert. They went into present-day New Mexico and spent the winter camped beside the Rio Grande. In the distance, they could see the Rocky Mountains, which stretch through the middle of New Mexico. In the spring, the explorers continued east onto the Great Plains. They never found any cities of gold, although a small group that went west became the first Europeans to see the Grand Canyon. Tired and disappointed, Coronado's expedition finally returned to Mexico.

If Coronado had traveled elsewhere in the Southwest Desert region, he would have seen other large landforms. Much of the Sonoran (soh•NOHR•ahn) Desert lies in southwestern Arizona. Part of the Chihuahuan (chee•WAH•wahn) Desert covers southern New Mexico. Nearly all of Nevada lies in the Great Basin, the largest desert region in the United States.

Coronado did not see the mostly desert Colorado Plateau of northern Arizona and New Mexico, either. Wide valleys, sharp cliffs, and deep canyons break this plateau's flat surface. Over millions of years, wind and water have shaped parts of the plateau into strange forms, such as mesas (MAY•sahz) and buttes (BYOOTS). A **mesa** is a hill or small plateau with a flat top and steep sides. A **butte** is a steep hill of rock with a flat top, like a mesa but smaller.

REVIEW Why did Coronado's expedition explore the Southwest Desert region?

Early Peoples of the Desert

As Coronado traveled across the Southwest Desert region, he met different groups of Native Americans. They and their ancestors had been living in this region for thousands of years.

At one time the only people who lived in the region's deserts were nomads. A **nomad** is a person who has no permanent home but moves from place to place. The deserts were too dry for people to stay in one location and grow crops. When their water supply ran out, they moved to another place.

Over time, however, several Native American groups began to build settlements in the desert. Among the earliest were the Hohokam (hoh•HOH•kahm). They settled in the Sonoran Desert about 2,000 years ago. The Hohokam built their villages near the Gila (HEE•lah) and Salt Rivers.

The Hohokam used sand and clay to make pottery, such as this jar shaped like a human.

The Hohokam learned that irrigation is the secret to living in the desert. They built dams and dug miles of irrigation canals. In their irrigated fields the Hohokam grew cotton, beans, squash, and corn.

Another Native American group settled north of where the Hohokam lived. They were the Anasazi (ah•nuh•SAH•zee)—the "Ancient Ones." They lived near what is today called the Four Corners. This is the area where Arizona, Colorado, New Mexico, and Utah meet.

The Anasazi built villages on mesas, on canyon floors, and even on the sides of high cliffs. Since few trees grew in the Four Corners' dry climate, the Anasazi built their villages out of stone or adobe (uh•DOH•bee). **Adobe** is a mixture of sandy clay and straw that is dried into bricks. Thick adobe walls kept the buildings warm in winter and cool in summer.

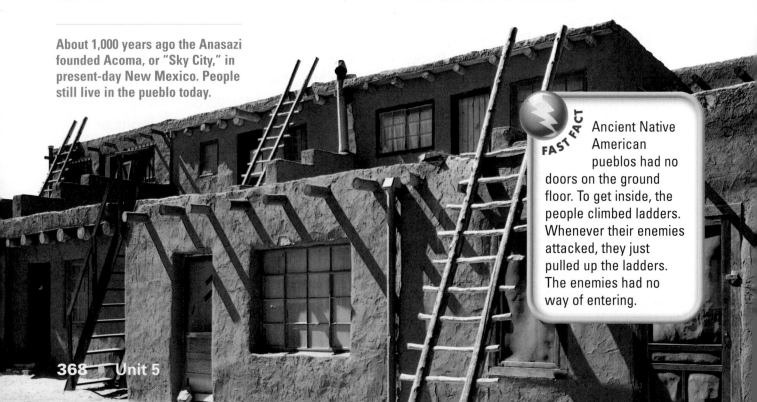

About 1,000 years ago the Anasazi founded Acoma, or "Sky City," in present-day New Mexico. People still live in the pueblo today.

FAST FACT Ancient Native American pueblos had no doors on the ground floor. To get inside, the people climbed ladders. Whenever their enemies attacked, they just pulled up the ladders. The enemies had no way of entering.

Analyze Primary Sources

This Navajo rock painting, or petroglyph, shows the arrival of Spanish settlers in the lands north of Mexico.

1 The Spanish brought the first horses into the region.

2 Spanish soldiers accompanied the settlers into the region.

3 The cross on this rider's cape shows that he is a priest.

◆ Why do you think early people in the desert painted on rocks instead of on paper?

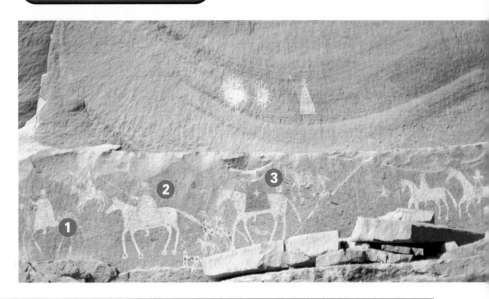

Some Anasazi villages were five or six stories high and had more than 800 rooms! As in today's apartment buildings, the rooms were built on top of other rooms. All the buildings were connected, and people used ladders to move between the levels. When the Spanish saw these adobe villages, they called them **pueblos** (PWEH•blohz). *Pueblo* is Spanish for "village."

Like the Hohokam, the Anasazi were farmers. They grew corn, squash, and beans on the flat lands between mesas. To get at the water beneath the soil, the Anasazi planted their seeds deep in the ground. They also dug holes and ditches to store water, and they dug canals to irrigate their fields.

No one knows what happened to the Hohokam. But experts think that many Anasazi moved to the Rio Grande valley in present-day New Mexico. They were probably the ancestors of the Pueblo who live there today.

REVIEW How were the Hohokam and the Anasazi able to grow crops in the desert?

MAKE INFERENCES

Native Americans and the Spanish

Many groups of Native Americans lived in what is now the Southwest Desert region. However, Spain eventually claimed all of the land. The Spanish called the entire area New Mexico.

By 1610 the Spanish were building a large settlement—the city of Santa Fe (SAN•tuh FAY). It was the capital of Spanish New Mexico. Today, Santa Fe is the capital of the state of New Mexico. It is the oldest capital city in the United States.

Spanish settlers built forts and ranches around Santa Fe. Many Native Americans were enslaved and forced to work without pay on the Spanish ranches.

Spain also built several **missions**, or religious settlements, in the Southwest. There, Catholic priests tried to get Native Americans to give up their own religion and become Christians. Many resisted but were forced to do so. Not all of the Native Americans spoke the same language. This made it difficult for them to unite against the Spanish. Some ran away from the missions. Others rebelled by attacking the Spanish.

In 1680, the Pueblo, a group of Native Americans living in New Mexico, united under a leader named Popé (poh•PAY). They drove the Spanish out of New Mexico and kept them out for 12 years. When the Spanish finally returned, they no longer tried to force the Pueblo to change their ways.

Despite their conflicts, the Spanish and the Native Americans learned from each other. The Spanish learned how to build adobe houses and how to use herbs as medicines. The Native Americans learned how to raise the cattle, horses, and sheep that the Spanish brought.

Over time, the missions became the center of Spanish society in the Southwest Desert region. A **society** is a group of people who have many things in common.

Spanish farms, ranches, and cities grew up around the missions.

REVIEW What did the Spanish learn from Native Americans?

The Southwest Desert States

In 1821 Mexico won its independence from Spain. As a result, the new Mexican government took control of all the lands in the Southwest Desert region.

As had happened in Texas, thousands of settlers from Mexico, Europe, and the United States soon headed to the Southwest Desert region. Many traveled on the Santa Fe Trail. This long overland trail led from Independence, Missouri, to Santa Fe. It served as a major trade route between the United States and the Mexican territories.

Then, in 1848, the United States fought and won a war with Mexico. As a result

The Spanish founded Mission San Xavier del Bac in the late 1600s. The settlement that grew up near the mission became the city of Tucson, Arizona.

Many Mexican holidays are celebrated in the Southwest Desert states. At some of these celebrations, dancers wear traditional Mexican costumes, which sometimes include sombreros (top). Some musicians play traditional Mexican instruments, too, such as maracas (above).

of this war, the United States gained most of the land in what is now the Southwest Desert region. A few years later the United States purchased from Mexico the rest of the land that makes up the region. All of present-day Arizona, Nevada, and New Mexico had become part of the United States.

Now even more settlers moved to the Southwest Desert region. By 1912 Arizona, Nevada, and New Mexico had joined the Union as states. After that the population of those states continued to grow.

Today Arizona, New Mexico, and Nevada have a mix of people and cultures. However, this region keeps much of its Spanish, Mexican, and Native American heritage. In all parts of the region are old adobe buildings and missions built by Spanish settlers. Even many newer buildings reflect the Spanish style—with thick adobe walls and flat, tiled roofs.

Because the Southwest Desert states are so close to Mexico, many people from that country have immigrated to the region—especially to New Mexico and Arizona. In some cities in the Southwest Desert states, more than half of the people trace their roots to Mexico. As a result, many people in the region speak Spanish as well as English.

Native American culture is a large part of the region's heritage today. More than 400,000 Native Americans now live in the Southwest Desert states. Many live and work in cities and towns, while others live on reservations. A **reservation** is land set aside by the government for use by Indians. On reservations, Indians govern themselves. In the state of Arizona alone, more than 200,000 Indians live on reservations. The Navajo reservation is the largest in the United States. It covers parts of Arizona, New Mexico, and Utah.

Inter-Tribal Ceremonial

For more than 80 years, Navajo, Hopi, Zuni, and many other Native American groups have gathered in Gallup, New Mexico, for a special celebration. Each year they hold the Inter-Tribal Ceremonial to remember their heritage. To start the event, Native Americans parade in traditional dress. For the next four days they perform ceremonial dances, display Indian artwork, and feast on Indian foods. They even have an all-Indian professional rodeo.

Like other Americans, Indians on reservations farm and run other businesses. They try to keep their heritage alive, too. They make traditional goods, such as weavings, silver and turquoise jewelry, and pottery. They hold cultural celebrations, such as the Inter-Tribal Ceremonial. Their children learn Indian languages as well as English in school.

REVIEW In what ways do people in the Southwest Desert states keep Spanish, Mexican, and Native American heritage alive?

LESSON 1 REVIEW

Summary Time Line

2000 Years Ago — 1525 — 1725 — 1925

1540 Coronado begins an expedition into the Southwest Desert region

1610 Santa Fe is built as Spain's colonial capital of New Mexico

1912 All of the Southwest states have joined the Union

 MAKE INFERENCES How were missions important to the settlement of the Southwest Desert region?

1 **BIG IDEA** How did people in the Southwest Desert region live long ago?

2 **VOCABULARY** Explain the difference between a **mesa** and a **butte** and tell where in the Southwest Desert states these landforms can be found.

3 **TIME LINE** By what year had all of the Southwest Desert states joined the Union?

4 **CULTURE** How do Native Americans in the Southwest Desert states keep their culture alive?

5 **CRITICAL THINKING—Evaluate** How do you think many Native Americans felt about the Spanish missions in the Southwest Desert region?

 PERFORMANCE—Stage a Ceremonial Work with a group, in the library or on the Internet, to learn about a Native American group in the Southwest Desert region. Use this information to plan a kind of inter-tribal ceremonial. Invite other classes to attend your event.

The Southwest Desert States Today

· LESSON ·

2

Finding enough water to meet their needs was a challenge for Native Americans and for other settlers in the Southwest Desert region. Today people in the region still face the same challenge. In recent years, however, new sources have brought more water to desert areas. This has helped the Southwest Desert states grow rapidly. It has also allowed people to use the region's rich natural resources in new ways.

MAKE INFERENCES

As you read, make inferences about ways that people in the Southwest Desert states manage their limited water resources.

BIG IDEA

Bringing more water to the Southwest Desert states has changed life there.

VOCABULARY

rain shadow
cloudburst
arroyo
aqueduct
migrant worker

Water in the Deserts

Like most natural resources, water is not distributed, or spread out, equally in the Southwest Desert states. Some parts of the region receive less than 10 inches (25 cm) of rain a year. Nevada gets less precipitation than any other state—about 9 inches (23 cm) per year.

Why are the Southwest Desert states so arid? The main reason is that mountains to the west of them—the Coast Ranges and the Sierra Nevada—keep moist air from reaching the deserts.

About 50 kinds of cactuses grow in the Sonoran Desert. The cactus plant stores water in its thick stem. The stored water helps the cactus survive in the dry, hot environment.

LOCATE IT

Sonoran Desert

ARIZONA

373

Clouds carrying moisture from the Pacific Ocean are blown against the mountains by the wind and then pushed up the western slopes. As the clouds rise, the air cools. Cool air cannot hold as much moisture as warm air can. As a result, the clouds drop most of their rain or snow on the western side of the mountains.

By the time the air reaches the other side of the mountains, little moisture remains in it. Because of this, places on the eastern side of the mountains, in the Southwest Desert region, receive little precipitation. They lie in the **rain shadow**, or the drier side of the mountains.

Because of the rain shadow effect, many rivers and streams in the Southwest Desert region are dry for much of the year. They fill with water only when mountain snows melt in the spring or after it has rained. Some desert areas might get half of their yearly precipitation in just one cloudburst. A **cloudburst** is a sudden, heavy rain.

When a cloudburst happens, not all of the rain can soak into the hard, sun-baked desert ground. Instead, the runoff fills nearby streams, rivers, or ancient arroyos (ah•ROH•yohz). An **arroyo** is a deep gully or ditch carved by running water. Sometimes there is enough water to cause a powerful flash flood.

REVIEW **Why are the Southwest Desert states so arid?** MAKE INFERENCES

Analyze Diagrams Places in a rain shadow usually receive very little precipitation. In the Southwest Desert region, the rain shadow effect created by the Coast Ranges and the Sierra Nevada has helped form several desert areas.

✦ What happens after winds push clouds up one side of the mountains?

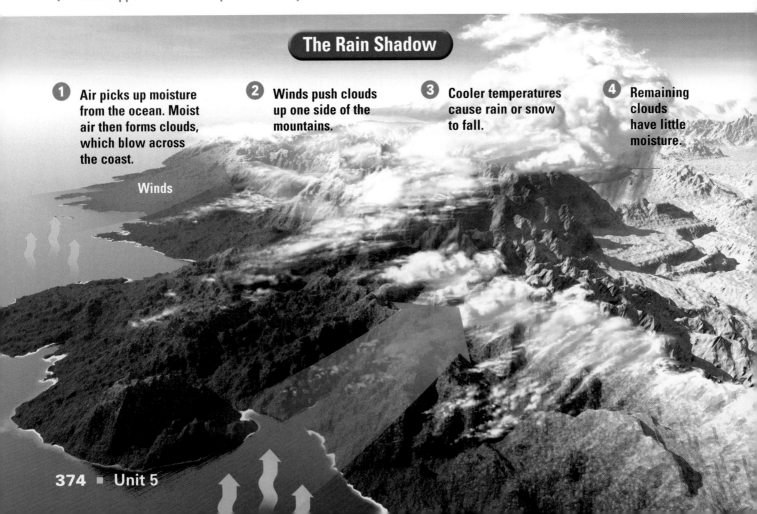

The Rain Shadow

1 Air picks up moisture from the ocean. Moist air then forms clouds, which blow across the coast.

Winds

2 Winds push clouds up one side of the mountains.

3 Cooler temperatures cause rain or snow to fall.

4 Remaining clouds have little moisture.

Irrigation in the Southwest Desert States

Human–Environment Interactions Hoover Dam and Lake Mead, along the Colorado River, provide much of Arizona's fresh water.

❖ What lake and rivers supply water for the Newlands Irrigation Project in Nevada?

New Sources of Water

Natural water supplies are scarce in the Southwest Desert states. People who live in the region try to make the most of the desert environment. They build dams and reservoirs and dig deep wells to create new sources of water. In many places, aqueducts (A•kwuh•duhkts) carry the water from those projects to places where it is needed. An **aqueduct** is a large pipe or canal built to carry water.

Every Southwest Desert state has several dam and reservoir projects to help control and save water supplies. The largest dam in the region is Hoover Dam. It was built across the Colorado River on the border between Arizona and Nevada and was completed in 1936. Hoover Dam stands about as tall as a 54-story building. Enough concrete was used in the dam to pave a two-lane highway from New York City to San Francisco, California!

Behind Hoover Dam lies Lake Mead, one of the world's largest reservoirs. Hoover Dam and Lake Mead provide water and electricity for millions of people in Arizona, Nevada, and California.

Both the Rio Grande and the Pecos Rivers in New Mexico also have dams on them. In Nevada, dams control the water flow of almost every river. The Newlands Irrigation Project, near Reno, is the state's largest irrigation project. Dams also cross Nevada's Humboldt, Walker, and Owyhee (oh•WY•hee) Rivers.

POINTS OF VIEW
Irrigation

SANDRA POSTEL, Director, Global Water Policy Project

❝Irrigation accounts for about four-fifths of the water used in much of the western United States. As water supplies become scarce, it is very important to use water more wisely and efficiently in agriculture.❞

SHELDON R. JONES, Director, Arizona Department of Agriculture

❝Any kind of adjustment in water allocations or agricultural access to water could be devastating to rural agricultural economies.❞

Analyze the Viewpoints

1. What is each person's viewpoint about using water for irrigation in the western United States?

2. **Make It Relevant** Choose the viewpoint above that you agree with most. Then, work with a partner to create a poster that supports this viewpoint. The poster should include an illustration and a slogan to catch people's attention. Display the poster on a classroom bulletin board.

People in the Southwest Desert region also dig wells deep beneath Earth's surface and pump out groundwater. The water supplied by reservoirs and wells has created important centers of agriculture in some parts of the Southwest Desert region. With irrigation, desert farms produce large amounts of cotton, lettuce, citrus fruits, hay, and chili peppers. Migrant workers harvest many of those crops. A **migrant worker** is someone who moves from farm to farm with the seasons, harvesting crops.

Although farming is possible in the Southwest Desert region, ranching is more important there. Livestock can graze in areas that are too dry for farming. In New Mexico, for example, large herds of cattle and sheep graze on the Great Plains and in the valleys of the Rocky Mountains. Herds of cattle also roam along the Humboldt River in eastern Nevada and in northeastern and central Arizona.

REVIEW How have people changed the desert to get enough water for their needs?

Grids of irrigation canals (right) cover parts of Arizona, supplying water to grow crops such as cantaloupes (below).

Growth in the Desert

Having a steady supply of water and electricity means that more people can live and work in the Southwest Desert states. The generally sunny climate has also attracted more people to this part of the Sun Belt. Many of them have come to find jobs in new industries there. As a result, the region's population and economy have been growing rapidly.

Growth has helped make service industries the largest part of the region's economy. Tourism is the leading industry in all three Southwest Desert states. Tourists come to visit the region's many national parks. Among the most popular are Grand Canyon and Petrified Forest National Parks in Arizona, Carlsbad Caverns in New Mexico, and Great Basin National Park in Nevada.

Manufacturing is a growing industry in the region, too. Factories in Las Vegas and Reno, Nevada, process foods and make concrete, appliances, and printed materials. Factories in Albuquerque, New Mexico, produce silicon chips for computers and telephones. Workers in the Phoenix and Tucson areas of Arizona manufacture computers, spacecraft, and satellites.

Mining is another large industry in the Southwest Desert states. Arizona mines produce about two-thirds of all the copper in the United States. Nevada ranks first in gold production and second in silver production. Many resources used to produce energy in the United States come from this region, too. Uranium, a mineral used to fuel nuclear power

Petrified Forest National Park

Understanding Places and Regions

A strange forest is in Arizona's Painted Desert. The trees in this forest are all dead, and they lie flat on the ground. They are petrified. This means their wood has been replaced by stone! These trees were buried in mud, sand, or ash millions of years ago. Water carried minerals into the buried trees. Over time, the minerals replaced the wood cells as they decayed, so the trees became stone. This forest of stone trees has been set aside as the Petrified Forest National Park.

plants, is mined in Arizona and New Mexico. New Mexico also produces large amounts of natural gas and petroleum.

Another employer in the Southwest Desert states is the United States government. In fact, the government either manages or owns nearly all of Nevada's land, and about half the land in Arizona and New Mexico. The government rents some of this public land to farmers, ranchers, and miners. Millions of acres are also set aside as national parks and forests.

Because it has so many telescopes, Tucson, Arizona, is known as the "Astronomy Capital of the World." Kitt Peak National Observatory there has the world's largest telescope.

LOCATE IT

ARIZONA

Kitt Peak National Observatory

The Southwest Desert region's flat, dry areas are also excellent places to build Air Force bases and testing areas for military weapons. The Los Alamos and Sandia National Laboratories, in New Mexico, are both world leaders in scientific research.

REVIEW **Why are the population and the economy of the Southwest Desert states growing so fast?**

Using and Conserving Water

So much growth happening so quickly has caused problems in the Southwest Desert states. Although people have created new sources of water in the desert, some worry that there may not be enough water to continue meeting the needs of this growing region. So they are working hard to conserve their water resources and use them wisely.

In many desert areas there are so many people now that they are using groundwater much faster than nature can put it back. In Tucson, for example, water levels in some wells dropped as much as 110 feet (34 m) in just ten years!

To help people use less groundwater, the Central Arizona Project was built. It uses canals, tunnels, pumping stations, and pipelines to carry water from Lake Mead in Nevada to desert cities such as Phoenix and Tucson.

New laws in the Southwest Desert states also help conserve water. People in the region are encouraged to design their yards with sand, rocks, cactuses,

Many people in the Southwest Desert states use cactuses and other desert plants along with colorful rocks and sand to landscape homes and businesses.

How Much Water?

USE	AMOUNT
Brushing teeth	1 to 2 gallons (4 to 8 L)
Flushing a toilet	5 to 7 gallons (19 to 26 L)
Running a dishwasher	9 to 12 gallons (34 to 45 L)
Taking a shower	15 to 30 gallons (57 to 114 L)
Washing dishes by hand	20 to 30 gallons (76 to 114 L)

Analyze Graphs Each American uses an average of about 140 gallons (530 L) of water a day.

✦ About how much water does a person use when taking a shower?

and other plants that do not require as much water as grass does.

In Arizona five water management areas have been formed. Leaders in each of these areas decide how much water cities and farms should use. Each water management area has also thought of ways to get people to conserve water. People are now being paid to put toilets that use less water in their homes.

People in Las Vegas, one of the country's fastest-growing cities, are also trying to use water wisely. Las Vegas leaders have passed several water-saving laws, such as forbidding builders to create new artificial lakes. Many of the city's golf courses and hotels that already have artificial lakes now recycle and reuse the water.

REVIEW Why is water conservation so important in the Southwest Desert states?

LESSON 2
REVIEW

MAKE INFERENCES Why have cities of the Southwest Desert states become the region's manufacturing centers?

❶ **BIG IDEA** How has bringing water to parts of the Southwest Desert states changed the region?

❷ **VOCABULARY** Use the terms **rain shadow** and **cloudburst** to describe the natural water supply in the Southwest Desert states.

❸ **ECONOMICS** Why do more people in the Southwest Desert states earn their living from ranching than from farming?

❹ **CIVICS AND GOVERNMENT** What kinds of laws have been passed in the Southwest Desert states to conserve water resources?

❺ **CRITICAL THINKING—Evaluate** Do you think the steps people in this region are taking to conserve water are effective? Why or why not?

PERFORMANCE—Draw a Landscape Plan Work with a partner to draw a plan for a desert garden. Decide how you would use sand, rocks, and desert plants instead of grass to landscape your garden. Share your drawing with the class and explain your garden's design.

·SKILLS·
READING

Predict a Likely Outcome

VOCABULARY

prediction

➡ WHY IT MATTERS

People often make **predictions**, or decide what they think will happen in the future. To predict a likely outcome, you use information that you have, as well as your past experiences.

➡ WHAT YOU NEED TO KNOW

You can take the following steps to predict a likely outcome.

Step 1 **Look at the information you already have on the topic.**

Step 2 **Gather any new information that relates to the topic.**

Step 3 **Look for patterns in these events or data.**

Step 4 **Make a prediction based on any patterns you discover and on your own experiences.**

➡ PRACTICE THE SKILL

You have read about why water is scarce in much of the Southwest Desert region. Some people in the region predict that there may not be enough water to meet all the needs of the people there in the future. Answer these questions to understand how people have made this prediction.

1 How is the population in the Southwest Desert states changing?

2 Are the region's natural water supplies changing?

3 What do you already know about using natural resources wisely?

4 What predictions can you make about the water supply in the Southwest Desert states?

➡ APPLY WHAT YOU LEARNED

Write several predictions about the ways deserts affect people in other parts of the world. Look at your predictions as you read the next lesson. Decide which of your predictions are correct and which ones are not. Compare your results with those of your classmates.

The Colorado River runs through three large desert regions. Irrigation projects along the river bring water to millions of acres of farmland there.

Deserts of the World

The deserts of Arizona, Nevada, and New Mexico are part of a much larger desert region called the North American Desert. It is just one of Earth's many large deserts. In fact, deserts cover about one-seventh of all the land on Earth.

When people hear the word *desert*, they usually think of a place that is hot and sandy. However, not all deserts are alike. Some desert areas have mountains, while others are perfectly flat. Some have rocky, stony soil, but others have miles and miles of sand. Although most deserts are hot, several are cold, such as the Gobi in central Asia. All deserts have only one thing in common—they do not have much water.

The Atacama Desert

The Atacama (a•tuh•KAH•muh) Desert is the world's driest desert. It stretches some 600 miles (965 km) along the Pacific Coast of South America from Peru to Chile. To the east of the desert are the Andes Mountains. Even though the Atacama hugs the coast, it averages less than one-half inch (1 cm) of rain each year. In parts of the Atacama, rain has never been recorded!

Unlike most deserts in the United States, the Atacama Desert has a cool climate. Its average temperature is 63°F (17°C).

The Atacama Desert has little vegetation. People often compare its landscape to that of the moon. One part of the desert is even called the Valley of the Moon.

Focus Skill **MAKE INFERENCES**

As you read, make inferences about life in desert regions around the world.

BIG IDEA

The deserts around the world are both alike and different.

VOCABULARY

sand dune

oasis

evaporation

desalinization

 FAST FACT The Atacama Desert closely resembles the landscapes of Mars and the moon. In fact, NASA chose the site to test the exploration vehicles it planned to use on both locations in space.

LOCATE IT

PERU

Atacama Desert

CHILE

Major Deserts of the World

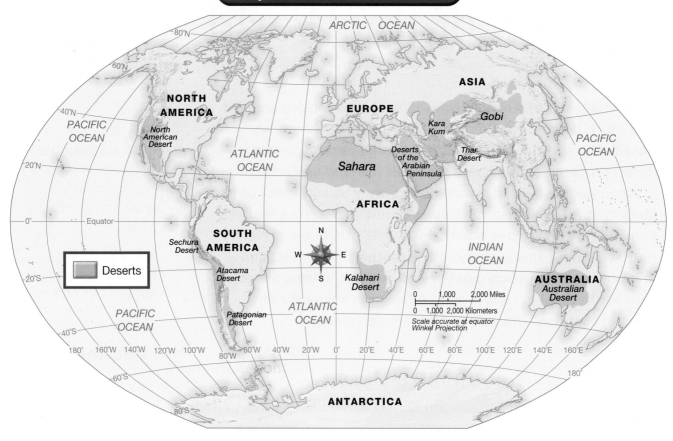

Regions   Large desert regions stretch across all Earth's continents except Antarctica and Europe.

❖ What major deserts are in Africa?

The temperatures stay cool because the air is cooled as it blows across the cold currents of the Pacific Ocean. Most of the air's moisture turns into a thick fog, which prevents much sunlight from reaching the Atacama Desert.

Because so little rain falls in this desert, there is very little plant or animal life. Sand and gravel cover most of its surface. Rugged mountain ranges rise from parts of the Atacama Desert floor.

Tarantulas live in desert areas such as the Atacama Desert.

Mines in the Atacama Desert produce copper, gold, silver, nickel, and lead. Mining companies have built a few towns in the Atacama to give their workers a place to live. Near these towns the companies have built irrigation systems to grow food for the miners. Much of the irrigation water comes from springs in the desert or from the Loa (LOH•uh) River. Dams on this river supply Atacama mining communities with hydroelectric power.

REVIEW What inferences can you make about the plants and animals that live in the Atacama Desert?

MAKE INFERENCES

The Sahara

The Sahara is the largest desert in the world. It covers 3½ million square miles (9 million sq km) of northern Africa. This means that the Sahara is about the same size as the United States.

Within the Sahara are a variety of landforms. There are flat plains covered with gravel, high plateaus scattered with rocks, and snow-capped mountain ranges. Most of the land in the Sahara is covered by great stretches of sand formations. This is because blowing sand often forms hill-like mounds called **sand dunes**. Some dunes can be 600 feet (183 m) high!

Like deserts in the United States, the Sahara lies in a rain shadow. The Atlas Mountains along the Mediterranean and Atlantic Coasts of northern Africa prevent moist winds from reaching the Sahara. As a result, most places in the Sahara get less than 5 inches (13 cm) of rain each year.

Temperatures in the Sahara can soar to 130°F (54°C) during the day. But the sands do not hold the day's heat. When the sun sets, the desert's temperatures can drop by as much as 80°F (27°C).

Although scarce, water can be found in the Sahara. The Nile and Niger Rivers both flow there. Away from these rivers, oases are the main source of water in the Sahara. An **oasis** is an area in a desert where there is water. Most of the water at an oasis comes from underground springs.

FAST FACT

Camels are well-adapted to travel in the Sahara. The hump on a camel's back stores fat. This fat is a source of energy for the camel when food and water are scarce. When camels do get water, they drink a lot—up to 50 gallons (190 L) in one hour!

Dakhla (DAH•kluh) Oasis in western Egypt has several springs. Hundreds of date palms and olive trees grow there.

LOCATE IT

EGYPT

Dakhla Oasis

383

People grow wheat, barley, olives, nuts, dates, figs, and citrus fruits at Saharan oases. Some people move between oases with their herds of goats, sheep, and other animals. They sell the animals' hides, meat, and wool to earn a living.

Camels are especially important for people in the desert. These animals provide wool, milk, hides, and meat. Often called ships of the desert, camels are excellent pack animals adapted to desert travel. For protection from sandy winds, they have two rows of thick eyelashes and nostrils that can clamp shut. They can also live up to two weeks without drinking water.

Like the Atacama Desert and deserts in the United States, the Sahara has important mineral resources. Huge amounts of oil and natural gas lie under the sands there. Valuable deposits of copper, iron ore, phosphate, and uranium also lie in the Sahara.

REVIEW **Where do most people in the Sahara get their water?**

The Negev

Northeast of the Sahara, Africa connects to Asia. Where the two continents meet lies the small country of Israel (IZ•ree•uhl). A little more than half of Israel's land is covered by a desert called the Negev (NEH•gev).

Like all deserts, the Negev is dry. Less than 4 inches (10 cm) of rain falls on the Negev in most years. Yet the Israelis have turned some of this dry land into valuable farmland.

Many of the Israelis' ideas about farming in the desert came from the Nabataeans (na•buh•TEE•uhnz). The Nabataean people lived in the Negev thousands of years ago. To raise crops, they collected in canals and tanks what little rain fell. The Nabataeans also put stones next to their plants. At night, when temperatures dropped, dew formed on the stones and dripped down into the soil around the plants.

These archaeologists are studying the ruins of settlements of people who lived in the Negev about 6,500 years ago.

LOCATE IT

ISRAEL

Negev

The Israelis today have built water storage tanks and irrigation canals, just as the Nabataeans did. They have even used some of the Nabataeans' old canals.

The Israelis also use new methods to farm in the Negev. They use canals, pipes, and tunnels to carry fresh water from the Sea of Galilee (GA•luh•lee) to the Negev. Using this water, Negev farmers grow citrus fruits, wheat, cotton, vegetables, and other crops.

To hold in moisture and prevent evaporation, the Israelis have also built greenhouses over some of their fields. **Evaporation** is the process of the sun's heat turning water into a gas form. Instruments measure moisture in the soil so farmers know when their plants need water. Underground pipes carry water to the plants' roots so that no water is lost by evaporation.

One method that the Israelis are using to increase their water supply actually uses evaporation. Heating seawater causes the water to evaporate, leaving the salt behind. The water vapor can then be

Drip irrigation delivers a precise amount of water to each plant in this greenhouse in the Negev. This system uses about one-fourth less water than sprinkler irrigation uses.

turned back into fresh water. This process of removing salt from water is called **desalinization** (dee•sa•luh•nuh•ZAY•shun). People in Israel are experimenting with the expensive process, but they are more hopeful about recycling wastewater for farming.

REVIEW What ideas about desert farming did the Israelis get from the Nabataeans?

LESSON 3
REVIEW

 MAKE INFERENCES How might life in cold deserts differ from life in hot deserts?

1. **BIG IDEA** How are deserts around the world and the ways people use them alike and different?

2. **VOCABULARY** Use the terms **sand dune** and **oasis** to write two questions about the Sahara.

3. **GEOGRAPHY** What are the largest and driest deserts in the world? Where are they?

4. **ECONOMICS** What are some ways people earn a living in deserts?

5. **CRITICAL THINKING—Evaluate** Why do you think the Israelis spend so much time and money to make the Negev fertile?

 PERFORMANCE—Design an Invention Work with a partner to design an invention that will use water efficiently, conserve water, or bring water to a desert. Draw and label your invention. Then use your drawing to explain your invention to your classmates.

11 Review and Test Preparation

 **Make Inferences**

Copy the following graphic organizer onto a separate sheet of paper. Use the information you have learned to make an inference about the Southwest Desert states.

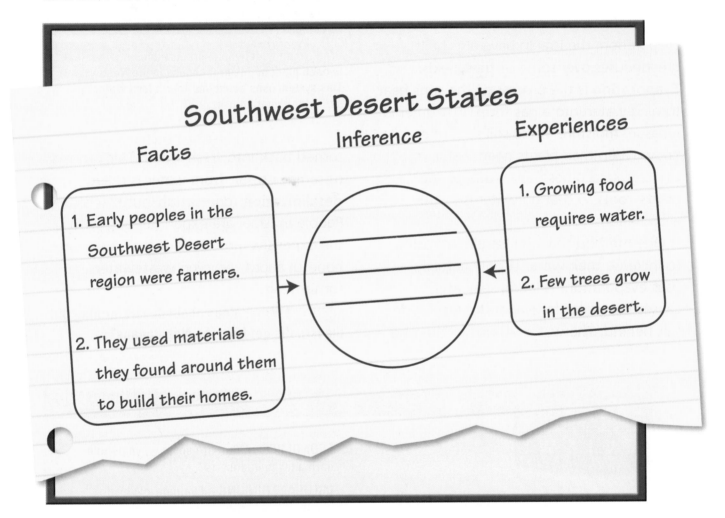

Southwest Desert States

Facts

1. Early peoples in the Southwest Desert region were farmers.

2. They used materials they found around them to build their homes.

Inference

Experiences

1. Growing food requires water.

2. Few trees grow in the desert.

THINK & WRITE

Write a Poem   Write a poem of four to six lines describing deserts. Your poem may be written in rhyme or free verse. Use strong nouns and verbs and a lot of adjectives.

Write an Explanation   Write a short paragraph explaining how much water you think you need every day for different activities, and why you need those amounts.

1540
Coronado begins his
expedition into the
Southwest Desert region

1912
All of the Southwest
Desert states have
joined the Union

1936
Hoover Dam is completed

USE THE TIME LINE

1 When was Hoover Dam completed?

2 Did Coronado explore the Southwest Desert region before or after the Hohokam settled in the Sonoran Desert?

USE VOCABULARY

Complete each sentence with the correct vocabulary term or terms.

adobe (p. 368)

pueblo (p. 369)

reservation (p. 371)

cloudburst (p. 374)

arroyo (p. 374)

oasis (p. 383)

3 Many homes in the Southwest Desert states today are made of sun-dried clay bricks called ____.

4 A person can live in a desert ____ because there is water here.

5 During a ____ in the desert, rainwater runs off the ground's hard surface and sometimes into an ____.

6 Today many Native Americans in the United States live on a ____.

RECALL FACTS

Answer these questions.

7 Who were two Native American groups to settle in the Southwest Desert region long ago?

8 Who claimed much of the Southwest Desert region for Spain?

9 How have people in the desert changed the region to meet their water needs?

Write the letter of the best choice.

10 What features do all deserts share?
A sand dunes
B hot temperatures
C mountains and plateaus
D dry climates

11 Mountains can help deserts form because they—
F are the source of many rivers.
G keep moist air from reaching the land.
H affect the flow of continents' rivers.
J contain many mineral resources.

THINK CRITICALLY

12 Would you want to live in a desert? Explain why or why not.

13 Water conservation is important in every part of the country. What can you do to conserve water?

14 Suppose that people had never worked out ways to get water to the desert. How would life in the Southwest Desert states be different today? How would the United States be different?

15 Why do you think migrant workers move from farm to farm with the seasons?

APPLY SKILLS

Predict a Likely Outcome

16 Make a list of the events that usually take place in your school each day of the week. Predict the events that are likely to take place next week. What steps did you follow to make these predictions?

SEATTLE, WASHINGTON

Located on a neck of land jutting into Puget Sound, Seattle is the largest city in Washington. The city is named after an Indian chief who befriended European explorers in the area. Seattle was once a sawmill center and a supply depot for the Alaskan gold rush. It quickly developed into one of the world's great seaports.

LOCATE IT

WASHINGTON

Seattle

12

Pacific States

❝ Seattle . . . covers the old frontier like frosting on a cake. ❞

—Winthrop Sargent,
The New Yorker, 1978

 Predict an Outcome

When you **predict an outcome,** you look at the way things were or are and decide what you think will happen in the future, or what will happen in another place.

As you read about the Pacific states, be sure to do the following.

- List facts about events, people, or places.
- Use that information to make predictions.
- Check to see if your predictions were correct.

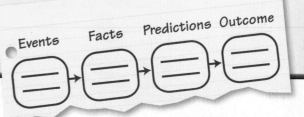

Events Facts Predictions Outcome

Heading to the Pacific

1800		1900		Present

PREDICT AN OUTCOME

As you read, make predictions about how the growth of the Pacific region affected the growth of the United States.

BIG IDEA

Read to discover how and why people crossed the continent to settle in the region along the Pacific Ocean.

VOCABULARY

forty-niner

telegraph

transcontinental railroad

labor

By the mid-1800s many Americans wanted the United States to stretch from sea to sea—from the Atlantic Ocean to the Pacific Ocean. To reach the Pacific, however, people had to cross steep mountains and sun-baked deserts. Still, thousands were willing to face such dangers because they believed life would be better for them in the Pacific region. For many, their dreams came true. They found fertile land and thick forests. Some even found gold. In time, the Pacific region became five states—California, Oregon, Washington, Alaska, and Hawaii.

Newcomers in the Oregon Country

For many pioneers heading west to the Pacific region, the Oregon Country was their destination. That is what people called the area that is now Oregon, Washington, and parts of other nearby states. For centuries beforehand, the Nez Perce (NEZ PERS), Chinook (shuh•NUK), and other Native American groups had been the only people living in the Oregon Country.

These museum buildings in the shape of covered wagons are in Oregon City, Oregon—the official end of the Oregon Trail.

LOCATE IT

Oregon City
OREGON

FAST FACT

The wagon journey to the Oregon Country usually took about six months. So many pioneers traveled the Oregon Trail that the ruts made by their wagon wheels can still be seen today.

END OF
The
OREGON
TRAIL
INTERPRETIVE CENTER
AND HISTORIC SITE

Many early settlers in the Oregon Country stopped at Fort Vancouver along the Columbia River in present-day Washington to rest and gather supplies.

Instead of farming, most of these Native Americans hunted animals, gathered plants in the forests, and caught fish in the rivers and ocean.

The first Europeans to come to the Oregon Country were fur trappers, hunters, and traders. They came from countries such as Russia, England, and France to hunt beavers and other animals in the region.

In the 1840s, Christian missionaries began to build settlements in the Oregon Country. They often sent letters to people back East describing their new homes. To many Americans, the Oregon Country sounded like a paradise. "[They] told us about the great Pacific Ocean, the Columbia River and the beautiful Willamette Valley, the great forests and the snow-capped mountains," remembered 14-year-old pioneer Martha Gay.

In 1843 the first wagon train brought about 1,000 settlers to the Oregon Country. Many more soon followed, including Martha Gay's family. The route they traveled became known as the Oregon Trail. Most pioneers using the trail started from Independence, Missouri, and traveled more than 2,000 miles (3,220 km) to the Oregon Country. Its green grasses, wooded hills, and large rivers were welcome sights to weary travelers.

Many pioneers in the Oregon Country started farms in the Willamette Valley and other fertile valleys between the Cascade Range and the Coast Ranges. The mild and rainy climate in the Oregon Country was good for growing many kinds of vegetables, nuts, and fruits. Families planted orchards of winter pears, apples, and cherries.

By 1859, Oregon had enough people to become a state, and Washington became a separate territory.

REVIEW How did most pioneers reach the Oregon Country?

Oregon winter pears

Miners rushed to California on sailing ships, but few passengers bought tickets to leave. Ships, like the ones shown above in San Francisco Harbor, were often abandoned. Others were made into hotels and stores.

Gold!

Fertile farmland attracted many settlers to the Oregon Country. Farther south, however, another resource soon brought even more people to the Pacific region—gold. Stretching across eastern California, the Sierra Nevada held huge deposits of this valuable mineral.

In 1848 workers in the Sierra Nevada foothills found gold nuggets near Sutter's Mill, a sawmill they were building. The news spread like wildfire. There was gold in California!

Thousands of people suddenly came down with "gold fever"—the dream of finding gold and getting rich. This fever set off a gold rush. Almost 100,000 people rushed to California with the hope of getting a share of the riches. These gold seekers were called **forty-niners** because the first of them arrived in California in 1849.

Some forty-niners traveled on the Oregon Trail. Others boarded ships at ports along the Atlantic Coast and sailed to California. Most miners came from the East. However, many also came from other countries, such as Germany, Australia, China, France, and Britain.

Not everyone who came to California found gold. In fact, most did not. Many unsuccessful miners went back East. Some became farmers or ranchers in the Central Valley, which lies between the

Forty-niners filled pans with earth, and used water to separate any gold from the rock and dirt.

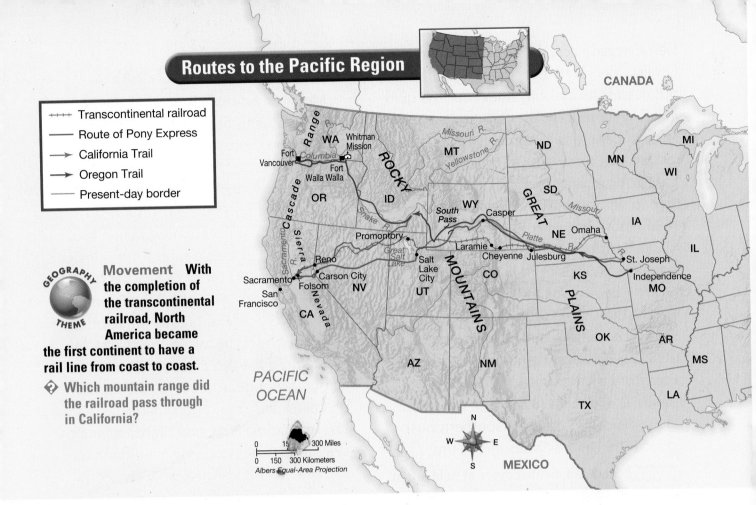

Routes to the Pacific Region

CANADA

Legend:
- ┼┼┼ Transcontinental railroad
- ─── Route of Pony Express
- ──▶ California Trail
- ──▶ Oregon Trail
- ─── Present-day border

Movement With the completion of the transcontinental railroad, North America became the first continent to have a rail line from coast to coast.

❓ Which mountain range did the railroad pass through in California?

Map labels: WA, Whitman Mission, Fort Vancouver, Columbia R., Fort Walla Walla, OR, ID, Snake R., Cascade Range, Sierra Nevada, Sacramento R., ROCKY, South Pass, WY, Casper, MT, Yellowstone R., Missouri R., ND, MN, MI, WI, SD, Promontory, Great Salt Lake, Salt Lake City, Laramie, Cheyenne, Julesburg, Platte R., NE, Omaha, Missouri R., IA, IL, Reno, Carson City, Folsom, NV, UT, MOUNTAINS, CO, KS, St. Joseph, Independence, MO, Sacramento, San Francisco, CA, GREAT PLAINS, OK, AR, MS, AZ, NM, TX, LA, PACIFIC OCEAN, MEXICO

Scale: 0 150 300 Miles / 0 150 300 Kilometers / Albers Equal-Area Projection

Compass: N W E S

An even faster form of communication—the telegraph—soon replaced the Pony Express. A **telegraph** is a machine that uses electricity to send messages over wires. Using a telegraph, people could send news from coast to coast in just minutes!

People now had a quick way to send messages across the country, but they still needed a faster and safer way to travel across the land. In 1862 the United States government agreed to plans to build a **transcontinental railroad**. It would be the first railroad to cross the North American continent, linking the East and West Coasts. Two companies were chosen to build the railroad. The Union Pacific would lay tracks west from

The Central Pacific Railroad met the Union Pacific Railroad on May 10, 1869.

Sierra Nevada and the Coast Ranges. Others opened hotels, stores, and other businesses. As a result, cities near the gold mines grew quickly. By 1850 California had enough people to become a state.

Gold was discovered in other parts of the Pacific region. In 1860 miners found gold in what is now Washington. In 1896, another gold rush occurred in the Alaska Territory. The United States had purchased Alaska from Russia in 1867.

Partly because of the gold strike in Alaska, the United States decided to acquire more new lands in the West. In 1898 the Hawaiian Islands also became a territory of the United States. These islands, 2,400 miles (3,862 km) off the California coast, were the southernmost part of the United States at the time.

REVIEW How did the discovery of gold affect the Pacific states?

PREDICT AN OUTCOME

Linking the Coasts

Many Americans lived along the Pacific Coast by 1860, but travel to and from the rest of the country remained difficult. Railroads reached only as far west as St. Joseph, Missouri, so horses and stage-coaches had to be used for the rest of the journey. Communication was slow, too. It would often take a month for a letter from the East to reach the Pacific region.

Beginning in 1860, the Pony Express mail delivery service greatly improved communication between the coasts. It operated like a relay race between St. Joseph and Sacramento, the capital of California. Young horseback riders carried the mail day and night, stopping only to change horses or hand the mail to the next rider. As a result, the Pony Express riders could deliver a mailbag from Missouri to California in 10 days.

The Pony Express

Analyze Primary Sources

The Pony Express had about 80 riders, 400 horses, and a station every 10 to 15 miles (16 to 24 km) from Missouri to California. There were 190 stations in all.

❶ This letter was sent from San Francisco to New York City by Pony Express.

❷ The services of the Pony Express were advertised on posters.

❸ Pony Express riders placed waterproof leather coverings over their saddles. Each covering had four locked pockets that held the mail.

◆ Why do you think the Pony Express mailbags had locks?

PONY EXPRESS !
CHANGE OF TIME! REDUCED RATES!
10 Days to San Francisco!
LETTERS
WILL BE RECEIVED AT THE
OFFICE, 84 BROADWAY,
NEW YORK,
Up to 4 P. M. every TUESDAY,
Up to 2½ P. M. every SATURDAY,
will be forwarded to connect with the PONY EXPRESS leaving ST. JOSEPH, Missouri,
every WEDNESDAY and SATURDAY at 11 P. M.
TELEGRAMS
For Express on the mornings of MONDAY and FRIDAY, to leave with PONY leaving St. Joseph, WEDNESDAYS and SATURDAYS.
EXPRESS CHARGES.
LETTERS weighing half ounce or under $1 00
every additional half ounce or fraction of an ounce 1 00
Letters to be enclosed in 10 cent Government Stamped Envelopes,
And all Express CHARGES Pre-paid.
PONY EXPRESS ENVELOPES For Sale at our Office.
WELLS, FARGO & CO., Ag'ts.

Omaha, Nebraska, through the Rockies. The Central Pacific would lay tracks east from Sacramento, California, through the Sierra Nevada.

Building the railroads was hard work. Tracks sometimes had to be laid on narrow ledges around steep mountainsides. Bridges had to be built across deep canyons, and tunnels often had to be dug or blasted through the mountains.

Both companies hired thousands of workers to do this **labor**, or work. Most of the Union Pacific's workers were immigrants from Ireland or other European countries. Most of the Central Pacific's workers were immigrants from China. The immigrants worked long hours at low pay.

On May 10, 1869, the two railroads met at Promontory, Utah. The whole country celebrated as the last spike, a solid gold

This engraved golden spike completed the first transcontinental railroad.

one, was driven in to complete the railroad. People and goods could now cross the country more easily and less expensively. A trip between New York City and San Francisco that once took months now took just 10 or 12 days.

People kept heading to the Pacific region, but now they came by train. Within 20 years after the transcontinental railroad started running, Washington Territory had enough people to become a state. It joined the Union in 1889. Seventy years later, in 1959, Alaska and Hawaii became the last two states of the United States.

REVIEW How did the transcontinental railroad affect travel to the Pacific region?

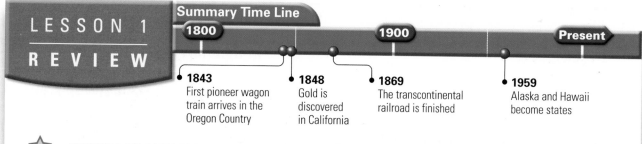

LESSON 1
REVIEW

Summary Time Line

1800 — 1900 — Present

1843
First pioneer wagon train arrives in the Oregon Country

1848
Gold is discovered in California

1869
The transcontinental railroad is finished

1959
Alaska and Hawaii become states

PREDICT AN OUTCOME Make a prediction about the ways the United States changed after gaining the Pacific states.

① **BIG IDEA** Why did many people settle in the Pacific region during the 1800s?

② **VOCABULARY** Describe the kind of **labor** that **forty-niners** did.

③ **TIME LINE** How many years after the first pioneer wagon train arrived in the Oregon Country was the transcontinental railroad finished?

④ **HISTORY** In what valley in Oregon did many early pioneers in the Pacific region settle?

⑤ **CRITICAL THINKING—Analyze** Why was it important for mail to travel quickly between the East and West Coasts?

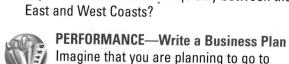

PERFORMANCE—Write a Business Plan
Imagine that you are planning to go to California during the gold rush to open a business. Work with a partner to write a business plan. Describe the business you will open and what good or service you will sell. Then share your plan with classmates, and explain why you think your business will be successful.

The Telegraph

During the 1830s an American inventor, Samuel F. B. Morse, experimented with sending messages by electricity along iron wires. To send messages along the wires, Morse invented a code system in which groups of dots and dashes stand for letters of the alphabet. On May 24, 1844, the first official telegraph message was transmitted: "What hath God wrought!" That first message indicated a fear of the new technology. That fear, however, would be replaced by hope as the telegraph linked the country, coast to coast, and opened up the world to communication by electricity.

FROM THE SMITHSONIAN INSTITUTION NATIONAL MUSEUM OF AMERICAN HISTORY

❶ To send a message by telegraph, this knob was pressed down for a short time to send a dot and for a longer time to send a dash.

❷ When the knob was pressed down, the message was sent through the electrical circuit.

❸ This metal strip acted as a spring to reopen the circuit.

Reaction to the telegraph:

"'We are one!' said the nations, and hand met hand, in a thrill electric from land to land."
—from "The Victory," a poem written in tribute to Samuel Morse, 1872

"At its very birth, the telegraph system became the handmaiden of commerce."
—*National Telegraph Review and Operator's Companion,* 1853

"The telegraph has become one of the essential means of commercial transactions."
—*St. Louis Republican,* 1847

"An entirely new and much-improved method of conducting diplomatic relations between one country and another has come into use with the telegraph wire and cable."
—Charles Bright in his book *Submarine Telegraphs,* 1898

"The demands for the telegraph have been constantly increasing; they have been spread over every civilized country in the world, and have become, by usage, absolutely necessary for the well-being of society."
—*The New York Times,* April 3, 1872

"How important an agent the telegraph has become in the transmission of business communications. It is every day coming more into use, and every day adding to its power to be useful."
—Laurence Turnbull in his book *The Electro-Magnetic Telegraph,* 1852

Analyze the Primary Source

1. How were messages sent through the telegraph?

2. What general opinion of the telegraph do most of the quotes express?

3. How do you think the telegraph was like the Internet today?

ACTIVITY

Write a Message   Look in reference books or use the Internet to learn about Morse code. Then write a short message in Morse code. Swap messages with a partner and translate each other's message.

RESEARCH

GO ONLINE Visit The Learning Site at **www.harcourtschool.com** to research other primary sources.

·SKILLS·

Use a Time Zone Map

VOCABULARY

time zone

▶ WHY IT MATTERS

The transcontinental railroad made it necessary to create a single way of keeping time. Before then, each town across the United States set its own time, using the sun as a guide. Clocks were set at noon when the sun was the highest in the sky. As Earth turns, however, it is noon in different places at different times.

Telling time by the sun was not a problem until people started using railroads to travel across the continent. Because the towns along the train routes all had their own times, it was impossible to make and keep schedules.

A group of people were asked to study the problem. They decided to divide Earth into 24 time zones—one for each hour of the day. A **time zone** is a region in which people use the same clock time. To figure out the time anywhere in the United States, you can use a time zone map like the one on page 399.

All the people in a time zone use the same time.

▶ WHAT YOU NEED TO KNOW

The United States has six time zones. From east to west, they are the eastern time zone, the central time zone, the mountain time zone, the Pacific time zone, the Alaska time zone, and the Hawaii-Aleutian time zone.

Earth rotates, or turns, from west to east, so time zones east of you always have a later time than your time zone has. Time zones west of you always have an earlier time than your time zone has.

Suppose you live in Atlanta, Georgia, and you want to call a friend in Butte, Montana, to wish her a happy birthday. It is 7:00 A.M. where you live. Would this be a good time to call your friend? To answer this question, find Atlanta and Butte on the time zone map. Atlanta is in the eastern time zone, while Butte is in the mountain time zone. Now look at the clock faces above those time zones on the map. You can see that it is two hours earlier in the mountain time zone than it is in the eastern time zone. Your friend probably would not want you to wake her up at 5:00 A.M. even to wish her a happy birthday!

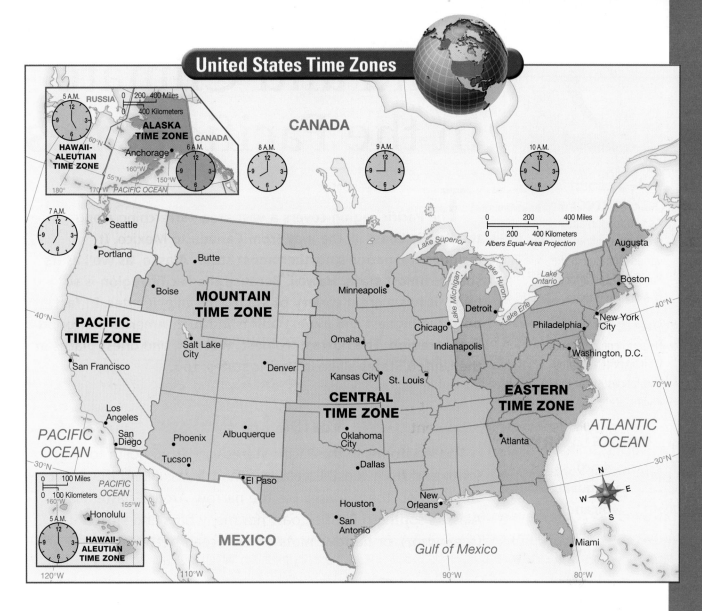

United States Time Zones

PRACTICE THE SKILL

Use the time zone map to answer these questions.

1. Imagine that you are in San Diego, California. Is it earlier, later, or the same time as in Chicago, Illinois?

2. If it is 4:00 P.M. in Dallas, Texas, what time is it in Boise, Idaho? in San Francisco, California?

3. In what time zone does our nation's capital lie?

4. In what time zone does each of the Pacific states lie?

APPLY WHAT YOU LEARNED

On the map, locate the area where you live. Look at a watch or a classroom clock. What time is it in your time zone? Now figure out the time for each of these cities.

Seattle, Washington
Honolulu, Hawaii
Anchorage, Alaska
Minneapolis, Minnesota
Washington, D.C.

Practice your map and globe skills with the **GeoSkills CD-ROM**.

Land and Climate in the Pacific States

The Pacific region covers a vast area—stretching along the Pacific Coast all the way from Canada to Mexico. It includes the nation's northernmost state, Alaska, as well as its southernmost state, Hawaii. Because the Pacific region is so huge, it has a great variety of landforms and climates. In fact, both the highest and lowest points in North America are found in this region. The hottest, coldest, wettest, and driest places in the United States all lie in Pacific states, too.

Varied Landforms

The landforms in the Pacific states vary from north to south and from coastal areas to inland areas. Along the Arctic Ocean in northern Alaska lies the narrow Arctic Coastal Plain. Alaska's southern Pacific Coast has many bays and **fjords** (fee•AWRDZ), or narrow inlets of the ocean between cliffs.

Sled dogs race across the snowy land below Mount McKinley, in Alaska.

FAST FACT

Though Alaska is the largest state, it has one of the smallest populations—only about 600,000 people live there. In fact, only Wyoming and Vermont have fewer people than Alaska does.

LOCATE IT

ALASKA
Mt. McKinley

Here the steep mountains of the Alaska Range go right down to the shore. Mount McKinley, North America's highest peak, is part of this range.

Farther south, the Coast Ranges shape nearly the entire coastline of Washington and Oregon. Together, these two states are sometimes called the Pacific Northwest. Inlets among the Coast Ranges create natural harbors there, including Puget (PYOO•juht) Sound in Washington.

The Coast Ranges also extend south along the California coast. California has several natural harbors, too. The largest are San Francisco Bay and San Diego Bay. Although northern California's coast is rugged and tree-covered, most of southern California has a sandy coastline with few trees.

Between the Coast Ranges to the west and the Sierra Nevada and the Cascade Range to the east lie several broad valleys, including the Willamette and Central Valleys. These valleys are the major agricultural centers for the Pacific states.

On the eastern sides of the Sierra Nevada and the Cascade Range are other landforms. The high Columbia Plateau lies in eastern Washington and Oregon. To its south, the Great Basin spreads along eastern California. Death Valley, part of the Great Basin, is the lowest place in the Western Hemisphere.

Like other Pacific states, much of Hawaii is mountainous. In fact, all of the Hawaiian Islands are actually the tops of mountains that rise from the ocean floor. Below the peaks, lush tropical forests cover much of the land.

REVIEW What landform shapes most of the Pacific Coast?

Elevations in the Pacific States

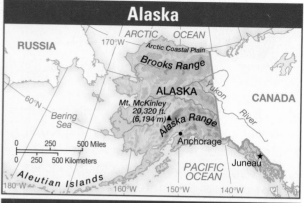

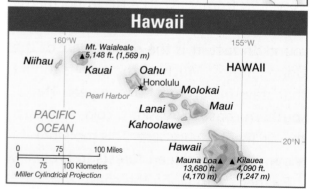

Regions Alaska is the nation's largest state.

❖ What three bodies of water surround Alaska?

Olympic National Park

Understanding Places and Regions

Olympic National Park in northwestern Washington is one of the few rain forest areas in the United States. As a result of average precipitation of up to 167 inches (424 cm) per year, forests of spruce, hemlock, fir, and maple trees thrive in the park. Ferns, thick mosses, and other plants cover the ground and climb up the sides of the trees.

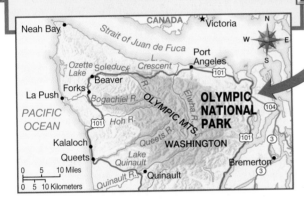

Varied Climates

Just as landforms vary in the Pacific states, so do climates. As with the land, the climate changes from north to south, as well as from west to east. In northern Alaska, the climate is bitterly cold year-round. In fact, it is the coldest part of the United States. Much of this area is tundra that stays frozen most of the year. The southern coast of Alaska is cold, too, but the air there is very wet. This moisture allows huge evergreen forests to grow.

Farther south along the coast, the climate gets milder, and coastal winds bring even heavier rains. Because of this moisture, some of the oldest, largest, and tallest trees in the world grow in the

mountains of the Pacific Northwest and in the Sierra Nevada of northern California. These are the coast redwoods and the giant sequoias (sih•KWOY•uhz). Some of these trees are 2,000 years old.

Fewer trees are found in the drier parts of the Pacific states. Eastern Washington and Oregon lie in the rain shadow of the western mountains, so they receive much less precipitation. Most of southeastern California has a desert climate. This area includes Death Valley, which is the hottest and driest place in the United States. It holds the national record for the longest time without rain—760 days.

In coastal southern California and in Hawaii, the temperatures are also warm, but not hot. Even though Hawaii lies in the tropics, the surrounding Pacific winds help cool the islands. Those same winds also bring heavy rains to parts of Hawaii. Its Mount Waialeale (wy•ah•lay•AH•lay) is the wettest place on Earth. It rains 335 days a year on this mountain!

REVIEW How do coastal climates differ from inland climates in the Pacific states?

PREDICT AN OUTCOME

A Shaky Land

Although the climate and landforms of the Pacific region are very different, all of the Pacific states share a common danger—earthquakes. An **earthquake** is a sudden shaking of the ground. It is caused by the movement and cracking of layers of rock deep inside Earth.

Each year many small earthquakes shake the Pacific states. Often people do not even feel them. Large earthquakes, however, can cause major damage. The shaking of the ground can cause buildings, bridges, and homes to fall down.

In recent years major earthquakes have hit several California cities, including San Francisco and Los Angeles. Buildings there are constructed to survive earthquakes, but damage still occurs. In 1964, the most powerful earthquake recorded in North America shook central Alaska.

It was so strong that parts of downtown Anchorage sank 30 feet (9 m).

The Pacific states share another common feature—mountains that were formed by volcanoes. A **volcano** is an opening in Earth's surface out of which hot gases, ash, and lava may pour. **Lava** is hot, melted rock. In fact, volcanoes formed the Hawaiian Islands. Today, two volcanoes in Hawaii, Mauna Loa (MOW•nuh LOH•uh) and Kilauea (kee•low•AY•uh), are active. An active volcano is one that is either erupting or likely to erupt.

How do volcanoes form mountains? When a volcano erupts, or begins to throw out lava, it blasts an opening in Earth called a **crater**. As more and more lava pours out of the crater, it cools and becomes hard. Over time, enough lava may pour out and cool to form a tall, cone-shaped mountain.

The earthquake that hit San Francisco (right) in 1906 nearly destroyed the city. In 1994 the earthquake that shook southern California (below) caused more than $20 billion in damage.

A Cross-Section Diagram of a Volcano

Steam, gas, and ash

Crater

Side eruption

Lava flow

Magma

Layers of rock

When a volcano erupts, the blast can sometimes tear down the mountain. Mount St. Helens, a volcano in Washington, erupted in 1980. A blast of steam, ash, and rock shot out thousands of feet into the air and spread for miles. About 230 square miles (596 sq km) of the mountain were destroyed. Its peak was lowered about 1,200 feet (366 m).

REVIEW **What are two dangers that the Pacific states share?**

Analyze Diagrams The energy released by the eruption of Mount St. Helens was equal to that of 10 million tons of dynamite.

From what parts of a volcano does lava spill out?

LESSON 2
REVIEW

 PREDICT AN OUTCOME What is a possible outcome of another eruption of Mount St. Helens?

1 BIG IDEA How are landforms and climates in the Pacific states alike and different?

2 VOCABULARY Use the terms **lava** and **crater** to describe a **volcano**.

3 GEOGRAPHY What are the highest, lowest, coldest, hottest, driest, and wettest places in the United States?

4 CRITICAL THINKING—Evaluate In which Pacific state would you most like to live? Why?

 PERFORMANCE—Play a Guessing Game Choose one place you have read about in this lesson. Find more information about it in books or on the Internet. List words that describe your place. Read your words to a classmate, and have him or her guess your chosen place. Then do the same for your classmate's list.

Living in the Pacific States

Millions of people now live in the Pacific states. Many of them are attracted to the region because of its different landscapes and climates. But just as those physical features are different, the ways people in the region use the land and water to earn a living can be different, too. As people use the natural resources of the Pacific states, they change the environment. Sometimes they can damage it. However, people can also work together to protect their environment.

PREDICT AN OUTCOME

As you read, make predictions about ways that people can affect the environment in the Pacific states.

BIG IDEA
Read to learn how people in the Pacific states use the region's natural resources.

VOCABULARY
ecosystem
oil slick
wetlands

Forests and Fish

The forests of the Pacific states have allowed the region to support a large lumber industry, particularly in the Pacific Northwest. Oregon has led the nation in lumber production every year since 1938. Oregon mills also turn out millions of tons of paper and paper products each year. Most of Alaska's lumber mills are in the southeastern corner of the state.

Some of Earth's largest and oldest trees grow in the Sequoia National Forest, in California. Once, after a giant sequoia was cut down, its leveled-off stump became a dance floor for 24 couples! Today, laws protect the giant sequoias from being cut down.

LOCATE IT

CALIFORNIA

Sequoia National Forest

Wood products are Oregon's leading manufactured goods.

In California, forests of Douglas fir and many other kinds of pine grow on the slopes of both the Coast Ranges and the Sierra Nevada.

At one time, the Pacific region and the rest of the country had so many forests that people often cut down trees faster than new ones could grow back. To help protect these resources, the United States set up national forests, such as California's Sequoia National Forest and Oregon's Willamette National Forest.

Lumber companies are allowed to cut a limited number of trees each year in some national forests. The companies also own forests where they raise trees to be cut. That way lumber industries will have raw materials for the future. In fact, more trees are now planted each year than are cut down.

Many people who live in the Pacific states also use rivers and the ocean to earn their living. Fishing is an important industry up and down the Pacific Coast. Alaska leads all other states in the amount of fish caught, especially salmon. Off the Washington coast, fishers harvest clams, oysters, and crabs. Along with a huge yearly salmon haul, Oregon fishers catch flounder and white sturgeon and bring up plenty of oysters, too. The ocean waters off of Oregon, California, and Hawaii also provide hundreds of thousands of tuna each year.

REVIEW **What products come from the ocean, rivers, and forests of the Pacific states?**

Alaskan king crabs

406

Dams and Irrigation

The waters of the Pacific states are important for reasons other than fishing. The large rivers there help produce huge amounts of electricity. Dams on the Columbia River and its tributaries produce most of the electricity in the Pacific Northwest. The Grand Coulee (KOO•lee) Dam in Washington makes more electricity than any other dam in the country.

Other dams in drier parts of the Pacific region provide water for irrigation. Dams and canals on the Sacramento and San Joaquin Rivers make up a huge irrigation system called the Central Valley Project. Such projects have helped California become the leading farming state. It ranks first in growing grapes, strawberries, tomatoes, and lettuce.

Dams have helped the region's economy. Yet every dam that is built affects a river's ecosystem. An **ecosystem** is all the living things in an area and their relationships with each other and the nonliving environment. When dams are built, they change the amount of water flowing through a river's channel. This change can affect the ecosystems both upstream and downstream.

The change to the ecosystems of many rivers in the Pacific Northwest caused by dams has affected Pacific salmon. Millions of salmon once followed the Columbia River upstream each year to lay their eggs in the place where they were born. But dams blocked the salmon's route upstream, and the number of salmon in the river fell sharply. To help solve the problem, people built fish ladders. A fish ladder is a group of pools of water set up like stair steps. Using the ladders, the salmon could "climb" up the dams. Some dams, like the Grand Coulee, are much too tall for fish ladders. In those areas salmon are raised in tanks and then are released into the river.

REVIEW **What needs do the dams in the Pacific states fill?**
PREDICT AN OUTCOME

Salmon in the Columbia River use this fish ladder to swim past the Rocky Reach Dam. They can jump over the walls that separate the pools.

The state of Washington is the country's leading manufacturer of jet airplanes.

Economic Leaders

Dams provide the power that factories need to run their machines. As a result, many cities in the Pacific states have become important manufacturing centers. Factories in Portland, Oregon, for example, turn out textiles, chemicals, and high-tech equipment. Wood products, computer software, ships, and airplanes are all produced in Seattle, Washington. In fact, many people around the world fly in airplanes made in and near Seattle. Much of the aluminum in these planes is manufactured near Seattle, too.

The country's leading manufacturing state, however, is California. Factories in the state manufacture many kinds of products. They make everything from computers, automobiles, and airplanes to CDs and movies. Hollywood, a part of Los Angeles, is the movie capital of the world. Silicon Valley, south of San Francisco, is one of the leading high-tech centers in the world.

Many of the goods produced in the Pacific states use the region's natural resources. Borax, a mineral found in the Mojave (muh•HAH•vee) Desert of California, is used to make such products as laundry soap and glass. Both petroleum and natural gas are found along the coasts of California and Alaska.

Service industries are the fastest-growing part of the economy of the Pacific states. Data processing, real estate, insurance, education, governments, and health care employ millions of people there. Many others work in shipping and trading industries in some of the large ports along the coast.

Tourism plays an important role in the Pacific region's economy, too. California's beaches, movie studios, and amusement parks have long been destinations for visitors to the region. Tourists also head for the mountains and rivers of the Pacific

Northwest and Alaska. In fact, Alaska now gets more visitors each year than it has residents! Tourism is also the largest industry in Hawaii.

It is also the region's wide variety of climates and landforms that attracts people. As Jeff Margulies, a teenager from New York, said during a trip to Oregon:

> 66 This place has everything! You can go snowboarding on Mount Hood in the middle of summer, and the same day you can go whitewater rafting. 99

REVIEW What are some of the products manufactured in and near Seattle?

DEMOCRATIC VALUES
The Common Good

CITIZENSHIP

Like people all over the United States, people in the Pacific states often volunteer their time, skills, and money for the common good of their communities. Many people in the Pacific states volunteer in stream teams to help clean up waterways. Some stream teams have adopted wetland areas. These volunteers pick up trash and plant grasses that are an important part of wetland ecosystems. They raise money to protect more wetlands and work with government leaders to help control pollution. In addition, stream teams share information on how all citizens can help protect water and wetland environments.

Analyze the Value

1 How do stream team volunteers work for the common good of their communities?

2 **Make It Relevant** Work in a group to think of a volunteer program you could start to help your community or environment. Share your ideas with the class.

Protecting the Environment

People who live in the Pacific states depend on the resources around them in many ways. At the same time, they have changed parts of the region, and sometimes accidents have happened that damaged the land and water. By working together, however, people in the Pacific states and across the United States have done much to protect the environment.

Prudhoe (PROO•doh) Bay, which lies on the Arctic Sea in northern Alaska, is at the center of one of the world's major oil-producing areas. The huge Trans-Alaska Pipeline carries oil from Prudhoe Bay south to Valdez (val•DEEZ). There it is loaded into oil tankers for shipment around the world. In 1989 one of those oil tankers crashed into a sharp, rocky reef, which tore holes in the ship. At that moment the most damaging oil spill in United States history began.

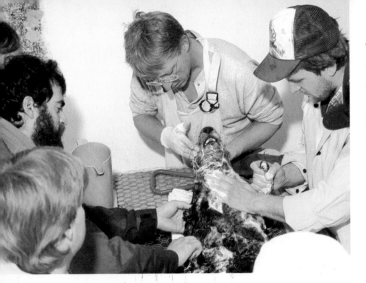

Over the next few hours, almost 11 million gallons (42 million L) of oil poured into Alaska's waters. Much of that oil floated to the top of the water and formed an oil slick. An **oil slick** is the film of oil that coats the water after an oil spill. Strong winds and high waves swept the oil onto land, covering the beaches.

The ship's owners hired workers to clean up the oil. But many volunteers also pitched in to help, including Billy Day. He saw that oil was polluting the beach where he lived, killing wildlife. So Day spent his own money to design a machine to wash the oil off the beach rocks.

Polluted water is a great danger to coastal environments. It can harm the animals that live along beaches and in coastal wetlands. **Wetlands** are low-lying lands where the water level is always near the surface of the land. In some places, people have dredged bays and filled in wetlands to get more land for building. This has damaged many coastal environments.

At the same time, people in the region have worked to pass laws that help protect the coasts. The United States has made some of its coastal areas into wildlife refuges. Other laws help protect wetlands from development, stop the dumping of wastes into oceans, control water pollution, and help prevent oil spills.

REVIEW **What actions have people taken to help protect the coastal environment?**

LESSON 3
REVIEW

 PREDICT AN OUTCOME What do you think experts predicted would happen to salmon after dams were built in the Pacific region?

1 **BIG IDEA** How do people in the Pacific states use natural resources to earn a living?

2 **VOCABULARY** How are **wetlands** an example of an **ecosystem**?

3 **CIVICS AND GOVERNMENT** What kinds of areas has the national government created to protect the natural resources of the Pacific region and the rest of the country?

4 **CRITICAL THINKING—Synthesize** Do you think a citizen has a duty to clean up someone else's mess? Why or why not?

 PERFORMANCE—Make a Mural Work with a group of classmates to make a mural that tells about living and working in the Pacific states. Include images of the region's natural resources and leading industries. Then explain your mural to the class. Tell what each part illustrates.

·SKILLS·

CITIZENSHIP

Act as a Responsible Citizen

VOCABULARY
responsibility

▶ WHY IT MATTERS

Citizens have many responsibilities to their country, state, and community. A **responsibility** is something that a person should do, like take part in the government and obey laws. When a responsible citizen sees a problem, he or she takes action to help solve it. Acting responsibly is an important part of being an active citizen.

▶ WHAT YOU NEED TO KNOW

Acting as a responsible citizen often requires some special thought. Here are some steps that you can follow to help you act responsibly.

Step 1 Identify a problem around you.

Step 2 Learn about the problem, and think of ways to solve it.

Step 3 Decide what you can do to help, either on your own or with other people. Then work to bring about change.

Step 4 Always look for safe solutions. If you cannot solve the problem yourself, get help from others, such as your family, a police officer, or a community official.

▶ PRACTICE THE SKILL

You just read about people who acted as responsible citizens by volunteering to help clean up an oil spill. One of those responsible citizens was Billy Day. Think about what he did to help.

1 What problem did Billy Day notice on the beach after the oil spill?

2 What actions did he take to solve the problem?

▶ APPLY WHAT YOU LEARNED

Read your local newspaper to find out about a problem facing your community, or identify a problem in your school or classroom. Use the steps to decide how you and your classmates can act as responsible citizens.

Billy Day used his rock-washing machine to wash oil off the beach rocks.

PREDICT AN OUTCOME

As you read, make predictions about the challenges faced by people living in the Pacific islands.

BIG IDEA

Location affects life in Hawaii and in other Pacific islands of the United States.

VOCABULARY

crossroads
monarch
produce

Diamond Head, an extinct volcano, towers over Honolulu's Waikiki Beach.

FAST FACT

The traditional Hawaiian greeting *aloha* means "hello," "good-bye," "love," and "friendship." It is a combination of *alo*, "to face," and *ha*, "the breath of life."

Americans in the Pacific

Millions of people live along the Pacific Coast. But many Americans also live on small islands in the middle of the Pacific Ocean. Because these islands lie thousands of miles from the United States mainland, the people who live there face special challenges. At the same time, the locations give the islands a mix of people from many backgrounds.

An Island State

Hawaii is the only state completely made up of islands. The word *Hawaii* means "big island." It refers to the state's largest island, Hawaii, as well as to the 131 other islands in the chain. People live on only 7 of Hawaii's islands. All the others are too small or windy or do not have fresh water.

The Hawaiian Islands are the tops of mountains, which were formed by volcanoes millions of years ago. Most of Hawaii's volcanoes are extinct, or do not erupt anymore. Diamond Head is one of these extinct volcanoes. It lies just outside Honolulu (hah•nuh•LOO•loo), Hawaii's capital and largest city. This city lies on Oahu (oh•AH•hoo), Hawaii's most crowded island. Honolulu's island location makes life there very different from life on the mainland. People in

Honolulu and the rest of Hawaii often pay more for most things. That is because most goods have to be imported from other places, adding to their costs.

Yet Hawaii's location near the middle of the Pacific Ocean has made it an important **crossroads**, a place that connects people, goods, and ideas. As such, Hawaii has attracted a mix of cultures. In fact, Hawaii is the only state that has two official languages—English and Hawaiian.

The Polynesians (pah•luh•NEE•zhunz) were the first people to come to Hawaii. They canoed to Hawaii from other Pacific islands more than 1,500 years ago.

In 1778 Captain James Cook became the first European to see Hawaii. After this British explorer returned to Europe with reports of Hawaii, trading ships soon began to visit the islands.

People from the United States started going to Hawaii during the 1800s. Some were missionaries who built schools and churches. Others came to set up sugarcane and pineapple plantations. Many Hawaiians and immigrants worked on the plantations. Most of the immigrants came from Asian countries bordering the Pacific Ocean, such as Japan, South Korea, and the Philippines.

By 1890 only about half of the people living in Hawaii had Polynesian ancestors. Soon, the Hawaiian **monarchs**, or kings and queens, began to lose power. Many plantation owners and business leaders wanted Hawaii to become a part of the United States. In 1898 Hawaii became a territory of the United States. Then in 1959 Hawaii became our fiftieth state.

REVIEW Why is Hawaii an important crossroads?

United States Pacific Islands

Guam

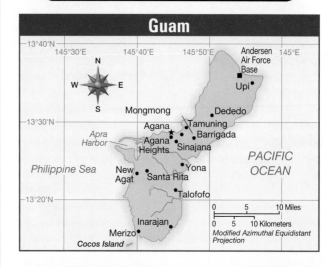

American Samoa

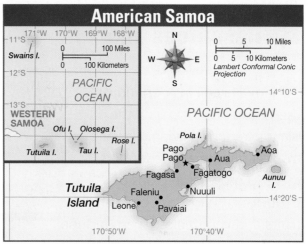

Hawaii

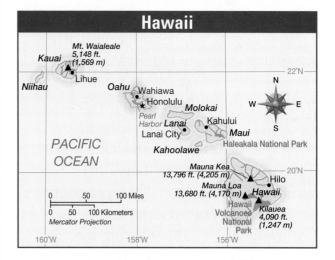

Regions Guam, American Samoa, and the islands that make up the state of Hawaii sit in the middle of the Pacific Ocean.

◆ On which island is Hawaii Volcanoes National Park?

Resources and Income

Many Hawaiians depend on the natural resources of the islands to earn a living. Hawaii's tropical climate allows farmers there to grow large crops of **produce** (PROH•doos), or fresh fruits and vegetables. These include such tropical fruits as pineapples, avocados, and bananas. Other important Hawaiian crops include sugarcane, coffee, macadamia nuts, and tropical flowers.

Hawaii has few minerals. It also has few factories, since transporting raw materials and finished products to and from the islands is so costly. One major industry on the islands, however, is food processing. Hawaii supplies most of the world's canned pineapple.

Because of Hawaii's location, the United States government has built many military bases there, especially for the navy. Nearly one-fifth of the people in the state work on those bases. On December 7, 1941, Japan attacked United States military bases at Pearl Harbor on the island of Oahu. This attack caused the United States to fight in World War II.

As a crossroads of the Pacific, Hawaii is also an important center for trade and banking. In Hawaii, most of those industries are based in Honolulu. Its many banks do business in cities all over the Pacific region. Tourism, however, is Hawaii's biggest source of income. Many tourists explore the tropical landscapes and beaches of the islands or visit Hawaii Volcanoes National Park.

REVIEW Why are there few factories in Hawaii? PREDICT AN OUTCOME

• HERITAGE •

The Hawaiian Luau and Hula

Many Hawaiians celebrate their Polynesian heritage with traditional feasts called luaus (LOO•owz). Usually luaus are held for special events such as the birth of a baby, a wedding, or a birthday.

Dancers wearing grass skirts and necklaces made of flowers, called leis (LAYZ), often perform the hula at luaus and other cultural celebrations. The hula is a Polynesian folk dance. The dancers' hand movements illustrate the words of a song.

Guam and American Samoa

Hawaii is not the only place in the Pacific where Americans live. Some live on the islands of Guam and American Samoa. Both are United States territories. Like Hawaii, Guam and American Samoa have warm weather all year. These islands, too, are the tops of underwater mountains formed by volcanoes.

Tourism and military bases are two of the largest sources of income for Guam and American Samoa. Many people on these islands work in hotels, restaurants, and other service industries. The few factories in both places mostly process coconuts, bananas, and other fruits and vegetables grown on the islands. Some islanders also earn a living fishing.

Guam and American Samoa have a mix of cultures, too. Like Hawaiians, natives of these other Pacific islands have Polynesian ancestors. However, many immigrants from Korea, China, Mexico, the United States, Australia, and Europe also make their homes there.

REVIEW **What are two Pacific island territories of the United States?**

Traditional huts in Guam and American Samoa have roofs made of woven palm leaves.

LESSON 4 REVIEW

 PREDICT AN OUTCOME What might happen to Hawaii's economy during a year of bad tropical storms?

1 BIG IDEA How has Hawaii's location affected its history and culture?

2 VOCABULARY Use the term **monarch** in a paragraph to describe Hawaii before it became a state.

3 CULTURE Why do all of the islands discussed in this lesson have a mix of people and cultures?

4 CRITICAL THINKING—Synthesize What role did agriculture play in the history of Hawaii?

PERFORMANCE—Prepare a Documentary Film Work with a group to write a script for a documentary film about Guam or American Samoa. Use the library or the Internet to find out more about these islands. Present your script to the class, and include maps and photographs to explain what your film would show.

PREDICT AN OUTCOME

As you read, make predictions about ways in which oceans connect people and places.

BIG IDEA
Read to learn about the world's oceans.

VOCABULARY

Pacific Rim
Ring of Fire

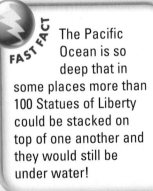

FAST FACT

The Pacific Ocean is so deep that in some places more than 100 Statues of Liberty could be stacked on top of one another and they would still be under water!

Oceans Around the World

The world's oceans—the Pacific Ocean, the Atlantic Ocean, the Indian Ocean, and the Arctic Ocean—cover nearly three-fourths of Earth's surface. For thousands of years, these oceans acted as barriers to trade and communication, very much as deserts and mountains did. People did not know that all of the oceans were connected. Today, however, people use oceans for travel and trade all over the world.

Pacific Ocean

The Pacific is Earth's largest ocean. All seven continents could fit over the Pacific Ocean, and there would still be room for another Asia! The Pacific extends from the Arctic Ocean in the north to the continent of Antarctica in the south. North and South America form the eastern edge of this great ocean, while Asia and Australia border the Pacific to the west.

The Pacific Ocean serves as a major trade route between countries that lie along its coast. In fact, much of the world's trade takes place between those countries. They are all part of a world region called the **Pacific Rim**. Because they all

Hong Kong, China, is one of the busiest ports in the world.

LOCATE IT

CHINA

Hong Kong

416

border the Pacific Ocean, many Pacific Rim countries have formed special trading partnerships. The United States, for example, has trade agreements with such Pacific Rim countries as Japan and Taiwan.

The Pacific Rim countries also share a common danger. They all are part of a region called the **Ring of Fire**. The Ring of Fire stretches along the western coast of the Americas and the eastern coast of Asia and into the southern Pacific Ocean. This region has many active volcanoes and thousands more that are not active. Places in the Ring of Fire frequently experience earthquakes, too. Japan, for example, experiences about 5,000 earthquakes a year!

REVIEW **Why do so many Pacific Rim countries trade with one another?**
PREDICT AN OUTCOME

Atlantic Ocean

The Atlantic Ocean stretches from the Arctic Ocean in the north to the continent of Antarctica in the south. North America and South America make up its western coastline, while Europe and Africa border the Atlantic on the east.

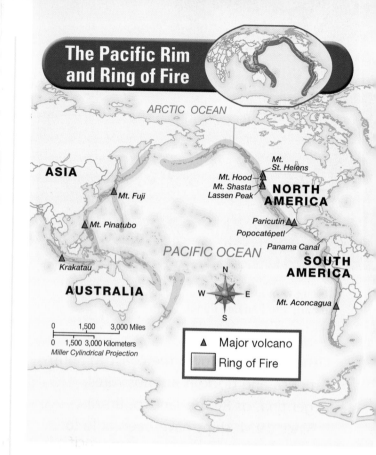

Regions   This map shows the Pacific Rim countries and the Ring of Fire.

❷ Which continents are part of the Pacific Rim?

Like the Pacific, the Atlantic Ocean is an important trade route for the world. Ships leaving our nation's Atlantic ports sail to African ports or to such European ports as Rotterdam in the Netherlands.

It took workers 10 years and about $380 million to build the Panama Canal.

Indian Ocean

The Indian Ocean is the third-largest ocean on Earth. Most of it lies south of the equator. The continents that border this ocean are Australia to the east, Asia to the north, and Africa to the west. Like the Atlantic and Pacific, the Indian Ocean has Antarctica as its southern border.

Sailing routes around and across the Indian Ocean have long connected coastal areas in Africa, Asia, and Australia. In 1498 Europeans began sailing around the tip of Africa to reach the Indian Ocean.

Today, trading ships sailing from the Atlantic Ocean to the Indian Ocean no longer have to make the long journey around Africa. They can reach the Indian Ocean from the Mediterranean Sea by sailing through the Suez (soo•ez) Canal in Egypt. This canal links the Mediterranean Sea to the Red Sea. Other ships on the Indian Ocean are huge tankers carrying much of the world's oil from the Persian Gulf.

REVIEW How can ships sail from the Atlantic Ocean to the Indian Ocean?

Other ships sail down the coast to South America and dock in Buenos Aires, Argentina, or Rio de Janeiro, Brazil.

Since 1914, ships have been able to travel quickly between the Atlantic and Pacific Oceans by using the Panama Canal. The canal cuts through a narrow isthmus that joins North America and South America. This route shortened the sea voyage between New York City and San Francisco by about 7,800 miles (12,500 km). However, the canal is too small for some of today's largest ships to use.

REVIEW What continents border the Atlantic Ocean?

Analyze Tables The world's largest fish, whale sharks, live in the Indian Ocean.

❧ Which ocean is deeper, the Indian or the Arctic?

Facts About the Oceans

Ocean	Area	Greatest Depth
Pacific	64,185,629 square miles (166,227,940 sq km)	35,837 ft (10,923 m)
Atlantic	33,424,006 square miles (86,561,490 sq km)	30,246 ft (9,219 m)
Indian	28,351,484 square miles (73,424,673 sq km)	24,460 ft (7,455 m)
Arctic	5,108,132 square miles (13,229,040 sq km)	18,456 ft (5,625 m)

On the Arctic Ocean, special ice-breaking ships cut through the ice, which can be 10 feet (3 m) thick.

Arctic Ocean

The Arctic Ocean is the smallest and northernmost of Earth's oceans. Most of its waters are ice-covered year-round. For this reason, it is perhaps the least-known body of water in the world.

For centuries, explorers tried to find a route through the Arctic Ocean from the Atlantic to the Pacific, but none succeeded. The harsh northern climate and the ice-covered waters made exploration of the Arctic Ocean too difficult and dangerous.

Today's technology, however, has greatly improved navigation on the Arctic Ocean. Guide planes and ice-breaking ships now travel with the trade ships sailing on the Arctic Ocean. The guide planes fly overhead, scouting out the easiest route through the ice. Then they radio this information to the ice-breaking ships. The ice-breaking ships move ahead of the trade ships and break a path through the thick ice.

REVIEW Why is the Arctic Ocean the least-known body of water in the world?

LESSON 5
REVIEW

PREDICT AN OUTCOME If the Suez Canal had not been built, how might trade around the Indian Ocean be different?

1 BIG IDEA How is the Arctic Ocean different from other oceans around the world?

2 VOCABULARY Use the terms **Pacific Rim** and **Ring of Fire** to describe the lands that border the Pacific Ocean.

3 GEOGRAPHY What shortcut can ships use to travel between the Atlantic and Pacific Oceans?

4 CRITICAL THINKING—Synthesize Why do you think European explorers first reached the Atlantic Coast of North America instead of the Pacific Coast?

PERFORMANCE—Create a Collage Choose a Pacific Rim country, and learn more about its coastal areas. Photocopy pictures from library books and magazines that show the country's port cities and the kinds of things people do along the coast. Create a collage, and write a caption for each picture.

12 Review and Test Preparation

 **Predict an Outcome**

Copy the following graphic organizer onto a separate sheet
of paper. Use the information you have learned to predict
outcomes of events in the Pacific states.

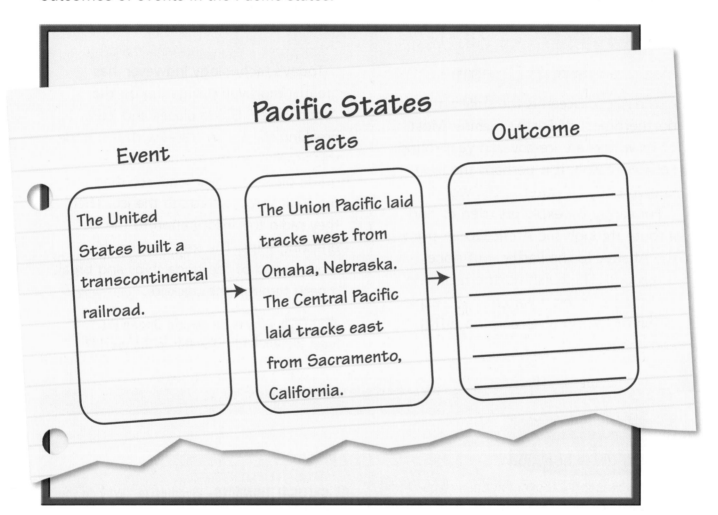

Pacific States

Event

The United States built a transcontinental railroad.

Facts

The Union Pacific laid tracks west from Omaha, Nebraska. The Central Pacific laid tracks east from Sacramento, California.

Outcome

THINK & WRITE

Write Interview Questions Imagine you are a newspaper reporter. You have been assigned to interview people after one of the earthquakes in California or Alaska. Write a list of questions that you would ask.

Write Riddles Create a riddle for each of the world's oceans. Write at least two clues for each riddle to help people solve it. End each of your riddles with this question: "Which ocean am I?"

1867
The United States buys
Alaska from Russia

1869
The transcontinental
railroad is finished

1941
Japanese attack
Pearl Harbor in Hawaii

1959
Alaska and Hawaii become states

USE THE TIME LINE

1 When was gold discovered in California?

2 How many years after the United States bought Alaska did Alaska become a state?

USE VOCABULARY

Match each term with the correct definition.

telegraph (p. 394)

fjord (p. 400)

earthquake (p. 403)

volcano (p. 403)

wetlands (p. 410)

monarch (p. 413)

Pacific Rim (p. 416)

3 a king or queen

4 a narrow inlet of the ocean between cliffs

5 a machine that uses electricity to send messages over wires

6 a sudden shaking of the ground

7 an opening in Earth's surface out of which hot gases, ash, and lava may pour

8 the countries that border the Pacific Ocean

RECALL FACTS

Answer these questions.

9 Why was the transcontinental railroad built? How did it change travel?

10 What causes earthquakes?

11 Which Pacific state has rain forest areas?

12 Which Pacific state leads the country in farming and manufacturing?

13 What is the capital and largest city in Hawaii?

14 Who were the first people to settle in Hawaii?

Write the letter of the best choice.

15 Which of the following carries oil from Prudhoe Bay to Valdez?
A Trans-Alaska Pipeline
B Central Valley Project
C Panama Canal
D transcontinental railroad

16 The United States territories of Guam and American Samoa lie in the—
F Atlantic Ocean.
G Pacific Ocean.
H Indian Ocean.
J Arctic Ocean.

THINK CRITICALLY

17 Would the threat of natural disasters, such as earthquakes or volcanic eruptions, stop you from living in a place that you like? Explain your answer.

18 Many people who lived near the oil spill in Alaska in 1989 believed that they should help clean up. Do you agree with their point of view? Explain.

APPLY SKILLS

Use a Time Zone Map

19 Look at the map on page 399. If it is 4:00 P.M. in Los Angeles, California, what time is it in Augusta, Maine?

Act as a Responsible Citizen

20 Watch the people around you. Identify a person who you think is acting as a responsible citizen. Explain why that person is responsible.

Hoover Dam

GET READY

Hoover Dam is located on the border between Arizona and Nevada. Built in the middle 1930s, the dam supplies electricity to millions of people in Arizona, Nevada, and California. It is also one of the most famous dams in the world. Hoover Dam is visited by more than one million people a year! Visitors can learn more about the dam by taking a tour. On a tour of Hoover Dam, you can see the Hoover Power Plant, learn about the dam's construction, and take in the grand scale of this impressive structure.

LOCATE IT

WHAT TO SEE

Hoover Dam stands in the Black Canyon on the Colorado River. It took thousands of workers to clear away rock and to build the dam. The amount of concrete that was used to build it could make a road from New York to California.

Visitors can watch the falling water that provides the power used to generate electricity.

Lake Mead was formed from the water held back by the dam. Many people use the lake for boating and recreation.

Each generator (left) can supply enough electricity for 100,000 people. The city of Los Angeles (right) uses electricity that is generated at the Hoover Power Plant.

TAKE A FIELD TRIP

GO ONLINE

A VIRTUAL TOUR
Visit The Learning Site at www.harcourtschool.com to take virtual tours of other places of interest in the United States.

Turner Le@rning®

A VIDEO TOUR
Check your media center or classroom library for a videotape tour of Hoover Dam.

5 Review and Test Preparation

VISUAL SUMMARY

Write a Letter Study the pictures and captions below to help you review Unit 5. Imagine that you live near one of the scenes and a friend lives near another. Write a letter to that friend to describe the place where you live and to compare it with the place where your friend lives.

USE VOCABULARY

For each pair of terms, write a sentence or two to explain how the terms are related.

1. **Continental Divide** (p. 344), **barrier** (p. 345)

2. **mission** (p. 369), **society** (p. 370)

3. **cloudburst** (p. 374), **arroyo** (p. 374)

4. **sand dune** (p. 383), **oasis** (p. 383)

5. **telegraph** (p. 394), **transcontinental railroad** (p. 394)

6. **volcano** (p. 403), **lava** (p. 403)

7. **ecosystem** (p. 407), **oil slick** (p. 410)

8. **Pacific Rim** (p. 416), **Ring of Fire** (p. 417)

RECALL FACTS

Answer these questions.

9. What areas did Lewis and Clark explore?

10. What happens to temperatures as the elevation increases?

11. How are rivers and dams important to the economy of the West?

12. How did the transcontinental railroad affect the West?

13. Why do people live on only seven of the Hawaiian Islands?

Write the letter of the best choice.

14. What is the largest desert in the world?
    A North American Desert
    B Sahara
    C Atacama Desert
    D Negev

15. Which of the following is **not** a Pacific island belonging to the United States?
    F American Samoa
    G Guam
    H Hawaii
    J Puerto Rico

Visual Summary

| 1200 | 1600 | 1650 | 1700 | 1750 |

1200s Native Americans settle at Mesa Verde, in Colorado. p. 368

1610 Spanish build the city of Santa Fe, in New Mexico. p. 369

1915 A motion picture industry starts in Hollywood, California. p. 408

HOLLYWOOD

THINK CRITICALLY

16 How have mountains and deserts affected transportation and settlement in the West?

17 What can you do to help clean up the environment where you live?

18 Why do you think Alaska and Hawaii were the last two states to join the United States?

19 How do you think people know that the Anasazi and Hohokam settled in the Southwest Desert about 2,000 years ago?

20 In what ways is the West a region of variety?

APPLY SKILLS

Use a Time Zone Map
Use the map on this page to answer the following questions.

21 What are the time zones in the West?

22 What is the difference in time between Hawaii and mainland Alaska?

23 Which states in the West are in more than one time zone?

24 Imagine that you are in San Francisco, California. Is it earlier, later, or the same time as in Butte, Montana?

25 If it is 4:00 P.M. in Seattle, Washington, what time is it in Denver, Colorado?

26 If you are in Cheyenne, Wyoming, and you need to call friends in Honolulu, Hawaii, at 9:00 A.M., what time should you make the call?

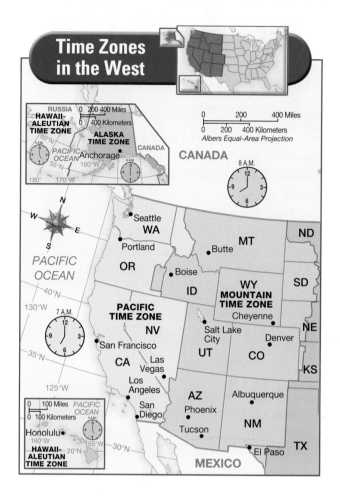

Time Zones in the West

1800	1850	1900	1950	Present

1923 Carlsbad Caverns National Park, in New Mexico, is established. p. 377

1941 Japan attacks the United States at Pearl Harbor, in Hawaii. p. 414

1971 Arches National Park, in Utah, is established. p. 355

425

Unit Activities

Visit The Learning Site at www.harcourtschool.com for additional activities.

Celebrate a Mexican Holiday

Work together to plan a classroom celebration of a Mexican holiday, such as those celebrated by many people in the West. First, research a holiday, such as Mexican Independence Day or Cinco de Mayo. Then plan the celebration. You may want to make colorful costumes, prepare traditional Mexican foods, or sing Mexican songs.

Design Postage Stamps

Work with a partner to design postage stamps that honor some of the people or events that you read about in Unit 5. Draw a design for each person or event on a sheet of paper. Then write a paragraph explaining why you chose to honor that person or event. Present your postage stamps to the class and share your paragraphs to explain each design. Finally, display your stamps on a bulletin board for everyone to see.

VISIT YOUR LIBRARY

■ *Sierra* by Diane Siebert. HarperCollins Publishers.

■ *Destination: Rocky Mountains* by Jonathan Grupper. National Geographic Society.

■ *Desert Trek: An Eye-Opening Journey Through the World's Driest Places* by Marie-Ange Le Roghais. Walker Publishing Company.

COMPLETE THE UNIT PROJECT

A 3-D Time Line   Work with a group of classmates to finish the Unit Project described on page 339. As a group, decide which five events discussed in the unit you will show on the time line. Then create a time line by writing the dates and captions for the events on large sheets of paper. Tape the time line to the floor, and use art materials to build three-dimensional models to illustrate the events. As your group presents its time line to the class, explain why the events are important to the history of the West.

Fireworks over
Bethlehem

Growth and Change

" A mind which really lays
hold of a subject is not easily
detached from it. "

—Ida Tarbell, 1857–1944

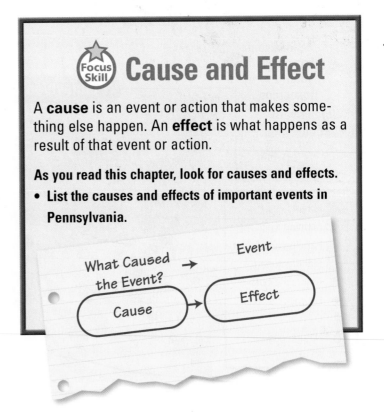

Focus Skill Cause and Effect

A **cause** is an event or action that makes something else happen. An **effect** is what happens as a
result of that event or action.

As you read this chapter, look for causes and effects.
• List the causes and effects of important events in
  Pennsylvania.

What Caused
the Event? → Event

Cause → Effect

Focus Skill **CAUSE AND EFFECT**

As you read, look for causes and effects of growing industries.

BIG IDEA
Pennsylvania's natural resources led to a strong economy in the late 1800s.

VOCABULARY

by-product
division of labor
industrialist
strike
human resource
capital resource

Growing Industries

During and after the Civil War, Pennsylvania continued to grow. More than ever before, the state's economy depended on natural resources.

Rich Natural Resources

On August 27, 1859, Edwin Drake found oil near Titusville, in northwestern Pennsylvania. Supplying oil and natural gas, a by-product of oil, became a big business. A **by-product** is something that is produced while making the main product.

In the 1860s, Williamsport was the center of the state's timber industry. Pennsylvania's forests were not then protected. Many trees were cut down before Governor Gifford Pinchot led the effort to save the forests.

Since colonial times, Pennsylvania coal was mined and used for fuel. The fuel helped run factories and railroads. Anthracite, or hard coal, was the main fuel for making iron products. In the 1840s, bituminous, or soft coal, was found in western Pennsylvania. Coke, a fuel made from soft coal, was used in steel factories, called mills.

REVIEW **What industries began because of Drake's discovery?**

Focus Skill **CAUSE AND EFFECT**

Pennsylvania Natural Resources

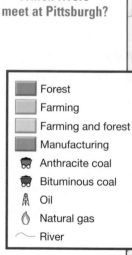

- Forest
- Farming
- Farming and forest
- Manufacturing
- Anthracite coal
- Bituminous coal
- Oil
- Natural gas
- River

In 1877, angry railroad workers started a fire on a bridge in Reading. The bell (right) comes from a locomotive used in the 1870s.

Workers Unite

For many people, working conditions were poor, and pay was low. Many workers were given one task to do over and over, all day long. This is called a **division of labor**, the sharing of large jobs so that each worker does only part of the work. Labor unions pushed for better working conditions and more money.

Pennsylvanians led the nation's labor movement. John Siney (SY•nee) started the first coal miners' union in 1868. Uriah Stevens (yoo•RY•uh STEE•vuhnz) and other Philadelphians formed a union called the Knights of Labor, in 1871. Ironworkers and steelworkers organized in 1876.

Industrialists, people who owned mines, mills, factories, and railroads, fought the labor unions. Franklin B. Gowen, president of the Philadelphia & Reading Railroad, hired people to break up the coal miners' union. This led to a bitter fight between workers and owners.

To improve working conditions, workers would sometimes strike. A **strike** is the stopping of work to make employers meet workers' demands.

The Great Railroad Strike of 1877 started in Pennsylvania. It was the first major strike in the nation. It started when railroad owners decided to lower workers' pay. The governor sent soldiers to end the strike. As a result, more than 32 people were killed in Pittsburgh and Reading.

In only two months, the strike spread to railroad workers in ten states. Partly because of the railroad strike, Terence V. Powderly led the Knights of Labor to open its membership to women in 1881 and to African Americans in 1883.

Industrialist George Westinghouse, a Pittsburgh inventor, improved railroad safety. His inventions, including air brakes, signals, and switches, made railroads safer for workers and travelers.

REVIEW What event led to the Great Railroad Strike? CAUSE AND EFFECT

The Iron and Steel Industries

The making of iron and steel products became Pennsylvania's largest industries. Many steel and iron mills were in the western part of the state. There were also mills in Bethlehem, Harrisburg, Lewistown, Carlisle, and Morrisville.

Pennsylvania's ironworking furnaces turned to making steel in 1873. In Chester, John Fritz invented a new process for making stronger steel tracks for the railroads. The steel industry moved west when bituminous coal, used in making steel, was found in western Pennsylvania.

Andrew Carnegie was a leader in the steel industry. He started out working in textile mills and for the railroads. In 1875, Carnegie built the first steel mill in Pittsburgh. When he sold Carnegie Steel Corporation, he used his wealth to help others. More than $56 million went to start public libraries in 2,500 communities across the nation.

Charles M. Schwab worked for Andrew Carnegie. In 1901, Carnegie sold his company to United States Steel, known as U.S. Steel. Schwab then became the new company's president. U.S. Steel was very successful. In its first year, U.S. Steel produced more than half of the nation's steel.

In 1904, Schwab founded Bethlehem Steel Company. The company became a leader in building warships during World War II. Bethlehem Steel delivered a ship a day during the war. Its products were used to make many bridges and buildings around the country.

REVIEW How did finding bituminous coal affect the steel industry? **CAUSE AND EFFECT**

The Homestead Steel Mill in southwestern Pennsylvania was one of several mills operating in the late 1800s.

Resources for Making Steel

Natural Resources	Human Resources	Capital Resources
Coal and iron deposits	Miners and steelworkers	Mining equipment, factories, railroads

Manufactured Products
Steel and steel products

Analyze Diagrams
Three kinds of resources are needed to make most products.

❖ Which kind of resource would safety equipment be?

Industry Uses Resources

Three kinds of resources are needed to make products—natural resources, **human resources**, or workers, and capital resources. **Capital resources** are the buildings, supplies, equipment, and money that a business uses. Pennsylvanians used these resources to build many industries.

Many people immigrated to the state to work. Before the Civil War, many came from northern Europe. In the late 1800s, immigrants came from eastern and central Europe. Starting about 1910, thousands of African Americans moved to northern cities from the South. This movement is known as the Great Migration.

By 1900, Pennsylvania led the nation's textile and leather industries. Other manufacturing included paper, soap, paint, and musical instruments. Factories also produced motorcycles and power tools.

Toy making was another industry. Factories in Erie and Girard made model trains. Several Pennsylvania companies made carousel (kar•uh•SEL) horses.

Many Pennsylvanians produced food products. H.J. Heinz founded a company that makes ketchup and other products. Milton Hershey started a successful chocolate company.

REVIEW What three kinds of resources are needed to make most products?

Carousel horses, such as this one, have been made in Pennsylvania since the late 1800s.

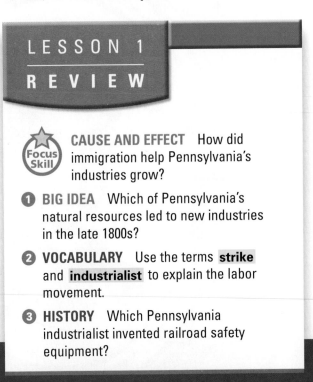

LESSON 1 REVIEW

⭐ **Focus Skill**

CAUSE AND EFFECT How did immigration help Pennsylvania's industries grow?

① **BIG IDEA** Which of Pennsylvania's natural resources led to new industries in the late 1800s?

② **VOCABULARY** Use the terms **strike** and **industrialist** to explain the labor movement.

③ **HISTORY** Which Pennsylvania industrialist invented railroad safety equipment?

CAUSE AND EFFECT

As you read, look for effects of industries on Pennsylvania society.

BIG IDEA

Social and economic changes affected Pennsylvania in the 1900s.

VOCABULARY

war bond
suffrage

A Changing World

The twentieth century was a time of social and economic change in Pennsylvania and the nation. In the early 1900s, events at home and around the world affected the state.

Into the Twentieth Century

Women were active in several social reform movements in Pennsylvania. Florence Kelley was a Philadelphia lawyer and social worker. Kelley improved working conditions for children and women. She worked hard to pass laws that gave women the right to vote in local, state, and national elections. Kelley also led the National Consumers League, a group that protected consumers. Isabel Darlington was the first woman to practice law in Pennsylvania's highest court.

Sarah C. F. Hallowell ran a newspaper called *The New Century*. Women did all the reporting, writing, and editing. At that time, many magazines did not include women's views on important issues. Author Ida Tarbell, from Erie, wrote a series of articles for *McClure's Magazine*. The articles focused on illegal actions by oil company industrialists. Even though women in Pennsylvania had new choices, they did not have the same rights as men.

REVIEW Which leader worked to protect consumers?

Florence Kelley

FAST FACT The Pennsylvania Women's Suffrage Association was founded in 1868. For the next 50 years, many Pennsylvania women worked to get the right to vote.

Ida Tarbell   1857–1944

Character Trait: Perseverance

From 1893 to 1906, Ida Tarbell was a writer and editor for *McClure's Magazine*. She also published the book *History of the Standard Oil Company*. In it, she took a close look at John D. Rockefeller's company. Tarbell discovered that Rockefeller had worked with the railroads so that his company could sell them more oil than the state's smaller oil refiners. As a result of Tarbell's work, the United States Supreme Court ordered changes in the oil industry.

37 USA
Ida M. Tarbell
2002

10 CENTS A COPY Stage Memories BY Clara Morris $1.00 A YEAR
McCLURE'S MAGAZINE FOR JANUARY

GO ONLINE **MULTIMEDIA BIOGRAPHIES**
Visit The Learning Site at www.harcourtschool.com
to learn about other famous people.

World War I

When the United States entered World War I in 1917, Pennsylvania's citizens helped the war effort. The state's shipyards, mills, and factories made products for the soldiers. Coal production increased to meet the needs of the United States Army and Navy. The state's economy improved as a result of the war. Pennsylvanians bought almost $3 billion worth of **war bonds**. These papers showed that the buyer had loaned money to the government to help pay for a war.

More than 300,000 Pennsylvanians fought in battles in Europe. General Tasker H. Bliss of Lewisburg was on the American Peace Commission.

After World War I, Congress approved the Nineteenth Amendment to the Constitution. It gave women **suffrage**, or the right to vote and hold public office.

Pennsylvania was the eighth state to pass the amendment. Women in the state had worked for their rights since the 1800s. Pennsylvanian Carrie Chapman Catt led the National American Women's Suffrage Association.

Not all of the changes after the war were good for Pennsylvanians. The demand for coal fell. In the 1920s, oil and gas replaced coal as the major fuel source. The shrinking market for coal caused economic problems.

Pennsylvanians began to suffer as industries changed. Many coal miners lost their jobs. Textile mill owners began to move their factories to the South, where costs were lower. Many textile workers lost their jobs. Farmers suffered when prices for their products dropped.

REVIEW How did the Nineteenth Amendment affect Pennsylvanians?
CAUSE AND EFFECT

The Great Depression and More Conflict

During the Great Depression in the 1930s, the economy weakened. Many people lost their jobs, and some people became homeless. Steel mills and coal mines lowered production. In 1932, nearly one-fourth of Philadelphia's workers did not have jobs. The next year, almost one-half were unemployed, or jobless.

Some people had to sell their homes, and many could not afford to buy food. Professionals, such as doctors and lawyers, could not collect money that was owed to them. Many people lost their savings.

State programs helped many people. Governor Gifford Pinchot hired workers to pave state roads. President Franklin D. Roosevelt's New Deal programs provided work for thousands of others.

During the Depression, many Mexican laborers worked on Philadelphia railroads. These workers were also hired to help out on Pennsylvania farms.

The United States entered World War II in December 1941. Oil, steel, food, and money from Pennsylvania helped the nation's war effort. Factories were making airplanes, tanks, and weapons. The Philadelphia Navy Yard built ships, including two of the largest steel battleships in the world.

The demand for Pennsylvania's products created millions of jobs. In turn, the new jobs made the state's economy much stronger.

More than one million people from Pennsylvania served in the military. There were 130 generals and admirals from the state. General George C. Marshall and commander of the Army Air Forces, Henry H. Arnold, both played key roles.

REVIEW How did high unemployment cause other economic problems?
 CAUSE AND EFFECT

Pennsylvania Governor Gifford Pinchot is shown supervising the work of a road-paving crew. The timetable (right) encourages people to buy war bonds to help pay for World War II.

PENNSYLVANIA RAILROAD

His Needs Come First!

BUY UNITED STATES WAR BONDS & STAMPS for Victory!

Each year, millions of crayons are manufactured in Easton, Pennsylvania.

Changing Industries

Over the years, the state's industries had polluted the air and water. Coal mines poured chemicals into rivers and streams. Smoke from iron and steel mills polluted the air and caused health problems for some people. In 1959, the Air Pollution Control Act gave the state the right to protect the air. Since 1967, the state and federal governments have spent almost $500 million on clean-up efforts. The Pennsylvania Department of Environmental Resources was created in 1968.

By the 1970s, other regions and nations were making steel at a lower cost. The demand for Pennsylvania's coal, iron, and steel dropped. Many mills shut down.

The Pennsylvania economy changed. Today, farming is a major industry that provides milk, eggs, chickens, fruits, and vegetables. Tourism also plays a major role.

Many visitors enjoy our state's historical sites and natural features.

Pennsylvania remains a leader in manufacturing. Companies around the state make machinery, electronic items, building materials, art supplies, and glass. Today, computer technology and biotechnology research are growing industries.

REVIEW How did problems in the steel industry affect the economy?

LESSON 2
REVIEW

Focus Skill **CAUSE AND EFFECT** How did wars affect Pennsylvania's economy?

❶ **BIG IDEA** How did the Great Depression affect Pennsylvania?

❷ **VOCABULARY** In a paragraph about equal rights, use the term **suffrage**.

❸ **ECONOMICS** What are two main industries in Pennsylvania today?

3

As you read, think about why people worked for change and how the changes affected the state.

BIG IDEA

African Americans worked to gain civil rights. Women worked together to improve their rights.

VOCABULARY

pesticide

Civil Rights and Social Changes

Social reform movements continued through the twentieth century in Pennsylvania and the nation. African Americans and women worked to gain civil rights. As suburbs were developed, many people left crowded cities.

Civil Rights

In the early 1900s, thousands of African Americans from the South moved north. They wanted to escape poor living conditions and laws that treated them unfairly. African Americans found jobs in the state's steel mills, coal mines, shipyards, and railroads. Some Pennsylvania workers did not like competing with African Americans for jobs and homes.

Racial tensions grew and sometimes resulted in violence. Some people were killed during protests in Chester and Philadelphia. The state's African American community came together to fight for their civil rights. African American churches became important meeting places. People gathered in churches to share information about jobs, education, and housing. In Philadelphia, Pittsburgh, and Harrisburg, more African Americans began to run their own businesses.

REVIEW Why did many African Americans move north? CAUSE AND EFFECT

The Mother Bethel African Methodist Episcopal (A.M.E.) Church in Philadelphia was one of the first churches in the city started by an African American.

Progress for African Americans

After World War II, African Americans continued to move north to work in Pittsburgh's steel mills and Philadelphia's shipyards. African American women also found work in the factories. These workers made up a large part of the city populations.

Working and living conditions for African Americans were still unfair. The struggle for civil rights continued through the twentieth century. In the 1960s, there were civil rights protests in the state.

In order to make change, some African Americans ran for political office. A growing number of African Americans were elected to city, state, and national governments.

In 1958, Robert N.C. Nix, Sr., became the first African American from Pennsylvania elected to the United States Congress. In 1977, K. Leroy Irvis became the first African American in the nation to serve as speaker of the house in a state legislature. In 1983, W. Wilson Goode, Sr., became Philadelphia's first African American mayor. By 1993, there were 18 African Americans

in the Pennsylvania General Assembly. By serving as elected officials, African Americans helped pass laws that improved civil rights.

REVIEW Why did some African Americans work within the political system?

CAUSE AND EFFECT

President Lyndon Johnson signed the Civil Rights Act on July 2, 1964. This important law (right) gave equal rights to African Americans.

The American Dream

In the 1950s and 1960s, there was a boom in suburban growth. In the early 1950s, William Levitt planned a suburb in Bucks County, Pennsylvania. He named the town Levittown and built small houses that young families could afford.

Many people were happy to leave crowded cities, such as Philadelphia. They gained a house with a yard in a quiet neighborhood. Levittown grew quickly. By the time the suburb was complete, there were more than 17,000 new homes.

The idea of owning a home in the suburbs became known as the American Dream. Pennsylvania's Levittown became a model for other suburbs around the country.

REVIEW **Where is Levittown?**

Women's Rights

During the 1960s and the 1970s, Pennsylvania's women began to have a larger role in state politics. In 1964, Genevieve Blatt ran for election to the United States Senate. Although she did not win the election, Blatt gained the respect of the state's Democratic party.

Pennsylvania women were active in the women's movement, a nationwide effort to win advances for American women. Many women's groups had headquarters in Philadelphia. In 1971, the Equal Rights Amendment was added to the state constitution. This law made it illegal to deny civil rights to women just because they are women. In the 1970s, rules were changed so that girls could play Little League baseball on the same teams as boys.

REVIEW **What was the women's movement?**

Levittown was a planned suburb with more than 17,000 single-family homes. Entrepreneur William Levitt purchased farmland in lower Bucks County (below left) and built homes, schools, churches, swimming pools, and shopping centers (below right).

No. 1

No. 2

The Levittowner
PRICE: $10,990 $67 A MONTH

NO CASH REQUIRED FROM VETERANS

No. 3

No. 4

Into a Modern World

Pennsylvanians have made many contributions to present-day life. Some citizens worked to develop computer technology. In 1925, Philadelphia member of Congress Clyde Kelly introduced the Airmail Act, which helped create the airline industry. Two years later, Governor Pinchot started the state's Bureau of Aeronautics. In the late 1930s, Philadelphia International Airport opened.

John R. Carson and Dr. Harry Davis helped develop the radio. The nation's first radio station, KDKA, broadcast from Pittsburgh in 1920.

Pennsylvania's women also made important contributions. Rachel Carson wrote *Silent Spring*. Her book focused on the dangers of **pesticides**, chemicals that kill harmful insects on crops. Carson discovered that pesticides also killed birds and other animals. Her book led to laws banning certain dangerous pesticides.

Author Pearl S. Buck was a civil rights and women's rights activist. Her novel *The Good Earth* won a Pulitzer Prize in 1932. She received the Nobel Prize for

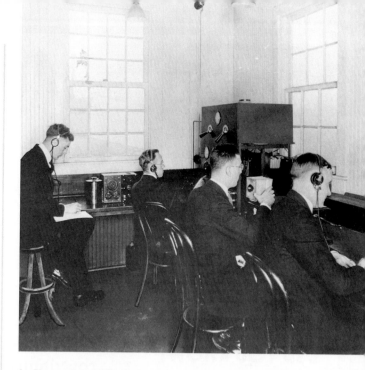

In November 1920, the country's first radio station, KDKA, broadcast results from the presidential election.

Literature in 1938. She was the first woman to win both awards.

Pennsylvanian Carl E. Stotz started Little League baseball in Williamsport in 1939. By 2000, there were Little League teams around the world. Williamsport hosts the Little League World Series each August.

REVIEW How did Pennsylvanians contribute to present-day society?

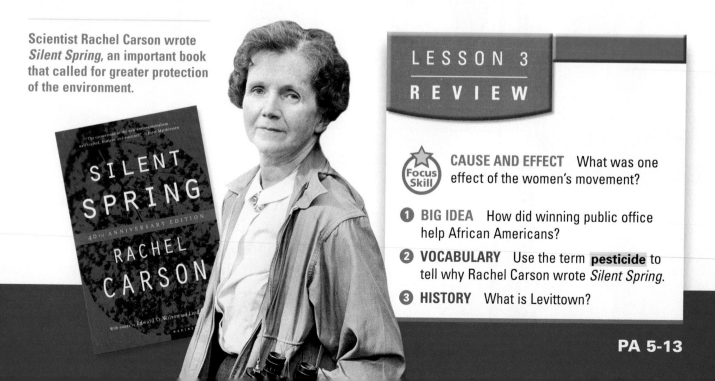

Scientist Rachel Carson wrote *Silent Spring,* an important book that called for greater protection of the environment.

LESSON 3 REVIEW

Focus Skill **CAUSE AND EFFECT** What was one effect of the women's movement?

❶ **BIG IDEA** How did winning public office help African Americans?

❷ **VOCABULARY** Use the term **pesticide** to tell why Rachel Carson wrote *Silent Spring*.

❸ **HISTORY** What is Levittown?

People Bringing Changes

DID YOU KNOW?

In 1946, scientists at the University of Pennsylvania announced the invention of the world's first digital computer, called ENIAC.

Pennsylvanians are proud of the many well-known people from their state. Each has contributed ideas and talents that have brought about positive changes. These people, and many others, have helped shape Pennsylvania's history.

Mary Lou Williams was one of the most important female jazz musicians of her time. She brought change to the jazz community as one of the few women to play the piano and to conduct the orchestra.

Min L. Matheson of Wilkes-Barre was one of the first women to fight to change working conditions in Pennsylvania factories. Along with the International Ladies' Garment Workers Union, or ILGWU, she improved conditions for textile workers.

Howard Zahniser was a leading conservationist who helped push the Wilderness Act of 1964 through Congress. This act protected 104 million acres of wilderness across the nation as public land.

Roberto Clemente was born in Puerto Rico. In 1955, he joined the Pittsburgh Pirates. For the next 18 years, Clemente was a role model for fair play and active in helping less fortunate people. For his contributions, Clemente was honored as the first Hispanic American in the National Baseball Hall of Fame.

ACTIVITY

Choose one of these leaders and design a postage stamp to honor him or her. Be sure to include information showing why they were important. Display your stamp in the classroom.

RESEARCH

Visit The Learning Site at **www.harcourtschool.com** to learn about other famous people.

Review and Test Preparation

Cause and Effect

(Focus Skill)

Copy the following graphic organizer onto a separate sheet of paper. Use it to show the effects of Edwin Drake's discovery of oil in 1859.

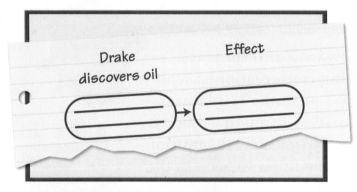

Drake discovers oil → Effect

THINK AND WRITE

Write a Paragraph Explain how one Pennsylvanian's contribution to modern culture has affected your life.

USE VOCABULARY

Write the word or words that correctly match each definition.

by-product (p. PA 5-2)   industrialist (p. PA 5-3)

human resource (p. PA 5-5) suffrage (p. PA 5-7)

pesticide (p. PA 5-13)

1. the right to vote

2. something that is produced while making the main product

3. owners of mines, mills, factories, and railroads

4. chemical used to protect crops from insects

5. workers

RECALL FACTS

Answer these questions.

6. What happened after World War I that caused economic problems in Pennsylvania?

7. How did industries hurt the environment of Pennsylvania?

Write the letter of the best choice.

8. Who was Ida Tarbell?
   A a Philadelphia lawyer
   B a writer for *McClure's Magazine*
   C a senator from Pennsylvania
   D a civil rights activist

THINK CRITICALLY

9. How did the state and federal governments help people during the Great Depression?

10. How did World War II affect the economy of Pennsylvania?

PERFORMANCE

Have a Debate Choose the point of view of either the workers or the industrialists about strikes. Make a list of reasons for your opinion. Partner with someone who has chosen the opposite position from yours. Conduct a debate before your classmates.

The United States Today

An Iroquois pouch,
1920

Flag court in Washington, D.C.

The United States Today

❝ The land has been the legacy
we cultivate an' reap,
The life has been the heritage
our fathers fought to keep . . . ❞

—Jim Fish, "Heritage," 1998

Preview the Content

Read the title and the Big Idea statement for each lesson.
Use them to develop a web for each chapter in this unit.

Preview the Vocabulary

Suffixes   A suffix is a word part added to the end of a root
word. Use the suffixes and the root words below to find a
meaning for each vocabulary word.

SUFFIX	ROOT WORD	VOCABULARY WORD	POSSIBLE MEANING
-ism (way of action or behavior)	**patriot** (one who loves a country)	**patriotism**	_____
-ment (the act, art, or process of)	**amend** (to change or revise)	**amendment**	_____

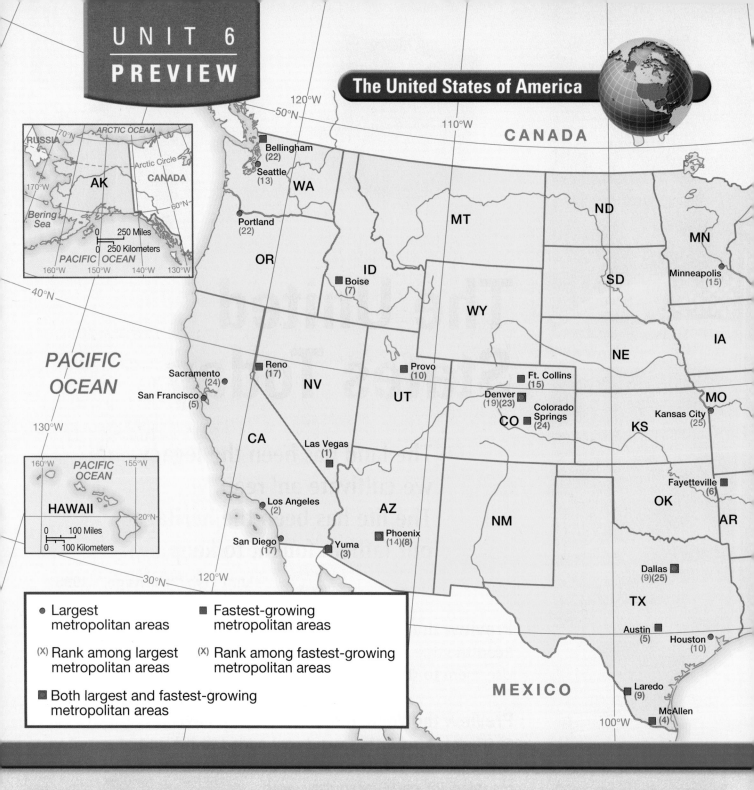

The United States of America

CANADA

ARCTIC OCEAN

RUSSIA

AK

CANADA

Bering Sea

PACIFIC OCEAN

0   250 Miles
0   250 Kilometers

Bellingham (22)
Seattle (13)
WA
Portland (22)
OR
Boise (7)
ID
MT
ND
MN
Minneapolis (15)
SD
WY
NE
IA
PACIFIC OCEAN
Reno (17)
NV
Provo (10)
UT
Ft. Collins (15)
Denver (19)(23)
Colorado Springs (24)
CO
KS
MO
Kansas City (25)
Sacramento (24)
San Francisco (5)
Las Vegas (1)
CA
Los Angeles (2)
San Diego (17)
Yuma (3)
AZ
Phoenix (14)(8)
NM
OK
Fayetteville (6)
AR
PACIFIC OCEAN
HAWAII
0   100 Miles
0   100 Kilometers
Dallas (9)(25)
TX
Austin (5)
Houston (10)
Laredo (9)
McAllen (4)
MEXICO

- Largest metropolitan areas
- Fastest-growing metropolitan areas
- (X) Rank among largest metropolitan areas
- (X) Rank among fastest-growing metropolitan areas
- Both largest and fastest-growing metropolitan areas

Americans share a belief in freedom. p. 448

People in the United States have rights and responsibilities. p. 449

The United States has a free enterprise economy. p. 454

CLEANERS
·DRY CLEANING · SHIRTS · SHOE REPAIR · LAUNDRY·

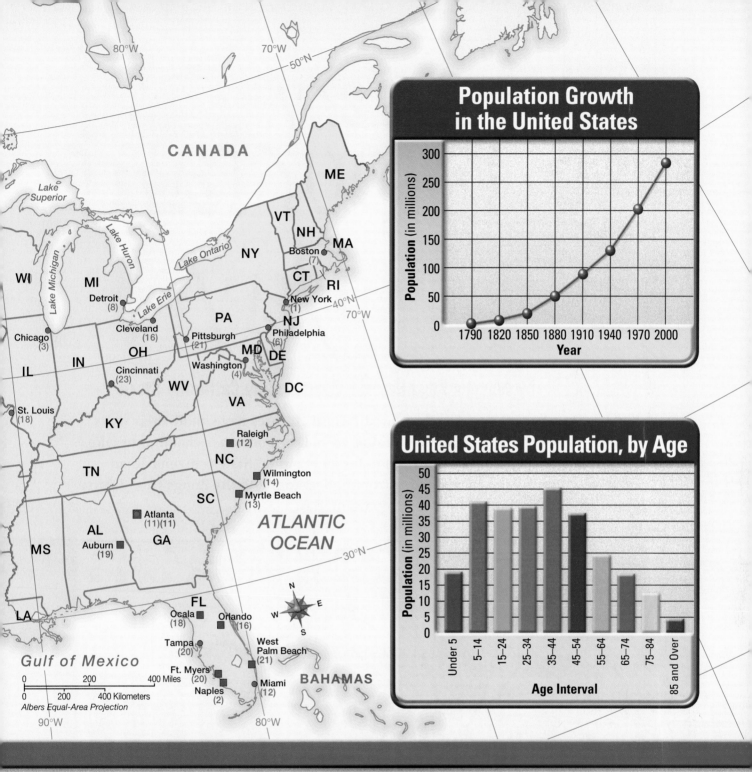

CANADA

Lake Superior

Lake Michigan

Lake Huron

Lake Ontario

Lake Erie

WI

MI
Detroit (8)

Chicago (3)

Cleveland (16)

IL

IN

OH

KY

TN

MS

AL
Auburn (19)

LA

St. Louis (18)

Cincinnati (23)

WV

Pittsburgh (21)

PA

Philadelphia (6)

NY

Boston (7)

New York (1)

VT

NH

MA

CT

RI

NJ

MD

DE

DC

Washington (4)

VA

NC
Raleigh (12)
Wilmington (14)
Myrtle Beach (13)

SC

GA
Atlanta (11)(11)

ME

ATLANTIC OCEAN

40°N

70°W

30°N

FL
Ocala (18)
Orlando (16)
Tampa (20)
West Palm Beach (21)
Ft. Myers (20)
Naples (2)
Miami (12)

Gulf of Mexico

BAHAMAS

0   200   400 Miles
0   200   400 Kilometers
Albers Equal-Area Projection

80°W
90°W

70°W
50°N

80°W

Population Growth in the United States

Population (in millions)

300
250
200
150
100
50
0

1790 1820 1850 1880 1910 1940 1970 2000

Year

United States Population, by Age

Population (in millions)

50
45
40
35
30
25
20
15
10
5
0

Under 5 | 5–14 | 15–24 | 25–34 | 35–44 | 45–54 | 55–64 | 65–74 | 75–84 | 85 and Over

Age Interval

One national government unites the 50 states. p. 466

Different levels of government serve citizens in the United States.   p. 476

The United States is a world leader. p. 488

A Very Important Day

by Maggie Rugg Herold • illustrated by Catherine Stock

On a snowy day, people from different cultures have made their ways to the courthouse. They have gathered in the courthouse chamber to take the final step in their journeys to become United States citizens. Read how families like the Castros from El Salvador and the Zengs from China feel on this snowy, but very important, day.

Soon the examiner appeared, and the room became quiet. "When I call your name," he said, "please come forward to receive your certificate."

Many names were called; many people went forward. Then, "Alvaro and Romelia Castro and children Marta, José, and Oscar."

The Castros approached the examiner. "Please sign here," he said to Alvaro. "And here," he said to Romelia. "These are your papers."

"Thank you," said Alvaro. "This is a proud moment."

The Castros returned to their seats. "The long journey from El Salvador has ended," Romelia whispered to her husband, and he squeezed her hand.

When the examiner had finished, he said, "Please open the door to relatives and friends."

People poured in. There were so many they filled the aisles and lined the walls at the back and sides of the chamber.

"Everyone please rise," said the examiner, and as everyone did, a judge entered the chamber.

"Your Honor," said the examiner, "these petitioners have qualified for citizenship in the United States of America."

"Then," said the judge, "will you repeat after me the oath of citizenship. Let us begin. 'I hereby declare, on oath . . .'"

"I hereby declare, on oath . . ."

Echoing the judge phrase by phrase, sentence by sentence, the many voices resounded as one, swearing loyalty to the United States of America.

"Congratulations," said the judge. "Those of you who can be, please be seated."

As the room became quiet again, the judge cleared his throat. "Two hundred nineteen of you from thirty-two countries have become United States citizens here today. You are carrying on a tradition that dates back to the earliest days of our country, for almost all Americans have come here from somewhere else. May citizenship enrich your lives as your lives enrich this country. Welcome. We are glad to have you. This is a very important day."

Everyone then rose and joined the judge in the Pledge of Allegiance.

petitioners people making a request
oath pledge

resounded rang out

Family and friends and strangers turned to one another. "Best wishes!" "I'm so happy for you." "You must be so proud." "Isn't it wonderful?" "What a day!" "Let me shake your hand." "Let me give you a kiss." "Let me give you a hug."

Zeng Yujin tore open the package from his friend Bailong. Inside he found small American flags, a dozen or so, enough to share with everyone in his family and with other new citizens surrounding him.

In a wave of excitement, they all made their way out of the chamber, through the hallway, and back to the courthouse door.

"Look!" they exclaimed, everybody talking at once. "The snow has stopped." "The sun is shining." "It will be easy to get home and go on celebrating." "This has become our country on this very important day!"

Analyze the Literature

1. Why do you think being a United States citizen is so special to many people?

2. How do you think citizenship will enrich these immigrants' lives and how will their lives enrich the United States?

READ A BOOK

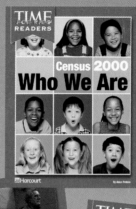

START THE UNIT PROJECT

A Cultural Fair As a class, plan a fair that celebrates the many cultures of the people of the United States. Small groups should select one cultural group to research. Talk with members of different cultural groups to learn about their customs. You will show what you have learned when you host your cultural fair.

USE TECHNOLOGY

Visit The Learning Site at **www.harcourtschool.com** for additional activities, primary sources, and other resources to use in this unit.

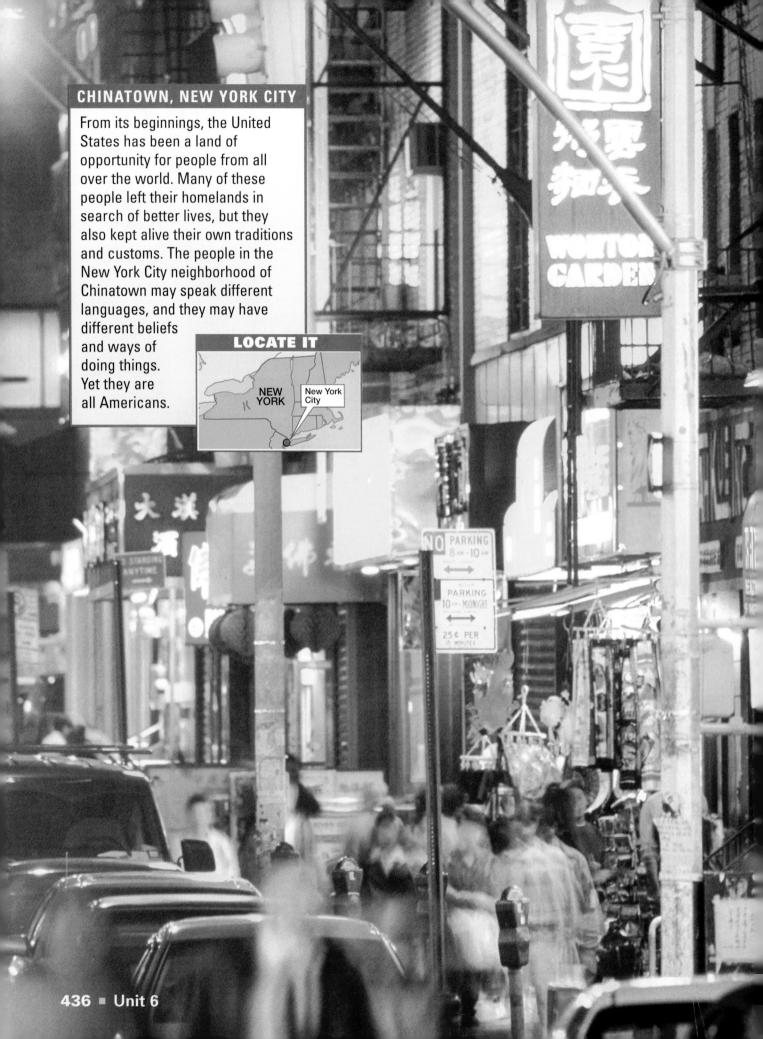

CHINATOWN, NEW YORK CITY

From its beginnings, the United States has been a land of opportunity for people from all over the world. Many of these people left their homelands in search of better lives, but they also kept alive their own traditions and customs. The people in the New York City neighborhood of Chinatown may speak different languages, and they may have different beliefs and ways of doing things. Yet they are all Americans.

LOCATE IT

NEW YORK

New York City

We the People

66 There is room for everybody in America. 99

—Michel Guillaume Jean de Crèvecoeur, "What Is an American?," 1782

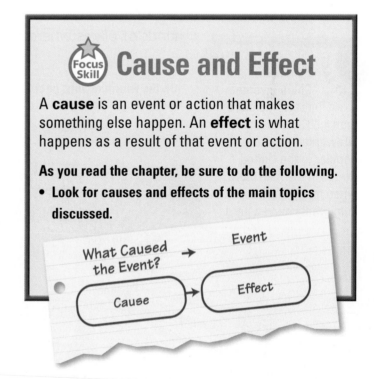

Focus Skill Cause and Effect

A **cause** is an event or action that makes something else happen. An **effect** is what happens as a result of that event or action.

As you read the chapter, be sure to do the following.
• **Look for causes and effects of the main topics discussed.**

What Caused the Event? → Event

Cause → Effect

CAUSE AND EFFECT

As you read, look for how people from different cultures came to live together in the United States.

BIG IDEA

There are different ways of life in the United States.

VOCABULARY

poverty

prejudice

motto

FAST FACT

People in China invented fireworks more than 1,000 years ago! Fireworks became popular in the United States in the mid-1800s, when many Chinese immigrants moved here.

Many Places, People, and Ways

The United States has a great variety of physical features. Each region of the country has different landforms, bodies of water, climates, and natural resources. The United States also has a great variety of people. From earliest times to today, people have come from many places around the world to live in the United States. Those people have brought their different cultures and traditions with them. By doing so, they have all contributed to the American way of life.

Where Americans Live

The United States is a huge country with countless physical, economic, and cultural regions. There are thousands of different cities, towns, and communities, too. People in the United States are free to choose to live in any of those places. However, the kinds of places where most people live have changed over time.

On the Fourth of July, people in Washington, D.C., and other cities across the nation watch fireworks. How do people in your community celebrate this holiday?

LOCATE IT

Washington, D.C.

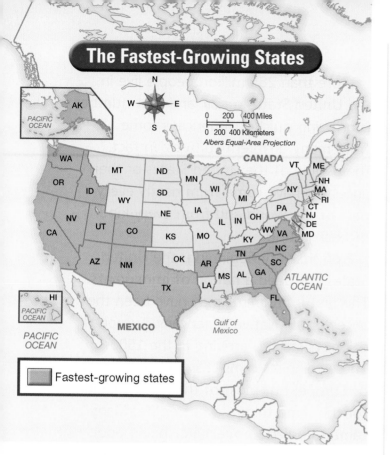

The Fastest-Growing States

0 200 400 Miles
0 200 400 Kilometers
Albers Equal-Area Projection

CANADA

ATLANTIC OCEAN

Gulf of Mexico

MEXICO

PACIFIC OCEAN

PACIFIC OCEAN

Fastest-growing states

GEOGRAPHY THEME

Regions About six out of ten people in the United States now live in the South or the West.

❖ Which South Central states are among the country's fastest-growing?

The first Europeans to come to what is now the United States settled mainly along major rivers near the Atlantic and Gulf Coasts. There they built farms and cities. Over time, settlers moved farther inland, where they built more farms and more cities. Much of the United States, however, remained rural.

In the late 1800s more and more people began moving to urban areas. By 1920 more people in the United States lived in urban regions than in rural regions. Much of

that urban growth took place in cities along the Atlantic and Pacific Coasts, along rivers, and along the shores of the Great Lakes. Today most of the largest cities in the United States are still located in those areas. More than half of all people in the United States now live in states that border the nation's coasts.

More recently, another change has been taking place in where Americans live. Many people have been leaving the central areas of cities and moving to suburban areas. The result has been the growth not only of suburbs but also of large metropolitan areas.

At the same time, the warm climate and resources of the Sun Belt have been attracting more people. Today the Sun Belt is one of the fastest-growing regions in the United States. In fact, Nevada and Arizona are now the two fastest-growing states. As in the rest of the country, most of the people in the Sun Belt live in or near large cities.

REVIEW Where do most people in the United States live today?

These students have different cultural backgrounds, but they are all Americans.

United States Immigration, 1900 and 2000

Number of People

16,000,000
14,000,000
12,000,000
10,000,000
8,000,000
6,000,000
4,000,000
2,000,000
0

Europe   Asia   Latin America

Regions of Origin

■ United States immigration, 1900
■ United States immigration, 2000

Analyze Graphs This graph shows some world regions from which large numbers of people immigrated to the United States in 1900 and 2000.

◈ How did the number of people immigrating from Europe change between 1900 and 2000?

The American People

More than 285 million people live in the United States today, and that number is growing quickly. Americans come from many different cultures. In fact, the people of the United States or their ancestors have come from nearly every part of the world and from every kind of background.

From its very beginnings the United States has been a nation of immigrants. The first immigrants may have been the ancestors of Native Americans. European colonists started arriving in the 1500s. These colonists came from different parts of Europe, but most of them were looking for the same thing—a better life. Many came to escape **poverty**, or being poor. Some wanted the chance to own their own land. Others came so they could freely follow their religious beliefs.

Not all people came to this country by choice, however. Most of the first Africans in the United States had been taken from their homes and sold into slavery.

Today, people still come to the United States from all over the world. An average of more than a million immigrants arrive in the United States each year. Most of those immigrants are from

These immigrants from Eastern Europe arrived in the United States in the early 1900s.

Latin America, Asia, or Africa. People from Mexico now make up the largest group of immigrants, followed by people from China and India. As in the past, many new immigrants have come to the United States to seek freedom or to escape poverty, war, or prejudice (PREH•juh•duhs) in their homelands. **Prejudice** is an unfair feeling of hatred or dislike for a group of people because of their background, race, or religion.

REVIEW What does it mean to say that the United States is a nation of immigrants?

Difficult Decisions

Even when life was hard in their old countries, most immigrants still had to make difficult decisions before coming to the United States. Should they stay in their home countries, where things are known? Or should they leave for a new life in an unknown land?

Rafael Muciño and his mother and brother faced such questions before they decided to leave Mexico, about 10 years ago. They could have stayed in the small town of Guanajuato (gwah•nah•WAH•toh), Mexico, with their friends and relatives. But life there was hard, without much hope of getting better. Even though Rafael was only 13 years old, he had to work to help the family earn enough money. He recalls,

> 66 It was a struggle to keep up my education. I wanted a good career, but it was hard for me to see the way ahead. 99

In hopes of making a better life for themselves, Rafael's family decided to move to the United States. They settled in Ohio, where Rafael and his brother went to school. Today Rafael is married and lives in Virginia. There he teaches Spanish and mathematics. Rafael feels his family made the right decision about coming to the United States. "It was difficult but worth it," he says. "I have a good future, and I am also able to help students find a good future for themselves. That is what makes me feel successful."

REVIEW What difficult decision do all immigrants sometimes have to make?

CAUSE AND EFFECT

Rafael Muciño (left) with his brother, Salvador, and his mother, Marta

---

Analyze Tables   This table shows the top five countries of origin of immigrants to the United States in a recent year.

◆ From which two countries did about the same number of immigrants come?

United States Immigrants, by Country of Birth

COUNTRY	NUMBER OF PEOPLE
Mexico	131,575
China	36,884
India	36,482
Philippines	34,466
Dominican Republic	20,387

Yo-Yo Ma   1955–

Character Trait: Self-Discipline

World-famous cellist Yo-Yo Ma was born in France, to Chinese parents. The family later moved to the United States, where Ma became a citizen. Yo-Yo Ma began playing the cello when he was four years old. The cello was taller than he was! To master his instrument, Ma needed self-discipline. He practiced many hours every day and still does so. Partly because Ma was raised in different cultures, he likes to play all kinds of music. Yo-Yo Ma wants people of all backgrounds "to come to concerts and be excited by the music they hear."

GO ONLINE

MULTIMEDIA BIOGRAPHIES
Visit The Learning Site at www.harcourtschool.com to learn about other famous people.

Special Ways

When people leave one country to settle in another, they often bring their customs and cultures with them. Some immigrants still speak the languages of the countries in which they were born. Some continue to wear clothing in the style of their homeland, to eat the same kinds of foods, and to listen to the same music.

In fact, many of the things Americans use each day first came from other places. These include some of the foods we eat. Spanish explorers brought the first oranges and grapes to the Americas. The English came here carrying bags of apple seeds, while Italian immigrants brought spaghetti. People from Mexico gave us tacos, and Chinese immigrants introduced us to egg rolls.

Many American holidays and customs came from other places, too. Do you trick people on April Fool's Day? English settlers brought this custom to North America. Do you color eggs at Easter? Immigrants from Ukraine, Russia, and Poland gave us this custom. Other holidays that came from other places include Chinese New Year, Cinco de Mayo, Mardi Gras, and St. Patrick's Day.

People from other places also brought new kinds of music, dance, and art to the United States. For example, banjos first came from West Africa and were later used in country and bluegrass music. Even the languages we speak are from other cultures and countries. Most

Many of the foods eaten in the United States have come from different cultures.

The National Puerto Rican Day parade takes place in New York City each June.

people in the United States speak English, but many of the words we use have come from other languages.

Have you ever noticed the words *E Pluribus Unum* on United States coins? This saying is Latin for "out of many, one." It has been our nation's motto for more than 200 years. A **motto** is a saying chosen to express the ideals of a nation, state, or group. "Out of many, one" helps define the American people and our country as a whole. The motto reminds us that, although the people of the United States come from many different places and cultures, we still live together as one people. Having many cultures mixed together means that Americans can enjoy richer lives. It also helps explain why people in the United States seem so different yet so alike in many ways.

REVIEW What kinds of things have immigrants brought to the United States?

LESSON 1 REVIEW

 CAUSE AND EFFECT What situations have caused many people to immigrate to the United States over the years?

1. **BIG IDEA** Why are there so many different ways of life in the United States?

2. **VOCABULARY** Name a synonym and an antonym for the term **poverty**.

3. **GEOGRAPHY** Which are the two fastest-growing states in the United States today?

4. **CULTURE** What holidays that came from other places are celebrated in the United States?

5. **CRITICAL THINKING—Apply** What hopes do you think immigrants today share with immigrants of the past?

 PERFORMANCE—Make a Collage Look in magazines for pictures of holidays, foods, and customs that have come to the United States from other countries. Use the pictures to make a collage. In a presentation explain the origins of the holidays, foods, and customs shown.

Read a Population Map

VOCABULARY

population density

▶ WHY IT MATTERS

Perhaps you live in a large city or in a suburb. Perhaps you live in a small town or rural area, where there are not many people. The world's population is not spread out evenly on Earth.

To understand how the population of a place is spread out, you can study a population map. Knowing how to read a population map can help you find out where most people live in a region, a country, or the world. Since a population map often shows how crowded a place is, it can also tell you something about what life is like there.

▶ WHAT YOU NEED TO KNOW

The map on page 445 is a population map of the United States. It uses colors to show population density (DEN•suh•tee). **Population density** tells how many people live in an area of a certain size. On this population map, the size is 1 square mile or 1 square kilometer.

To find the population density of a certain place, look to see which color covers that place on the map. Then find that color in the map key. It will tell you how many people per square mile or square kilometer live there. For example, the area around Charlotte, North Carolina, is brown. This means that there are between 50 and 250 people per square mile in the Charlotte area.

Cities such as New York City (below) are crowded with people. Few people live in the rural areas of Virginia (left).

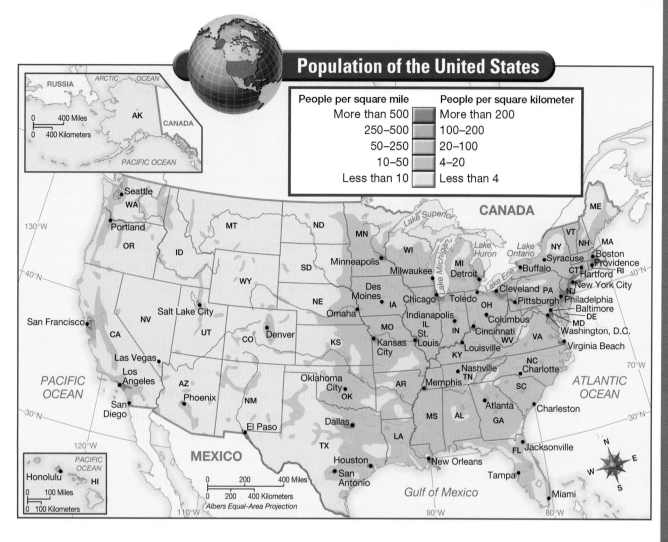

Population of the United States

People per square mile
- More than 500
- 250–500
- 50–250
- 10–50
- Less than 10

People per square kilometer
- More than 200
- 100–200
- 20–100
- 4–20
- Less than 4

▶ PRACTICE THE SKILL

Use the population density map on this page to answer these questions.

1 Which color on the map stands for the areas that are the most crowded? the least crowded?

2 If an area of the map is colored green, what is the population density there?

3 Which area of the country is the most crowded?

4 Do more people live along the Atlantic Coast or the Pacific Coast?

5 Why do you think many of the coastal cities on the map are colored red?

▶ APPLY WHAT YOU LEARNED

Use an encyclopedia or an atlas to find a population map of your state. What is the population density of the place where you live? Which parts of your state are the most and least crowded? Write a paragraph explaining how these different population densities may affect the way people live in those areas of your state. Then share your paragraph with your classmates.

Practice your map and globe skills with the **GeoSkills CD-ROM**.

2

CAUSE AND EFFECT

As you read, look for ways in which government and belief in freedom affect the ways that Americans live.

BIG IDEA

Sharing a way of life helps unite people living in the United States.

VOCABULARY

patriotism
monument
democracy
majority rule

FAST FACT

Little League baseball started in Pennsylvania in 1939 with three teams. Today about 3 million children in countries all around the world play in its leagues.

A United Country

What is an American? Ask a hundred people, and you will get a hundred different answers. That is because Americans are different from one another in so many ways—whether we were born here or came from far away. Sometimes we speak different languages and eat different foods. We often have different customs. Yet in many important ways, Americans also have much in common.

Americans Share Things

Americans share a way of life. We learn about one another from television, newspapers, magazines, and the Internet. We go to school together. We go to many of the same movies. We like certain sports. All of these things help bring us together as a people.

Americans are united when they rise together before a baseball game to sing the national anthem. Americans feel pride and **patriotism** (PAY•tree•uh•tih•zuhm), or love of country,

Members of this Little League baseball team celebrate their victory with their coach.

Veterans Day

Veterans Day is a holiday that honors all veterans, or people who have served in the armed forces, in the United States. On November 11, Americans celebrate this holiday with parades and speeches. Each Veterans Day, the President leads a ceremony at the Tomb of the Unknowns at Arlington National Cemetery in Virginia. The tomb holds the remains of unidentified soldiers killed in World War I, World War II, and the Korean War, but it honors all the men and women who have given their lives in our country's wars.

when they salute the flag as it passes by in a parade. They promise to be loyal to the United States when they say the Pledge of Allegiance.

Americans also share their country's history, or past. One Russian immigrant remembered how reading about the history of the United States made him feel a part of America. He said,

> ❝As I read . . . it dawned on me gradually what was meant by *my country*. The people all desiring noble things and striving for them together.❞

One way that people remember their country's history is to celebrate its holidays. One of the most important holidays in the United States is Independence Day, or the Fourth of July. On that date in 1776, the 13 American colonies declared their independence from British rule.

Although Independence Day was celebrated for many years after 1776, it was

not made an official holiday until 1941. Today millions of Americans get together each July 4 to celebrate this holiday.

Analyze Tables Most government holidays are observed throughout the country.

◆ Which holiday is observed on the first Monday in September?

United States Government Holidays

HOLIDAY	OBSERVED
New Year's Day	January 1
Martin Luther King, Jr., Day	third Monday in January
Presidents' Day	third Monday in February
Memorial Day	last Monday in May
Independence Day	July 4
Labor Day	first Monday in September
Columbus Day	second Monday in October
Veterans Day	November 11
Thanksgiving	fourth Thursday in November
Christmas	December 25

This citizen is casting her vote on a computer. Why is voting important in a democracy?

Sharing Certain Beliefs

Americans share many beliefs, and a deep belief in freedom is one of the most important to them. Americans believe in freedom of religion, freedom to work, freedom to say what they want, freedom to go where they like, and freedom to meet with other people.

Freedom has always attracted people from other places to the United States. One immigrant told family members who had stayed in Europe, "If you wish to see our whole family living in a country [with] freedom of speech . . . if you wish to be really happy and independent, then come here."

Americans share their government, too. The main job of a government is to make and carry out laws. Laws help people live together in order and safety. They help settle disagreements and unite people.

In the United States our government is a democracy (dih•MAH•kruh•see). A **democracy** is a form of government in which the people rule by making decisions themselves and by electing leaders to make decisions for them. In a democracy people are free to make choices about their lives and their government. They often make their choices by voting.

People also remember their country's history by visiting its monuments. A **monument** is something that is built to remind people of the past. Millions of people visit Mount Rushmore National Memorial in South Dakota every year to remember four Presidents of the United States. Washington, D.C., has many important monuments, such as the Vietnam Veterans Memorial, that honor Americans and historic events. When people visit the Statue of Liberty National Monument in New York Harbor, they remember that the United States offers freedom to people all over the world.

REVIEW What are some ways people remember their country's history?

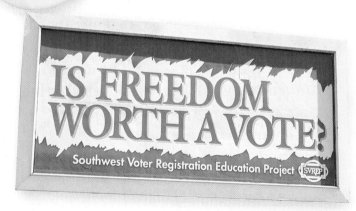

IS FREEDOM WORTH A VOTE?
Southwest Voter Registration Education Project SVREP

What do you usually do when you and your friends cannot decide which of two games to play? You most likely vote. You and your friends agree to play the game that gets the most votes, or the majority. This way of deciding is called **majority rule**. Democracy is based on majority rule. In the United States each citizen over 18 gets one vote. Majority rule is a way to make choices that most people agree with and that are fair to most people.

But *all* people in the United States have certain rights—even people who do not agree with the majority. The majority cannot make decisions that take away those rights. For example, all people in this country are free to say what they think about the government. All are free to worship as they please. All have the right to a fair trial. The leaders who helped start our nation designed our government to make sure that these rights would forever be protected.

REVIEW In a democracy, who makes the decisions about the laws for all the people?
CAUSE AND EFFECT

DEMOCRATIC VALUES
Rights of Citizens

Citizens of the United States have many rights. People are automatically citizens of the United States if they were born here or if at least one parent is a citizen of the United States. Many people from other countries also want to become citizens of the United States. To do so, they must meet certain requirements.

First, they must live in the United States for three to five years. Then, they must apply for citizenship and pass a test to show that they understand United States history and government. Finally, they must take part in a ceremony in which they promise to be loyal to the United States. At the same time, they must also give up citizenship in their old countries. In return, they receive all the benefits and freedoms that our government guarantees its citizens.

Analyze the Value

1. Which people are automatically citizens of the United States?
2. What are some requirements for people to become citizens of the United States?
3. **Make It Relevant** Work together with a group to list other requirements that you think people seeking United States citizenship should have to meet.

Sharing Responsibilities

People in the United States enjoy many rights, but they also have many responsibilities, or things they should do. Some responsibilities, such as obeying traffic signs and going to school, are required by law. Other responsibilities are things that good citizens do by choice. These things include voting, learning about the country, working hard, and treating others fairly.

In order for a democracy to work, the government needs active, involved citizens. Many people participate in making our country work by volunteering.

Have you ever seen an Adopt-A-Highway sign? These signs mean that people have promised to keep a certain stretch of road clean. When necessary, the volunteers pick up any litter near the road. Some even plant flowers.

Many people also volunteer in schools, libraries, and museums. Others help sick or elderly people. Habitat for Humanity is a group of volunteers who work together to build homes for needy

More than 1 million volunteers help keep America beautiful through the Adopt-A-Highway program.

families. Recently the group completed a new house for Brenda Ferebee of Brooklyn, New York. "It's not just a house," she says. "It's a home."

Volunteers also help in emergencies. Often these volunteers are professional firefighters,

More than 500,000 volunteers help athletes of all abilities train and compete in the Special Olympics every year.

Exhausted firefighters gather after the attack on the World Trade Center in New York City.

doctors, and nurses who donate their time and talents to help victims of natural disasters such as earthquakes, floods, and fires.

Americans also help one another after other kinds of disasters. On September 11, 2001, enemies of the United States flew planes into the twin towers at the World Trade Center in New York City and into the Pentagon near Washington, D.C. Another plane crashed into a field in Pennsylvania. Thousands of people were killed. Firefighters, police officers, doctors, construction workers,

and other citizens from all over the country donated their time and skills to help these places and the survivors recover from the attacks.

Volunteering and helping one another in times of need can bring people together. Sharing responsibility for the well-being of a community can also bring people together. By working together, Americans can share their different ideas. By sharing their ideas, they can find ways to solve problems.

REVIEW How does sharing responsibilities help unite Americans?

LESSON 2
REVIEW

CAUSE AND EFFECT How do the rights that people have in the United States affect their responsibilities as citizens?

1 **BIG IDEA** What helps unite people living in the United States?

2 **VOCABULARY** What does each word in the term **majority rule** mean?

3 **CIVICS AND GOVERNMENT** How do Americans make decisions about their government?

4 **CRITICAL THINKING—Evaluate** What are some ways you can be a responsible citizen even though you are not old enough to vote?

PERFORMANCE—Plan a Patriotic Celebration Plan a celebration of our rights and freedoms in the United States. With classmates, find patriotic poems, speeches, and music. Choose several poems and speeches to read aloud and some songs to sing. Invite other classes to participate in your celebration.

Determine Points of View

▶ WHY IT MATTERS

Artists and photographers very often have their own feelings about an event or a situation. They use their artwork to share their feelings and beliefs and to express certain points of view. If you learn to look for an artist's point of view, you will have a better idea of why he or she took the photo or painted the picture. Then you may learn more about the picture's meaning.

▶ WHAT YOU NEED TO KNOW

Look at the painting on page 453. American artist Norman Rockwell painted it in 1943. He called the painting *Freedom of Speech*. It illustrates a town meeting in a small New England community. It not only illustrates freedom of speech but also tells how Rockwell felt about that freedom.

To help you determine Rockwell's and other artists' points of view, you can follow these steps.

Step 1 **Think about how the work of art makes you feel. Your own feelings can help you better understand the artist's point of view.**

Step 2 **Study the details to help you understand the artist's point of view. Look at colors, faces, clothing, actions, and background.**

Step 3 **Decide what point of view the artist wants to show you. Think about all the details together.**

Step 4 **Think about how the work of art shows the artist's point of view.**

Have you ever visited an art museum? How did the works displayed there make you feel?

Norman Rockwell (above) painted *Freedom of Speech* (left) after hearing President Franklin Delano Roosevelt give a speech. In the speech, Roosevelt expressed his hope for the future.

▶ PRACTICE THE SKILL

Use the steps on page 452 to answer these questions about Rockwell's point of view in *Freedom of Speech.*

1 How does the painting make you feel?

2 What do the expressions of the speaker and listeners in the painting tell you?

3 How might your feelings change if someone in the picture were frowning, shouting, or shaking a fist?

4 What does the clothing of the people in the painting tell you about Rockwell's point of view?

5 What point of view do you think Rockwell wanted to express in this painting?

▶ APPLY WHAT YOU LEARNED

Look in books, magazines, or newspapers to find a photograph or painting that gives you strong feelings. Follow the steps on page 452 to describe how the picture makes you feel. What did the artist show to make you feel as you do? What do you think was the artist's point of view? Do you agree with this point of view? Why or why not? Share the picture and your feelings about it with your classmates.

Focus Skill

CAUSE AND EFFECT

As you read, look for the effects that the economy of the United States has on peoples' opportunities.

BIG IDEA

Learn about the economy of the United States and how it works.

VOCABULARY

human resource
capital resource
factors of production
profit
interest
wholesale trade
retail trade
global economy

The United States Economy

People in the United States share many beliefs, rights, and responsibilities. We are also united in another way—by our nation's economy. The free enterprise economy of the United States affects the lives of all Americans, and it offers us many economic opportunities and choices. We can decide what products to buy, what services to use, where we want to work, what kind of jobs we can try to get, and what kinds of businesses we may start.

A Free Enterprise Economy

Because the United States has a free enterprise economy, people can decide for themselves what kinds of businesses to operate. For the most part, they can run their businesses the way they want. The government does not tell them what goods to produce or what services to offer.

However, the government does control certain business practices. For example, it requires businesses to limit pollution and to provide safe environments for workers. There are laws that limit the number of hours people can work each day, too.

People in the United States, such as this butcher, have opportunities to earn their living in many ways.

This young person saw a demand for walking the dogs in her neighborhood. She started a dog-walking business to supply the service people wanted.

Do you need someone to walk your dog? Call Robin at 865-555-3297

Other laws set a minimum wage, or the least amount of money that workers can earn per hour. Our government also has laws about products in order to help protect consumers.

To produce any good or provide any service, a business needs three different kinds of resources. It must have workers, or **human resources**. It must have natural resources, such as water, minerals, and fuel. It must also have capital resources. **Capital resources** are the money, buildings, machines, and tools needed to run a business. Together, these human, natural, and capital resources are called the **factors of production**. A person must think about each of the factors of production before starting a business.

The goal of most businesses is to make a **profit**, or the money a business earns after everything is paid for. In order to make a profit, a business owner must decide how many goods to produce or services to offer and how much to charge for them.

If the demand for a good or service is high and the supply is low, prices generally rise. For example, if there are only a few copies of a popular computer game, the price of that game is likely to rise. If the demand falls or the supply is greater than the demand, then the price generally falls.

If a computer game costs $1,000, very few people will be willing to buy it, because the price is too high. The manufacturer may stop producing the game or even go out of business. Or the manufacturer might decide to lower the price of the game. If the price is lowered to $50, more people will be able to buy it. Demand for the product will rise, and the company will produce more of it. If this high demand continues, the supply may become lower. So, once again, prices may rise.

REVIEW What kinds of resources does a business need in order to provide a product or service? CAUSE AND EFFECT

This bank teller is providing a service by helping the customer deposit money in her bank account.

A Changing Economy

The economy of the United States is changing all the time. Early in our country's history, agriculture was the leading economic activity. Then, during the late 1800s, manufacturing began to replace farming as the leading industry. By the beginning of the 1900s, the United States was the world's leading manufacturing country. It remains so today.

However, service industries now make up the largest part of our nation's economy. In fact, about one-third of all workers here have service jobs. They may be doctors, lawyers, or teachers. Or they may work in restaurants or repair cars. If workers in government, stores, and other kinds of service industries are included, then about four out of every five workers have service jobs.

People who work in banks are part of the nation's financial service industries. Workers in financial industries are concerned with lending, handling, and collecting money. Banks, for example, pay interest to people who put money into them. **Interest** is the money a bank or borrower pays for the use of money. In turn, the banks lend that money to other people and charge interest on the money borrowed. People often put money in banks to save for an important purchase, such as a house or a car, or to pay for college in the future.

A Savings Account Statement

Analyze Primary Sources

A person who has a savings account in a bank, usually receives a statement every month.

❶ The beginning balance is the amount of money that was in the account at the beginning of the month.

❷ Deposits are the amounts of money that were put into the bank.

❸ The statement shows the total amount of interest earned that month.

❹ Withdrawals are the amounts of money that were taken out of the bank.

❺ The ending balance is the amount of money in the account at the end of the month.

BANK
MARYLAND
STATEMENT PERIOD
4/09/99 – 5/06/99

PAGE 1 OF 1
3160278648
0 ENCLOSURES

E CROLAND
4243 MILL
ROAD
BALTIMORE, MD 21202

YOUR MONEY MARKET SAVINGS ACCOUNT 3160278648

BEGINNING BALANCE	DEPOSITS AND OTHER ADDITIONS	INTEREST PAID	CHECKS	WITHDRAWALS AND OTHER DEDUCTIONS	TAXPAYER ID # 522-9339
3,897.16	558.00	9.98	295.72	75.00	5/06/99 BALANCE 4,094.42

DEPOSITS AND OTHER ADDITIONS

	AMOUNT
	558.00
TOTAL	558.00

DATE	EXPLANATION
5/04	DEPOSIT

❖ Why do you think it is important for people to understand a bank statement?

The Internet

The Internet is a communication system that links computers around the world. The United States government set up the Internet in 1968 for military communications. In 1972 electronic mail was introduced, and 20 years later the World Wide Web came into use. Today millions of Americans "go online," or connect to the Internet and the World Wide Web through phone or cable lines. They can send messages, search distant libraries, listen to music, shop, and do much more on the Internet.

Another large service industry in the United States today is trade. There are two main categories of trade industries—wholesale trade and retail trade. **Wholesale trade** is made up of businesses that buy large amounts of goods from producers and then sell them to other businesses. For example, a company may buy huge crops of apples and then sell them to grocery stores all over the country. **Retail trade** is made up of businesses that buy goods and sell them directly to consumers. Bookstores and supermarkets are just two examples of retail businesses in the United States.

Many economic experts call the time in which we live the "Information Age." More information is available today than ever before, and more technology is available to help people organize, share, and use information. People receive and send information through television, videos, radios, movies, telephones, fax machines, and the Internet. As a result, thousands of people in the United States have jobs producing and using these forms of communication and information-processing technology.

REVIEW How has our nation's economy changed since the 1800s?

Analyze Graphs This pictograph shows the income provided in a recent year by major industries in the United States.

❖ About how much income do wholesale and retail trade industries provide each year?

United States Economy

INDUSTRY	INCOME
Agriculture, forestry, fishing, and mining	$ $
Manufacturing and construction	$ $ $ $ $ $ $ $ $ $ $ $ $ $ $ $
Wholesale and retail trade	$ $ $ $ $ $ $ $ $ $ $
Finance, insurance, and real estate	$ $ $ $ $ $ $ $ $ $ $ $ $ $
Government	$ $ $ $ $ $ $ $ $ $
Transportation and public utilities	$ $ $ $ $ $
Other service industries	$ $
$ = $100 billion	

A Global Economy

Advances in technology have helped the United States take part in the global economy. The **global economy** is the world market in which companies from different countries buy and sell goods and services.

Just as different regions of the United States depend on one another for goods and services, different regions of the world are interdependent, too. All around the world, countries exchange their raw materials, finished products, and services.

American crops, such as wheat, corn, and soybeans, are exported to markets all over the world. So are manufactured goods such as computers, chemicals, and automobiles. At the same time, the United States imports many goods from other countries. For example, many electronic products and clothing items come from Japan and Taiwan.

Our nation's automobile industry is a good example of global interdependence. Automobile manufacturers need many different materials to produce a car. These materials come from different regions of

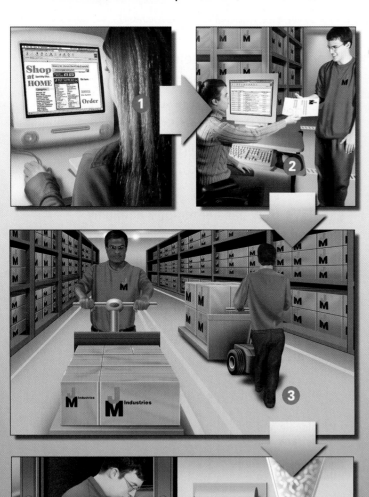

A CLOSER LOOK
E-Commerce

Many people today do their shopping by computer. Doing business this way is called *e-commerce*, which is short for *electronic commerce*.

❶ Using a computer at home, a consumer places an order for a product on a company's Web site on the Internet.

❷ Computer operators at the business site record the order and send it to the computers at their company's warehouse.

❸ Warehouse workers print the order, locate the items ordered, pack them, and send them to the company's shipping department.

❹ Consumers' orders are shipped from the warehouse on a daily schedule.

❺ The mail service or a company driver delivers the product to the consumer who ordered it.

◈ Where are the ordered items packed for shipment?

Analyze Graphs The United States trades almost $2,000 billion in goods and services each year with countries around the world.

❖ Which country is our nation's top trading partner in both exports and imports?

Leading United States Trading Partners

Trade (in billions of dollars)

Canada China Germany Japan Mexico
Country

■ U.S. exports to
■ U.S. imports from

the United States as well as from other countries. Steel to build the cars' frames may come from the Great Lakes states, from Appalachia, or from South Korea. Glass for the windows may be made in California or Mexico. Electronic parts may come from Japan. Leather for the seats may be shipped from South American countries. Once these materials reach factories in the United States, workers put them together to build complete cars that will be sold all over the world.

Today the United States' most important international trading partners are Canada, Mexico, Japan, China, and Germany. Our nation depends on these and other countries in many ways. For example, many companies from other countries have built factories in the

United States. In fact, people in other countries own more than 12,000 businesses in the United States. These businesses create thousands of jobs for American workers.

REVIEW What does it mean for a country to be part of the global economy?

LESSON 3
REVIEW

CAUSE AND EFFECT How do supply and demand affect prices?

❶ **BIG IDEA** What kind of economy does the United States have, and how does it work?

❷ **VOCABULARY** Compare and contrast the meanings of **wholesale trade** and **retail trade**.

❸ **CIVICS AND GOVERNMENT** In what ways does our government control businesses?

❹ **ECONOMICS** How does the United States economy depend on other countries?

❺ **CRITICAL THINKING—Apply** What part do you and your family play in the economy of the United States?

❻ **CRITICAL THINKING—Hypothesize** Imagine that computers and the Internet had not been invented. How do you think the economy of the United States would be different today?

 PERFORMANCE—Conduct a Survey Work with a group of classmates to conduct a consumer survey of your school. Ask students how they spent money in the past week—what products or services they bought. Organize into categories the information you collect, and share your findings with the class.

Make Economic Choices

▶ WHY IT MATTERS

You make economic choices every day. Whenever you eat in a restaurant, buy something in a supermarket, or go to the dentist, you are a consumer.

Some economic choices, such as which flavor of ice cream to buy, are easy to make. Others, such as choosing a doctor or deciding which computer to buy, are more difficult. Like most consumers, you may not have enough money to buy everything you want at exactly the moment you want it.

To buy one thing, you may have to give up the chance to buy something else.

Giving up one thing to get another is called a **trade-off**. For example, you may choose to give up buying a new game in order to have enough money to buy a gift for someone. What you give up in order to get something else is called the **opportunity cost**. Giving up something does not mean that it has no value. It means that, at the time, something else has more value to you.

Knowing about trade-offs and opportunity costs can help you make thoughtful economic decisions. It will help you be a more careful consumer and will help you spend your money wisely.

Every time you buy something in a store, you are making an economic choice.

WHAT YOU NEED TO KNOW

Making wise economic choices requires some special thought and information. Here are some steps that can help you make those choices.

Step 1 Identify what you want to buy.

Step 2 Figure out how much money you have right now and how much you can spend on the product you want.

Step 3 Think about trade-offs and opportunity costs. Decide whether you want the product enough to give up buying something else.

PRACTICE THE SKILL

Imagine that you just earned $25 for doing chores for a neighbor. You want to buy a new flashlight for your camping trip next week. However, you also want to buy a T-shirt you saw at the mall. You have to make an economic choice. Use the steps above to decide.

1 What do you want to buy?

2 How much money do you have for the items?

3 How much does each product you want to buy cost? Do you have enough money to buy both items?

4 What are the advantages of buying either the flashlight or the T-shirt?

5 What would be the opportunity cost of each of your economic decisions?

6 Which product will you buy? Why did you make this economic choice?

APPLY WHAT YOU LEARNED

Suppose you are the mayor of your city or town. You have to decide whether to spend money to build a bike path or to build a basketball court in the park. The city does not have enough money to pay for both projects. Explain to a partner the trade-offs and opportunity costs of your choices. What economic choice would you make?

CITIZENSHIP SKILLS

13 Review and Test Preparation

Cause and Effect

Copy the following graphic organizer onto a separate sheet of paper. Use the information you have learned to show that you understand the causes and effects of important facts about the United States today.

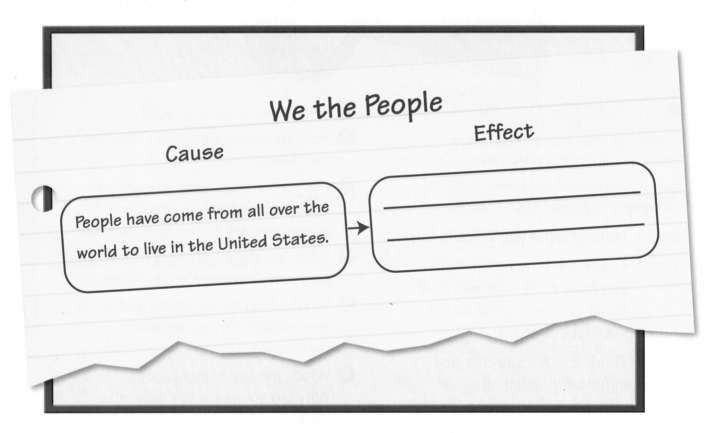

We the People

Cause

Effect

People have come from all over the world to live in the United States.

THINK & WRITE

Explain Differences   Suppose a visitor asked you to explain why there are so many different customs and ways of life in the United States. Write a paragraph or two to explain why there are differences. Tell how those differences affect your life.

Write a Letter   Imagine that you are an immigrant who has recently come to live in the United States. Write a letter to a friend in your old country. Describe the many things Americans share. Be sure to tell about rights and responsibilities.

Use Vocabulary

Choose the term that matches each definition.

prejudice (p. 441)

patriotism (p. 446)

monument (p. 448)

democracy (p. 448)

majority rule (p. 449)

profit (p. 455)

interest (p. 456)

1 In the United States our government is a ____.

2 ____ is an unfair feeling of hatred or dislike for a group of people because of their background, race, or religion.

3 A ____ is the money a business earns after everything is paid for.

4 Love of country is called ____.

5 A ____ is something that is built to remind people of the past.

6 When decisions are made by voting, people follow ____.

Recall Facts

Answer these questions.

7 Most people came to North America by choice. Which group did not?

8 What is the government's main job?

9 In what ways is our nation's automobile industry a good example of global interdependence?

Write the letter of the best choice.

10 Why do most immigrants come to the United States?
- **A** to buy products at lower prices
- **B** to work as farmers
- **C** to make difficult decisions
- **D** to make better lives for themselves

11 Which of the following is **not** a responsibility of citizenship in the United States?
- **F** opening a business
- **G** learning about the country
- **H** voting in elections
- **J** obeying laws

12 An example of a financial service industry is—
- **A** a farm.
- **B** a factory.
- **C** a bank.
- **D** a mine.

Think Critically

13 Is majority rule always the best way to decide things? Explain your answer.

14 If you were going to open a business in your community, what product or service would you supply? What demand would it meet?

Apply Skills

Read a Population Map

15 Look at the population map on page 445. How does the population density vary in Maine?

Determine Points of View

16 Find a painting or photograph that you like in this book. Tell what it shows, and describe the artist's point of view.

Make Economic Choices

17 Imagine that you have $5 to spend. You want to buy a magazine, but you also want to rent a movie. You do not have enough money for both. How would you make this economic choice?

THE UNITED STATES HOUSE OF REPRESENTATIVES, WASHINGTON, D.C.

Our national government is based in Washington, D.C. The members of Congress, who make the laws for the nation, work there in the Capitol building. The two parts of Congress usually meet in separate groups. Sometimes they meet in a joint session, mainly to hear an address by the President or a foreign official. Here, Congress gathers to hear President George W. Bush speak.

LOCATE IT

Washington, D.C.

IN GOD WE T

Our Country's Government

" No man is good enough
to govern another man
without that other's
consent. "

—Abraham Lincoln, 1854, Peoria, Illinois

 **Point of View**

When you determine **point of view**, you try
to figure out what feeling or opinion a person
expresses about an event, a person, a place,
or a situation.

As you read this chapter, be sure to do the following.
- **Identify things people say, write, paint, or
  photograph.**
- **List details, such as word choices, faces,
  backgrounds, and colors.**
- **Use that information to determine each person's
  point of view about the subject.**

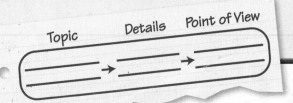

Topic   Details   Point of View

POINT OF VIEW
As you read, think about ways in which the United States government unites the people in the 50 states.

BIG IDEA
As United States citizens we share many important things.

VOCABULARY
federal
Constitution
republic
legislative branch
executive branch
judicial branch
checks and balances
veto

A Plan of Government

Our nation's early leaders believed in self-government. That is, they wanted the people of the United States to govern themselves. In the Declaration of Independence, Thomas Jefferson explained that "Governments are instituted among Men, deriving their just Powers from the Consent of the Governed." Jefferson meant that a government gets its power from the people. This is the basic idea that unites all Americans under one national, or **federal**, government.

A Written Plan of Unity

The early leaders of the United States had to figure out a plan for a federal government that would unite the states as one nation. In 1787, fifty-five representatives gathered in Philadelphia to decide how the government should work.

This painting shows the representatives of the United States who wrote the Constitution.

The United States Constitution has 4,400 words. It is the oldest and the shortest written constitution of any government in the world.

Among them were several of the same leaders who had met 11 years earlier to write the Declaration of Independence, including George Washington and Benjamin Franklin. After months of heated debates, the leaders came up with a plan for our country's federal government—the United States **Constitution**.

The Constitution makes the United States a **republic**, a form of government in which the people elect representatives to govern the country. The Constitution also describes the rights that people in the United States have. Everyone must obey the Constitution—leaders and citizens alike. As the Constitution states, it is the "supreme law of the land."

The Constitution explains how our government works, too. It sets up three branches, or parts, of the federal government. Each branch of government has a separate job to do. Each branch is just as important as the other two.

REVIEW What document is the plan for our federal government?

• HERITAGE •

The National Archives

The Declaration of Independence and the Constitution are important parts of our nation's heritage. Both documents are held at the National Archives (AR•kyvz) Building in Washington, D.C. Created in 1934, the National Archives preserves the most valuable records of the United States government. For safety, the Constitution and the Declaration of Independence are sealed in heavy, airtight cases.

The Legislative Branch

One branch of government is the legislative (LEH•juhs•lay•tiv) branch. The main job of the **legislative branch** of government is to make laws. In the federal government this branch is called Congress. Congress meets in the Capitol building in Washington, D.C. There, members of Congress make laws for the whole nation.

Congress is made up of two parts. One part is the Senate, which is made up of 100 senators. Each state's voters elect two senators to represent them in the Senate.

The other part of Congress is the House of Representatives, sometimes called the House for short. Like senators, members of the House are elected by the voters in each state. However, the number of representatives a state elects depends on how many people live there. States with large populations, such as California and Texas, have the most representatives.

The Presidential Seal

Analyze Primary Sources

All important documents signed by the President are stamped with the Presidential Seal.

1 Our nation's motto, *E Pluribus Unum,* means "Out of many, one."

2 The bald eagle, a bird known for its strength and freedom, is a symbol of the United States.

3 In one claw the eagle holds an olive branch—a symbol of peace.

4 In the other claw the eagle holds arrows to show that the United States wants peace but is willing to fight if necessary.

◈ What do you think the stars that circle the eagle represent?

Congress makes laws that touch the lives of all Americans. A member of Congress once said that the United States is "a government of the people" and that "Congress is the people." He was saying how important the legislative branch is in a representative democracy.

REVIEW What is the main job of the legislative branch of the federal government?

POINT OF VIEW

The Executive Branch

The second branch of the federal government is called the executive (ig•ZEH•kyuh•tiv) branch. The main job of the **executive branch** is to see that the laws passed by Congress are carried out. The executive branch often suggests laws to Congress as well.

In the federal government, the head of the executive branch is the President. The President oversees the day-to-day business of the federal government and directs the workers who run it. Voters elect a President every four years.

The Constitution is very specific about the President's powers. It even gives the exact oath the President must swear before taking office. In the oath, the President pledges to

> **66** preserve, protect, and defend the Constitution of the United States. **99**

The President has one of the most important and difficult jobs in the world. The President deals with other countries on behalf of the United States. The President is also the leader of the United States military.

REVIEW What is the main job of the executive branch of the federal government?

A CLOSER LOOK
Washington, D.C.

Washington, D.C., has many of our nation's important museums, monuments, and government buildings. Many are on or near the National Mall, an area which serves as the nation's "town common."

1. The members of Congress meet and vote on laws at the U.S. Capitol building.
2. The President lives and works in the White House.
3. The Smithsonian Institution runs many museums and educational programs.
4. The Washington Monument honors George Washington, our nation's first President.
5. The Jefferson Memorial honors Thomas Jefferson, the third U.S. President and an author of the Declaration of Independence.
6. The Lincoln Memorial honors Abraham Lincoln, who was President during the Civil War.

? Why do you think there are so many important buildings on and near the National Mall?

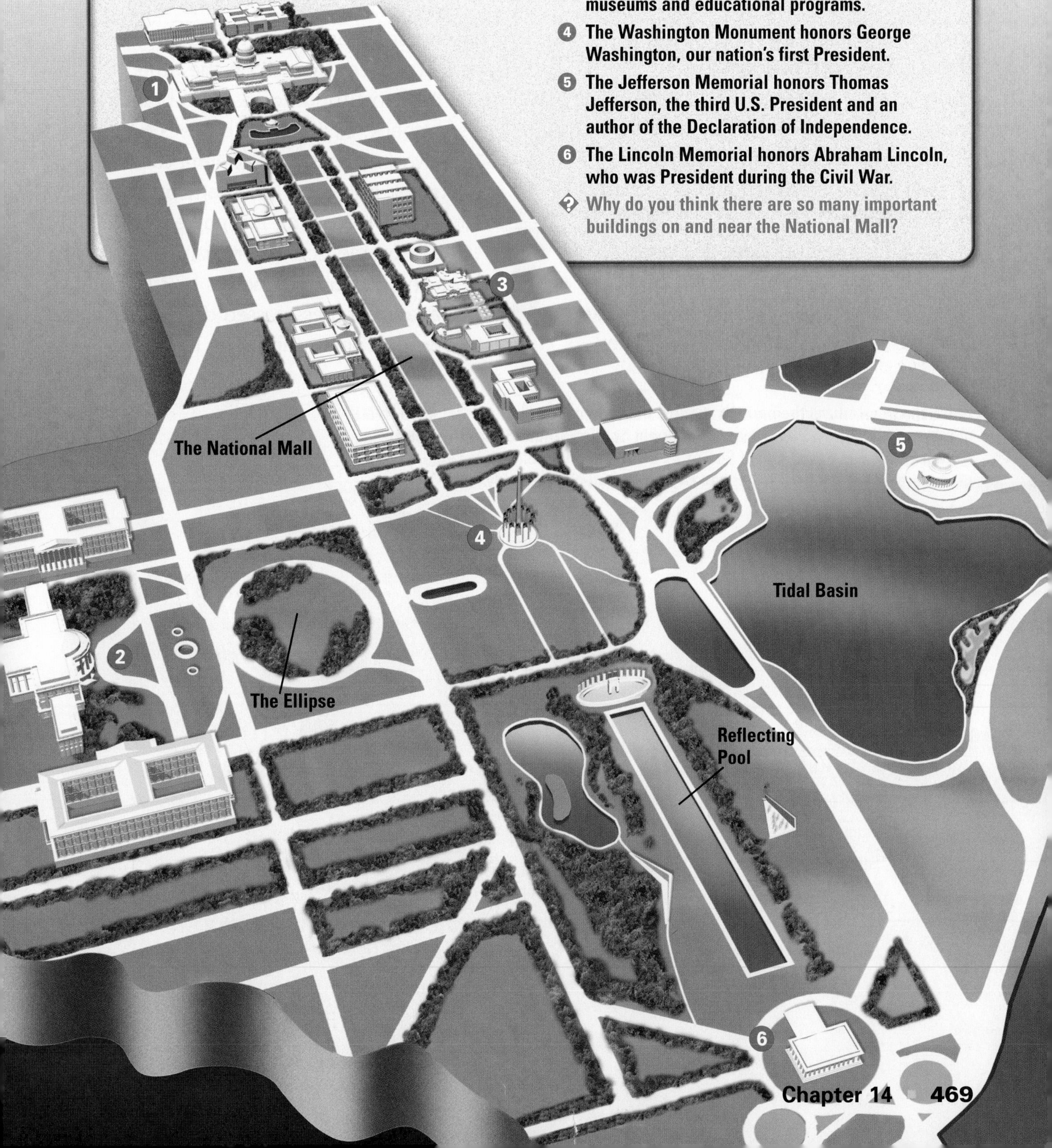

1
2
3
4
5
6
The National Mall
The Ellipse
Tidal Basin
Reflecting Pool

The Judicial Branch

The judicial (ju•DIH•shuhl) branch is the third branch of the national government. The main job of the judicial branch is to see that laws are carried out fairly.

The judicial branch is made up of all the federal courts. It includes the most important court in the country—the Supreme Court. Nine judges, called justices, serve on the Supreme Court for life. They are chosen by the President and approved by the Senate.

The Supreme Court decides cases about the rights and freedoms of all citizens. In these cases the justices make sure that the Constitution is followed. They must decide if laws passed by Congress or the states and actions taken by the President agree with the Constitution.

REVIEW What is the main job of the judicial branch of the federal government?

Working Together

The three branches of the federal government work together. At the same time, each branch keeps watch on the other two. The Constitution gives each branch ways to check, or limit, the power of the other two branches. This system, called checks and balances, keeps any one branch from becoming too powerful.

The Supreme Court, for example, can check the power of Congress by ruling that a law Congress passed does not follow the Constitution. The President

The Supreme Court is the nation's highest court. It makes the final decision in all matters of law. Shown below are ❶ Antonin Scalia ❷ Ruth Bader Ginsburg ❸ John Paul Stevens ❹ David Souter ❺ William Rehnquist ❻ Clarence Thomas ❼ Sandra Day O'Connor ❽ Stephen Breyer ❾ Anthony Kennedy.

Branches of the United States Government

LEGISLATIVE BRANCH	EXECUTIVE BRANCH	JUDICIAL BRANCH
• Makes laws for the country • Prints and coins money • Oversees the United States Postal Service	• Carries out laws • Meets with leaders of other countries • Leads the military	• Makes sure laws follow the Constitution • Decides court cases about the rights and freedoms of all citizens

Analyze Charts **This chart shows the three branches of the United States government and some of the main powers of each branch.**

◆ **Which branch of the federal government leads the military?**

can **veto**, or reject, a law Congress proposes. In turn, Congress can check both the President and the Supreme Court. By a majority vote, Congress can cancel a President's veto. Congress can also reject a person chosen for the Supreme Court.

The federal government helps unite American citizens. It makes laws for everyone to obey. It also sets up common ways of doing things. For example, Congress has the right to print and coin money. That way, Americans can use the same money in every state.

The federal government has many important powers. But another group has just as much power—the voters of the United States. Citizens of the United States have the right to choose their own leaders and to help make decisions about our government and country.

REVIEW **Why is it important for the branches of government to keep a watch on one another?**

LESSON 1
REVIEW

 POINT OF VIEW Look at the painting on page 466. What do you think the artist's point of view was?

1 **BIG IDEA** What are two important things we share as American citizens?

2 **VOCABULARY** What clues can you use to remember the meaning of the term **checks and balances**?

3 **CIVICS AND GOVERNMENT** How is the United States a republic?

4 **CIVICS AND GOVERNMENT** What are the three branches of the federal government?

5 **CRITICAL THINKING—Hypothesize** What do you think would happen if each state made its own money?

 PERFORMANCE—Write a Summary Look in newspapers for articles about the federal government. Select one article, and write a summary of it, explaining how the article illustrates a responsibility of the nation's government. Present your summary to the class.

Benjamin Banneker
Mathematician, Scientist

Born in 1731 in Maryland, Benjamin Banneker was one of the leading scholars of the 1700s. A free African American, he attended a Quaker school. Banneker had a great curiosity to learn about many subjects and taught himself advanced mathematics and astronomy.

 FROM THE MARYLAND HISTORICAL SOCIETY AND THE LIBRARY OF CONGRESS

Benjamin Banneker worked to end slavery. In 1791, he sent a copy of his yearly *Almanac* to Thomas Jefferson and attached a letter, to which Jefferson replied.

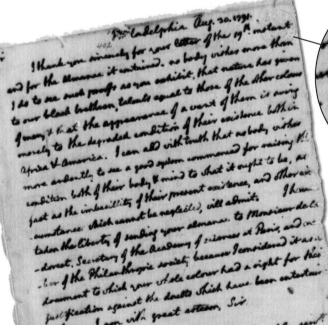

In his letter, Banneker reminded Jefferson, "One Universal Father endowed us all with the same faculties."

Analyze the Primary Source

1 What do you think motivated Benjamin Banneker to learn about many subjects?

2 What role did Banneker play in planning Washington, D.C.?

3 What was in Banneker's *Almanac*?

Benjamin Banneker's
PENNSYLVANIA, DELAWARE, MARY-
LAND, AND VIRGINIA

ALMANAC,

FOR THE

YEAR of our LORD 1795;

Being the Third after Leap-Year.

BANNAKER.

PHILADELPHIA:

Printed for WILLIAM GIBBONS, Cherry Street

Banneker was one of two surveyors whose maps guided the building of Washington, D.C.

The *Almanac* included information about ocean tides, astronomy, and medicinal herbs.

ACTIVITY

Prepare an Interview Imagine you are a reporter for a national newspaper. You are going to interview Benjamin Banneker about his *Almanac*. Write a list of the questions you will ask Banneker. Share your questions with your class.

RESEARCH

Visit The Learning Site at **www.harcourtschool.com** to research other primary sources.

Read a Flow Chart

VOCABULARY

bill
flow chart

▶ WHY IT MATTERS

The United States Constitution outlines how the federal government works. It also explains the steps the government must follow for a bill to become a law. A **bill** is a plan for a new law. You can read the Constitution to learn exactly what must happen for a bill to become a law. However, the steps in this process may be difficult to understand by just reading about them.

Sometimes a process is easier to understand when it is explained in a flow chart. A **flow chart** is a drawing that shows the order in which things happen. The arrows on a flow chart help you read the steps in the correct order.

President George W. Bush signed a bill on May 29, 2001, to build a World War II Memorial in Washington, D.C.

▶ WHAT YOU NEED TO KNOW

The flow chart on page 475 shows how a bill becomes a law in the federal government. To read and understand this and other flow charts, you can follow these steps.

Step 1 Read the flow chart's title. It tells you what process is explained.

Step 2 Trace the direction of the arrows. The arrows show you the order of the steps in the process. Notice the step that comes first, and what must happen before the next step can occur.

Step 3 Read the entire chart, paying close attention to the order of the steps in the process. Notice that sometimes one step can lead to more than one possible outcome.

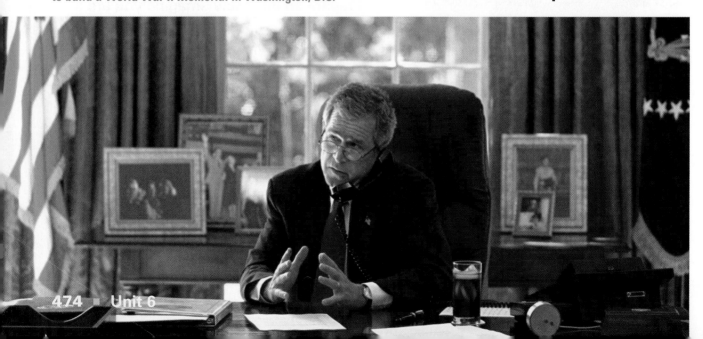

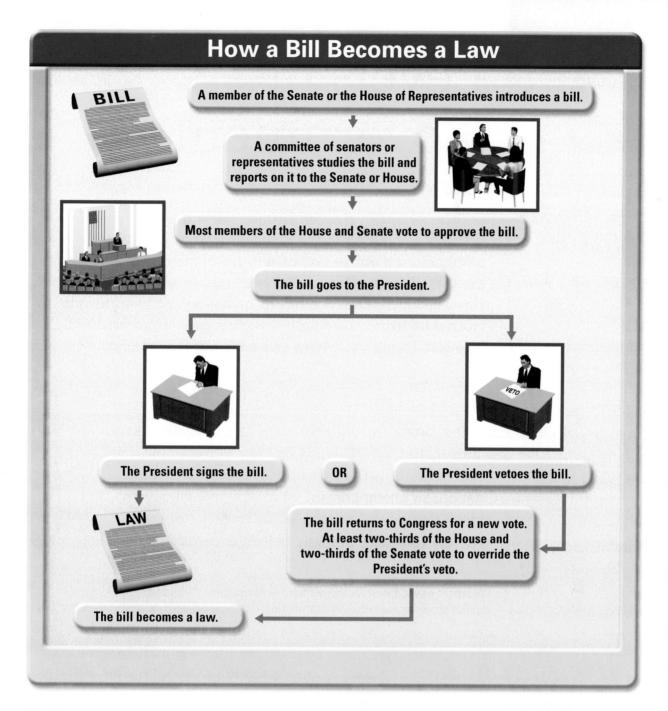

How a Bill Becomes a Law

BILL

A member of the Senate or the House of Representatives introduces a bill.

A committee of senators or representatives studies the bill and reports on it to the Senate or House.

Most members of the House and Senate vote to approve the bill.

The bill goes to the President.

The President signs the bill.   OR   The President vetoes the bill.

LAW

The bill returns to Congress for a new vote. At least two-thirds of the House and two-thirds of the Senate vote to override the President's veto.

The bill becomes a law.

▶ PRACTICE THE SKILL

Use the flow chart above to answer these questions.

1. Who may introduce a bill?

2. What happens before the bill is sent to the President?

3. If the President signs the bill, what happens?

4. How can a bill become a law after the President vetoes it?

▶ APPLY WHAT YOU LEARNED

Work with a partner to make a flow chart that explains to younger students how something works. Write each step on a strip of paper. Then paste the strips in order onto a sheet of posterboard, and connect the steps with arrows. Give your flow chart a title. You may also wish to illustrate each of its steps. Then use the flow chart to teach a group of younger students.

2

Levels of Government

POINT OF VIEW

As you read, look for ways you think each level of the United States government works to solve different kinds of problems.

BIG IDEA

Read to learn about the different levels of government in the United States.

VOCABULARY

state legislature
governor
jury
municipal
city manager
budget

The writers of the Constitution knew that the federal government needed to share responsibilities with states and communities if our system of self-government was to work. In the United States there are three levels of government—federal, state, and local. Each one has its own laws and helps people work together to solve problems. Each level of government, however, handles problems of a different size or kind.

The Federal Government

The federal government takes care of issues and problems that affect the entire country. For example, the United States needs a military to protect the whole nation. So one important job of the federal government is to make sure that all the branches of our military forces are properly trained and equipped.

Navy jet pilots, Coast Guard workers, and rangers in national parks work for the federal government.

POINT CABREW

The federal government has the right to call on these armed forces to protect American citizens when necessary. If there is an emergency, such as a hurricane, an earthquake, or a tornado, the federal government can send the military to help communities recover.

The federal government provides many services, such as printing and coining the money we use and overseeing the country's postal service. It also supports national parks, forests, seashores, historic sites, and wildlife refuges. In addition, the federal government helps people protect and clean up the environment and builds and repairs interstate highways.

The federal government also runs programs that help children, people who are ill, and people who are elderly. Many older people in the United States use a federal program called Medicare to help them pay the costs of health care. Many also depend on the Social Security program. Most people who work pay money into Social Security. Then, when they retire, they receive monthly payments from Social Security.

Delivering the mail (above) is a responsibility of the federal government. The first United States postage stamps (top) were issued in 1847.

To provide these and other services, the federal government has many departments and agencies. For example, the Department of the Treasury prints and coins our money, while the United States Postal Service delivers the nation's mail.

Some Responsibilities of Government

Federal Government
- Print and coin money
- Declare war and make peace
- Oversee trade between states and with other countries
- Oversee the nation's military
- Make immigration laws
- Admit new states

Shared Powers
- Collect money from citizens to pay for government
- Provide for the public health and welfare
- Set up court systems

State Governments
- Set up public schools
- Set up local governments
- Oversee trade within the state
- Set qualifications for voting
- Conduct elections

Analyze Charts This chart shows some responsibilities of the federal and state governments. Both levels of government share certain responsibilities.

❖ Which level of government can set up public schools?

The Department of Transportation makes sure that cars, airplanes, trains, and ships are used safely in the United States. The National Aeronautics and Space Administration conducts space explorations. According to the government, the purpose of the federal Department of Education is "to ensure equal access to education and promote educational excellence for all Americans."

REVIEW What is the job of the federal government?

State Governments

Just like the federal government, state governments provide many services and help people solve many problems. State governments build and manage state highways and state parks. They oversee public schools and state colleges and universities. They also help people in their state who do not have enough money to pay for food, shelter, health care, or other basic needs.

Santa Fe has been the capital of New Mexico since 1610. New Mexico's round capitol building was designed to look like the Indian Sun symbol, or Zia symbol, which also appears on the state flag.

LOCATE IT

Santa Fe

NEW MEXICO

State governments have the same three branches as the federal government does. In state government, the **state legislature** (LEH•juhs•lay•cher) is the legislative branch. The voters in a state elect representatives to their state legislature. These representatives make laws for all the people of the state.

Every state also has a **governor**, who is the head of the state executive branch. This branch sees that all state laws are carried out. State courts, which form the state judicial branch, make sure that state laws are fair. They also settle disputes between people and judge people accused of breaking state laws. In many cases, juries make those decisions. A **jury** is a group of citizens who decide who is right in a dispute or whether a person accused of a crime is guilty. If a person is found guilty, the courts decide how the person will be punished.

REVIEW **What kind of services do you think state governments should provide?**

POINT OF VIEW

Local Governments

Local governments provide services and take care of matters that are important to people in specific communities. They often make decisions about transportation and land use in that community. They provide police and fire protection and sometimes hospitals and clinics. They manage garbage collection and public utilities, such as water and electricity. Local governments also build and repair county and city roads and streets. They run local schools, libraries, museums, and parks, too.

Local governments decide where traffic lights are needed and repair the lights when necessary.

There are two main kinds of local government in the United States—county and **municipal** (myu•NIH•suh•puhl), or city, governments. In their own areas, these local governments make laws and see that those laws are obeyed.

Many counties in the United States are governed by an elected group of people called the board of county commissioners. This group often does the work of both the legislative and executive bra[n]ch of county government. It makes the county and oversees county

Other elected officials in a county may include a sheriff and a supervisor of elections. The sheriff's job is to protect people and make sure laws are obeyed. The supervisor of elections makes sure that all elections are fair.

Cities have various forms of municipal government. Many cities have a council-mayor form. Voters in these cities elect a mayor to head the executive branch and a city council that makes up the legislative branch.

Other cities have a council-manager form of government. In these cities, the city council, and sometimes a mayor, hires a **city manager** to oversee the day-to-day operations of the city government. Larger cities also have their own courts to decide about traffic, parking, and other matters important to the community.

REVIEW **What are the two main kinds of local government in the United States?**

Paying for Government Services

People get many services from local, state, and federal governments. Those services cost money to provide. Government employees, such as police officers, judges, trash collectors, and teachers, must get paid. Taking care of such things as schools, streets, and parks costs money, too.

People pay for government services when they pay taxes. Each level of government collects taxes from citizens. People often pay taxes on the money they earn at their jobs and on the property they own. When they buy things, people may also pay a sales tax. Paying taxes is a responsibility shared by all people in the United States. Citizens must pay taxes in order for the country to run smoothly.

Taxes help pay for many services, such as fire and police protection.

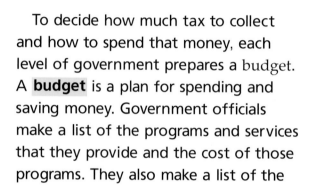

Analyze Primary Sources

The federal government prints about 37 million bills per day. About half of them are $1 bills.

1. Every United States bill has a serial number to keep track of the money that is printed.

2. The $1 bill has a portrait of the first President of the United States, George Washington.

3. The seal of the Department of the Treasury is stamped on each bill.

◆ Why do you think many of the bills printed in the United States are $1 bills?

To decide how much tax to collect and how to spend that money, each level of government prepares a budget. A **budget** is a plan for spending and saving money. Government officials make a list of the programs and services that they provide and the cost of those programs. They also make a list of the amount of money the government expects to receive that year from taxes and other sources. Then the officials decide how the money will be divided among the different programs and services throughout the year.

REVIEW How do governments pay for the services they provide?

LESSON 2
REVIEW

 POINT OF VIEW What point of view do you think the government is expressing when it says that its job is "to ensure equal access to education and to promote educational excellence for all Americans"?

1. **BIG IDEA** What are the levels of government in the United States?

2. **VOCABULARY** Explain why serving on **juries** and paying taxes are responsibilities that all Americans share.

3. **CIVICS AND GOVERNMENT** What are the differences between a mayor, a city council, and a city manager?

4. **ECONOMICS** How are budgets important to each level of government in the United States?

5. **CRITICAL THINKING—Hypothesize** What might happen if a level of government did not take care of its share of responsibilities?

 PERFORMANCE—Write a Letter Think of a problem in your state that you would like to help the governor solve. Write a letter to the governor, explaining the problem and offering possible solutions. Read your letter to the class. Then mail it. When you receive a response, share that as well.

3

POINT OF VIEW
As you read, think of ways in which the rights of United States citizens are an important part of our democracy.

BIG IDEA
United States citizens have many important rights.

VOCABULARY
amendment
general election
candidate
campaign
ballot
petition
civil rights

United States Citizenship

In 1863 President Abraham Lincoln gave one of the most powerful speeches ever given by an American leader. In it, Lincoln said that our nation has a "government of the people, by the people, for the people." Like the writers of the Constitution, President Lincoln knew that a democracy depends on the people's willingness to accept their rights and responsibilities as citizens.

The Bill of Rights

Not long after the first states approved the Constitution, it was changed. Ten **amendments**, or changes, were added to the Constitution to protect people's rights. These ten amendments, called the Bill of Rights, describe freedoms that the government cannot take away. The Bill of Rights also lists actions that the government is not allowed to take.

Because of freedom of the press, people in the United States can learn about what is happening in the country and the rest of the world.

The Bill of Rights states that no citizen of the United States can "be deprived of life, liberty, or property, without due process of law." This means that people have the right to fair treatment under the law. According to the Bill of Rights, people accused of crimes or serious wrongdoings have the right to a fair public trial by a jury. They do not have to speak against themselves in court, and they can have a lawyer speak for them. They cannot be put on trial twice for the same crime or be given "cruel or unusual" punishment. All of these and other rights that are part of due process of law are listed in the Fifth Amendment through the Eighth Amendment to the United States Constitution.

Analyze the Value

❶ What is due process of law?

❷ What kind of trial are citizens guaranteed by the Bill of Rights?

❸ **Make It Relevant** With a partner, discuss why a fair public trial by a jury is important. Share your ideas with the class.

The scales of justice (left), a symbol of the judicial system, stand for fair treatment. In a trial (above), lawyers present the facts of a case to a jury.

The First Amendment is perhaps the best known of the ten amendments. It guarantees the freedoms that are such an important part of our daily lives. The First Amendment states that people in the United States have freedom of religion, freedom of speech, and freedom of the press. It also says that people can hold meetings to discuss problems and share information, and that they can ask the government to hear their complaints.

The Bill of Rights also protects other, equally important rights, such as the right to a fair public trial. It guarantees that the government cannot search people's homes or take their property without a very good reason. The Bill of Rights also says that the federal government can do only those things that are listed in the Constitution. All other rights and powers belong to the states or the people. As extra protection, another amendment says that people have many other rights that are not listed in detail in the Constitution.

REVIEW Why is the Bill of Rights an important part of the Constitution? **POINT OF VIEW**

Voting and Elections

One right that is very important to Americans is the right to vote. In a democracy, the power to rule comes from the people. Citizens of the United States can exercise this power by voting for the people they think will be the best leaders.

Most of these government leaders are elected by voters in a general election. A **general election** is an election in which the voters choose the people who will represent them in government. The people who run for office in an election are called **candidates**. Usually there are two or more candidates for each office. Before an election most candidates carry on **campaigns** to get people to vote for them. During a campaign a candidate sometimes runs advertisements on television and the radio, displays signs, makes speeches, and talks with voters.

So that voters can make a choice on election day, the names of all the candidates running for office are listed on a ballot. A **ballot** is a sheet of paper or some other method that is used to record a vote. All votes are secret, so citizens feel free to choose the candidates they think will best represent them.

In addition to voting, many citizens volunteer to work in political campaigns or even run for office themselves. Citizens can also work for change by writing a petition (puh•TIH•shuhn) describing what they want done. A **petition** is a signed request for action. By signing a petition, people show that they support what it asks for. If enough citizens sign the petition, it will be listed on the ballot and voted on in the next election.

REVIEW **What power are American citizens using when they vote?** 🔵Focus Skill **POINT OF VIEW**

State representatives select candidates for national elections.

Dr. Martin Luther King, Jr., addressed a huge crowd of civil rights supporters during the 1963 march in Washington, D.C.

The Civil Rights Movement

The right to vote is just one of the many rights guaranteed to citizens of the United States. However, some groups of people in the United States did not always share in those rights. For many years, African Americans, Asian Americans, Hispanic Americans, Native Americans, and others were often denied those rights. They often did not get the same freedoms or opportunities as other Americans. They could not get certain jobs or live in certain neighborhoods. Their children often had to go to schools that were not as good as the schools for most other American children.

Over time, many people worked hard to end these unfair ways. Their work became known as the Civil Rights movement. **Civil rights** are the rights of citizens to equal treatment under the law.

One of the movement's leaders was Dr. Martin Luther King, Jr., an African American minister who was originally from Georgia. He encouraged African Americans to use peaceful ways to gain their civil rights. He and millions of other people made speeches and took part in marches and protests to show their support for civil rights.

In 1963 King and other civil rights leaders organized a march in Washington, D.C. More than 250,000 people took part in it. In a speech there, King told the marchers of his hopes for equality in the United States. He said,

> **❝I have a dream that my four little children will one day live in a nation where they will not be judged by the color of their skin, but by the content of their character. ❞**

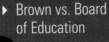

EXPANDING CIVIL RIGHTS IN AMERICA 1954-PRESENT

1954

▶ Brown vs. Board of Education

1964

▶ The Civil Rights Act of 1964 is passed

About a year after the march in Washington, Congress passed the Civil Rights Act of 1964. This law states that all Americans have the right to use public places and services. It also says that employers cannot refuse to hire people because of their race, religion, national origin, or gender. The next year, Congress passed the Voting Rights Act. That law helps make sure that all Americans can vote in free and fair elections.

Following the lead of the African American Civil Rights movement, other groups also worked for equal rights. Native Americans formed the American Indian Movement (AIM) to work for their rights. By 1975 Native American tribes were allowed for the first time to run their own businesses and health and educational programs.

To help improve the lives of migrant farm workers, Cesar Chavez helped form

• BIOGRAPHY •

Cesar Chavez 1927–1993

Character Trait: Citizenship

When Cesar Chavez was 15 years old, he had to quit school to become a migrant worker and help earn money for his family in California. Like other migrant workers at the time, Chavez was often treated unfairly and was paid poorly.

In 1965 Cesar Chavez and the United Farm Workers led a grape pickers' strike in California. They asked Americans to boycott, or refuse to buy, grapes as a form of protest. With the support of the country, the farm workers succeeded in getting more pay and better working conditions. "Together," Chavez said, "all things are possible." For his work, Cesar Chavez was awarded the Presidential Medal of Freedom in 1993. It is our nation's highest civilian honor for patriotism and public service.

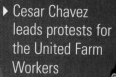

▸ The Voting Rights Act of 1965 is passed

▸ Cesar Chavez leads protests for the United Farm Workers

▸ The American Indian Movement is founded

▸ The Americans with Disabilities Act is passed

a group that later became the United Farm Workers (UFW). This group helped get better wages and working conditions for farm workers, many of whom were Mexican Americans.

By the 1960s many women had jobs outside the home, but they often earned less than men who had the same kinds of jobs. Like other groups, women began to work together for equal rights. New laws were passed saying that employers must treat men and women equally.

Other people, such as Justin Dart, worked hard to get the Americans with Disabilities Act (ADA) passed in 1990.

This law says that Americans with disabilities must have the same rights and opportunities as other citizens.

Protecting the rights of all citizens to equal treatment under the law has been a long and difficult struggle. Throughout the history of the United States, many people have been willing to fight and die to secure those civil rights. Citizens today have a responsibility to see that those rights are preserved for future generations of Americans.

REVIEW **What is the Civil Rights movement?**

LESSON 3 REVIEW

POINT OF VIEW How were the people who took part in the march in Washington in 1963 expressing a point of view?

1 BIG IDEA What are some of the important rights United States citizens have?

2 VOCABULARY What do **candidates** often do during a **campaign**?

3 CIVICS AND GOVERNMENT What is the Bill of Rights?

4 HISTORY How has the Civil Rights movement worked to meet its goals?

5 CRITICAL THINKING—Evaluate Why is voting both a right and a responsibility?

PERFORMANCE—Write a Petition Working in a group, identify a change you want to make in your school. Write a petition describing what you want done, and ask students and teachers to sign it. Then ask permission to present your petition to the school principal.

POINT OF VIEW
As you read, think about the many responsibilities the United States has as a world leader.

BIG IDEA
The United States works with nations around the world.

VOCABULARY

alliance
negotiation
foreign aid

The United States and the World

The United States is a wealthy, powerful, and democratic nation. Because of this, the United States plays a special role among the countries of the world. The United States also works with countries around the world to help in times of need and to solve international problems.

A World Leader

Countries in many parts of the world today look to the United States for leadership and for help in solving problems and conflicts. To make sure that peaceful relations are maintained around the world, the United States sometimes makes treaties or forms alliances with other countries. An **alliance** is a partnership between countries or groups of people. Often these alliances or treaties are made to avoid or end wars. Other agreements are economic ones about trading goods, services, or information.

Representatives from more than 180 countries meet in the United Nations headquarters in New York City. By providing its members opportunities to discuss problems, the United Nations can bring peace and understanding. The seal of the United Nations is shown at the left.

The United States sent medical supplies, food, and workers to help Central America recover from a recent hurricane (above). A volunteer for the Peace Corps teaches a group of students in Africa (top).

To help solve world problems, the United States often leads **negotiations**, or talks, between countries involved in a conflict. Through such negotiations, the United States can sometimes help countries around the world find peaceful solutions to their conflicts. If negotiations fail, however, the United States must sometimes use its military strength to help restore peace.

Even though the United States is a world leader, it cannot solve all problems alone. To help settle many conflicts between countries, the United States works with international organizations, such as the United Nations. More than 180 countries around the world belong to the United Nations.

REVIEW Why does the United States make treaties and form alliances?

 POINT OF VIEW

Helping the World

Some world problems, such as poverty, hunger, and disease, require other kinds of help from the United States. To address those problems, the United States often provides foreign aid. **Foreign aid** is the money, goods, and services that one country gives another.

Every year the United States gives millions of dollars in foreign aid to countries around the world. The United States sends food, medicine, and many other goods to different countries. It also sends experts, such as doctors, teachers, and scientists, to those countries to help. Some of these experts belong to a United States organization called the Peace Corps. It trains and sends volunteers to countries that ask for help to improve people's living conditions.

Disaster relief is another kind of foreign aid that the United States provides. The United States sends this kind of help to countries suffering from natural disasters, such as earthquakes or floods. Recently, a powerful tsunami hit Asian countries, causing the loss of many lives and millions of dollars worth of damage. The United States sent food, clothing, and medical workers to help the countries recover.

The United States also cooperates with other countries to take care of matters affecting the entire world. Protecting Earth's environment, stopping the spread of diseases, and making scientific advances are important to all people, regardless of where they live.

In the area of space exploration, the United States formed a partnership with several nations to build the International Space Station. All the countries provided materials, tools, and people to work on the station. The space station is the site of many scientific experiments.

Another important world scientific project operates in Antarctica. In 1959 the United States and many other countries signed a treaty that set aside the entire continent of Antarctica as an international scientific zone. In this way, the world has pledged to protect Antarctica and to share the continent peacefully.

REVIEW **What kinds of world problems does the United States address with foreign aid?**

The Role of the United States

Since the beginning of the United States, our nation's leaders have given much thought to the role the United States should play in world affairs. In 1796, when our first President, George Washington, was leaving office, he gave a farewell speech.

• GEOGRAPHY •

Antarctica
Understanding Places and Regions

Antarctica is the coldest and windiest place on Earth. A thick sheet of ice covers nearly the entire continent year-round. Because of these harsh conditions, Antarctica has no permanent settlements. But the continent's mostly untouched environment makes it perfect for scientific research. Scientists from all over the world work together in Antarctica. In fact, the entire continent is an international scientific zone.

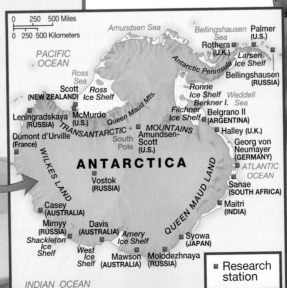

0 250 500 Miles
0 250 500 Kilometers

Amundsen Sea
Bellingshausen Sea
Palmer (U.S.)
Rothera (U.K.)
Larsen Ice Shelf
PACIFIC OCEAN
Antarctic Peninsula
Bellingshausen (RUSSIA)
Ross Sea
Ronne Ice Shelf
Weddell Sea
Berkner I.
Scott (NEW ZEALAND)
Ross Ice Shelf
Filchner Ice Shelf
Belgrano II (ARGENTINA)
Leningradskaya (RUSSIA)
McMurdo (U.S.)
Queen Maud Mts.
TRANSANTARCTIC
Halley (U.K.)
Dumont d'Urville (France)
MOUNTAINS
South Pole
Amundsen-Scott (U.S.)
Georg von Neumayer (GERMANY)
WILKES LAND
ANTARCTICA
ATLANTIC OCEAN
Vostok (RUSSIA)
Sanae (SOUTH AFRICA)
QUEEN MAUD LAND
Maitri (INDIA)
Casey (AUSTRALIA)
Mirnyy (RUSSIA)
Davis (AUSTRALIA)
Amery Ice Shelf
Syowa (JAPAN)
Shackleton Ice Shelf
West Ice Shelf
Mawson (AUSTRALIA)
Molodezhnaya (RUSSIA)
■ Research station
INDIAN OCEAN

In it, Washington gave advice to his fellow citizens about the future of the young nation and its dealings with the world. He said, "Observe good faith and justice toward all nations. Cultivate peace and harmony with all."

The United States is rich in natural resources and has a strong economy. Our technology and industries are among the most advanced of all nations. Most important, citizens of the United States are free to make decisions about their economy and their government. All of these factors will help the United States remain a world leader in the future.

Throughout the history of the United States, its citizens have faced many decisions about events in this country and around the world. In facing those challenges, they have helped shape the future of the world. As the United States and the world continue to change over time, so will the role of the United States in world affairs.

In 2001, when President George W. Bush took the oath of office, he said,

> **We have a place, all of us, in a long story . . . the story of a power that went into the world to protect but not possess, to defend but not to conquer. It is the American story . . . and even after nearly 225 years, we have a long way yet to travel.**

REVIEW How can the United States continue to be a world leader?

LESSON 4
REVIEW

 POINT OF VIEW What viewpoint do you think President Bush was expressing in the quotation above?

❶ **BIG IDEA** What are some ways in which the United States helps solve international problems today?

❷ **VOCABULARY** How do you think the meaning of the term **alliance** relates to the meaning of the term *ally*?

❸ **HISTORY** By a treaty in 1959, what continent did nations around the world agree to share for scientific purposes?

❹ **CRITICAL THINKING—Evaluate** Many experts say that the idea of democracy is one of the most important "products" that the United States exports. What do you think that statement means?

 PERFORMANCE—Conduct a Debate Conduct a class debate about the role the United States should play in world affairs in the future. Use examples from the past to support your arguments in the debate. You may wish to invite other classes to attend the debate.

14 Review and Test Preparation

⭐(Focus Skill) Point of View

Copy the following graphic organizer onto a separate sheet of paper. Use the information you have learned to describe the different points of view expressed in this chapter.

Our Country's Government

Topic	Details	Point of View
"Governments are instituted among Men, deriving their just Powers from the Consent of the Governed." —President Thomas Jefferson →	_____ →	_____

THINK & WRITE

Write an Explanation Suppose a person from another country asks you about the rights you have as a United States citizen. Explain some of the rights guaranteed by the Constitution, and tell why they are important.

Write an Editorial Write an editorial for your local newspaper, urging its readers to be good citizens. Explain why it is important to continue to preserve the rights that United States citizens have.

USE VOCABULARY

For each group of terms, write a sentence or two that explains how the terms are related.

1 **Constitution** (p. 467), **amendment** (p. 482)

2 **general election** (p. 484), **campaign** (p. 484), **candidate** (p. 484)

3 **petition** (p. 484), **ballot** (p. 484)

4 **alliance** (p. 488), **negotiation** (p. 489), **foreign aid** (p. 489)

RECALL FACTS

Answer these questions.

5 What does each branch of the United States government do?

6 What are three rights that all United States citizens have?

7 Who were some of the leaders in the fight for civil rights in the United States?

8 What role does the United States have in helping to solve world problems?

Write the letter of the best choice.

9 What two parts make up the United States Congress?
  A the President and the Supreme Court
  B the President and the Senate
  C the Senate and the House of Representatives
  D the Supreme Court and the House of Representatives

10 The system by which each branch of government keeps watch on the other two branches is called—
  F checks and balances.
  G veto.
  H due process of law.
  J international trade.

11 Citizens of the United States are guaranteed freedom of speech under the—
  A Declaration of Independence.
  B Pledge of Allegiance.
  C National Anthem.
  D Bill of Rights.

12 To what international organization do more than 180 countries around the world belong?
  F the International Space Station
  G the United Nations
  H the Peace Corps
  J the United States Congress

THINK CRITICALLY

13 Why do you think it is important to know about a candidate who is running for office?

14 Why do you think accepting the responsibilities of citizenship is as important as enjoying the rights of citizenship?

15 Think about ways in which tax money is spent in your community. How might your life be different without those tax funds?

16 If you had the chance to meet the President, what would you say? What questions would you ask? Explain your reasons.

17 Why do you think United States citizens may have different views about the role that the nation should play in world affairs?

APPLY SKILLS

Use a Flow Chart

18 Think about something you do often. List the steps you follow when performing the task. Then make a flow chart, placing the steps in order.

CHART AND GRAPH SKILLS

VISIT

THE STATUE OF LIBERTY

The Statue of Liberty was a gift of friendship from the people of France to the people of the United States. Installed in New York Harbor in 1886, the statue welcomed new arrivals who sailed to the United States. For those immigrants, the Statue of Liberty meant freedom and the start of a new life on American soil.

The statue continues to represent American values of freedom and democracy. For this reason, millions of people visit the Statue of Liberty each year. From the observation platform, you can see the statue's interior. On the promenade, you can look out over New York Harbor and imagine how immigrants felt as they saw America for the very first time.

LOCATE IT

NEW YORK

Statue of Liberty

NEW JERSEY

There are seven rays on the statue's crown. They represent the seven seas and the seven continents of the world.

A ferryboat transports visitors to the Statue of Liberty.

You can see the inside framework of the statue.

The statue marks Independence Day, July 4, 1776.

Many people from around the world visit the Statue of Liberty each year.

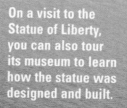

On a visit to the Statue of Liberty, you can also tour its museum to learn how the statue was designed and built.

TAKE A FIELD TRIP

GO ONLINE

A VIRTUAL TOUR
Visit The Learning Site at **www.harcourtschool.com** to find virtual tours of other United States historical sites.

CNN Turner Le@rning

A VIDEO TOUR
Check your media center or classroom library for a videotape tour of the Statue of Liberty.

6 Review and Test Preparation

VISUAL SUMMARY

Write a Paragraph   Study the pictures and captions below to help you review Unit 6. Then write a letter to a fourth grader in another country explaining how these pictures illustrate life in the United States today.

USE VOCABULARY

Write the term that correctly matches each definition.

motto (p. 443), **amendment** (p. 482)

democracy (p. 448), **civil rights** (p. 485)

global economy (p. 458), **alliance** (p. 488)

1 the world market in which companies from different countries buy and sell goods and services

2 a partnership between countries or groups of people

3 the rights of citizens to equal treatment under the law

4 a saying chosen to express the ideals of a nation, state, or group

RECALL FACTS

Answer these questions.

5 Why have people immigrated to the United States over the years?

6 What features make our government a democracy?

7 What is the goal of nearly every business?

8 What are the three levels of government in the United States?

9 What is the most important court in the United States?

Write the letter of the best choice.

10 The largest parts of the United States economy are—
  A agricultural industries.
  B mining industries.
  C service industries.
  D manufacturing industries.

11 Which of the following is ***not*** a right listed in the First Amendment to the United States Constitution?
  F freedom of speech
  G the right to due process of law
  H freedom of religion
  J the right to gather and hold meetings

Visual Summary

Americans share a belief in freedom.
p. 448

People in the United States have rights and responsibilities.   p. 449

The United States has a free enterprise economy.   p. 454

12 The United States Congress makes up the—
 A military branch.
 B executive branch.
 C judicial branch.
 D legislative branch.

THINK CRITICALLY

13 Why do you think many immigrants want to keep their native cultures and traditions in their new countries?

14 What kind of job would you like to have in the future? Why?

15 How might your life be different if the United States was not part of the global economy?

16 What kinds of things unite people in the United States?

17 In which state would you most like to live? Explain your answer.

APPLY SKILLS

Read a Population Map
Use the population map on this page to answer the following questions.

18 What is the population density in and around San Francisco?

19 Which city has a higher population density, Bakersfield or Palm Springs?

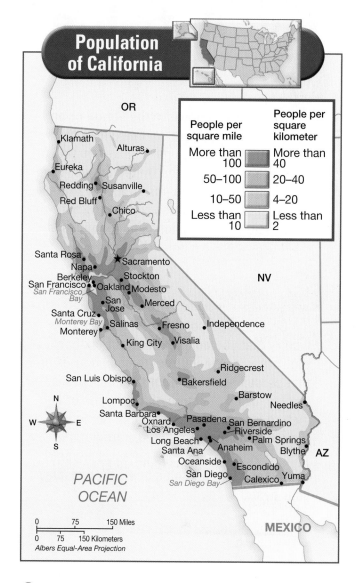

Population of California

People per square mile		People per square kilometer
More than 100		More than 40
50–100		20–40
10–50		4–20
Less than 10		Less than 2

0   75   150 Miles
0   75   150 Kilometers
Albers Equal-Area Projection

20 Which parts of California have very large areas of land with low population density? Why do you think so few people live in those places?

One national government unites the 50 states.   p. 466

Different levels of government serve citizens of the United States.   p. 476

The United States is a world leader.   p. 488

497

Unit Activities

GO ONLINE Visit The Learning Site at www.harcourtschool.com for additional activities.

Design Currency

Look through books in the library or on the Internet for pictures of currency used around the world. Compare those you find to the currency used in the United States. Then work with a partner to design a coin and a bill for new United States currency. Share your designs and explain them to the class.

Honor a Hero

Choose a person from United States history that you admire. Use your textbook, the library, or the Internet to find pictures of that person and to learn more about his or her life. Draw a picture of the person or a picture of a scene showing that person in action. Add words or phrases around the picture that tell about the person's life and what made that person a hero. Then display your poster in the classroom.

VISIT YOUR LIBRARY

- *Immigrants: Coming to America* by Gare Thompson. Children's Press.

- *Kids' Guide: State Government* by Ernestine Giesecke. Heinemann Library.

- *Uncle Sam and Old Glory: Symbols of America* by Delno C. and Jean M. West. Atheneum Books for Young Readers.

COMPLETE THE UNIT PROJECT

A Cultural Fair Work with a small group to complete the Unit Project described on page 435. Select a cultural group in the United States to celebrate in a cultural fair of the United States. Use your textbook, books from the library, the Internet, and interviews with family or community members to learn more about your chosen group. Find out about their customs and traditions, such as foods, clothing, holidays, and languages. Make a display for the cultural fair and decide with your classmates how the displays will be presented. You may want to invite another class to your fair.

Pennsylvania Today

❝ **You have responsibilities as a global citizen.** ❞

—August Wilson, 1987

The Roberto Clemente Bridge, Pittsburgh

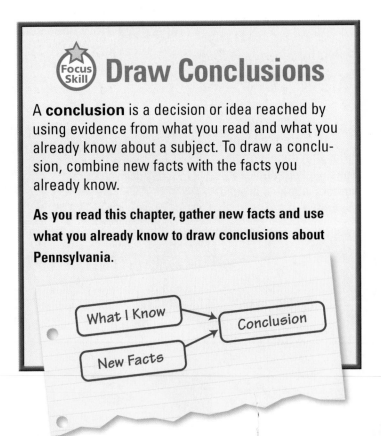

⭐ **Focus Skill** **Draw Conclusions**

A **conclusion** is a decision or idea reached by using evidence from what you read and what you already know about a subject. To draw a conclusion, combine new facts with the facts you already know.

As you read this chapter, gather new facts and use what you already know to draw conclusions about Pennsylvania.

What I Know → Conclusion
New Facts →

DRAW CONCLUSIONS

As you read, draw conclusions about Pennsylvania's modern economy.

BIG IDEA

Pennsylvania's economy today is diverse.

VOCABULARY

marketplace
producer
scarcity
incentive
interest

A Modern Economy

Pennsylvanians make good use of the marketplace, or the sale of goods and services. By making and selling many products, the state's citizens strengthen the economy.

The Marketplace of Today

In Pennsylvania's marketplace, consumers buy from producers, or people who make goods and provide services. Many factors affect the trade of goods and services. One of these factors is product demand. If a producer makes a product that people want or need, it will be easy to sell. If demand for a product is low, it will be more difficult to sell.

Scarcity, or limited supply, also affects the marketplace. If many consumers want an item that has a limited supply, producers can charge more money for it. For example, Amish quilts are scarce because they are made by hand. People who want to buy an Amish quilt must pay more for it than they would for one made in a factory.

REVIEW How does scarcity affect selling prices?
 DRAW CONCLUSIONS

FAST FACT Throughout Pennsylvania, there are many farms that supply fresh fruits and vegetables to farmers' markets around the state.

SWEET YELLOW PEPPERS $3.99 lb

FRESH RED PEPPERS $3.00 lb

BUTTER LETTUCE 79¢

FRESH CILANTRO 70¢

FRESH MINT OR DILL 1.00 bunch

FRESH ITALIAN PARSLEY

SWEET SALAD ONION 1.75 bunch

FRESH FENNEL 1.75 EA

Economic Choices

The marketplace is driven by consumer choices. Think about the choices you make when you shop. How do you decide whether to buy now or later?

Governments must make similar economic choices. In the past, coal mined in Pennsylvania helped the state because it could be sold in areas that did not have it. In recent years, many cities and towns have turned to fuel sources other than coal. As a result, some Pennsylvania communities have developed different fuel sources. State officials expect that as fuels such as coal and oil become scarcer, new fuel sources will be needed.

Some communities give **incentives**, or special rewards, to attract businesses to their communities. Pennsylvania has recently offered incentives to companies that make products and do research for

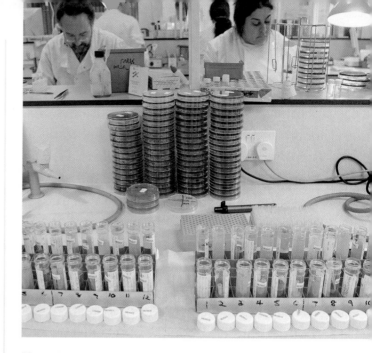

Many companies in Pennsylvania do medical research.

health care. These companies will expand their businesses and create more jobs for people in Pennsylvania.

REVIEW **Why do some communities offer incentives to businesses?**

Global, State, and Local Economies

Today, many companies do business all around the world. International trade is an important part of Pennsylvania's economy. In a recent year, the state exported more than $16 billion worth of goods to more than 200 countries. Canada and Mexico are the state's two largest foreign trading partners. Farm products are the most commonly traded goods. Chemicals, machinery, and high-tech products are also bought and sold.

Geographic differences affect the state's economy today. The economy of western Pennsylvania depends mainly on agriculture. Pittsburgh continues to lead the state in iron and steel production.

In many areas, tourism is important. Thousands of people visit cities, such as Harrisburg and Hershey, every year to learn about our state's history and cultural heritage. Philadelphia and other historic sites are also popular tourist attractions.

Although coal plays a smaller role in the state's economy than it once did, coal mining is still a major industry. Manufacturing has always been important to the state. Today, Pennsylvania is a leading maker of cement products, chemicals, and electronics. Allegheny, Philadelphia, and Montgomery Counties are the main centers of manufacturing.

Many people throughout the state work in retail stores. Many others have jobs with high-tech companies, hospitals, or colleges. State College, the town where Penn State University is located, has become a large metropolitan region. Many people work there.

REVIEW Which countries are Pennsylvania's leading foreign trading partners?

Analyze Graphs The bar graph below shows the number of people who work in various industries in Pennsylvania.

◆ Which industry has the greatest number of employees?

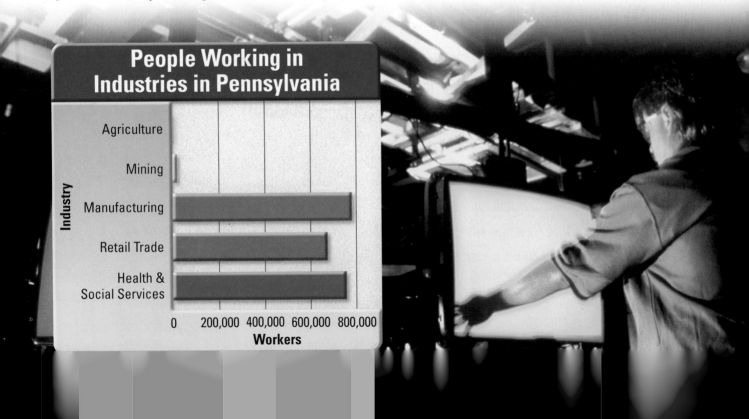

People Working in Industries in Pennsylvania

Industry

- Agriculture
- Mining
- Manufacturing
- Retail Trade
- Health & Social Services

0   200,000 400,000 600,000 800,000
Workers

Like adults, children can earn interest on their money by putting it in a bank. The state quarter (below) features a keystone and the state motto, Virtue, Liberty, Independence.

Saving Money

If you save your money in a bank, the bank will pay you interest. **Interest** is money a bank or borrower pays for the use of money. The longer money stays in the bank, the more interest is earned. When a bank lends money, the borrower pays interest to the bank. You can use a bank to save money that you earn from a job or an allowance.

Some people earn money by investing in businesses. If the company does well, the investment grows larger. Many Pennsylvania businesses were built up by investors who believed that those companies would be successful.

REVIEW Why is it good to save money in a bank? DRAW CONCLUSIONS

LESSON 1
REVIEW

Focus Skill **DRAW CONCLUSIONS** Why are farm products the most commonly traded goods?

① **BIG IDEA** How is Pennsylvania's economy today different from its economy in the past?

② **VOCABULARY** Write a sentence that explains how **incentives** affect economic choices.

③ **ECONOMICS** Why do some people invest in businesses?

2

Levels of Government

DRAW CONCLUSIONS

As you read, draw conclusions about the role of government in Pennsylvania.

BIG IDEA

Pennsylvania's governments serve and protect its citizens.

VOCABULARY

limited government
unlimited government
preamble
commonwealth

Our government makes laws and makes sure that those laws are obeyed. The government also provides services to citizens. People living in Pennsylvania have three levels of government—national, state, and local.

Governments by the People

Each level of government in Pennsylvania has its own responsibilities. The different powers and duties of each are written into laws by the citizens. The result is **limited government**. When citizens participate in the lawmaking process, the power of their leaders is limited.

When rulers make laws without considering what citizens want, the result is **unlimited government**. People must obey laws even if they are unfair. People with no say in their government cannot make changes when they want them.

REVIEW Why do you think Pennsylvanians choose to have limited government? DRAW CONCLUSIONS

FAST FACT When the Pennsylvania General Assembly opens a new session in January, family members attend the ceremony. There are 50 state senators and 203 representatives in the General Assembly.

Seven justices serve on the Pennsylvania Supreme Court. They meet in Philadelphia, Pittsburgh, and Harrisburg.

Levels and Branches of Government

The federal, or national, government is responsible for issues that affect citizens in every state. State government serves the needs of citizens of a single state. Elected state officials make decisions about public schools and hospitals. Local governments meet the needs of their communities, such as fire and police protection.

Like the federal government, our state government has three branches. The legislative branch writes laws. The executive branch enforces laws. The judicial branch decides if laws are fair and punishes lawbreakers.

The General Assembly is the law-making, or legislative, branch. It meets in the State House in Harrisburg. The legislature has two parts—the senate and the house of representatives. Members of the General Assembly are elected to office. General Assembly has 50 senators and 203 representatives.

Voters elect a governor to head the executive branch. The executive branch makes sure that laws made by the legislature are carried out. Voters also elect a lieutenant (loo•TEH•nuhnt) governor to help the governor run the executive branch.

The judicial branch is headed by the Pennsylvania Supreme Court. The supreme court has seven judges, called justices. They decide cases about the fairness of state laws and review decisions made by lower courts.

The three branches make sure that no single branch becomes too powerful. Because the power of each branch is limited, this system is known as checks and balances.

REVIEW **What are the three branches of government?**

Students can learn about government by participating in mock elections. In a mock election, these students vote for a presidential candidate.

A Plan for Government

Our state constitution has changed several times since 1776. The current constitution was adopted in 1968. The **preamble**, or opening section of the constitution, shows that the state respects individual freedoms and religious freedom. It reads:

> 66 We the people of the Commonwealth of Pennsylvania, grateful to Almighty God for the blessings of civil and religious liberty, and humbly invoking [calling upon] His guidance, do ordain [approve] and establish this constitution. 99

Pennsylvania is a **commonwealth**—a state founded by law for the common good of its citizens. The constitution shapes our state and local governments. It also gives the General Assembly certain powers over local governments.

The General Assembly defines areas in Pennsylvania as cities, counties, boroughs, school districts, and townships. Each has a different form of local government. Large cities, such as Philadelphia and Pittsburgh, have governments headed by a mayor. Boroughs and smaller cities are managed by a council and a mayor.

Cities, boroughs, and townships have certain duties. They provide public services, such as fire and police protection. Local governments also help manage emergencies.

REVIEW What are some public services that local governments provide to citizens?

The Pike County Courthouse in the northeast part of the state is one of many local courthouses throughout Pennsylvania.

PIKE COUNTY COURT HOUSE

The Flight 93 National Memorial in Shanksville honors the passengers and crew members who lost their lives on September 11, 2001. The Shanksville fire chief (left) rings the bell of remembrance during a ceremony on September 11, 2005.

Citizens' Responsibilities

Citizens have a responsibility to vote in elections. Voting lets the public make decisions about important issues. Elected officials pay attention to how citizens vote. Citizens use their votes to have a say in government.

To vote in Pennsylvania, you must be at least 18 years old, be a United States citizen, and have lived in Pennsylvania for at least 30 days before the election. Citizens must fill out a voter registration form at least 30 days before Election Day. Citizens who will be away from home on Election Day can vote by using an absentee ballot.

Citizens also have a responsibility to help the government pay for public services. Citizens do this by paying taxes. If people think their taxes are unfair, they can speak up and ask for change. Citizens may also decide to serve their community in special ways. This may include serving in the United States military or the National Guard. Pennsylvania's National Guard helps the state in times of emergencies or during natural disasters.

On September 11, 2001, an emergency happened. United Airlines Flight 93 crashed in a field near Shanksville, Pennsylvania. Terrorists had hijacked the plane, but a group of brave passengers tried to take over the plane. They prevented the plane from crashing into a building in Washington, D.C. The Flight 93 National Memorial now marks the site where the plane went down.

REVIEW What are some responsibilities of citizenship? **DRAW CONCLUSIONS**

Citizens' Participation

There are many good reasons for people to participate in government and community life. One important reason is to make sure that people's interests are heard at all levels of government.

Citizens and officials must also make sure that the interests of their state are protected. For example, the federal government might pass laws that affect industries in our state. If a federal law is not good for Pennsylvania's citizens, state and local officials will take action to protect those people.

Participation in the community goes far beyond voting. It includes helping your neighbors, cleaning up the community, and doing volunteer work for others who need help.

Being a citizen is like being part of a family. Just as a family is stronger when every family member helps out, a community is stronger when everyone takes an active role.

Participation helps members of certain groups who are in the minority. For

By volunteering to help someone in need, you can participate in an important community effort.

example, the immigrant population of Pennsylvania has grown in recent years. Political groups have formed to help these immigrants get what they need, such as newspapers in their own languages.

REVIEW **How can participating in the community help members of minority groups?**

Young people and adults volunteer together to install a gate on the Capital Greenbelt, a walking trail that circles Harrisburg.

Media helps people learn about current events.

Citizenship in an Information Age

Citizens need information about their communities and governments to make good decisions. Radio, newspapers, magazines, television, and the Internet all provide information about important issues and events. Each of these **media** sources affects many people.

Often the goal of the media is to affect how people think or act. Many businesses use all kinds of media to sell products. If consumers like an advertisement, they may be more likely to buy the product.

Media can also affect the way people think and vote. Responsible citizens listen to different points of view. Freedom of the press means that the media can present facts, ideas, and opinions without government approval.

You have many media choices to help you learn about your local, state, and national governments. To be a responsible citizen, you should gain information from several media sources. In this way, you can decide what is best for your community.

REVIEW What is freedom of the press?

LESSON 3 REVIEW

DRAW CONCLUSIONS How are citizens' rights different from their responsibilities?

❶ **BIG IDEA** How can Pennsylvanians be responsible citizens?

❷ **VOCABULARY** Write a sentence telling one way that the **media** keeps people informed.

❸ **CIVICS AND GOVERNMENT** Why is it important for citizens to vote?

The Pennsylvania State Capitol

DID YOU KNOW?

The large round area beneath the dome, or rotunda, is lit by almost 4,000 lights.

Harrisburg, Pennsylvania is the third city to serve as the state capital. The capital was moved from Philadelphia to Lancaster in 1799, and then to Harrisburg in 1812. The original Harrisburg capitol building was destroyed in a fire in 1897. The five-story capitol building that stands today was finished in 1906. At its dedication, President Theodore Roosevelt declared the building "the most beautiful state capitol in the nation".

The House Chamber, known as the Hall of the House, is larger than two basketball courts and is four-stories high. It is filled with stained glass windows, murals of Pennsylvania history, and original wooden desks. Legislative assemblies use this ceremonial mace (left) as a symbol of the government's authority.

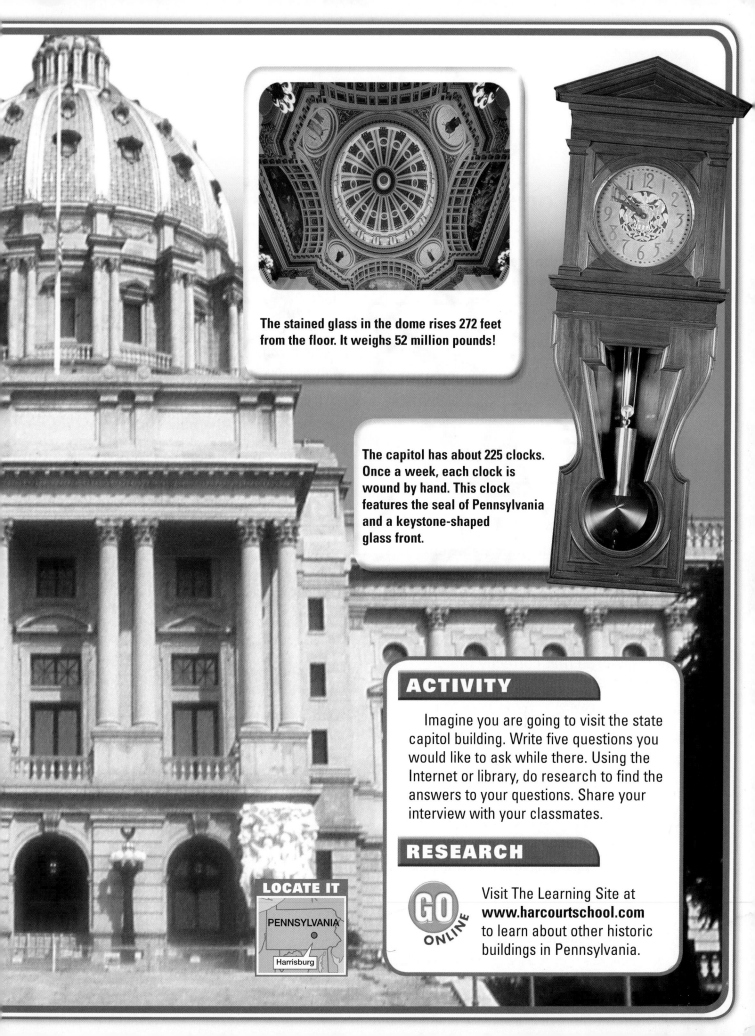

The stained glass in the dome rises 272 feet from the floor. It weighs 52 million pounds!

The capitol has about 225 clocks. Once a week, each clock is wound by hand. This clock features the seal of Pennsylvania and a keystone-shaped glass front.

ACTIVITY

Imagine you are going to visit the state capitol building. Write five questions you would like to ask while there. Using the Internet or library, do research to find the answers to your questions. Share your interview with your classmates.

RESEARCH

GO ONLINE

Visit The Learning Site at **www.harcourtschool.com** to learn about other historic buildings in Pennsylvania.

LOCATE IT

PENNSYLVANIA

Harrisburg

Review and Test Preparation

Draw Conclusions
(Focus Skill)

Fill in the flow chart with facts and conclusions about the way that Pennsylvania's limited government works.

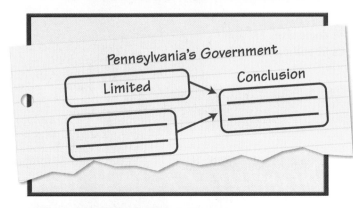

Pennsylvania's Government

Limited

Conclusion

THINK AND WRITE

Write a Letter Write to your state senator, telling him or her about a community project that you would like to begin.

USE VOCABULARY

Write the words that correctly match each definition.

marketplace (p. PA 6-2)   **incentive** (p. PA 6-3)

interest (p. PA 6-5)   **limited government** (p. PA 6-6)

preamble (p. PA 6-8)

1 the opening section of the constitution

2 money a bank or borrower pays for the use of money

3 when citizens participate in the lawmaking process

4 special rewards

5 the sale of goods and services

RECALL FACTS

Answer these questions.

6 How does scarcity affect prices?

7 What products are made in Pennsylvania today?

8 How do governments pay for services?

9 What are the three branches of our state government?

10 What is the media?

Write the letter of the best choice.

11 A producer is
  A someone who buys a product.
  B someone who makes goods or provides services.
  C someone who grows crops.
  D someone who works for the government.

THINK CRITICALLY

12 Why is it important to participate in government and community life?

PERFORMANCE

Create a Chart Learn about the economy in your community. Find out what businesses employ a large group of people. Make an illustrated chart that shows the major economic activities of your area.

For Your Reference

Almanac

Biographical Dictionary

Gazetteer

Glossary

Index

Almanac

Facts About the United States

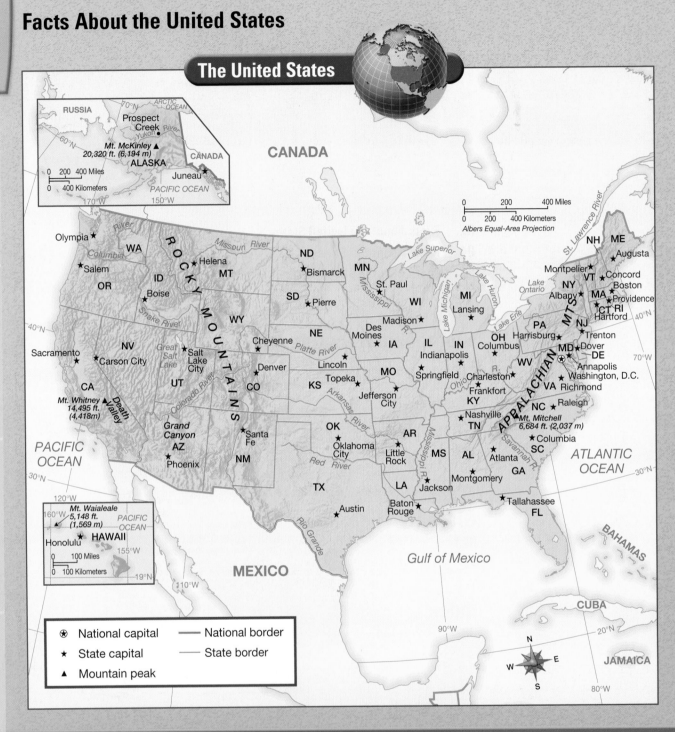

The United States

RUSSIA

Prospect
Creek
Mt. McKinley ▲
20,320 ft. (6,194 m)
ALASKA
Juneau
ARCTIC OCEAN
CANADA
PACIFIC OCEAN

0 200 400 Miles
0 400 Kilometers

CANADA

0 200 400 Miles
0 200 400 Kilometers
Albers Equal-Area Projection

Olympia ★
WA
Columbia River
Salem ★
OR
Helena ★
MT
ID
Boise ★
ROCKY MOUNTAINS
Missouri River
ND
Bismarck ★
SD
Pierre ★
WY
NE
Cheyenne ★
Snake River
MN
St. Paul ★
WI
Madison ★
Lake Superior
Lake Michigan
Lake Huron
MI
Lansing ★
NH
Montpelier ★
VT
ME
Augusta ★
Concord ★
Boston
St. Lawrence River
Lake Ontario
Lake Erie
NY
Albany ★
MA
Providence
CT RI
Hartford

NV
Sacramento ★
Carson City ★
CA
Mt. Whitney ▲
14,495 ft.
(4,418m)
Death Valley
Great Salt Lake
Salt Lake City ★
UT
Denver ★
CO
Colorado River
Platte River
IA
Des Moines ★
IL
Springfield ★
IN
Indianapolis ★
OH
Columbus ★
Harrisburg ★
PA
WV
Charleston ★
Ohio R.
Frankfort ★
KY
VA
Richmond ★
APPALACHIAN MTS
NJ
Trenton ★
MD
Dover ★
DE
Annapolis ★
Washington, D.C. ⊛
70°W
40°N

Lincoln ★
Topeka ★
KS
MO
Jefferson City ★
Arkansas River

Grand Canyon
AZ
Phoenix ★
Santa Fe ★
NM
OK
Oklahoma City ★
AR
Little Rock ★
Red River
TN
Nashville ★
Mt. Mitchell
6,684 ft. (2,037 m)
NC
Raleigh ★
Columbia ★
SC
Savannah R.
MS
AL
Atlanta ★
GA
ATLANTIC OCEAN
30°N

PACIFIC OCEAN
30°N

Mt. Waialeale
5,148 ft.
(1,569 m)
PACIFIC OCEAN
Honolulu
HAWAII
160°W
155°W
19°N
0 100 Miles
0 100 Kilometers

MEXICO
TX
Austin ★
Rio Grande
LA
Baton Rouge ★
Jackson ★
Montgomery ★
Tallahassee ★
FL
Mississippi R.
Gulf of Mexico
BAHAMAS
CUBA
JAMAICA
90°W
20°N
80°W

Legend:
- ⊛ National capital
- ★ State capital
- ▲ Mountain peak
- —— National border
- —— State border

N W E S

Washington, D.C.,
became the nation's
capital in 1800.

The United States

LAND	SIZE	CLIMATE	POPULATION*	LEADING PRODUCTS
Highest Point: Mt. McKinley, in Alaska 20,320 feet (6,194 m) Lowest Point: Death Valley, in California 282 feet (86 m) below sea level Largest Freshwater Lake: Lake Superior, 31,800 square miles (82,362 sq. km) Deepest Lake: Crater Lake in Oregon 1,932 feet (589 m) deep	Area: 3,615,292 square miles (9,363,563 sq. km) Geographic center: near Castle Rock, Butte County, South Dakota	Highest Recorded Temperature: 134°F (57°C) at Death Valley, in California, on July 10, 1913 Lowest Recorded Temperature: -80°F (-62°C) at Prospect Creek, Alaska, on January 23, 1971 Rainiest Place: Mt. Waialeale, in Hawaii average yearly rainfall of 460 inches (1,168 cm) Driest Place: Death Valley, in California average yearly rainfall of 2 inches (5 cm)	288,368,698	Farming: Beef cattle, chickens, corn, cotton, eggs, hogs, milk, soybeans, wheat Fishing: Crabs, salmon, shrimp Manufacturing: Airplanes, cars and trucks, chemicals, clothing, computers, electronic equipment, gasoline, machinery, medicines, metal products, paper, plastics, printed materials, processed foods Mining: Coal, natural gas, oil

*latest available population figures

The 50 states are divided into 3,092 counties. The courthouse for Rice County, Kansas, is shown to the left. More than half of the country's population lives in 50 metropolitan areas. Los Angeles (right) is one of the largest of these.

State Flag	State	Year of Statehood	Population*	Area (sq. mi.)	Capital	Origin of State Name
	Alabama	1819	4,486,508	50,750	Montgomery	Choctaw, *alba ayamule*, "one who clears land and gathers food from it"
	Alaska	1959	643,786	570,374	Juneau	Aleut, *alayeska*, "great land"
	Arizona	1912	5,456,453	113,642	Phoenix	Papago, *arizonac*, "place of the small spring"
	Arkansas	1836	2,710,079	52,075	Little Rock	Quapaw, "the downstream people"
	California	1850	35,116,033	155,973	Sacramento	Spanish, a fictional island
	Colorado	1876	4,506,542	103,730	Denver	Spanish, "red land" or "red earth"
	Connecticut	1788	3,460,503	4,845	Hartford	Mohican, *quinnitukqut*, "at the long tidal river"
	Delaware	1787	807,385	1,955	Dover	Named for Lord de la Warr
	Florida	1845	16,713,149	54,153	Tallahassee	Spanish, "filled with flowers"
	Georgia	1788	8,560,310	57,919	Atlanta	Named for King George II of England
	Hawaii	1959	1,244,898	6,450	Honolulu	Polynesian, *hawaiki* or *owykee*, "homeland"
	Idaho	1890	1,341,131	82,751	Boise	Invented name with unknown meaning

State Flag	State	Year of Statehood	Population*	Area (sq. mi.)	Capital	Origin of State Name
	Illinois	1818	12,600,620	55,593	Springfield	Algonquin, *iliniwek*, "men" or "warriors"
	Indiana	1816	6,159,068	35,870	Indianapolis	*Indian* + *a*, "land of the Indians"
	Iowa	1846	2,936,760	55,875	Des Moines	Dakota, *ayuba*, "beautiful land"
	Kansas	1861	2,715,884	81,823	Topeka	Sioux, "land of the south wind people"
	Kentucky	1792	4,092,891	39,732	Frankfort	Iroquoian, *ken-tah-ten*, "land of tomorrow"
	Louisiana	1812	4,482,646	43,566	Baton Rouge	Named for King Louis XIV of France
	Maine	1820	1,294,464	30,865	Augusta	Named after a French province
	Maryland	1788	5,458,137	9,775	Annapolis	Named for Henrietta Maria, Queen Consort of Charles I of England
	Massachusetts	1788	6,427,801	7,838	Boston	Massachusett tribe of Native Americans, "at the big hill" or "place of the big hill"
	Michigan	1837	10,050,446	56,809	Lansing	Ojibwa, "large lake"
	Minnesota	1858	5,019,720	79,617	St. Paul	Dakota Sioux, "sky-blue water"
	Mississippi	1817	2,871,782	46,914	Jackson	Indian word meaning "great waters" or "father of waters"
	Missouri	1821	5,672,579	68,898	Jefferson City	Named after the Missouri Indian tribe. *Missouri* means "town of the large canoes."

* lastest available population figures

State Flag	State	Year of Statehood	Population*	Area (sq. mi.)	Capital	Origin of State Name
	Montana	1889	909,453	145,566	Helena	Spanish, "mountainous"
	Nebraska	1867	1,729,180	76,878	Lincoln	From an Oto Indian word meaning "flat water"
	Nevada	1864	2,173,491	109,806	Carson City	Spanish, "snowy" or "snowed upon"
	New Hampshire	1788	1,275,056	8,969	Concord	Named for Hampshire County, England
	New Jersey	1787	8,590,300	7,419	Trenton	Named for the Isle of Jersey
	New Mexico	1912	1,855,059	121,365	Santa Fe	Named by Spanish explorers from Mexico
	New York	1788	19,157,532	47,224	Albany	Named after the Duke of York
	North Carolina	1789	8,320,146	48,718	Raleigh	Named after King Charles II of England
	North Dakota	1889	634,110	70,704	Bismarck	Sioux, *dakota*, "friend" or "ally"
	Ohio	1803	11,421,267	40,953	Columbus	Iroquois, *oheo*, "great water"
	Oklahoma	1907	3,493,714	68,679	Oklahoma City	Choctaw, "red people"
	Oregon	1859	3,521,515	96,003	Salem	Unknown; generally accepted that it was taken from the writings of Maj. Robert Rogers, an English army officer
	Pennsylvania	1787	12,335,091	44,820	Harrisburg	*Penn* + *sylvania*, meaning "Penn's woods"

State Flag	State	Year of Statehood	Population*	Area (sq. mi.)	Capital	Origin of State Name
	Rhode Island	1790	1,069,725	1,045	Providence	From the Greek island of Rhodes
	South Carolina	1788	4,107,183	30,111	Columbia	Named after King Charles II of England
	South Dakota	1889	761,063	75,898	Pierre	Sioux, *dakota*, "friend" or "ally"
	Tennessee	1796	5,797,289	41,220	Nashville	Name of a Cherokee village
	Texas	1845	21,779,893	261,914	Austin	Native American, *tejas*, "friend" or "ally"
	Utah	1896	2,316,256	82,168	Salt Lake City	From the Ute tribe, meaning "people of the mountains"
	Vermont	1791	616,592	9,249	Montpelier	French, *vert*, "green," and *mont*, "mountain"
	Virginia	1788	7,293,542	39,598	Richmond	Named after Queen Elizabeth I of England
	Washington	1889	6,068,996	66,582	Olympia	Named for George Washington
	West Virginia	1863	1,801,873	24,087	Charleston	From the English-named state of Virginia
	Wisconsin	1848	5,441,196	54,314	Madison	Possibly Algonquian, "the place where we live"
	Wyoming	1890	498,703	97,105	Cheyenne	From Delaware Indian word meaning "land of vast plains"
	District of Columbia		570,898	67		Named after Christopher Columbus

* lastest available population figures

Almanac

Facts About the Presidents

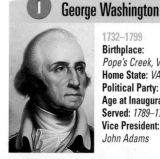

1 George Washington

1732–1799
Birthplace:
Pope's Creek, VA
Home State: *VA*
Political Party: *Federalist*
Age at Inauguration: *57*
Served: *1789–1797*
Vice President:
John Adams

2 John Adams

1735–1826
Birthplace: *Braintree, MA*
Home State: *MA*
Political Party: *Federalist*
Age at Inauguration: *61*
Served: *1797–1801*
Vice President:
Thomas Jefferson

3 Thomas Jefferson

1743–1826
Birthplace:
Albemarle County, VA
Home State: *VA*
Political Party:
Democratic-Republican
Age at Inauguration: *57*
Served: *1801–1809*
Vice Presidents:
Aaron Burr,
George Clinton

4 James Madison

1751–1836
Birthplace:
Port Conway, VA
Home State: *VA*
Political Party:
Democratic-Republican
Age at Inauguration: *57*
Served: *1809–1817*
Vice Presidents:
George Clinton,
Elbridge Gerry

5 James Monroe

1758–1831
Birthplace:
Westmoreland County, VA
Home State: *VA*
Political Party:
Democratic-Republican
Age at Inauguration: *58*
Served: *1817–1825*
Vice President:
Daniel D. Tompkins

6 John Quincy Adams

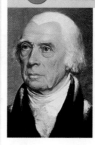

1767–1848
Birthplace: *Braintree, MA*
Home State: *MA*
Political Party:
Democratic-Republican
Age at Inauguration: *57*
Served: *1825–1829*
Vice President:
John C. Calhoun

7 Andrew Jackson

1767–1845
Birthplace:
Waxhaw settlement, SC
Home State: *TN*
Political Party:
Democratic
Age at Inauguration: *61*
Served: *1829–1837*
Vice Presidents:
John C. Calhoun,
Martin Van Buren

8 Martin Van Buren

1782–1862
Birthplace: *Kinderhook, NY*
Home State: *NY*
Political Party:
Democratic
Age at Inauguration: *54*
Served: *1837–1841*
Vice President:
Richard M. Johnson

9 William H. Harrison

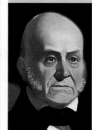

1773–1841
Birthplace: *Berkeley, VA*
Home State: *OH*
Political Party: *Whig*
Age at Inauguration: *68*
Served: *1841*
Vice President:
John Tyler

10 John Tyler

1790–1862
Birthplace: *Greenway, VA*
Home State: *VA*
Political Party: *Whig*
Age at Inauguration: *51*
Served: *1841–1845*
Vice President: *none*

11 James K. Polk

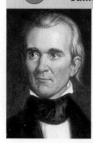

1795–1849
Birthplace:
Mecklenburg County, NC
Home State: *TN*
Political Party:
Democratic
Age at Inauguration: *49*
Served: *1845–1849*
Vice President:
George M. Dallas

12 Zachary Taylor

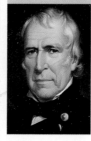

1784–1850
Birthplace:
Orange County, VA
Home State: *LA*
Political Party: *Whig*
Age at Inauguration: *64*
Served: *1849–1850*
Vice President:
Millard Fillmore

13 Millard Fillmore

1800–1874
Birthplace:
Cayuga County, NY
Home State: *NY*
Political Party: *Whig*
Age at Inauguration: *50*
Served: *1850–1853*
Vice President: *none*

Home State refers to the state of residence when elected.

14 Franklin Pierce

1804–1869
Birthplace: *Hillsboro, NH*
Home State: *NH*
Political Party:
Democratic
Age at Inauguration: *48*
Served: *1853–1857*
Vice President:
William R. King

15 James Buchanan

1791–1868
Birthplace:
Cove Gap, PA
Home State: *PA*
Political Party:
Democratic
Age at Inauguration: *65*
Served: *1857–1861*
Vice President:
John C. Breckinridge

16 Abraham Lincoln

1809–1865
Birthplace:
Hardin County, KY
Home State: *IL*
Political Party:
Republican
Age at Inauguration: *52*
Served: *1861–1865*
Vice Presidents:
Hannibal Hamlin,
Andrew Johnson

17 Andrew Johnson

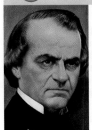

1808–1875
Birthplace: *Raleigh, NC*
Home State: *TN*
Political Party:
National Union
Age at Inauguration: *56*
Served: *1865–1869*
Vice President: *none*

18 Ulysses S. Grant

1822–1885
Birthplace:
Point Pleasant, OH
Home State: *IL*
Political Party:
Republican
Age at Inauguration: *46*
Served: *1869–1877*
Vice Presidents:
Schuyler Colfax,
Henry Wilson

19 Rutherford B. Hayes

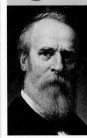

1822-1893
Birthplace:
Delaware, OH
Home State: *OH*
Political Party:
Republican
Age at Inauguration: *54*
Served: *1877–1881*
Vice President:
William A. Wheeler

20 James A. Garfield

1831–1881
Birthplace: *Orange, OH*
Home State: *OH*
Political Party:
Republican
Age at Inauguration: *49*
Served: *1881*
Vice President:
Chester A. Arthur

21 Chester A. Arthur

1829–1886
Birthplace: *Fairfield, VT*
Home State: *NY*
Political Party:
Republican
Age at Inauguration: *51*
Served: *1881–1885*
Vice President: *none*

22 Grover Cleveland

1837–1908
Birthplace: *Caldwell, NJ*
Home State: *NY*
Political Party:
Democratic
Age at Inauguration: *47*
Served: *1885–1889*
Vice President:
Thomas A. Hendricks

23 Benjamin Harrison

1833–1901
Birthplace: *North Bend,*
OH
Home State: *IN*
Political Party:
Republican
Age at Inauguration: *55*
Served: *1889–1893*
Vice President:
Levi P. Morton

24 Grover Cleveland

1837–1908
Birthplace: *Caldwell, NJ*
Home State: *NY*
Political Party:
Democratic
Age at Inauguration: *55*
Served: *1893–1897*
Vice President:
Adlai E. Stevenson

25 William McKinley

1843–1901
Birthplace: *Niles, OH*
Home State: *OH*
Political Party:
Republican
Age at Inauguration: *54*
Served: *1897–1901*
Vice Presidents:
Garret A. Hobart,
Theodore Roosevelt

26 Theodore Roosevelt

1858–1919
Birthplace: *New York, NY*
Home State: *NY*
Political Party:
Republican
Age at Inauguration: *42*
Served: *1901–1909*
Vice President:
Charles W. Fairbanks

27 William H. Taft

1857–1930
Birthplace: *Cincinnati, OH*
Home State: *OH*
Political Party:
Republican
Age at Inauguration: *51*
Served: *1909–1913*
Vice President:
James S. Sherman

28 Woodrow Wilson

1856–1924
Birthplace: *Staunton, VA*
Home State: *NJ*
Political Party:
Democratic
Age at Inauguration: *56*
Served: *1913–1921*
Vice President:
Thomas R. Marshall

29 Warren G. Harding

1865–1923
Birthplace:
Blooming Grove, OH
Home State: *OH*
Political Party:
Republican
Age at Inauguration: *55*
Served: *1921–1923*
Vice President:
Calvin Coolidge

30 Calvin Coolidge

1872–1933
Birthplace:
Plymouth Notch, VT
Home State: *MA*
Political Party:
Republican
Age at Inauguration: *51*
Served: *1923–1929*
Vice President:
Charles G. Dawes

31 Herbert Hoover

1874–1964
Birthplace: *West Branch, IA*
Home State: *CA*
Political Party:
Republican
Age at Inauguration: *54*
Served: *1929–1933*
Vice President:
Charles Curtis

32 Franklin D. Roosevelt

1882–1945
Birthplace: *Hyde Park, NY*
Home State: *NY*
Political Party:
Democratic
Age at Inauguration: *51*
Served: *1933–1945*
Vice Presidents:
John N. Garner,
Henry A. Wallace,
Harry S. Truman

33 Harry S. Truman

1884–1972
Birthplace: *Lamar, MO*
Home State: *MO*
Political Party:
Democratic
Age at Inauguration: *60*
Served: *1945–1953*
Vice President:
Alben W. Barkley

34 Dwight D. Eisenhower

1890–1969
Birthplace: *Denison, TX*
Home State: *NY*
Political Party:
Republican
Age at Inauguration: *62*
Served: *1953–1961*
Vice President:
Richard M. Nixon

35 John F. Kennedy

1917–1963
Birthplace: *Brookline, MA*
Home State: *MA*
Political Party:
Democratic
Age at Inauguration: *43*
Served: *1961–1963*
Vice President:
Lyndon B. Johnson

36 Lyndon B. Johnson

1908–1973
Birthplace:
near Stonewall, TX
Home State: *TX*
Political Party:
Democratic
Age at Inauguration: *55*
Served: *1963–1969*
Vice President:
Hubert H. Humphrey

37 Richard M. Nixon

1913–1994
Birthplace: *Yorba Linda, CA*
Home State: *NY*
Political Party:
Republican
Age at Inauguration: *56*
Served: *1969–1974*
Vice Presidents:
Spiro T. Agnew,
Gerald R. Ford

38 Gerald R. Ford

1913–
Birthplace: *Omaha, NE*
Home State: *MI*
Political Party:
Republican
Age at Inauguration: *61*
Served: *1974–1977*
Vice President:
Nelson A. Rockefeller

39 Jimmy Carter

1924–
Birthplace: *Plains, GA*
Home State: *GA*
Political Party:
Democratic
Age at Inauguration: *52*
Served: *1977–1981*
Vice President:
Walter F. Mondale

40 Ronald W. Reagan

1911–2004
Birthplace: *Tampico, IL*
Home State: *CA*
Political Party:
Republican
Age at Inauguration: *69*
Served: *1981–1989*
Vice President:
George Herbert Walker Bush

41 George Bush

1924–
Birthplace: *Milton, MA*
Home State: *TX*
Political Party:
Republican
Age at Inauguration: *64*
Served: *1989–1993*
Vice President:
James Danforth Quayle

42 William Clinton

1946–
Birthplace: *Hope, AR*
Home State: *AR*
Political Party:
Democratic
Age at Inauguration: *46*
Served: *1993–2001*
Vice President:
Albert Gore, Jr.

43 George W. Bush

1946–
Birthplace: *New Haven, CT*
Home State: *TX*
Political Party:
Republican
Age at Inauguration: *54*
Served: *2001–*
Vice President:
Richard Cheney

Biographical Dictionary

The Biographical Dictionary lists many of the important people introduced in this book. The page number tells where the main discussion of each person starts. See the Index for other page references.

A

Allen, Richard *1760–1831* An African American minister who founded the Free African Society in Philadelphia. p. PA 4–8

Armstrong, Louis *1900–1971* A noted trumpeter and singer who helped make jazz popular in the 1920s. p. 235

Armstrong, Neil *1930–* An American astronaut who was one of the first people to set foot on the moon. p. 241

Austin, Stephen F. *1793–1836* An American pioneer, known as "The Father of Texas." He helped lead Texas in its fight for independence from Mexico in 1836. The city of Austin is named for him. p. 233

B

Bates, Katharine Lee *1859–1929* An American poet and educator who wrote "America the Beautiful." p. 91

Boone, Daniel *1734–1820* One of the first American pioneers to cross the Appalachian Mountains. p. 174

Bradford, William *1590–1657* Leader of the Plymouth Colony for 30 years. Much of what is known about the colony comes from his journals. p. 102

Breyer, Stephen *1938–* United States Supreme Court justice. p. 470

Brûlé, Étienne (bru•LAY ay•tee•EN) *1592–1632* A French explorer who followed the Susquehanna River to the Chesapeake Bay. p. PA 2–8

Buchanan, James *1791–1868* 15th U.S. President and former Congressman from Pennsylvania. p. PA 4–11

Bush, George W. *1946–* 43rd U.S. President and former governor of Texas. He is the son of 41st President George H. W. Bush. p. 474

C

Carnegie, Andrew *1835–1919* A leader in the early U.S. steel industry based in Pennsylvania who was well known for his gifts of money to schools and libraries. p. 138, p. PA 5–4

Carson, Rachel *1907–1964* A biologist who has been called the mother of the modern environmental movement. p. PA 5–13

Cather, Willa *1873–1947* An American novelist who wrote several books about pioneer life on the Great Plains. p. 297

Catto, Octavius *1839–1871* An African American who fought for civil rights. p. PA 4–9

Champlain, Samuel de (sham•PLAYN) *1567?–1635* A French explorer who explored and mapped much of New England. Lake Champlain is named in his honor. p. 109

Chavez, Cesar *1927–1993* A Mexican-American civil rights leader and organizer of the United Farm Workers. p. 486

Clark, William *1770–1838* An American explorer who, with Meriwether Lewis, explored the Louisiana Territory and lands west of the Rocky Mountains. p. 343

Clemens, Samuel *1835–1910* An American writer who wrote many stories and books under the pen name Mark Twain. p. 284

Columbus, Christopher *1451–1506* An Italian-born Spanish explorer who, in 1492, sailed west from Spain looking for a new route to Asia. Instead he reached islands near the Americas, lands that were unknown to Europeans. p. 22

Cook, James *1728–1779* An English sea captain and explorer who was the first European to see Hawaii. p. 413

Coronado, Francisco Vásquez de (kawr•oh•NAH•doh) *1510?–1554* A Spanish explorer who led an expedition from Mexico City into what is now the southwestern United States in search of gold. p. 366

D

Dart, Justin *1930–2002* A civil rights leader who helped get the Americans with Disabilities Act (ADA) passed in 1990. p. 487

Davis, Jefferson *1808–1889* President of the Confederate States of America from 1861 to 1865. p. 204

Disney, Walt *1901–1966* An American cartoonist who created many popular cartoon characters, animated movies, and theme parks. p. 210

Drake, Edwin *1819–1880* An oil driller who found oil near Titusville, Pennsylvania. p. PA 5–2

F

Fitch, John *1743–1798* A Philadelphia inventor who designed a steamboat in 1787. p. PA 4–3

Flagler, Henry *1830–1913* An American business leader who built a railroad south through the Florida Keys, linking Miami to Key West. p. 217

Ford, Henry *1863–1947* An American automobile manufacturer who produced cars at a low cost by using assembly lines. p. 280

Franklin, Benjamin *1706–1790* An American leader who helped write the Declaration of Independence and the Constitution. He was also a respected scientist, inventor, and business leader. p. 129

Fulton, Robert *1765–1815* An American engineer and inventor who, in 1807, built the *Clermont*, the country's first money-making steamboat. p. 284

G

Ginsburg, Ruth Bader *1933–* United States Supreme Court justice. p. 470

H

Holme, Thomas *1625–1695* An Irish civil engineer who drew maps of Philadelphia and Pennsylvania. p. PA 3–4

Hudson, Henry *?–1611* An English explorer who sailed up the Hudson River, claiming much of present-day New York for Holland. p. 126, p. PA 2–8

I

Inglis, Charles *1743–1816* A religious leader and Loyalist during the American Revolution. p. 130

J

Jefferson, Thomas *1743–1826* 3rd U.S. President and the main writer of the Declaration of Independence. p. 131

Jenney, William *1832–1907* An American engineer who developed the use of steel frames to build tall buildings. p. 279

Joliet, Louis (zhohl•YAY) *1645–1700* A French fur trader and cartographer who, with Jacques Marquette, explored parts of the Great Lakes and the Mississippi River for France. p. 269

Jones, Absalom *1746–1818* An African American minister who founded the Free African Society in Philadelphia. p. PA 4–8

K

Kelley, Florence *1859–1932* A Philadelphia lawyer who worked for improvements for women and children. p. PA 5–6

Kennedy, Anthony *1936–* United States Supreme Court justice. p. 470

King, Martin Luther, Jr. *1929–1968* An African American civil rights leader who worked for integration in nonviolent ways. He won the Nobel Peace Prize in 1964. p. 485

L

La Salle, René-Robert Cavelier, Sieur de (luh•SAL) *1643–1687* A French explorer who found the mouth of the Mississippi River and claimed the whole Mississippi Valley for France. p. 231

Lewis, Meriwether *1774–1809* An American explorer who, with William Clark, explored the Louisiana Territory and lands west of the Rocky Mountains. p. 343

Lincoln, Abraham *1809–1865* 16th U.S. President; he served during the Civil War and ended slavery. p. 204

Louis XIV *1638–1715* King of France, for whom Louisiana was named. p. 232

M

Ma, Yo-Yo *1955–* A well-known American cello player. p. 442

Marquette, Jacques (mar•KET, ZHAHK) *1637–1675* A Catholic priest who knew several Indian languages. With Louis Joliet, he explored parts of the Great Lakes and the Mississippi River for France. p. 269

McCoy, Elijah *1844–1929* An African American inventor who developed a device to oil steam engines while the engines remained in motion. p. 137

McCoy, Joseph G. *1837–1915* A cattle trader and entrepreneur who built stockyards near the railroad at Abilene, Kansas. This led to the growth of a major cattle ranching industry in the Great Plains states. p. 307

Melville, Herman *1819–1891* A well-known American writer. p. 25

Moran, Thomas *1837–1926* An American artist well known for his watercolors of wilderness areas in the western United States. p. 335

Mott, Lucretia *1793–1880* A Quaker minister who was active in the abolitionist movement. p. PA 4–8

Muir, John (MYOOR) *1838–1914* An American naturalist and conservation leader known as "The Father of Our National Parks System." p. 33

N

Nix, Robert N.C. *1905–1987* Pennsylvania's first African American congressman. p. PA 5–11

O

O'Connor, Sandra Day *1930–* First woman to be appointed to the United States Supreme Court. p. 470

P

Paine, Thomas *1737–1809* The author of a widely read pamphlet called *Common Sense*, in which he called for a revolution to make the American colonies independent from Britain. p. 130

Penn, Hannah *1671–1727* William Penn's second wife, who was proprietor of the Pennsylvania colony for fifteen years. p. PA 3–5

Penn, William *1644–1718* An English Quaker who founded Pennsylvania and made the colony a refuge for settlers who wanted religious freedom. p. 127, p. PA 3–2

Pike, Zebulon *1779–1813* An American explorer who explored the southwestern part of the Louisiana Territory and southern Rocky Mountains. p. 344

Pinchot, Gifford *1865–1946* The governor of Pennsylvania during the 1920s and early 1930s. p. PA 5–2

Pocahontas *1595?–1617* A Powhatan Indian princess who helped maintain peace between English colonists and Native Americans. She was a friend to the settlers at Jamestown, in present-day Virginia. p. 172

Ponce de León, Juan (PAHN•say day lay•OHN) *1460–1521* A Spanish explorer who, in 1513, was the first European to land on the North American mainland. He named what is now Florida. p. 200

Potter, Beatrix *1866–1943* A British author of popular children's books. p. 119

Powell, John Wesley *1834–1902* An American geologist who was one of the first people to explore the Grand Canyon. p. 41

Powhatan (pow•uh•TAN) *1550?–1618* A chief of a federation of Indian tribes that lived in the area of present-day Virginia. p. 172

R

Rehnquist, William *1924–2005* United States Supreme Court justice. p. 470

Rockwell, Norman *1894–1978* An American painter and illustrator who is best known for his paintings of everyday activities of American people. His illustrations often appeared on the covers of the *Saturday Evening Post*. p. 452

Roosevelt, Franklin Delano *1882–1945* 32nd U.S. President; he served during the Depression and World War II. p. 453

Roosevelt, Theodore *1858–1919* 26th U.S. President; he worked to protect the nation's natural resources and wilderness areas. p. 317

Rush, Benjamin *1745–1813* A Philadelphia doctor, writer, and educator who opposed slavery. p. PA 3–8

S

Sable, Jean Baptiste du (SAH•bluh, ZHAHN bah•TEEST doo) *1750?–1818* A French trader from Haiti who founded the settlement that became the city of Chicago, Illinois. p. 269

Sacagawea (sak•uh•juh•WEE•uh) *1786?–1812?* A Shoshone woman who acted as an interpreter and guide for the Lewis and Clark expedition. p. 343

Scalia, Antonin *1936–* United States Supreme Court justice. p. 470

Schwab, Charles *1862–1939* A Pennsylvania industrialist who founded the Bethlehem Steel Company. p. PA 5–4

Seattle *1790?–1866* A chief of several Indian tribes in the Puget Sound area, for whom Seattle, Washington, was named. p. 388

Siney, John (SY•nee) *1831–1879* A Pennsylvania coal miner who started the first coal miners' union. p. PA 5–3

Slater, Samuel *1768–1835* A business leader who helped bring an industrial economy to the United States by opening the country's first factory—a textile mill in Rhode Island. p. 104

Smith, John *1580–1631* An English explorer who explored the northeast coast of what is now the United States and named the area New England. He also helped found the colony of Jamestown, in what is now Virginia. p. 100, p. PA 2–8

Soto, Hernando de (SOH•toh, air•NAHN•doh day) *1500–1542* A Spanish explorer who in 1539 began an expedition through nine present-day southeastern states, claiming all of the land for Spain. p. 201

Souter, David *1939–* United States Supreme Court justice. p. 470

Stevens, John Paul *1920–* United States Supreme Court justice. p. 470

Stuyvesant, Peter (STY•vuh•suhnt) *1592–1672* A Dutch colonial governor who ruled New Netherland. p. PA 2–10

Swartz, Anthoni An African man who lived in New Sweden in the 1600s. p. PA 2–12

T

Tarbell, Ida *1857–1944* A journalist who wrote about illegal activity in the oil industry. p. PA 5–7

Thomas, Clarence *1948–* United States Supreme Court justice. p. 470

V

Vespucci, Amerigo (veh•SPOO•chee, uh•MAIR•ih•goh) *1454–1512* An Italian explorer who made several voyages from Europe to what many people thought was Asia. He determined that he had landed on another continent, which was later called America in his honor. p. 25

W

Washington, George *1732–1799* 1st U.S. President and leader of the Continental army during the American Revolution. p. 64

Westinghouse, George *1846–1914* A Pittsburgh inventor who made railroads safer. p. PA 5–3

Wilmot, David *1814–1868* A Pennsylvania congressman who introduced a famous antislavery bill. p. PA 4–10

Y

York *1800s* An enslaved African who was an important member of the Lewis and Clark expedition. He was an acclaimed hero when the expedition returned home. p. 343

The Gazetteer is a geographical dictionary that will help you locate places discussed in this book. The page number tells where each place appears on a map.

A

Abilene A city in central Kansas. (39°N, 97°W) p. 307

Adirondack Mountains (a•duh•RAHN•dak) A range of the Appalachian Mountains in northeastern New York. p. 92

Agana (ah•GAHN•yah) The capital of Guam. (13°N, 145°E) p. 413

Akron A city in northeastern Ohio. (41°N, 81°W) p. 277

Alabama River A river in the southeastern United States. p. 40

Alaska Range A mountain range in southern Alaska. p. 401

Albany (AWL•buh•nee) The capital of New York. (42°N, 74°W) p. 137

Albuquerque (AL•buh•ker•kee) The largest city in New Mexico. (35°N, 106°W) p. 367

Aleutian Islands (uh•LOO•shuhn) A chain of islands extending west from the Alaska Peninsula. p. 401

Allegheny Mountains (a•luh•GAY•nee) A range of the Appalachian Mountains in western Pennsylvania. p. 92

Allegheny Plateau A physical region in Pennsylvania. p. PA 1–7

Allegheny River A river in the northeastern United States. p. 92

Allentown A town in eastern Pennsylvania. (40°N, 75°W) p. PA 1–9

Alps A mountain range in south-central Europe. p. 357

Altoona A town in central Pennsylvania. (40°N, 78°W) p. PA 1–9

Amarillo A city in the Texas Panhandle. (35°N, 102°W) p. 240

Amazon rain forest A tropical forest in South America, located mainly in Brazil. p. 289

Amazon River A river in South America; the second-longest river in the world. p. 287

American Samoa An island territory of the United States in the western Pacific Ocean. p. 413

Amistad National Recreation Area A national park surrounding a reservoir along the Rio Grande in Texas. (29°N, 101°W) p. 245

Amsterdam The capital of the Netherlands. (52°N, 4°E) p. 150

Anchorage (ANG•kuh•rij) The largest city in Alaska. (57°N, 145°W) p. 401

Andes Mountains (AN•deez) A mountain range in South America; the longest chain of mountains on Earth. p. 357

Annapolis (uh•NA•puh•luhs) The capital of Maryland. (39°N, 76°W) p. 478

Antarctica One of the world's seven continents. p. 490

Appalachian Mountains (a•puh•LAY•chee•uhn) A mountain range in the eastern United States. p. 31

Appalachian National Scenic Trail A trail extending from Mt. Katahdin, in Maine, to Springer Mountain, in Georgia. p. 29

Aquinnah A town located on the southeast coast of Massachusetts. p. 100

Arabian Peninsula A peninsula in southwestern Asia bordered by the Red Sea, the Persian Gulf, and the Arabian Sea. p. 80

Arabian Sea A sea located west of India and east of the Arabian Peninsula; forms the southern border of southwestern Asia. p. 80

Arctic Coastal Plain A narrow plain in northern Alaska, along the coast of the Arctic Ocean. p. 401

Arctic Ocean One of the world's four oceans. p. 23

Argentina A country in southern South America, along the Atlantic Ocean. p. 321

Arkansas River A tributary of the Mississippi River. p. 40

Asheville A city in western North Carolina. (36°N, 83°W) p. 183

Asia One of the world's seven continents. p. 23

Atacama Desert (ah•tah•KAH•mah) A desert region in South America; the driest desert in the world. p. 382

Athens The capital of Greece. (8°N, 4°E) p. 151

Atlanta The capital of the state of Georgia. (34°N, 84°W) p. 211

Atlantic Ocean One of the world's four oceans. p. 23

Atlas Mountains A mountain range in northern Africa. p. 357

Augusta The capital of Maine. (44°N, 70°W) p. 92

Austin The capital of Texas. (30°N, 97°W) p. 164

Australia One of the world's seven continents; a country filling the continent of Australia. p. 323

B

Badlands An area of barren land in southwestern South Dakota and northwestern Nebraska. p. 260

Bangor A city in northeastern Maine. (45°N, 69°W) p. 110

Baltic Sea A sea in northern Europe that is part of the Atlantic Ocean. p. 83

Baltimore The largest city in Maryland. (39°N, 76°W) p. 143

Baton Rouge (BA•tuhn ROOZH) The capital of Louisiana. (30°N, 91°W) p. 240

Bay of Bengal An inlet of the Indian Ocean that runs alongside eastern India. p. 80

Bering Sea A sea separating Alaska and Russia. p. 401

Bering Strait A narrow strip of water separating Asia from North America. p. A14

Bethlehem A town in northeastern Pennsylvania. (40°N, 75°W) p. PA 1–9

Big Bend National Park A national park along the Rio Grande in Texas. (29°N, 103°W) p. 228

Big Cypress Swamp A swamp that covers part of southern Florida. p. 216

Billings A city in south-central Montana. (46°N, 109°W) p. 352

Biloxi A port city in Mississippi. (30°N, 89°W) p. 212

Birmingham A city in central Alabama. (33°N, 87°W) p. 207

Bismarck The capital of North Dakota. (47°N, 101°W) p. 260

Bitterroot Range A range of the Rocky Mountains running between Montana and Idaho. p. 345

Black Hills A group of mountains in western South Dakota and northeastern Wyoming. p. 317

Blacktail Butte A peak of the Rocky Mountains in Wyoming, with an elevation of 7,688 feet (2,343 m). (43°N, 110°W) p. 340

Blue Ridge Mountains A mountain range in the Appalachian Mountains. p. 165

Boise The capital of Idaho. (43°N, 116°W) p. 332

Bolivia A country in western South America. p. 361

Boston The capital of Massachusetts. (42°N, 71°W) p. 92

Brazil The largest country in South America. p. 289

Brazos River A river that flows through Texas. p. 40

British Columbia A province of western Canada along the Pacific Ocean. p. A18

Brooks Range A mountain range in northern Alaska. p. 401

Brownsville A city in southern Texas. (26°N, 97°W) p. 240

Buenos Aires (BWAY•nohs EYE•rays) The capital of Argentina. (35°S, 58°W) p. 151

Buffalo A city in western New York. (43°N, 79°W) p. 137

Butte A city in southwestern Montana. (46°N, 112°W) p. 332

C

Cairo A city in southern Illinois, located where the Ohio River joins the Mississippi River. (37°N, 89°W) p. 282

Cape Canaveral (kuh•NAV•ruhl) A cape on the Atlantic coast of Florida. (28°N, 80°W) p. 215

Cape Cod A cape on the southeastern coast of Massachusetts. p. 101

Cape Hatteras (HA•tuh•ruhs) A cape on Hatteras Island, in North Carolina. (35°N, 76°W) p. 164

Caribbean Sea (kair•uh•BEE•uhn) A part of the Atlantic Ocean bounded by the West Indies and Central and South America. p. 218

Carson City The capital of Nevada. (39°N, 120°W) p. 332

Cascade Range A mountain range in the northwestern United States. p. 31

Catskill Mountains An Appalachian Mountain range in southeastern New York. p. 92

Cedar Breaks Canyon A canyon of the Colorado Plateau in Utah. (37°N, 113°W) p. 32

Central America The southernmost part of the continent of North America. p. A8

Central Arizona Project An engineering project that uses canals, tunnels, and pipelines to carry water from the Colorado River to desert lands in Arizona. p. 375

Central Plains The eastern part of the Interior Plains. p. 305

Central Valley A large valley in central California. p. 401

Chang Jiang (CHANG jee•AHNG) The longest river in Asia. p. 287

Charleston (SC) A port city in South Carolina. (33°N, 80°W) p. 207

Charleston (WV) The capital of West Virginia. (38°N, 81°W) p. 164

Charlotte The largest city in North Carolina. (35°N, 81°W) p. 164

Chattanooga (cha•tuh•NOO•guh) A city in southeastern Tennessee. (35°N, 85°W) p. 164

Chesapeake Bay (CHEH•suh•peek) A bay on the Atlantic coast of the United States. Its lower section is in Virginia and its upper section is in Maryland. p. 164

Cheyenne (shy•AN) The capital of Wyoming. (41°N, 105°W) p. 332

Chicago A city in Illinois; the third-largest city in the United States. (42°N, 88°W) p. 266

Chihuahuan Desert (chee•WAH•wahn) A desert region that covers part of Mexico, New Mexico, and Texas; part of the North American Desert. p. 367

Chile A country on the southwestern coast of South America. p. 381

China A country in eastern Asia. p. 79

Cincinnati (sin•suh•NA•tee) A city in southern Ohio. (39°N, 84°W) p. 89

Ciudad Juárez (SEE•oo•dahd HWAR•ays) A city in northern Mexico, near El Paso, Texas. (31°N, 106°W) p. 244

Cleveland A city in northern Ohio. (41°N, 82°W) p. 89

Coast Ranges The mountain ranges that stretch along the Pacific coast of North America. p. 31

Coastal Plain One of the major plains in the United States, located along the coasts of the Atlantic Ocean and the Gulf of Mexico. p. 31, p. PA 1–7

Colorado Plateau A plateau in the southwestern United States; covers most of northern New Mexico and Arizona. p. 31

Colorado River A river in the southwestern United States. p. 40

Columbia The capital of South Carolina. (34°N, 81°W) p. 174

Columbia Plateau A plateau located to the east of the Cascade Range. p. 31

Columbia River A river in the northwestern United States and southwestern Canada. p. 40

Columbus The capital of Ohio. (40°N, 83°W) p. 89

Concord The capital of New Hampshire. (43°N, 71°W) p. 92

Connecticut River The longest river in New England. p. 40

Continental Divide A ridge that divides eastern and western North America and extends from northwestern Canada to South America. p. 345

Corpus Christi (KAWR•puhs KRIS•tee) A city in southeastern Texas. (28°N, 97°W) p. 164

Council Bluffs A city in Iowa, along the Missouri River on the Iowa–Nebraska state line. (41°N, 96°W) p. 296

Cuba An island country, located south of the Florida Keys of the United States. p. 216

Cumberland Gap A pass through the Appalachian Mountains in Tennessee. p. 174

GAZETTEER

GAZETTEER

D

Dakhla Oasis (DAH•kluh) An oasis in the Sahara region of Egypt. (26°N, 29°E) p. 383

Dallas A city in northeastern Texas. (33°N, 97°W) p. 164

Dauphin Island A small barrier island in Mobile Bay, off the coast of Alabama. (30°N, 88°W) p. 214

Daytona Beach A city in eastern Florida. (29°N, 81°W) p. 165

Death Valley The lowest point in the Western Hemisphere, located in the Mojave Desert in California. (36°N, 117°W) p. 47

Delaware Bay A bay on the coast of the Atlantic Ocean, located between New Jersey and Delaware. p. 92

Delaware River A river in the northeastern United States. p. 40

Denver The capital of Colorado. (40°N, 105°W) p. 352

Des Moines (dih MOYN) The capital of Iowa. (41°N, 94°W) p. 260

Detroit The largest city in Michigan. (42°N, 83°W) p. 277

Dodge City A city in southern Kansas which was a major railroad center on the Santa Fe Trail. (38°N, 100°W) p. 307

Dover The capital of Delaware. (39°N, 76°W) p. 92

Duluth (duh•LOOTH) The third-largest city in Minnesota. (47°N, 92°W) p. 277

E

East China Sea The part of the China Sea north of Taiwan. p. 287

Eastport A port city on Moose Island in Maine; the easternmost city in the United States. (45°N, 67°W) p. 100

Egypt A country in northeastern Africa. p. 286

El Chamizal (sha•muh•ZAHL) A tract of land on the Rio Grande, adjoining El Paso, Texas. This land was the source of a border conflict between the United States and Mexico after the Rio Grande changed its course. The land was ceded to Mexico by the United States in 1963. p. 244

El Paso A city in western Texas. (32°N, 106°W) p. 244

Ellsworth A city in central Kansas. (39°N, 98°W) p. 307

England The largest part of the United Kingdom; also called Britain. p. 118

Equator An imaginary line that circles Earth halfway between the North Pole and the South Pole. The line divides Earth into the Northern Hemisphere and the Southern Hemisphere. p. 26

Erie A city in northwestern Pennsylvania. (42°N, 80°W) p. 137

Erie Canal A waterway that connects Lake Erie with the Hudson River and the Atlantic Ocean. p. 137

Erie Plain A physical region in Pennsylvania. p. PA 1–7

Europe One of the world's seven continents. p. 23

European Plain A large region of plains stretching across northern Europe. p. 321

Everglades A large area of wetlands in southern Florida. p. 216

F

Fargo A city in eastern North Dakota. (47°N, 97°W) p. 316

Flagstaff A city in north-central Arizona. (35°N, 112°W) p. 367

Florida Bay The body of water located between the southern tip of Florida and the Florida Keys. p. 216

Florida Keys A chain of islands off the southern tip of the Florida Peninsula. p. 216

Fort Bragg A town in North Carolina that is the site of a training camp for the U.S. Marine Corps. (35°N, 79°W) p. 189

Fort Smith A city in western Arkansas. (35°N, 94°W) p. 240

Fort Wayne A city in northeastern Indiana. (41°N, 85°W) p. 260

Fort Worth A city in north-central Texas. (33°N, 97°W) p. 240

Framingham A suburban town located 20 miles west of Boston, Massachusetts. (42°N, 71°W) p. 61

France A country in western Europe. p. 82

Frankfort The capital of Kentucky. (38°N, 85°W) p. 164

Front Range A mountain range of the Rocky Mountains in Wyoming and Colorado. p. 345

G

Gallup A city in northwestern New Mexico. (35°N, 108°W) p. 332

Galveston A city on Galveston Island, in Texas. (29°N, 95°W) p. 240

Ganges River (GAN•jeez) A river in India that flows into the Bay of Bengal. p. 287

Gary A city in northwestern Indiana. (41°N, 87°W) p. 277

Germany A country in western Europe. p. 83

Gila River (HEE•lah) A river in the southwestern United States. p. 40

Glenwood Canyon A canyon in Colorado. p. 86

Gobi (GOH•bee) A desert region in central Asia. p. 382

Grand Canyon A canyon in northwestern Arizona, formed by the Colorado River. p. 41

Grand Rapids A city in western Michigan. (43°N, 86°W) p. 277

Grand Teton The highest peak of the Teton Range of the Rocky Mountains in Wyoming. It has an elevation of 13,766 feet (4,196 m). (44°N, 111°W) p. 332

Great Barrier Reef A coral reef along Australia's eastern Pacific coast; the longest coral reef in the world; site of the Great Barrier Reef Marine Park. p. 194

Great Basin An area of low, dry land in the western United States, including parts of Nevada, Utah, California, Idaho, Wyoming, and Oregon. p. 31

Great Lakes A chain of five lakes, located in central North America; the largest group of freshwater lakes in the world. p. 277

Great Plains The western part of the Interior Plains of the United States. p. 305

Great Salt Lake The largest lake in the Great Basin, located in Utah. p. 40

Great Smoky Mountains A mountain range in the Appalachian Mountains. p. 190

Great Smoky Mountains National Park A national park in Tennessee and North Carolina, along the Great Smoky Mountains. (35°N, 83°W) p. 190

Greece A country in southern Europe, made up of several peninsulas and islands. p. 224

Green Bay A city in eastern Wisconsin. (45°N, 88°W) p. 277

Green Mountains An Appalachian Mountain range in the northeastern United States, which extends from Canada through Vermont and into Massachusetts. p. 92

Greensboro A city in north-central North Carolina. (36°N, 80°W) p. 165

Greenville (MS) A city in western Mississippi. (33°N, 90°W) p. 212

Greenville (SC) A city in northwestern South Carolina. (35°N, 82°W) p. 257

Guadalupe Peak (gwah•dah•LOO•pay) A peak of the Guadalupe Mountains, with an elevation of 8,749 feet (2,667 m). (32°N, 105°W) p. 232

Guam (GWAHM) An island territory of the United States in the western Pacific Ocean. p. 413

Gulf of Mexico A body of water off the southeastern coast of North America; it is bounded by the United States, Cuba, and Mexico. p. 31

Gulfport A port city in southern Mississippi, on the Gulf of Mexico. (30°N, 89°W) p. 212

H

Hampton Roads A port city in eastern Virginia on the Chesapeake Bay. (37°N, 76°W) p. 186

Harrisburg The capital of Pennsylvania. (40°N, 77°W) p. 140, p. PA 1–5

Hartford The capital of Connecticut. (42°N, 73°W) p. 92

Havana The capital of Cuba. (23°N, 82°W) p. 201

Havre de Grace A city in eastern Maryland. (39°N, 76°W) p. 173

Hawaii The largest of the eight major Hawaiian Islands. p. 413

Hawkshead A town in northwestern England. (54°N, 3°W) p. 118

Helena (HEH•luh•nuh) The capital of Montana. (46°N, 112°W) p. 332

Hilton Head Island A barrier island off the coast of South Carolina. (32°N, 81°W) p. 165

Himalayas (hih•muh•LAY•uhz) A mountain range in southern Asia. p. 357

Hong Kong A port city in southeastern China. (22°N, 114°E) p. 416

Honolulu (hah•nuh•LOO•loo) The capital of Hawaii. (21°N, 158°W) p. 413

Honshu Island An island in central Japan. p. 80

Hoover Dam A dam on the Colorado River on the Nevada–Arizona state line. (36°N, 114°W) p. 422

Houston The largest city in Texas. (30°N, 95°W) p. 240

Hudson River A river in the northeastern United States. p. 40

Humboldt River A river in Nevada. p. 375

Huntsville A city in northern Alabama. (35°N, 87°W) p. 164

I

Illinois River A river in Illinois. p. 40

Illinois Waterway A waterway that connects Lake Michigan with the Illinois River. p. 277

India A country in southern Asia. p. 220

Indian Ocean One of the world's four oceans. p. 23

Indianapolis (in•dee•uh•NA•puh•luhs) The capital of Indiana. (40°N, 86°W) p. 260

Interior Plains One of the major plains regions of the United States, located between the Appalachian Mountains and the Rocky Mountains; includes the Central Plains and the Great Plains. p. 31

Ireland A country in western Europe, located in the British Isles. p. 83

Israel (IZ•ree•uhl) A country on the eastern coast of the Mediterranean Sea. p. 384

Italy A country in southern Europe, on the Mediterranean Sea. p. 83

J

Jackson The capital of Mississippi. (32°N, 90°W) p. 212

Jacksonville A port city in northeastern Florida. (30°N, 82°W) p. 165

James River A river in central Virginia. p. 40

Jamestown The first permanent English settlement in America, located on the James River. (37°N, 77°W) p. 172

Japan An island country in eastern Asia. p. 154

Jefferson City The capital of Missouri. (38°N, 92°W) p. 316

Juneau (JOO•noh) The capital of Alaska. (55°N, 120°W) p. 401

K

Kansas City The largest city in Missouri, located on the Missouri River on the Kansas–Missouri state line. (39°N, 94°W) p. 314

Kauai (kah•WAH•ee) The fourth-largest of the eight major Hawaiian Islands. p. 413

Key Largo The largest island in the Florida Keys. p. 216

Key West A city in southwestern Florida, on the island of Key West. (24°N, 82°W) p. 216

Kilauea (kee•lah•WAY•ah) An active volcano on the island of Hawaii. It has an elevation of 4,090 feet (1,247 m). (19°N, 155°W) p. 413

GAZETTEER

Kitt Peak   Mount Elbert

GAZETTEER

Kitt Peak A mountain in the Quinlan Mountains of Arizona; it has an elevation of 6,880 feet (2,097 m). (32°N, 111°W) p. 378

Knoxville A city in eastern Tennessee. (36°N, 84°W) p. 183

Kruger National Park The largest national park in South Africa. (25°S, 31°E) p. 192

L

La Paz The capital of Bolivia; the highest capital city in the world. (16°S, 68°W) p. 361

Lagos (LAY•gahs) A port city in Nigeria. (6°N, 3°E) p. 151

Lake Champlain (sham•PLAYN) A large lake on the New York–Vermont state line. p. 109

Lake Erie The fourth-largest of the Great Lakes, bordering New York, Pennsylvania, Ohio, Michigan, and Canada. p. 277

Lake Huron The second-largest of the Great Lakes, bordering Michigan and Canada. p. 277

Lake Itasca (eye•TAS•kuh) A lake in northern Minnesota; the source of the Mississippi River. p. 282

Lake Mead A reservoir on the Colorado River, formed by Hoover Dam. p. 422

Lake Michigan The third-largest of the Great Lakes, bordering Michigan, Indiana, Illinois, and Wisconsin. p. 277

Lake Okeechobee (oh•kuh •CHOH•bee) The largest lake in the southern United States, located in southern Florida along the northern edge of the Everglades. p. 216

Lake Ontario The smallest of the Great Lakes, bordering New York and Canada. p. 277

Lake Superior The largest of the Great Lakes, bordering Michigan, Wisconsin, Minnesota, and Canada. p. 277

Lakshadweep Islands (luhk•SHAHD•weep) A group of islands off the southwestern coast of India, in the Arabian Sea. p. 220

Lancaster A city in southeastern Pennsylvania. (40°N, 76°W) p. 140, p. PA 1–9

Lansing The capital of Michigan. (43°N, 85°W) p. 260

Laramie A city in southern Wyoming. (41°N, 108°W) p. 352

Laredo A city in southern Texas, located on the Rio Grande. (27°N, 99°W) p. 244

Las Vegas The largest city in Nevada. (36°N, 115°W) p. 332

Levittown A town in eastern Pennsylvania. (40°N, 74°W) p. PA 1–9

Lexington A city in north-central Kentucky. (38°N, 84°W) p. 164

Lincoln The capital of Nebraska. (41°N, 97°W) p. 260

Little Rock The capital of Arkansas. (35°N, 92°W) p. 164

Long Island An island located east of New York City and south of Connecticut. p. 143

Long Island Sound The body of water separating Connecticut and Long Island, New York. p. 137

Los Angeles The largest city in California; the second-largest city in the United States. (34°N, 118°W) p. 332

Louisville The largest city in Kentucky. (38°N, 86°W) p. 164

M

Madison The capital of Wisconsin. (43°N, 89°W) p. 260

Mammoth Cave A system of caves in south-central Kentucky; the largest cave system in the world. (37°N, 86°W) p. 164

Manomet A town located on the coast of Massachusetts. p. 100

Marquette A city in northwestern Michigan. (46°N, 87°W) p. 277

Mashpee A town located on Cape Cod in Massachusetts. (41°N, 70°W) p. 100

Massachusetts Bay An inlet of the Atlantic Ocean on the coast of Massachusetts. p. 101

Maui (MOW•ee) The second-largest of the eight major Hawaiian Islands. p. 45

Mauna Loa (MOW•nah LOH•uh) An active volcano on the island of Hawaii, with an elevation of 13,769 feet (4,169 m). (19°N, 155°W) p. 413

Mediterranean Sea (meh•duh•tuh•RAY•nee•uhn) The sea south of Europe, north of Africa, and west of Asia. p. 83

Memphis The largest city in Tennessee. (35°N, 90°W) p. 164

Merritt Island A barrier island off the coast of southeastern Florida. (28°N, 80°W) p. 215

Mesabi Range (muh•SAH•bee) An area of low hills in northeastern Minnesota. p. 260

Mexico City The capital of Mexico. (19°N, 99°W) p. 152

Miami A city in southern Florida. (26°N, 80°W) p. 74

Miami Beach A city on a barrier island off the coast of southern Florida. (26°N, 80°W) p. 198

Middle West One of the four large regions of the United States. p. 260

Milwaukee (mil•WAW•kee) The largest city in Wisconsin. (43°N, 88°W) p. 277

Minneapolis (mih•nee•A•puh•luhs) The largest city in Minnesota. (45°N, 93°W) p. 282

Mississippi Delta The landform at the mouth of the Mississippi River, created by silt deposited by the river. p. 42

Mississippi River A river that flows from Minnesota to the Gulf of Mexico; the longest river in the United States. p. 282

Missouri River A tributary of the Mississippi River; it flows from Montana to St. Louis, Missouri. p. 40

Mobile A port city in southern Alabama. (30°N, 88°W) p. 164

Mojave Desert (moh•HAH•vee) A large desert area between the southern Sierra Nevada and the Colorado River. p. 401

Monongahela River (muh•nahng•guh•HEE•luh) A river that flows through Pennsylvania and West Virginia. p. 92

Montgomery The capital of Alabama. (32°N, 86°W) p. 164

Montpelier (mahnt•PEEL•yuhr) The capital of Vermont. (44°N, 72°W) p. 92

Mount Elbert A mountain in Colorado, with an elevation of 14,433 feet (4,399 m). (39°N, 106°W) p. 332

R18 ▪ Reference

Mount Everest The highest point on Earth, with an elevation of 29,028 feet (8,848 m); part of the Himalayas in Nepal. (28°N, 87°E) p. 356

Mount Hood A mountain in Oregon, with an elevation of 11,235 feet (3,424 m). (45°N, 122°W) p. 401

Mount McKinley The highest point in North America, with an elevation of 20,320 feet (6,194 m); located in the Alaska Range. (57°N, 150°W) p. 400

Mount Mitchell The highest point in the eastern United States, with an elevation of 6,684 feet (2,037 m), located in the Appalachian Mountains of North Carolina. (36°N, 82°W) p. 165

Mount Rainier (ruh•NIR) The highest point in the Cascade Range, in Washington, with an elevation of 14,410 feet (4,392 m). (47°N, 122°W). p. 34

Mount Rushmore A mountain in the Black Hills of South Dakota, with an elevation of 5,600 feet (1,707 m). (44°N, 103°W) p. 317

Mount St. Helens A volcano in the Cascade Range, in Washington, that erupted in 1980. It has an elevation of 8,364 feet (2,549 m). (46°N, 122°W) p. 401

Mount Waialeale (wy•ah•lay•AH•lay) A mountain on the island of Kauai, in Hawaii, with an elevation of 5,208 feet (1,587 m); the rainiest place in the United States. (22°N, 159°W) p. 401

Mount Washington A mountain in the White Mountains, in New Hampshire, with an elevation of 6,288 feet (1,917 m). (44°N, 71°W) p. 92

Mount Whitney The highest point in the continental United States, with an elevation of 14,495 feet (4,418 m); located in the Sierra Nevada, in California. (37°N, 118°W) p. 401

Myrtle Beach A resort city on the northeastern coast of South Carolina. (34°N, 79°W) p. 257

N

Nashville The capital of Tennessee. (36°N, 87°W) p. 183

Natchez A city in southwestern Mississippi, located on the Mississippi River. (31°N, 91°W) p. 212

Negev (NEH•gev) A desert region in southern Israel. p. 384

Nepal (nuh•PAHL) A country in southern Asia, between India and China. p. 356

Netherlands A country on the northern coast of central Europe, on the North Sea. p. 150

New Orleans (AWR•lee•uhnz) The largest city in Louisiana. (30°N, 90°W) p. 234

New York City The largest city in the United States. (41°N, 74°W) p. 143

New York State Barge Canal System A system of canals that links the Great Lakes with the Hudson River and the Atlantic Ocean. p. 137

Newark The largest city in New Jersey. (41°N, 74°W) p. 143

Newfane A small town in southeastern Vermont between the Connecticut River and the Green Mountains. (43°N, 73°W) p. 112

Newlands Irrigation Project An engineering project on Lake Tahoe and the Truckee and Carson Rivers in Nevada, used to move water to the state's desert lands. p. 375

Newport A city in southeastern Rhode Island, on the Massachusetts–Rhode Island state line. (41°N, 71°W) p. 161

Niagara Falls (ny•AG•ruh) The large series of waterfalls on the Niagara River. (43°N, 79°W) p. 137

Niagara River A river in western New York, which forms part of the United States–Canada border. p. 137

Niger River A river in western Africa. p. A7

Nigeria A country along the western Atlantic coast of Africa. p. 249

Nile River A river in northeastern Africa; the longest river in the world. p. 287

Norfolk (NAWR•fohk) A port city in Virginia. (37°N, 76°W) p. 165

North America One of the world's seven continents. p. 23

North American Desert A desert region in western North America. p. 382

North Pole The northernmost point on Earth. (90°N) p. 26

North Sea A part of the Atlantic Ocean, located east of Great Britain and west of Denmark. p. 287

Northeast One of the four large regions of the United States. p. 92

Northwest Territory A former territory of the United States, made up of the lands west of Pennsylvania, north of the Ohio River, east of the Mississippi River, and south of the Great Lakes; later became the six Great Lakes states. p. 270

Nuevo Laredo (NWAY•voh luh•RAY•doh) A city in northern Mexico, on the Rio Grande opposite Laredo, Texas. (27°N, 99°W) p. 244

Nullarbor Plain A narrow coastal plain along the southern Pacific coast of Australia. p. 321

O

Oahu (oh•AH•hoo) The third-largest of the eight major Hawaiian Islands. p. 413

Oak Bluffs A town located on the island of Martha's Vineyard off the coast of Massachusetts. (41°N, 70°W) p. 11

Ogallala (oh•guh•LAHL•uh) A city in western Nebraska. (41°N, 102°W) p. 307

Ohio River A tributary of the Mississippi River. p. 40

Okefenokee Swamp (oh•kee•fuh•NOH•kee) A swamp that covers part of southeastern Georgia and northern Florida. p. 254

Oklahoma City The capital of Oklahoma. (35°N, 98°W) p. 164

Olympia (oh•LIM•pee•uh) The capital of Washington. (47°N, 123°W) p. 332

Olympic National Park A national park in Washington that has some of the few rain forest areas in the United States. (48°N, 124°W) p. 402

Omaha The largest city in Nebraska. (41°N, 96°W) p. 307

Oregon City A city in northwestern Oregon; the official end of the Oregon Trail. (45°N, 123°W) p. 390

Oregon Trail A former overland route to the Oregon Country, extending from the Missouri River northwest to the Columbia River in Oregon. p. 394

Orlando A city in central Florida. (28°N, 81°W) p. 165

Ottawa A city in northwestern Ohio. (41°N, 84°W) p. 89

Ouachita Mountains (WAH•shuh•tah) A mountain range in western Arkansas and southeastern Oklahoma. p. 164

Outer Banks A chain of sand islands and peninsulas along the coast of North Carolina. p. 164

Ozark Plateau (OH•zark) A plateau extending from southeastern Missouri across Arkansas and into Oklahoma. p. 31

P

Pacific Ocean One of the world's four oceans. p. 23

Pacific Rim A region of the world that includes the countries that border the Pacific Ocean. p. 417

Paducah (puh•DOO•kuh) A city in western Kentucky; located where the Tennessee River joins the Ohio River. (37°N, 87°W) p. 183

Pago Pago (PAH•goh PAH•goh) The capital of American Samoa. (14°S, 171°W) p. 413

Painted Desert A desert region in Arizona. p. 366

Palenque National Park (pah•LENG•kay) A national park in southern Mexico at the site of an ancient Mayan city. (18°N, 92°W) p. 195

Pampas (PAM•pahz) A plains region in central South America. p. 321

Panama Canal A canal across the Isthmus of Panama, connecting the Atlantic Ocean and the Pacific Ocean. p. 417

Paris The capital of France. (48°N, 2°E) p. 82

Pascagoula (pas•kuh•GOO•luh) A port city in southern Mississippi. (30°N, 88°W) p. 212

Pawtucket A city in northeastern Rhode Island; the site of the first textile mill in the United States. (42°N, 71°W) p. 161

Pearl Harbor An inlet on the southern coast of Oahu, Hawaii; the Japanese attacked an American naval base there on December 7, 1941. p. 413

Pecos River (PAY•kohs) A river that flows through eastern New Mexico and western Texas. p. 40

Penn Hills p. PA 1–9

Pennsylvania A state located in the northeast region of the United States. (39–42°N, 80–75°W) p. PA 1–3

Peru A country in western South America. p. 381

Petrified Forest A once-forested region in Arizona's Painted Desert, in which all the trees are dead and have turned to stone. (35°N, 110°W) p. 377

Philadelphia The largest city in Pennsylvania. (40°N, 75°W) p. 124, p. PA 1–9

Phoenix (FEE•niks) The capital of Arizona. (33°N, 112°W) p. 73

Piedmont (PEED•mahnt) A region of high land that lies east of the Appalachian Mountains. p. 31, p. PA 1–7

Pierre (PIR) The capital of South Dakota. (44°N, 100°W) p. 260

Pikes Peak A peak of the Rocky Mountains in east-central Colorado, with an elevation of 14,110 feet (4,301 m). (39°N, 105°W) p. 344

Pittsburgh A city in southwestern Pennsylvania. (40°N, 80°W) p. 38, p. PA 1–9

Platte River A river that flows through central Nebraska and is a tributary of the Missouri River. p. 40

Plymouth (PLIH•muhth) A town on Plymouth Bay in Massachusetts; the site of the first settlement built by the Pilgrims in 1620. (42°N, 71°W) p. 101

Pocono Mountains (POH•kuh•noh) An Appalachian Mountain range in eastern Pennsylvania. p. 92

Poland A country in eastern Europe. p. 322

Portland The largest city in Oregon. (45°N, 123°W) p. 332

Potomac River (puh•TOH•muhk) A river in the eastern United States. p. 64

Prime meridian An imaginary line that divides Earth into the Eastern Hemisphere and the Western Hemisphere. p. 26

Providence (PRAH•vuh•duhns) The capital of Rhode Island. (42°N, 71°W) p. 105

Puerto Rico (PWAIR•toh REE•koh) A commonwealth of the United States, located southeast of Florida, in the Caribbean Sea. p. 218

Puget Sound (PYOO•juht) An inlet of the Pacific Ocean in northwestern Washington. p. 332

Q

Quidnick A city in central Rhode Island. (41°N, 71°W) p. 161

R

Raleigh (RAH•lee) The capital of North Carolina. (36°N, 79°W) p. 174

Reading A town in eastern Pennsylvania. (40°N, 75°W) p. PA 1-9

Red River A tributary of the Mississippi River. p. 40

Red River Valley A fertile valley in eastern North Dakota along the Red River. p. 58

Reno (REE•noh) The second-largest city in Nevada. (39°N, 120°W) p. 332

Rhine River A river in western Europe. p. 287

Richmond The capital of Virginia. (38°N, 77°W) p. 174

Ridge and Valley A physical region in Pennsylvania. p. PA 1–7

Ring of Fire An area of volcanic activity and earthquakes surrounding the Pacific Ocean. p. 417

Rio de Janeiro (REE•oh DAY zhuh•NAY•roh) A port city in southwestern Brazil. (22°S, 43°W) p. 223

Rio Grande (REE•oh GRAND) The river that forms the Texas–Mexico border. p. 244

Rochester A city in western New York. (43°N, 77°W) p. 137

Rock Hill A city in north-central South Carolina. (35°N, 81°W) p. 257

Rocky Mountains A mountain range that extends through the western United States into Canada. p. 31

Russia A country in northeastern Europe and northern Asia. p. 250

S

Sabine River A river that forms part of the Texas–Louisiana border. p. 40

Sacramento (sa•kruh•MEN•toh) The capital of California. (39°N, 122°W) p. 394

Sacramento River A river in northwestern California. p. 40

Sahara (suh•HAR•uh) A desert region in northern Africa; the largest desert in the world. p. 382

St. Andrews A town in eastern Canada, near the Maine–Canada border. (45°, 67°W) p. 120

St. Augustine (AW•guh•steen) A city on the Atlantic coast of Florida; the oldest city founded by Europeans in the United States. (30°N, 81°W) p. 200

St. Croix (SAYNT KROY) The southernmost of the three major United States Virgin Islands. p. 218

St. Helena Island An island off the coast of South Carolina. p. 166

St. John The westernmost of the three major United States Virgin Islands. p. 218

St. Johns River A river in northeastern Florida. p. 165

St. Joseph A city in northwestern Missouri. (40°N, 95°W) p. 394

St. Lawrence River A river that forms part of the border between Canada and the United States. p. 40

St. Lawrence Seaway A waterway that connects Lake Ontario with the St. Lawrence River and the Atlantic Ocean. p. 137

St. Louis The largest city in Missouri. (38°N, 90°W) p. 326

St. Paul The capital of Minnesota. (45°N, 93°W) p. 260

St. Thomas The easternmost of the three major United States Virgin Islands. p. 218

Salem (SAY•luhm) The capital of Oregon. (45°N, 123°W) p. 332

Salt Lake City The capital of Utah. (41°N, 112°W) p. 345

San Antonio A city in central Texas. (29°N, 98°W) p. 233

San Diego A city in southern California. (33°N, 118°W) p. 399

San Francisco A city in northern California. (38°N, 124°W) p. 401

San Francisco Bay A bay on the northern coast of California. p. 401

San Joaquin River (SAN wah•KEEN) A river in central California. p. 401

San Jose (san hoh•ZAY) A city in western California. (37°N, 122°W) p. 332

San Juan (SAN HWAHN) The capital of Puerto Rico. (18°N, 66°W) p. 218

Sand Hills A region of sand dunes and grasslands covering about one-fourth of Nebraska. p. 294

Santa Fe (SAN•tah FAY) The capital of New Mexico. (35°N, 106°W) p. 332

Santorini (san•toh•REE•nee) One of the Greek islands in the Aegean Sea. p. 224

Saudi Arabia A country that occupies most of the Arabian Peninsula. p. 248

Savannah (suh•VA•nuh) The oldest city in Georgia. (32°N, 81°W) p. 165

Savannah River A river that forms the border between Georgia and South Carolina. p. 40

Scranton (SKRAN•tuhn) A city in northeastern Pennsylvania. (41°N, 75°W) p. 140, p. PA 1–9

Seattle (see•AT•uhl) The largest city in Washington. (47°N, 122°W) p. 388

Sequoia National Forest A national forest on the western side of the Sierra Nevada in California. (37°N, 119°W) p. 405

Shanghai (SHANG•hy) A port city on the East China Sea, located near the mouth of the Chang Jiang. (25°N, 125°E) p. 151

Shenandoah Valley (sheh•nuhn•DOH•uh) A valley that lies between the Blue Ridge Mountains and the Allegheny Mountains in Virginia and West Virginia. p. 165

Shreveport A city in northwestern Louisiana. (33°N, 94°W) p. 240

Siberia A region in north-central Asia, mostly in Russia. p. 80

Sierra Nevada (see•AIR•ah nuh•VA•duh) A mountain range in eastern California. p. 31

Snake River A river in the western United States. p. 40

Sonoran Desert (soh•NAWR•uhn) A part of the North American Desert; located in southwestern Arizona. p. 373

South One of the four large regions of the United States. p. 164

South Africa A country at the southern tip of Africa. p. 192

South America One of the world's seven continents. p. 23

South Pass A pass through the Rocky Mountains near where the states of Wyoming, Utah, and Colorado meet. p. 345

South Pole The southernmost point on Earth. (90°S) p. 26

Spain A country in southwestern Europe. p. 83

Spartanburg A city in northern South Carolina. (35°N, 82°W) p. 257

Spokane A city in eastern Washington. (48°N, 117°W) p. 332

Springfield (IL) The capital of Illinois. (40°N, 90°W) p. 260

Springfield (OH) A city in west-central Ohio. (40°N, 84°W) p. 89

State College A town in central Pennsylvania. (40°N, 77°W) p. PA 1–9

Straits of Florida A narrow waterway separating the Florida Keys and Cuba. p. 216

Susquehanna River (suhs•kwuh•HA•nuh) A river in Pennsylvania. p. 40

Sweden A country in northern Europe, along the Baltic Sea. p. 83

Switzerland A country in central Europe, in the Alps. p. 358

T

Tacoma A city in Washington. (47°N, 123°W) p. 401

Taiwan (ty•WAHN) An island country off the southeastern coast of China. p. 80

Tallahassee (ta•luh•HA•see) The capital of Florida. (30°N, 84°W) p. 165

Tampa A city in west-central Florida. (28°N, 82°W) p. 165

Tennessee River A tributary of the Ohio River. p. 183

Tenterfield A town in southeastern Australia. (29°S, 148°E) p. 119

GAZETTEER

Teton Range A range of the Rocky Mountains in Wyoming. p. 345

Tokyo (TOH•kee•oh) The capital of Japan. (34°N, 140°E) p. 154

Toledo A city in northern Ohio. (42°N, 84°W) p. 401

Topeka The capital of Kansas. (39°N, 96°W) p. 307

Trenton The capital of New Jersey. (40°N, 74°W) p. 92

Tucson A city in southern Arizona. (32°N, 111°W) p. 367

Tulsa (TUHL•suh) A city in northeastern Oklahoma. (36°N, 96°W) p. 240

Tupelo A city in northeastern Mississippi. (34°N, 89°W) p. 212

United Kingdom A European country made up of four kingdoms in the British Isles—England, Scotland, Wales, and Northern Ireland. p. 83

Ural Mountains (YOOR•uhl) A mountain range that runs north and south between Asia and Europe. p. 357

Valdez (val•DEEZ) A port city in southern Alaska. (61°N, 146°W) p. 332

Varanasi (vuh•RA•nuh•see) A city in India along the Ganges River. (25°N, 83°E) p. 288

Virgin Islands A group of islands between the Caribbean Sea and the Atlantic Ocean that are United States territories. p. 218

Virginia Beach A city and ocean resort in Virginia. (37°N, 76°W) p. 165

W

Wabash River (WAW•bash) A river in Indiana and Illinois that empties into the Ohio River. p. 40

Waiehu (wah•ee•AY•hoo) A town on the island of Maui in Hawaii. (21°N, 156°W) p. 45

Washington, D.C. The capital of the United States. (39°N, 77°W) p. 64

Welland Ship Canal (WEH•luhnd) A ship waterway that connects Lake Erie and Lake Ontario; part of the St. Lawrence Seaway. p. 137

West One of the four large regions of the United States. p. 332

White Mountains A mountain range of the Appalachian Mountains in northern New Hampshire. p. 92

Wichita (WIH•chih•taw) A city in southern Kansas. (37°N, 97°W) p. 260

Wilderness Road A former pioneer road that began in Tennessee and crossed the Appalachian Mountains into Kentucky. p. 174

Wilkes-Barre A town in northeastern Pennsylvania. (41°N, 75°W) p. PA 1–9

Willa Cather Memorial Prairie An area of prairie in Nebraska, set aside as a national memorial. (40°N, 98°W) p. 297

Willamette Valley A valley in Oregon between the Coast Ranges and the Cascade Range. p. 401

Wilmington A city in eastern Delaware. (40°N, 76°W) p. 92

Wisconsin River A river in Wisconsin that empties into the Mississippi River. p. 260

Wolong Natural Reserve (WOH•lahng) A national park in central China for preserving the habitat of giant pandas. p. 193

Woodstock A city in east-central Vermont. (43°N, 72°W) p. 99

Yangshuo (yang•JOH) A city in southern China. (23°N, 109°E) p. 79

Yellowstone National Park The first national park in the United States, which covers parts of Idaho, Wyoming, and Montana. (45°N, 111°W) p. 332

Yellowstone River A river in the northwestern United States. p. 332

York A city in south-central Pennsylvania. (40°N, 76°W) p. 140, p. PA 1–9

Yosemite National Park A national park located in the Sierra Nevada of eastern California. (38°N, 118°W) p. 20

Yucatán Peninsula (yoo•kah•TAHN) A peninsula extending from the eastern coast of Central America. p. A9

Yukon River (YOO•kahn) A river that flows through Alaska and the southwestern Yukon Territory in Canada. p. 40

Z

Zanesville A city in east-central Ohio. (40°N, 82°W) p. 89

GAZETTEER

Glossary

The Glossary contains important social studies words and their definitions. Each word is respelled as it would be in a dictionary. When you see this mark ´ after a syllable, pronounce that syllable with more force than the other syllables. The page number at the end of the definition tells where to find the word in your book.

add, āce, câre, pälm; end, ēqual; it, īce; odd, ōpen, ôrder; tŏŏk, pōōl; up, bûrn; yōō as *u* in *fuse*; oil; pout; ə as *a* in *above*, *e* in *sicken*, *i* in *possible*, *o* in *melon*, *u* in *circus*; check; ring; thin; this; zh as in *vision*

A

abolish (ə•bä´lish) To end. p. 204

abolitionist (a•bə•´li•sh•nist) Someone who opposed slavery. p. PA 3–8

absolute location (ab´sə•lōōt lō•kā´shən) An exact position on Earth's surface. p. 26

adapt (ə•dapt´) To change in order to make more useful, such as fitting one's way of living into a new environment. p. 300

adobe (ə•dō´bē) A mixture of sandy clay and straw that is dried into bricks. p. 368

aerospace (âr´ō•spās) Having to do with the building and testing of equipment for air and space travel. p. 240

agriculture (a´gri•kəl•chər) Farming. p. 67

alliance (ə•lī´ənts) A partnership between countries or groups of people. p. 488

ally (a´lī) A partner in an alliance; a friend, especially in times of war. p 269

aluminum (ə•lōō´mə•nəm) A metal used to make things that need to be strong and lightweight. p. 183

amendment (ə•mend´mənt) A change or an addition to the Constitution. p. 482

analyze (a´nəl•īz) To break something into its parts and look closely at how those parts connect with one another. p. 5

ancestor (an´ses•tər) A family member from long ago. p. 25

apprentice (ə•´pren•təs) Someone who works for others in order to learn a trade. p. PA 2–13

aqueduct (a´kwə•dəkt) A large pipe or structure built to carry water. p. 375

arid (ar´əd) Dry. p. 242

arroyo (a•roh´yō) A deep, water-carved gully or ditch. p. 374

assassinate (ə•´sa•sən•´āt) To murder in a sudden attack. p. PA 4–13

assembly line (ə•sem´blē līn) A line of workers and machines along which a product moves as it is put together one step at a time. p. 280

B

ballot (ba´lət) A sheet of paper or some other method used to mark a secret vote. p. 484

barge (bärj) A large, flat-bottomed boat used on rivers and other inland waterways. p. 285

barrier (bar´ē•ər) Something that blocks the way or makes it hard to move from place to place. p. 345

barrier island (bar´ē•ər ī´lənd) A low, narrow island that is near a coast. p. 214

bartering (bär´tər•ing) The trading of one kind of good or service for another without using money. p. 361

basin (bā´sən) Low, bowl-shaped land with higher ground all around it. p. 31

bayou (bī´ōō or bī´ō) A slow-moving body of water. p. 232

bill (bil) A written plan for a new law. p. 474

blizzard (bliz´ərd) A snowstorm driven by strong, freezing winds. p. 308

boomtown (bōōm´toun) A town that grew up quickly, almost overnight. p. 346

borough (bər•´ō or bə•´rō) A self-governing town that is bigger than a village. p. PA 1–11

budget (bu´jət) A plan for spending and saving money. p. 481

butte (byōōt) A steep hill or rock with a flat top, like a mesa but smaller. p. 367

by-product (bī•´prä•dəkt) Something that is produced while making the main product. p. PA 5–2

C

campaign (kam•pān´) To carry out a series of actions, such as running advertisements on television, displaying signs, making speeches, and talking with voters, with the goal of getting elected to office. p. 484

canal (kə•nal´) A waterway dug across the land. p. 135

candidate (kan´də•dāt or ka´nə•dət) A person who is running for office in an election. p. 484

canyon (kan´yən) A deep, narrow valley with steep sides. p. 32

cape (kāp) A point of land that reaches out into the ocean. p. 101

capital resource (kap´ə•təl rē´sôrs) The money, a building, a machine, or a tool needed to run a business. p. 455, p. PA 5–5

cardinal directions (kär´də•nəl də•rek´shənz) The four main directions: north, south, east, and west. A3

cartographer (kär•tä´grə•fər) A person who makes maps. p. 269

cash crop (kash krop) A crop people raise to sell to others rather than to use themselves. p. 203

cause (kôz) Something that makes something else happen. p. 78

century (sen´chə•rē) A period of 100 years. p. 106

channel (chan´nəl) The deepest part of a river or other body of water. p. 38

charter (chär•tər) A written document. p. PA 3–3

checks and balances (cheks and ba´lən•sez) A system that gives each branch of government different powers so that each branch can keep the powers of the others from becoming too great. p. 470

chronology (krə•nä´lə•jē) A record of events in the order in which they happened. p. 4

citizen (sit´ə•zən) A member of a country, state, city, or town. p. 9

city manager (si´tē ma´ni•jər) A person hired by a city council or mayor to oversee the day-to-day operations of the city government. p. 480

civics (si´viks) The study of the rights and duties of citizens. p. 9

civil rights (si´vəl rīts) The rights of citizens to equal treatment. p. 485

civil war (si´vəl wôr) A war between groups of people in the same country. p. 204

classify (kla´sə•fī) To put into groups. p. 54

climate (klī´mət) The kind of weather a place has over a long time. p. 44

cloudburst (kloud´bûrst) A sudden, heavy rain. p. 374

coastal plain (kōs´təl plān) Low land that lies along an ocean or other large body of water. p. 30

colonist (kä´lə•nist) A person who lives in a colony. p. 103

colony (kä´lə•nē) A settlement started by people who leave their own country to live in another land. p. 102

command economy (kə•´mand i•kä´nə•mē) An economy in which the government controls production. p. PA 4–2

common (kä´mən) An empty field in the center of a town, often used as a public park. p. 113

commonwealth (käm´ən•welth) A territory that governs itself. p. 218, p. PA 6–8

commute (kə•myōot´) To travel back and forth. p. 145

compass rose (kum´pəs rōz) The direction marker on a map. A3

competition (käm•pə•ti´shən) In business, the contest among companies to get the most customers or sell the most products. p. 138

compromise (käm´prə•mīz) The settlement of a disagreement, with each side giving up some of what it wants in order to make an agreement. p. 244

Confederacy (kən•fe´də•rə•sē) The Confederate States of America, a new country that was formed by Southern states that seceded from the Union after Abraham Lincoln was elected President in 1860. p. 204

confederation (kən•fe•də•rā´shən) A loosely united group of governments working together. p. 127, p. PA 2–7

conflict (kän´flikt) A disagreement between two or more people or groups. p. 243

consequence (kän´sə•kwens) Something that happens because of an earlier action. p. 291

conservation (kän•sər•vā´shən) The protecting of natural resources and the using of them wisely. p. 52

Constitution (kän•stə•tōō´shən) The plan for the federal government. It describes the rights that people in the United States have, and it is the "supreme law of the land." p. 467

consumer (kən•sōō´mər) A person who buys a product or service. p. 318

continent (kän´tə•nənt) One of the seven largest land areas on Earth. p. 23

Continental Divide (kän•tə•nen´təl də•vīd´) An imaginary line that runs north and south along the highest points of the Rocky Mountains. Rivers flow west or east from this line. p. 344

cooperate (kō•o´pə•rāt) To work together. p. 116

coral (kôr´əl) A stony material formed in tropical waters by the skeletons of tiny sea animals. p. 194

county (koun´tē) A part of a state, usually larger than a city, that has its own government. p. 62

county seat (koun´tē sēt) A town or city that is the center of government for a county. p. 62

crater (krāt´ər) An opening in Earth's surface created when a volcano erupts and begins to throw out lava. p. 403

crossroads (krôs´rōds) Any place that connects people, goods, and ideas. p. 413

crude oil (krōōd oil) Petroleum pumped from the ground. p. 239

culture (kul´chər) The way of life of a group of people. pp. 10, 65

currency (kər´ən•sē) Money. p. 82

custom (kus´təm) A usual way of doing things. p. 68

cutaway diagram (ku´tə•wā dī´ə•gram) A diagram that shows the outside and inside of an object at the same time. p. 348

cyclone (sī´klōn) An intense tropical storm with strong winds and heavy rains, such as a hurricane. p. 221

GLOSSARY

D

decade (de´kād) A period of ten years. p. 106

declaration (de•klə•rā´shən) An official statement. p. 131

deforestation (dē•fôr•ist•ā´shən) The clearing of forestland by cutting down all the trees. p. 289

delegate (de•li•gət *or* de•li•gāt) An elected representative. p. PA 3–10

delta (del´tə) The triangle-shaped land at a river's mouth. p. 42

demand (di•mand´) A desire for a good or service by people who are willing to pay for it. p. 315

democracy (di•mä´krə•sē) A form of government in which the people rule and are free to make choices about their lives and their government. p. 448

desalinization (dē•sal•ə•ni•zā´shən) The process of removing salt from water. p. 385

diverse economy (dī•vûrs´ i•kä´nə•mē) An economy that is based on many kinds of industries. p. 236

division of labor (də•´vi•zhən uv lā´bər) The sharing of large jobs so that each worker does only part of the work. p. PA 5–3

drainage basin (drā´nij bā´sən) The land drained by a river system. p. 40

dredge (drej) To dig out the bottom and sides of a waterway to make it deeper and wider. p. 240

drought (drout) A long period of little or no rain. p. 48

dugout (dəg•´aut) A canoe made from trees. p. PA 2–3

E

earthquake (ûrth´kwāk) A sudden shaking of the ground caused by the movement and cracking of rock deep inside Earth. p. 403

economics (e•kə•näm´iks *or* ē•kə•näm´iks) The study of how people provide and use goods and services. p. 8

economy (i•kä´nə•mē) The way people in a state, a region, or a country use resources to meet their needs. pp. 8, 67

ecosystem (ē´kō•sis•təm) The relationship between living things and their nonliving environment, and their working together as a unit. p. 407

effect (i•fekt´) That which happens because of an earlier action. p. 78

elevation (e•lə•vā´shən) The height of the land in relation to sea level. p. 34

emancipation (i•´man(t)•sə•´pā•shən) Freedom from someone else's power. p. PA 3–8

endangered (in•dān´jərd) Being threatened with extinction. p. 193

entrepreneur (än•trə•prə•nûr´) A person who sets up a new business. p. 307

equator (i•kwā´tər) An imaginary line that circles Earth halfway between the North Pole and the South Pole. The line divides Earth into the Northern Hemisphere and the Southern Hemisphere. p. 22

erosion (i•rō´zhən) The gradual wearing away of Earth's surface. p. 41

estancia (i•stän´sē•a) A large ranch in South America or in other Spanish-speaking areas. p. 321

ethnic group (eth´nik grōōp) A group made up of people from the same country, people of the same race, or people with a common way of life. p. 68

evaporation (i•va•pə•rā´shən) The process of the sun's heat turning water into a gas form. p. 385

evidence (e´və•dəns) Proof. p. 4

executive branch (ig•ze´kyə•tiv branch) A branch of government whose main job is to see that laws passed by the legislative branch are carried out. p. 468

expedition (ek•spə•di´shən) A journey into an area to learn more about it. p. 231

export (ek´spôrt) A good shipped from one country to another, most often to be sold. p. 208

extended family (ik•´stend•əd fam•lē) Children, parents, aunts, uncles, cousins, and grandparents. p. PA 2–6

extinct (ik•stingkt´) No longer in existence, which is what happens to a living thing when all of its kind have died out. p. 194

F

fact (fakt) A statement that can be checked and proved to be true. p. 133

factors of production (fak´tərz uv prə•duk´shən) The human, natural, and capital resources that a business needs to produce goods or services. p. 455

fall line (fôl līn) A place where a river drops from higher to lower land. p. 173

federal (fed´ər•əl) National. p. 466

fertilizer (fûr´təl•ī•zər) Matter added to the soil to make it more productive to help crops grow. p. 207

fish farm (fish färm) A closed-off area of water in which people raise fish. p. 121

fjord (fē•ôrd´) A narrow inlet of the ocean between cliffs. p. 400

flatboat (flat´bōt) A large boat with a flat bottom and square ends. p. 283

floodplain (flud´plān) The low, flat land along a river. p. 42

flow chart (flō chärt) A diagram that shows the order in which things happen. p. 474

food processing (fōōd pro´ses•ing) The cooking, canning, drying, or freezing of food and the preparing of it for market. p. 207

foreign aid (fôr´•ən ād) Money, goods, or services that one country gives to another. p. 489

forty-niner (fôr•te•ni´nər) A person who went to California in 1849 to search for gold. p. 392

free enterprise (frē en´tər•prīz) A kind of economy in which people own and run their own businesses with only limited control by the government. p. 318

freight (frāt) Goods that are transported. p. 285

frontier (frən•tir´) The land beyond the settled part of a country. p. 270

fuel (fyoo´əl) A natural resource, such as coal, oil, or natural gas, burned to make heat or energy. p. 52

G

gaucho (gou´chō) A skilled rider who lived on the open land of the Pampas of South America and who hunted cattle for food and hides. Today a gaucho is a ranch hand on an estancia. p. 321

general election (jen´ər•əl i•lek´shən) An election in which the voters choose the people who will represent them in government. p. 484

generation (je•nə•rā´shən) The average time between the birth of parents and the birth of their children. p. 130

geographer (jē•ä´gra•fər) A person whose work is to study geography. p. 2

geography (jē•äg´rə•fē) The study of Earth's surface and the ways people use it. p. 2

geyser (gī´zər) A spring that shoots steam and hot water into the air. p. 355

glacier (glā´shər) A huge, slow-moving mass of ice. p. 109

global economy (glō´•bəl i•kä´nə•mē) The world market in which companies from different countries buy and sell goods and services. p. 458

government (guv´ərn•mənt) A system for deciding what is best for a group of people. It protects the group members and settles disagreements among them. The main job of government is to make and carry out laws. pp. 9, 61

governor (guv´ər•nər) The head of the executive branch of state government. p. 479

grid system (grid sis´təm) On a map, the system of lines that cross each other to form a pattern of squares used to locate places. A2

groundwater (ground´wô•tər) Water beneath Earth's surface. p. 38

growing season (grō´ing sē´zən) The time during which the weather is warm enough for plants to grow. p. 202

gulf (gəlf) A part of an ocean or sea extending into the land. p. 24

H

habitat (ha´bə•tat) A region where a plant or animal naturally grows or lives. p. 193

hailstorm (hāl´stôrm) A storm that drops hail, or lumps of ice. p. 308

harbor (här´bər) Part of a body of water where ships can dock safely. p. 103

hemisphere (he´mə•sfir) Half of a sphere, such as a ball or a globe; a half of Earth. p. 22

heritage (her´ə•tij) A way of life, a set of customs, or a belief that has come from previous generations and continues today. pp. 10, 81

high-tech (hī tek) Having to do with inventing, building, or using computers and other kinds of electronic equipment. p. 188

historian (hi•stôr´ē•ən) A person whose work is to study the past. p. 4

history (his´tə•rē) The events of the past. p. 4

hub (həb) A city where trains or planes stop on their way to other places. p. 187

human feature (hyoo´mən fē´chər) A structure, such as a building or a highway, that has been made by people. p. 2

human resource (hyoo´mən rē´sôrs) A worker and the ideas and skills that he or she brings to his or her job. p. 455, p. PA 5–5

humidity (hyoo•mi´də•tē) The amount of moisture in the air. p. 46

hurricane (hûr´ə•kān) A huge tropical storm with heavy rains and winds of at least 74 miles (119 km) per hour. p. 48

hydroelectric power (hī•drō•i•lek´trik pou´ər) Electricity made by waterpower. p. 182

I

immigrant (i´mi•grənt) A person who comes from some other place to live in a country. p. 143

import (im´pôrt) A good brought into one country from another country, most often to be sold. p. 208

incentive (in•´sen•tiv) A special reward. p. PA 6–3

indentured servant (in•´den(t)•shərd sər•vənt) Someone who got a paid passage to the colonies in exchange for a work contract. p. PA 2–11

independence (in•də•pen´dəns) Freedom to govern oneself or freedom from control by others. p. 130

industrial economy (in•dus´trē•əl i•kä´nə•mē) An economy in which factories and machines manufacture most goods. p. 104

industrialist (in•´dəs•trē•əl•list) Someone who owns mines, mills, factories, or railroads. p. PA 5–3

industry (in´dus•trē) All the businesses that make one kind of product or provide one kind of service. p. 67

inlet (in´let *or* in´lət) A narrow strip of water leading into the land from a larger body of water. p. 230

inset map (in´set map) A small map within a larger map. A3

interact (in•tər•akt´) To act upon one another. p. 2

interchangeable parts (in•tər•chān´jə•bəl pärts) Identical copies of parts made by machines so that if one part breaks, an identical one can be installed. p. 280

GLOSSARY

interdependence (in•tər•di•pen´dəns) Depending on one another for resources and products. p. 75

interest (in´tə•rəst) The money a bank or a borrower pays for the use of money. p. 456, p. PA 6–5

intermediate directions (in•tər•mē´dē•it də•rek´shənz) The directions between the cardinal directions: northeast, southeast, southwest, and northwest. A3

international trade (in•tər•na´shən•əl trād) Trade among nations. p. 208

irrigation (ir•ə•gā´shən) The use of canals, ditches, or pipes to move water to dry areas. p. 243

isthmus (is´məs) A narrow piece of land that connects two larger land areas. p. 24

J

judicial branch (jōō•di´shəl branch) A branch of the government whose main job is to see that laws are carried out fairly. p. 470

jury (jōōr´ē) A group of citizens who decide whether a person accused of a crime or other wrongdoings should be found guilty or not guilty. p. 479

K

keelboat (kēl´bōt) A flat-bottomed boat with pointed ends and sometimes a sail, which can be poled or sailed up a river against the current. p. 283, p. PA 3–6

keystone (kē´•stōn) The middle stone at the top of an arch that locks the other stones in place. p. PA 1–4

L

labor (lā´bər) Work. p. 395

labor union (lā´bər yün•yən) A group that aims to improve the workplace. p. PA 4–6

land grant (land grant) A gift of land. p. 232

land use (land yōōs) The way in which most of the land in a place is used. p. 70

landform (land´fôrm) One of the shapes that make up Earth's surface, such as mountains, hills, or plains. p. 28

lava (lä´və) Hot, melted rock that comes from a volcano. p. 403

legend (lej´ənd) A story that has come down from the past; part of it may or may not be true. p. 224

legislative branch (le´jəs•lā•tiv branch) The law-making branch of government. In the federal government it is called Congress. p. 467

limited government (li•mət•əd gə•vər(n)•mənt) A government in which citizens participate in the lawmaking process. p. PA 6–6

line graph (līn graf) A graph that uses a line to show changes over time. p. 178

lines of latitude (līnz uv la´tə•tōōd) The set of imaginary lines on a globe or a map that run east and west. They are used to tell how far north or south of the equator a place is. p. 26

lines of longitude (līnz uv lon´jə•tōōd) The set of imaginary lines on a globe or a map that run north and south. They are used to tell how far east or west of the prime meridian a place is. p. 26

location (lō•kā´shən) The place or site where something can be found. p. 2

locator (lō´kā•tər) A small map or globe that shows where a place on a main map is located in a state, in a country, or in the world. A2

lock (läk) A part of a canal in which the water level can be raised or lowered to bring ships to the level of the next part of the canal. p. 136

longhouse (lȯn´•hau̇s) A long, narrow building with a curved roof. p. PA 2–6

M

mainland (mān´land) The continent or the part of a continent nearest to an island. p. 214

majority rule (mə•jȯr´ə•tē rōōl) A way of deciding something in which whoever or whatever gets the most votes wins. p. 449

manufacturing (man•yə•fak´chə•ring) The making of goods from raw materials by hand or by machinery. p. 67

map key (map kē) The part of a map that explains what the symbols on the map stand for. A2

map scale (map skāl) The part of a map that compares a distance on the map to a distance in the real world. A3

map title (map tī´təl) The words that tell you the subject of a map. A2

market economy (mär´kət i•kä´nə•mē) An economy in which people decide which goods and services to produce. p. PA 4–2

marsh (märsh) Low, wet land where cattails, tall grasses, and other similar plants grow. p. 171

mass production (mas prə•duk´shən) A way of manufacturing in which many items that are identical can be made quickly and cheaply. p. 279

meat packing (mēt pak´ing) The preparing of meat for market. p. 315

media (mē•dē•ə) Radio, newspapers, magazines, television, and the Internet. p. PA 6–13

megalopolis (me•gə•lä´pə•ləs) A huge urban region formed when two or more metropolitan areas grow together. p. 143

meridian (mə•ri´dē•ən) A line of longitude. p. 26

mesa (mā´sa) A hill or small plateau with a flat top and steep sides. p. 367

metropolitan area (me•trə•pä´lə•tən âr´ē•ə) A large city together with its suburbs. p. 143

migrant worker (mī´grənt wur´kər) Someone who moves from farm to farm with the seasons, harvesting crops. p. 376

migration (mī•grā´shən) The movement of many people who leave one country or region to settle in another. p. 283

mileage (mī´lij) The distance between two places. p. 140

mileage table (mī´lij tā´bəl) A table that gives the number of miles between the listed cities. p. 141

millennium (mi•len´ē•əm) A period of 1,000 years. p. 107

mineral (min´rəl) A natural substance found in rocks. p. 51

mission (mish´ən) A religious settlement. p. 369

modify (mäd´ə•fī) To change. p. 73

monarch (mä´närk) A king or queen. p. 413

monsoon (män•sōōn´) A seasonal wind of the Indian Ocean and southern Asia. p. 221

monument (män´yə•mənt) Something that is built in remembrance of a person or event. p. 448

motto (mät´ō) A saying chosen to express the ideals of a nation, state, or group. p. 443

mountain range (moun´tən rānj) A group of connected mountains. p. 28

mouth (mouth) The place where a river empties into a larger body of water. p. 39

municipal (myōō•ni´sə•pəl) Having to do with a local government, such as a town or city. p. 479

natural resource (nach´ə•rəl rē´sôrs) Something found in nature that people can use. p. 49

natural vegetation (nach´ə•rəl ve•jə•tā´shən) The plant life that grows naturally in an area. p. 66

navigable (na´vi•gə•bəl) Deep and wide enough for ships to use. p. 135

negotiation (ni•gō•shē•ā´shən) A talk with another person, group, or country involved in a conflict in order to work out an agreement. p. 489

neutral (nü•trəl) Taking no side in a war. p. PA 3–9

nomad (nō´mad) A person who has no permanent home but moves from place to place. p. 368

nonrenewable (non•ri•nōō´ə•bel) Not able to be made again quickly by nature or by people. p. 52

O

oasis (ō•ā´səs) An area in a desert where there is water. p. 383

occupation (äk•yōō•pā´shən) The work that a person does for a living. p. 188

oil slick (oil slik) The film of oil that coats the water after an oil spill. p. 410

opinion (ə•pin´yən) A statement that tells what the person who makes it thinks or believes. It cannot be proved. p. 133

opportunity cost (ä•pər•tōō´nə•tē kôst) That which you give up to get something else. p. 460

oral history (ôr´əl his´tə•rē) Accounts that tell the experiences of people who did not have a written language or who did not write down what happened. p. 4

ordinance (ôr´dən•əns) An order or a law. p. 270

ore (ôr) Rock that contains enough of one or more kinds of minerals to be mined. p. 279

P

Pacific Rim (pə•si´fik rim) A world region that includes the states and countries that border the Pacific Ocean. p. 417

paddy (pad´ē) A rice field. p. 288

palisade (pa•lə•´sād) A fence made of tall wooden poles. p. PA 2–6

parallels (par´ə•lelz) Lines that are always the same distance apart, such as lines of latitude. p. 26

pass (pas) An opening between high mountains. p. 174

patriotism (pā´trē•ə•ti•zem) Love of country. p. 446

peninsula (pə•nin´sə•lə) Land almost entirely surrounded by water. p. 30

pesticide (pes•tə•sīd) A chemical used to kill harmful insects on crops. p. PA 5–13

petition (pə•ti´shən) A signed request for action. p. 484

petrochemical (pe•trō•ke´mi•kəl) A chemical made from oil or natural gas. p. 249

petroleum (pə•trō´lē•əm) Oil. p. 238

physical feature (fiz´i•kəl fē´chər) A feature, such as a landform, body of water, or resource, that has been formed by nature. p. 2

piedmont (pēd´mänt) An area at or near the foot of a mountain. p. 29

pioneer (pī•ə•nir´) A person who first settles a new place. p. 174

plantation (plan•tā´shən) A huge farm where tobacco, cotton, rice, sugarcane, or indigo were the main crops grown. p. 202

plateau (pla•tō´) An area of high, mostly flat land that rises above the surrounding land. p. 30

point of view (point uv vyōō) A person's set of beliefs that have been shaped by factors such as whether that person is old or young, male or female, rich or poor. p. 5

political party (pə•´li•ti•kəl pär´tē) A group of people with the same point of view about many issues. p. PA 5–10

pollution (pə•lōō´shən) The act of making a natural resource, such as air, soil, or water, dirty or unsafe to use. p. 53

population (pop•yə•lā´shən) The number of people who live in a place. p. 72

population density (pop•yə•lā´shən den´sə•tē) The average number of people living in an area of a certain size, usually 1 square mile or 1 square kilometer. p. 444

port (pôrt) A trading center where ships are loaded and unloaded. p. 129

poverty (pä´vər•tē) The condition of being very poor. p. 440

prairie (prâr´ē) An area of flat or rolling land covered mostly with wildflowers and grasses. p. 297

preamble (prē•´am•bəl) The opening section of the constitution. p. PA 6–8

precipitation (pri•si•pə•tā´shən) Any form of water such as rain, sleet, or snow, that falls to Earth's surface. p. 44

prediction (pri•dik´shən) Looking at the way things are and saying what you think will happen in the future. p. 380

prejudice (pre´jə•dəs) An unfair feeling of hatred or dislike for a group because of its background, race, or religion. p. 441

primary source (prī´mer•ē sôrs) A record made by people who saw or took part in an event. p. 6

prime meridian (prīm mə•rid´ē•ən) An imaginary line that divides Earth into the Eastern Hemisphere and the Western Hemisphere. p. 23

produce (prō´dōōs) Fresh fruits and vegetables. p. 413

producer (prō•´dü•sər) Someone who makes goods and provides services. p. PA 6–2

product (prod´əkt) Something that people make or grow, usually to sell. p. 50

profit (prä´fət) In a business, money left over after all costs have been paid. p. 455

proprietor (pruh pry´uh ter) The owner of a land grant. p. PA 3–3

public land (pub´lik land) Land that is owned by the government. p. 355

pueblo (pwe´blō) An adobe village. p. 369

pulp (pulp) A soft mixture of ground-up wood chips and chemicals that is used to make paper. p. 207

Q

quarry (kwôr´ē) A large, open pit cut into the ground from which stone is mined. p. 110

R

rain forest (rān fôr´əst) A wet area, usually warm, where tall trees, vines, and other plants grow close together. p. 80

rain shadow (rān sha´dō) On a mountain, the drier side that receives little or no precipitation. p. 374

rapids (ra´pəds) A rocky place in a river w... sudden drop in elevation causes fast-moving o... dangerous water. p. 135

ratify (ra•tə•´fī) To vote to accept. p. PA 3–13

raw material (rô mə•tir´ē•əl) A resource in its natural state, such as a mineral, that can be used to manufacture a product. p. 208

reclaim (ri•klām´) To return something, such as land, to its natural condition. p. 184

recreation (rek•rē•ā´shən) Any form of amusement or relaxation. p. 119

recycle (rē•sī´kəl) To use again. p. 52

reef (rēf) A ridge of rocks, sand, or coral near the surface of the sea. p. 194

refinery (ri•fī´nər•ē) A factory that turns crude oil into useful products, such as gasoline and other fuels. p. 239

region (rē´jən) An area with at least one feature that makes it different from other areas. pp. 2, 60

relative location (re´lə•tiv lō•kā´shən) The position of a place in relation to other places on Earth. p. 24

relief (ri•lēf´) Differences in elevation. p. 34

renewable (ri•nōō´ə•bəl) Able to be made or grown again by nature or people. p. 52

representation (re•pri•zen•tā´shən) Acting or speaking on behalf of someone or something else. p. 130

republic (ri•pub´lik) A form of government in which people elect representatives to govern the country. p. 467

reservation (re•zər•vā´shən) Land set aside by the government for use by American Indians. On reservations, Indians govern themselves. p. 371

reservoir (re´zə•vwär) A lake formed by the water held back by a dam and used to store water. p. 182

resolve (ri•zälv´) To settle a conflict or problem. p. 247

resort (ri•zôrt´) A place where people go to relax and have fun. p. 191

responsibility (ri•spän•sə•bi´lə•tē) Something that a person should do. p. 411

retail trade (rē´tāl trād) A service industry made up of businesses that buy goods and sell them directly to consumers. p. 457

revolution (rev•ə•lōō´shən) A large, sudden change in government or in people's lives. p. 131

Ring of Fire (ring uv fīr) A world region that stretches along the western coast of the Americas, the eastern coast of Asia, and into the southern Pacific Ocean. It has many volcanoes and frequently experiences earthquakes. p. 417

river system (ri´vər sis´təm) A river and its tributaries. p. 39

runoff (run´ôf) Surface water that does not soak into the ground. p. 245

rural (rōōr´əl) Of or like a country region. p. 61

GLOSSARY

... mound formed by

...-made object that orbits

...ndant. p. 50

...) Limited supply. p. PA 6–2

...al) The level of the surface of the
...29

sec...si•sēd´) To leave the Union. p. 204

secondary source (se´kən•der•ē sôrs) A record of an event written by someone who was not there at the time. p. 7

self-sufficient (self sə•fish´ənt) Able to do everything for oneself, with no help from other people. p. 299

service industry (sər´vəs in´dəs•trē) An industry in which workers are paid to do things for other people. p. 68

skyscraper (skī´skrā•pər) A very tall steel-framed building. p. 279

slavery (slā´vər•ē) The practice of making one person the property of another person. p. 201

social reform (sō•shəl ri•´fôrm) Change to improve society. p. PA 4–8

society (sə•sī´ə•tē) A group of people who have many things in common. pp. 10, 370

sod (sod) A layer of soil held together by the roots of grasses. p. 299

source (sôrs) The place where a river begins. p. 38

specialize (spe´shə•līz) To work at only one kind of job. p. 121

state legislature (stāt le´jəs•lā•chər) The legislative branch of state government. p. 479

station (stā´shən) A large sheep or cattle ranch in Australia. p. 323

steamboat (stēm´bōt) A boat powered by a steam engine that turns a large paddle wheel. p. 283

steppes (stepz) A large region of dry, grassy plains in northern central Asia. p. 80

strait (strāt) A narrow channel that connects two larger bodies of water. p. 24

strike (strīk) The stopping of work to make employers meet workers' demands. p. PA 5–3

suburb (sub´ərb) A town or small city built near a larger city. p. 60

suffrage (su´frij) The right to vote. p. 347, p. PA 5–7

Sun Belt (sun belt) A wide area of the southern part of the United States that has a mild climate all year. p. 209

supply (sə•plī´) A product or service that a business offers for sale. p. 319

survey (sər•vā´) To measure, especially land. p. 270

swamp (swämp) A low, wet area where trees and bushes grow, usually covered by shallow water at least part of the year. p. 210

T

technology (tek•nä´lə•jē) The use of new ideas to make tools and machines. p. 77

telegraph (te´lə•graf) A machine that used electricity to send messages over wires. p. 394

tepee (tē´pē) A cone-shaped tent made of poles and covered with animal skins. p. 300

terrace (ter´əs) A flat "shelf" dug into a mountainside to make farming there possible. p. 360

territory (ter´ə•tôr•ē) An area owned and governed by a country. p. 218

textile mill (tek´stīl mil) A factory in which fibers such as cotton and wool are woven into textiles, or cloth. p. 104

timberline (tim´bər•līn) On a mountain, the elevation above which the temperatures are too low for trees to grow. p. 353

time line (tīm līn) A diagram that shows the order in which events took place and the amount of time that passed between them. p. 106

time zone (tīm zōn) A region in which people use the same clock time. p. 398

tornado (tôr•nā´dō) A funnel-shaped, spinning windstorm, sometimes called a cyclone or twister. p. 47

tourism (toor´iz•əm) Traveling to a place for pleasure. p. 75

township (toun´ship) A square section of land in the Northwest Territory measuring 6 miles (about 10 km) on each side; each township was divided into 36 smaller squares of land to be sold to settlers. p. 270

trade (trād) The buying or selling of goods. p. 77

trade-off (trād´ôf) Giving up one thing to get another. p. 460

tradition (trə•dish´ən) A custom, a way of life, or an idea that has been handed down from the past. p. 82

traditional economy (trə•dish•nəl i•kä´nə•mē) An economy that changes little over time. p. PA 4–2

transcontinental railroad (trans•kon•tə•nen´təl rāl´rōd) A railroad that crosses an entire continent, such as the one completed in 1869 linking the East and West Coasts of North America. p. 394

treaty (trē´tē) An agreement between countries or groups of people. p. 128

tributary (trib´yə•ter•ē) A stream or river that flows into a larger stream or river. p. 39

tropics (trop´iks) A band of warm climate that circles Earth near the equator. p. 219

tundra (tun´drə) A large, flat, treeless plain that stays frozen most of the year. p. 79

turnpike (tərn´pīk) A road that drivers must pay to use. p. 139

U

unemployment (un•im•ploi´mənt) The state of being without a job. p. 153

GLOSSARY

Union (yōōn´yən) The United States of America. p. 204

unlimited government (ən•li•mə•təd guv´ərn•mənt) A government in which rulers make laws without considering what citizens want. p. PA 6–6

urban (ûr´bən) Of or like a city region. p. 60

urban growth (ûr´bən grōth) The growth of cities. p. 145

urban sprawl (ûr´bən sprôl) The spreading of urban areas and the growth of new centers of business and shopping. p. 154

urbanization (ûr•bə•nə•zā´shən) The growth of the proportion of people living in cities compared with that of people in rural areas. p. 315

V

veto (vē´tō) To reject a bill and to try to stop it from becoming a law. p. 471

volcano (vol•kā´nō) An opening in Earth's surface out of which hot gases, ash, and lava may pour. p. 403

volunteer (vä•lən•tir´) A person who offers to do something without pay. p. 115

W

wagon train (wa´gən trān) A group of wagons, each pulled by horses, mules, or oxen. p. 345

war bond (wår bänd) A paper showing that the buyer loaned money to the government to help pay for a war. p. PA 5–7

waterpower (wô´tər•pou•ər) Energy produced by rushing water. p. 173

waterway (wô´tər•wā) A body of water that boats can use. p. 135

wealth (welth) Riches. p. 248

wetlands (wet´landz) Low-lying land where the water level is always near or above the surface of the land. p. 410

wholesale trade (hōl´•sāl trād) A service industry made up of businesses that buy large amounts of goods from producers and then sell them to other businesses. p. 457

wildlife refuge (wīld´līf re´fyōōj) An area of land set aside to protect animals and other living things. p. 193

windbreak (wind´brāk) Rows of large trees or bushes planted between fields to help block the wind and prevent soil erosion. p. 309

windbreak

B

INDEX

INDEX

INDEX

INDEX

INDEX

INDEX

INDEX

INDEX

INDEX

For permission to reprint copyrighted material, grateful acknowledgment is made to the following sources:

Atheneum Books for Young Readers, an imprint of Simon & Schuster Children's Publishing Division: Cover illustration by Christopher Manson from *Uncle Sam and Old Glory* by Delno C. West and Jean M. West. Illustration copyright © 2000 by Christopher Manson.

Digital Scanning, Inc.: Cover illustration from *Life on the Mississippi* by Mark Twain. Illustration © 2000 by DSI digital reproduction. Originally published by Dawson Brothers, 1883.

Dutton Children's Books, an imprint of Penguin Putnam Books for Young Readers, a division of Penguin Putnam Inc.: Cover illustration by Stacey Schuett from *Purple Mountain Majesties* by Barbara Younger. Illustration copyright © 1998 by Stacey Schuett.

Jim Fish, Ozona, TX: From "Heritage" by Jim Fish. Text © 1998 by Jim Fish.

Harcourt, Inc.: Cover illustration by Greg Shed from *Squanto's Journey: The Story of the First Thanksgiving* by Joseph Bruchac. Illustration copyright © 2000 by Greg Shed. From *A River Ran Wild* by Lynne Cherry. Copyright © 1992 by Lynne Cherry. Cover illustration by Barry Moser from *Appalachia: The Voices of Sleeping Birds* by Cynthia Rylant. Illustration copyright © 1991 by Pennyroyal Press, Inc.

HarperCollins Publishers: From *A Very Important Day* by Maggie Rugg Herold, illustrated by Catherine Stock. Text copyright © 1995 by Maggie Rugg Herold; illustrations copyright © 1995 by Catherine Stock. From *Heartland* by Diane Siebert. Text copyright © 1989 by Diane Siebert. From *Mississippi* by Diane Siebert, illustrated by Greg Harlin. Text copyright © 2001 by Diane Siebert; illustrations copyright © 2001 by Greg Harlin. Cover illustration by Wendell Minor from *Sierra* by Diane Siebert. Illustration copyright © 1991 by Wendell Minor. From *Pioneer Girl: Growing Up on the Prairie* by Andrea Warren. Text copyright © 1998 by Andrea Warren.

Holiday House, Inc.: Cover illustration by Samuel Byrd from *A Picture Book of Harriet Tubman* by David A. Adler. Illustration copyright © 1992 by Samuel Byrd.

Henry Holt and Company, LLC: Cover illustration by Ib Ohlsson from *It Happened in America: True Stories from the Fifty States* by Lila Perl. Illustration copyright © 1992 by Ib Ohlsson.

Houghton Mifflin Company: Cover illustration from *Alice Ramsey's Grand Adventure* by Don Brown. Copyright © 1997 by Don Brown.

Pantheon Books, an imprint of Random House Children's Books, a division of Random House, Inc.: from "This Newly Created World," translated by Paul Radin from *The Road of Life and Death: A Ritual Drama of the American Indians* by Paul Radin.

Raincoast Books: Cover illustration by Henry Ripplinger from *If you're not from the prairie…* by David Bouchard. Illustration copyright © 1993 by Henry Ripplinger.

Scholastic Inc.: From *Grand Canyon: Exploring a Natural Wonder* by Wendell Minor, back cover photograph by Geoff Parker. Text, illustrations, and photograph copyright © 1998 by Wendell Minor; back cover photograph copyright © 1998 by Geoff Parker. Published by The Blue Sky Press/Scholastic Inc.

Simon & Schuster Books for Young Readers, an imprint of Simon & Schuster Children's Publishing Division: Cover illustration from *The Amazing Impossible Erie Canal* by Cheryl Harness. Copyright © 1995 by Cheryl Harness. Cover illustration from *Mark Twain and the Queens of the Mississippi* by Cheryl Harness. Copyright © 1998 by Cheryl Harness.

Walker and Company, Inc.: Cover illustration from *Desert Trek: An Eye-Opening Journey Through the World's Driest Places* by Marie-Ange le Rochais. Copyright © 1999 by l'école des loisirs, Paris.

WGBH: "Building Big–Wonders of the World– Golden Gate Bridge" at http://www.pbs.org/wgbh/buildingbig/wonder/structure/goldengate_bridge.html. Copyright © 2000 by WGBH Educational Foundation.

PLACEMENT KEY: (t) top; (b) bottom; (l) left; (c) center; (r) right; (bg) background; (i) inset

ILLUSTRATION CREDITS

Pages 76-77 Don Foley; 102-103 Luigi Galante; 136 Stephen Durke; 144 Jim Effler; 144-145 Jim Effler; 182-183 Studio Liddell; 208-209 Dale Gustafson; 243 Chuck Carter; 269 Jacqueline Scardova; 278 Dick Gage; 353 Uldis Klavins; 374 Sebastian Quiggley; 404 Stephen Durke; 455 Monotype Composition; 458 Jeff Mangiat; 469 Studio Liddell; PA 2-7 (cr) Luigi Galante; PA 2-13 (tr) Luigi Galante; PA 2-4 (tr) Luigi Galante; PA 2-14 (bg) Anthony Morse; PA 2-6 (tc) Gino D'Achille.

All maps by MapQuest.com

PHOTO CREDITS

Cover: Independence Hall: Frank Baker/Index Stock Imagery, Flag: Comstock, Map: maps.com/Index Stock Imagery, Mountain Laurel: Photodisc/Media Bakery, Delaware River: Jeff Greenberg/AgeFoto Stock, Harrisburg: Comstock/Media Bakery.

TITLE PAGE AND TABLE OF CONTENTS

i (fg) Blair Seitz; i (bg) Harcourt; ii Blair Seitz; iv David Muir/Masterfile; v Michael Freeman; vi Jim Strawser/Grant Heilman, G. Kidd/Earth Scenes; vii Harcourt; viii Smithsonian Institution; ix Terry Heffernan

INTRODUCTION

1 G. L. French/H. Armstrong Roberts, Inc. 3 (tr) Superstock 3 (bl) Jim Steinberg/Photo Researchers 3 (br) David Young-Wolff/PhotoEdit/PictureQuest 3 (cl) Jan Stromme/Bruce Coleman, Inc. 3 (cr) Jeffrey Muir Hamilton/Stock, Boston/PictureQuest 4 (c) Associated Press, AP/Wide World Photos 4 (b) The Indianapolis News 5 ((tr) to (br) #1, #3, #4 Bob Daemmrich Photos; #2 Randy Mallory; #5 Texas State Library and Archives Commission 5 (bl) H. Armstrong Roberts 6 (l) The Bancroft Library, University of California, Berkeley 6 (c) Hulton/Archive 6 (bl) The Bancroft Library, The University of California, Berkeley 7 (l) M. Schneiders/H. Armstrong Roberts 7 (r) Courtesy of PBS 7 (inset tr) Hulton/Archive 7 (inset br) Michael T. Sedam/Corbis 8 all photos Harcourt

9 (t) Harcourt 9 (b) Bettmann/Corbis 10 (l) Ken Highfill/Photo Researchers 10 (r) Bob Daemmrich Photos/Stock, Boston/PictureQuest

UNIT 1
UNIT OPENER, Pages 20-21 (bg) D. Carriere/H. Armstrong Roberts, 22 (bl) Doug Wilson/Black Star; 24 (b) Doug Wilson/Black Star; 24 (b) Doug Wilson/Black Star; 25 (tc) Jon Feingersh/Corbis Stockmarket; 28 (bg) Jim Wark/Kieffer Nature Stock; 29 (tr) Lee Foster/Words & Pictures/PictureQuest; 30 (b) Kevin Horan/Tony Stone Images; 30 (tc) Michael Pohuski/FoodPix; 32 (b) Ricxhard Sisk/Panoramic Images; 33 (t) Ric Ergenbright/Ric Ergenbright Photography; 34 (b) Cliff Leight/PictureQuest; 36 (b) US Geological Survey; 36 (l) (br) (c) US Geological Survey/Pennsylvania State University; 36 (tr) Bob Daemmrich/Stock Boston/PictureQuest; 37 (t)Library of Congress; 37 (r) (c) US Geological Survey, Pennsylvania State University Library; 38-39 (bg) C.E. Mitchell/BlackStar; 41 (b) John Coletti/Index Stock; 41 (c) Corbis; 42 (b) Yann Arthus-Bertrand/Corbis; 43 (t) Cindy Roever; 44 (bg) Eric Haase/Contact Press Images/PictureQuest; 45 (t) David Olsen/Tony Stone Images; 47 (c) Stockbyte/PictureQuest; 47 (b) Thia Konig/Tony Stone Images; 48 (t) Burton McNeely/Image Bank; 49 (b) Greig Cranna/StockBoston/PictureQuest; 50(l) John Keiffer; 51 (b) J. A. Kraulis/Masterfile; 52 (br) IFA/eStock Photography/PictureQuest; 52 (bl) Photo courtesy of Photocommunications Department, Southern Illinois University Carbondale; 53 (tr) John Elk III/StockBoston; 54-55 (bg) Rick Ergenbright/Corbis; 58-59 (bg) Annie Griffiths Belt/Corbis; 60 (b) Ken O'Donoghue; 60 (br) Massachusetts Executive Office of Environmental Affairs; 61 (t) The MetroWest Daily News, Framingham, MA; 62 (tc) Bernalillo County Sheriff's Dept., New Mexico; 64 (t) Joseph Sohm, Visions of America/Corbis Images; 65 (b) Ron Sanford/Stockmarket; 67 (b) Mark Gibson/Index Stock Imagery/PictureQuest; 68 (b) Sylvain Grandadam/Tony Stone Images; 69 (tl) AFP/Corbis; 70 (bl) David R. Frazier Photo Library; 72-73 (b) Joseph Sohm/PictureQuest; 73 (cr) Courtesy: Arizona Historical Society/Tucson #2297; 74 (b) Christopher Brown/PictureQuest; 75 (br) Jeff Greenberg/PictureQuest; 75 (tc) Bill Lisenby/Corbis; 75 (tr) Inset Felicia Martinez/PictureQuest; 79 (b) Bill Bachmann/PhotoEdit; 80 (cl) Jacques Langevin/Corbis Sygma; 81 (bl) Charlotte Thege/Das Fotoarchiv; 81 (tc) Garry Adams/PictureQuest; 82 (b) Corbis Images Page 86 (c) David Sailors Photography; 86-87 (bg) Richard Cummins/Corbis; 87 (b) Jack Olson Photography; 87 (t) Steven J. Brown; 88 (bl) Photo Library International/Corbis; 88 (bc) Kart Weatherly/Corbis; 88 (br) David Ball/Getty Images; 89 (bl) Alan Oddie/Photo Edit; 89 (bc) David Ball/Tony Stone Images; 89 (br) Nikos Desyllas/SuperStock, Inc.; 90 (bl) Ken Karp; PA 1-1 © David Muench/CORBIS; PA 1-3 Bob Krist/Corbis; PA 1-5 (tr) Blair Seitz; PA 1-5 (inset) Associated Press, AP; PA 1-6 PA Department of Environmental Protection; PA 1-9 Tom Rosenthal/Superstock; PA 1-10 Harcourt; PA 1-11 (t) Corbis; PA 1-12 (tr) Marta Urban, Pennsylvania German Fraktur Artist; PA 1-12 (bl) Dexter Press; PA 1-13 (tl) ODUNDE, Inc.;